Also by John Szwed

Jazz 101: A Complete Guide to Learning and Loving Jazz
Space Is the Place: The Lives and Times of Sun Ra

So What

THE LIFE OF MILES DAVIS

JOHN SZWED

SIMON & SCHUSTER

New York · London · Toronto · Sydney · Singapore

SIMON & SCHUSTER
Rockefeller Center
1230 Avenue of the Americas
New York, NY 10020

Copyright © 2002 by John Szwed
All rights reserved,
including the right of reproduction
in whole or in part in any form.

SIMON & SCHUSTER and colophon are registered trademarks
of Simon & Schuster, Inc.

For information regarding special discounts for bulk purchases, please contact
Simon &Schuster Special Sales at 1-800-456-6798 or business@simonandschuster.com

Designed by Lauren Simonetti

Manufactured in the United States of America

10 9 8 7 6 5 4 3 2 1

Library of Congress Cataloging-in-Publication Data

Szwed, John.
So what : the life of Miles Davis / John Szwed
p. cm.
Includes bibliographical references, discography, and index.
1. Davis, Miles. 2. Jazz musicians—United States—Biography. I. Title.
ML419.D39 S98 2002
788.9'2165'092—dc21
[B]
2002026803

Excerpt on p. 182 from *Collected Poems* by Frank O'Hara,
copyright © 1971 by Maureen Granville-Smith, Administratrix of the
Estate of Frank O'Hara. Used by permission of Alfred A. Knopf,
a division of Random House, Inc.

ISBN 0-684-85982-3

To
Roger D. Abrahams
Dan Rose
Robert Farris Thompson

Contents

Vamp

Put that down. Put it all down. And listen, don't you try to
make me into a nice guy.

Miles Davis

ONE NIGHT while I was having a drink with a friend in a SoHo bar in New
York City, an acquaintance of his joined us, and I was introduced to him
as someone who was thinking of writing a biography of Miles Davis. He
immediately launched into a Miles story, one that was hysterically funny,
but one that also seemed highly improbable. When I asked where he had
heard the story, he threw up his hands in mock horror: "You want attri-
bution? This is *Miles* I'm talking about—he belongs to everyone!" It was
only the first of many such encounters, every one of which reiterated a
basic lesson about writing about Miles Davis: stories about him are
legion, many of them dramatic, and all of them accompanied by strong
emotions. That's the good news. The bad news is that many of them
never happened. All of which is to say that his life is now, as it was when
he was alive, in the realm of legend.

Part of his legendary status, of course, stems from his unwillingness to
be forthcoming about himself throughout most of his life; in fact, that
reticence was central to his mystique. Davis claimed not to be able to
remember much of his youth, and in the name of change, chose to forget
many of his past accomplishments. Writers, as well as the public, looked
for some kind of revelation in the few crimped and guarded interviews
he did chose to give. But Davis was difficult to approach, quick to anger,
and often oblique or contradictory in what he did say. It is no wonder
that the interviews that were published nearly always quoted other
interviews. Yet in the effort to piece together a full portrait of the man,
they sometimes unwittingly repeated errors in the process. Some sense of
the dimension of these problems can be grasped when Miles denied the
truth of the some of the stories presented in early interviews with him.

When he was not asked further about these denials, the information he claimed to be false continued to be repeated, and so seemed to be confirmed in everything written about him.

Miles' life as a whole is not easy to grasp, and the meaning of it, with or without his help, is resistant to quick interpretations. This is not to say that any life is easy to fathom and render into words. Novelist Martin Amis put it this way: "The trouble with life . . . is its amorphousness, its ridiculous fluidity. Look at it: thinly plotted, largely themeless, sentimental and ineluctably trite. The dialogue is poor, or at least violently uneven. The twists are either predictable or sensationalist. And it's always the same beginning; and the same ending." What makes the problem worse in our own time is that celebrity biographies serve the function once served by novels, their authors bent on creating organic, convincing narratives that explain everything their subjects have ever done or said, even if it means reading their minds to explain their behavior—he wondered, she thought—with speculation taking over where there are no facts to help, leaping across the gaps, forgetting that no life is ever led the way a biographer's story line is written. In biographical writing, the urge to fill in the blanks, thicken the story line, provide missing motivation, and heat up the significance is hard to resist, and it has turned more than one biographer into a novelist.

A word, then, about the intentions of this book. There already exist several biographies of Miles Davis, as well as his autobiography and a memoir from his collaborator. I found all of them interesting and useful, drew on them in my writing, and strongly recommend them to anyone seriously interested in Miles' life and work. Why then am I writing yet another Davis biography? One answer is that there is still more to be known and a number of misunderstandings to be corrected. To do this, I have gone back to the transcripts of Davis' interviews conducted by his autobiographer, Quincy Troupe (housed in the Schomburg Library in New York City), in search of material not used in *Miles: The Autobiography*, or looking to highlight what was used in the autobiography in different ways. (Although I was not able to quote directly from those interviews, I have paraphrased their contents.) I have also examined and drawn on Alex Haley's extensive notes (also at the Schomburg) for his *Playboy* interview with Miles, as well as on the Teo Macero Collection at the New York Public Library of Performing Arts at Lincoln Center. Numerous people were also interviewed for this book, especially those family members—like Davis' brother, Vernon, common-law wife, Irene, and son, Gregory—and fellow musicians, such as Allen Eager and Stan Levey, who had not been spoken to for previous publications. In addition, I've drawn freely (and with thanks) on Davis' published interviews, especially some of those not so well known or in other languages than English. I hope that readers will find here some new information on Davis' youth, his stay at Juilliard, his time in Detroit, his lovers, his music, his business affairs, and the man himself.

A second answer to why another biography on Miles Davis is that this is not a biography in the contemporary sense, as it does not attempt to track down every event or person in his life. Nor is it strictly a musical study, especially because not all of his music is discussed. (I have, however, attempted to make the case for some of Davis' early recordings with Charlie Parker, which are often passed over, as well as for some of his mid-1970s recordings, which even his biographers don't like.) What I am attempting to do in this book might better be described as a meditation on Miles Davis' life, one that looks at the variety of meanings that were (and continue to be) projected onto him. Davis embodied a large array of such meanings, many of them apparently contradictory, and he created a public self that was at times even larger and more complex than that of the private person.

Those are my reasons, and readers will be the judge of whether this book is worthwhile. But for certain, mine is not the last word, and I would be surprised, even distressed, if what I have done or not done doesn't spark yet another Davis biography. After all, it is now eleven years since his death, and Miles seems omnipresent. We speak of him in the present tense, his first name used not so much to demonstrate personal familiarity as it is to acknowledge the pervasiveness of his influence. He is a haunting specter at jazz festivals: Miles Davis tributes outdraw newer musicians' performances, and such acolytes as Wayne Shorter, Chick Corea, Keith Jarrett, John McLaughlin, and Joe Zawinul are now the stars of the music. Trumpet players copy his playing. Musicians and fans lapse into his vocal rasp to make a point. A Mercedes-Benz TV ad portrays a string of animals and people lined up to board Noah's ark, each carrying some important piece of Western culture to preserve—a painting by van Gogh, a musical score by Mozart, a computer—and Miles' *Birth of the Cool*. The entire side of a twenty-story building in New York City is covered with a sulking black-and-white portrait of Miles with Apple Computer colloquially urging its market to "Think Different." Jack Nicholson dedicates his Academy Award to him. The president and CEO of one the largest banks tells his executives that he wants the bank to function like Davis' quintet and emblazons Miles' picture against the cool night blue of its credit cards.

His music continues to express hipness (as on the soundtracks to films like *Lenny* and even in the anachronistic posters and albums that dot the screen in *The Talented Mr. Ripley*), and just as often it signals a certain delicacy and romanticism (albeit a *white* delicacy and romanticism, given the films in which his music is used: *Pleasantville, Jerry Maguire, Runaway Bride*). And his records do better than when he was alive—*Kind of Blue* sells over 5,000 copies a week in the United States alone. His life has inspired fictions such as Walter Ellis' *Prince of Darkness*, Herbert Simmons' *Man Walking on Eggshells*, as well as Leo Penn's 1966 film *A Man Called Adam* and Robert Lepage's 1991 theater piece *Needles and Opium*, which pairs Jean Cocteau's and Miles' careers in the arts and drugs.

As they once said of his mentor, Charlie Parker: Miles lives.

CHAPTER ONE

And to see the cool way of that nigger—why he wouldn't give me the road if I hadn't shoved him out o' the way.

MARK TWAIN, HUCKLEBERRY FINN

HE WAS BORN ON MAY 26, 1926, in Alton, Illinois, on the Mississippi River. This single stroke of fate was enough to augur greatness for Miles Dewey Davis III, for the history books say that this is the artery along which the blood of the jazz ancestors flowed north from New Orleans to Chicago. Never mind that the river flows nowhere near Chicago, for in the mythic geography of jazz, the Mississippi is its Liffey or its Styx, its Thames or its Seine, the line that bisects the land into West and East Coasts, the pendulum that passes over the heartland. For black folks, it was the nexus between the North and the South, a means of escape, and often in song, a symbol of a mighty race. For white folks, too, the river was emblematically black. Mark Twain spoke of its "mulatto complexion," and for T. S. Eliot, himself born in St. Louis, the Mississippi was sometimes a "strong, brown god—sullen, untamed and intractable"; at other times, just a "river with its cargo of dead Negroes, cows and chicken coops."

Davis' father, Miles II, was born in 1900 in Pine Bluff, Arkansas, into a family of six sons and three daughters. His grandfather Miles Davis I had come from Georgia and married Mary Frances from Arkansas, and later a second wife, Ivy, who was the grandmother Miles knew as he was growing up. His grandfather was an accountant and a farmer whose land was in Noble Lake, Arkansas, southwest of the Mississippi delta, where he raised crops of sugarcane, watermelon, and corn. It was on this farm that young Miles III spent summers visiting his grandparents, playing with two stepuncles (Ed and John, children from his grandmother's previous marriage, who were only a year older and a year younger than he was), and riding a horse that his grandfather gave him when he was seven. Like many other African American children, Miles first experienced southern culture with his grandparents, helping with chores, listening to folk songs and blues played by his cousins and their neighbors, hearing the collective moans coming from backwoods houses of worship, or moving through groves of trees that local folk said were inhabited by the spirits of the dead.

Though Miles' father had not gone to high school, he passed an equivalency test and then entered Arkansas Baptist College and graduated with honors. He enrolled in Lincoln University for predentistry training and went on to Northwestern University's School of Dentistry, where he was one of only four black students, and earned a D.D.S. with honors. While he attended Arkansas Baptist, he met Miles' mother, Cleota H. Henry. She was the only child of Leon and Hattie Henry, born in 1901 and raised in North Little Rock. They were married after he completed his dental training.

The plan had been for Miles' father to open an office in Belleville, Illinois, after graduation, but Alton had a greater need for a black dentist, and once Dr. Davis visited the town, he decided to settle there. The river was a constant presence in Alton, even though much of it was hidden by levees. At highwater levels, nearby fields were flooded, and the dense trees that grew at the river's edge peeked up through water; it was the kind of place where Huckleberry Finn and Jim could have hidden their skiff. Alton was a town of grand houses rising up on the hills and bluffs on the north side, which the poorer families could see from their homes in the gullies below. It was a center of river commerce, of old families, and culture, but it was also a town in which farmers in coveralls, straw hats, and brogans moved sullenly through the streets when they came to town on Saturdays. Alton was the site of the last Lincoln-Douglas debate in 1858 and a stop on the Underground Railway. Yet it was also the place where Elijah P. Lovejoy, the abolitionist editor of the *Alton Observer*, was lynched in 1837.

The Davises' first child, Dorothy Mae, was born in Alton in 1924, two years before Miles III. Three years later, his father saw a chance to expand his practice into a specialization in oral surgery, and the Davis family moved downriver twenty-three miles to East St. Louis, Illinois, a much larger town with only one black dentist. The opportunities were real enough, but East St. Louis was a city with a troubled history that would doom it to fighting for its survival for years to come.

East St. Louis had begun with promise in the late eighteenth century as a ferry point to Missouri, and the sheer volume of activity in the area made it possible for St. Louis to become known as the Gateway to the West. East St. Louis lay in a floodplain, below the water level of the Mississippi, but its critical location close to river traffic and the major coal mines nearby made it a midwestern commercial and railroad center by the mid-1800s. After Chicago, it was the site of the second largest stockyard and railroad yard in the United States, where meat-packing companies like Hunter's, Swift, and Armour were based, along with a number of chemical and manufacturing companies. But most of the industrial and commercial development occurred outside the city limits, with some of the companies even being incorporated as their own cities. The result was a weak tax base that by 1920 made East St. Louis one of the poorest cities in America.

There was a southern feel to the wide streets, the large houses, and the many shotgun shacks. The areas in which black folks lived were divided into distinct neighborhoods, such as Rush City in the southwest, beyond the tracks, where the people were rural, kept farm animals, and still used oil lamps; the more sophisticated Polack Town in the Northeast; Goose Hill, next to the stockyard; and South End. Still, East St. Louis was a country town, filled with Arkansippians. "Upcountry," some called it, hip country. After 1900, the businesses around East St. Louis demanded new laborers as the city developed rapidly, and recruitment of foreign workers and black people in the South changed the profile of the population. Railroads brought great numbers of black people to town, sometimes to stay, sometimes to move on to Chicago or Detroit. Since local businesses at times used the new black workers as strikebreakers, racial tensions increased, and by 1917 had reached the point that skirmishes broke out between whites and blacks. Then, beginning in the evening of May 28, 1917, antiblack riots erupted; by the time they ended in July, hundreds of people had been wounded or injured, at least nine whites and thirty-nine blacks were dead, and hundreds of buildings had been burned. Many blacks escaped across city lines, hid in the basement of the post office, or fled across the bridge to St. Louis. Thousands of other black folks left the city, never to return. Outrage over the event sent shock waves across the United States, with state and federal investigations following. Black leaders such as W. E. B. DuBois, Madame C. J. Walker, Marcus Garvey, and Ida B. Wells became involved in the fallout.

With the Great Depression, many businesses moved away from the town or shut down. But demand for military production in World War II brought East St. Louis back to life, a new influx of cheap labor filling the town, raising its population to a peak of 80,000 in 1945, one-third of whom were black.

When they first moved to East St. Louis, the Davises lived in three rooms behind the dental office on the second floor of a brick building at 3 North Fifteenth Street at Broadway, over Daut's Drugstore. Fifteenth and Broadway was the black business and social center of the city, and within a few doors either way was the Ringside pool room, the Jolly Corner lounge, and the offices of a physician, Dr. John Eubanks. Across the street was the Peppermint Lounge and Restaurant. (On Friday and Saturday nights, young Miles could sit in his window and hear music of all sorts rising up from the street.) A service station was on one corner, a grocery on another, a hat shop next door to it. St. Augustine's Catholic School was just down the street, as was the Broadway Theater, a Greek restaurant, and the Southern, the only hotel in town for blacks. Within a few blocks south were more nightclubs and churches, the John Robinson School, the Paul Laurence Dunbar Elementary School, and O'Connor's hardware store. If you kept walking south, there were people who still raised chickens, hogs, and horses in their backyards.

Fifteenth and Broadway may have been the focus of black life in East St. Louis, but it was not entirely African American. There was also a large Armenian population that owned dry-cleaning shops, liquor stores, bars, and restaurants. A number of their stores and homes were located on the same block as Dr. Davis' office. A scattering of Germans and Greeks also lived in the neighborhood. The south side of town below nearby Missouri Avenue was largely black, and north of it was white.

In 1929, only two years after they'd moved to East St. Louis, the Depression hit, the same year that Miles' brother, Vernon, was born on November 3. Almost immediately, Dr. Davis' income fell when his working-class patients, black and white, were laid off and unable to pay him in cash. "They used to pay my father in script, the pink relief slips the government provided the out-of-work, or with stolen hams and cheese from the packing houses," Vernon Davis said. "We got so sick of ham and cheese: ham-and-cheese sandwiches, ham-and-cheese casseroles, ham-and-cheese what-have-you. But Father didn't make any real money until World War II." Paid in cash or not, Dr. Davis worked six days a week, seldom finishing with his patients before nine o'clock, just before the children were ready for bed.

The Davises were upper-middle-class people, even if they were not wealthy in the beginning, and they maintained certain standards in their home. They employed both a maid and a cook, and Dr. Davis insisted that all cooking be done from scratch—he had come from a family in which everyone cooked (his sister Josephine was head cook at a Works Progress Administration center during the Depression). And he himself always cooked his specialties—spaghetti and meatballs, oxtail stew, chili—on Saturdays, the night when he came home early. The Davises dressed in the latest fashions, Dr. Davis always in suits with a waistcoat, Mrs. Davis in furs and hats she designed and had made for her. The children were just as fashionable. Miles years later remembered the clothing his father bought him when he first began to wear long pants—Thom McCann boots, a yellow striped shirt, a tie, a gray double-breasted jacket, a cap, and a leather change purse. Vernon claimed that Miles' sense of fashion came from his mother: "He always dressed sharp, in vicuña coats, sharkskin suits, nothing but the best."

There were fifteen or so families with whom the Davises had close ties, people like the Hancocks (a physician and his family), the Summers (a lawyer's family), the Quinns (Mr. Quinn was a former principal of Lincoln High School), the Millers (Mr. Miller was then the current principal of Lincoln High School), the Smiths, and the Eubanks. On holidays like the Fourth of July, Labor Day, and New Year's, they took turns spending time at different houses. Dr. and Mrs. Davis were members of various social groups such as the Charleston Club, and they were active in community and church affairs. Sundays were family days, with services at St. Paul's Baptist Church (where Nat Turner's granddaughter Fanny was the organist), followed by ice-cream sundaes together at the drugstore downstairs. Some evenings they took the children to the Opera House in Kiel Auditorium, where they had season tickets, to see Vladimir Golschmann conduct the St. Louis Symphony and to hear soloists such as Rachmaninoff, Horowitz, and Prokofiev.

Dorothy and Miles started in Catholic schools when they moved from Alton, but then went on to public schools—first John Robinson Elementary School, then Attucks Elementary School and Lincoln High School. The black schools in East St. Louis were underfunded, in disrepair, always short of books and teachers, and for the rest of his life Miles recalled the condition of the toilets in the schools as a bitter emblem of life in his hometown. Though the schools had been legally desegregated in Illinois for many years, in practice most remained racially separate, so all three Davis children attended black schools. Yet "we weren't fooled," Vernon said. "Keeping white and black people separate was a joke. There were people in East St. Louis who came up from the South who weren't white there, but they became white here. There were students in school who were blue-eyed, with light skin and blonde hair, but they were black because they had people in their families who were black."

The Davises felt more comfortable with the Armenians they lived among, because they saw them as less prejudiced than other whites they knew. Miles' first best friend was an Armenian boy named Leo, who died in a fire when he was six. Both Miles and Vernon started school speaking some Armenian, but the teachers stopped them because most of what they knew were curse words. All three Davis children had white friends through high school. Among their other white neighbors was Mr. Blanke, a Jewish shopkeeper who impressed the Davis children with his worldliness and the fact that he could speak seven languages, which, he explained to them, he needed in order to survive in different countries.

Miles had been the baby of the family for three years, and he later complained that when Vernon was born, they dressed and cared for him "like a baby" until he was four, "his feet never touching the floor" as he was passed from mother to sister to grandmother and his mother's friends. Dorothy and her friends played with Vernon as if he were their doll, Miles said, bathing him and dressing him. He especially resented his maternal grandmother's attention to Vernon, and when Miles teased him, his grandmother hit him with a switch. Many times he wished that his grandmother would die (and when she did, he said he was terrified that he had caused it). Miles was determined that they were not going to raise him the same way—like a girl. And he made an effort to teach Vernon manly things like baseball and cursing—all in vain, he said.

The three children were close when they were young, talking and playing together, and entertaining each other. Several nights a week they staged a talent show for themselves, with Vernon and Dorothy singing pop songs and working up new routines based on dances like the Suzy-Q or the Snake Hips. Miles sat in front of them and acted as director, judge, and audience. When the children were a little older, their parents asked them to perform for their guests, Dorothy playing piano and Miles the trumpet, while Vernon danced or twirled the baton.

Miles felt that his parents were too strict with them as they grew up, not allowing them to hang out on the corner or go near pool halls and bars. He suffered the most: "I couldn't fool around. I knew that whatever I did, if it wasn't good, my father was going to strangle me." Yet it was his mother who did most of the punishing.

My mother would whip the shit out of me at the drop of a hat. She was into whipping so much that one time, when she couldn't do it because she was sick or something, she told my father to do it. He took me into a room, closed the door, and told me to scream like he was beating me. "Make some noise, like you're getting beat," I remember him saying. And then me screaming at the top of my lungs and him sitting there looking at me all steely-eyed. That was some funny shit, man. But now that I think about it, I would have almost preferred his whipping me to the way he used to look right through me like I was nothing. When he did that, he made me *feel* like I was nothing. That feeling was worse than a whipping could ever have been.

When Miles wrote in his autobiography that it was he who got the brunt of his mother's punishment, Vernon disagreed:

I don't know what Miles was talking about in his book: all three of us children were disciplined. Sometimes all together. We'd hide under the bed when Mother came after us to switch us, and then we got it again when our father came home. Miles may have been jealous, maybe because he sometimes had to baby-sit me, but he never showed it when he was living at home. Miles always wanted to be a tough guy.

Whatever else Miles might have said about it, Vernon added, Miles and his mother were always very close, as were they all. "He and I were like *Jack Armstrong, the All-American Boy*—the radio program we listened to every day after school. We were raised properly, with good manners and speech and respect. Miles wasn't always the way he appeared later." Even when he and Miles were apart in later years, Vernon said that he knew what his brother was thinking.

A few years after they came to East St. Louis, the Davises moved several blocks away from the office, to the corner of Seventeenth Street and Kansas Avenue. There, in a white thirteen-room house with red awnings, a garage, a large yard, a garden, and hedges, the children had the second floor to themselves. Diagonally across from them was a base-ball diamond where Miles played, and a few blocks down was Lincoln Park, one of the few city parks open to black people, with clay tennis courts, indoor and outdoor swimming pools, and summer jazz concerts played by local bands.

Miles was a skinny little child, quiet and shy, who kept his head down, avoiding eye contact, but a good boy who did well at school and enjoyed sports, strolling by the shops on Broadway, playing in the railroad yards, or wandering along the river and watching the barges and riverboats. He was seldom in trouble, though he and another boy, Millard Curtis, played hooky from school a few times, bringing a bag of biscuits and syrup or potted ham and crackers along with them, the two then climbing up to the catwalk at the bottom of a billboard. Miles once managed to climb a water tower and fell in, but got out by himself, and he and Vernon never told their parents. When he was twelve, he started his father's new Lin-coln Zephyr when no one was home and backed it out of the garage—into a telephone pole.

At age thirteen, Miles proudly began a paper route, delivering the *Chicago Defender*, the premier African American newspaper in the nation. It was the only day job he ever had, and later in life it was the only part of his youth that he enjoyed talking about. He told tales of close escapes from dogs, of meeting new people, and of the freedom it gave him to explore the town (though he managed to stay away from the rougher areas, like Goose Hill). He spent his earnings on candy, barbe-cue, and phonograph records.

As he moved into his teen years, he played stickball and baseball, and like other boys his age in East St. Louis, he began to be drawn to boxing. Though he and his friends did not train or enter the ring—never going beyond wrestling or playful punches to the chest—it occupied their thoughts and shaped their images of themselves. Boxing was popular in East St. Louis among black men, though to most it did not represent a possible means of economic and social mobility. Nor was it a metaphor for a kind of art or intellectual activity. Rather, it was a stance, a way of moving in your clothes, a way of being a man. This was important to Miles, because his size and color made him the object of a certain kind of abuse. Like many other people in black communities of the time, he had several nicknames, both positive and negative. His parents called him Junior, his friends called him Little Davis or Little Doc Davis, and some people called him Buckwheat, a name that stuck to him even when he returned home for visits after he became nationally known.

Miles remembered his mother as beautiful and stylish and described her as looking "East Indian." (Vernon said that one promoter recommended billing Miles himself as an Indian, and another thought he was Mexican.) She was beautiful not only physically, but in attitude. "Mother was a *lady*," Miles would say, in every sense of that word, especially as it was denied black women in the South. Yet she was also cold and distant, "blank-faced . . . no expression," he said, and could withdraw from being touched. His father was dignified and imposing, and a man who moved easily in high society. He was a decent golfer, and Miles caddied for him when he played tournaments in St. Louis with other black professionals and visiting stars such as Joe Louis. Most impressive to Miles was the way in which his father dealt with the law. Once when he was stopped by white police on the highway, his father pulled out his honorary sheriff's badge and said, "I've got one of those, too. What do you want?"

Behind the family's social manners and affluent surface, however, were volatility and deep antagonism. Their mother and father fought openly for years. Much of their lives were spent apart, Dr. Davis' long hours of work, his many interests, and his involvement with local political affairs keeping him away from home; and when they were together, anything could set them off—dressing for a party, a visit from relatives, dinnertime. Once in a fit of anger, his mother threw an iron at his father, just missing his head. Following an argument on another occasion, she locked him out of the house, and he punched through the glass door that separated them and broke her teeth. Miles recalled being upset by this, and crying out that now they would have to spend even more time together while his father fixed her teeth.

Dr. Davis was a gambler and had lost as much as $250,000 according to Mrs. Davis. This was a source of constant friction. They also fought over Miles. "When I was eleven," Miles remembered, "my mother said, 'Spank Miles,' and my father would say, 'For what?' She'd say, 'He's crazy'; he'd say, 'Remember that.'" Miles often found himself having to stand between them to prevent violence. Their verbal combativeness spread to the children: "Miles, Vernon, and Dorothy Mae all cursed like sailors," a girlfriend said. "Miles, especially, was an expert on profanity even though he used it as descriptive terms, as adjectives." (Miles said that the first thing his father said when he got up every morning was "Shit!")

It was in their teens that Dorothy noticed that Vernon was often seen with a group of gay men in town and told Miles. The two of them kept it a secret as best they could, but when their mother and father eventually found out, their marriage developed yet another line of fracture.

The precarious civility within the family was not helped by the move of Dr. Davis' sister Corrine to East St. Louis. While she was working in Chicago as a bank teller, she had developed an interest in fortune-telling and clairvoyance and decided to open up shop as a psychic and palm reader downstate. Once she was set up in East St. Louis, with a sign outside her shop reading "Dr. Corrine, Reader, Healer" and her diploma in metaphysics hanging on the wall, she did well, with both white and black clients who came to her for readings. She was popular with the Davis children, since she entertained them and read their personalities (Miles, she said, was connected to infinity, and as a Gemini was the kind of person who was "flighty and changed his mood quickly"). But Aunt Corrine didn't like Mrs. Davis and once, exercising her spiritual powers, told Dr. Davis that Dorothy was not his child (Miles and Vernon scoffed at this, saying that Dorothy was the only member of his family who really looked like their father). This, added to rumors that Dr. Davis was a ladies' man, was unsettling.

The breaking point for them came just before the war, when Cleota accused her husband of having an affair with a woman in his office. They separated, with Dr. Davis moving over to St. Louis, the children staying with their mother. When their parents divorced a short time later, Miles took it badly, arguing with his mother, chafing at her efforts to advise him, and once even slapping her. Some might have said that he seemed to be assuming his father's role, and Vernon said that "sometimes Miles would say something to me, and I'd say, 'My god, you sound just like Daddy!'" But he believed that Miles was more complex than that: "Parts of Mother and Father were mixed in Miles. That was his Gemini quality." Though Miles sometimes blamed his mother more than his father, he also understood his father's failings. Years later, while commenting to an interviewer on why he never wanted to go into dentistry after he worked in his father's office, he homed in on what caused the divorce:

> That's when I said, never again. Because you don't do anything. You just sit there, people come in, you fix their teeth or you operate on them and that's it. You go to the office and do the same thing. I'm not like that. I have to be finding out things. And it's so weird, to say you're a doctor in a black community. Women say, shit, my daughter's going out with such and such a person and his father's a doctor. What does that mean? That means that he's gonna be in an office all day, he's gonna make love to his secretary. I seen my father.

A few years later, Dr. Davis bought a farm of 160 acres in the rolling hills of Millstadt, eight miles south of East St. Louis, which he named Mary Frances Manor after his mother. There, he bred Landrace hogs—an English breed—and Chester White swine, keeping cows and as many as fifteen horses (which he and other horsemen rode as entertainment at halftime at local football games). Whether driving his luxury cars or sitting on the porch of his white colonial house with its gardens and guesthouse overlooking a lake, he was the consummate gentleman farmer. As the first black person in a largely German American farm community, Dr. Davis faced harassing phone calls and stones thrown at the house in the dark. But eventually the community accepted him, at least tacitly, by his resistance to the threats and by the success of his farm. Soon he was buying prize animals, including a boar from the farms of Winston Churchill, or holding annual auctions on the farm that drew breeders from across the country. Dr. Davis became involved in local politics, and while he was fighting for a fire department to be established in Millstadt, he made an unsuccessful run for state representative of Illinois. Miles also recalled him as being a Garveyite, or at least sympathetic to the separatist cause of Marcus Garvey and opposed to the integrationist ideology of the National Association for the Advancement of Colored People (though Vernon said that he had never heard his father mention Garvey).

Miles loved the farm. He had his own horse there and loved to spend days riding across the fields, walking among the livestock, or hearing his trumpet ring out across the lake. (In later years, musicians often dropped by the farm to see him. Charlie Parker once came by, and Vernon remembered him wearing a suit as he walked through the pig pens and the barn, then looking at Miles and saying, "So *this* is why you're like you are.")

The battling between the Davises didn't cease after the separation. Any contact between husband and wife seemed to set them off. And later, when Mrs. Davis' cousin died and left her money, giving her some independence, things seemed to grow even worse. (At one point, Dr. Davis became so angry with his wife that he stopped giving her the money they had agreed on, cutting it in half. When he refused to pay more than half of Dorothy's tuition to Fisk University, Miles, then sixteen years old, paid the rest from his music earnings.) The only thing that could bring his parents together, according to Vernon, was Miles' drug addiction in later years.

The Davises were aggressive about their children's success, though Miles said his father urged him to do whatever he wanted as long as he succeeded, while his mother was more focused in her aspirations. Dr. Davis encouraged Miles and Vernon in the arts, and once they began to show some interest in drawing, even gave them a few lessons. But their mother wanted both of the boys to be dentists ("Artists don't make money," Vernon recalled her telling them again and again), and Dorothy to be a teacher, which she later became, in the Chicago school system. "But my mother was never impressed with Miles' music. Even years later when I'd say, 'That's your son on the radio,' she'd say, 'Is it?' and keep right on dusting. We finally got mother to go to a nightclub to hear Miles play. He played so well, but she just sat there and listened and said nothing."

From age nine on, Miles wanted to play the trumpet because he liked the way men looked playing it. But his mother thought the violin, an instrument she had played, was a better choice. Yet the trumpet was destined to win out because the St. Louis area was famous for its trumpet players, who had learned their instrument in the marching bands of the black fraternities and social clubs and had gone on to become professionals in concert and dance halls, on riverboats and in nightclubs. When Miles was ten, Dr. John Eubanks gave him his first horn, a cornet, which seemed to fit his small hands and short arms better than the longer trumpet, and it was Eubanks' uncle, Horace, who gave Miles his first instruction on the horn, at the end of his paper route every day. Although the lessons were informal, they were enough to allow him to learn "Stardust," the Hoagy Carmichael hit that every dance band trumpet player had mastered by the late 1930s, and by the time summer came, he was made bugler at Boy Scout camp.

Miles became consumed by music, listening late at night in bed to live radio broadcasts from across the country, often not getting to sleep until five in the morning, then trying to hear the fifteen-minute *Harlem Rhythms* program at 8:45 in the morning and still get to school by 9:00. He spent afternoons practicing, ordering music through the mail, teaching himself harmony from George A. Gibbs' *Modern Chord Construction and Analysis*, or shopping for used jukebox phonograph records for a dime apiece. (Among the records he recalled buying were Coleman Hawkins' "Woody 'n' You," Jay McShann's "Hootie Blues" and "Swingmatism," Lester Young's "Sometimes I'm Happy," Art Tatum's "Get Happy," Duke Ellington's "J. B. Blues," and others by Albert Ammons,

Billy Eckstine, Dizzy Gillespie, Jimmie Lunceford, Boyd Raeburn, and Charlie Christian with Benny Goodman. His brother remembered Miles also looking for records with Buddy Rich on drums and those with Helen Forrest singing with Benny Goodman.)

He began formal music lessons in the sixth grade at the Attucks Grade School with Elwood C. Buchanan, Sr., a professional musician who visited each elementary school one day a week to give instruction. It was Buchanan who urged Miles' father to buy him his own horn, and on Miles' thirteenth birthday his gift was a new trumpet.

Buchanan was an African American educator in the Booker T. Washington mold. He played the trumpet himself on the riverboats and in local bands, making part of his living from it, and he was serious about the study of music. If a boy took up a musical instrument, he was entering an African American tradition of commitment, masculinity, and passion. It allowed for no other interests of the same magnitude. He even discouraged Miles from playing baseball for fear that he'd be hit in the mouth. As a trumpet player himself, Buchanan put special attention to the embouchure—the technique of the lips, breathing, the use of the tongue—and fingering, and he stressed self-control and discipline. Students were pitted against each other competitively, and mistakes were openly mocked by the others. Criticism from the teacher was intense and praise stinting. When Buchanan once told him that he couldn't hear him when he was playing in the band, Miles said he almost cried. (He salved himself by thinking, "They play loud, but I got the soul.") It was widely reported that Davis came in second or third in school trumpet competitions behind whites who were inferior musicians, but Miles insisted this wasn't true, just something that writers made up. Buchanan himself said that "he received all first awards with my band groups that competed in the Illinois State High School Music Association concerts."

Miles had heard classical trumpet soloists with the St. Louis Symphony and knew that what they played went beyond what he was learning. So once a week he crossed over to St. Louis and paid $2.50 for a half-hour lesson with Joseph Gustat, the principal trumpeter with the symphony and a teacher who had trained many of the area's trumpeters, including Elwood Buchanan. Gustat insisted that his students use a mouthpiece designed by Gustav Heim, the trumpeter who had preceded him in the first chair with the symphony, and then went on to play for the Boston Symphony. It was an unusually thin mouthpiece that produced a round, big sound rather than a high, bright one, and some claim that it was the source of a distinctive St. Louis trumpet sound.

Gustat was a technician who demanded a legitimate tone and proper technique from his students, and the kind of teacher who thought bleeding lips were part of the learning process. But Miles was impressed by Gustat's ability to play an entire C scale with one valve down by lip strength alone or run a chromatic scale spread over two octaves seventeen times on a single breath. When Miles first played for him, Gustat told him that he was the worst trumpet player he'd ever heard. But Miles took the criticism in stride and worked all the harder, practicing longer, working on the fundamentals, learning to play without vibrato in the classical manner. Vernon Davis described him as tirelessly searching for perfection on the horn, though often in conflict with his mother's aspirations:

> Miles would be practicing down in the basement the same thing over and over. He practiced long tones, slowly, looking for quality. "Why does he keep doing that," Mother asked. "It's practicing, Mother," Vernon said. "Why doesn't he sound like Louis Armstrong?" She loved Armstrong and Ellington's music. Mother told him that he should play something you can whistle. Not bebop, all up in the air. Years later, he was talking to her after a concert where he'd played "Someday My Prince Will Come." He said, "Was that all right with you, Mother?"

His first chance to play music with others was also his first job as a professional: he played a dance with a trio of Horace Eubanks (whose alto saxophonist tone and vibrato, Miles said, made him sound like someone out of Guy Lombardo's sax section), and a pianist and a drummer, reading melodies from sheet music like "Auld Lang Syne," "Honeysuckle Rose," "Body and Soul," "Maria Elena," and their big number, "Nagasaki." Little Davis made six dollars playing for "white people" in Belleville, the county headquarters of the Ku Klux Klan. Soon Miles was pestering these older musicians about when he could begin playing a solo without reading music.

After school, friends from the school band like Raleigh McDonald, Elbert "Red" Bonner, Duck Waters, and Frank Gully came over to the Davises' because Miles had sheet music and exercise books, and they sat out on the back porch jiving, playing cards, listening to records, practicing parts for the high school band, and showing off for girls who walked by. Miles sometimes rehearsed an eighteen-piece dance band he squeezed into their basement, using instrumental parts he painstakingly copied off popular dance band records. The band never worked publicly, and to keep them together, Miles sometimes had to pay some of them to come, but it established him as a serious musician among his friends.

"Miles always had a learning attitude," according to Vernon. "He taught two other students to play the trumpet while he was in high school."

Vernon was also interested in music and had been twirling the baton since he was six or seven. When he was nine, Miles recommended him to Mr. Buchanan, who then made him the drum major in the high school band. (Later, Vernon took up the trumpet himself, practicing with Miles and playing duets with him, and went on to study trumpet at the American Conservatory of Music in Chicago, even playing a few times with the Sun Ra Arkestra.)

Miles and some of his friends next formed a small band that played once in a while in Huff's Summer Garden, a nightspot with a better clientele and close enough to their house that Miles' father allowed him to play there. While the more seasoned musicians entertained those inside the bar and on the dance floor, Miles and his friends played current pop hits like "In the Mood" and "Tuxedo Junction" in the outdoor garden with its big pool of goldfish, surrounded by tables with umbrellas.

Louis Armstrong and Roy Eldridge were the favorites of most young trumpet players in those days, but when Miles began playing, it was Harry James who fascinated him. James was a handsome bandleader, a movie star, and a horse breeder who was married to Betty Grable, the quintessential pinup girl of World War II Hollywood. After he saw a photo of James in a velvet-collared jacket, Miles got his mother to sew velvet collars on all his jackets. When he saw James dressed in a green tab-collar shirt and a brown knit tie, he rushed straight to Boyd's men's store in St. Louis to match it, but with no luck.

Miles' playing impressed a slightly older trumpet player named Clark Terry, who began to drop by the Davis house when Miles was fourteen and asked his parents if Miles could go with him to jam sessions at the Moonlight Inn. There they'd sometimes play from six in the evening to six the next morning. Miles followed Terry's lead of practicing from a clarinet exercise book, and then from books of piano études, in order to increase his speed and articulation. When they played together, Miles would tease Terry by repeating whatever he had just played. On weekends, he and Terry might go to Ned Love's in Centreville, a big barn of a place with a large stage, where a house rhythm section was always on hand and jam sessions lasted until well into the morning. The level of the playing was high enough that musicians like tenor saxophonist Jimmy Forrest (of "Night Train" fame) dropped by when he was home from touring with the Andy Kirk band. These sessions were deeply communal affairs but also highly competitive, with the musicians being challenged by an audience that cheered them on like athletes, with cries for them to "work." These were ritualized events where sweat was a visible sign of commitment and soul and the musicians playing until they dropped. They played jazz, not what East St. Louis musicians called "funky butt," the music of the working folk that others might call rhythm and blues.

Miles came from a remarkably successful family. Among his father's brothers was a journalist who had studied at Harvard and in Germany, a nationally known minister, and an undertaker; on his mother's side, her uncle William Pickens was president of the NAACP; and his father had three college degrees. It was all very intimidating to a boy whose choice of a profession seemed downwardly mobile at best to his family. Still, music seemed a natural choice for Miles, not only because he was good at it, but also because to him it made practical sense in the American racial arena:

> I just got onto the trumpet and studied and played. It would have been that or something else; a lot of black people think that to keep from being Jim Crowed and shit like that you have to be a professional man and know a bit of something. But then if you want an engineer or an architect or something, who do you get? You don't go to a black man.

Years later, shortly after his father died, Miles reflected on his father's profession and the costs of being a black professional:

> I got to thinking about my father the other night. . . . I thought about how he spent his whole life trying to be better than the "niggers"—and I started crying. He could have been a musician, too, you know—I have slave ancestors that played string music on the plantations—but that wasn't what my grandfather wanted for him. He thought there were more important things to do than entertain white folks.

With Buchanan's encouragement, Miles began to work on developing what he called "a Midwestern sound, a round sound with no attitude in it . . . a voice with not too much tremolo and not too much bass." He had studied classical music and jazz and also absorbed country, blues, and church music:

I also remember how the music used to sound down there in Arkansas, when I was visiting my grandfather, especially at the Saturday night church. . . . I guess I was about six or seven. We'd be walking on these dark country roads at night and all of a sudden this music would seem to come out of nowhere. . . . A man and a woman singing and talking about getting *down!* . . . That *kind* of sound in music, that blues, church back-road funk kind of thing, that Southern, Midwestern, rural sound and rhythm. I think it started getting into my blood on them spook-filled Arkansas back-roads after dark when the owls came out hooting. So when I started taking lessons I might have already had some idea of what I wanted my music to sound like.

He was beginning to play the trumpet with a vocal quality that disguised its valve-and-piston mechanical nature and erased the instrument's heritage of war and heraldry, the masculine identity attached to its history. He had found a way to personalize the instrument, return breath and voice to it, and in doing so he converged on a style of music that had often been identified with white players from the Midwest like cornetist Bix Beiderbecke, a style rooted in lieder and European brass bands. But Miles' playing was also deeply inflected by the blues: he could signify with a single note, make it sing with the phrasing and the declamatory quality of some blues singers, or murmur with the small vibrato and introspective phrasing of others. Or he could make that note shimmer and hang in the air like the steel-string stroke of a blues guitarist.

In the story of jazz, St. Louis takes a backseat to New Orleans, New York, and Chicago. In jazz history, St. Louis is designated a ragtime town, the place where Scott Joplin and Tom Turpin first played and wrote rags and where Joplin would write his first opera, A *Guest of Honor.* But things are not that simple. The New Orleans bands, like the riverboats themselves, wintered in New Orleans and came north to dock and operate from St. Louis all summer. St. Louis regularly got to hear New Orleans musicians like Fate Marable, Louis Armstrong, and Red Allen on those boats and off them. New Orleanians like drummer Zutty Singleton and Jelly Roll Morton recorded with local St. Louis bands, and area musicians such as Charlie Creath, Dewey Jackson, and Elwood C. Buchanan, Sr., were heard on the boats when they reached New Orleans. What these riverboat musicians played was often fairly simple, a music for dancing, but they played it well, gracefully and easily, laying a basis for the jazz to come. By the early 1900s, St. Louis may have been the center of ragtime, but it was also primed for the development of jazz.

The St. Louis area was also rich in the blues. It was there, after all, that W. C. Handy first heard the blues from "shabby guitarists" singing a song called "East St. Louis Blues." It was also where Ma Rainey heard her first blues and where some of the first blues in sheet music form was published. By the late 1920s, the St. Louis area had resident blues performers such as Lonnie Johnson, Roosevelt Sykes, Henry Townsend, Peetie Wheatstraw, and Walter Davis. Although ragtime and the blues were at times competing crazes, the blues could also be heard played inside rags. And some blues bands in the St. Louis area used harmonicas and trombones together with two guitars for a music very close to jazz.

East St. Louis may have been a poor sister city to a cultural and economic metropolis like St. Louis in many ways, yet black people in that part of Illinois never saw themselves as its second-class citizens. Missouri had been a slave state, and what with St. Louis' blue laws—a strange state government system that ran the city's school boards and the police from Jefferson City—the residents of East St. Louis reassured themselves by seeing the folks across the river as somewhat behind the times. East St. Louis clubs stayed open after those in St. Louis closed, and whites felt free to cross the river to drink and party in black-owned bars in an environment reminiscent of New Orleans. Musicians moved easily between one town and the other, and East St. Louis was a stopping-off point for instrumentalists traveling on the trains running between the South and Chicago or Detroit. "East Boogie" was the name given it by some, a blues town, a gangster town, with its own red-light district, distinct music and food, and a remarkable array of nightclubs and bars—places like Ned Love's, the Barrel, Red Top, the Harlem Club, Ruby's Lounge, the Red Inn, El Patio, the Mellow Cellar, the Paris Lounge, the Blue Note, La Casa, the Blue Flame Club, Club Manhattan, the Town Talk Tavern, the Cotton Club, and the Sportsman Lounge.

In 1942, Clark Terry introduced Miles to a pianist named Emmanuel St. Claire Brooks (often called Duke, for his knowledge of the Ellington repertoire). Brooks played with Terry in a band supported by one of the anti-Depression measures sponsored by the National Recovery Administration, and which rehearsed daily and played in the parks and for public functions. Brooks played in the fleet-fingered Nat "King" Cole style, and sometimes worked with the great bassist Jimmy Blanton at the Red Inn.

During high school lunchtimes, Miles walked several blocks to Brooks' mother's house, where he learned harmony at the piano in the room off the back porch where Brooks slept. Often Miles had heard other musicians say, "Little Davis, you can't get any jobs because you play too modern," so he saw in Brooks someone who could understand what he was doing and asked him to help form their own band. Soon, Miles, Brooks, and a drummer, Nick Haywood, were playing as a trio in places like the cocktail lounge at the Carver Bowling Alley, copying Benny Goodman's Trio on tunes like "Air Mail Special."

Until he was sixteen, Miles had shown little interest in girls. Outside of his family—mostly without his parents' knowledge—he was moving in a world of musicians, prostitutes, gamblers, and hustlers of various stripes, dressing and acting as if he were much older, even though he never drank more than the occasional glass of wine. But he also stuck close to the orbit of the high school band, kept up with his schoolwork, never dated, and when he went to house parties he hung around with the boys. Then, in 1942, he suddenly became aware of Irene Cawthon, a senior with bright eyes, delicate features, tiny feet, and long, straight hair. "What attracted Miles to me," said Irene, "was that I was very visible."

> I was in glee club, cheering squad, drill team, elected as the Most Classy person in my class. A basketball player who was also in the band—Carlos Faulkner—told me that "Little Doc" Davis wanted to talk with me. I had never even heard of him. So I said, "Well, tell him to come see me, and I'll have a Snickers bar with him." So the next day there was Miles waiting at the door of my typing class, with a Snickers for me. After that we'd wait for each other at the door of the school every day. . . . We were inseparable.

They did everything together from then on, meeting before and after school and calling each other at all hours. Irene had a part-time job at Klein's Department Store in St. Louis, and when the store was open evenings, Miles took a trolley across the bridge and waited for her outside. Between her work and his, they had money, dressed well, and attracted attention. But this was not a relationship that pleased his father. She was two years older than Miles, and Irene was literally from the wrong side of the tracks: Goose Hill, a neighborhood near the stockyards, where you could see the workers from the killing floors—the slaughterhouses—leaving work with their coveralls stained with blood, where Miles recalled the smell of "burnt meat and hair . . . the smell of death." Irene's father was dead, and her mother—a beautiful woman, polite and graceful—had remarried. Still, they were not the kind of people Dr. Davis had in mind for Miles' future. Nonetheless, he put up with it, and when Irene invited Miles to her senior prom, his father allowed him to use the car for the first time. Miles bought her a huge rose corsage that almost covered her left shoulder. "Everything had to be big with Miles," she said. Yet as musical as he was, Miles hadn't learned how to dance and had no interest in learning. Irene was graceful enough that she made Miles look good on the floor.

They became lovers, wherever and whenever they could, Miles slipping money to Irene's younger brother to leave them alone in her house. Then they became something more than lovers—dreaming of a life together, a future they could share. Irene knew that Miles was gifted, and she pushed him to make himself more visible, to present himself in the best possible way:

> Miles was like a sponge. He absorbed everything around him. He was young, talented, and beautiful, and I believed that he would be famous. But he was afraid to try out for anything. He had never taken part in trumpet competitions, and never really tried to reach higher.

She even coached him on his stage manner. "Miles always played with his trumpet pointed down. I tried to get him to hold it higher, but he said he could hear himself better that way." She was not alone in trying to bring Miles out. Elwood Buchanan had been unsuccessful at convincing him to try out for Eddie Randle's Blue Devils, one of the most popular dance bands in St. Louis. Randle's band was often compared to Al Cooper's Savoy Sultans of Harlem, a group with rhythmic drive and a great feeling for the blues. The Blue Devils also had a history of fine musicians passing through on their way to national acclaim—Jimmy Forrest and Ernie Wilkins, for example, and some exceptional trumpet players, such as Clark Terry and the legendary Levi Madison—and Randle himself was a trumpet player who had come up playing on the riverboats. Irene, too, kept daring him to call Randle, telling him he should be playing somewhere other than those smoky little clubs where his father allowed him to play in East St. Louis. Finally, early in 1943, he made the call, and Randle agreed to a tryout. When the night came for his audition, Irene carried his trumpet to make sure he would go through with it. Together, they went over to the Castle Ballroom in St. Louis where Randle's band was appearing, and Miles auditioned in front of the evening's audience.

The older musicians in the band saw Miles as just a kid and were surprised when he was hired. But Randle said that "Miles came prepared with the fundamentals, the ability to read music at first sight, technical skills, and the like." And Miles held his own, gaining respect for his thoughtful solos played with a beautiful tone. On Miles' first night with the band, Randle said that he was scared to death. Seated in the trumpet section between Randle and Irving Wood, he found himself worrying not about how to play a solo but how to attack a note, how to "play from his stomach"—phrasing long passages with one breath, and with a huffing motion that pushed the sound forward—as well as with the subtleties of emphasis and volume that make an instrumental section sound as one horn. Randle's group was the house band at the Rhumboogie, a club located in the Elks Club, where they had a weekly job either alternating with eastern bands like Cab Calloway's, or playing for dancers and drinkers at the bar who sipped from the half-pint bottles the club sold, and providing music for exotic dancers, and comedian-singers like Butterbeans and Suzie or Fred and Sled. There, from ten to four in the morning, Little Davis held his own, even with some of his teachers sitting in the audience.

The Rhumboogie drew visiting musicians after their own gigs were over, and one night shortly after Miles' audition, saxophonist Sonny Stitt and trumpeter Howard McGhee dropped by and asked to sit in. Stitt and McGhee were two of the earliest players to embrace bebop, and though often passed over by audiences in favor of Charlie "Yardbird" Parker and Dizzy Gillespie, they were known to hip musicians as famished and classy contenders in their own right, who on a good night could eat you alive. Eddie Randle recalled that moment:

> Howard started playing—Howard played nice trumpet—Stitt played some. And I said, "OK, Miles." And then it was Miles' turn to play. Miles was a youngster, his knees was knocking! I laughed, I said, "Miles didn't need any drummer. His knees was keeping time." He didn't realize it, but at that time he was, as the guys used to say, cutting heads thin. He was growing out of this world. He was good and he didn't know it. He had a beautiful sound.

Sonny Stitt was impressed too and later came around to the Davis house to teach him some "little licks" and try to enlist him in the Tiny Bradshaw band that he was traveling with. But when Miles' mother refused to let him drop out of school, he "cried like a baby," according to Stitt. Miles and his mother argued for days, and she urged him to wait and get a good job at the post office instead of becoming a musician. When he told her to leave him alone, she slapped him, and he slapped her back. "Just because you're my mother doesn't mean that I should believe everything you tell me. And I'm not asking you nothing. If I want to know something I'll go ask my father—that's manly and stuff." But his father rejected the idea as well.

Other visiting musicians were equally impressed by Miles and wanted him in their bands: Illinois Jacquet later also offered him a job, as did McKinney's Cotton Pickers. When Lester Young played the Club Riviera in St. Louis, Miles sat in with him and was encouraged by how good he sounded with him. (The pianist with Young at that time remembered that Davis "had that man walking on eggshells sound" even then.) Miles, like most other musicians his age, was drawn to the bebop that was beginning to emerge in the East. He had first seen Charlie Parker in St. Louis at the Riviera Club, and when he spoke to him briefly, Parker told him to look him up when he got to New York City. Randle saw where Miles was headed musically, and he begged him not to sacrifice that beautiful tone for technique, for playing only with flash. "When he played with Parker he lost some of his sound, but he got it back eventually."

Because he was the only member of the band without a day job, Miles was given the responsibility of organizing rehearsals, and soon he was rehearsing music for the routines of the singers and dancers who worked the floor show at the club. His mother never went to nightclubs, so Miles returned nights from playing in the Rhumboogie and told her about the acts—singing for her, showing her the two-step, getting her to laugh by telling her about the bawdy songs and jokes. He was sixteen years old, making between $85 and $125 a week, driving his father's car to the club, and owned ten suits that he'd picked up in pawnshops. When the suits he bought weren't in the latest fashion, he'd make small changes in them, like cutting the pockets off the vests and moving them to different places. At a time when many younger black men were wearing long coats with a one-button roll, high-rise peg pants with little cuffs, white-on-white shirts with huge, roll collars, all of it topped off with pearl-gray double-breasted overcoats called six-button Bennys, Miles and his friends dressed more conservatively. Their jackets were cut short, and their shirts had collars so stiff with starch that they'd chafe their necks if they turned their heads too fast. Their nails were coated with clear polish, their shoes had a hard, deep shine, and they walked a little dip walk and called themselves *el gatos*. They were sharp and clean.

Miles was drawn to fashionable actors and musicians, like Cary Grant and Walter Pidgeon. But Fred Astaire and the duke of Windsor were his models: he wanted notches in his lapels just like the duke wore, and with Astaire, it was his small size and his movement that fascinated him. For Miles, looks and playing were so closely allied that after gigs, he often asked not, "How'd I play?" (because he knew), but, "How'd I look?" Clothes, especially shoes, competed with music for his attention.

He was astonished when women sent him notes on the bandstand or tried to pick him up. Years later, he became convinced that they were attracted to him because he was innocent and didn't know anything about sex. But at the time, he didn't know what to make of it and remained loyal to Irene.

Irene and Miles began to make plans to leave East St. Louis to go to New York City together. She had studied dance since she was seven, and Katherine Dunham was the only black dancer she had ever heard of and the only one with a school and a dance company. She fantasized studying with Dunham and touring with her company, though Miles warned her that African American dancers were not allowed to perform anywhere but nightclubs. Miles wanted nothing except to learn about the new jazz and to play with Dizzy Gillespie and Charlie Parker, and for that, New York City was the only place to be. A local piano prodigy he knew, Eugene Haynes, had been accepted into the Juilliard School of Music in New York the year before, so that began to look like a possibility that might be acceptable to his parents. His mother wanted him to go to Fisk, like his sister, and told him that Fisk had a fine music department and that he could sing with the Fisk Jubilee Singers. Again, it was Irene who urged Miles on, writing away to Juilliard for him for applications and brochures.

Miles bought a copy of the The 1944 Esquire Jazz Book, the first of a series of annuals the magazine produced. He pored over photos of Duke Ellington and Cab Calloway hanging out with Orson Welles, shots of Oscar Pettiford, Louis Armstrong, Coleman Hawkins, Billie Holiday, Sidney Bechet, Lionel Hampton, and the Esquire All-American Band—all of them looking stylish and at ease. There were no pictures or bios or critics' choices of young beboppers, for the book was all about hot jazz, the old-style jazz. Although there was a "Historical Chart of Jazz Influences," it stopped at swing. Still, the message was clear: New York City was the place to be. Miles showed it to his mother again and again, as if it were a catalogue of new bicycles or BB guns, and disingenuously asked her where all of this was happening.

He finished his senior year in January 1944, although graduation was not until June. He was seventeen and making plans to leave for his audition for Juilliard, when Irene told him that she was pregnant. Miles' father was furious. He told Miles that she was not the kind of person he should marry and that she would only be a distraction from his studies. Aunt Corrine joined in against her, calling her "a hussy" and casting spiritualist doubt about the baby's being Miles' child. Only his mother thought that their getting married was the right thing to do. Miles argued with his father, telling him that he loved Irene and that it was his responsibility as a man to marry her. But his father refused to give him the legal permission he needed to marry her at his age. Their baby was born in June 1944, a girl they named Cheryl.

Almost halfway through 1944, Miles was recommended as a one-week replacement for trumpeter Thomas Jefferson in Adam Lambert's Six Brown Cats, a swing group from New Orleans that included singer Joe Williams and was working its way north, playing next in Springfield for dancing and strippers' and comedians' acts. It was Miles' first trip that far north and an opportunity to see more of Illinois. For the first time, he saw just how much East St. Louis was surrounded by country. The farm fields seemed to stretch on forever, the roads as flat and straight as a ruler, most of them running nowhere he wanted to go.

He was back in East St. Louis just in time to hear that Billy Eckstine had organized a band of young beboppers and was bringing them to St. Louis for two weeks. Eckstine had recently made a splash as a barrel-voiced baritone singer with the Earl Hines Band, where he had a number of rhythm and blues hits. Still, his reputation rested on only a couple of singles that folks had heard on the radio. Musicians traveling through the Midwest passed on stories of what was happening in the music, but without magazines or movies that covered black music, it was difficult to imagine what was going on in the East or even in Chicago. When Eckstine reached town, it was clear that he was much more than a singer. With his jacket cut low on his neck to accentuate the high roll of the collars on his tailored shirts, a stickpin studded with the monogram "BE" piercing his silk cravats (which earned him the nickname "B"), his pants a miracle of high rise, drape, and taper, he was the model for a certain kind of postwar black man: handsome, debonair, a lover of beautiful women and choice wines, a crossover star with a loyal interracial audience, and a fighter. He was quick to slap a woman or punch a man— white or black, he didn't care—or to leave a nightclub a message by ripping the strings out of a poorly tuned piano when the band was leaving. He took no stuff from nobody.

After a successful year as a solo singer in 1943 (billed as Billy X-Stine on 52nd Street in New York City, and later as "the Sepia Sinatra"), he formed his band using as many of the musicians who had been with Hines as he could get. With arrangements by people like Count Basie, Boyd Raeburn, Tadd Dameron, Budd Johnson, and Gil Fuller to build on, with Dizzy Gillespie as musical director, Art Blakey on drums, Charlie Parker, Lucky Thompson, Leo Parker, and Gene Ammons among the saxophonists, and with vocals by himself and Sarah Vaughan, they hit the road in the spring for a tour of the South and the Midwest. They were excited by the music they were playing, and although they were an odd assemblage of individualists—some of whom were very difficult— they were all deadly serious about their work. Each of the sections of the band rehearsed on its own, and Dizzy Gillespie and Charlie Parker worked out their own ideas back in their hotel rooms.

By summer, the Eckstine band was booked into the Plantation Club in St. Louis, a popular gangster-owned nightspot for whites (a club that Miles always remembered as being located next to a hospital for heart disease that would not accept blacks as patients). But the band's engagement ended the first week when a few of the musicians disregarded some of the town's Jim Crow codes. B, for one, insisted on coming in through the front door, and Charlie Parker on one occasion walked through the club, drinking water from each table, then breaking the glasses on the floor to relieve the waiters of the problem of having to wash them. But the band was quickly picked up by a posh black nightspot, the Club Riviera, where Eckstine spent the days rehearsing the band's new book and the nights putting it on display.

Miles had heard Eckstine's first recordings on jukeboxes—the sophisticated "Good Jelly Blues" and the roaring "I Stay in the Mood for You"—and though it was only a studio band backing B's vocals, the hip phrasing of the brass section, its raucous shaken notes, and Dizzy Gillespie's solo on "Mood" (which seemed to come soaring from out of a cloud of chords) were thrilling. ("It was like being in a box of firm titties," Miles later said.) They played with youthful energy and a restless anticipation that marked the way they attacked every note. Live, Eckstine's road band was amazing: the soloists lined up on the side of the stage for their moment at the lone microphone, like batters waiting their turns at the plate. Some joked and mugged for the audience and each other, some distanced themselves in an almost trancelike state of relaxed indifference, and others came out like boxers muscling aside their inferiors. It was this band, more than Dizzy Gillespie's and Charlie Parker's, that introduced many to bebop.

On the first night, Miles and his friend Bobby Danzig showed up four hours early at the Riviera, hoping to hear a rehearsal or meet some musicians. Some nights Miles sat beside Art Blakey's tom-toms, begging him to let him sit in with the trumpet section. One evening, one of the trumpet players, Buddy Anderson, began to hemorrhage from tuberculosis on the bandstand and was rushed to the hospital. In the confusion that followed, Dizzy Gillespie approached the boy with the trumpet case and asked him if he had a union card. "I knew all the parts anyway," said Miles, "I was there every night. Shit, I knew the saxophone parts. That's the difference between a dedicated musician and one that bullshits, the guy who's just carrying a case." It could have been a scene out of a Broadway musical—that waiting-in-the-wings/star-is-born moment—except that Eckstine said that Miles was terrible. And even Miles admitted he had trouble reading the band's book when what he really wanted to do was listen to Parker's and Gillespie's solos. He was good enough to finish out the week with the band, but not good enough to be asked to go with them when they left for Chicago.

Meanwhile, Miles had graduated from high school, though in absentia since he was playing out of town. And soon he would be leaving East St. Louis for New York City, for Juilliard, and for life in the bebop business.

CHAPTER TWO

The real fever of the place will begin to take hold upon him. The subtle, insidious wine of New York will begin to intoxicate him. . . . He will stay on until the town becomes all in all to him; until the very streets are his chums and certain buildings and corners are his best friends. Then he is hopeless, and to live elsewhere would be death.

PAUL LAURENCE DUNBAR,
THE SPORT OF THE GODS

They were my best times—in St. Louis and the first part of my being in New York on Fifty-second Street.

MILES DAVIS

IN LATE SEPTEMBER 1944, Miles took a train to New York City in time to arrive at Juilliard a few days before the entrance examinations and his audition. His parents had called ahead and asked Eugene Haynes to meet him at Penn Station and help him get settled. Miles spent his first week at the Claremont Hotel, which Juilliard recommended because it was located near the school in Harlem, at 122nd Street and Broadway. It was also a hotel favored by professional musicians, so many that they said you could put together a band for a rehearsal just by knocking on doors.

Far from what he expected, New York was quiet, and even rustic in places. The streets were smooth, and cars and taxis were sparse. Someone lucky enough to own a car with good tires and a wartime gas ration card could park anywhere. North of his hotel, hills seemed to rise up from nowhere, and rock outcroppings dotted the landscape. Near Columbia University there was a cliff with an almost European vista of flat red and black rooftops, and from Riverside Drive you could see far up the lordly Hudson.

Miles arrived in New York at a moment when hopes were high for a quick ending to the war. After the Allied landings at Normandy, you could believe that it was already over, for the streets of Harlem were full of people, and restaurants like the Red Rooster were packed, nightspots like the Apollo Theatre were always filled, just as were the after-hours clubs like Minton's and Monroe's. The Savoy, that classic American dance hall, was still in full flower—the biggest in the world, they said, with box seats, and a lobby with carpeting and armchairs. Though some white people still went there, it was essentially a black dance hall, a center of the community where some folks danced, some talked and drank, others dozed or did needlepoint.

"Oh man, I was so excited when I first came. I used to walk in the rain. I'd never seen a place like that before. Subways. All sorts of pastry." Yet there was also a hint of homesickness about those first days in Manhattan: even before he began his fabled search for saxophonist Charlie Parker, Miles walked all through Central Park looking for the place where the horses were stabled.

On September 30, he found long lines ahead of him at Juilliard, for the school was expanding wildly, some twenty times larger than it had been ten years before. He took his examinations and for his audition played "Youth Dauntless," a florid composition written by Herbert Lincoln Clarke, soloist for the Sousa Band, and said to be the greatest of the concert band cornetists. Juilliard had some of the most musically talented individuals in America, and he was there with students like Ned Rorem and Robert Craft. Miles passed all of the requirements and enrolled as an orchestral instrument major with a minor concentration in piano. Larry Rivers, then a saxophonist but one of the more important figurative painters of the fifties, was in Miles' music dictation class that fall, and when he and Miles both arrived early for class, they'd find an empty practice room, and Miles would show him some of the chords he'd been working on, or some progressions he'd picked up from Charlie Parker.

Miles and I would prepare for the exam by going outside to smoke some marijuana. We were convinced it improved our hearing, and we gulped down the smoke and the myth in big draughts. On the other hand, we didn't do badly on those tests. Put that in your pipe and poke it.

Miles' real interest was in the private lessons he had with William Vacchiano, then principal trumpet with the New York Philharmonic and on his way to becoming one of the most influential teachers in the music world. Though they came from opposite ends of the musical spectrum, Miles respected classical playing, and he already knew what to expect after his studies in St. Louis. Vacchiano admired Harry James as much as Miles did. He himself had once played with Paul Whiteman's Orchestra and had taught jazz players before Davis; Mercer Ellington, for one, had been his student between 1938 and 1940. Vacchiano began by taking Davis back through the fundamentals with emphasis on tone quality and moderation of volume. Miles later claimed that they argued over what and how he should be taught. But Vacchiano remembers only that he quickly recognized Davis' special talent, that he was always a good student—polite, cooperative, and willing—and that he had no complaints about Miles.

Though he went to classes, studied, and practiced, Miles was not deeply involved in the school's activities and usually left right after class. "Miles was very thin and quiet," according to Larry Rivers, "and—which seems amazing in the light of his subsequent public image—shy. It seemed I was the only white person at the school that he spoke to. I would invite him to some function or other; he always refused." Some nights Miles was downtown visiting with his father's older brother, Ferd. Davis' mother disapproved of his uncle, believing him to be an alcoholic, and tried to keep Miles away from him, but in vain.

After his first week in New York, Dr. Davis had arranged for Miles to move into a kitchenette farther uptown at 149th Street, some thirty blocks or three subway stops from Juilliard. It was small, but there was enough room for a rented piano on which Miles could practice. With his tuition and rent paid and an allowance from home of $40 a week, he was able to eat where he wanted, take an occasional taxi, and enjoy the new music that was beginning to flower in the city.

It was the atomic age of music. We were dropping bombs on Japan and Max Roach was dropping musical bombs. It was a crazy era because everybody was sort of wild at the time.

ROBERT ORR

Miles spent his nights in the clubs of Manhattan, a witness to the beginnings of bebop, the most radical form of jazz that America had yet heard. It was a music that tracked the turbulent wartime experience of strikes, dislocation, military service, and persistent discrimination, but it also had all the makings of a high art, one that expressed a new generation of black Americans' sense of their own power and destiny. True, bop had a silly name reflecting its public reception as something strange coming out of the black community; many of the musicians who first played it were migrants from the South and the Southwest unknown to most jazz fans. These musicians' abilities were developed within an urban framework of local intellectual activity and political thinking, and they often presented themselves as artistes-bohemians, even as they simultaneously parodied those roles. Dizzy Gillespie, for example, at times appeared dressed in a long, flowing bow tie *à la Bohème*, with beret, goatee, and horn-rimmed glasses, speaking in the arcane vocabulary of the hip. Bebop compositions were titled "Anthropology," "Ornithology," and "Epistrophy" alongside others such as "Oop-Pop-a-Da," "Emanon," and "In the Land of Oo-Bla-Dee." Traditional intellectuals—those, that is, with institutional approval—were caught napping by this music. If they listened to anything other than modern classical music, it was to Louis Armstrong, Bessie Smith, New Orleans funeral parade music, work songs, Paul Robeson's spirituals, Pete Seeger, Josh White, and, for that matter, any other music that seemed to reflect the experiences of America's proletariat. But bebop? It seemed musically, and maybe even politically, too far out.

To swing devotees, bop was a musical affront, a calculated provocation. (The great blues singer Jimmy Rushing once defined bebop caustically: "You know the obbligatos the instrumentalists play behind singers while they're singing a song? Bebop is the obbligato without the singer *or* the song!") Outside of a small number of people in a few key cities, most who had heard it thought bop was a mysterious derailment of jazz by a group of strange young musicians. Its fans, however, called it "revolutionary," "innovative," and "modern." And in retrospect, bop does seem to be an extraordinarily distinctive style of jazz. On the other hand, its development took place during a 1942–1944 ban on recording ordered by the United Federation of Musicians in protest over records being played on radio without fees being paid, and the resulting absence of any of the new music on record made the transition from swing to bebop appear less inevitable than it actually might have been. Some of those on the scene who were listening hard saw bop coming, even before the early

1940s, in the slowly accumulating innovations of swing musicians like Lester Young, Roy Eldridge, Coleman Hawkins, Charlie Christian, and Art Tatum. The playing of those musicians suggested the need to go beyond the recurrent melodies and formulaic harmonic structure of pop tunes to a music freed of the needs of dancers.

Bebop bands were small groups of five or six, but unlike the rhythm and blues bands that they closely resembled and with which they often shared players, they were not stripped-down swing bands, with a trumpet and a saxophone representing the brass and the reed sections. The horns of the bebop bands were organized differently, occasionally in counterpoint, but more typically playing in unison.

Younger players had begun to tinker with pop tunes, sometimes by retaining their older harmonic structures and putting new melodies over them, or by radically paraphrasing the older ones. Staples like "Sweet Georgia Brown" (later the theme song of the Harlem Globetrotters) could be turned into a cascading, start-and-stop display piece like "Hollywood Stampede" by Coleman Hawkins in 1943; stripped down to its skeleton, it would emerge as Thelonious Monk's "Bright Mississippi" in 1964. But instead of simply following the phrasing used by pop singers or heard in swing riff melodies (those evenly and symmetrically placed one- or two-bar repeated fragments that made up Glenn Miller's "In the Mood" or Benny Goodman's "Stomping at the Savoy"), bop melodic phrases were longer and less repetitious, but at the same time unevenly structured and irregularly placed.

The new bop melodies were more angular than pop songs and older jazz tunes, and the intervals between their notes were wider. Passing tones (the notes not strictly part of the chords being played or about to be played) were typically left hanging unresolved, without moving on to the notes of the next chord. In the playing of the greatest of the boppers, like Charlie Parker, musical phrases were asymmetrical and often quite distinct and separate from each other. Parker might, for example, begin playing in the lower register, leap upward without warning, then let the melody tumble downward. Yet once the syntax of his music was grasped, his solos seemed coherent, even organic.

It was also an era of great experimentation with harmony, bebop players often knowing the work of current classical composers like Igor Stravinsky, Béla Bartók, and Stefan Wolpe. Chords were extended or altered, one laid on top of another, and new chords were added to existing ones to create complexity and motion in harmonic structure. In the reharmonizations of a pianist like Thelonious Monk, the chords seem blunt and desiccated, but also freshly minted and free of the clichés of pop songs.

But it was in the rhythm of bebop where the giddiness of creation was most strongly felt. Just as the melodies of bop seemed broken up, so was the rhythm, such that on a first hearing of this music, both rhythm and melody seemed erratic or disorganized. Even the rests—the brief moments of silence in bop melody lines—were used rhythmically. These pauses sprang up in surprising places, not at those moments of quiet usually left at the ends of phrases in pop songs and the blues. When this kind of staggered use of silence occurred along with offbeat accents and sudden shifts of speed in the melody, at the same time as it was played over the steady beat of the bass and the jagged snare drum accents and erratic "bombs" dropped on the bass drum, fleeting moments of polymeter, or multiple rhythms, could be heard.

What made bop feel even wilder and more of a break with the past was the sheer virtuosity of its players: Charlie Parker's zigzag lightning melody lines, the relentless flow and power of Bud Powell's right hand on the piano, Dizzy Gillespie's soaring, aggressive solos, and J. J. Johnson's elevation of the trombone to the solo status of the trumpet by sheer technique and speed. The bebop players had found within themselves the resources to intensify swing and go beyond it, to what was previously thought to be musically impossible.

Most of America was under the spell of swing in the 1930s. But when bebop emerged, it was seen as New York City's own. Its musicians may have come from Missouri, North Carolina, Illinois, and all those other border states of culture, but it was a music wired to New York's vernacular speech and gestures, its end-of-war nervous energy, the sharp, quick turns of taxis on the prowl, and the crisscrossing of streets that Piet Mondrian caught in his painting *Broadway Boogie-Woogie*.

Once intellectuals were forced to confront bop, they were fiercely split over its importance. Simone de Beauvoir, for example, visited New York City in 1947, and though she was in love with the jazz she had known before the war, bebop to her was abstract expressionism without meaning or content, jazz with only its rhythms still intact. All she heard in it was a "breathless, exasperated expression of New York's restlessness." When she and Richard Wright dropped into a nightclub in Harlem where bop was being played, they may have been hearing Parker, or Gillespie, or even Miles Davis for that matter (she thought the musicians not worthy of mention). But she and Wright found it unbearable and left within half an hour. Younger writers like Jack Kerouac, on the other hand, found that same sense of abstraction in bebop exhilarating, seeing it as part of the great abstraction that was New York City. Abstract art, abstract war—Kerouac listed them all—abstract classical music, abstract advertising, abstract baseball, abstract drama, abstract novels, and "Abstract modern jazz soft-sound tenor horns blowing, sweet, distant, rowel, up-going, go-baby-to-New York in a rush of things."

After the end of prohibition, 52nd Street between Fifth and Seventh Avenues became the focus of jazz in New York City, an area that reached its zenith in the mid-forties. By the time Miles came to New York, what they simply called the Street was open to every form of jazz, from dixieland to bebop. He might have seen Art Hodes at Jimmy Ryan's, Slam Stewart at the Three Deuces, Erroll Garner at Tandelayo's, and Coleman Hawkins, that epicurean of all styles, at the Downbeat, where he was resident for almost a year. And there were other clubs—Kelly's Stable, the Hickory House, the Famous Door, and the Onyx—the last still surviving from its days as an upstairs speakeasy. Most of these nightspots were small, just the ground floors or basements of brownstones that could hold something like 135 people. They were dark, hot, and smoky, with crowded bars, tiny bandstands, tiny kitchens, tiny everything. But they managed to mix musicians of every style on the same program, and any night's audience was dotted with musicians, both amateur and professional, who might join those on the stage. With the doors open in warm weather, the music spilled out onto the sidewalk and drew in an odd mixture of jazz cognoscenti, servicemen on furlough, dealers in narcotics, Long Island farm boys, people who drifted in from other nearby strip and variety clubs, the slumming wealthy, and police of various sorts, checking for drugs and the musicians' cabaret cards (permits to perform, issued by the police). The police were a presence on the sidewalks as well. Musicians hanging outside the clubs during breaks were forced to identify themselves, and couples walking on the sidewalk—especially interracial couples, common in this area—were warned to keep moving. Blacks may have been accepted in this oasis of midtown New York racialism, but they were not encouraged unless they were celebrities like Joe Louis or Lena Horne.

As disreputable as the 52nd Street clubs sometimes were, with mob connections of all sorts, they offered an intimacy and a chamberlike setting perfect for acoustic music and for the shouted badinage that sometimes went on between musicians and audience. It was possible for those sitting close to the band to hear sounds that even now escape recording technology: the sizzle of the rivets or chains that sustain the whoosh of the ride cymbal, the dry click of stick on closed high-hat cymbals, the swish and spin of brushes on a snare drum, the medicine-ball-in-the-stomach thump of the bass drum, the depth and natural volume of the piano, the woodiness of the string bass, and the mix of humid air and sound emerging from the horns.

More than just showplaces for bands and singers, these clubs were also the sites at which jazz musicians came to maturity, classrooms where mistakes were made, triumphs witnessed, careers launched or buried. Many musicians spent the larger part of their adult lives in these places, drank in them, avoided the military draft board, found lovers and mates, confronted enemies, and met their ends—by acclaim, failure, beatings, drugs, whatever.

It was at one of these places, the Spotlite, the only black-managed club on 52nd Street, that the bass player W. O. Smith recalled seeing the Charlie Parker group in the winter of 1944. Onstage with Parker were pianist Al Haig, Max Roach on drums, guitarist Teddy Walters, and Curly Russell on bass. And standing well hidden behind one of the other musicians, with his back to the audience, his muted horn pointed toward the curtain behind the band, was a young man they said was a student named Miles Davis.

In December, Irene came to Manhattan, leaving their new daughter, Cheryl, in the care of Miles' mother in East St. Louis. Just after she arrived, Irene moved with Miles to a larger apartment in a brownstone on 147th Street between Broadway and Riverside Drive, owned by Bob Bell, an East St. Louis guitar player who had married well and whose wife had set him up in business. At Broadway and 147th, the Bells also owned a cocktail lounge, a restaurant, and a soda parlor. Irene and Miles were taken into the Bells' care, invited to dinner, given rides in their car, and taken to the horse races. It was the Bells who gave Irene her first job in New York as one of their cashiers.

For the first time, they could live as if they were married, and they spent most of their time together. Before Miles left for class, they had breakfast in a luncheonette, and then sometimes sat for a while on a park bench on Riverside Drive. After classes, Irene and Miles met for ice-cream sodas at Bell's soda parlor (the inspiration for Miles' composition, "Sippin' at Bells"). On weekends they took the subway all over the city or walked through Central Park. When Miles wasn't in class, he practiced for hours, always asking Irene if she wanted to go shopping so that she would have something to do. "There was never a minute when he didn't hear music in his head," according to Irene. "He carried his trumpet mouthpiece wherever he went, and when he fell asleep each night, his feet still were moving to a rhythm."

"We didn't have much money," Irene said, "but New York had wonderful produce, and every night for dinner I made corn bread and greens and other things, all from fresh ingredients." The building she and Miles lived in was popular with musicians like Lucky Thompson and Freddie Webster, who were their neighbors upstairs. Later, Charlie Parker moved into their building, sharing a room upstairs with Stan Levey, a drummer from Philadelphia. After Parker first tasted Irene's cooking, he began dropping in for dinner every night, eating his share and most of theirs, until they had to ask him to stop. Parker was infamous for his appetites, his sexual tastes, his mooching, begging, trickery, lies, and the ease with which he borrowed or stole his friends' clothes or horns and then pawned them. When he came by their apartment, he might show up with hustlers, prostitutes, or anyone else he had run into on the street; he might be so high that he'd be sick or pass out on the floor; worse yet, drug dealers started turning up at the apartment, sent there by Bird, expecting to be paid. Miles was determined to maintain a normal family and to keep Irene innocent of the chaos of a musician's day-to-day existence, even if it meant keeping Parker away from her. Still, Irene always found him kind and respectful: "Whenever I saw Bird, he had a group of people with him. But he always stopped to say hello, and was nice to me."

At the end of his first term at Juilliard, Miles had done well considering all that he was trying to juggle at eighteen years of age. He received a B in music theory, a B+ in sight singing, A in dictation, B- in piano, B- in trumpet, A in orchestra, and a D in music history, for a B average.

One of the first people in New York City to befriend Miles was his upstairs neighbor Freddie Webster, a trumpet player from Cleveland whom Miles had first met in St. Louis when he came through town with the Jimmie Lunceford Orchestra. Webster had worked with famous bands like Earl Hines' and Benny Carter's, and when Miles saw him first in New York, he was with John Kirby's "biggest little band in the land," a polite and disciplined swing group very popular among café society folk downtown. Webster played in the kind of warm, spare manner that Miles was trying to cultivate, and he lived in high style, dressed to the nines, women trailing after him wherever he went, and maintaining a serious heroin habit. Almost every day, Freddie and Miles ran into each other in the apartment building and talked music for hours, Miles sharing with him whatever he was learning at Juilliard. (Drummer Connie Kay recalled Miles playing in a trio with Sir Charles Thompson and himself, and when Webster came into the club, "he showed Miles how to get those . . . big tones Miles uses now.") They shared money when one or the other was short, and Freddie began to ease Miles into the New York music scene, from time to time recommending him as his replacement in John Kirby's and drummer Sid Catlett's bands. (Two years later, when Webster died at age thirty from a dose of impure heroin that it was said vengeful drug dealers had intended for alto saxophonist Sonny Stitt, Davis was deeply shaken. "Why Webs?")

When Dizzy Gillespie and Charlie Parker were booked into the Three Deuces from March to July 1945, Freddie and Miles were there night after night. Charlie Parker by himself was astonishing, his musical ideas seemingly limitless (Miles said that "Bird used to play forty different styles"), finding rhythmic and harmonic solutions to musical problems at a dazzling rate of speed. When he was paired with Gillespie, the results were phantasmagorical: they improvised together almost telepathically, notes pouring forth with the fire of collective invention. They lived to play every night, inciting each other to risk everything to reach what Gillespie called "the height of perfection in our music." And it was *their* music, a music of black people, but also one that broke with their past (Parker went so far as to say that bebop had nothing to do with jazz), and rested finally on what a few musicians had come to know and feel.

Their audience knew that what it was hearing was historic. Creativity such as Parker's and Gillespie's happens maybe once in a lifetime. Miles and Freddie Webster were well aware of the level and speed of innovation in front of them and brought music manuscript paper along with them to the club every night to jot down whatever Dizzy was playing (Parker was too fast to transcribe, Miles said), and when the paper ran out, they wrote on matchbook covers and napkins. It was a bebop obsession, the sort of all-consuming world building that young people can find themselves engaged in. Though many of its players were addicted to heroin and other substances, bebop was nonetheless a scholarly enterprise that required intelligence and commitment, and Miles thrived on it:

We really studied. . . . If a door squeaked, we would call out the exact pitch. And every time I heard the chord of G, for example, my fingers automatically took the position for C-sharp on the horn—the flatted fifth—whether I was playing or not.

Freddie Webster and I used to go down every night to hear Diz. If we missed a night, we missed something. . . . Stand up at the bar, throw up a quarter, and name the note that it came down on. That shit be going so fast; and we'd be testing ourselves.

Saxophonist Gerry Mulligan knew Miles during this period and had the same studious relation to him:

Miles and I used to spend a lot of time talking about . . . the mechanics of music. He was particularly interested in chord progressions. He loved to make alterations . . . loved to make changes in chord progressions and try different things, you know, then how to apply that to a line so that the line flowed. And how to deal with it melodically.

It was not unusual for jazz musicians to invert time, night for day, but Miles tried to work both sides of the clock, getting by on a couple of hours of sleep, fighting the boredom in classes, trying to keep from yawning while singing in choir. Following classes, he went home to see Irene and practice, and have supper. Then, with his trumpet in a leather bag beneath his arm, he'd head downtown to see who was playing. After midnight, when the clubs closed, he went uptown to Minton's Playhouse where the after-hours crowd gathered. Pianist Sadik Hakim remembered "walking with him from 52nd to 107th Street through Central Park, singing chords, changes, every night."

Minton's was easy to spot on West 118th Street. It was located in the Hotel Cecil, and a long awning stretched from the door to the street in the manner of the swank clubs downtown. After their work elsewhere in the evening, the first thing arriving musicians saw was a tap dancer such as Baby Laurence or the legendary Groundhog, dancing on the street for change tossed to him by the hustlers and gamblers drawn to the club. Inside, above the bandstand, was a mural of a group of white and black musicians jamming in a bedroom by the light of a kerosene lamp, a scene that pointed back to the club's origins in the 1930s, when saxophonist Henry Minton first opened it. Minton's quickly came to be a kind of musicians' social club where food, drink, gossip, and music were shared. In 1941 it was taken over by the band leader Teddy Hill, who installed a house band made up of musicians who had once played in his own group, young modernists like drummer Kenny Clarke, Thelonious Monk, and trumpeter Joe Guy. The club then gradually became the center for the music that would later come to be known as bebop, and eased out the swing musicians who had once held forth there. It was a different music, and they were musicians with new attitudes. Not everyone welcomed the change. In "The Golden Age, Time Past," a 1959 essay in *Esquire* that depicted the old Minton's in mythic proportions, Ralph Ellison bitterly complained of the players of this new jazz

> that the performing artist can be completely and absolutely free of the obligations of the entertainer, and that they could play jazz with dignity only by frowning and treating the audience with aggressive contempt; and that to be in control, artistically and politically, one must be so cool as to quench one's own human fire.

In April 1945, Miles received his first call to record. It was a rhythm and blues date for Savoy Records with Herbie Fields' band accompanying Rubberlegs Williams. Williams was a former vaudeville dancer and comedian turned raw-edged blues singer who a few months earlier had cut the infamous "I Want Every Bit of It." That session was memorable for two reasons: first, Charlie Parker and Dizzy Gillespie were recording together for the first time; and second, Williams was flying behind three tabs of Benzedrine that Parker had whimsically dropped into the singer's coffee as they were beginning to record. Herbie Fields was a saxophonist (and Juilliard student) who had just joined the Lionel Hampton band, the first white musician ever to play in that group (he sometimes wore makeup to pass as black on stage). Though he was not listed on the record, Hampton insisted that he played drums in Fields' band on that session, and he described Miles as "kind of a roaming cat in those days. He had to heed the call of his feel, his sound." The producer of the record was Teddy Reig, a big ball of a man who loved bop and took every opportunity to record its musicians: "I threw Miles into that date because Bird asked me to do what I could for him. Miles was a very nervous young man at that date. He had Freddie Webster, his idol, there to calm him down. After each take, Freddie would go over it with him."

The owner of Savoy Records was Herman Lubinsky, and though he lived and died by recordings aimed at the eastern urban black community, he was having trouble grasping the new music bubbling up all around him. He was suspicious of the musicians he recorded, and counted on his artists and repertoire man, Reig, to organize the sessions:

Herman didn't understand Miles at all. He pulled me aside and said, "Look, this is not a school! We don't have to have guys on the date with the trumpet player, trying to refresh his memory. We're in the record business; this ain't a goddamn university." Naturally, Miles hated Herman with a passion.

These were rather straightforward blues recordings, but Miles felt that he hadn't played well. He told journalist George Hoeffer, "I was too nervous to play, and I only performed in the ensembles, no fills." Though that was not precisely true—Davis did have several obbligatos—he played softly and back from the mike. He warmed up to the task slowly over the first few takes of two of the pieces, "That's the Stuff You Gotta Watch" and "Bring It on Home," and by the last (and issued) take of the tunes, there was no question that he was a bebop musician—if a somewhat insecure one.

When the school term ended, Miles' grades had plummeted, the consequences of missed classes and exams: he received five Fs, one D, a B- for trumpet once again, and no grades for several other courses. Miles was looking for some way to avoid returning home, so he enrolled in summer school at Juilliard, and Irene went back to East St. Louis to be with Cheryl. But now Miles was even less involved in his studies ("I did the whole summer program in one day"—analyses of Mozart's Requiem in D Minor and Paul Hindemith's 1922 *Kleine Kammermusik* for wind quintet). The instruction seemed so slow to him—"stretched out," was the way he put it—while the music on the Street and at Minton's seemed to be accelerating into a new phase every night. (Vibraphonist Milt Jackson used to say that you could get a Ph.D. in music after just one set at Minton's.) But to succeed in the direction that Juilliard was pointing him, he would have to "play white":

> I was going to have to act like a white man toward music. The direction, you know what I mean, so I left. Because there was certain things you had to do, or a certain way you had to play to get in there, to be with them. And I didn't come all the way from St. Louis just to be with a white orchestra.

Once a fellow brass student tried to have some fun with him: "He was with the Metropolitan Opera House orchestra, and he tried to make me play 'Body and Soul' so that he could laugh at my tone. What he was really doing was calling me 'Nigger,' putting down the jazzy tone." Later, Miles would say, "Now they all have that tone, and if you play like Harry James you can't get a job."

He bridled at the fact that Juilliard had no interest in what he was learning in the clubs; worse, he noted the teachers seemed to have no idea of the importance of what black music had achieved. The professor in his music history class, for example, Ruth Van Doren, once lectured on the blues as the product of suffering under slavery. It was a progressive point of view and a discussion rare for any music class at the time, but Miles said that he objected because it was an oversimplification of black history.

> So they were sad, and that's where the blues came from, their sadness. . . .
> I stood up and said, "I'm from East St. Louis and my father is rich, he's a dentist, and I play the blues. My father didn't never pick no cotton and I didn't wake up this morning sad and start playing the blues. There's more to it than that."

Yet he was ambivalent about his studies. He told the musicians he met that he was studying at Juilliard, and he shared what he was learning with Gillespie, Webster, and others. And only one page after he criticized Juilliard in his autobiography, he chastised older black jazz musicians who rejected music education because "it would make you play like you were white." He then went on to speak of the advantages of studying classical music. Years later, he said that when he was at Juilliard, he walked around with Stravinsky's scores in his pockets. Some of this ambivalence came from the fact that there was no real future for a person of color in classical music, a point he made in his autobiography: "I knew that no white symphony orchestra was going to hire a little black motherfucker like me, no matter how good I was or how much music I knew."

Miles began hanging out at clubs where he felt his chances of being allowed to play were good. Saxophonist Budd Johnson recalled that Miles often played so poorly that other musicians would threaten to leave the stand if he sat in. "That's how bad he sounded. This hurt his feelings, you know." But Miles persisted. While Coleman Hawkins was at the Down Beat, Miles was there every night, apprenticing himself to the master. Al McKibbon was the bassist with that group:

> Miles . . . was at Juilliard at the time. He used to come in with his horn and he'd sit up on the bandstand and he'd listen to us play, watch what Monk was doing. And sometimes Monk would hit something strange and he'd figure it out on his horn, but he'd never play. He would just sit and listen and laugh to himself.

Joe Guy was the trumpeter with Hawkins, but when he failed to show up, which was often, Miles grew braver and offered to play for free. Billie Holiday was alternating sets with Hawkins, and Miles sometimes stayed to see her or ran over to the Spotlite to see if he could play with Eddie "Lockjaw" Davis, who later gave him his first professional job playing in New York.

It was in Billie Holiday's dressing room after one of those sets that Miles had his first taste of cocaine. He told Stan Levey that it did nothing for him.

Miles' heart was no longer in his studies, and for the three courses he took that summer he received a B, a D, and no credit for the third. And yet he feared that if he were no longer in school, he would have no excuse to be in New York and would be forced to move back to East St. Louis. Freddie Webster warned him that he had come too far for that and there was no returning. "Man, you know if you go back to St. Louis, and them booges and crackers there, you're going to get mad and . . . you might get killed."

The time seemed right for him to make his own way. With the war over, New York was flooded with returning GIs, and work for musicians was increasing. Charlie Parker had also been hinting that he would hire him for a new group he was thinking about. Miles had to tell his father about his plans, but since Dr. Davis knew nothing about Dizzy, Bird, Monk, and bebop, he felt he had to go home and explain it all to him face to face.

> He had a patient and he looked up and said, "What the fuck are you doing here?" I said, "I'll tell you when you get through." And then I told him. I couldn't call him on the phone and say, "Yardbird Parker," you know? Because like if I failed they wouldn't beat me up or anything, they would kill me. Because a Davis isn't supposed to be dumb.

Over the years, Miles' account of that meeting with his father became more elaborate and sentimental, with his father accepting his break with school and giving him his blessing, but it was likely to have been much more of a disappointment than he allowed.

When he returned to New York, Miles joined Local 802 of the Musicians' Union of New York City on September 4, and in October he became a member of the Charlie Parker group, playing first at the Three Deuces and then moving down the street to the Spotlite. This was what he had dreamed of in Illinois, what every young musician of his day dreamed about. But it was also something of a nightmare. Parker was such a volatile and exhilarating player, moving in a blur of notes—sometimes as fast as ten a second—and *loud,* so fast and loud that he could make everyone else seem as if they were thinking in slow motion. When Parker played, everyone expected to be surprised. His musical ideas seemed to be coming from out of nowhere, and the collective reflex was, "What was *that?*" But it was not Parker alone who was so intimidating to young musicians. Behind him, drummer Max Roach was creating a firestorm, sticks moving so fast that they were a blur, his rhythms crisscrossing Parker's, his voice hoarse from screaming over the music, "Blow, baby, blow!" There was no room for mistakes in this music, no time to think ahead, no allowance for coasting.

Some said Miles was not up to this band, that Parker should go back to Gillespie, or that he should use Fats Navarro, that baroque magician of bebop who, a few said, was even better than Dizzy, or even the young Kenny Dorham, whose every solo bristled with energy. Novelist Gilbert Sorrentino articulated the response to Davis among many in the audience at the time:

> He was incredibly shy, and, since his striving toward a trumpet style different from either Gillespie's or Fats Navarro's was far from perfected, he was simply tolerated by the audience. As I recall, the listeners used his solo time to go to the bathroom, buy a beer, talk to friends, etc. This was something that was, of course, rude and stupid, since what Miles was doing was very new, and very different from anyone else—he was in the process of transition from bop to "cool," and in the process was tortured by the inadequacies of his playing. He probably hit more clinkers than any other trumpeter of his time, and when he played with Bird it was ridiculous. I cannot think of any other instrumentalist of that time who sounded so bad.

Bird, however, heard something in what Miles was playing, something deep in his calculated lyricism, his unadorned sound, the choice of notes, the flow of his phrases. Yet life in the vortex of Parker's group was nonetheless a daunting experience. Miles was plagued with doubts about everything. Was he good enough? Could he play this music? How did he look playing? ("I couldn't figure out how to keep time, whether to tap my toes inside my shoe, or tap the whole shoe!") Bad enough that he had to follow him, but Bird would sometimes leave while Miles was playing and not come back for a long time. And when he came back, he'd complain that Miles was playing too loud. ("But I know he was out for coke, and coke makes everything too loud. I was playing with a mute.") When he *was* there, he had to play with him on the ensembles, and that itself was frightening:

> I used to play under Bird all the time. When Bird would play a melody, I'd play just under him and let him lead the note, swing the note. The only thing that I'd add would be a larger sound. I used to quit every night. I'd say, "What do you need me for?"

Regardless, Miles was able to put a proud front on things, telling anyone who would listen that New York was not *that* impressive. He'd say that before he came to New York, he thought everyone would be more advanced, but now he knew that St. Louis musicians—most of them unknown—were better than those in New York City, or even those in Chicago, that he had learned more in the Eddie Randle band than he ever gotten from Juilliard.

The other musicians in the Parker band had never seen anyone like Davis before. Stan Levey, himself something of an outsider—white, Jewish, and a professional boxer recently converted to drummer—summed it up:

> He was a middle-class guy, well-dressed. He wore Brooks Brothers suits and we were in rags. He had his own horse at home. He had walking-around money, but no day gig. He went to a school we'd never heard of. He was shy, but he was arrogant. When Bird and Dizzy were playing at the Three Deuces, he came in and said to Dizzy at intermission, "I can play anything you can play!" Diz said, "Yeah, but an octave lower." Miles was a smart-mouth. We were always telling him, "Shut up, Junior, you don't know what you're talking about."

With Irene out of town, Miles roomed with Levey off and on over the next two years. It was the boxer Levey who introduced Miles to training, taking him with him to Stillman's gym, or to Sugar Ray Robinson's. Miles loved that scene—the acrid smell of it, the crowd that hung out there, the brutal discipline of the place—and he became a convert. For many years afterward, he skipped rope, did floor exercises, and worked the speed bag with bebop phrasing and triple-tongue rhythms ("tataka-tataka-tataka"), and for breath and endurance, he threw himself into the heavy bag with bass drum explosions.

Like many would-be bohemians before him, Miles sought to distance himself from his middle-class background by identifying with the rootless of the streets and the nighthawks of the clubs, and seeking their respect. He subjected himself to possible humiliations and dangers against which he had always been protected at home. The things he could see only from a safe distance in East St. Louis, the people he knew who existed but was not allowed to know, all of this was now something he witnessed as a participant observer. But he remained an enigma to other musicians, especially to Levey: "His father was wealthy enough to support him, send him to school. Yet he's here sharing a single room with a white drummer. He's hanging out with irresponsible jazz freaks and druggies." The gap between what he had been in East St. Louis only a little over a year ago and what he was becoming in New York City was widening fast. As Levey put it, "It bothered him that he loved it so—the life, the music, everything." Singer Annie Ross said that "when Miles was new in town, he seemed bewildered, with a look of fear—you can see it in pictures of him from then—but he was sweet and soft, not cynical at all."

Miles recorded for the first time with Charlie Parker for Savoy Records on November 26, 1945, on what was also Bird's first recording as a leader. Teddy Reig was again the producer for the date, and he was excited: "[Bird] played with so much authority! He'd play things and all the guys like John Lewis, Miles, Dizzy, would run to the piano to check the harmonic progressions to determine whether he was crazy or right. And he was always right! He'd turn away and laugh." Yet it was an unusually chaotic and strange session. Bud Powell was the pianist chosen for the date, but as he wasn't available at the last minute, Bird brought Dizzy in to play piano (and, according to pianist Sadik Hakim—who was also known as Argonne Thornton—himself as well, but since he wasn't a member of the Musicians' Union, they used the pseudonym "Hen Gates" for both men on the label (which made matters even more confusing since Hen Gates was the professional name of a Philadelphia pianist, Jimmy Foreman). Ross Russell, the owner of a rival record company,

Dial, accused Reig of laying out "a table of assorted drugs, a regular smorgasbord. . . . The musicians were free to use whatever they wanted. That was the setting: flying high and making all that great music." But Reig tells it differently. For him, a man accustomed to recording under the worst of conditions, the day's work was exasperating:

> If you had been at this session you'd be lucky to remember anything. I was like a policeman on duty—where's Miles, where's Bird, where's Dizzy? The only one who tended to be normal was Curly [Russell]. Max stood around and took it all in. To him it was a floor show!

The first two Parker compositions they recorded were blues, "Billie's Bounce" and "Now's the Time" (the latter's melody was later turned into "The Hucklebuck," a rhythm and blues song that became a hit for singer Paul Williams), and the third was "Thrivin' on a Riff" (sometimes recorded by others under the title of "Anthropology"), a melody based on the shifting harmonic structure of the Gershwin tune "I Got Rhythm." As they began to record, Parker's horn was giving him trouble, so he went up to 48th Street to get it repaired (accompanied by Reig, to make sure that he came back). Meanwhile, the musicians who remained partied on, and when Parker and Reig returned, Reig said that "Miles wasn't worth three dead flies." There was still one record left to cut, "KoKo," an improvisation for Parker modeled on the chord progressions of "Cherokee," a pop tune beloved of jazz musicians because of its challenging key change at the bridge. Davis was unable to play the short arranged introduction because it was new to him, so Dizzy Gillespie filled in for the opening and the closing parts on the trumpet, then moved back to the piano for the rest of the record. Miles Davis thus missed out on a piece considered one of the most important in jazz history.

The session ran well beyond the union's three-hour limit, what with mechanical problems with Parker's saxophone, friends drifting through the studio, and breaks to send out for refreshments and sundries. There were stories of other distractions. It was said, for example, that Miles fell asleep on the floor of the studio while they were recording and that Reig himself was asleep in the engineer's booth.

Jazz history has not looked kindly on Davis' work on these recordings, and the long shadow thrown by Parker (and, more distantly, by Dizzy Gillespie) continues to obscure what he achieved at this early age. Sadik Hakim said that Miles was nervous throughout the session, and with the felt mute he was using he couldn't be heard even six feet away. The anonymous *Down Beat* writer who was the first to review the 78 rpm single of "Billie's Bounce" and "Now's the Time" complained that "the trumpet man, whoever the misled kid is, plays Gillespie in the same manner as a majority of the kids who copy their idol—with most of the faults, lack of order and meaning, the complete adherence to technical acrobatics." Many later critics have heard his playing as insecure, and unstable, a scared nineteen-year-old, in over his head. John Mehegan, the liner-note writer for the first LP to contain all of the material recorded that day, dismissed Davis brutally: "Lugubrious, unswinging, no ideas, ludicrous." Even Davis' biographers have been less than enthusiastic about these solos. Weird theories have developed about them: one has it that it was Dizzy Gillespie who was playing in the style of Davis on take three of "Billie's Bounce"; another one says that it was Gillespie playing like himself on "Thrivin' on a Riff." Adding insult to injury, trumpeter Benny Bailey claimed that Miles' solo on the issued take of "Billie's Bounce" was a note-for-note copy of a solo that he had heard Freddie Webster play on that tune.

Because of the availability of a number of alternative takes on which Miles performed that day, it's now easier to judge Davis' early playing fairly. Despite the session's problems—or because of them—the Parker group recorded five takes of "Billie's Bounce," four of "Now's the Time," and three of "Thrivin' on a Riff."

Before the invention of recording tape, takes were multiple recordings of the same piece, usually made at the same session, one after the other. Though this custom began as a means of ensuring that there would be at least one acceptable version available in case of mechanical failure in the record pressing process, takes also provided a way with jazz to choose the best or most definitive version from several improvisations. Takes were not viewed as opportunities for practice, however; they were seen as artworks in themselves, as versions of some platonic ideal sensed or dreamed of, or of a perfect work revealed as the takes began to accumulate. In jazz, these versions often take on lives of their own, offering a glimpse inside the otherwise sacrosanct walls of the studio. For many years, takes were something hoarded by record companies or collectors who, once they got hold of them, endlessly argued over their merits like monks in possession of relics. Only when an artist died did the companies release takes, either as a gesture to the artist's greatness or as a way to make more money from the dead, depending on who you ask. When Charlie Parker died suddenly at the age of thirty-four, for example, there was a larger market for his recordings, and both Dial and Savoy had plenty of takes for the asking, so many that they have been surfacing ever since, as completed works, scraps, or aborted starts. Takes that were interrupted are especially interesting, as they often offer evidence of self-criticism, the artist unable to bear preserving what was going onto record. The Argentine novelist Julio Cotázar once meditated on the danger sensed in these interrupted works of art by recalling that in some of Parker's takes, you suddenly hear him cry out, "Hold it!" Sometimes Duke Jordan or Max Roach continue playing as if neither believe the music has been stopped. Then, afterward, there is the ominous mechanical silence of the engineer ending the recording.

> Strange power of the record, which can open for us the workshop of the artist, let us attend his successes and failures. How many takes are there in the world? This edited one can't be the best; in its turn the atom bomb could someday be the equivalent of Bird's "Hold it!", the great silence. But will there be other usable takes, afterwards?

The takes of the November 26 Savoy session are particularly revealing for Davis. On the three versions of "Billie's Bounce" on which he appears, for instance, there is a common shape to all of his solos, but each of them also shows him making changes and refining his line. Perhaps his most effective take, number three, finds him measuring his phrases with care, placing notes for their rhythmic value and enhancing the overall direction of the two choruses he plays, and adding a distinctive vibrato to the ending of each long note he holds. If Parker's solos on these blues show him to possess a grand and complex rhythmic sensibility articulated with an often anguished tone, Davis is his opposite: muted, choosing only a few notes, worrying the small details, playing against the harmonic structure, playing against the blues, even playing against Parker. (In jazz, playing *against* others is equally as important as playing *with* them. This is what Ralph Ellison called the cruel contradiction implicit in the music: the individual finding personal identity both against and within the group.)

Once the listener steps back from Parker's bravura stance and surrenders to Davis' version of an alternate musical reality, even his clichés (such as a repeated pair of notes on almost every take of all three tunes, or a heavily emphasized, Monkish use of diminished fifths) reveal a distinctive stylistic logic at work. It was a logic that should have been apparent to listeners at least by 1958, when pianist Red Garland played a harmonized version of one of Davis' solos on "Now's the Time" (take four) near the end of his own improvisation with Davis' band on "Straight, No Chaser" (on the album *Milestones*). Most jazz trumpet players' styles can ultimately be traced to Louis Armstrong's swaggering, red-hot, aim-for-the-roof flash, what they used to call playing hell-for-leather. But Davis, like saxophonist Lester Young, was drawn to another side of Armstrong: those cool, green, quarter-note lines, notes carefully chosen and spaced, delivered slightly off or behind the beat, and relaxed, as if Louis were playing in a different world of time. On this recording session, face-to-face with Parker and Gillespie, the two greatest innovators of their time, Miles Davis was able to organize this alternate approach and present himself as an independent thinker, as a possessor of a distinct aesthetic. It was no small achievement.

In December, Parker left for California with Dizzy Gillespie and other musicians to play Hollywood for an eight-week run, and Miles went home for Christmas. But he was restless and bored, uncomfortable back at his mother's house. So when Benny Carter's big band played the Riviera in St. Louis in January 1946 and Freddie Trainer, one of the trumpet players, was sent over to ask Miles to join as fourth trumpet, he leaped at the chance. Carter was returning to the band's home base in Los Angeles, and Miles saw it as an opportunity to hear Parker and Gillespie play together. Mrs. Davis made a point of asking Trainer detailed questions about the trip, and she was reassured when she realized that she and his mother were old acquaintances and that Miles would be rooming with Benny Carter and his wife.

Carter had a sophisticated swing band that was popular with the Hollywood crowd. Stars like Lana Turner and Kay Starr were in the audience whenever they played, and Jackie Coogan and Mickey Rooney regularly sat in on drums. Trombonist Al Grey was in that band, and he recalled that Miles was a good soloist who kept to himself and practiced all day long in his room. Benny Carter remembered Miles as "quiet and cooperative."

When Davis arrived in Los Angeles, Parker and Gillespie were already settled in. During the day, they were making a number of bebop, novelty, and rhythm and blues records. At night "Dizzy Gillespie and his Rebopers" were something of a curiosity, with local musicians and the more adventuresome movie stars seeking them out at Billy Berg's Swing

Club, one of the first white-owned clubs in Los Angeles that welcomed black customers. In spite of the fact that Parker was sick, drinking heavily, and in constant search of a regular source of heroin, his playing made instant converts of many musicians in the audience. Miles and other members of Carter's band regularly sat in at Berg's, and then after hours they went down to the Finale in Little Tokyo, an unlicensed black-run club set up in the headquarters of a Japanese cultural society abandoned after the internment of its members in camps. The word spread quickly, and soon musicians like Stan Getz, Gerry Mulligan, Sonny Criss, and Shorty Rogers were gathering there as well. (Bill Green, a saxophonist on the scene at the time, recalled hearing Miles at the Finale one night and asking him to describe how he went about playing jazz. "Well, Bill, I take one note that I like, and I add another"—he started walking off. "And another and another"—until he disappeared.)

Still, in the long run, bebop did not sit well with Billy Berg's customers, and attendance fell off by February. "They were flummoxed" by the music, as pianist Al Haig put it. Gillespie was hurt by their reaction: "They thought we were just playing ugly on purpose. They were so very, *very* hostile! They were *very* square. Man, they used to stare at us *so* tough!"

With no other work offered, the Gillespie band prepared to leave together for New York ("If I ever get back alive to the Apple," Dizzy said, "I'll never leave it"). But Parker, in the grip of his habit, sold his train ticket at the last minute for drug money, and the band left without him.

Most nights, Bird continued to show up at the Finale, where Miles dutifully came to jam with him, until the union fined him for working two gigs on the same night. As spring came, Miles began looking for a graceful way out of Benny Carter's group. The big band swing arrangements were beginning to seem stale and square to him compared to what he was hearing elsewhere. At his midnight sessions, he was meeting young, inventive musicians like Charles Mingus, Red Callendar, Sonny Criss, and Art and Addison Farmer and learning new ways of thinking about music.

Meanwhile, Charlie Parker had agreed to do a recording session for Dial Records, a tiny new company that was attempting to specialize in jazz, ethnic music, and avant-garde classical composers like Arnold Schoenberg. The musicians were to be Davis, Lucky Thompson, Dodo Marmarosa on piano, guitarist Arvin Garrison, bassist Red Callendar, and Roy Porter on drums. Rehearsals were set to begin at the Finale after Parker finished playing at 2 A.M. But then Bird disappeared for an hour and a half, and when he returned, it was obvious that he had not yet written any music for the session. Arguments broke out over what they might play, and anxieties were running so high that Red Callendar bowed out. The next day, Dial owner Ross Russell hastily replaced him with local bassist Victor MacMillan.

The session began at one in the afternoon on a rainy March 28 at Radio Recorders Studios just across the street from Forest Lawn Cemetery in Glendale. When Parker arrived, he surprised everyone by assuming control, rehearsing for real, picking tempos, and playing parts of his new compositions for each of them to learn by ear. This method of modeling the music treated the written page as if it were defective and instead counted on the musicians to grasp Parker's intentions and rise to them, bringing whatever they could to the process. Miles was fascinated by its possibilities.

Parker started the first tune in his usual manner: he hummed the line to himself, rattled the saxophone's keys in rhythm, then instead of counting 1-2-3-4, gave a little jump and landed on his left foot, then his right, then left and right again, running in tempo, and they were off.

First recorded was "Moose the Mooche," an original piece Parker had worked up in the car on the way to the session and named after a Central Avenue shoeshine stand owner and Parker's principal drug supplier in Los Angeles. "Yardbird Suite" followed, a melody Parker had written for Jay McShann's Orchestra under the title of "What Price Love." The third piece was "Ornithology," a composition formed on the harmonics of "How High the Moon," but one that also used a melodic phrase Parker had played in an earlier recorded solo on McShann's "The Jumpin' Blues."

Bird had been paid for four new compositions, and when it became clear that he had only three, Ross Russell suggested they try Dizzy Gillespie's "Night in Tunisia," which had recently been recorded by the Boyd Raeburn band. This was the piece that gave them trouble. Though on record it lasts only a few seconds over three minutes, it took them more than two hours and five takes to get through it. When they tried it, according to Roy Porter, they hit a snag with the interlude—a twelve-bar passage, plus a four-bar break for Parker that led into his solo. (A break in jazz is that moment when the other instruments all stop for a few bars to allow the soloist to sail across the empty expanses without a chordal or rhythmic net beneath him.) What Parker played during that break was so astonishing in its rhythmic and harmonic flash, its speed, and its recklessness that the rhythm section failed several times to come in correctly behind him once he moved into the body of his solo. Miles finally solved the problem by standing near the piano, covering his ears, concentrating as he counted off the beats, and bringing his hand down as a signal when the band should start again.

Eight hours after they began, they had recorded what would turn out to be four of the most discussed pieces in the history of jazz. It was music that was supremely aware of the rules being broken and shimmering with the thrill of seeing new ideas work. Miles was nonetheless angry at himself for playing what he thought of as poorly and for not sounding like himself, even though he had played with a mute to set himself apart (as well as to keep out of the limelight). Though the music was rehearsed at the last minute and Davis was put in the impossible position of filling Dizzy Gillespie's shoes and yet not sounding like him, what he did play was enough to get him a "New Star" award (along with Thompson and Mamarosa) in *Down Beat* magazine's critics' poll later that year.

Miles finally gave his notice to Benny Carter, who seemed concerned about turning him loose on his own and offered him some money if he needed it. Miles then briefly moved in with Lucky Thompson and his wife. His father was still sending him money, but the life he was leading was expensive. He was out every night, attempting to dress in the latest styles, and was also supposed to be supporting a wife and child. Seriously short of money for the first time in his life, Miles pawned his trumpet.

Next, he moved in with trumpet player Howard McGhee and his girlfriend, and it was through her that he met a woman who was often seen in the company of actor George Raft and other celebrities and was rumored to be a call girl. She became interested in Miles, treating him almost maternally. He had brought only summer clothes to California, and when cool weather came on, she bought him several cashmere sweaters and offered him money. When he turned down her gifts, an incredulous McGhee chided him: "We can't play. The black union don't want us because we're too modern. The white union don't like us because we're too black. And here's a white woman . . . wants to give you some money and you say 'no'?" Miles finally accepted some of her gifts, but he was uncomfortable with the idea, not the least because she was white.

Now at loose ends, he began rehearsing with an experimental big band that bassist Charles Mingus had organized, playing music that seemed unlike anything he'd ever heard before. It was strange, he said, but strange in the same way that Duke Ellington's music could be strange, with ordinary harmonies left unresolved or melodies angling off in strange directions. But not much was offered to him musically in Los Angeles for which he was paid. So when he received a call from Irene that she was pregnant with their second child, he began to look for some way back east that would not involve asking his father for more money. Meanwhile, Billy Eckstine's band had arrived in Los Angeles in September, and Miles' reputation was now strong enough that Eckstine offered him a chance to replace Fats Navarro as soloist in the trumpet section, a position first held by Dizzy Gillespie. The pay was $170 a week—whether they worked or not. Miles accepted and joined them for the trip back to New York City.

Life in the big bands was always difficult and never as glamorous as the tuxedos, stage lights, and mirrored balls in the dance halls would suggest. Bands were loosely strung together groups of men, most of whom shared little more than music, and on long and arduous trips their personal habits and problems, their differences in ages and backgrounds, could make for chaotic life. The bands were paternalistic at best, despotic at worst, and could make demands on individuals that were brutally unrealistic. The younger members especially were given rapid and harsh educations, suffering pranks and abuses that could be crippling. Though Miles was twenty years old, with one child and another on the way, he looked so young (and so "pretty," he said) that he was questioned about his age at bars and teased about his privileged childhood and sheltered life. But Eckstine was no surrogate father to his musicians; at best, he played the older, more worldly brother. Though he was not the greatest trumpet player and trombonist, as a singer, he had the potential of being a star on records, radio, and in the movies. But it was the musician's life he loved, and he wanted to be seen with his ace sidemen on and off the stand.

Eckstine seemed ambivalent about Miles (he called him "Dick"). He went out of his way to tell others that he was not a good musician, and Miles said that B often forced him to run errands for him, while he sat with beautiful women.

B would call out, "Where's Miles!" and make me go get his suits, or make sure his shoes were shined or send me out to get him some cigarettes . . .

used to make me sit on a Coke box when I first joined the trumpet section. And all because he was the bandleader and I was the youngest guy in the band, a kid, and how this was making me pay some dues because he was the leader and could do this kind of shit to me.

It was while he was in this band that Davis said he had his first serious encounters with drugs. Hobart Dotson, one of the trumpet players, gave him a rock of cocaine (which Dotson referred to as "Miles' Dick"); shortly afterward Miles did liquid cocaine with trumpeter Fats Navarro by means of drops in the nose and sniffing soaked cotton. "All I know is that all of a sudden everything seemed to brighten up, and I felt this sudden burst of energy." Heroin was next, and this time he was introduced to it by Gene Ammons, a saxophonist who would later suffer some of the harshest penalties ever given for drug use, spending eleven of his twenty-eight adult years in prison. But for now, at least, Miles did not consider himself an addict. In fact, he claimed that he was too naive at the time to know what addiction was.

The Eckstine band made a few records while they were in Los Angeles, but their live performances were not drawing large enough crowds to keep a band of their size together. Big bands were on their way out, and B's idea of balancing pop songs with an advanced form of jazz was not working. A postwar recession had set in, and music was one of the first things hurt by it. In New York, even Billie Holiday and Sidney Bechet were sometimes playing to empty rooms on 52nd Street.

Some members of the band recorded a couple of singles in October, one each accompanying vocalists Earl Coleman and Ann Hathaway, but the records remained unissued for forty years. Miles played several short solos and obbligatos behind the singers, and though he sometimes seemed to be straining to complicate the music by choosing notes outside the usual blues chords, his playing was nicely compatible with that of Gene Ammons, the other horn soloist on the records.

Meanwhile, Charlie Parker's behavior had become so bizarre that he had been arrested and placed in a state mental hospital some seventy miles north of Los Angeles, where Miles went to visit him.

I was out [in Los Angeles] in 1946, when Bird got sick. . . . They had put him in Camarillo. I went up to see him. He was sedated, but he knew I was there. They had him behind a wire fence, and it was real dark. I stayed there and talked to him, and he didn't say nothin'. . . . When you give an artist like that shock treatment—and that's what they did—you know, your fingers don't move anymore.

After Eckstine's band set out for the East, they got only as far as Chicago, where they took a break before going on to New York. Miles went home to see his parents, Irene, Cheryl, and his new son, Gregory. When he returned to Chicago, he took Irene and Vernon along with him, and he and Vernon went to a concert of the Chicago Symphony Orchestra. It was an evening heavy with Beethoven, and Miles brought a pocket-sized student score along with him to follow (he pointed out to Vernon that the conductor had cut several bars of music). For a few nights, Miles played at jam sessions at clubs on the Southside with Sonny Stitt or Gene Ammons, and Irene noticed that all the musicians seemed to be nodding. Miles told her that they were high and explained to her how drugs worked on people. He never told her, however, that he was among the users. Once before, while he was still studying at Juilliard, he had asked her to try some marijuana. But when her heart started beating fast, he panicked and afterward avoided mentioning drugs.

The band moved on to Boston and New York and broke up in February 1947 for lack of work. Almost immediately, Miles picked up a recording session with Illinois Jacquet's group, then joined Dizzy Gillespie's new big band for a few weeks at Hunts Point Palace in the Bronx. The trumpet section was made up of Dizzy, Miles, Freddie Webster, Kenny Dorham, and Fats Navarro, all the greatest of the bop horn players, and each night found them reveling in their collective brilliance. But when Charlie Parker asked him to join a new quintet he was putting together with Max Roach, Tommy Potter, and Duke Jordan, Miles left Dizzy's band without a second thought. There were only a few rehearsals, at either Teddy Reig's apartment or Max's mother's house, and most of those Parker missed. When he was there, he was unwilling to assume direction. According to Duke Jordan, "He'd hand a piece of music to Miles and say you do this and you do that. He didn't tell us how to play or try to direct the group. He expected us to know what to play. But he didn't mind hurting your feelings about the music."

On May 8, Parker had another session with Savoy Records, and from the recordings that resulted, it was clear that Davis' role in the group had become more important. On "Chasing the Bird," for example, the interplay between trumpet and saxophone on the melody line puts him on an equal footing with Parker. Instead of their usual unison, the two horns wind around and through each other in a heterophonic style that reaches back to the origins of jazz. "Donna Lee," another of the four pieces recorded that day, was by Davis, his first recorded composition. Unfortunately for Miles, credit for the piece was given to Charlie Parker on the record jacket. Miles later claimed the tune and said that the record company had made a mistake but that he had been paid for it. But other questions have since been raised about the composition's origins.

"Donna Lee" is a pure bebop melody, perhaps *the* quintessentially pure bop melody: fast, relentlessly flowing, difficult to play, and largely based on the harmonic structure and melodic contours of an older pop tune, "Back Home Again in Indiana." Many of the most celebrated bebop melodies, like "Anthropology" and "Ornithology," borrow their harmonic structure from other well-known tunes. Musicologists have variously called this method countermelody, or a silent theme, or a melodic contrafact (an allusion to the medieval practice of replacing the words of a song with new words); some have described this method as a form of homage or parody by means of irony and signifying. But whatever else they may be, these bebop themes conceptually set one song against another, and the tension that results opens up new possibilities for invention. In the case of "Donna Lee," however, Miles apparently had more than just "Indiana" in mind, for his new melody also alludes to another song, "On the Banks of the Wabash." Those in the know at the time might have noticed that the melody of "Donna Lee" also sounded very similar to a solo recorded by Fats Navarro on a record called "Ice Freezes Red." And others said that they had heard lines similar to the melody of "Donna Lee" improvised many times by Charlie Parker when he played "Indiana."

"Donna Lee" was indeed ironic, and maybe too quintessentially bebop as well, since it is such a strong melodic line that the improvised solos that follow it on records made later by others often sound weak by comparison. And it may also be too fast and too difficult, as the various takes of the tune show that Miles had problems playing it that day in the studio, and he never recorded it again.

That summer, when Coleman Hawkins was booked at the Three Deuces, Miles tried to be there every evening to sit in with the man who brought the tenor saxophone into jazz. He never tired of hearing Hawkins answer requests for his jukebox hit "Body and Soul." Thelonious Monk was the pianist, and Miles studied Monk's music and asked him for help with harmony. The band tolerated him because he was serious, and Hawkins treated Miles like a son, selling him his hardly used stylish suits, ties, and shirts for virtually nothing. When he hired Miles for a group that recorded two singles in June, Davis was formally connected to a musician whose career extended almost to the beginnings of jazz.

On August 14, Teddy Reig scheduled the first recording session under Miles' name. It should have been a moment of triumph, but Webster's recent death shadowed the session. Reig later revealed that "I had promised Freddie Webster that I would try to help Miles. Give Miles credit; he had put up with a lot working with Bird and really, like we owed him this date because of all the shit he took. Since Miles was com-paratively unknown, I felt that Bird's presence would help carry him over." Parker played the session using the tenor saxophone instead of his usual alto, and since he was still under contact with Dial Records, some assumed that he was attempting to disguise himself. But Savoy claimed to have signed Parker before Dial, and in any case—bad luck again for Davis—Savoy ultimately issued the records under Parker's name.

Still, Miles was excited by the contract and called home several times to tell everyone about it. He was always in touch with his parents, and his sister and brother, and now he was calling several times a day. Reig said that Miles took the sessions very seriously, choosing the musicians (Max Roach on drums, Nelson Boyd on bass, and pianist John Lewis), rehears-ing them for two days before they recorded, with Parker borrowing tenor saxophones from different people each day. John Lewis brought his com-position "Milestones" to the session, and Miles had written three new pieces of music: "Little Willie Leaps" (based on the harmonic structure of "All God's Children Got Rhythm"), "Half Nelson" (named for Nelson Boyd, and built on the chord structure of Tadd Dameron's "Ladybird"), and "Sippin' at Bells," a blues, and what a blues it was, so dense with chords (eighteen of them, within twelve bars) that only a formalist would recognize it. Dizzy Gillespie said that the younger musicians saw the blues as too down-home, too southern for their taste, and complicated it by creating new harmonic changes—"a thousand changes in one bar." Miles seldom reflected publicly on his past work, but ten years later, he looked back and commented on his tendency in the beginning to complicate simple forms:

> You don't learn to play the blues. You just play. I don't even think about harmony. It just comes. You learn where to put the notes so they'll sound right. You just don't do [it] because it's a funny chord. I used to change things because I wanted to hear them—substitute progressions and things. Now I have better taste.

There was a chamberlike balance and grace to this music, with Miles paying great attention to getting his own sound right. The tempos were moderate, set to Miles' taste, Parker responding by playing within Davis' orbit. Davis seemed at ease, happy to be playing in midrange, and so relaxed as he threaded his way through the chords that some might have called *this* the beginnings of cool jazz.

In August, Parker's quintet played to full houses at the Three Deuces, and no wonder, for their experimentation on the bandstand was visceral and ecstatic. "Bird would go out of meter, shifting the starting places," Duke Jordan said, "and you were expected to keep on playing what you were playing. For a while I had trouble doing that and followed him, and put everyone out of meter." But Miles described it this way:

> He used to turn the rhythm section around every night. Say we would be playing a blues. Bird would start on the eleventh bar. As the rhythm section stayed where they were, then Bird would play in such a way that it made the rhythm section sound like it was on 1 and 3 instead of 2 and 4. . . . Every time he would do this, Max would scream at Duke not to try and follow Bird. He wanted Duke to stay where he was, because he wouldn't have been able to keep up with Bird and would have fucked up the rhythm. Duke did this a lot when he didn't listen. See, when Bird went off like that on one of his incredible solos all the rhythm section had to do was stay where they were and play some straight shit. Eventually Bird would come back to where the rhythm was, right on time. It was like he had planned it in his mind. . . . You had to be ready for anything.

After every set, they were surrounded by fans and musicians asking, "How do you do that?" "What was that tune?" "What book did you get that out of?" Parker usually just laughed and walked away from them. In a year in which the most popular records in America were inane songs like Hoagy Carmichael's "Huggin' and Chalkin'," Count Basie's cover version of Jack McVae's "Open the Door, Richard," or Ted Weems' "Heartaches" (which featured a whistler), Parker's music had the sound of destiny in it.

It was not only the audience that was awed by what he was playing; the rest of the band was hopelessly enthralled as well. Miles heard Parker playing with hard, short bursts of breath that would leave Max Roach "between the beats," while the bassist and pianist were completely lost— "like everybody else, only more lost."

When Bird played like that, it was like hearing music for the first time. I'd never heard anybody play like that. Later Sonny Rollins and I would try to do things like that, and me and Trane, those short, hard bursts of musical phrases. But when Bird played like that, he was outrageous. . . . He was notorious in the way he played combinations of notes and musical phrases. The average musician would try to develop something more logically, but not Bird. Everything he played—when he was on and *really* playing—was terrifying, and I was there every night! . . . It was unreal.

The braver musicians asked to sit in, but Parker usually said no, since most of them couldn't keep up with him. But he loved to play on other musicians' gigs, and whenever Dizzy and he were both working the Street, Gillespie tried to get Bird to join him during intermissions. Sometimes he did. Sometimes he would not come back, and his musicians had to search the clubs for him.

Unlike many other musicians who were using, Bird seldom played badly when he was sick from drugs or the lack of them. He just played differently. Despite their apparent codependency, Parker was often distant from the rest of the group. He called rehearsals and then didn't show, leaving them to rehearse on their own. Then he turned up at the performance at the last minute and played faultlessly whatever they had rehearsed. The message was both clear and infuriating: it was not he who needed to rehearse, it was they. Miles especially felt that he was not up to Parker's standards. He knew he was not playing Parker's music at the level Bird wanted and felt that everyone else knew it. Max Roach, for example, said, "When Kenny Dorham joined the band, the band, to me, actually began to grow as far as playing the figures that Bird had written. I think that Kenny came much closer to dealing with them than Miles did."

Parker was not one to hang out with the other musicians in the group. Miles said that he never talked to Parker for more than fifteen minutes at a time—and that was usually when Parker refused to pay him. The weight of responsibility for rehearsing the band was also beginning to irritate Miles, especially since Parker resisted change.

Bird didn't tell me anything. I did all the work. . . . I rehearsed the band, the foundation, so that he could play what he could play against. The chords that he and Dizzy were playing, to me, were like, sacred. If you didn't play the right chord, what's the use of being in the [bebop] movement? So I had the rhythm section play the right chords, and play the right substitute chords, leading to this and to that.

"He never did talk about music. I always even had to show Duke Jordan, the pianist, the chords." Miles felt they needed a pianist who used bigger, fuller harmony and stayed out of the soloists' way; he told Bird that he wanted to replace Jordan with John Lewis. Lewis was a serious, scholarly person, classically trained, an elegant pianist who used musical space as carefully as Davis did. But Parker called him a "classical musician," and his response to Miles' suggestion was, "You're getting too big for your britches, Miles. If you don't like it, get your own group." On top of everything else, Miles resented Parker's new girlfriend, Doris Sydnor, who, he felt, was attempting to control the band and usurp his own position of musical director.

This was the summer that the Esso Building went up at Rockefeller Center, and by fall, its shadow darkened the blue door of the Deuces. It was only the first sign that midtown Manhattan was on the way to being transformed by financial interests that would soon disperse jazz clubs into other neighborhoods.

The annual *Esquire Jazz Book* for 1947 picked Miles in a poll of the critics as a "New Star," along with musicians like Trummy Young, Sonny Stitt, Lucky Thompson, Dodo Marmarosa, Ray Brown, Milt Jackson, Tadd Dameron, Boyd Raeburn, and Sarah Vaughn. Although Miles often scoffed at such awards, this one, he later said, meant the most to him. Unfortunately, the award was announced in a volume that itself became very controversial. The new editor of the *Book* was also the manager of Eddie Condon, a dixieland guitarist who was a well-known enemy of bebop; so when the 1947 book appeared, many were shocked to see that despite the critics' poll, it had turned away from the new music and was filled with photos of white musicians and articles about older forms of jazz. Something of an organized protest followed. Miles signed a letter along with Louis Armstrong, Coleman Hawkins, Roy Eldridge, Dizzy, Sarah Vaughan, Nat "King" Cole, Billie Holiday, Duke Ellington, Ella Fitzgerald, and twenty-four other musicians objecting to what they saw as a reactionary and Jim Crow view of their music. It was to be the last of the annual jazz books from *Esquire*.

When Irene returned to New York with Cheryl and Gregory, Miles found them a two-bedroom apartment in Jamaica, Queens, with a fenced-in lawn for the children. To her it seemed like a fresh start:

> Miles came home right after work, like other husbands, only at a different time. He'd get on the subway and come straight home, in the middle of the night. First thing he'd do was get Gregory up, and just sit him in front of him and look at him. Little Gregory was so sleepy, that if Miles turned away for a minute, Gregory would toddle off to bed.
>
> Miles loved that child so much . . . he'd take baths with him, and fix his hair with a little rag on his head.

Davis was now twenty-one, in the front line of the most innovative musical group in the United States, as well as being a father and a husband. But Irene was well aware of the kind of domestic strife he had grown up in: "I told him I'd kill him if he ever did to me what his father did to his mother."

Though he described his stay at Juilliard negatively, he continued to study on his own, checking out music scores, going to see Martha Graham dance to John Cage's music, practicing difficult études from a clarinet exercise book, and meeting as many of the pantheon of jazz as he could. On sunny Saturday afternoons, he often borrowed a bicycle, put Gregory on the back, and peddled over to Billie Holiday's house, where they talked and drank gin. Billie reminded Miles of his mother, with her light brown skin, long hair, and regal carriage. Gregory remembers only that his father said that Miss Holiday was very fond of him, that she played with him and never wanted him to leave. It was a strange suburban pastoral: Miles and Billie were drawn together by their commitment to a music perpetually under commercial assault, but also by their common need for family, Billie longing for the children she would never have and Miles for the family he seemed on the verge of losing.

Miles ended 1947 with three recording sessions with Charlie Parker for Dial in October, November, and December in New York City and one other for Savoy in Detroit. His playing on these records shows him coming more to the front (though still often in a mute) in a much more assured and coequal role with Parker. The tempos are generally faster, the melody lines more fragmented and abstract, and new ideas spring forth on almost every record. Though there were still doubters, hereafter Miles Davis could justifiably lay claim to being one of the creators of bebop. And when, in 1949, Ross Russell brought together some of the first recordings Miles had made with Parker on a 12-inch long-playing record titled *The Bird Blows the Blues,* Miles found himself on the first jazz LP ever issued of new recordings, as well as the first jazz LP on a 12-inch record.

On a winter's eve in Chicago in early 1948, Miles, Tommy Potter, Max Roach, and Duke Jordan took the El to a club called the Argyle on the north side of Chicago, the white side. They arrived early, as it was the opening night for the new Charlie Parker Quintet. The band set up and waited. But Bird wasn't there. Meanwhile, the owner—Jack Ruby, a colorful character in his own right, destined to play a small but well-etched role in American history—began to grow angry, pacing through the club and muttering to himself. The house was packed and growing more restless by the minute. Miles slipped over to the phone booth and called his sister to let her know he was in town, just in case they were fired. He was wondering to himself why audiences sat through the music they were playing, much less why they put up with Parker's behavior—or for that matter, why Parker put up with him since Bird complained that no one could play his music correctly.

But the word was out that something exceptional was happening with this saxophonist, and the people were there. And suddenly Parker was too, a couple of hours late, so high on Nembutal that he couldn't find the bandstand. From the first note, the band knew they were in trouble because Bird nodded off asleep on his feet. Even worse, he woke up, say, in the middle of "Embraceable You"—and started playing "Cherokee," then spinning off into "Donna Lee," with Duke Jordan following him. Next, Parker would be out when his turn came to solo. Nothing seemed to wake him, not Max's purposefully loud solos, not Miles' trumpet pointed in his ear. Parker had forgotten his own rule: never take barbiturates and play chromatics. (The sleeping pill of choice was contraindicated when one was sailing loose from chords at superhuman tempos.) Max thought it was all very funny, but Miles felt as if the blame for this madness was resting on him, that he was the one at whom the audience was staring.

After the first set, Bird disappeared and was later found asleep in the phone booth, his pants wet and a stream of urine flowing out the door.

This was the second time that this had happened in his club, said Ruby, and the last. He fired them at the end of the evening. Now they were stranded in Chicago with no money and no way to get home. Parker went to the union building for help and banged on the president's desk when he didn't get it. But the president was sick of Parker's antics as well. He pulled a pistol from his desk drawer and threw him out of his office. Miles' sister took him in that morning and gave him train fare back east. Several years later, Parker would run into Miles and ask, "Why didn't you wake me up in Chicago?"

Parker's fame was spreading, along with his infamy, and his performances were attended by fans who treated him as a god, as well as by musicians who offered any number of personal services to have him teach them. His solos were recorded covertly at clubs, pored over and analyzed by his acolytes. At the same time, his behavior was becoming increasingly erratic. Drug dealers trailed after him wherever he went. Excess and constant partying were beginning to take their toll on his performance. He told Duke Jordan that "if you do something out of the ordinary between sets, when you come back to play, you will have different thoughts, and it will come out in your playing." Something out of the ordinary could mean rolling along on an overturned trash can in the alley, sleeping out in the middle of Dewey Square between sets, or God knows what else. Miles, who claimed to have always seen Parker for what he was, was nonetheless shocked by his capacity for cruelty, his sexual voracity, and the way in which he treated the women around him, and was reaching the point where he could not stand to be with him. Nonetheless, he stayed with Parker for the first half of 1948, traveling with the quintet to Chicago and Detroit from December to March, then with them on Norman Granz' Jazz at the Philharmonic tour of the East and the Midwest through much of April and May. At the end of the tour, Parker refused to pay the band. Max Roach, who could forgive Parker a lot, said that he could understand Parker's position because he had been acting as their teacher. But Miles was livid: "I got two kids, everyday I'm borrowing like a dollar. I'm buying potatoes and cabbage, fatback, and enough for a little cornbread. It cost me about $1.50—onions and carrots and stuff like that. And he told me, 'You will not get a penny, Junior.'" When Miles finally threatened him with a beer bottle, Bird gave him $20.

He would play with Parker off and on for the rest of the year and sometime after, and even record with him a few more times, but the spell had been broken.

CHAPTER THREE

What a thing is Man, this lauded demi-god! Does he not lack
the very powers he has most need of? And if he should soar in
joy, or sink in sorrow, is he not halted and returned to his
cold, dull consciousness at the very moment he was longing
to be lost in the vastness of infinity?

JOHANN WOLFGANG VON GOETHE,
THE SORROWS OF YOUNG WERTHER

The outstanding thing about Miles Davis is not his style but
its genuine, though elusive content. . . . Of late, Davis has
added to these approaches an almost funereal legato style in
the middle and lower registers. These young-Werther rumina-
tions most clearly reveal the content of Davis' music—a view
of things that is brooding, melancholy, perhaps self-pitying,
and extremely close to the sentimental. It is, except for certain aspects of Johnny Hodges and Sidney Bechet, a new flavor in jazz.

WHITNEY BALLIETT, *DINOSAURS IN THE MORNING*

"What had jazz done to him!"

IRENE CAWTHON DAVIS

SOMETIME IN LATE 1947, Miles was stopped one evening on 52nd Street
by a thin white man in a cap and workers' clothes. Miles had seen him in
the clubs, munching salted radishes from a paper bag. What he wanted
from Miles was permission to make a big band arrangement of "Donna

Lee." He was Gil Evans, an arranger for the Claude Thornhill Orchestra. The Thornhill band was something of an anomaly. In a time when dance bands were unambiguously either sweet or hot, Thornhill's had French horns, tuba, flutes, and brass muted in hats, playing together with an almost delicate combination of French impressionism, chinoiserie, and pop song melodrama. What Evans was up to with the Thornhill band when he ran into Davis was simply outrageous: he was attempting to bring bebop sensibilities into this almost fastidiously aristocratic orchestra. Miles had already heard Thornhill's recording of "Robbins' Nest," an Evans arrangement of a piece written by Illinois Jacquet and Sir Charles Thompson for the disk jockey Freddy Robbins. Davis was struck by the sonority of the "bell-like chords" they produced and how relaxed their melody lines were—as if the whole band was playing a written-out bebop solo. Miles told a *Down Beat* reporter a few years later that "Thornhill had the greatest band, the one with Lee Konitz, during these modern times. The one exception was the Billy Eckstine band with Bird." Davis was not alone in his regard for this group. Thelonious Monk and Duke Ellington were also fans of its music. Miles told Evans that he could use "Donna Lee," if in return, Miles could see copies of Evans' arrangements of tunes like "Robbins' Nest."

Evans had drifted into New York in 1946, drawn, like Miles, to the flame of bebop. He stayed with friends until he found his own place, a storage space behind the Asia Laundry on West 55th Street, near Fifth Avenue, then an area of old buildings and warehouses. His room was little more than an unheated basement with all the pipes in the building running through it. He had a bed, an upright piano, a phonograph, hot plate, refrigerator, desk, and a few chairs. It was as close to the action as he could get, and he soon found his place becoming the center of a nightly gathering of a new kind of New York musician. The door was literally always open, and people came and went, sharing the piano and the bed, living a life of the arts in a fishbowl. Almost any night you might have seen Max Roach and Charlie Parker, singer Blossom Dearie and pianist John Lewis, musicians from the Claude Thornhill band like Billy Exiner, Barry Galbraith, Gerry Mulligan, and Joel Shulman, and arrangers like Dave Lambert, George Russell, Johnny Carisi, and John Benson Brooks. Arrangers in jazz are a special breed, operating somewhere between composers and improvisers, recomposing music that already exists, creating variations on themes, erecting frameworks with which to highlight soloists, yet always with a style identifiable as their own. Most of them then were self-taught, drawing their ideas from any place they found them, unafraid to venture into the classics or the world of pop. Paul Hindemith and Charlie Parker? Stefan Wolpe and Duke Ellington? Maurice Ravel and George Gershwin? It all made perfect sense to them.

In his basement salon, Evans was the senior member. When Miles first met him, he was thirty-five, and Davis, like most of the others who dropped in, was barely twenty-one. To them, Evans was a teacher and a scholar with a taste for modern painting and music. He brought home scores and records of contemporary classical music and set an example for serious study of music. Arranger George Russell recalls that Gil, like many others of them, was then under the spell of Stravinsky's *Le Sacre du Printemps* and, for that matter, everything that the city had to offer:

> New York City was ablaze with the most exciting things happening, not only in jazz, but in music in general, in sculpture—it was exploding. Anywhere you went you could tap into the energy. We thought it was an enormously wonderful time, and that it would go on forever.
>
> We all hung out at Gil's apartment under the St. Regis Hotel. I'd go there nightly for a few hours, especially when Bird was staying there. Gil would get Bird, John Lewis and I together and take us over to Juilliard to hear Robert Craft preparing a concert of Hindemith, or to hear Dimitri Mitropoulos rehearse. Gil inspired us to reach for the impossible.

Davis also remembered Evans introducing him to the music of John Cage in 1948 and loaning him recordings by the iconoclastic composer Harry Partch, most likely "Dark Brother" and "U.S. Highball." The first was several paragraphs of a Thomas Wolfe essay set to sliding microtonal chords and arrhythmic drumming, the second a montaged epic of America as seen by hoboes, scored for two vocalist-narrators, modified guitar, and three microtonal instruments of Partch's own making—chromelodeon (a retuned harmonium), kithara (an elaborated harp), and double canon (a form of zither)—all of which he had overdubbed on the recording, producing the sound of desert winds and a slithering, rushing train. This was a liberating experience, Miles said, giving him confidence to go beyond the rules of music.

When Miles began to drop in on the gatherings at Gil's, Gerry Mulligan and Evans had been toying for some time with the idea of writing for a Thornhill-type band, only a hipper, smaller, more focused version, with room for soloists and freedom of movement. It would be an arranger's band, an experimental unit to let them hear in rehearsal new ideas by Carisi, Mulligan, Evans, and Lewis. Nine instruments seemed to be the minimum to get the sound they wanted: six horns and a three-piece rhythm section—a nonet. The idea was to break with the conventional dance band formation of rhythm, saxophones, and brass. Instead, they would spread the sounds and instrumental colors across the orchestra by means of a high-register grouping of trumpet and alto saxophone, a middle group of trombone and French horn, and a low section with tuba and baritone saxophone. This meshed with some ideas about writing for bands that Miles had shared with Charles Mingus back in 1946. Davis thought of the different instruments as if they were a vocal group, one in which each voice could be distinctly heard within a chord. Such an orchestra would have the kind of vocal sound that Duke Ellington managed to get. Miles was also thinking cross-over. The problem with bebop, he thought, was that it was not being fully appreciated and needed to be slowed down to be understood by a broader audience, especially a white audience. "Bird and Diz played this hip, real fast thing, and if you weren't a fast listener, you couldn't catch the humor or the feeling in their music."

It was Miles who took the lead in bringing the band into existence:

Nobody else [but the people I chose] could play those instruments. I wanted Sonny Stitt [on alto saxophone], but Sonny was in jail, you know. And Lee Konitz could play a lot of notes and it wouldn't bother you. . . . Bird would have just shoved them down your throat. Bird was raw.

Not all of the band members shared this view. Mulligan, for one, saw what they were doing as an extension of what they had heard in Charlie Parker's quintets:

What it was, was a bunch of people who appreciated Bird, were influenced by Bird, loved what Bird was doing, and we each applied the lessons from Bird in different ways. But it was because we loved what was going on, it wasn't inaccessible to us, and we weren't thinking about making it that accessible to other people.

Gil, in fact, had first conceived of this group as being built around Charlie Parker, but Bird had no interest in giving up being a soloist in order to become a lead voice in an ensemble. Yet once the group was formed, many musicians heard the nonet's music as an extension of what Miles had been doing. More to the point, once they heard him in a musical setting created to complement his own style, it helped them to appreciate the role he played in Parker's group. Evans recognized that Davis' primary contribution was in the development of his own sound, a mod-

ern trumpet sound "suitable for the ideas he wanted to express." For
Mulligan, Miles "was the perfect lead voice, because of the way he
approached melodies. And so it was very easy for me to write for Miles. I
understood his melodic sense:

> Miles dominated that band completely; the whole nature of the interpre-
> tation was his. That was why we were always afraid to get another trum-
> pet player; it would have been ideal, actually, to have a second trumpet.
> We thought about it but never did it.

Davis assumed the job of organizing rehearsals, making phone calls,
and getting work for the nonet, and it was his name that it would come
to be known by. When they began looking for players, some of the former
members of the Thornhill band were obvious choices: tuba player Bill
Barber, alto saxophonist Lee Konitz, French hornist Junior Collins, and
baritone saxophonist Gerry Mulligan. The trombonist would be J. J.
Johnson, Al McKibbon would play bass, Max Roach drums, and John
Lewis—whom Miles wrote and asked to come back from Paris to play
with them—would be the pianist.

Off and on for the next several months, Miles rehearsed the band,
with the personnel changing depending on who was around and not
working. "Miles did most of the organizing," Mulligan said.

> We did most of the writing, but, left to us, we might not have even ever
> gotten around to getting the thing into rehearsal, we would keep talking
> about it. And, surely if we had gotten into calling rehearsals, we wouldn't
> have called a lot of the people that Miles did, and it was to some, to a great
> extent, what some of the people did that Miles brought in, that made the
> thing gel the way it did as a band. Most notably, Max Roach, who was
> absolutely perfect in that band.

In September, 1948, they found their first paying job, two weeks at a
former chicken restaurant called the Royal Roost, the first of several new
clubs associated with modern jazz that began to open along Broadway
between 47th and 53rd Streets. The nonet would alternate each evening
with Count Basie's band, with Friday night radio broadcasts announced
by disc jockey Symphony Sid Torin. As the opening night approached,
Miles had most of the regulars set, but J. J. Johnson wasn't available. His
job went to Mike Zwerin, a college student not back at school yet; Miles
had heard him one night sitting in at Minton's. Some of the other members of the band were annoyed at Miles' hiring a musician they didn't

know, and for Zwerin, the gig was as much a test of character as it was of music:

> He came over as I packed up about three. I slunk into a cool slouch. . . . We were both wearing shades. No eyes to be seen. "You got eyes to make a rehearsal tomorrow?" Miles asked me. "I guess so." I acted as though I didn't give one shit for his stupid rehearsal. "Nola's. Four." Miles made it absolutely clear that he could not care less if I showed up or not.

When the first night arrived, Zwerin remembered, the Roost was packed. Out front a sign announced, "Miles Davis Band, Arrangements by Gerry Mulligan, Gil Evans, and John Lewis." Miles sat on a small stool near the tuba and trombone. No one announced the tunes or directed the band, and different musicians took turns setting the tempos. "Miles was pleasant and relaxed but seemed unsure of how to be a boss," Zwerin said. "It was his first time as a leader. He relied quite a bit on Evans to give musical instructions to the players." The whole engagement was casual, or "loose and sloppy," according to Lee Konitz, who said they had not rehearsed enough and the personnel were too fluid. "Everybody was ill at ease and trying to make this new kind of band work." Bill Barber already had a job at the Ziegfeld Theater every night, but since it was near the Roost, Miles agreed to his coming in late every night. The music they played was limited to a handful of arrangements, so they had to repeat some songs a couple of times a night. The audience throughout their two-week stay was respectful but not excited. It was not the kind of music they expected from a big band, nor was it the way they were used to hearing bebop. Like so many other signal moments in jazz history, there was no press there to document the occasion. But musicians who heard it were impressed. The band took pride when the whole trumpet section of the Gene Krupa Orchestra came to hear them. And Count Basie, himself no modernist, told a journalist, "Those slow things sounded strange and good. I didn't always know what they were doing, but I listened, and I liked it."

Among the audience at the Roost was Pete Rugolo, an arranger with Stan Kenton's band who had recently been given the job of signing jazz groups with Capitol Records, a new recording company located in Hollywood. He had already signed Tadd Dameron and Lennie Tristano. Although another recording ban had been called by the Musicians' Union that would last for most of 1948, Rugolo arranged for the nonet to be recorded as soon as it was over. On January 5, 1949, Miles signed a contract with Capitol, and on January 21 the group went into the studios of radio station WMGM on Fifth Avenue for the first four of the twelve single records contracted for.

The band huddled around Miles while they recorded Gerry Mulligan's "Jeru" (Miles' nickname for him) and George Wallington's "Godchild," both arranged by Mulligan; "Budo" (Bud Powell's "Hallucinations," retitled, and claimed by Miles in both his and Powell's names) and "Move," written by Denzil Best and arranged by John Lewis. The session was remembered as being "tense, hectic, and filled with headaches for all concerned—much last-minute planning preceded it, and the seeking, searching experimentation continued throughout." "Move," for example, was a popular jam tune among boppers, with a jagged, rhythmic melody, but Lewis' arrangement softened its nervous edges with its voicing and light phrasing and by introducing a tranquil countermelody against the trumpet and saxophone melody. With only three minutes to record with, give or take, everyone made the most of it. Davis' solo was concise and to the point. (He had written out the introductory and concluding phrases of his solos to ensure continuity in the short times in which he had to play). Max Roach's drum breaks hinted of nostalgia for the conventions of big band drumming, but the independent tuba line, the interplay of the horns, and the restraint of the rhythm section signaled that a radical alternative to the swing band was being introduced.

They were back in the studios on April 22 to record "Venus de Milo" by Mulligan, "Boplicity" by Evans and Davis, "Rouge" by John Lewis, and "Israel" by John Carisi. And almost a year later, on March 9, 1950, they would return to the studio for "Moon Dreams," a pop tune arranged by Evans, "Rocker" by Mulligan, "Darn That Dream," another pop tune, sung by Kenny Hagood, and "Deception" by Davis himself. Since "Deception" was based on pianist George Shearing's "Conception," some may have taken lightly Davis' role in reshaping it. But what he did with it offers clues for understanding his working methods for years to come. Miles extended each of the A parts of the composition by two bars to a total of fourteen, then eliminated the harmonic structure of five of the last fourteen bars, replacing it with a pedal—a single repeated note from the bass—that creates the effect of the melody floating free of the harmony and even free of the rhythm. (Vibraphonist Teddy Charles says that by putting this interlude into Shearing's "Conception"—and later, doing much the same to "Dear Old Stockholm"—Miles created pieces that were not played very often because they were too difficult.)

It was not until 1954 that all of these sessions were grouped together on record, when eight of the compositions were issued on a 10-inch LP under the title *Birth of the Cool*. If what was meant by "cool" was understatement, a softer attack, a quieter and smoother flow of rhythm, and lower volume and vibrato, then cool music had been around at least since the 1920s with musicians such as Bix Beiderbecke, Frank Trumbauer, and Red Nichols. In the 1930s, it was a style that could be heard in the music of Red Norvo and John Kirby, and most pointedly in the playing of Lester Young, a saxophonist whose style helped usher in bebop. (Young had underscored the long history of his own style by pointing back to Frank Trumbauer as an inspiration. Miles himself, on being asked if he ever listened to Bix Beiderbecke, also made a similar connection when he answered, "No, but I listened to Bobby Hackett, and *he* listened to Bix.") Even in the 1940s, the musicians associated with Lennie Tristano were creating a form of bebop that had an equal claim on cool. If, on the other hand, Davis' music was being labeled "cool" in order to emphasize its existence as a counterforce to bebop, that made more sense, for it was what he intended. As he put it, "After a while, what was happening around New York became sickening, because everybody was playing the clichés that people had played five years before, and they thought that made them 'mod-ren' musicians. I really couldn't stand to hear most of those guys."

Miles may have been the driving force behind the band, but there were grumblings about his leadership. His method of directing was indirect and nonverbal, and added to the work habits that sometimes kept Gil Evans from finishing arrangements, the band was often unsure of what to do next. Tensions built up in the group, according to Mulligan, and Miles was not willing to deal with them:

> John Lewis got really upset with Miles, for a number of reasons, not the least of which was when the band became a working entity, Miles refused to assume control. He thought if you got problems, they'll solve themselves. You know, things don't work themselves out in bands. Somebody has to make it come together, and I suppose that being Miles' first band, he hadn't come to grips with that, so the first band, when it went out to play in clubs—this is not a problem when you're a recording band or a rehearsal band—but when a band plays night after night in clubs, then you start running into whole new sets of problems. About phrasing, and playing together, and so on . . . somebody has to lay down the rules: . . . if there's a choice, somebody has to make the choice.

John Lewis would keep trying to tell him, "Miles, you went out and got the gig for this. This is not a rehearsal band any more. If you want to be the leader, then you've got to be the leader." Miles would say, "Bullshit, man. Problems have got to take care of themselves."

Then there was Miles' casual way with credits and money. The arrangers who wrote the band's book did so for the pleasure of hearing their music without any regard for money. But when Miles received advances of $150 a side for each single record and small royalties began to come in, they wanted their share. According to Mulligan, "John . . . was [also] upset because it became Miles' band, and those of us that had written the music never got paid for the charts. We never got any money from the record company when the things were recorded. Miles assumed ownership."

But no one denied that the nonet was an artistic success, and even now, fifty years later, it's obvious that this music was fresh and filled with surprises. Miles said at the time that "Boplicity" was his own favorite recording and claimed the melody while giving Evans credit for the harmonization (though, on the advice of his father, Davis registered the composition under his mother's maiden name, to make sure his rights were protected). He later commented that the reason that other bands hadn't played it was that the "top line isn't interesting. The harmonization is, but not the tune itself."

For years, he continued to say that the nonet was one of his favorite bands, though he was critical of it for being more interested in writing than in recording and getting work:

> We made twelve sides altogether with the group. Some of them were so bad that I asked Capitol not to release them, but they did anyway. And those sessions were so much trouble! Everyone in the band was nervous. And at every rehearsal, there were these little cliques. Gerry was always looking at me so that I wouldn't play anything fast. He didn't like to play fast then and Max was about to drive him nuts. A couple of the guys were studying composition and they'd always have their heads together. Everyone was tense.

Yet five years after the last of the singles was recorded, Miles told jazz writer Nat Hentoff that he would like to do a similar session with a full brass section, anticipating the Columbia recordings with Gil Evans' arrangements.

Today, some suggest that this band was the first of a series of strategic errors that Davis made that ultimately led him away from jazz. This music, they say, was too academic, or too commercial, maybe too European—that is to say, too white—and it failed to swing in any real jazz sense. But the concept of swing is notoriously complex and far from agreed on or even understood. On the nonet's approach to rhythm, for example, Gerry Mulligan once quoted Mel Powell, the pianist and arranger with Benny Goodman's band between 1941 and 1943:

> He said the first impact of Benny Goodman's band in the 1930s was people saying how could all these guys play ahead of the beat, on top and ahead of it and make it swing? It didn't sound like they were playing out of rhythm or anything. And when *our* date came along, he said, it was the complete opposite; how could we lay so far back, play so far behind the beat together, and sound like we were swinging and not slow down?

Although the 78 rpm singles that resulted from these sessions did not sell well and the group played publically only once, these musicians knew they were doing something special, that they were crossing lines. For one thing, it was a racially integrated band, and that had a certain cachet. But to some black musicians outside the band, it was an affront for Davis to hire whites. Times were tight for musicians during the recording ban, and some let him know their objections. But he was unmoved:

> So I just told them that if a guy could play as good as Lee Konitz played—that's who they were mad about most, because there were a lot of black alto players around—I would hire him every time, and I wouldn't give a damn if he was green with red breath.

Some black musicians also disparaged the cool music that developed in the wake of this band—Dizzy Gillespie, for example—though he made an exception for Miles: "Miles wasn't cool like that, anyway. Miles is from that part of St. Louis where blues comes from. Just part of his music is played like that, cool. They copped that part—the cool—but let the rest, the blues, go, or they missed it."

Much of the influence of this band was with white musicians, to be sure, many of whom were located on the West Coast—Shorty Rogers, Dave Pell, and especially Marty Paich, who used a band very similar to the *Birth of the Cool* group behind Jeri Southern on her 1958 recording, *Southern Breeze*. His band even quotes from the Davis recordings on "Isn't This a Lovely Day." "It got to be traditional awfully fast to do a date with French horn and tuba," Gil Evans joked some years later. Both Gil Evans and John Carisi also continued to write for similar groups on recordings made in the 1950s for RCA under the title of the Jazz Workshop. But this influence did not stop at race lines. Alto saxophonist Sonny Criss, an African American, recorded with a similar group on his 1968 album, *Sonny's Dream*. And the musicians in Davis' group themselves went on to change jazz in a myriad of ways that nonetheless recall the original band. John Lewis formed the Modern Jazz Quartet, which used forms borrowed from European classical music as well as from jazz, and played everything with a delicate touch. Gerry Mulligan created a pianoless quartet characterized by the subtle use of counterpoint. Lee Konitz continued to participate in the experiments that Lennie Tristano was carrying out in New York. J. J. Johnson wrote a number of extended compositions that expanded ideas about what a jazz band could play. And French hornist Gunther Schuller developed the concept of the third stream, a music with the orchestral complexity of advanced contemporary classical music, but played with an improvisational feel.

As soon as the stay at the Roost ended, Miles went back in the studio to record with Parker for Savoy, and by December the Parker quintet was playing the Roost as well. It was there that Norman Granz approached Bird about again taking the quintet on a tour with the Jazz at the Philharmonic, the first jazz spectacular, a traveling company of musicians whose careers Granz was in effect managing. Miles was appalled by the idea. Aside from his bad experience with Parker on the last tour, he didn't like the artistic concept behind the JATP. Granz had a reputation for raising the income and accommodations of jazz musicians who worked for him, but he did it by packaging the jam session for theater presentation and pushing the music toward the kind of overheated histrionics that was then associated with rhythm and blues: honking saxophones, screaming trumpets, hysterical call-and-response solo exchanges, and raw physicality. The players he used had a variety of styles and came from different historical periods, but were encouraged to play together regardless of compatibility. Miles found the idea distasteful and feared that Parker's participation in it would weaken the music.

I knew every chord that [Parker] and Dizzy played. Every night, we're listening for it and trying to learn how to play it. And then Norman Granz comes in and ruins everything by taking Bird to Jazz at the Philharmonic. He ruined the [bebop] movement. There's no more Diz and Bird, there's no more, "I have to have the right piano player, I have to have the right drummer," there's no more development.

I felt like he'd broken a silent code, you know what I mean? That it would hurt [the progress of] the music. So I told Max, "I'm not going. You do what you want to do." And Max said, "I'm not either."

Bird then went on his own, playing with the tour's rhythm section, some of whom still had one foot in swing music. As far as Miles was concerned, that alone confirmed that he had been right not to go.

By the early months of 1949, Miles' visibility was increasing rapidly. Not yet twenty-three years old, he had placed high in a readers' poll in *Metronome* magazine, and following that, recorded with the Metronome All-Stars, a band made up of the poll's winners. Sitting in the trumpet section alongside Dizzy Gillespie and Fats Navarro, the three trumpeters traded short phrases in the same solo space, and it was difficult to tell who was who. Miles played high and fast and as aggressively as the others. Here, if nowhere else, it was clear that he *could* play like them but was apparently choosing not to do so.

Just after the first nonet recording session, Miles joined the ten-piece house band at the Royal Roost which was led by pianist Tadd Dameron, one of the few arrangers who knew how to adapt bebop to big bands successfully. Though Fats Navarro was their usual trumpet player, Davis played with them in February and then recorded with them in April. Miles can also be heard on live recordings from the club, for the second time as the lead trumpet of a large ensemble, and taking well-constructed solos spaced by silences that drummer Kenny Clarke enthusiastically filled. In March, Davis appeared on a CBS-TV show called *Adventures in Jazz,* one of several specials at the time that paired boppers with dixieland players in a mock battle of the bands. Miles soloed briefly against Max Kaminsky on "Billie's Bounce."

It was sometime in early 1949 that Miles said that Duke Ellington asked to see him at his office in the Brill Building and told him he wanted to include him in his plans for the fall. It was a great moment for Miles, but because he had hopes for the *Birth of the Cool* group, he had to say no.

Looking back, Miles later said that in early 1950, Gil Evans went into a writing slump. But it was worse than that: Evans was using drugs more often and may even have had a breakdown. Gil simply said he spent those years waiting for Miles. Whatever the case, despite their affinity for one another, each of them found himself in his own form of difficulty, and they drifted apart for the next four or five years.

> If these [jazz]men's lives are often tormented, it's because instead of keeping death at a distance, like other artists, they are always mindful of the marriage of existence and death.
>
> SIMONE DE BEAUVOIR, *AMERICA DAY BY DAY*

In February 1948, Dizzy Gillespie had taken a remarkable big band into the Salle Pleyel, a concert hall in Paris. The group was flush with young talent, primed to play the erratic rhythms and surprise harmonies of bop. Few people in France had heard bop played by a large band, and no one was ready for Gillespie's group. Stark, explosive pieces like "Things to Come" were shocking enough, but Gillespie had also brought along Chano Pozo, a Cuban conga drummer who had grown up playing in the services of the Abakwa, a religion with ancient roots in Nigeria. When Gillespie played the "Afro-Cuban Suite," the jazz sections suddenly gave way to Pozo leading the band in choral chants in a Nigerian-Cuban creole language. The audience was at first stunned into silence and then erupted into shouting—pro and con. If this was music that was capable of bewildering American audiences, for the French, who had been cut off from developments in American jazz over the previous seven war years, it was even more confusing. Bebop, they had been led to believe, was the height of urbanity and sophistication.

Liberation of the French from the Nazis had meant release from the fear of being forced to labor for the Germans, as well as the lifting of curfews and bans on music and theater. It also meant the end of food rationing and the return of exiled teachers, stationery, foreign films, and phonograph records. The craze among French youth for American jazz had continued through the war and had taken on new meaning under Nazi occupation. But for most of the young, dixieland and swing were still new, and only among some of the *zazous* of St-Germain-des-Prés (the young hipsters who drew their name from the sounds of Cab Calloways's scat singing) had bebop taken hold. The arrival of bop set off a critical war between traditionalists and boppers even more spirited than the one already under way in the United States. Many French traditionalists chose to ignore bop, treating it as an aberration caused by black intellectuals who, they said, had been warped by drugs and American culture. But with liberation, American GIs visiting French clubs wanted to hear the kind of music they had heard on V-discs and radio broadcasts from Armed Forces Radio. Bebop was sending a frisson through postwar France, a shock much like the one that followed their discovery of film noir once American movies began to be seen there again. Bop was separating intellectuals from one another and dividing age groups into warring camps. The *querelle de bebop* was on.

Nonetheless, jazz continued to thrive in postwar France, and by the end of 1949, the critic Charles Delauney organized the largest jazz spectacle ever staged anywhere, one that would bring together both sides of the bebop debate and draw musicians from virtually every country where jazz was popular. Kenny Clarke, the drummer with Dizzy Gillespie's big band, had stayed on to live in Paris when Gillespie left for the United States, and when he heard that the festival wanted some other American boppers in addition to Parker, he suggested Tadd Dameron. When Dameron was offered a spot on the program, he proposed using Miles Davis and alto saxophonist James Moody (already living in Paris) as the horns for his band, with Clarke as the drummer. (The choice of a bass player he left to the producers, and it turned out to be another American expatriate in Paris, Barney Spieler.)

Miles was excited by the idea of going to Europe and taking his first plane trip. He had a new suit fashioned for the occasion, especially after the ultrahip saxophonist Dexter Gordon had made fun of his conservative tastes. The only serious difference in the new suit was its wide shoulders, but in the fashion of the times, such small distinctions meant everything. Irene wanted to go with him to Paris, but Miles told her that traveling with a bunch of musicians was not a good idea. So she and the children saw him off at the airport on May 7, the day before the opening concert.

When Miles arrived in France he checked into a hotel on the Place de l'Etoile, and the next day rehearsed and performed at the Salle Pleyel, where their quintet followed Sidney Bechet, the boogie-woogie pianist

Pete Johnson, a jam session that included Don Byas, Hot Lips Page, and others, and preceded the Charlie Parker Quintet. Parker was the star of the festival, but his onstage and offstage behavior became something of a scandal. Instead of acknowledging applause, he quickly turned and counted off the next piece; when a member of the audience gave him a rose, he ate it; during an interview with a British journalist, he answered every question with a quote from the *Rubáiyát*.

Pianist Henri Renaud recalled that Miles' first of several appearances at the festival was also something of a surprise for Parisian jazz fans. They had already heard Parker's recordings and been thrilled by them, but found those with Davis on them disappointing. This was not the bravura display of trumpet technique and harmonic sophistication that they had heard from Gillespie. If Dizzy was bebop, what was this? Renaud said,

> Many musicians had been stunned by Dizzy Gillespie's appearance in Paris the year before, and so saw Miles as somehow not the real thing—no vibrato, no flurries of fast notes, no stratospheric soaring. . . . But slowly, Miles became the talk of Paris. To some, his technique, his harmonic sense, his choice of notes, that moody sound, meant that he was the real avant-garde of jazz.

Live in Paris, Miles sounded louder, clearer, and higher than they had thought he was capable of playing. He even said that the whole French experience "pushed things up a notch." Some parts of those concerts were broadcast on radio and then recorded by Renaud, and hearing them today is a surprise to those who only know Miles' nonet recordings from the same period. On slow ballads like "Don't Blame Me," he was melodically inventive and risky. "The young musicians were amazed by the chords Tadd Dameron was playing," Renaud said. "And by the fact that Miles could play with him." Dameron seemed to pull chords from out of the air, changing their progression at will. At rehearsals, Tadd "fed Miles some original melody lines," British guitarist Ivor Mairants observed, "which Miles at first considered 'impossible to play,' but eventually performed."

Onstage, Miles was poised and assured. He announced songs, set the pattern of solos, and as far as the audience was concerned was the leader. On the last night, he was chosen to be part of a blues jam with Sidney Bechet, Toots Thielemans, Parker, Max Roach, and the other stars of the festival. (Miles allowed that he had never heard Sidney Bechet before, but that Bechet's playing reminded him of Duke Ellington's lead alto saxophonist, Johnny Hodges.) For the first time in his life as a big name musician, he was playing without Charlie Parker, and being admired for himself and what he could do.

Wherever Miles went during his ten days in Paris, a young man named Boris Vian seemed always to be nearby. Vian was one of the better-known characters of postwar Paris, a dynamo of boundless energy and crazed talent. On the humdrum train of everyday life, someone once said, it's Boris who pulls the emergency brake and stops the routine in the middle of anywhere. Boris specialized in everything. He was an engineer, a part-time surrealist and pataphysician, jazz trumpet player, pop songwriter, singer, novelist, translator of Raymond Chandler and Nelson Algren, opera composer, and author of the notorious pulp fiction, *I Spit on Your Grave* (which Vian claimed he had translated from the work of a black American named Vernon Sullivan, although it was later discovered that Vian had written it himself). He was also one of the first jazz disc jockeys, and his record programs in France even reached New York City on station WNEW in 1948 and 1949.

Boris and his two brothers played late-hour sets in small clubs with Claude Abadie's orchestra, an amateur traditional jazz group. Vian also wrote articles for the then somewhat reactionary magazine *Jazz-Hot*, arguing the line of the so-called mouldy figs—the side of the jazz divide that held that anything after swing (and sometimes even swing itself) was a decadent form of music (Bix Beiderbecke was Vian's man). But when Boris first heard Miles' solo on Charlie Parker's "Now's the Time," the connection between bebop and the music of the 1920s that had eluded him was made clear. Now Vian changed sides with a vengeance, mocking the jazz controversy by likening it to the arguments that had gone on between Nazis and communists. In the 1948 Christmas issue of *Jazz-Hot*, he published a short parody in which Goebbels visits Vian and they greet each other with "Heil Gillespie" and "Heil Parker" salutes. While smoking weed, Goebbels tutors Vian in propaganda and the hip manner in which to order food: "Une poule au riz-bop . . . du riz-bop au curry-bop, avec pain riz-bop et du thelonious."

Shortly before Miles reached Paris, Vian announced himself as Davis' defender, and was already arguing for him as one of the greatest jazz musicians of all time. In one of the first articles written about Davis anywhere ("Miles Davis: The Ears of a Faun"), Vian said that Miles's brilliance stemmed from his total relaxation, the logic of his melodies and his use of space, his sound—"nude, vulnerable, almost no vibrato, totally calm, but . . . excitingly vehement"—and his sense of rhythmic structure and balance.

It was at one of the rehearsals for the festival in Paris that Vian introduced Davis to Juliette Greco, whom Miles would later describe as "the first woman that I loved as an equal human being." Born to a Corsican family, Greco grew up in Paris during the war, was a member of the underground Resistance in her teens, and had come to be known as the queen of the *zazous*. It was her dark slacks and long straight hair that set the mode for postwar French women (Simone de Beauvoir never forgave her for being the first woman after the war to wear her hair that way). You could always find Greco amid the new underground, hanging out in bars in the cellars of the Latin Quarter, places like the Rhumerie Martiniquaise, Café Flore, Club St-Germain, the Montana Bar, Les Deux Magots, Brasserie Lipp, but most often in Tabou, a *cave*, a basement, with African masks on the walls, which opened in 1945. Greco was beginning to develop into a singer and actress, and when Miles first met her, she was reading poetry at the Tabou and acting in Jean Cocteau's film *Orpheus*. (After her success in that film, she appeared in a string of French and American movies, including *The Sun Also Rises, The Roots of Heaven, Naked Earth*, and *The Big Gamble*.)

The attraction between Miles and Juliette was part exoticism, part the delight in being beautiful, being young geniuses together. "She told me that she didn't like men but that she liked me. After that we were together all the time." Nicole Barclay, the wife of club owner and record producer Eddie Barclay, warned Miles that Greco was an existentialist. He wasn't sure what that meant (who was?), but he was fascinated by her—her dark eyes and hair, the shape of her nose. He called her his "Gypsy girl." Their relationship was sensual, based on touch, gesture, and few words (neither spoke the other's language). They walked together through Paris, drank in cafés, and mixed with writers, intellectuals, and artists. For the first time in his life, Miles said, he was drawn away from music, and for the first time he found himself able to look at things, to feel them, to be in love with a place and a time, the smell of Paris, of cologne, of coffee, all of it almost tropical in its richness and intensity.

Miles told Kenny Clarke that he had never felt so free in his life as when he walked along the Seine, drinking wine, unnoticed by anyone. Or when he walked into a restaurant without bothering to know whether they would serve him. (When Miles was in Paris some years later, he ran into the French pianist René Urtreger, and as they passed each other, he whispered in René's ear, "Freedom!") Almost everywhere he went, fans gathered around him, especially women. At one point, one of them ran up and asked for an autograph, handing him her program open to a picture of Hot Lips Page, a very different looking trumpet player who had come to fame with Count Basie's Orchestra in the 1930s. Miles signed it with Page's name. Then, as she began to recognize him, he signed Page's name again to another picture of Page next to one of himself. It was an incident that would be repeated over and over throughout his life when fans sometimes confused him with his younger musicians or roadies. He never ceased to enjoy the wicked possibilities for humor in these little racial scenes.

Greco introduced Miles to Jean-Paul Sartre, and the two men were intrigued by what they shared in common. Sartre was a short man who took amphetamines, loved boxing and jazz, and had once wanted to be a jazz pianist and singer. In fact, he was a good enough pianist to teach students, though his taste at the time ran less to jazz and more to spirituals, light swing, and pop tunes. (In *Nausea*, a novel he came to regret having written, Sartre's protagonist compares life unfavorably to art by rhapsodizing over the "jazz tune" "Some of These Days," by Sophie Tucker.) Sartre was helping Greco plan her first nightclub act and gave her one of his own songs, which she added to a repertoire written by other literati such as Françoise Sagan, Raymond Queneau, and François Mauriac.

Miles and Sartre chatted through an interpreter (possibly Vian's wife, Michelle), mostly showbiz talk, Sartre telling him about his woes with American producers who were proceeding with an unauthorized American adaptation of his play *Les Mains Salées*, set to open in New Haven, Connecticut, as *Red Gloves* with Charles Boyer in the lead, until Sartre's attorneys put a stop to it. Later, recalling his nights with Sartre, Miles would laughingly claim—perhaps with some justification—that he should have gotten at least *some* of the credit for existentialism. Vian also brought Sartre to see Charlie Parker play at the St. Germain. When he introduced them, Parker said to Sartre, "I like your playing very much." (Even today, the French still puzzle over the meaning of that remark.)

When the time came for Miles to leave, Juliette urged him to stay, as did Sartre and Kenny Clarke, but he had obligations, a wife and two children, the final stage of the recordings of the nonet, and a heroin habit in the making. Once he was back in New York, Miles never wrote to Juliette, but asked about her of anyone he met who might have run into her. (Henri Renaud said when he met Miles, the first thing he said to him was, "You French? You must know Juliette.") Later, when one of Greco's films opened in the United States, Miles went to see it and was stunned to see that Greco's character had a picture of him on her dresser. Was it a signal to him? A message to come back? But still, he never wrote.

They would see each other from time to time over the years. Yet when Greco published her autobiography, *Jujube*, in 1983, it was for the most part silent on Miles Davis. In the huge cast of characters that populates her book, he appears only once: it is the 1950s; she is in New York and visits Birdland, where she sees Miles and the members of the Modern Jazz Quartet. They talk late into the night, and she invites them all for dinner to her suite at the Waldorf Astoria Hotel the next evening. When the maître d' brings the dinner up, the musicians sense his disapproval— in the language of the times, they "feel a draft." At five in the morning, long after the guests have gone home, Greco receives a call:

> It was Miles Davis. "If you don't want to ruin your reputation and your career in America, come to see us at our place, but don't ever be seen with us at yours. Do what I'm asking of you: I don't want you to be called a 'nigger's whore.' I like you very much, you know, but you have to understand that you're not in Paris, but in the U.S. of A."
>
> Greco cried out of sadness and rage. She also cried over the insult against her and over those who suffer under oppression. She would see them on the sly. Some day they would declare their friendship to her and Miles would play for her alone and would make her taste fried chicken which he would prepare himself in the sweetness of a liberty regained if only for a few hours.

In Davis' autobiography, Greco takes up fewer than three pages. His account of their meeting at the Waldorf is strangely different from hers. He is still in love with her, desperate to see her, when she calls and asks him to come to her suite. He takes drummer Art Taylor along with him, "just in case." "That way, I could control the situation as best I could." The appearance of two black men at the front desk calling on a French movie star shocks the clerks. When they reach her door and she rushes into his arms, he "goes into his black pimp role . . . mainly because I was scared." He demands money from her and then leaves abruptly without an explanation.

In New York, Miles was faced with the responsibilities of a family again, and if he expected that his triumph in Paris would put him in demand in the

United States, he was sorely disappointed. There was even less work offered to him now than before he left. The postwar recession of late 1949 and 1950 hit just as the public was becoming interested in new forms of rhythm and blues, and together they were enough to push bebop out of the spotlight. Bop was beginning to be looked on as a cause of the decline in jazz, and *bebopper* was on the verge of becoming a synonym for juvenile delinquent. In New York, people were still debating whether bop was jazz. Charlie Parker said no; Dizzy Gillespie said yes. In an interview with *Down Beat* reporter Pat Harris, Davis went to some pains to agree with Gillespie. Surprisingly, he also defended dixieland music and said that bop was just one form of many styles in jazz. He insisted that all modern jazz musicians had been influenced by earlier forms of jazz and illustrated his point by saying that while he was in Paris, he heard Sidney Bechet play a musical figure that he'd first heard from Charlie Parker when they were recording "KoKo." When he asked Bechet about it, Sidney told him it was from an "old New Orleans march" ("High Society").

Despite disappointments, Miles was still basking in the glow of the sweet life he had experienced during his short stay in Paris. In the same *Down Beat* interview, he said, "What I would like to do is to spend eight months in Paris and four months here. Eight months a year where you're accepted for what you can do, and four months here because—well, it's hard to leave all this." Whether "all this" included his family, or drugs, music, and at least some affinity for his country of birth was not clear.

He moved his family to 173rd Street in nearby St. Albans, Queens, bought an almost new blue Dodge convertible on time payment, and once again tried to maintain normal family life. But this was not the way it was to be. Jazz lived alone or nowhere, dressed up every night, walked into clubs with a horn under its arm, made itself known. Jazz had no day job, no wife or child. Jazz could drift over to Nola's Studios and find someone to jam with, and never have to go home for dinner or explain itself. Yet here was Miles, out of work most of the time, depressed, and living the life of the square in the suburbs. It was all too much.

He began commuting daily back and forth to Harlem, going to the gym, having breakfast with Lester Young whenever he was in town, and hanging out with a new generation of musicians who had been drawn to bebop and were now deep into drugs. "When we first came to New York everyone was so bright and eager," Irene said. "Then suddenly everyone was nodding." Heroin had spread across Harlem, and the best of the younger musicians had given themselves to drugs. Cocaine had begun to circulate outside Spanish Harlem, and Miles was using both.

For some time he'd been snorting diluted heroin and cocaine, but with only short-term highs, and if he missed a day, he'd be hit with aches, fever, and chills; a gradual weakness took over, and his nose was constantly streaming. A friend told him that he had a habit and that inhaling was an expensive waste of the drug, so he began injecting it. First, he got high alone, but he hated the idea of becoming a junkie who roamed the streets with the drug as his only friend. He moved instead into one of those small circles of users who "roomed" with each other—regularly getting high together someplace in the city, borrowing and stealing from each other, bound together in a strange comitatus, a fellowship of the needle in the name of bebop.

Miles' behavior changed quickly. He became withdrawn, distant, passive, asexual. The transformation was so rapid and profound that at first Irene suspected him of being with other women, then discovered it was drugs:

> Miles began coming home later and later in the evening. I accused him of drugs, because I'd found a spot of blood on his shirt. He grabbed the shirt out of my hand and said nothing. I got him an appointment with a psychiatrist, and he went once. But he never went again because he said the psychiatrist was crazy.

Miles' daily commutes to Manhattan were becoming shopping trips for narcotics. "My mother was a country girl at the time," their son Gregory said, "and she could see the deterioration of his character. I remember my mother trying to hide his shoes from him so that he wouldn't be able to go out to cop." And when Miles was at home, his depression deepened:

> Irene and I didn't have any kind of family life anyway. We didn't have a whole lot of money to do things with, with the two kids and ourselves to feed and all. We didn't go anywhere. Sometimes I used to stare in space for two hours just thinking about music. . . . I basically left Irene sitting at home with the kids because I didn't want to be there. One of the reasons I didn't want to be there was that I felt so bad that I couldn't hardly face my family. Irene had such confidence and faith in me. . . . But Irene knew. It was all there in her eyes.

"One Thanksgiving we didn't have the money for a turkey," Irene said, "so we bought as big a chicken as we could, and Miles told the children, 'See the turkey?' When Easter Sunday came, I asked Miles to pick up some dye for Easter eggs. But when I brought the children home from church, Miles had just drawn on the eggs with a pencil."

Smack, junk, skag, horse, shit, H. It had as many names as an ancient god, which for some it seemed to be. Heroin was the ultimate high. It could remove the constant knot from your stomach, or make you think you'd always had one there before you'd used it. It was not so much that it could bring you euphoria and erase the day-to-day concerns of family and job, but it could take away the surprises and lower emotions. St. Louis hipster Ollie Matheus recalled Charlie Parker's praise for his drug of choice: "Bird says it's like a loan. You consolidate all your loans into one payment; that's a junkie. All of life's problems are one problem." Like driving in a fast car—something Miles would soon grow to love— heroin narrowed the emotional and visual fields to only the moment. It gave a crystalline vision of the music, slowing the music down as well, stopping and holding up to the light those beautiful bop melodies that otherwise could fly by so fast that they left nothing but vapor trails. Before club gigs or recording dates, the musicians could be seen fanning out across the city looking to score—up to the roof of a place in Hell's Kitchen, into a Spanish restaurant on Eighth Avenue, uptown to a certain corner. A musician prepares.

With Miles, a certain remoteness also set in; his attention span shortened, and his distance from others increased. The drug itself became the object of his affection. In an insecure and capricious world, it was something he could count on to work, and work again and again, forming a ritual of return that in itself stabilized and gave solace. Beyond that, it was the key to the door of the restricted club of those who know. Pianist Walter Davis described the exclusivity of drugs this way:

> I just know that when you got high at that time, you were further into the clique. . . . It was in to be doing that. [When somebody was playing well] conversation went like this: you would always hear somebody say, "Who the hell is that?" Guy say, "Well, that's such and so," and the next question would be, "Does he get high?" You say, "Yeah, he gets high as a motherfucker."

Heroin was emblematic for some musicians, a sign of alienation from a certain kind of society. It was, after all, a crime to use it. For Miles, it signified that he was not a square—or a dentist. Yet like all other junkies, life for him was now built around drugs. He had to find them, had to cop, score, deal. He had to protect himself against rip-offs of all sorts, everything from impure product to bad counts. He had to watch his transactions like any middle-class man of commerce, and make sure that he timed every part of the process correctly so that he wasn't nodding during the set, wasted before the gig, or arrested. Heroin took time, labor, and planning, and when he traveled anywhere, the problems were compounded: where to cop, and where to go if he got sick? He would ultimately declare that heroin was boring—the waiting, living in the present, all those rituals of use—but for now it was the cost of feeling safe for the moment.

Heroin is an illusory drug, its continuous use a source of physical pain, disappointment, and heartbreak, each hit less satisfying than the previous one, until a nostalgia for the first time drives the urge. Miles soon hit bottom, and went so low that he saw something in himself that he could never forget. He had crossed the line, and even when he was off drugs, the experience haunted him. He constructed a vision of his experience that changed him from a "nice, quiet, honest, caring person into someone who was the complete opposite." It was simplistic but in a sense true. He was pawning his horn (renting Art Farmer's trumpet when he could), begging others for money, lying, cheating, and stealing from those closest to him.

Irene, desperate, turned to anyone whom she thought might help her. "Once I went to Birdland to talk to Charlie Parker about Miles using drugs, and he was sympathetic, and seemed surprised that Miles was using. He said he'd give him a good talking to." When nothing else worked, she called Miles' father to tell him that she had no way of coping with drugs. Though he never mentioned how his father reacted, his sister said, "When Miles put that needle into himself, he put it into the whole family." Miles did recall the disgrace of being discovered in the gutter on Broadway by Clark Terry, of being fed and put to bed in Terry's room, only then to steal his clothes and radio and pawn his trumpet. When Pauline, Terry's wife, called Miles' father to tell him what was happening to his son, his father turned on Clark, blaming him and other musicians in New York.

Babs Gonzales, consummate hipster and bebop singer (and, some would say, not always reliable raconteur), tells of an evening in Chicago during this period where Miles, his brother, Vernon, and another man were setting up a small-time drug-dealing scam in order to trick a hometown man into giving them $300 for drugs, which they would use to pay the hotel bill. But the mark spotted what they were up to, and Miles and Vernon were put out of the hotel.

Reflecting back on his worst days on heroin, Miles would later say that he had become a pimp in order to survive. "Under heroin, you could pimp yourself, your mother, anyone," he told a girlfriend later. If he was a "pimp" it was not in the sense that white people use the term, as a noun, as someone in The Life, a man who runs women on the streets for profit. He was a pimp only in that he took gifts from women who lived by selling sex, as well as from those who didn't. "Player" might be the better term, a ladies' man, one who manipulates women to support his habit or his lifestyle. But Miles could also play at being the mackman, using pimp talk to flirt with women, as well as talking with the kind of verbal aggressiveness that kept men at bay. The conceit or fantasy of living off women was not uncommon among some men, something you could find in Ralph Ellison's *Invisible Man* and in the ambivalent claims made by Charles Mingus about himself in his autobiography, *Beneath the Underdog* (though those who knew Mingus also denied that he ever pimped women). As an upper-middle-class young man, the role of the pimp fascinated Miles—the walk, the talk, the dress, the attitude of the wily trickster in control of every situation, the black businessman operating outside the reach of white commerce. Yet years later, when he was cast in the role of a pimp on the television show *Miami Vice*, he complained about it, to his brother's amusement.

He boasted in his autobiography that between 1951 and 1952, "I had a whole stable of bitches out on the street for me." Yet he quickly added, "It wasn't like people thought it was; these women wanted someone to be with and they liked being with me. I took them to dinner and shit like that. . . . I just treated the prostitutes like they were anybody else. I respected them and they would give me money to get off in return. The women thought I was handsome and for the first time in my life, I began to think that I was, too. We were more like a family than anything."

He explained that the women

wouldn't give me their money. They just give me money to take them out. They made a lot of money . . . screwin'. They didn't give all their money to me, they just said, "Miles, take me out. I don't like people I don't like, I like you, take me out . . ." That's like a family they like to be in. I know, I can understand that.

I was getting by with the help of women; every time I really needed something during this period I had to go to women to get it. If it hadn't been for the women who supported me, I don't know how I would have made it without stealing every day like a lot of junkies were doing. But even with their support, I did some things I was sorry for later.

Miles never glamorized the drug experience or turned it into a horror story. And if, like other junkies, he developed a tale of decline and self-destruction, it was at least a minimalist narrative as sparse as his speech and his playing. For much of his time under heroin, he was not fully addicted, though he suffered flulike symptoms, malaise, headaches, and weakness. It was a matter of pride to him that he not be seen nodding. Other symptoms of drug use—like mood swings, forgetfulness, and unhappiness—he hoped would be treated as merely part of his character.

Thinking he might find work (and drugs) more easily if he were living in Manhattan again, Miles moved his family into the Hotel America on 48th Street, where Clark Terry, singer Betty Carter, and a number of other musicians stayed. "Betty worshipped Miles," Irene said, so Miles talked Betty into letting the children and Irene move in with her and share the rent. Irene had recently found a job in the Admissions Department at the Brooklyn Jewish Hospital. Since Betty sang in clubs at night, she could take care of the children during the day.

In the last part of 1949, Miles played at a few high-profile events: a Town Hall concert with Erroll Garner, Lennie Tristano, Charlie Parker, and Harry Belafonte; two weeks with the Bud Powell group at the Orchid Club (the old Onyx); a short stay at the Hi-Note Club in Chicago; and a Christmas Day "Stars of Modern Jazz" concert at Carnegie Hall. But work was otherwise hard to come by, and he whiled away some of the days in rehearsal bands organized by Gene Roland and Tadd Dameron. In January 1950, he went to Chicago and Detroit to do a few guest spots with tenor saxophonist Wardell Gray, who had come in from California. While he was in Chicago, Miles' father continued to send him money, but now through his brother, Vernon, to make sure it wasn't spent on drugs. But before the month was over, Miles asked Vernon to let him have $100 so that he could loan it to Wardell, who needed it to get home. Vernon was suspicious about how the money might be used and never got his money back.

Miles returned to New York in March to finish the last of the *Birth of the Cool* sessions and in May he recorded with a small group accompanying

Sarah Vaughan on four singles she made for Columbia Records. On ballads like "It Might as Well Be Spring" he wove obbligatos softly through her lines, complementing them perfectly. He was filling the same role Freddie Webster had played on her records four years before.

Changing musical tastes, police closings of clubs, and real estate speculation in midtown Manhattan began to drive rents out of the reach of club owners, and jazz lost out to strip clubs and bars without entertainment. But the area still had appeal for musicians and audiences. It was near restaurants like Lindy's and Jack Dempsey's, the Arcadia and Roseland Ballrooms, the CBS recording studios, and the Nola Studios, the largest rehearsal hall in New York City. And the Roost had enough success with bebop to encourage a few new clubs to spring up nearby—Bop City, and most notably, Birdland, which opened just before Christmas in 1949.

Birdland was located below street level at 1678 Broadway just off the corner of 52nd Street, where the lettering on an awning proclaimed, "The Jazz Corner of the World." It was a big room that could hold 500 people, with a long bar, tables, booths, and a fenced-in "bullpen"—a drinkless area where teenagers sometimes were allowed in to watch. Birdland was the closest thing to a pure jazz club at the time, a place where new bands were born, new alliances formed, and modern musicians felt at home. But it was also a site of drug dealing, hustling of various sorts, and violence. Irving Levy and Morris Primack were the owners of Birdland, though it was operated by Oscar Goodstein, who took tickets and tended bar. Levy himself was stabbed to death in front of the club (in what the papers called "the bebop killing") and was replaced by his brother Morris, who succeeded so well that he went on to open other clubs like the Down Beat, the Round Table, and the Embers. Morris would later own Roulette Records and the Strawberries chain of record stores, and through his mob ties and criminal activities, was finally convicted in 1988 of extortion and sentenced to federal prison. The Birdland management were *starkers*, tough guys. Charles Mingus recalled seeing Irving Levy kicking musicians downstairs—"'Get down the stairs, nigger,' you know?" For musicians who worked there five sets a night, six nights a week, it was hard and sometimes even dangerous work.

Miles became a regular at Birdland, bringing a band in for a few days, sitting in on the Monday night jam sessions, or just sitting at the bar. It was a scene he found strangely comfortable: the gruff, hipper-than-thou Symphony Sid who emceed the late sets for radio; the miniature doorman Pee Wee Marquette (who could blow cigar smoke in your face or insult you in his stage introductions if your tips weren't right); and the thuggish Mo Levy. For much of the first half of 1950, Birdland was virtually Davis' only source of work, but it was one that would give him notoriety. A certain kind of celebrity was drawn to Birdland, where Miles was the most interesting and stylish fixture. The *Journal-American* columnist Dorothy Kilgallen was a regular, and often seen chatting with Miles. Ava Gardner always dropped in when she was in town and, in later years, came in one night with Richard Burton and Elizabeth Taylor. Gardner, who had worked with Juliette Greco in *The Sun Also Rises,* went back to the dressing room between sets to see Miles. Not every celebrity left happy: British novelist Kingsley Amis came by one evening in 1958, and later wrote in his *Memoirs* that he had tried to forget what he heard, but "the sound of Miles Davis' trumpet, introverted, gloomy, sour in both senses, refuses to go away. I had heard the future, and it sounded horrible."

As quickly as Davis' fame spread in New York, his life away from the bandstand began to unravel. He had fallen behind in his rent at the hotel, the loan company was trying to repossess his car, and Irene learned that she was pregnant again—with a child that Miles doubted was his own. In July, he put his family in the car and drove back to East St. Louis, only to be humiliated by having his car towed from in front of his father's house almost as soon as they arrived. Irene, Miles, and the children then moved in with Miles' mother in Chicago, where she had bought property and was living part of the time, and where his sister, Dorothy, was teaching and Vernon was studying music.

In Chicago, Miles met Johnny Bratton, a flashy welterweight boxer from Arkansas who had made the city his home base. Bratton was a year younger than Miles, and they were similar in physique and tastes, though the fighter dressed a bit flashier, with brilliantined hair and a fondness for purple shirts. He was a classy and graceful fighter and took on some of the best boxers, like Ike Williams and Beau Jack. When Sugar Ray Robinson moved up to middleweight status in 1951, Bratton took the welterweight title and held it for a few months until the Cuban Hawk, Kid Gavilan, took it away from him. According to Irene, "Miles became friends with Johnny, and started getting really serious about boxing while we were in Chicago."

Miles and I went out with Johnny a few times, and he drove us around town in his new convertible. One time the cops stopped him for speeding when we were with him, but let him go when they recognized him. "It's Honey Boy Bratton!" Miles was really impressed by that. When he got back to New York City he began to train hard.

Bratton fought professionally for eleven years, but his career ended badly, and he wound up living in his car, then homeless, and finally in and out of mental hospitals. But it was said he was a sharp dresser even to the end.

When Irene give birth to Miles IV, their second son, Davis returned to New York to join Billy Eckstine in August, 1950, for a tour with a small group B was assembling—the All-American All-Stars—and wound up at a big concert with the George Shearing Quintet at the Shrine Auditorium in Los Angeles on September 15. As they were on their way to the plane at the Burbank airport after that concert, drummer Art Blakey suggested they make a drug run by a house he knew. As they did, the police followed them and arrested Davis and Blakey for possession of heroin capsules. In his autobiography, Davis says that he was off heroin at the time, and that Blakey had testified against him in order for him to get himself off from drug charges. But saxophonist Hadley Caliman was in the county jail when Art and Miles were put in his cell, and he recalls it differently:

I see this real black guy there with his hair standing straight up on his head. He had this hair straightener on his hair. And I see it's Miles Davis. . . . Miles was trying to wean off. Everybody who is hooked tried to wean off. They had to have a good friend, straight like Art Blakey, who could put it in his pocket and keep it. So when the police busted 'em, Miles ain't got nothin' but the marks [on his arms] and Art Blakey got the shit. So Art Blakey gets busted for possession. He's like doling it out to Miles so he won't go hog wild.

New prisoners were given a rough initiation on their first day and tricked by inmates into believing that they might be killed by one of the crazed prisoners. Miles took the teasing badly, Caliman said: "He was very soft. He cried a little bit. He didn't like the fact that he was incarcerated with these thugs." Irene said that

Miles always tried to talk himself out of things. He once got away with giving a cop money for a speeding ticket. He got off from a drug arrest in Harlem once by joking with the officers, telling them they held their guns too high. . . . So in California he tried to buy his way out of it and there he got charged with bribery. He called his father, and he got him a lawyer who was a family friend, but he let it come to trial. And while he was in jail, he got over drugs for a while.

When he was released on bail, Miles stayed with Dexter Gordon, then moved into a hotel, waiting for the trial to begin. When he went to court in November, Irene told him to "dress well, wash your face, and they'll know you didn't do it." It was over quickly, the jury voting ten to two in his favor, and he was released (Irene said that "a little lady on the jury told him that she knew he couldn't do anything like that"). But only days later *Down Beat* editorialized on the subject of drugs in the music business, with Davis and Blakey singled out as examples. After such national attention, both men began to have even greater problems finding work.

Miles returned to East St. Louis to wait until December, when he was booked into the Hi-Note Club on the north side of the Loop in Chicago, playing opposite Billie Holiday. On the opening day of his engagement, December 22, the temperature fell to 15°F below zero, and the streets were jammed with traffic following a nearby chemical plant explosion. Miles arrived without a band but picked up a local bassist and a drummer, and Holiday agreed to share her pianist, Carl Drinkard, though she was notorious for jealously keeping her musicians to herself. After being paid each night, Miles and two of the musicians bought heroin, then went to one of their apartments or Miles' hotel room, where they got high and worked on music for the next night in the club. According to Drinkard, Miles would "shoot up just as often as his money would allow him. You space it according to how much your money will allow you. Nobody ever really has as much as they want." Miles' father was still supporting him, now sending him $75 a week and paying for his phone calls, which allowed him to stay at good hotels for $28 a week and still afford heroin at a dollar a cap.

Miles was finishing his last week at the Hi-Note as 1951 began, when he received a call from Bob Weinstock, who had been calling for him around St. Louis to offer him a $750 advance to record for his new company, Prestige, whenever Miles got back to New York. Then Charlie Parker called asking him to record with him for Verve records. *Metronome* magazine's readers had meanwhile voted him the top jazz trumpet player of 1950. With the drug charges behind him, things seemed to be looking up.

Weinstock was typical of the small record company owners who operated outside the mainstream. Much like Ross Russell of Dial, he had
started as a jazz fan, became a record collector, then sold records by mail
order, and moved on to owning his own shop in Manhattan, the Jazz
Corner, selling mostly dixieland and swing. From there, he began to
make records, mostly of dixieland revivalists. One of his customers,
Kenny Clarke, first took him to hear bebop at the Royal Roost. Then
Ross Russell invited Weinstock to come to the Dial session where
"Embraceable You" and "Don't Blame Me" were recorded, and it was
there that he met Miles. At that session, it occurred to Weinstock that
he could record bebop and maybe sign some of the rising stars: "I
couldn't get Bird, and Dizzy was tied up with RCA. But Miles and Lee
Konitz, they could be the Bird and Dizzy of the future." Weinstock asked
Miles to have a drink with him after the session, but when Miles said
he'd rather have ice cream, they went out for ice cream.

It was an odd relationship, this bebop recording business. The big
record companies wanted nothing to do with marginal music and low
sales, much less to contend with junkies and musical eccentrics. But the
small labels took chances, putting up with the craziness, documenting a
new art form in the making, in return paying as little as possible and tying
the musicians to long-term contracts, and—like the rest of the recording
business—paying for recording expenses out of the musicians' earnings.
Weinstock once offered this glimpse of his dealings with Davis:

> We'd get into these staring sessions. He'd ask for more money, and I
> wouldn't answer. Then, I'd look at him and he'd look at me; we'd just
> stand there. We went through this a lot. I'd give him the money, but I'd
> always say, "Okay, that means we have to do another album." He'd say, "I
> don't want to do another album." I'd say, "And I want better people than
> the last!" So that's how those sessions with Milt Jackson and Monk came
> about. Those were some of our best sessions, because before he'd get the
> money—this was part of the game—I'd make him think real hard about
> who he was going to get.

It was cockroach capitalism, filled with potential for strife and resent-
ment of all kinds, compounded by whites owning the companies and
blacks by and large supplying the music. It was business as usual, only
worse.

During this time, Miles became friends with Jackie McLean, a young alto saxophonist who still lived at home with his mother in Harlem but played with great maturity and with a sound that marked him off from all the other altoists of his time. He had been around the bebop scene since he was a child, staring in the club windows on 52nd Street, watching Bird, Miles, Max. He had been hanging around Bud Powell of late, practicing with him, and it was Bud who sent him downtown to sit in with Miles because the word was out that Davis was looking for an alto saxophonist. Jackie went down to Birdland, and afterward Miles asked him to come over to his place and bring his music. McLean took his saxophone and some of his compositions such as "Dig," and after an afternoon of jamming, Miles asked him if he wanted to play at Birdland with him in January.

He and Miles became close friends, wandering through the city, watching the characters on the train as they took the long subway trip from uptown to 42nd Street to go to the movies. McLean remembers them seeing *Union Station* together, and both of them trying to act like William Holden, dressed sharp, his hat snapped down low, tough, and smart. "Miles was fun to be with," McLean said, "but there was a provocative side to him. He often said things in interviews that I know he didn't mean." "More than anything, he wanted to be a superstar, to be with the cream of society. . . . He looked and acted like money. But sometimes he didn't have any, and he had to come uptown and he and I borrowed it from my father."

On January 17, 1951, Miles recorded at three sessions in a single day in New York: first, there were four singles with Charlie Parker for Verve; then, as a pianist, he cut "I Know" for Prestige under Sonny Rollins' name; finally, he did four more records of his own with Prestige—"Morpheus," backed by "Down," and "Whispering" on the other side of "Blue Room." Five years later, British writer Alun Morgan asked him about that latter session: "You know that record of 'Blue Room,' made in 1951, Miles? What happened there? Did you play piano or trumpet on that or what?" Miles implied that the problem was drugs: "Hell man, I was playing badly on that date. I was . . . you know." On the other hand, on the occasion of another interview, he told François Postif, "At that period, you see, between 1951 and 1953, I was out of work for much of the time and it may be that it affected my playing."

Miles had just recorded with the Metronome All-Stars for Capitol Records and was writing lead sheets for record companies (that is, transcribing music from recordings for copyrights), and was again rooming with Stan Levey, when in February, he opened the latest issue of *Ebony* and found an article by Cab Calloway titled, "Is Dope Killing Our Musicians?" Calloway warned readers that drugs had swept across the black community and that a generation of addicted jazz musicians was doomed unless they sought help. Though he mentioned no names, he managed to comment on "one young trumpeter, recently picked up on the West Coast for possession of heroin." In case anyone might have missed the point, a rogues' gallery of junkies' pictures was also included: Miles, Billie Holiday, Fats Navarro, Gene Krupa, Eddie Haywood, John Simmons, Howard McGhee, Art Blakey, and Dexter Gordon. Miles was hurt and embarrassed by the article and claimed that he as well as the others were not able to work for a long time afterward. The music press, meanwhile, documented his decline with the euphemisms that those in the know understood. Miles was "sick"; he was suffering from "personal problems." *Metronome* editor Barry Ulanov would call Miles' playing "feeble again," only a year after *Metronome* picked him as "Influence of the Year," and "Venus de Milo" as one of their "Records of the Year." Leonard Feather in *Melody Maker* would say that Miles was at a "standstill," "his career slipping away from him," and guessed that he had performed publicly for no more than five or six weeks in 1951 (and most of that, though Feather did not mention it, was at Birdland where his problems were tolerated).

In spite of the dire tone of these observers, Miles could still surprise. In March, for instance, he played well on recordings of a very different sort from those of his own. Lee Konitz put three of Lennie Tristano's disciples together with Davis and Max Roach, unifying the two wings of cool jazz, and using "Odjenar" and "Ezz-thetic," two complex and unusual compositions by George Russell, as the bridge between them. Miles seemed comfortable on both and may have improvised the countermelody on the latter. Konitz recalls that session rather self-effacingly:

> I always felt I could relate to Miles' group, but I was too nervous to play with the quintet in 1951, the recording date with Miles. Miles was interested in Tristano's music. I had written something called "Hi Beck" and we rehearsed that a few times. He said, "That's it with that one," so I played it on the album alone.

In October, Miles recorded for Prestige at a session that was one of the first to use microgroove technology for recording directly to 10-inch LPs, the musicians (including Sonny Rollins and Jackie McLean) now extending their playing time well beyond the three-minute limits they were used to working with. ("Bluing," for example, ran over nine minutes.) The level of musicianship on the record was exceptionally high, with Miles playing as if he were driven to make known everything he had not been able to say publicly over the last year. Most of the session was issued as *Dig*, a record that Jackie McLean would later say was the first real step beyond bebop.

Somehow, despite the blur and spin of his life under the sway of dope, Miles managed to pull himself up when he was in the studio or the club. But away from music, he wandered the streets, becoming one of those characters who stood on corners nodding, maybe reading a newspaper upside down as they waited for a bicycle rider to come past and hand them something. He went by other young musicians' houses, maybe practicing a bit, or getting high if their mothers were at work and there was no one at home, or wandering from room to room in hotels and staying with anyone who'd put up with him. He had pawned everything of value and used the pawn slips to borrow from club owners. He had hit up everyone he knew for money, turned to his friends among the prostitutes for comfort, and made some vain efforts to pull himself out of the chaos into which he had drifted. When he asked boxing trainer Bobby McQuillen at Gleason's Gym to take him on, Bobby told him he never trained anyone who was using.

One night while Miles was on the bandstand at the Downbeat Club on 53rd Street, he suddenly put down his horn, turned to Jackie McLean, and said, "Take it out for me, my father's here." He and his father spoke for a minute by the door; there was some talk with the club owner about loans made to Miles; money was exchanged. Miles returned to the stand only to tell Jackie to "Get J. J. I got to go home with my father," and then left so quickly he forgot his trumpet.

CHAPTER FOUR

> First they steal your money, then they start with your life and
> characteristics, and then your jokes, and then your dreams—
> they steal everything.
>
> MILES DAVIS

IT WAS CHRISTMAS IN EAST ST. LOUIS, 1951, and Miles had sworn off
drugs, pledged never to touch them again, and though he seemed to be
the same Junior he was when he first left home, his parents were frantic.
Nothing had prepared them for this, and their only hope was to keep
constant watch on him. Out on the farm, the maid kept track of him
when his father was at work, and when friends visited him at his
mother's house, she stood guard at the door. Ollie Matheus said, "When
I would go over to Miles' house to pick him up, his mother would search
me better than the cops ever did before I could come in the house. I
mean she'd go through the things in my pants and around my cuffs. They
really tried to take care of him, but when Miles and Bird would come
home, the junkies would come out of the woodwork. Their idols were
there."

Within days of coming back home Miles was out to the bars and
nightclubs, even playing some with Jimmy Forrest's band at the Barrel-
house in St. Louis. It was there that he met and became involved with
the daughter of one of the executives of Buster Brown Shoes, a St. Louis
society girl. Miles' father objected to his dating a white girl, and Miles
wasn't permitted to visit her at her home, so the only place they could
meet was at his mother's. "One day," Vernon said, "this girl came over to
see Miles at our mother's house, and she wouldn't let her in. 'If Miles is
not good enough to go into her house, she's not coming in here,' she
said. The girl would be sitting out in the cab crying, and we'd beg

Mother: 'You can't leave that girl out there!' Then finally, she gave up and let her in."

Some nights he slipped out to visit the housing projects in East St. Louis to buy heroin, using small amounts of money he had gotten from his father—$10 to $20 at a time, barely enough to score, but not enough to arouse suspicion. But the day came when he had to have more, when he went up to his father's office and asked for it, and Dr. Davis refused him—perhaps the first time he had ever denied his son. Dorothy had told Dr. Davis that Miles was still using drugs. Miles began screaming at his father, cursing him in front of a waiting room of patients. Dr. Davis calmly picked up the phone and called the sheriff's office in Belleville and had his son arrested. "He was in the Belleville jail for two weeks," according to Vernon. "We took him cookies and things, but he was there alone in that cell, shivering and sweating." It was his second experience with cold turkey.

Miles was released from jail when he promised his father that he was serious about getting help and agreed to commit himself for treatment at the Lexington Prison Hospital. "Narco," as its inmates called it, was located on a thousand acres of farmland in Kentucky and was a government-run drug treatment facility for prisoners as well as for voluntarily admitted patients. Miles knew about Lexington because any number of musicians had been there—Tadd Dameron, Dexter Gordon, Sonny Stitt, Anita O'Day—so many that they always had a first-rate prison band on hand, with an exceptional book of arrangements. Miles, his father, and his father's new wife, Josephine (whom he had married in 1947), drove down to Lexington, and when they arrived, word spread quickly. Red Rodney, a trumpeter who'd played with Charlie Parker, rushed out to meet him, but Miles had changed his mind and had already left.

The decision to volunteer for therapy was not as simple as it appeared. First, it was necessary to have a hearing before a Kentucky magistrate to be committed to the prison hospital with a "key"—the right to leave whenever one wanted. Addicts had to confess to drug use, make a pledge to break the habit, and then be sentenced. Once inside, the user would be required to do kitchen or farm work and give up normal privileges. At the last minute, Miles was unable to convict himself and face the humiliation, and he convinced his father that his time in the Belleville jail had cured him. With his father's money, he took a train back to New York.

From May through the first week of August, in 1952, Miles was booked into a package tour, "Jumping with Symphony Sid," with Sid Torin as the emcee, and an all-star group called Jazz, Inc. Miles and Sid clashed throughout the tour—no small matter, since Sid was close to Mo Levy, and there were stories about musicians who had crossed Sid being beaten (or worse) by hard men. Miles accused Sid of skimming, of taking more of the profits than he acknowedged to the musicians. At one point during the tour, they opened George Wein's new but short-lived Storyville club in New Haven, and after a week of trouble with Davis, Sid said to Wein, "Don't pay Miles nothing." Miles turned to George and said, "George, give me $19." When Wein balked, Miles said, "OK, then give me $5." Then, "Give me $1, George . . . give me 50 cents . . . give me a cent."

Miles was in particularly bad shape on this tour, and Sid claimed that when they were in Toronto, Davis tried to get a dentist to pull a tooth in hopes of getting some drugs for the pain. Charles Mingus' wife, Celia, remembered Miles coming by their place one night that winter, looking for a "loan." Everything he had he had sold or pawned, and he was getting by on what his girlfriends gave him, while the cops rousted him on the street to look for needle marks.

On January 30, 1953, Miles set up a recording session for Prestige with a sextet including Jimmy Heath and Sonny Rollins on tenor saxophones. Heath gave Miles a composition of his own for them to record, but at the last minute, Miles replaced Heath with Charlie Parker on tenor because Bird was badly in need of money. Miles had already missed the rehearsal for the session according to producer Ira Gitler, and was late for the recording, as were Parker and Rollins. Bird was drinking most of the gin intended for everyone, and Miles was not playing well, coasting through the session. Gitler could see the whole session beginning to unravel: "I took a calculated risk in an effort to jar him. 'Man, you're not playing shit,' I said, coming out of the control room after another incomplete take. This from a young 24-year-old who was in a room full of idols." Miles began to pack up his horn, "Cat says I'm not playing shit." Gitler began to plead with him, and Miles went back to work. The engineer left at five o'clock, and another came on, but the studio closed at six. On "Well You Needn't," Miles spoiled a few takes, so with fifteen minutes left they tried recording "'Round Midnight" instead, to fill the leftover space on the record, doing it slow and long to stretch it out, and they finished by six. Afterward, Jimmy Heath complained that the piece he had given Miles when he thought he would be recording with him came out under the title given it by Ira Gitler, "Serpent's Tooth," and Jimmy never received credit for it.

Miles did not always have such difficulties recording. On May 19, for example, he recorded two singles for Prestige with just himself and a trio of John Lewis, Percy Heath, and Max Roach (Kenny Clarke was booked to be the drummer but failed to show up). Davis' playing was faultless, showing the kind of relaxed creativity that he would be credited with several years later by those who had not yet caught up with him. All four pieces were first takes: "When Lights Are Low" (which Miles tried to convince producer Ira Gitler was his own composition rather than Benny Carter's, because no one knew the tune's original bridge and they had to make up a new one); "Miles Ahead" was a revised and more com-pact version of the original "Milestones" (neither of them was the tune later recorded under those titles for Columbia Records); and the other two pieces were Miles' "Tune Up" (which Eddie Vinson also claimed to have composed) and "Smooch," a slow mood piece co-credited to Charles Mingus, since John Lewis left the studio early and was replaced on piano by bassist Mingus.

In the first half of 1953, Miles survived by doing several other record sessions for Blue Note and Prestige, some of which were rather chaotic, with musicians slipping out for drugs in the middle of the session or not showing up at all. He did a few dates at Birdland, but not much else— which at least kept him from running into Irene, who was back in New York with the children, and who sometimes came to the clubs hoping to find him and make him pay for the children's support.

Typical of the only work he was getting was a weekend jam in June at the office and performance space of Debut Records that Max and Charles Mingus ran, where Miles, Mingus, Max, Monk, altoist Gigi Gyrce, Hank Mobley, and Oscar Pettiford were playing before a few fans. When someone suggested "Memories of You," a tune not everyone knew, Miles said he'd call out the chords for them. But he called out wrong chords to confuse them, leaving them all angry. When they started the next set and Miles took his first solo, Monk came up behind him, went through Miles' pockets looking for cigarettes and matches, lit up, and put them back in his pocket. Celia Mingus said, "It was like a vaudeville act. And Miles—Miles wasn't going to give them the satisfac-tion of missing a note."

June, 1953: it was nothing more than a chance meeting with Max Roach, Max greeting him, "What's happening?" The usual, but as Miles turned to walk off, Roach slipped two hundred dollars into his pocket. It was this humiliation that drove Miles to call his father and ask him to send him a ticket so that he could come home. He needed help.

But walks around the farm and rides on horseback always sounded better than they were when he was there, and within a week the tedium set in, the dreariness of feeling his life running backward. There was nothing there for him now except the quiet. And it was only days before they found out he was home—the dealers, the visiting musicians, the local junkies. So when Max called in August and said that he and Charles Mingus were driving west to California in the new Oldsmobile that Max's girlfriend had bought him, Miles invited them to stop off on the way and spend the night at his father's farm. They talked about music, New York, the scene; slept in the silk pajamas that Dr. Davis provided for guests; and the next morning Miles left with them. Mingus, being the lightest skinned of the three, was appointed to go into white-run restaurants along the way to get food to take out, but he began to argue about this and insisted on taking a stand for civil rights . . . in the middle of Oklahoma or somewhere. Miles and Max finally calmed him down, and Mingus got the sandwiches to go, but the three of them then argued and joked about race and white people the rest of the way across the country.

Miles stayed in California for almost three months, living off his father's money, playing one or two gigs, getting into fights, and drifting deeper into drugs. Out of boredom one day, he went along with a friend who was delivering a gift of jewelry to one of the Katherine Dunham dancers who was appearing at Ciro's. She was Frances Taylor, a ballet dancer from Chicago who had made the transition to the folk-inspired modern dance of Dunham's company. Max had been telling Miles about an exceptionally beautiful woman he wanted him to meet, and later when Max arranged for them all to go out together one evening, she turned out to be the same Frances Taylor. This time when she saw Miles —"dressed like a model," he said—in a Brooks Brothers madras jacket, white denim shirt, pleated silk trousers, and his hair processed, he caught her sneaking looks at him. He wrote his name and phone number on a piece of paper and passed it to her, saying, "Now you don't have to stare." But Miles was not going to stay in LA much longer. His habit was outstripping his means, and once again he had to ask his father for money so that he could come home.

Along with Miles' other problems, a new trumpet player had surfaced on the West Coast to much acclaim. Miles had heard about him from Charlie Parker, who had hired him at an audition at the Tiffany Club in Los Angeles and given him his imprimatur, just as he had once done for Miles. ("That little white cat is kinda Bixelated . . . reminds me of some of those Bix records my Mama used to get for me . . . sweet, gentle, yet direct and honest.") It was easy to tease Miles about him, and everyone from Miles' tailor to Bird had his turn ("Hey Miles, there's a little white cat on the coast who's gonna eat you up!"). But Miles wasn't prepared for Chet Baker's sudden ascendancy to fame when he won the *Down Beat* poll as the best trumpet player of 1953.

Although Baker was white and working class, an Okie who had drifted to southern California with other midwestern families in the 1930s, there were striking similarities between him and Davis. He was taller than Miles, but he was also slim and handsome. Though he was no serious dresser—preferring white T-shirts and wrinkled khakis—whatever he wore looked good on him, and photographers chased him as if he were a model. And then there was his name: jazz musicians in the thirties and forties had cheerful nicknames such as Bird, Klook, Dizzy, Zoot, or Lucky. By the fifties, they were more often known by their given names—Art, Dave, or Stan, names that hit on the downbeat and stayed there. "Miles" and "Chet" were perfect for the recondite but confidential *entre nous* tone that hip observers assumed when declaiming on the actions of their idols ("Miles, man, he . . .").

Both of them loved fast cars (though Baker preferred the big ones, especially Cadillac convertibles with fins) and dogs (Miles' was named Milo, Baker's was called Bix). Both were junkies, though the variety and volume of drugs Baker consumed were unparalled, and ultimately the cause of his exile and decline. Both projected within and across gender lines, threatening some men, attracting others, and although their allegiance to heterosexuality was pronounced, the swath they cut through women went so far beyond conventional male codes that some questioned the nature of their appetites. They were both obsessed with music and served it with a passion that overshadowed everything else in their lives. (The mouthpiece that Davis always carried with him was the only thing that he would allow to ruin the line of his suit, and Baker concealed a broken tooth from photographers for years, fearing that replacing it might ruin his sound.)

Baker and Davis were equally drawn to popular songs for their purity and directness of emotion, and they knew how to turn them into jazz without crushing their beauty or their innocence. They both saw that despite the naive optimism of most pop songs, they were essentially sad; in fact, they formed a long chain of shared anguish, one song linked to another in the deep consciousness of their audience, and both men were devoted to excavating these sites of romantic ruin.

Miles had begun to be attracted to show tunes, and if his passion to make them safe for jazz had left some hip people wondering, Chet Baker pushed the matter even further by actually singing those songs, often choosing songs usually associated with women. True, Baker sang them without affect, slightly on the flat side, unadorned, without vibrato—the way he played—but he gave them a new context, framing them like res-cued objets d'art on display in an unsavory environment.

Both of them were ceaselessly fascinating to their audiences, their behavior, real and imagined, generating endless tales. But there similari-ties ceased: if Miles stories ended with a devastating zinger, the hero as cruel commentator on the human condition, Chet stories just ended with a sad comment on his squandered career.

The appearance of Chet Baker on the scene at this moment called the critics out and made it clear where jazz stood, how it was regarded in the mirror of modernity, and underscored how Davis was ultimately to be judged. Jazz critics were high modernists, looking for originality, influ-ence, a certain toughness of self-expression in their heroes. And if any jazz musicians dared to honor pop music with straight faces, to cloak themselves in fashion and make their appeal to women paramount, they were inviting critical contempt.

Back home again on the farm, at the end of November, 1953, Miles made another stab at breaking his habit. In an interview that was not published until many years later, he described the ordeal:

> I made up my mind I was getting off dope. I was sick and tired of it. You know you can get tired of anything. You can even get tired of being afraid.
>
>   I laid down and stared at the ceiling and cursed everybody I didn't like, I was kicking it the hard way. It was like having a bad case of flu only worse. I lay in a cold sweat, my nose and eyes ran. I threw up everything I

tried to eat. My pores opened up and I smelled like chicken soup. Then it was over.

His account was uncharacteristically elaborate and romanticized, and in his autobiography it was even more so. It begins like this: desperate, he took the bus home to East St. Louis and again turned to his father for help. On a slow walk out in the pasture, his father said to him: "If you were with a woman and the woman left you, I would know what to tell you; you could get another woman. But this you have to do by yourself, you know that, because you've been around drugs all your life. You know what you have to do." His father turned and walked away from him. Afterward, Miles locked himself in the guest house and stayed until he kicked the habit: "You feel like you could die and if somebody could guarantee that you would die in two seconds, then you would take it. You would take the gift of death over this torture of life." For the next seven or eight days, he lay there sweating, aching, sending the maid away when she brought him food, hoping to die. (He was not entirely alone, however. His St. Louis society girlfriend came by, and they made love, but he said he failed to enjoy it.) "Then one day it was over, just like that. Over. Finally over. I felt better, good and pure. I walked outside into the clean, sweet air over to my father's house and when he saw me he had this big smile on his face and we just hugged each other and cried."

But it was not over. The *Autobiography* misleads the reader as he undoubtedly misled himself, ending Chapter 8 with an image of him contemplating a life free of drugs. Most writers on Davis' life have been eager to take him at his word, not reading the first few paragraphs of the next chapter, where he makes it clear that he was still addicted.

From late December, 1953, to March, 1954, Miles lived in Detroit where he had found work playing at the Blue Bird Inn, an older club that drew mostly black audiences and had a tradition of a house band that invited musicians to sit in and play whatever they wanted. The club had recently begun a policy of hiring nationally known guest stars to play with the house band for a month at a time. Throughout the early 1950s, the band was led by saxophonist Billy Mitchell, with Elvin Jones on drums, Tommy Flanagan or Barry Harris on piano, along with various bass players. In 1953, just before Miles arrived, the club had been taken over by a group of new owners that included Clarence Eddins, a local numbers boss whom Miles knew from various adventures on the road. While

Miles was at the Blue Bird, he was said to be working more for drugs than for money, and though he denied it, rumors persisted that he was in debt to the club. Whatever was happening, Miles' drug habit was pulling him further under. At one point, Miles became so desperate for stability that he called his father and asked him if he could marry Irene, but then changed his mind. Carl Hill, the doorman at the Blue Bird Inn, remembers Miles at that time:

> When Miles first came to the Blue Bird . . . he was strung out and living in Sunnie Wilson's hotel on Grand River and the [Grand] Boulevard. . . . It was in the winter and Miles walked from the hotel to the Blue Bird, and the joint was packed; everybody was waiting for Miles Davis. So when he came in he had on this grimy white shirt and a navy blue sweater and Clarence told him to go home and put on a tie. . . . So Miles went outside and took a shoelace out of his shoe and tied it up under his shirt and said: "How do you like this, boss?" and went on the bandstand and played.

Miles' existence in Detroit was especially chaotic even within a life that was never particularly orderly. Sleeping late in the day in a darkened room, eating virtually nothing, drinking cognac, he spent much of the time waiting, usually for his daily care package from his man Freddie Frue—"Frue with the Do." At night he assumed the role of the vampire of Motor City, his damaged but still beautiful self turning up everywhere, hanging out with the prostitutes, indulging his deeper fantasies by watching them make love to each other, or sitting alone in bars, saying nothing, looking bad, becoming legend. "He used to come in the bar," bluesman John Lee Hooker recalls. "He was wild. He was a very young man then. . . . He wasn't a mean man, he just didn't like bein' around a lot of people." One Miles story from those days in Detroit has particular staying power. As told by painter Prophet Jennings, it begins with a tragic figure coming in from those dark, rain-slicked streets:

> I remember one night, one time, Max Roach and Clifford Brown . . . they were playing at a club in Detroit—the Crystal Lounge. . . . So, this particular night we're at the Crystal Lounge and Max Roach and him had set the stage on fire. Now, Miles, he was—you know, he was staying around Detroit at this time. It was raining like a motherfucker, so this particular night, Brownie—we called him Brownie—he had just come off the stage. That stage was a burning inferno. Clifford Brown had set that motherfucker on fire. . . . The door opened and in walked Miles. He had his coat

turned up and it was raining. . . . He went over to Clifford Brown and asked for Clifford's trumpet. He reached in his inside coat pocket, took out his mouthpiece, put it in Clifford's trumpet. . . . Now, the stage was still on fire. It was still burning. . . . Miles got up on that stand with the support of the piano to hold his ass up. He put that motherfucking trumpet to his mouth and that motherfucker played "My Funny Valentine." Clifford Brown stood up there and looked at him and just shook his head. . . . That little black motherfucker, behind all that fire, he made people cry. . . . When he got through playing and took his mouthpiece out, he put it back in his coat, gave Brownie his trumpet, and split. That's what he did. I saw this. I was *there!*

Miles denied the story, yet if not true in every detail, overall it seems right. Lonnie Hillyer, a young admirer who regularly loaned Miles a trumpet (and whose mother demanded that Miles return it every night right after the gig), recalls Miles working at a dance in Detroit: "And he started to play a ballad. The people just stopped dancing and crowded all around him, listening to this cat play this ballad. You know? Miles STOPPED people from dancing, and I'll never forget that as long as I live."

As was Miles' wont, he drifted between mobsters and socialites, his raggedy romantic image giving him entrée to both ends of the spectrum. Two women took it on themselves to care for him. One, a woman of substance, a designer—he didn't want to reveal her name, because she was so prominent—tried to help him and took him to a mental hospital to see a psychiatrist. In his first session, he was asked if he ever masturbated as a way of coping with his addiction. He was so shocked and appalled by the suggestion that he never went back. The other woman, who also remains nameless in his autobiography but because he could not remember her name, was younger, someone he said he "abused" to the point that Clarence Eddins warned him to leave her alone.

So here's this big gangster motherfucker, got his boys all around everywhere. He's got guns and shit in his pocket and I'm getting an attitude with him, right? . . . He looked at me like he's one second away from killing my ass. . . . He studied me like a scroungy dog that had crawled in out of the streets. "Man, you're fucking pathetic, a pitiful, miserable motherfucker who don't even deserve to live."

Miles was so afraid, he said, that he would never go back to the Blue Bird after he left Detroit for fear they might kill him.

Davis returned to New York early in March, 1954, and called up Alfred Lion at Blue Note records and Bob Weinstock at Prestige and asked to be recorded again. Horace Silver was living in the same hotel as Miles on 25th Street, the Arlington. He had an upright piano in his room, and Miles came by to play it and to talk to him about his plans for their upcoming recording session, showing him the voicings he wanted, suggesting how much space he wanted in the piano's accompaniment. Miles had pawned his trumpet, had nothing to practice on, and had been renting one for ten dollars a night from Art Farmer, who always came along with it to make sure it didn't disappear.

On March 6, Miles recorded six tunes for Blue Note with a rhythm section of Silver, Percy Heath, and Art Blakey. They were the first recordings he had done for almost a year, and whatever his other difficulties, the assuredness with which he approached this material was striking. If no one had understood it before, it was becoming clear that Davis was rebuilding the jazz trumpet tradition from a different set of principles from those that guided the hot players of the past. There was a softness to his attack on "Take-off" and a considered approach to note choice new to trumpet playing, one that found him landing on unexpected notes again and again, all of it at a high speed of execution. "Take-off" and "The Leap" recalled the harmonic direction Davis had taken with the Birth of the Cool band on tunes like "Deception," alternating a series of chord progressions with moments of harmonic and rhythmic suspension, the trumpet soloing over a repeated single chord—a device somewhere between an old-time break, an interlude, and what would soon be called modality in jazz. Jazz had from its beginnings hinted at what might happen if the melody broke loose from harmony. Jelly Roll Morton had even insisted that breaks were part of the definition of jazz. Now musicians were exploring the possibility of detaching melody and harmony more openly, and moving toward a more pronounced break with harmonic constraints. Some were even wondering what would happen if that "release" from "tension," as they put it, become permanent.

Jules Colomby, a hipster and sometime trumpet player who worked for Bob Weinstock, was present on March 15 at Beltone Studios for the session that created three-quarters of the album Blue Haze for Prestige. Colomby remembers it as an important occasion:

Miles' personal life may not have been always so together, but the music was fantastic. He was always thinking, and he could write something in his head and later on sketch an arrangement in seconds. Everyone revered him even then, because he was considered a master. At the sessions, Miles was in charge, but not in a take-charge kind of way.

Another observer in the studio that day was David X. Young, a painter who had recently talked Prestige into hiring him to put art on its album covers instead of the simple, almost generic graphics Prestige had been using. He did his first cover for free, and then asked for $50 each. Weinstock offered him $100 for three. "Weinstock ran everything by himself," said Young:

> He had taken a bus across the country and stopped at record stores along the way, and set up his own distribution. Since his records were selling well in Harlem, Weinstock was cautious about what I put on the covers. When I painted a skull for one of them, he objected to it. He thought it wouldn't sell to blacks because they would think it was voodoo.

Young was assigned the cover of the Davis session, and when he turned up at the Beltone Studios that day, no sooner had he set up a music stand as an easel with art supplies and sketch pad than he found the musicians' connection sitting beside him, setting up a music stand on which he was rolling joints. After several hours, the group had finished all the music it had prepared, and there was still not enough for an album. "We got a half hour left," Weinstock said. "Play a funky blues." Midway into it, Weinstock cut it off, saying, "Too funky!" They tried again; he cut it off once more. "Not funky enough." Miles said, "What do you want, Mr. Eisenhower?" Art Blakey got up, sputtering, and switched off all the lights in the studio with a sweep of his arm, and they recorded "Blue Haze"—nothing more than Davis improvising a blues over a bare bass line—in the dark. Percy Heath mused that, "All we need now is for someone to say 'motherfucker!'"—a reference to Miles' habit of sometimes talking while the mikes were on so that the comments ended up on the records. (In Miles' autobiography, there is a yet another version of the light dimming, where someone says, "'If we turn out the lights we won't be able to see Miles or Art.' That shit was funny. They said that because Art and I are so dark.")

Almost a month later, Miles was recording again, and this time the studio was in optometrist-turned-engineer Rudy Van Gelder's parents' living room in Hackensack. The band now included alto saxophonist

Davey Schildkraut, who had just come from a tour with the bombastic Stan Kenton band. (For his part, Schildkraut said he didn't play his best because on the way to the New Jersey studios, Bob Weinstock kept making remarks about how bad he thought the Kenton band was.) Part of what they recorded there wound up on the album *Blue Haze*, and part of it on another album, *Walkin'*, along with the recordings made at Miles' next session, on April 29. Kenny Clarke was on drums because Miles wanted to play quieter and needed Clarke's brush work behind him. And quiet it was. With a cup mute in and the horn's bell close to the microphone, he got a distinctive sound on several ballads, and then launched one of his signature tunes, "Solar."

Before they recorded on March 29, a rehearsal in the form of a concert was held at a small record store; and that time, the band included trombonist J. J. Johnson, tenor saxophonist Lucky Thompson, Horace Silver, Percy Heath, and Kenny Clarke. When the day to record came, Jules Colomby was again present:

> We drove in two cars across the bridge to Jersey, where Weinstock and Van Gelder were waiting at the studio. Horace sat down at the piano, Percy stood near the control booth window, and Miles just walked back and forth. Then Miles motioned to Bob, and said, "Hey, I don't have my horn."
>
> At that point, Weinstock turned white—he turned white-on-white. Here, after all that money to set the date up, Miles shows without his horn. It was like dropping a bomb.
>
> So I said to Miles, "I've got a trumpet in the trunk of my car. It's an old Buescher I've had since I was 13." Miles said, "Bring it in." I walked to the car knowing the horn was full of leaks, and I thought, "How in the world is he going to play it?" Miles warmed up by just going over the valves with his fingers, to see if they were loose. Then he counted off the tempo to "Walkin'" without saying a word. It was just a blues, and everyone knew the tune. Miles played and I couldn't believe how beautiful he could make that trumpet sound. Forget about take two, it was one of the best records he'd ever made. The band just went right into "Blue 'n' Boogie," an uptempo blues that Dizzy wrote.

Lucky Thompson had agreed to provide four arrangements for this session, but since Weinstock did not pay for rehearsals, they were not tried out before they got to the studio. For some reason, they did not work out, and two long blues were recorded instead. Miles took seven improvised choruses on "Walkin'," with a poise and a sense of self-control that were new to his playing and to jazz. The listener can hear him waiting calmly for ideas before he plays and working those silences into the fabric of his solo. The effect is one of hearing him think, with the audible thought process itself becoming part of the music. The other musicians almost rise to his level, their solos not just part of the usual melody-solo-melody format but played in an order that builds dramatically, one solo upon the other. (Lucky Thompson plays one of his finest solos on record—so fine, bassist Percy Heath recalls, that he wouldn't stop: "Miles came up behind him, but he didn't get it. Weinstock showed him the stopwatch, but he kept on playing. So it had to be turned into a part 1–part 2, two-sided 78 rpm single record.") A year later, Miles told Nat Hentoff that of the records he had made recently, only *Walkin'* "and the one with Sonny Rollins" [*Dig* on Prestige in 1951] were the best. "The rest sound too much alike."

"Walkin'" is widely revered as the recording that opened up a new style of jazz, one that would come to be called hard bop for its use of stronger, more interactive drumming, funky and soulful melodies, and a reassertion of the primacy of the blues. It is a music that rejected the reserve of cool jazz and reclaimed the principles of bebop in a more recognizable and accessible African American form. This was a music that appeared around the time of the Supreme Court's decision in *Brown* v. *Board of Education* on separate but equal schools, and was part of what writer Amiri Baraka called the anti-assimilationist sound. That period between the mid-1950s and the mid-1960s was an era in which the resources of jazz were being consolidated and refined and the range of its sources broadened. Some of the jazz of this period reached across class and age lines and unified black audiences. Young people could see this music as "bad" in much the same sense that James Brown used the word, and older people could see its links to black tradition. As a name for all of the musics that surfaced in this period, "hard bop" is simplistic. Yet, in a world that often welcomes the simple, Miles Davis has come to be seen as an originator of yet a fourth style of jazz.

Despite Miles' alleged fears of Detroit gangsters, he was back in that town at the Blue Bird again between August 14 and October 2. Those stays in Detroit paid off, as he felt that he was gradually weaned away from heroin because of its poor quality—so poor, drummer Philly Joe Jones said, that in Detroit you might as well buy yourself a Hershey bar and save your money because heroin was cut and would gradually increase your tolerance. Whatever was the mix of sheer will and inferior drug quality, Miles no longer needed heroin. In fact, for years afterward, he became physically ill whenever he saw someone using it. Cocaine? That was another story.

Near the end of 1954, Davis was called for induction into military service. The draft was a constant subject of conversation at the time among musicians, and they had a veritable armory of methods for escaping it, ranging from chemical potions to freak diets and scripts for feigning madness. Dizzy told Miles that if he wanted to be sure to be rejected, he should take his horn with him once he stripped for the physical exam— that would do it! Irene is sure that he went that day, but military records say that he failed to report for induction on October 27. Whatever happened, he was dismissed from military service as an "administrative reject."

On Christmas Eve 1954, Miles had scheduled a recording session at Rudy Van Gelder's with vibraphonist Milt Jackson, Thelonious Monk, Percy Heath, and Kenny Clarke—a group that Prestige called the Modern Jazz Giants. Giants, indeed. A session like this could be the stuff of legends in years to come, every surviving take or scrap of gossip examined as a clue to some hidden truth. Or a clash of titans. Engineer Van Gelder recalls that while they were rehearsing "Bags' Groove," Miles told Monk, "During my solo, lay out [that is, don't play]." Miles, as he usually did when he recorded, sat on a chair, pointing the bell of his horn at the floor. When he began his solo, Monk stood up next to him. After the take, Miles asked him why he had done that. "I don't have to sit down to lay out," Monk replied. But Ira Gitler remembers that when he was laying out—or "strolling"—Monk said, "Rudy, where's the bathroom," and ruined a take.

From accounts like these, stories spread that Monk and Miles had gotten into a fight, but Monk scoffed at the idea: "Miles got killed if he hit me." "Miles liked to accompany people on the piano," said bassist Percy Heath. "He told all his piano players to stroll (not just Monk) and it *was* Miles' record date. Miles always bragged about showing piano players things—he knew how he wanted things to sound. He wouldn't criticize your playing, though he'd show you things." Still, the stories continued. In one of the most bizarre, "Outside the Capsule," jazz critic André Hodeir's Joycean science-fiction meditation on "Bags' Groove," a group of archaeologists and government agents in the distant future discover the record, identify it as a sacred artifact, and pore over it for its spiritual and ritualistic significance.

Fighting or not, there is an audible tension in this music, especially evident in the playing of Davis and Monk, though Monk's solos are some of the most calculatingly idiosyncratic in jazz history, and Davis, despite his discomfort with Monk's accompaniment, seems to be affected by his surroundings, and at moments sounds positively Monkian himself.

Irene was sick of trying to track down Miles to get money from him for child support, and early in 1955 she hired Maxwell T. Cohen, Billie Holiday's lawyer, the man who handled the Charlie Parker estate, and the force behind the lawsuit that brought an end to the cabaret card. When she told Miles what she was doing, he told her, "You're just giving another white man some money." "I didn't know they were going to arrest him and put him on Riker's Island," Irene said of Miles. "I just thought he had the money and would pay me. When I heard that he was in jail, I cried and cried." Bob Weinstock visited him while he was there, and said that when he left, Miles was screaming, "Get me out of here!" Weinstock and attorney Harold Lovett found the money to bail him out on the third day, and at the same time passed on the news to him that Charlie Parker had just died.

Parker's passing was no surprise to Davis, who knew what condition he was in and blamed his death on Parker's "greediness." But meeting Lovett was a fateful encounter. He was the first lawyer whom Miles felt he could trust. Lovett was a stylishly dressed, flamboyant, and aggressive lawyer whom Miles jokingly accused of trying to act like him (though there were those who thought Lovett made Miles look like a choirboy). They became friends, and for years Lovett was Miles' companion at concerts or the fights and his defender at some of his worst moments. Lovett had a girlfriend who lived down the street from Miles, and whenever he wanted Harold to stop by, Miles put a white mannequin in his window as a signal of distress.

Once Miles was out of jail, Lovett talked Mingus and Roach into letting him make a record under his own name for Debut because he needed money so badly. Mingus had planned to record Miles a year before, playing on "Miles Apart" and "Miles Milieu," two compositions by saxophonist John LaPorta, but the rhythm figures proved too difficult for Mingus, and the session was scrapped. This time the arrangements were by Mingus and Teo Macero, one of the more interesting composers within Mingus' circle, and on July 9, Miles, Mingus, Elvin Jones, Britt Woodman, and Teddy Charles went into the studio to record a few singles to be called *Blue Moods*. But there was trouble when Miles refused to walk two blocks to the studio because he had been promised a ride. And once he got the ride, he told the driver, "I hope I won't have to hit Mingus in the mouth." (The *Metronome 1957 Yearbook* picked *Blue Moods* as one of the best jazz records of 1956.)

In an interview he did with Nat Hentoff, titled "A Trumpeter in the Midst of a Comeback Makes a Very Frank Appraisal of Today's Jazz Scene," Miles let loose with barbed opinions that ranged across the entire jazz scene: the West Coast players wrote good arrangements but couldn't solo; Basie's band wouldn't be so good if it weren't for Neal Hefti's arrangements; Billy Eckstine needed someone like Sinatra to tell him what kind of songs to sing; big band playing will ruin you for soloing; jazz has to swing (i.e., make you tap your foot), and Brubeck didn't swing, but Benny Goodman did; and he referred to the arrangements he played with Mingus (and Teo Macero) as "depressing," as "tired modern paintings." It was the kind of diatribe that Miles could usually get away with, but Mingus was so provoked that he wrote a response to him in *Down Beat* under the title, "An Open Letter to Miles Davis." Like much of Mingus' writing, it rambled and revisited a lot of old battles. He defended Charlie Parker as a loving father, praised Dave Brubeck for his honesty, lauded Monk's style of accompaniment, and claimed the right for himself to play whatever he wanted. He took Miles to task for his hypocrisy, anger, and lack of respect. "What's happening to us disciples of Bird?" he groaned.

Soon after returning from army service in 1946, record producer George Avakian got to know Miles, and starting in 1952, whenever Miles ran into Avakian he would try to talk the producer into signing him with Columbia because he knew it was the leading company for LP record production and because Columbia promoted its artists aggressively. "Every time I saw him, he'd ask me to sign him. I lived near him, and he'd come by to hang out. He'd tell me that he'd been asking me to sign him 'for years': at first it was two years, then it was four years, then six years."

One problem was that Miles was signed to Prestige Records through 1957. Another was that his addiction made him unreliable and forced him to look for work outside New York in places where his difficulties were not as yet well known. And a third problem was that he had no regular band. But Miles had a plan for his own promotion that was hard for Avakian to resist: "Miles suggested that I tell [Prestige president] Bob Weinstock that if he'd allow Miles to record with Columbia while he was still under contact with them, and hold the masters until the contract ran out, then Prestige could benefit from the publicity that Columbia would generate when his first records for them were released. It was a wild idea, but just might work."

The Newport Jazz Festival was in its second year in July 1955 and beginning to hit its stride. The musicians who gathered there spanned all styles and periods of jazz, bringing with them a greater array of live music than even the most devoted fans had ever been exposed to before. Erroll Garner was there, and so were Woody Herman, Roy Eldridge, Coleman Hawkins, and Louis Armstrong; Max Roach, Clifford Brown, Chet Baker, Dave Brubeck, Count Basie, Lester Young, Lee Konitz, Dinah Washington, and Charles Mingus. It was as if they were announcing the arrival of the golden age of jazz.

On the night of Sunday July 17, Duke Ellington was the master of ceremonies when the Modern Jazz Quartet took the stand, followed by a small group led by Count Basie with Lester Young. Most of the crowd was probably there to see Dave Brubeck's quartet, which was then at its peak of popularity, but there was a twenty-minute jam session scheduled before they came on to allow for stage changes. The program listed Zoot Sims, Gerry Mulligan, Thelonious Monk, and the rhythm section of the Modern Jazz Quartet for the short set. But at the last second, the festival's director, George Wein, added Miles Davis to the group. Wein thought Miles was something special, "a melodic bebopper, a bebop Bobby Hackett," a player who could reach a larger audience than most other musicians. Each of the horn players was featured one at a time with the rhythm section, and when Davis' turn came, he strode on stage in a white seersucker sport coat and a small black bow tie, looking sharp and serious, if a bit nervous. The Newport sound system was not very good that year, and the crowds were grumbling about not being able to hear anything. Miles opened by jamming his horn against the mike, so that he was the *only* thing folks could hear at the back of the festival grounds. The tune was Monk's own "Hackensack," and Miles grasped the direction of Monk's aggressive leading chords and breezed through the composition as if he had been playing it for years. He and Monk next shared the solos on "'Round Midnight," with Miles comfortably making the melody his own. Then they ended Miles' part of the program with "Now's the Time," his solo hewing closer to traditional blues than it had on his original recording with Charlie Parker. Later, it would be said that the solo he took on "'Round Midnight" riveted the audience and for the first time showed them how much he had matured musically. Avakian doesn't remember it that way, and the Voice of America recording of the concert reveals rather tepid applause. Yet Avakian's brother Aram whispered to him that night that he should sign Davis now, before he became a hit. Miles later said he didn't understand what the fuss was about: he was playing the way he always had. And in a sense that was true. But over the past five years, he had gained the reputation of an unreliable junkie who blew gigs, missed notes, and couldn't hold a band together. Now his faultless playing and his clean looks forced the start of a grudging reevaluation, especially on the part of a press that was not inclined to forgive.

But triumphant moments were often short-lived for Miles. Before the evening was over, Elaine Lorillard, doyenne of Newport society and one of the organizers of the festival, had enraged him by referring to him at an après-festival party at one of the waterfront estates as "the boy who played so beautifully." And then, in the limo back to New York, Monk told him that he hadn't played "'Round Midnight" correctly. "So what?" Miles replied. He didn't like the way Monk had accompanied him and suggested that Monk was jealous of the reception he had received. At that point, Monk angrily got out of the car and walked on alone to the mainland ferry.

On Tuesday July 19, Miles met with Avakian for lunch, bringing along his friend Lee Kraft and his lawyer, Harold Lovett. Bob Weinstock had bought the idea of Miles recording for Prestige and Columbia simultaneously. As part of the arrangement for signing with Columbia, Miles was asked to form a group that would still be together a year and a half later, when the Columbia records were released. Miles said the group he had been playing with for the past week was the one he wanted: tenor saxophonist Sonny Rollins, and a rhythm section of pianist Red Garland, drummer Philly Joe Jones, and bassist Paul Chambers. Avakian next insisted that Jack Whittemore of the Shaw Agency become Miles' agent. Miles then proposed a $2,000 advance against royalties, which, along with his payments for sessions, would guarantee him $4,000 a year.

But Sonny Rollins was not ready to resume playing, so Miles turned to Cannonball Adderley, an alto saxophonist who had arrived in New York City from Florida that summer, where some were calling him "the new Bird." The second night that he was in town, he sat in with Oscar Petti-ford's band at the Cafe Bohemia, and Dizzy, Miles, and J. J. Johnson had all come by to sit in with him. Truth be told, Cannon was no Parker, yet Miles thought he brought a strong blues feel into whatever music he interpreted and would fit comfortably into his quintet. But Adderley had a teaching job in Florida and needed to return home by September or lose his tenure.

Miles rehearsed briefly in Chicago with John Gilmore, the pyrotech-nic tenor saxophonist who played with the Sun Ra Arkestra. Gilmore, like a handful of other younger saxophonists, had been pushing the horn to new limits. The saxophone was invented relatively late in the history of musical instruments, and though its capacities were still being discov-ered, it had already moved well beyond what most other horns were capable of playing in jazz. The saxophone offered the potential for play-ing an enormous variety of tones, many of which lay well outside the Western aesthetic. It was possible to play it with intense vocalized artic-ulation, new extremes of vibrato, alternate ways of producing the same tone, overblowing, and the so-called false upper register developed among stomping, bar-walking rhythm and blues saxophonists. Tenor sax-ophones, especially, were able to honk, howl, scream, cry, pop, growl, and tongue-slap tones, and Gilmore had taken the horn further in this direction than anyone else at the time. But he was not what Davis was looking for.

Philly Joe Jones put in a call for John Coltrane to come up to New York to rehearse with the Davis group because Coltrane had worked with Jones and Red Garland in Philadelphia. Once Coltrane arrived, it was clear that he knew their repertoire and wouldn't be starting from scratch. Davis had heard Coltrane over the years, had kept up with his progress, and was excited by the idea of adding him. (Irene recalled that Miles first met Coltrane at a warehouse where he was very impressed at how much weight he could lift.)

But once Trane joined the band, there were questions of compatibil-ity. He was musically mercurial, often changing directions without warn-ing in the middle of solos, and he was studious, laboriously so, running scales and chords in the kitchens of the clubs during breaks. But he was also shy, and even reticent in the studio; he kept backing away from the mike and often had to be pushed back to it. He was sometimes unsure of what he was supposed to be doing with the band. Davis was not much help, because he was annoyed by Coltrane's questions about what he *shouldn't* play and refused to answer him. Miles later said, "My silence and evil looks probably turned him off." For those who might have thought that Davis' stage behavior was only an affectation, Coltrane's response to it must have been a revelation:

> Miles is a strange guy; he doesn't talk much and he rarely discusses music. You always have the impression that he's in a bad mood, and that what concerns others doesn't interest him or move him. It's very difficult, under those conditions, to know exactly what to do, and maybe that's the reason I just ended up doing what I wanted.

And what did it feel like to have Davis leave them alone on the bandstand?

> Miles' reactions are completely unpredictable: he'll play with us for a few measures, then—you never know when—he'll leave us on our own. And if you ask him something about music, you never know how he's going to take it. You always have to listen carefully to stay in the same mood as he!

Beyond the interpersonal problems of the group, there was a generally negative reaction by audience and critics to the direction that Coltrane was taking. Like John Gilmore and a number of other younger players, Coltrane was beginning to question the fundamentals of the music—playing with a reduced number of chords, perhaps playing on only one chord, recognizing the possibility of equality among all twelve tones of the octave so that all chords and melodies could be contained in one chord; or playing between the notes, shattering and splitting them into shards that hinted at secrets yet to be revealed about music. Coltrane had begun by placing one chord on top of the other like the beboppers, but he was now attempting to play through all of the stacked-up chords at the same time in a manner that Ira Gitler called "sheets of sound." All this Coltrane did with a sound that had a desiccated, unromantic, flat-earth quality in which one might hear purity, pain, and universal truth, or a sour, undisciplined yawp, depending on one's inclinations.

Davis' fans were often skeptical of Coltrane, and some critics outdid one another to find new metaphors of distaste: musical nonsense, anti-jazz, playing while eating peanut butter sandwiches . . . For Miles Davis to hire him was not a great public relations move. Even Vernon was put off by his choice: "I told Miles, 'You can't use that boy . . . everything he plays is unresolved.' Miles said, 'If he plays with me, he'll resolve things.' But he didn't. Everything he played was hung out there on the clothesline, and it's still out there." Miles was aware of how others would react to the addition of Coltrane, but hiring him was a risk he was prepared to take.

When I first recorded Trane, the guy from the record company [Bob Weinstock of Prestige] said, "Miles, who is that out there playing saxophone?" I said, "Man, just record the shit. You want us to play, we'll play, if not we'll go home." I mean, Trane was a big thing to be dropping on people! That was hard shit to just think of!

Coltrane said he had always wanted to play like Miles, but once he was with him, he found that what Davis played wouldn't work on the saxophone, and he went in a different direction, filling up spaces, extending his solos further and further out. A certain amount of tension developed between the two of them, and on the length of Coltrane's solos, drummer Jimmy Cobb recalled that "Miles would say to him, 'Can't you play 27 choruses instead of 28?'" When Coltrane explained his long solos by saying that he couldn't find a way to stop, Miles suggested that "you might try taking the horn out of your mouth." But Coltrane continued to play for long stretches of time, "because Miles sensed that he was working on something." Still, there were times when the audience hooted or whistled during his solos, and at the Apollo Theatre, they threw money at him and jeered, until the management turned the lights out on him. "Then he'd go off in the corner and practice," Cobb said. For Coltrane it was a rare learning opportunity, and a space in which to explore his own potential: "Miles' band is the one band where you had to be able to read music but there wasn't any music"—that is, you had to be able to play in the abstract, but also in a professional and disciplined manner.

What Miles was hoping to accomplish finally depended on his having the best rhythm section in jazz. First, there was Joseph Rudolph Jones from Philadelphia, nicknamed Philly Joe to distinguish him from the great swing drummer Jo Jones from Chicago (you have to be hip, Amiri Baraka once said, to have a city use your name). Before he was drafted in World War II, Philly Joe had been a truck driver and a tap dancer—good enough as a dancer that Honi Coles had informally trained him. In the tradition of the great dancer-drummers, he had also become a drummer good enough to play in an army band while he was serving as a military policeman. When he returned from the army at the end of 1944, he arrived just in time to see whites and blacks clashing in the streets of Philadelphia. The charismatic black leader Father Divine was spearheading demonstrations to get African Americans their share of wartime jobs, and white men returning from the war saw blacks' claims for equal rights as a threat to their economic welfare. When the Philadelphia transportation workers' union struck over integration, riots followed, and President Franklin Delano Roosevelt seized the Philadelphia Transit Company under the War Powers Act and promised the use of the militia to keep it running. Eight black men were picked to be the first to integrate the company, and Philly Joe was among them. He had passed an intelligence test and a physical examination, and on August 1, 1944, he became the first black trolley driver in Philadelphia history. But he also continued his drumming, playing with Fats Navarro, Dexter Gordon, and other musicians who came to town, and stories persist about Philly Joe's playing sets in South Philadelphia clubs during his breaks on the route while the passengers waited outside in the trolley car.

Jones left Philadelphia for New York in the late forties and worked his way through the clubs, strip houses, and dance halls. He could dance, do dialect bits, and mimic anyone. His Dracula routine epitomized what was becoming known as sick comedy ("Shut up and drink your blood"). Lenny Bruce was always cracked up by it and worked his own version into his act. But as a drummer, Joe embodied the best of what came before him: he launched every piece he played with God's own sense of time, cracking a stick against the snare drum's rim on the fourth beat of every bar like a well-timed heart, working the ride cymbal with such consistency that it seemed as natural as breathing, until without warning he shifted into double time, setting up a crosscurrent that could suck the unsuspecting musician under, then just as quickly stepping back to calm the waters and leave the hapless player thrashing. Jones' drumming was filled with swells and dips of volume and melodic outbreaks as he crisscrossed the kit from tom-tom to snare. And through it all, he was a vision of sartorial splendor behind the gleaming bundles of the drum set, his face animated dramatically. Philly Joe could *play*.

Miles first worked with Philly Joe barnstorming across the Midwest, Jones traveling ahead to scout up local sidemen to make up a band, Miles following, arriving just before the gig, walking into the club at the last minute. Joe was an addict, had done time for it, and could often be unreliable, but Miles kept his eye on him. Jones dressed immaculately, often tailoring his own suits (a skill he had picked up in the slam). Miles found Joe's antics endlessly hilarious, one of his favorite routines being check-out time at a hotel, where Joe invariably met with the manager to argue his bill down, insisting that he hadn't stayed as many days as the manager said or complaining about the quality of the mattress. Later, Miles joked that he had gotten a hernia laughing so hard at Philly Joe.

Though Miles seldom told his musicians how to play, drummers were the exception. He involved himself directly in Jones' playing, telling him not to play a rhythmic figure *with* him but *after* him, or changing the way he played the ride cymbal, the device that carried the basic beat of jazz:

> And I listen to the top cymbal to hear whether he plays it even or not. He may not play it like I want him to play it, but he can be taught how to play it if he plays even. I changed Joe's top cymbal beat. He was kind of reluc-tant at first, but I changed it so it could sound more ad lib than straight dang-di-di-dang-di-di-dang: I changed it to dang-di-di-dang-di-di-di-di-dang, and you can play off that with your snare drum.

Philly Joe would put up with him messing with the rhythm because Davis himself was such an exceptionally rhythmic player. As he put it:

> Miles had this real uncanny sense of time and rhythm, real different from anybody I've ever met. . . . I could never lose him, and he could never lose me. I always knew where he was. As much as I like to play melody in things on the drums, I could get with Miles and go into *anything,* just like he does with me; he never stays with the drummer; he goes way out.

Pianist Red Garland joined Miles in early 1955, after Philly Joe sug-gested both Ray Bryant and Red as possible pianists, Miles got a chance to hear Garland in Boston and asked him to join his group. After he was with the band, Garland in turn proposed Coltrane as their saxophonist. Davis heard things in Red's playing that he also heard in the playing of another pianist he admired, Ahmad Jamal, and Miles encouraged that side of him—the way Garland moved the root of the chord away from the bottom to create a more ambiguous harmony, or his use of block chords, what was sometimes called locked-hands style, the notes of the chord voiced closely together and distributed between the two hands. (On his 1956 recording of "You're My Everything," Miles can be heard asking Garland to play in that style. Miles also featured him on "Ahmad's Blues.") Garland loved show tunes, ballads, and the blues, and he was responsible for adding many of them to Miles' book for live perfor-mances. It didn't hurt that Garland had once been a boxer, and as a pro-fessional welterweight in the 1940s had fought more than thirty fights, one of them an exhibition with Sugar Ray Robinson.

Paul Laurence Dunbar Chambers, Jr., was the bassist, born in Pittsburgh and raised in Detroit. A baby-faced but big man, he kept time with a supple and strong beat and was also able to create interesting solos, sometimes using the bow. He was musically educated, had worked in singing groups and classical music, and his previous experience with Red Garland and Philly Joe gave Miles a rhythm section ready-made for his group.

Miles' quintet was sometimes known as a band of boxers, but it was also a group of unreliable drinkers and junkies. Red often came late to gigs; Chambers was frequently drunk, even passing out while he ate. And Joe and John were usually high. Stories of Davis' problems with this band were legion. Miles may have been the only member of the band free of heroin at the time, and he spent much of his time on the road keeping watch over them, trailing after them, keeping them away from the cops, getting them fed, or sobering them up. Miles sometimes wrote out checks to Philly Joe with sardonic notes on them saying that they were for dope. Unbeknown to the band, he even kept a stash of heroin in case of an emergency with one of them. Jimmy Heath was with another group on tour along with the Davis band and witnessed some of their travails. "Paul was proceeding to get as drunk and as high as he could," Jimmy said, every show.

> We had to play three or four shows during the day, and he was getting messed up at every show. Miles would play "So What" faster and faster every time he'd think Paul was drunk just to show him up and try to get him to straighten up. At one show, he says, "You're drunk, Paul, you're drunk!" And Paul says, "No, I ain't drunk." He's slobbering all over himself and everything, so Miles brought this food to make him eat so he would sober up enough to play the next set. Miles, as small as he was, and Paul was a big guy. Miles was the band leader and he's paying the man, and he showed his authority physically.

Coltrane may or may not have been the worst of the lot, but he bothered Miles the most because he was the most visible, and in some ways the most important, of his musicians. Miles saw Trane slipping deeper into trouble night after night. During a stay at Storyville in Boston, Coltrane was in particularly bad shape, nodding off on the bandstand, showing up late most nights, or not at all, his clothes sometimes filthy and foul. Miles' quintet was alternating sets at the club with the Australian Jazz Quartet, a band whose short-lived reputation was built on polite, chamberlike renderings of jazz standards with bassoon, bass clarinet, flute, and the like. Miles sat at a table with his tailor, Charlie David-son, seething over Coltrane's tardiness:

> Coltrane had already missed one night, he was late again, and Miles was fuming. "Charlie, I can't put up with this shit anymore. That mother-fucker . . . !" The other band is getting near the end of their set. *Australians*, right? Whiter than white. Coltrane walks in—high, looking awful. Miles says to Coltrane, "If you do this to me again, motherfucker, I'm going to sell you to the Australian Jazz Quartet!"

They were all high, but Philly Joe could be higher than anybody, and Miles was forced to monitor his every move, trying to hold down the quantities of dope he was consuming and keeping him from drinking with the customers. Joe could gorge himself on junk and drink until he overdosed, with his skin turning gray, his breathing shallow; then get put in a tub and iced down, taken to the bandstand and propped up on the drum stool, and still play as if nothing had happened. And it was not just Philly Joe. One night Miles told Philly to go next door and get the band ready to play. "What band?" Philly said. Paul was in the bathroom next door covered with ice cubes, and when Joe lifted him up, Paul was ready to fight him. When Miles got to the club, there was no one there but Trane, and he was in no shape to play. No one had a clue where Red was. Even when things were at their best, the performance might come apart if Philly Joe got interested in some woman in the audience and started playing to her. Coltrane, on the other hand, saw nothing at all but the music he was playing.

Winter in Quebec City, snowed in, Paul goes up to two white women in their seventies in the club, and says, "What are you two girls doing after the show?" Philly turned to Miles and said, "This motherfucker is crazy, Miles! What's wrong with him?" Suddenly Miles was sick of the whole scene. He got on the phone and called one of his Upper West Side pros-titute friends. "Get out of there," she said, and wired him money for the whole band to come back to New York.

In October 1955, Miles had an operation on his larynx for the removal of polyps. As he was recovering, he began talking too soon—at a rehearsal, he recalled—and damaged his voice still further. It had already been impaired from playing the trumpet, he thought, just as Louis Armstrong's and Dizzy Gillespie's voices had been. (Stories nonetheless persist that he ravaged his voice while in a shouting match with some music industry figure, like Don Friedman or Morris Levy.) If he had been shy about speaking publicly before, his self-consciousness about his voice now made him more so, and he spoke less and less. When he did speak, he often was not heard and had to whistle to get attention. Worse, some thought he was drunk or high, and over the phone he was often mistaken for a woman.

Though he continued in the life of a working musician—hustling club gigs, looking for small concerts—a series of events was slowly moving Miles toward something bigger: a few well-placed figures in the media began to pay attention to him—Steve Allen, for one, then a popular TV comedian and talk show host with a reputation for going beyond the philistinism of the usual programming by having guests such as Lenny Bruce or Jack Kerouac. Allen booked Miles for an appearance on his show on October 18 and also asked him to perform at a benefit Allen was hosting on October 15 at Carnegie Hall for the Red Cross of Israel. Davis' rise was also aided by the revitalization of the music business that followed the development of the long-playing record. Jazz itself was coming to be viewed as something a bit more sophisticated, more adult, an alternative to classical music and pop and especially to the new rock and roll that many in the bigger record companies found unsavory.

George Avakian also began to see Davis in a different light as he moved from being merely a cult figure, a bebopper, toward becoming a musician who could create an entirely new audience playing a melodic jazz—"an easy-listening modern jazz," as Avakian put it—a music that was easier for an audience that knew nothing about jazz to grasp. But Miles would still carry with him the mystique of having played with Charlie Parker. Avakian's plan was to record both sides of Davis, starting first with his working quintet, under circumstances that would better capture his jazz qualities for the hard-core fans. Since Prestige would be simultaneously promoting its own records with the same group, Columbia would also showcase Davis in a more dramatic and mainstream setting, reaching more people in the process. He would be given star treatment, including professional photographers and publicists. Avakian's assessment of Davis' potential was shared by others at Columbia. When he first took Debbie

Ishlon, the Columbia publicist, to hear Miles at the Cafe Bohemia, she immediately declared that with his Italian suits, Cole Porter tunes, and seductive use of the mute, she could get him into *Newsweek* or *Time*.

The Davis quintet entered Columbia's Studio D on October 26, 1955, and began recording tunes, some of which would appear on Miles' first Columbia album, to be called *'Round About Midnight*, recalling Miles' performance of the Thelonious Monk composition that summer at Newport. Avakian told Davis to hold back recording the title tune for Prestige in the meantime. Columbia was then pioneering in the editing of recordings, and all of the material recorded that first day was edited to get the best solos onto the takes to be released (as a result, the same solo can sometimes be heard on different takes). After two more sessions in June and September 1956, *'Round About Midnight* was finished; the songs were sequenced as if each side of the LP were a set at a club, with ballads and fast tunes pacing each other. The band had matured rapidly, and the tunes on the recording flowed together as if it were a concept album, or as if they had all been written by the same person, or rewritten to fit together. (When the album was issued on March 3, 1957, it outsold all five of the Davis quintet recordings for Prestige combined.)

Miles was now seeing Susan Garvin, a woman in New York City whom he called Lazy Susan, and named a composition for her. He was also visited sometimes by his St. Louis girlfriend. Both of these women, he said, kept him in money. He had also become closer to his prostitute friend from Texas on the Upper West Side, who looked out for his well-being, helped keep him off drugs, and often bailed him out of financial troubles.

Jean Bach, a rising New York radio personality from Milwaukee society by way of Vassar, first met Miles in the middle of 1952 at a benefit at the Ritz-Carlton Hotel in Boston, where he had been brought as a guest by Charlie Bourgeois of the Storyville club:

> When I first saw Miles I thought he was gay, the way he moved and dressed—he was dressed so meticulously, and he was *too* good looking. He

asked me to dance, and I was surprised at how well he could dance. He knew how to do the Peabody! It was a dance you couldn't do without practicing. Most musicians can't dance anyway, but Miles was very graceful. He was very different from other jazz musicians in many ways. He was witty, charming, and always able to come up with some unusual point of view.

Though Miles found mixing it up at the bottom of the social order thrilling, he could be protective of women like Jean from the other end of society. "I had a small birthday gift for Miles, and I was carrying it on the subway when I ran into Philly Joe Jones. When I told him about the gift, he offered to take it to Miles for me. Late that night I got a call from Miles warning me that I should stay away from people like Joe."

Davis was then living at 881 Tenth Avenue, a spacious, loftlike apartment of the kind that most people of color couldn't get in those days, and Miles' children often stayed with him on weekends, then went back to Irene's apartment in Brooklyn. "He took great pride in their clothes," Jean said, "and was very proud of them. He was beginning to entertain at home. I went to a party at his apartment in 1957, where the guests were mostly musicians and their wives, all of them sitting rather stiffly around the edge of the room. A butler had been hired for the occasion, and Miles was acting the perfect host, seeing that everyone had what they wanted. Another time I was there a musician dropped by with a six-pack of beer, and Miles scolded him for bringing alcohol into his house while there were children there." "But there was always this kind of sadness about him," Jean told writer Stanley Crouch.

> It was there and very penetrating. You knew he'd been hurt by something or was sunk in some kind of deep melancholy. Miles could withdraw into his sadness and it could seem as if he wouldn't be able to come out of it. His unhappiness could trap him and hold him down. It really could. Depression was one of his struggles.

Any number of things were troubling him. He worried about Vernon's homosexuality and the trouble some of his aggressive behavior had gotten him into in East St. Louis, and he wondered what all that might mean about himself. He told Jean that he had read a magazine article on the traits of gay people, and he feared that he might have some of the ones they described—a receding hairline, for example, or a certain type of fingernail. At the other end of things, he had been living for a while with a young white girl, possibly a teenager, whom he had met through Gerry Gray, the original "Satin Doll," celebrated in a song by Duke

Ellington, and one of the dancers in Sammy Davis, Jr.'s musical *Mr. Wonderful*. The girl had become pregnant, and when she miscarried, Miles visited her in the hospital and brought her a book of Paul Laurence Dunbar's collected poetry.

Race was something he seldom forgot—or was allowed to forget. Beyond the predictable racial hassles with whites, there were black musicians who called him Little Inky. He would not abide racial insults and once punched out Paul Chambers for calling him a "black bastard." These slights were something he expected, and when they didn't come, he might probe for them. Miles dropped by Jean's apartment one day while TV writer and producer Goodman Ace was visiting. Miles sat down across from him, and seeing Goodman had cigars in his pocket—though he wasn't smoking because Jean preferred him not to—Miles asked for one, lit up, puffed on it a few times, and handed it back to him: "You finish it." Small tests for racism like this would recur many times in the years to come, sometimes with a shared bottle of Heineken, a joint, or merely to see if a journalist, fan, or would-be lover was willing to touch the muscles in his lips or finger the scar from an operation.

Composer David Amram met Miles during a time when he was playing French horn with Charles Mingus at the Cafe Bohemia in the fall of 1955, and Miles, Monk, Max, and Sonny Rollins all dropped in to hear Mingus. The Bohemia had a reputation for its seriousness as a club. Its owner, Jimmy Garofalo, had been known to literally jump over the bar and beat up people if they were making noise. And when Miles himself played there, Amram was in the club every night:

> Cecil Taylor and I became friends going down to hear Miles every night. After the set was over, Miles would usually walk out onto the street during the break. And when he walked by, lots of times people were so scared of him they would just kind of sit there in awe. But he saw Cecil and I every night, so about the third night when he came by he gave us both a high five. And then a few more nights, the same thing between each set. So after a while he came by one night and he was slapping me the high five and he kind of gave a signal with a little move of his head to join him. So he started out and I walked out with him. We walked about five blocks without saying a word, and then he finally said, "Where are you going?" And I said, "I don't know, Miles. I was just following you." He cracked up laughing! And at that moment I saw the humorous side of him and his

appreciation of humor and the absurdity of life that I think a lot of people never even imagined was part of him.

Amram had ambitions to compose symphonic music in a contemporary vein, one that drew on jazz, and Miles asked him if he had heard *Birth of the Cool:*

> I told him that was one of the major musical moments in my life, hearing that. Not just the French horn part, but as someone who wants to write symphony music using what I knew as a jazz player—that opened up the door. And he began to talk about Junior Collins, who was the improvising horn player of that group. Then we went back to the club, but I would continue to go down and hear him, and sometimes we would have a conversation. And I found out how interested he was in all kinds of music, including some of the old jazz masters, a lot of whom people weren't that aware of. People like trumpeter Joe Guy. And he started talking about all the great musicians from St. Louis, and people that most musicians even didn't know about that he was constantly discovering. A lot of the people he talked about—musicians, players, composers, writers, artists—weren't on a list of the top ten. He didn't judge things by the label. He judged them by what they *were* and what he felt about them. And that's something I think was consistent in his life, and also confused people because they never could understand what they thought was his constant changing of styles and changing interests was because he had such broad interest in so many things and was so perceptive.

Miles was usually willing to respond to any request for an interview from jazz writer Leonard Feather, in part because Feather had defended him against other music critics and because he had given him exposure in his regular columns in both the United States and England. In 1955 Feather conducted a "Musicians' Musicans Poll" for the 1956 *Encyclopedia Yearbook of Jazz,* which he was editing. Miles agreed to participate and provided an unusually large list:

> Trumpets: Louis Armstrong, Roy Eldridge, Dizzy Gillespie, Bobby Hackett, Harry James, Clark Terry, Freddie Webster. New Stars: Clifford Brown, Donald Byrd, and Kenny Dorham.
>
> Trombones: J. J. Johnson and Bill Harris.
>
> Alto saxophones: Charlie Parker, Lee Konitz. New Star: Cannonball Adderley.

Tenor saxophones: Lester Young, Sonny Rollins. New Star: John Coltrane.

Baritone saxophone: Harry Carney, Gerry Mulligan.

Clarinet: Benny Goodman, Artie Shaw. New Star: Tony Scott.

Flute: Bud Shank.

Vibes: Lionel Hampton, Milt Jackson.

Guitar: Charlie Christian.

Bass: Oscar Pettiford, Ray Brown. New Star: Paul Chambers.

Drums: Art Blakey, Max Roach. New Star: Philly Joe Jones.

Miscellaneous Instrument: Ray Nance, violin; Jimmy Smith, organ.

Male singers: Frank Sinatra, Al Hibbler. New Star: Bobby Short.

Female singers: Carmen McRae, Jeri Southern.

Arranger: Billy Strayhorn, Gil Evans. New Star: John Lewis.

Big band: Duke Ellington. New Star: Sauter-Finnegan.

Combo: Modern Jazz Quartet. New Stars: Art Blakey's Jazz Messengers.

Piano: Art Tatum, Bud Powell, Dizzy Gillespie. New Star: Ahmad Jamal.

It was a judicious and wide-ranging list for the time, especially in his choice of trumpet players. At least some eyebrows at the time must have been raised by his choosing so many white musicians. But perhaps the only real surprises were the Sauter-Finnegan Band, a rather glitzy and short-lived group, and the inclusion of Dizzy Gillespie as a pianist. (Gillespie had served as Miles' piano teacher, and Davis was always quick to credit him.) The previous year Nat Hentoff had also asked Davis about his favorite musicians, and his list then was similar except that it included even more white musicians—such as Lennie Tristano, Nelson Riddle, Stan Getz, and Bob Brookmeyer.

The presence of Ahmad Jamal on Miles' list for Feather pointed again to his newfound fascination with a pianist his brother and sister had introduced him to in Chicago. Jamal seemed to have ignored the influence of Bud Powell and the bebop pianists, and played with a clarity and austerity that was unique and fresh. More than that, he was reversing the basic premise of the piano trio: it was *he* who was often accompanying the drums and the bass. He left extraordinary space in his playing for the rhythm to shine through and, if necessary, stretched the music out of shape by means of vamps, repeated bass figures, and even interludes that realigned the harmonic underpinnings of conventional songs. Jamal approached every song as a distinct composition, with something unique always located within it. He varied his rhythms, often switching between the conventional swing four-beat and the two-beat identified with older jazz. In everything he played, there was a lightness of touch and a respect for dynamics that were out of sync with his times, and which sometimes left him vulnerable to charges of being nothing more than a cocktail pianist.

Cannonball Adderley early on drew attention to Jamal's influence on Miles:

> Miles, for example, depends more on the rhythm section than he used to. For a long time, of course, Miles has been the type of soloist who implies a lot of things, and Jamal's influence made him even more aware of his being on the right side of this as far as he's concerned. Miles has also become fonder of tags and transitory passages since listening to Ahmad. There is one specific thing Ahmad does that Miles likes his band to do— it's a left hand thing the pianist plays [repeated single eighth notes, separated by a beat or a beat and a half] that keeps the time alive regardless of how slow the tempo is. Gil Evans now uses it a lot. It's almost like shoving the beat.

On March 16, 1956, Miles did a short, quickly thrown-together recording session for Prestige with Sonny Rollins, Paul Chambers, Art Taylor, and Tommy Flanagan on piano. Flanagan recalls Miles pulling a sketch of the chords for Dave Brubeck's "In Your Own Sweet Way" out of his back pocket. "I remember him telling me how to voice the intro. He always knows exactly what he wants. It makes him easy to work with. If you don't play what he wants, he tells you. . . . 'Play block chords, but not like Milt Buckner. In the style of Ahmad Jamal.' Dave Brubeck commented that Miles always played an E-natural in the eighth bar of 'In Your Own Sweet Way,' even though it had been written with an E-flat. When I asked Miles why he played that, he said, 'Why did you write that?' Now some musicians play it that way . . . or both ways."

In order to complete his contractual obligations to Prestige, Miles asked to record as much as possible at several sessions, an idea that was agreeable to Bob Weinstock. So on November 16, 1955, and on May 5 and October 26, 1956, Miles' new quintet recorded thirty-one tunes, which were used to make up five albums: *Miles*, *Workin'*, *Steamin'*, *Relaxin'*, and *Cookin'*. Since these were all first takes (save one), there is often a club-like feeling about the albums with their mix of show tunes, blues, and bebop favorites. Davis alone is the soloist on some ballads, ushering in a long series yet to come of stark, lonely songs full of long stretches of silence and played softly in the mute. John Coltrane's hard-edged showers of notes on these recordings have led critics to speak of him as a foil to Davis' introspection. And he is that, sometimes exploding out of the quiet left in Davis' wake, exploring the possibilities of every chord with a feverish rigor. The rhythm section functions so flawlessly and effortlessly behind them that the listener scarcely notices that the group is often playing tunes with simplified harmonic structures. Philly Joe changes the rhythmic texture behind each soloist, often drifting into the group's trademark use of two-beat, which in any other setting at the time would have seemed outré.

These recordings were made quickly, under rough conditions, and sometimes with little regard for union rules. But the results were brilliantly evocative of what this band sounded like live. Adding to the flavor was Miles' practice of leaving traces of studio talk on the records, especially on *Relaxin'*. On the opener, "If I Were a Bell," Miles responds to an unheard question from producer Weinstock by saying, "I'll play it and tell you what it is later." When "Woody 'n' You" comes to an end, Miles asks if that take is okay, and Weinstock jokes that it isn't. When Miles asks why, Coltrane is heard in the background asking for the beer opener. Red Garland's introduction to "You're My Everything" is interrupted by Miles' directions for him to play it in block chords. The grain of Miles' voice adds a raw, spontaneous, ever mysterious quality to the performances, transforming them from the classically pure recorded documents that 1950s listeners expected, into moments of drama and vérité.

Throughout 1956 Leonard Bernstein had been giving talks and performances on CBS TV's *Omnibus* show on Sunday afternoons that were so successful that Columbia made recorded versions of some of them, including the program called *What Is Jazz*. Bernstein used samples from the Columbia catalogue to illustrate his points—Leadbelly, Duke Ellington, Turk Murphy, Pete Johnson, Machito, Bessie Smith, and Louis Armstrong among them. But when he recorded the program, he decided to illustrate the rapid evolution of jazz by having several groups play "Sweet Sue" in different styles. Beginning with a group led by Buck Clayton to represent older jazz, he moved on to Boyd Raeburn's Orchestra for swing. Bernstein wanted to end with examples of what he thought of as serious jazz, one of which was arranged and played by Teo Macero with the Don Butterfield Sextet. But when he heard it, Bernstein's reaction was "too lugubrious . . . get Miles." Macero then sketched out an introduction for Miles' group, and they improvised the rest. (On the boxed set *Miles Davis and John Coltrane: The Complete Columbia Recordings 1955–1961*, Bernstein can be heard telling Miles to play the first two notes of "Sweet Sue" so listeners will know what he's doing, and then he can play anything he likes.) Although it was only a short excerpt on the *What Is Jazz* LP, this was the first recording by Davis that Columbia released.

In the mid-1950s, interest in modern classical music began to intersect with developments in new forms of jazz composition. It was a natural outgrowth of the first generations of musicians and fans who had been exposed to both jazz and classical music through schools and the media, but it was also brought about by a new group of jazz musicians who, like Miles Davis, had trained in conservatories. There had been gestures in this direction before, with composers like Stravinsky occasionally slumming in the jazz neighborhood, or Benny Goodman commissioning a composer to write something for him. But this was serious: classical tradition bringing formal refinement to jazz, with jazz bestowing the chic of the contemporary on classical heads. In retrospect, it may sound either contrived or the next obvious step in music, but at the time, it was a rather giddy and daring fusion—something akin to what Katherine Hepburn said of the pairing of Fred Astaire and Ginger Rogers: she gave him sex, and he gave her class.

With those *Birth of the Cool* recordings still ringing in his ears, John Lewis formed the Modern Jazz Society in 1955 to perform new works geared to younger musicians. Next he expanded the idea with former Davis bandmate Gunther Schuller by forming the Jazz and Classical Music Society to perform contemporary and seldom-heard older classical music, as well as to encourage new forms of composition in jazz. Together they sponsored a concert at Town Hall in 1955 and planned a second one for 1956 featuring the premier of Schuller's *Symphony in Brass and Percussion*. But when Dimitri Mitropoulos scheduled a performance of it for a New York Philharmonic concert, Lewis and Schuller cancelled their event. It was a long shot that any company would ever record such music. But Avakian saw that since rehearsals were already underway for the concert, a recording could be produced without the overtime required when musicians are suddenly confronted in the studio by difficult new music. In addition, both Mitropoulos and Davis were under contract to Columbia.

Two of the pieces recorded in October were John Lewis' "Three Little Feelings," a composition that manages to sound classical while drawing on the blues, and J. J. Johnson's "Poem for Brass," a stately work in four movements and seven sections. Schuller recommended Davis as the soloist for both. Since Miles had recently been trying out the flugelhorn (played with a trumpet mouthpiece), the brass sonorities of these two pieces encouraged him to use the bigger horn. He played both horns on Lewis' piece, then flugelhorn alone on Johnson's, navigating the unusual forms of the two pieces with ease and grace.

When Miles attended the recording of Schuller's symphony, conducted by Mitropoulos, he glimpsed that there might be an opportunity for him to be a classical player after all. He asked George Avakian to "ask him if I could play with his band sometime."

Miles had heard my wife, Anahid Ajemian, premier the Kurt Weill violin concerto with Mitropoulos and thought I had an inside connection with him. So after the first hour of recording I introduced him to the Maestro as the principal soloist for the other side of the proposed LP [*Music for Brass*], adding (as Miles had asked me to in a stage whisper before Mitropoulos came into the control room to listen to a playback), that Miles hoped one day to perform with the New York Philharmonic. Mitropoulos nodded, and said "perhaps," the perfect answer. Miles was pleased and never mentioned it again.

Schuller would ultimately call such projects as *Music for Brass* "third stream," a music free of barriers, classical played with greater freedom and jazz given new harmonic and formal resources. As benign as it now sounds, both classical and jazz coteries at that moment looked on such projects with suspicion, if not contempt. Purists were everywhere then, and they all thought their own particular stream was about to be poisoned. And there, in the middle of it all, stood Miles Davis: bebopper, quintessential cool jazz musician, barely turned hard bopper, now a creator of yet another style of music, all within ten years of playing. A few years later he would characteristically distance himself from this music by saying that listening to third-stream music was "like a woman I don't like, walking naked in front of me."

In the beginning of November, Miles left his band for Paris on a three-week tour of Europe arranged by Morris Levy as part of what was billed as the Birdland All Stars: the Modern Jazz Quartet, Lester Young, Bud Powell, and a French rhythm section of René Urtreger on piano, bassist Pierre Michelot, and Christian Garros on drums. On November 1, the French rhythm section was scheduled for its first meeting and rehearsal with Miles in a cold, dark cellar in the Fourteenth Arrondissement. When the musicians arrived, according to Urtreger, Miles fanatics were already hiding in dark corners of the room. Miles entered straight from the airport, dressed in a beige raincoat (which he kept on the whole time), with two friends of Urtreger from the film industry, Marcel Romano and Etienne Becker:

> Miles said "Hello," took out his trumpet, blew a couple of notes, and, right away, without the usual politesse, attacked his composition "Tune Up" in a very fast tempo. I and the two others reacted almost immediately and were able to follow him. When it was over, he said "Okay." with his broken voice (which was a surprise to us), and went away with Marcel and Etienne, straight to his hotel room to get some sleep. . . . I believe it was a kind of test. He didn't play "Tune Up" by accident—he could have chosen any jazz standard—he wanted to know if an unknown (to him) French rhythm section could play and follow him in the style he played at this time.

Miles liked the trio, but warned Urtreger to stay "absolutely clean of drugs" while he was playing with him. Miles and René shared rooms in hotels as they traveled for almost a month across western and northern Europe, Miles happy, joking, keeping an eye on René's drug habit, and chatting with René about his band in New York ("Man, I've got a tenor player in the quintet. His name is Coltrane. He plays funny, man!"). Miles seemed at ease, coasting a bit on his solo stints with the rhythm section, then becoming more expansive and wider-ranging when he played along with the Modern Jazz Quartet and Lester Young.

At their first concert at the Salle Pleyel in Paris, Miles noticed a pretty young woman behind the curtain on the stage and asked her why she was there. She told him she was listening to her brother play (and keeping an eye on him, René added: it was his sister Jeannette, who treated him very maternally since their mother had died in a Nazi camp during the war). Miles and Jeannette soon became lovers:

> He was very handsome, not like he became. . . . But what really attracted me was that he made me laugh and was a great musician. The first thing I said to him was that he played like an angel. And he was very modest, like all great musicians: "Are you sure?" he asked.

When the band went out on the road, Miles pestered René every day: "Let's call Jeannette." "Let's write a postcard to Jeannette." When they went back to Paris, René said, "Jeannette and I and Miles went out to restaurants, and Miles really seemed to enjoy being in Paris with Jeannette and her friends." It was an affair that continued for two or three years, with Jeannette coming to New York to visit him. Throughout the tour, Miles never saw Juliette Greco. "It was like something that was completely past and forgotten," he said.

CHAPTER FIVE

My name's my color.

MILES DAVIS

MILES WAS UNCHARACTERISTICALLY SENTIMENTAL about Christmas—the home-cooked food, gifts, the gathered relatives, putting toys together for the children the night before. For just a moment, he could step out of the centrifuge of hustlers and hipsters and into a still place where he could once again be his mother's son. A day or two later, he could be back to haunting the streets, but it never occurred to him not to spend Christmas Day with his family in Illinois if he could. He usually managed to get himself booked into Chicago for Christmas week, and when he couldn't, he'd try to book his band without him somewhere else to keep his musicians employed. In 1956, the whole band had a week at the Crown Propeller club in Chicago during Christmas.

Now only thirty years old, his records popping up one after the other on two different labels (with heavy advertising to support them), Davis started off 1957 with a shocker: during a stay at the Preview's Modern Jazz Room in Chicago, he announced to several lounging journalists that he might quit jazz. "I've had it. This is no sudden decision. I've been thinking about it for a long time and after I close here I'm calling it quits." He said he had offers to be a musical director at a record company or a teacher at Howard University. He didn't need the money. He was disgusted with the business. He was sick of jazz and was beginning even to dislike the word.

Though John Coltrane and Philly Joe Jones were not mentioned as the source of his grief, he fired both of them for their erratic behavior during a stay at the Cafe Bohemia in April and replaced them with Sonny Rollins and Art Taylor. His anger with Coltrane had reached the point that one night, he punched him while Thelonious Monk looked on. Monk immediately offered John a job with his group.

Davis' playing on the *Music for Brass* recording had convinced George Avakian that if he recorded Davis in a similar setting but without playing classical music, Miles could reach a much larger audience. Avakian proposed that they might expand on the *Birth of the Cool* nonet, but Miles said he wasn't interested in going backward. George then suggested that Miles might record with a band close to the size of the one Gunther Schuller had just used for *Music for Brass* and offered him either Gil Evans or Schuller as possible arrangers for the project. Miles chose Evans, who was also Avakian's preference, as he had already worked with him in recording Claude Thornhill's music, as well as on albums with Pearl Bailey and Johnny Mathis.

Avakian took Miles and Gil Evans to lunch at Lindy's, the restaurant of choice among showbiz folk, to plan the record. "I remember that Milton Berle, Henny Youngman, and a bunch of comics were seated nearby," George said, "staring at the three of us, making jokes about this strange-looking trio." They had lunch together again the next day to talk further, and Avakian presented his "Miles Ahead" concept—a publicity ploy, Miles "ahead" of everyone, moving "ahead." He left the choice of music up to Evans and Davis, except that there would have to be a composition called "Miles Ahead" that would anchor the 12-inch LP album, and could also be issued as a 45 rpm single. A cover photo would be chosen that would tell the story of the record's title.

Gil picked all of the songs to be recorded, except for Miles' choices of Ahmad Jamal's "New Rhumba" and Dave Brubeck's "The Duke," which Miles had heard on Brubeck's solo record for Columbia, *Brubeck Plays Brubeck*. (George Gershwin's "Summertime" was also on their list but was not recorded.) Miles was originally credited with the composition of "Miles Ahead," though the 1996 reissue more accurately co-credits Evans; "New Rhumba" is an orchestration of Jamal's own recording of this piece, including his piano solo; and Doris Day's "I Don't Wanna Be Kissed" was also recorded by Jamal under the title of "Medley" in 1955; "Springsville" already existed in an arrangement by Johnny Carisi; and Gil himself had previously arranged his own composition, "Blues for Pablo" and Leo Delibes' "The Maids of Cadiz" for an earlier recording. The other pieces were compositions by Bobby Troup, Kurt Weill, and J. J. Johnson. Altogether, it was an astonishing array of music to appear on one record.

The 12-inch LP record was brand new, though the recording industry had been working on it for at least thirty years. There had been 16-inch radio program transcription records before, developed for recording shows and sending them to stations across the country, but they were too big for home use and played for only fourteen and a half minutes a side. When it became possible to get seventeen minutes on one side of a record, Columbia decided to develop the format for public sale. Classical 12-inch LPs were the first produced, because pop and jazz were thought of as suitable only for singles, four 78 rpm record singles could fill one side of a 10-inch LP, and that was thought to be enough. The problem now was how to program music for this expanded format. Avakian decided to follow the 16-inch radio program transcription practice of placing a particularly strong performance—a "grabber"—at the beginning of the recording and another attention-getter at the end of the side to induce listeners to turn the record over. The same pattern would be repeated on the other side. With a single record, approximately three minutes had been the limit within which a composition or song had to be completed, but the LP allowed greater length for single pieces. At first, recorded tracks were only modestly lengthened, but a theme or a drama was often programmed to unfold across the entire recording, linking each track together to express a particular mood or create a personal statement. Miles Davis, along with Frank Sinatra, was one of the first to be offered this treatment, and it gave him a commercial edge that very few jazz musicians would ever have.

When Gil prepared the arrangements for *Miles Ahead*, he got the idea of running them together so that they formed something of a suite, or a *Konzertstück*. The model for this may have been Michel Legrand's *I Love Paris* album for Columbia, where one song segued into another. But Evans went further and wrote bridging passages that made the album seem more of a single work.

The orchestra that Evans used was large for a jazz album, nineteen pieces, all of them stellar figures in studio and club work. And despite Miles' wish to avoid recreating *Birth of the Cool*, the arrangements often seem like extensions of the original idea. In fact, Lee Konitz, Johnny Carisi, Bill Barber, and some of the original people were in the band. Evans later said that the recording was as good as it was because each musician already understood the idiom within which he was working. These were plush surroundings in which to feature a single jazz musician, but not unprecedented; Dizzy Gillespie, Charlie Parker, and Clifford Brown had all made records with string sections, and broadened their audience by doing so. What's more, the Davis-Evans record appeared at a time when Bobby Hackett's recordings with Jackie Gleason were high on the hit charts. But while presenting jazz soloists in such a setting might seem like an obvious move, the tension that has always existed in jazz between small, improvised group recordings and heavily orchestrated, preplanned music presents a tricky course to navigate: a move too successful and too far away from jazz tradition could be disastrous with fans.

Stereo recording was in its experimental stages in 1957, and Columbia had been loaned a new test model Ampex two-track recorder to try out, so they decided to record Davis' album in two formats—the usual mono and the new stereo. Another innovative move was the use of overdubbing, still relatively rare at that time. Miles was having trouble with some of the parts and was becoming upset with himself, and overdubbing meant that he would not have to play during some portions of a recording and would add his part later. Recording more than one take may have been standard procedure for 78 rpm recording, but new technology now made it unnecessary for the orchestra to play along with the soloist each time, allowing producers to put the best orchestral versions together with the best solo versions. (Davis' overdubbing on *Miles Ahead* occurred three months after the orchestra had recorded its part on "Springsville," "Miles Ahead," "New Rhumba," and "I Don't Wanna Be Kissed.")

The amount of editing in this album—the number of takes and overdubs involved—was extraordinary for the time, and all the more remarkable because the state of the technology required cutting and splicing the tape by hand, something the engineers had been warned against by Ampex, the tape's manufacturer, for fear the tapes would deteriorate or separate, and clicks would be heard at the point of every edit. Still, the Columbia engineering department finally decided to allow some splicing, and by the time the record was completed, there was only one unedited take left from those sessions. Miles, along with Dave Brubeck, was one of the first artists to submit to such editing processes, and he continued to be one of the most edited musicians. But as Gil Evans often said, Miles always edited himself as he played anyway.

Since Evans had recomposed the tunes much as an improviser might do—rephrasing melodies, adding countermelodies, altering original harmonies, and varying tempos—the material could seem as though it had all been written by the same composer. On Delibes' "The Maids of Cadiz," for example, he changed the mood of the original composition by radically altering the instrumentation, changing the harmonies, switching the meter from 3/4 to 4/4, slowing the tempo, and adding in some twenty-nine bars (over half the composition) of new material. On his own composition, "Blues for Pablo," Evans borrowed and transformed some portions of Manuel de Falla's *The Three-Cornered Hat*, as well as some unidentified Spanish folk material, and worked them into his own composed melodies. All of his arrangements keep Davis' flugelhorn focused and square in the center, and with the edits in place, the record has a continuity and flow that few other albums have ever achieved.

Miles was also part of the process. Art Taylor dropped by Davis' Tenth Avenue place several nights after the quintet played, and watched Gil and Miles working on scores until daybreak.

> It was very exciting. . . . I would just sit around with magazines listening to what they're doing, watching. . . . "Man, take that out." "Put this in here." "Maybe we could try that." "No, I don't know if that'll work." It was like trial and error. They were putting this music together. It was very serious and very intense.

The sessions went slowly because of Evans' perfectionism and his practice of continual rehearsal in the studio, and sometimes it seemed as if it would go on forever. Some of the trumpet players complained that their parts were too difficult and their lips were giving out. Without the musicians knowing it, Avakian began recording the rehearsals, fearing they might otherwise never complete a satisfactory take of an entire performance, and unlabeled sections of the music began to accumulate on tape. By the time they were finished, Evans had written the arrangements, rehearsed them, in some cases taught them to the musicians, conducted them during recording, directed the engineer, and worked on the editing. For this, he received the usual payment for arrangers, $500 an arrangement, with no royalties or residuals. But then record companies had never seen an arranger quite like Gil Evans.

The photo selected for the cover of *Miles Ahead* was one of a fashionable woman in a sailboat—it was generic, corny, and very white. Once the record was out, Miles became annoyed and went to his publicity agent at Columbia, Debbie Ishlon (whom he later said he was sleeping with) and asked her if he couldn't get it changed. She told him to take the problem to Avakian. Why a white woman? he asked George. Why not a black woman? Avakian suggested that they replace the cover photo with one of Miles himself. Columbia was known for the speed at which it could get LPs on the market (the cast recording of the Broadway show *Kismet* was in stores three days after it was recorded and one week after the show opened). Columbia would print large quantities of covers in advance because they were cheaper when ordered that way, but would press records only as they were needed. The covers could then be thrown away if the sales were low. Avakian explained to Davis that if they had to change the cover now, they would have to stop shipment of the record for at least six weeks and everyone would lose money. So Miles agreed to release the record in the existing cover and then to change it once the new ones were printed. Once it was out, the record took off: Columbia sold some 75,000 to 100,000 copies (the break-even sales point for its LPs at that time was 15,000 to 20,000 copies) before the cover was changed to one with a picture of Miles.

There was more confusion and multiple versions of this record yet to come in the future. The first CD issue of *Miles Ahead* was produced by Teo Macero and was "electronically rechanneled for stereo" (a mono recording was reworked in fake stereo, or produced from newly found original stereo tapes, depending on whom you talk to). But the versions used this time were different, and inferior, most said, to those on the original LP issue, and the bridging passages between songs were eliminated. The second CD release was produced by George Avakian, again, and was sold as in the original mono, using the original takes, but some of the tracks were still in fake stereo, with at least one new mix ("I Don't Wanna Be Kissed" was corrected for mistakes in Miles' part). Some of the connecting passages were remixed, and one of them was entirely new, added in to connect the sections of the music that were previously separated by being on different sides of the LP. In 1997 *Miles Ahead* was reissued again, now with newly discovered true stereo versions of the mono takes and with the original interludes restored.

Miles Ahead was a success in every way. It sold well, making Columbia a leader in creating concept albums in LP format, with albums as entities in themselves, not just as collections of singles. And it established Davis as a popular entertainer, no longer merely a colleague of Charlie Parker or simply the leader of a post-bop quintet, but a new kind of jazz musician, a modernist capable of reaching an audience to which beboppers had never had access.

When Miles' first check for 'Round About Midnight came in, he used it to buy a Mercedes 190 SL, a blue, gull-wing, two-seater sport car, from a showroom floor. He said it had been winking at him every time he passed the showroom on upper Broadway.

At Birdland one night, Mo Levy introduced Miles to Beverly Bentley, a small, green-eyed blonde, at first glance as close to a southern belle as it was possible to be, post–Gone with the Wind. Beverly had originally come to New York from Atlanta by way of Kentucky and Florida to work on the Arthur Godfrey Show on television. She worked her way through TV, doing commercials, becoming a "weather girl," then studying method acting and finding roles in Off-Broadway plays like Jean Giraudoux's Tiger at the Gate, or Broadway productions such as Romanoff and Juliet. When they met, she had just finished working in Elia Kazan's film A Face in the Crowd.

Beverly was drawn to Miles for his humor, his charm, the twilight world he moved in, his sheer physical beauty, and the brilliance of his music. He had developed an interest in theater and film and had memberships to the Beekman Theater and the Museum of Modern Art Film Series ("He loved Westerns," Bentley said, "and he often compared women to horses"). Beverly and her place in that world were especially attractive to him. She introduced him to new styles of acting and played him records by Bessie Smith (she had them all) and folk-blues singers like Leadbelly. (Once Beverly sang him "Funky Butt," a song by Buddy Bolden, the New Orleans trumpet player who was said to be the first jazz musician, and Miles immediately recognized it as a riff that Bird used to play.)

He often cooked for her, using recipes he'd learned from home such as his father's chili:

bacon grease

3 large cloves of garlic

1 green, 1 red pepper

2 pounds ground lean chuck

2 teaspoons cumin

½ jar of mustard

½ shot glass of vinegar

2 teaspoons of chili powder

dashes of salt and pepper

pinto or kidney beans

1 can of tomatoes

1 can of beef broth

serve over linguini

He gave her recordings by Khachaturian, Bloch, Debussy, and Ravel and bought her clothes from Jax, one of the chicest women's shops in the city. Miles responded to her southern sense of class, her openness and grace, and called her "Lady Bentley" and himself "Lady Bentley's lover." They had become lovers, and, like his involvement with other white women, it was a relationship that in those times and in that city was daring, even in hip circles (the editor of *Confidential* magazine joked to her one night at Birdland that he could ruin her career by exposing her as dating a black man), and one never entirely free of danger.

To Beverly, "Miles was an odd combination of many things. He was insecure, and didn't want to go anywhere he wasn't known, so the jazz clubs were his main nighttime entertainment. He didn't like to go out to eat, and often cooked at home. He could get very upset—very paranoiac—when anyone stared at him in a club. But he was also very vain. He thought his legs were too thin; and he wished he had soft hair, like his brother Vernon's." He supported her in her career and came to her plays, and she urged him to step out and take his place at the front of the jazz world. "Miles felt he was destined to be great, but I had to encourage him, to push him to ask for more money for his performances. . . . When I had the role of Carrie Bliss in *The Big Knife* I suggested Miles to the director as someone who could do the music for the play. It turned out that Miles was too busy, and he suggested David Amram, and when that didn't happen, they used Billy Taylor's recording of 'Satin Doll' for the play's theme."

Miles was completely off heroin by 1957 but deeply into cocaine and alcohol, and Beverly found herself having to keep track of his condition. "He could be very loving, but when he was using coke he lied—though he always told the truth sooner or later—and became violent. He tried to get me to use cocaine one night at Birdland, but I flushed it down the toilet. He was also drinking scotch with milk, which was bad, because he was lactose sensitive. Whenever Miles called home, his father always asked to speak to me. He'd plead with me, 'Please take care of my boy, and keep him off heroin.'"

Meanwhile, as he wrote in his autobiography, Frances Taylor had "reentered my life." She had come to New York to appear in Sammy Davis, Jr.'s Broadway musical Mr. Wonderful, and she and Miles ran into each other on the corner of 52nd and Broadway. Taking his cue from a song from South Pacific, Miles said, "Now that I found you, I'll never let you go." Frances was small and doll-like, and projected a mixture of innocence and elegance that turned heads wherever she went. She had traveled abroad many times, spoke several languages, loved classical music, and was widely read. "She was cool and wasn't in competition with anything because she had a lot of confidence in herself," Miles said—all the characteristics he sought for himself. She was in the process of getting a divorce from another Dunham dancer, Jean-Pierre Durand, with whom she had a young child, and Miles pursued her relentlessly, picking her up for lunch at rehearsals, waiting for her when she was finished for the day, and finally asking her to move in with him.

Frances had been raised in Chicago and had studied classical ballet from childhood. As she was finishing high school, she caught the attention of Katherine Dunham and was accepted into the Dunham School of Dance (just as Irene Cawthon had once hoped to be). To move from dancing bourrées on point to mastering Dunham's deep Afrocentric, folk-based aesthetic was no simple matter, but Dunham saw the elegance and grace with which Frances moved and began to work her into her company. When she and Miles met, she had appeared in Porgy and Bess and Carmen Jones and was about to premier as one of the featured dancers of West Side Story. In fact, on opening night in September 1957, she would be awarded the company's "gypsy robe" for being the outstanding dancer in the cast.

Miles loved Frances' dancing, her legs, the way she moved, and he boasted about her to everyone. He was there to see her perform on opening night of West Side Story, and for many nights afterward. She was overwhelmed by his attention, and their lovemaking, and moved into his Tenth Avenue apartment with him. "Then one night in March he picked me up at the stage door after the performance, and he said to me, 'A woman should be with her man. I want you out of West Side Story.' I was in total shock . . . as was Jerome Robbins when I told him that I would have to leave. But Jerome later said to Miles, 'You know, since she's not in West Side, since you've taken her out of the Broadway show, can she at least do the movie?' And Miles told me, 'I'll give you my answer when we get home.' And his line was: 'You think I'm gonna let you do the movie?'" Frances was devastated, but also deeply in love with Miles: she left the show and gave up her career at its peak.

Life with Miles could be wonderful at times but also grindingly wearisome. "He was an incredible lover," but he might also disappear for days. Or he could be reclusive and refuse to go anywhere. And when they traveled, she had to see to the arrangements while he waited outside since he feared being turned away because of his color. When they were in Europe, he could relax some and was easier to be with. But when they returned to the United States, his fears returned.

Miles said that he "cut everyone else loose and was just with her during this time." But he continued to see Beverly Bentley, and when she went to Spain in 1958 to take a role in Mike Todd's film *The Scent of Mystery*, Miles seemed distraught, and sent her telegrams asking her to come home to be with him for two or three days—"It's on me. I'm rich. We are relatives" (both of them claimed some Cherokee ancestry). In one telegram he asked her to marry him ("You are my Beverly Davis").

When she returned from Spain, he began seeing her again and explained Frances' and her six-year-old son's presence in his apartment as something he was doing to protect her from her ex-husband. He kept Beverly a secret from Frances, however, and when he and Frances were married in December 1960, Miles told Beverly that he had to do it because Frances' father demanded it. In a sense, that was true, because Maceo Taylor confronted him on a number of occasions, wanting to know just what his daughter's future was with him and urging him to marry her. But Miles and Beverly nonetheless continued to see each other. When Miles' father died in May 1962, she even accompanied him to East St. Louis, though Miles staged the event carefully, asking her to stay at the hotel so as not to upset his mother. But Frances was also at the funeral, as was Irene, who said Miles kept his head down throughout the service until she walked past and he recognized her feet.

Beverly and Miles continued their relationship off and on for the next few years, until she met Norman Mailer, and they were married in late 1963. Mailer knew that she had been seeing Davis, which added to his fascination with her. To him, Miles was the incarnation of hip, and according to Mailer's biographer, Mary Dearborn—"with his lean, chiseled good looks and his ultracool manner he was distinctly a sex symbol as well, appealing to white women as well as black; rumor had it that he was omnivorously sexual. Norman was beginning to see blackness as the ultimate in Hip—a connection he would make powerfully, and often objectionably, over the next few years." Beverly said that Miles is one of the inspirations for Mailer's notorious essay "The White Negro," in which he laid out white male fantasies about black male sexuality and violence under the guise of a homespun existentialism.

Given the richness of his fantasies, it's no surprise that Mailer was also "insecure and jealous of Miles and all the black musicians who were around me," according to Bentley. In Mailer's 1964 novel, *An American Dream*, one of the characters, Shago Martin, is a thinly disguised Miles Davis: Martin is a violent black jazz singer, pimp, and former lover of Cherry, a character modeled on Beverly (Bentley's photo actually appears among others' in the photomontage on the book jacket). Cherry is the lover of Stephen Rojack, the Mailerian protagonist, who at one point in the novel brutally beats and almost kills Martin in a jealous rage over his coolness and perceived sexual superiority.

Though Miles and Norman were cordial—Miles, for example, recommended David Amram to Norman as a composer for a project Norman was working on—there are those who remember moments of tension between them. In May 1964, for example, a party was held at the Village Vanguard to celebrate the publication of Mailer's *An American Dream*. Miles turned up as a surprise guest, possibly invited by Vanguard owner Max Gordon, though Norman assumed he was there to see Beverly and challenged him. The two had a staring match, but nothing more occurred. Norman's obsession with Beverly's relationship with Miles would haunt her right into her divorce proceedings, when in an effort to discredit her, Mailer's lawyer included Davis on a list of names of men with whom he tried to associate her as their mistress.

When Jeannette Urtreger came over from France to see Miles in New York later in 1958, she was angered to find that "he had fallen back into his old habits . . . he was paranoid . . . and he was drinking again." Drinking, but it was cocaine that was driving his behavior. Though cocaine lacked the flashpoint, the explosion of pleasure that came with a hit of heroin, Miles said that it gave him energy and a sense of confidence about music and sex:

> Cocaine is a good drug for making love and making you decide quicker what you want to do. If you play a trumpet or any instrument, any drug like that, or brandy, will help you make up your mind quicker about certain things. So will firecrackers, but you can't snort a firecracker.

Since Miles seldom recorded with singers, disliked even accompanying them for a single song in a club, it came as a surprise to many that his own playing had been shaped by a certain type of singer he loved: quiet, slow-burning, low-vibrato, understated singers, chanteuses, really, with a taste for show tunes . . . singers who sounded the way he played. Blossom Dearie was one—a small, sweet-voiced soprano who had worked her way through singing groups in the big band era, sang with King Pleasure on his hit recording "Moody's Mood for Love," worked with Annie Ross, then moved to Paris where she formed the Blue Stars singing group and married Belgian saxophonist Bobby Jaspar. Miles was impressed by Dearie's insistence on having a club completely quiet when she sang and her willingness to chastise noisy audiences. It was her version of "Surrey with the Fringe on Top" that led him to record it a year after she first did it, though it was also a song that Ahmad Jamal had recorded a few years earlier. (When Miles reformed his quintet in the fall of 1957, he used Bobby Jaspar on reeds.)

Jeri Southern was another singer he admired. A pianist turned song interpreter, she had a smoky, soft voice and opened her sets with slow ballads (which did not always sit well with jazz audiences—she was actually hissed at a 1956 Carnegie Hall concert she did with Sarah Vaughan and Count Basie's band). In the 1950s she worked hip nightspots like Birdland, or the Den at the Duane (Hotel) on Madison Avenue when Lenny Bruce and Nichols and May were also appearing there.

Shirley Horn was also one of Miles' favorites. She first met him in 1961 when he called her out of the blue and asked her to come to New York City "to meet some very important people." When she arrived at his house, she was stunned to find all of his children singing her songs: he had been playing her first album over and over. "Miles took over when I got to New York, and I'm not easily taken over. But he immediately made me feel like family." He became her chaperone, uncle, and manager, and the first stop was the Village Vanguard, where he insisted that owner Max Gordon allow her to open for him. "I was completely overwhelmed. I had never been in a nightclub, and there I was in the Village Vanguard, in New York City, playing my twenty-minute sets before that wonderful band." Miles was protective, keeping her away from the bar, on her for smoking, and steering her around some of the more unsavory figures in the jazz life. But he also wanted her to sit in with them on piano for a blues: "I was scared to death. I was taking the piano bench away from Wynton Kelly, who I adored! He was trying to get to the bar, but I kept saying, 'No, don't leave me!'"

Miles and I didn't talk much about the music then, but he liked the slow way I did ballads. He had that same sense of space. Playing like that makes you think: you take a bite and you savor it. They used to say of my singing, "Never try to find the one" [the down beat]. And Miles was the same way.

Davis faced a crisis in September when he fired Red Garland for missing gigs, Art Taylor quit in anger over Miles' criticism of his playing, and Sonny Rollins left to form his own group. But before he could form a new band, the French producer Marcel Romano offered him three weeks of concerts across Europe in late November and early December, all of which would be documented in a short film, a sort of nuts-and-bolts view of musicians new to one another coming together to play. Without enough money to bring over American musicians, Romano lined up Barney Wilen, a young tenor saxophonist from a wealthy and cultured background in Nice, who was then attracting attention; France's best bebop pianist and bassist, René Urtreger and Pierre Michelot; and Miles' old friend Kenny Clarke on drums. The tour didn't work out quite as planned, but there were still two concerts in Paris, others in Brussels, Amsterdam, and Stuttgart, and a few weeks at the Club St. Germain on the Rue St. Benoît. When the plane landed at Orly, Romano was there to greet Miles with an idea to make up for the missing gigs: a young director named Louis Malle had just finished his first dramatic film, *Ascenseur pour l'échafaud* (*Lift to the Gallows* in the United Kingdom and *Frantic* in the United States), starring Jeanne Moreau and Maurice Ronet, and he was looking for someone to do a jazz score for it. Was Miles interested? He told Romano that he'd never done anything like that, but if he liked the film, he'd try it.

Ever since he had heard the score for *A Streetcar Named Desire* in 1952, Miles had been fascinated by Alex North's film music. That was the moment at which North broke with Hollywood's tradition of using nineteenth-century European-derived methods for scoring films and instead began using a kind of simulated jazz for *Streetcar*, weaving trumpet and bassoon lines together over slithering rhythms and quasi-modal themes as the music drifted out from the doorway of the Four Deuces café in New Orleans. Characters in the film were given distinct themes to identify them; then the themes were overlapped and worked against each other, underlining their interrelationships and conflicts. Music such as North's would later be associated in the minds of viewers with film noir of the 1940s and 1950s, even though none of those films' scores sounded anything like North's. Miles talked the *Streetcar* score up to everyone; he told his brother, Vernon, "Fuck jazz! Alex North is the man."

Miles' first concert on this trip to Paris was at the Olympia on November 30, 1957. But rumors were rampant that no one had seen him in Paris, and as of concert time, the audience was anxiously whispering among themselves.

> The Olympia Theatre was sold out that night, but by curtain time Miles' whereabouts were still a mystery. Finally, the curtain went up, revealing [the band] all set up. They started playing "Walkin'" and sounded fine. But no Miles Davis. Barney took a tenor solo, and as he was finishing, backing away from the microphone, Miles appeared from the wings, and arrived at the mike without breaking his stride, just in time to start playing—strong. It was an entrance worthy of Nijinsky. If his choreography was good, his playing was perfect that night. He had recently made his "comeback" and was really putting the pots on. He was serious, and he was trying hard instead of just catting.

So wrote Mike Zwerin, who hadn't seen Davis since he played with the *Birth of the Cool* band.

The next night was a concert for television. Recordings from both evenings show Miles energized, playing brightly in the upper register, merrily quoting from other songs, and blissfully riding the rhythm section through the blues. Urtreger said that their repertoire included "Tune Up," "Bye Bye Blackbird," "Four," "Walkin'," "All of You," "Half Nelson," "What's New?" "Dig," "Oleo," and "'Round Midnight" ("He showed me some chords on 'Midnight' that I still play"), and that Miles seemed happy with the band. Yet Barney Wilen told Mike Zwerin that Miles had growled at him in the middle of a saxophone solo to "stop playing those terrible notes." Wilen thought it was funny and kept on playing. Later, he remembered, "If we were unfortunate enough to lack inspiration, he'd plug up both his ears. Nastily. So we were careful." René Urtreger's recollection is more equivocal: "Difficult to say about Miles and Barney Wilen. Barney was very young, and was acting as the 'great tenor player,' with cool attitude, dark glasses, etc. And Miles was not too gentle about that. Miles, like many jazzmen—famous or not—was able to change his opinion about somebody very quickly: one day, you're the top; next day you're shit."

Marcel Romano meanwhile began to make arrangements for the film score commission. Louis Malle was a big fan of Miles—in fact, there was already a Miles Davis album cover visible in one of the shots in the film. Plus, he admired the score that John Lewis had just done that year for Roger Vadim's *Sait-on jamais?* (titled *No Sun in Venice* in the United

States). But Malle was looking for something else—a film score that would play against characters rather than underline or run parallel to them (a murder scene, for example, was to be accompanied by a gentle, balladlike theme rather than one that was violent or loud). What excited him was not the use of jazz for its own sake, but the creation of a score that would be totally improvised. (At the time he thought his would be the first film with an improvised score, with the musicians responding to the images on the screen, but he later learned that French guitarist Django Reinhardt had already done just that for some short films.)

Malle's movie was a near-noir about adultery, a bungled murder, and the tangled results that followed. It offered the director a chance to film a new postwar France in the making—convertibles zipping down highways, glitzy shops, office buildings. He wanted to submit the film for the Prix Louis Dullac, and that meant that the music had to be completed quickly—in four days, to be precise, including time for mixing. Malle said that Miles was concerned about not having his New York musicians with him, but after viewing the film and discussing it, he said he could do it. "Malle organized a showing," according to Romano:

> The film crew was there. I narrated the film to Miles [in English], "live." The actor which left a deep impression on him was Lino Ventura [in the role of the inspector]. Miles kept saying, "That guy's good." He quickly said yes to the idea. I believe they had a piano carried into his hotel room. He worked on some music themes. Then they lunched together to speak about the film.

Miles was back with Jeannette Urtreger, again trying to experience Paris through her eyes, feeling that same Francophile rush of freedom, committing the same delicious fallacy as all travelers who feel that they understand a country because they have slept with one of its citizens. Jeannette, on the other hand, saw things he missed:

> In Paris, he was completely relaxed, he felt good, as if he was on vacation, because he didn't feel the racism in France—though there was latent racism everywhere. . . . It was very complicated to be with a black person in Paris—like in America—at the time. There are certain people who said terrible things. My older sister was unhappy about it, but I said, "Listen, this is a man who brings me chocolate ice cream every morning for breakfast!"

Malle rented a sound studio on the Champs-Elysées for the session on September 4, and they began rather casually at 9:00 P.M., with Jeanne

Moreau passing out drinks from a makeshift bar. Miles had not told the band that he'd already been to a screening, so they were surprised by his sure sense of what was going to happen. They began to record the score, René Urtreger recalls, by watching twenty- to thirty-second clips and putting music to them. Davis had brought in nothing more than a few chord progressions for them to work from. "Miles had seen the film . . . and he knew more or less what kind of 'atmosphere' was needed." For one scene, for example, they decided that there would only be bass and drums behind the horns. "During one sequence he asked me *not* to play, because he wanted to improvise on the chords of 'Sweet Georgia Brown' at a very fast tempo with Klook [Kenny Clarke] on brushes, and he didn't want the original theme recognized (without the piano harmony, he said, the tune became a little more 'abstract')."

"What was typical of this session," said bassist Pierre Michelot, "was the absence of a specific theme. This was new for the period, especially with the soundtrack for a film. In most cases there was only the barest minimum of instructions: play two chords only, for example, D-minor and C7—four bars for each, with no specific length to the piece."

Louis Malle was very nervous because he wanted to win the Dullac award, but Miles told him to be cool, because he knew what he wanted; he had been working it all out in his head. Jeannette had witnessed the process the day before: "At four in the afternoon we had rested for a while, when he got up and went to the bathroom naked, carrying his trumpet. He played a few notes, and said, 'This is the bass line I want Pierre to play!'"

As far as Miles was concerned, it was only a matter of looking at the images and putting music to them. In one scene, for example, a man climbs out a window, using a grappling hook and a rope to pull himself up to his lover's husband's office on the floor above. Once there, he has to walk across a long office as he approaches his intended victim. For this, Miles chose to use a single repeated note on the bass. But Malle wanted some tension as the man walked toward him, so Davis told Kenny Clarke to play swells of sound on a cymbal. Miles thought the whole process was easy because he had gone to so many movies as a child and had seen French films in Paris and New York. The only problems occurred when the actors did not move in consistent rhythms, especially Jeanne Moreau. ("The bitch didn't know how to walk in rhythm," he told Beverly Bentley when he got back to New York.)

Kenny Clarke described Miles' scoring method this way:

He said, "Wait a Minute, right here! Stop! Right here." And he'd say, "We play this, and this right here"—'cause this seemed really to go with the scene and it was really well thought out. And we did the music to the film right then and there. . . . It turned out beautiful. Miles really put it together wonderfully. And I mean, it all happened on the spur of the moment, you know. After about three hours, it was over.

Michelot remembers Malle as expressing what he wanted in a non-musical fashion, but in a way that he got him what he wanted:

For example, I remember that for one sequence he wanted only bass and drums, which we did, but he thought we had stayed too close to the onscreen image. He explained that music ought to be in counterpoint to the image. This obviously explains how he came to use certain takes for sequences other than the ones they were recorded for in the beginning.

Malle sought the sense of risk that improvisation could give his film and wanted the audience to feel the tension in the music independent of the film. "I insisted that in *Ascenseur* the music be more important than the image in several places. And I would have preferred in some scenes that the image were more neutral in order to bring out the importance of the music more strongly." (Because Malle thought of music as so much a part of the film, he had doubts about the music being issued as a record-ing. He was convinced that a successful soundtrack album was usually a sign that the music was ineffective in the film it accompanied.)

There are only eighteen minutes of music in the film, but nonetheless the music seems to penetrate every scene, holding it all together:

It was not like a lot of film music, emphasizing or trying to add to the emo-tion that is implicit in the images and the rest of the soundtrack. It was a counterpoint, it was elegiac—and it was somewhat detached. But it also cre-ated a certain mood for the film. I remember the opening scene; the Miles Davis trumpet gave it a tone which added tremendously to the first images.

Davis' muted trumpet on this soundtrack—rather than the usual accor-dion or violin—signals that something foreign had entered French film at the time, much as it had in the nouveau hip culture of St-Germain-des-Prés, and suggests that this film might be seen as something more than just a con-ventional thriller or a statement about the amorality of postwar France.

Boris Vian also became involved with the film score, since he was artistic director for Philips Records and was planning to issue the score as an LP. In his liner notes, he injected a characteristic romantic tone: Miles had hurt his lip, Boris claimed, and a piece of skin had come off and stuck to the mouthpiece, producing "a strange sonority" during the recording of "Diner au motel": "And as some painters owe the plastic quality of their work to some accident, in the same way, Miles willingly greeted this 'unheard of' element of music ('unheard of' in the literal sense of the word)." Yet René Urtreger recalled that Vian was not at the recording session and that the lip story was "pure fiction."

Malle said that he tried to work with Davis again. He wanted to use him for his next film, *Les Amants* (*The Lovers*), this time alone, because he could not think of any other musicians whom he felt as strongly about. But it was not to happen, because "he had become very difficult and wanted to do it with a whole orchestra, twenty musicians, with arrangements. It could have been very interesting, but it would have meant doing it in New York, and that was beyond the possibilities of a French budget at that time."

Ascenseur pour l'échafaud did win the Prix Louis Dullac in 1957, and Miles' contribution to the film was widely acknowledged in the European press, with his name appearing on the movie's posters. Yet his role in the film was never fully acknowledged in the United States. First, the soundtrack was buried in an odd anthology record called *Jazz Track*, which mixed together several different sessions, and then Miles was not invited to the American premier of the film: "They had a press party when they brought the picture over here. I was not invited, until somebody reminded them. Then I was invited. I had a hard time. I couldn't have said what I really felt."

Over the next three weeks Miles played the Club St-Germain, where the audience was surprised by the changes in him since his last time in Paris: there were no introductions, acknowledgments, stage chatter, nothing but music. "Miles' playing," according to Urtreger, "was at a high level. But, like many jazz stars of this period, he didn't take many risks during the concerts. In clubs, however, we really had fun. He enjoyed playing with the group at night. He especially worked well with Kenny Clarke, liked being with him, even laughed with him onstage. He let the rest of us—the 'kids'—play as long as we wanted. The crowds were fantastically happy."

> One night at the club, after hours, everybody had left. It was about 3 A.M. We had a few drinks, and I went to the piano and played the Fantasie-Impromptue in C# Minor by Chopin. When it was finished, Miles said, "René, I'd have my right arm cut off if I could write that." He had tears in his eyes.

In Amsterdam on December 8, unknown to them, they were recorded at a concert they played in the Concertgebouw. René said, "There were microphones set up for a future 'pirate' recording, but we didn't know that at the time." Miles went on to Stuttgart on December 18 for a solo spot with the Erwin Lehn Orchestra for a television show called *Treffpunkt Jazz*. On the bits of the show still available on film and audiotape, Miles can be heard playing a swing version of "Walkin'" on which he shows his familiarity with big band conventions and even quotes a lick from the old Benny Goodman hit "And the Angels Sing." For the occasion, instead of a tie he wore a short Italian silk scarf that Jeannette had given him, one he was often seen wearing for several years to come.

Miles left Europe on December 20, just in time to join Frances, Cheryl, Gregory, and Miles IV in Illinois for Christmas and to play at the Sutherland Lounge in Chicago with his reformed sextet of Garland, Chambers, Jones, Cannonball Adderley, and John Coltrane, now forgiven, and back again.

> The idea I had for this working sextet was to keep what we already had going . . . and add the blues voice of Cannonball Adderley into this mixture and then to stretch everything out. I felt that Cannonball's blues-rooted alto sax up against Trane's harmonic chordal way of playing, his more free-form approach, would create a new kind of sound, because Coltrane's voice was already going in a new direction. And then I wanted to give that musical mixture more space, using the concepts I had picked up from what Ahmad Jamal did. I heard my trumpet voice kind of floating over and cutting through all of this mixture, and I felt that if we could do it right, the music would have all the tension up in it.

When Miles was in Paris in December, he ran into Allen Eager, who was rooming with poet Gregory Corso at the Beat Hotel. Eager, a white bebop tenor saxophonist, was one of the first jazz musicians to be called "cool." He was a jazz phenomenon, a player like Miles who violated the laws of chance that produced musicians. Eager was raised in the Bronx, in a family that ran the Premier, a borscht belt Catskills hotel in Fallsburgh, New York. As a teenager, he had gone on the road with dance bands and had found his way into the bop scene in the late 1940s, recording with Coleman Hawkins, playing with Tadd Dameron for a year at the Royal Roost, working with Howard McGhee and Oscar Pettiford. He became one of the few white musicians that a black bebop band would call for a gig. Away from music, Eager was a ski instructor, taught horseback riding, and drove racing cars, once even winning first place in the GT division at Sebring.

It was an era when a few very rich women like Doris Duke and Barbara Hutton sought out jazz musicians for a connection to a way of life otherwise denied them. Certain musicians moved easily among the rich, and Eager was one of them, often appearing in the society columns through his association with heiress Peggy Mellon Hitchcock. Later, he might be found with Timothy Leary at his Millbrook, New York, quarters, or sitting in with Frank Zappa in the 1970s. Eager, a stylish dresser, advised Miles on clothing, and referred him to Joe Eula, at the house of Halston, who designed a suit for Miles that was made up by Joe Emsley, a tailor who understood the slim look that Miles craved. And it was Eager who introduced Miles to Peggy Hitchcock and other ladies of high society, and who took him up to Luigi Chinetti's auto showroom on Eleventh Avenue in Manhattan, where Miles immediately fell in love with a room full of red Formula I racers. It was a place he would return to over the years, even after Chinetti moved to Greenwich, Connecticut, a place where he could spend hours discussing motors, watching the mechanics, and sitting in the cars. Davis had recently replaced his Mercedes with a Jaguar, but complained that it didn't give him the power he needed when he turned onto the West Side Highway off 96th Street. Unable to afford a new Ferrari at the time, he bought a used white one (with twelve cylinders, Miles liked to remind people) for $8,500. Eager taught him how to shift gears and drive a sports car, and on the day he went to try out the Ferrari, Eager was with Miles when his Jaguar was hit from behind by a bread delivery truck. It was a minor accident, small enough that it amused Eager, but Miles was furious. He threatened to put Eager out of the car and to kill the other driver, whom he had by the throat. "Miles was shy and oversensitive," Eager thought, "but he could also be arrogant—because he was the best."

In February 1958, Columbia recorded Miles' sextet and produced *Milestones*, an album whose title tune suggested new possibilities in jazz composition and improvisation. Built on two scales, with a simple melody rocking back and forth on one of them and a staggered melody floating on the other, it all seems straightforward enough. But the two scales do not connect with each other in any obvious way, so that the improvisers were forced to guard against becoming comfortable with whatever they'd been developing when the other scale came along to interupt them.

This session produced some of the finest examples of post-bop that jazz would ever hear, and made up an album that again sounded like a world-class group playing a live set. Yet all did not go well while they were recording. Red Garland walked out during an argument with Miles, who then had to fill in on piano on "Sid's Ahead" (a tune also known as "Weirdo"). Confusion also developed over the tune called "Milestones," since Miles had already recorded a different tune under the same name. The producer suggested that he change this second "Milestones" to "Milestones #5" when new copies were pressed. But that was unacceptable to Miles, who wanted it changed to "Miles."

Davis' son Gregory was now twelve, and Miles began to take him with him to clubs where he was performing. He enjoyed introducing him to musicians, some of whom—Allan Eager and Philly Joe, especially— occasionally took Gregory out with them for a day around New York. Gregory was the only one of his children Miles ever took to gigs, where he sat near the bandstand at his own table, thrilled by it all: "I used to sit there and shake all over. It would hit me like a bomb. I would be so impressed and so shaken by this, and wonder, where did it come from, and how are they doing this? It dawned on me—this man is really this great! And it gave him a purpose, too, I guess. To see me in the audience gave him a little more inspiration." Once, when Gregory was fourteen, they drove the Ferrari to Philadelphia, where Miles' was playing for a week, and on the way down he taught Gregory how to drive, to shift and corner like a race car driver. After a couple of nights, Miles had a day off, and he decided to go back to New York City.

He was feeling melancholy because he missed Beverly, so he said "I'm taking the train back to New York, I'll be back tomorrow morning." He drove to the train station, parked the car, and inside the station he gave me some money and the keys, and said, "You can lock it up and take a cab or you can take it back to the motel." That's the kind of man he was: "That's my boy!" And I'm driving this Ferrari through the middle of Philadelphia, and the police were looking, and it's —'No, Bill this couldn't be true—a young, black kid driving this red Ferrari? We're imagining things!'

Miles wanted to treat him like a man, give him whatever he needed to defend himself in the world. Gregory was a timid, sweet boy, and when he had moved with his mother to 33 Troy Avenue in Bedford-Stuyvesant, a tough neighborhood in Brooklyn, he was picked on and provoked to fight. Irene asked Miles to do something before he got hurt.

My father got me a private trainer, Johnny Greenwich, and from age twelve I started to go to the gym every day after school. And when I was living with father I did road work every morning at 5 A.M., come home, drink some tea and honey and get ready for school. Philly Joe and my father pushed me into boxing because that was one of their greatest loves.

"He was a proud father. He especially liked my sister. I remember times when a guy would come to the door to take her out somewhere, and if he didn't have a tie on, he'd say, 'You come here to take my daughter out? Now you better go back and put on a tie!'" They had a gym in the basement, and Gregory and his brother Miles would give demonstrations for anyone their father brought around. "'Yeah! Let me see that left hook again.' He'd show us off to people like Coltrane. 'Throw that combination you learned!'"

When I got into boxing seriously, I was in a club and won my little smokers—I won them all. But my father couldn't deal with the fact that I might get hurt. . . . He couldn't sit there and see me in a combative situation. "No, Philly Joe, *you* go!" When I won my first trophy my father gave it to Philly Joe.

Gregory continued to box as he grew up and was the most successful member of his army team while he was stationed in Germany during the Vietnam War.

There were trumpet lessons too: "Father would give me certain patterns to work on and ask me to write them out and play them. If I made a mistake he'd say, 'I don't want to see this anymore. . . . It's got to be clear, and I want to see this done right.' Or he might say, 'I know you haven't been practicing, I can tell by your lip.' But mostly he sent me to other people for lessons, like Bill Hardman of Art Blakey's band."

"We lived in a great house. I mean he really provided for us at that time. Before . . . when he was on drugs, my mother had to really prod him to do it. But when we were living with him, he really, really provided. We were clothed from Saks Fifth Avenue, and we went to private schools."

Word got around that Miles needed a new pianist, and George Russell recommended Bill Evans, whom Russell had worked with on a number of projects. Among jazz musicians, Evans was something else, and nothing like the stereotype: he was quiet, like Coltrane; he read philosophy, studied Zen and Japanese art, was eloquent on subjects like the poetry of William Blake; and now here he was, white in a black band . . . *the* black band, most would have said. When Evans first joined them, Miles told him (in order "to see what he could do") that to keep his job, he would have to "fuck the band." Evans considered the meaning of this proposal for a few minutes, Davis said, and then told him that as much as he'd like to make everyone happy, he couldn't get behind that. It was classic Miles, of course, and whether it ever happened or not, this anecdote has been seen by some to bear considerable weight in understanding Davis' wicked sense of humor.

Miles saw Bill Evans as taking Ahmad Jamal's playing in a new direction ("If I could play like Ahmad and Bill combined with one hand," he told Nat Hentoff, "they could take the other one off"). Evans (whom Miles called "Moe") came over to Miles' apartment often, and they talked for hours, discussing a wide range of music, Bill playing chords and modes, Miles maybe playing a chord for him and asking him what he would do with it. A small sense of those conversations can be gathered in a remark Evans once made to writer Dan Morgenstern: "I remember discussing Brahms with Miles Davis once. . . . He said that he couldn't enjoy it. And I said, 'If you can just get past the stylistic thing that puts you off, you'd find a great treasure there.' I don't know if it had any effect or not; we never talked about it again."

When Evans brought him Arturo Benedetti Michelangeli's 1957 recording of Ravel's Piano Concerto in G it became something of an obsession with Miles, and he proselytized about it for years to come ("When he plays something it sounds like he'll never play it again"). Though he mentioned only the use of modulation in this piece, like Ravel's other piano concerto, it was a work that showed the influence of early jazz. Evans also urged Miles to hear Ravel's string quartet and other records by Khachaturian and Rachmaninoff, and once he had listened to them, they often spent hours analyzing the scores. These were composers who were not difficult for Miles to appreciate. He had heard them all played at concerts of the St. Louis Symphony Orchestra, and each had something with which he could sympathize: Rachmaninoff, for example, was somewhat out of favor in his own time, writing with simplicity and transparent harmonic structure, under a veil of melancholy; and Khachaturian was then very popular, his brassy, folkish ballets favorites for displaying the possibilities of early stereo recordings.

Miles was not always generous in praising his musicians after they had left his band—even John Coltrane—but he never stinted in his acknowledgment of Evans. Saxophonist Dave Liebman recalled Miles' deep respect for Evans as the person "who opened the doors for him musically. The whole 'So What' fourth voicing, for example. I think Bill was very special to him. He said to me, 'I used to call Bill up and tell him to leave the phone off the hook; just leave it off and play for me because I loved the way he played.'"

What Evans got from working with Davis, above all, was coming to understand the role of technique in creativity, and Evans recognized the importance of maturity in Davis' playing:

> Miles is . . . more or less a late arriver. You could hear him building his abilities from the beginning, very consciously, very aware of every note he played, theoretically, motifically and everything. I know Miles has spoken about how he didn't have the kind of facility that a lot of other trumpet players had for fast tempos and all this stuff, and Bird would tell him, "Just get out there and do it!" There are always a lot of early-arrivers who have great facility. [Miles] had to go through a longer, laborious, digging, analytical process, finally arriving at something which is far more precious.

In May, the sextet recorded three compositions that Miles would feature nightly for the next eight or nine years—"Stella by Starlight," "Fran-Dance," and "On Green Dolphin Street"—which were all released within a few months as one side of *Jazz Track*. The studio's piano was out of tune, but Evans negotiated around it and minimized the problem. In the year he was with the Davis group, Evans said that Miles made suggestions to him about what he should play only four or five times, and two of those suggestions were on this session. Davis changed the original sheet music's bass line to "On Green Dolphin Street" and gave Evans specific chords to play on "Fran-Dance."

Today, this music has the sound of classic ballads, coming straight from the roots of jazz. But at the time, these recordings had the power to shock. When *Jazz Track* reached France, for example, a letter from CBS International complained that on side 2, tracks 1 and 2 ("Stella" and "Fran-Dance"), one of the saxophone solos was "off," and that the quality control department had checked to make sure that there was no mechanical distortion in the tracks. Teo Macero wrote back that "nothing was wrong, and John Coltrane is a great musician." Others, however, were deeply moved by these ballads. Classical composer George Rochberg, for example, inserted a quotation from "Stella by Starlight" into his 1965 *Music for the Magic Theater*, side by side with other musical quotes from Webern, Varèse, Beethoven, and Mozart.

Cannonball Adderley once talked about the experience of playing with the Davis sextet. When he first joined the group, he said,

> There were certain things that I did that Miles didn't like and he is out-spoken enough to tell you when he doesn't like something. . . . At first it didn't hurt me but it shocked me. I'd think I played something that was nice and he'd say, "Yeah, why you got to play all that? That ain't got noth-ing to do with it. Man, you playin' all them notes that don't mean nothin." When you play a note it should mean something.

But there was always something to learn from Miles. For example, his choice of notes was such that a single note could often suggest several chords at once: "Coltrane and I call it the 'implied reference,' the things Miles does. He can play three notes and he can make them work out so well." As with his other musicians, Davis' example forced Adderley to rethink the basics of what he was doing in a jazz ensemble. "I used to use the solo as a secondary thing, more or less, to the band," said Adderley. "The ensembles were the thing; cleanliness, the ensembles, all the fun-damentals of music. And listening to Miles—who is not a good trumpet player but a great soloist—you know what I mean. All of a sudden the fundamentals don't mean that much to me because he's so brilliant oth-erwise. A solo is like the way he thinks about the composition and the solo became *the* thing . . . he's tired of *tunes*. You know, he says, 'You play the melody, then everybody blows and you play the melody and the tune is ended and that's a jazz performance.'" "He thinks a solo can be a com-position if it's expressed the right way."

By summer, Columbia steered Davis toward recordings that could solid-ify and reinforce his successes: a record with French composer and arranger Michel Legrand (*Legrand Jazz*), on which four of Miles' musi-cians played, including Bill Evans, and a live recording from the New-port Jazz Festival with the whole sextet (*Miles Davis at Newport 1958*). Avakian, meanwhile, had left Columbia to start a new record company for Warner Bros., and Miles' new producer was Calvin Lampley, a classical pianist and the first black producer to work with white artists. He proposed that Davis and Gil Evans follow up *Miles Ahead* by collaborating on an instrumental version of George Gershwin's 1935 opera, *Porgy and Bess*. It certainly seemed timely. Samuel L. Goldwyn's film version was in production, and two years before, Bethlehem Records had recorded the opera using virtually its entire roster of jazz artists. Just the year before, saxophonist Buddy Collette had recorded his own version, as did Louis Armstrong and Ella Fitzgerald. There were still other recordings by Sammy Davis, Jr., Diahann Carroll, Harry Belafonte, and Lena Horne, and even trumpeters Rex Stewart and Cootie Williams, not to mention the planned re-releases of earlier cast recordings. And given Columbia's big success with LPs of Broadway shows, the idea made good sense. But when Lampley called him with his suggestion, Miles seemed uninterested:

> He said, "Cal, I'm sitting here trying to think of doing something with my wife and you're calling me with this shit," and hung up! Uh-oh, I guess I blew that. Then ten days later he called me and said, "Cal, that *Porgy and Bess* idea's a good one—let's get started."

But to some at the time, it might have seemed a very peculiar choice, since every stage production of the show had been met by protests from one or another African American group who found the idea of a musical written by white men on black folk life in South Carolina to be objectionable for any number of reasons. In a time in which stereotyped roles in films and television shows like *Amos 'n' Andy* were widely criticized, the Robert Breen production for the American National Theatre and Academy, which was touring the United States, Europe, and even Russia, was being greeted ambivalently at best. Still, the Gershwin brothers had already been accepted into jazz tradition and their songs were part of the repertoire. Al Tinney, the musical director at Monroe's Playhouse in Harlem (one of the sites of bebop's birth), had been part of the cast of the original production of *Porgy and Bess* and had worked closely with George Gershwin on staging the show. Even Duke Ellington, who had condemned the earliest version of the show, was enthusiastic about the 1950s production. Miles had seen Frances Taylor in the New York production; Raleigh McDonald, his friend from his high school band days, had toured with the Breen production; and the Columbia producer who suggested the idea was African American. Miles saw no problems with it.

In July and August, Gil Evans and Davis recorded *Porgy and Bess*, and though the results were as heavily edited, overdubbed, and spliced together as *Miles Ahead*, Lampley worked in smaller units of music and recorded fewer rehearsals (though he left Columbia to work for Warner Bros. before the record was finished, and Irving Townsend completed the postproduction work). There were still some rough spots in the finished product, such as some mistakes in "Gone, Gone, Gone," but Miles told Jimmy Heath that they didn't bother him because the feeling was right.

> Gil Evans used to ask me, "You can be playing a whole number—chords, breaks, everything—but have you thought about the tempo?" . . . When we did *Porgy and Bess*, we would get into serious shit—about this. His face would change. *"What tempo is it?"* All the time I'd been playin' in tune, but . . . see the tempo is the *whole thing* in music. *The whole goddamn thing.*

As with the other Evans-Davis recordings, everything had to be worked up from scratch in the studio, the musicians playing an unfamiliar score, and this time not all of them were used to playing under Evans' direction or even with each other. The score was difficult to read and to play, especially as there was no piano part, and some sections of the band had to function like a keyboard. There were also problems in the mechanics of recording. Since this was an early stereo session, it was not always clear where the musicians should be placed in the studio so as to avoid time lags from one side of the orchestra to the other on the final tape.

Once the record was completed, it was obvious that Davis and Gil Evans had departed from the spirit of the opera. Far from the pseudo-folk/pop songs of Gershwin's original, this was big band jazz, put together to maintain a flow and a certain sensibility, with the original order of the songs changed, their tempos and harmonic structures altered, and their programmatic quality stripped away. Even the integrity of many of the original tunes was affected. Gershwin's melody on "Summertime" is stated only at the beginning of Evans' arrangement, while the counter-melody he wrote continues throughout. In a similar way, "Buzzard Song" disappears quickly, and instead a bass and tuba line becomes the melody. "I Got Plenty of Nuttin'" was dropped completely, but its bridge turns up as the introduction to "It Ain't Necessarily So." A bit of theme from the unused "Requiem" finds its way into "Summertime." Sometimes even the mood of the originals is radically changed: "Summertime," no longer a lullaby, enters with an urbane stride; "Prayer" hints at the blues; and "Gone, Gone, Gone" becomes deeply solemn. And sitting in the middle of the album is a ringer, Evans' own composition, "Gone," which turns out to be a setting for the kind of drums-and-trumpet interplay that Miles wanted whenever he had a great rhythm section.

Davis' trumpet playing throughout is as vocalized as it would ever be, full of choked tones, half-sighs, and holy laughs. Despite the orchestral frame placed around him, there was a sense of new freedom here, one incited by the frame itself, a thinning out of harmonic density that would later be called modal music. Miles said the hardest piece he ever had to play was "Bess, You Is My Woman," "because the melody repeats over and over. It was necessary to play along with the orchestration under it, phrasing it so it sounds like you—like a Frank Sinatra and a Roberta Flack might do." In fact, when vocalist Roberta Flack first heard the record, she said she could hear him "playing the words." "And that other passage with just two chords," Miles said, "gives you a lot more freedom and space to hear things." At times sonic clouds drift by in the tradition of Claude Thornhill, but at other moments bass lines rumble under-neath, instrumental cries and shouts ricochet across the band, and Evans' use of distinctive instrumentalists provides richness of detail.

It was a meeting of folk, pop, jazz, and art musics, a challenge to the theories of high modernism in a single record. And it was a recording that even Ira Gershwin liked. (Much later, "Here Come de Honey Man" somehow found its way onto the bootleg recording of the Beach Boys' *Smile,* with a note identifying it as a rare Beach Boys instrumental called "Holidays.")

Irving Townsend came up with an idea for Columbia to throw a party in September to call attention to the success that it was having with jazz records. The musicians would be Duke Ellington's Orchestra and the Miles Davis Sextet, along with singers Billie Holiday and Jimmy Rushing. The twist on this public relations party was that it would be held in the lofty Persian Room of the Plaza Hotel on 58th Street in New York City, thereby highlighting the seriousness and importance of jazz, in much the way George Wein had done when he first took jazz to Newport, Rhode Island, only a few years earlier. Formal invitations were sent out for a gathering at teatime on September 9, and in fact that room was usually reserved for receptions and high teas accompanied by small salon ensem-bles. With the heavyweight artists and the grand setting, the afternoon was declared a success, another cultural beachhead taken. But Ralph Elli-son, the author of *Invisible Man* and one of Columbia Records' guests that day, saw this as a generational battle for the future of jazz, with Davis as an impudent upstart. He wrote to his friend Albert Murray that

I finally saw that . . . poor, evil, lost little Miles Davis, who on this occasion sounded like he just couldn't get it together. Nor did Coltrane help with his badly executed velocity exercises. These cats have gotten lost, man. They're trying to get hold of something by fucking up the blues.

Murray responded to Ellison in kind:

I cannot understand for the life of me what these guys are finding so *revolutionary* in Gil Evans–Miles Davis' *Miles Ahead* and *Porgy and Bess*. It's nice and pleasant but other than that all I can hear is a bunch of studio musicians playing decadent exercises in orchestration based on Ellington's old pastel period. . . . Gil Evans, my ass. This guy caint [*sic*] even beat Lenny Bernstein.

The affair at the Plaza was recorded, but more as a historical document, with no thought of commercial release. But by 1967, some interest had developed in releasing part of the material along with some other scattered recordings under the title of *Oleo*: there would be Monk's "Straight, No Chaser," "If I Were a Bell," Sonny Rollins' "Oleo," along with "Sweet Sue" and "Love for Sale" from other recording sessions. But by that time, Cannonball Adderley had become something of a jazz star himself and didn't want to settle for union scale for his performances, so the release was canceled. The music recorded that day in September finally did appear in 1973 under the title *Jazz at the Plaza*, with "Straight, No Chaser" erroneously being given the same title as the album in the notes. And according to Bill Evans, when the musicians finally got their money for the recording, they discovered that they had been paid at the 1958 scale.

Miles' earnings from royalties and advances were beginning to accumulate, and the demand for the Davis group was getting them into the best clubs. Miles had turned his image around so completely that he was now beginning to make demands on his bookers and employers. The first was that he no longer wanted to follow the five sets a night, 40 minutes on–20 minutes off policy of nightclubs, which allowed the clubs to maximize drink orders and customer turnover. Next, he challenged the practice of concert promoters who paid only half the price of the first concert for a second performance. Finally, there was the Davis theory of booking: if you didn't want to play a gig, ask for four or five times what it was worth, and maybe they'd pay it. And then maybe you'd want to play.

Throughout his stay with the Davis band, Bill Evans had to bear the criticisms leveled at Miles for replacing Red Garland with a white player who didn't swing. With the civil rights movement underway, black domains of influence were being identified and marked off as various forms of cultural nationalism began to emerge. There was talk about "soul," a distinctive cultural feature of blackness, something all whites lacked; and the presence of a white musician—especially one with such an original and lyrical approach—in the premier black jazz band was difficult for many to fathom. And Miles was not beyond having fun at Bill's expense as well. (Jimmy Cobb recalls Evans joining in an argument between Davis, Coltrane, and Adderley, and having Miles tell him that he didn't need his "white opinions.") Adderley said that Bill told Miles that he was making him uncomfortable, because "Miles used to mess with him; not about his music or anything, but he used to call him 'whitey' and stuff like that, so Bill put in his notice." But when Evans left that summer, he explained his decision more in terms of career choices than racial questions:

> I have heard a great deal about the disparity between Miles and his music. For instance, Miles says that he's prejudiced, which he probably is in a certain way since he is bitter and hurt, but he doesn't live in a prejudiced way. He certainly recognizes talent where he finds it.

Publicly, Miles had always defended hiring Evans in no uncertain terms, as Bill was aware:

> It was more of an issue with the fans. The guys in the band defended me staunchly. We were playing black clubs, and guys would come up and say, "What's the white guy doing there?" They said, "Miles *wants* him there—he's *supposed* to be there!"

> At the time I thought I was inadequate. I wanted to play more so that I could see where I was going. I felt exhausted in every way—physically, mentally, and spiritually. I don't know why. Maybe it was the road. But I think the time I worked with Miles was probably the most beneficial I've spent in years, not only musically but personally. It did me a lot of good.

When Evans formed a new trio with drummer Paul Motian and bassist Scott LaFaro, Miles for the first time allowed his words to be used for promotion of a record, appearing on the cover of *Everybody Digs Bill Evans* ("I've sure learned a lot from Bill Evans. He plays the piano the way it should be played"). And Motian said that the Evans trio had made plans to record with Davis, until bassist LaFaro was killed in an automobile accident.

Jazz up to this point had been on what seemed to be a stable evolutionary path, following its own logic, its own distinct aesthetic. People might not have been able to say exactly what jazz was, but they could usually distinguish it from classical and popular music. The music's audience had grown with it for almost a half-century and generally knew what to expect from it, even when changes occurred. There were established rules for what was acceptable and successful in jazz performance, and when a group of musicians took the stage, they already knew how to begin, where to take the performance, and how to end it. Bebop had made the ground rules a bit less clear, but jazz still had a linear pulse that when added to harmony and melody, created a cycle of climaxes and repeats that helped listeners to locate themselves comfortably within a performance.

In 1959 the mainstream of jazz was flowing nicely: Louis Armstrong recorded with Duke Ellington, affirming the wholeness of the tradition. Dave Brubeck had just made *Time Out*, an album of compositions with unusual meters (for jazz, at least). It was experimental music, but mildly so, and his quartet still sounded friendly to those who followed him. Cannonball Adderley recorded *The Cannonball Adderley Quintet in San Francisco* that year, which became one of the most popular albums of soul jazz, a revitalization of black folk elements and rhythm patterns that were beginning to be called funk. Charles Mingus recorded *Mingus Ah Um*, which showed how such folk and soul elements could be used not just for popular amusement, but also in compositions of great seriousness and emotional power. Many other musicians at this time were busy recording jazz versions of Broadway and private-eye TV show scores: *Gypsy, Flower Drum Song, Peter Gunn*, and *77 Sunset Strip*. America as a whole thought of jazz as a single style of music.

But different directions were beginning to be taken as several revolutionary albums appeared in 1959, each producing its own distinctive form of shock. First, John Coltrane recorded *Giant Steps* with his own quartet, music that might have seemed to the casual listener to be merely bebop of a very high order. The title piece was played extraordinarily fast, with constant chord changes (a new chord appearing on every other beat) and a melody whose odd intervals appeared to be designed to make life difficult for its tenor soloist. In fact, it *was* difficult, and Coltrane's virtuoso performance drew attention to both the exhilaration and the tedium that the principles underlying bebop could produce. Coltrane played with a constant stream of notes, relentlessly navigating the guides and barriers that the chords presented—a bebop tour de force, to be sure, but also a statement about the exhaustion of what was once a bold idea. As if to underline the point, something that could not have been more different was buried in the album: "Naima" was a slow, meditative piece built on a single chord—a single note, really—repeated over and over by the bassist, a fulcrum on which the entire composition was raised. It was a sign that Coltrane was beginning to use static and open forms of harmony by means of minimal scales and drones, even at the same time as he was testing the limits of bop.

Ornette Coleman took things even further with his 1959 album, *The Shape of Jazz to Come:* he liberated his musicians from improvising on the chordal patterns that had traditionally determined what could be played, and was edging toward eliminating the cycles of repeats, returns to the beginning, and even the endings. Like some modern poets, Coleman let the limits of breath determine the phrase and the line. And his richly developed melodies often ignored conventional chord patterns, as well as traditional pitch and tonality.

There were two paradoxical tendencies at work in jazz at this point: to simplify and to complicate the existing vocabulary of music. On the one hand was a compulsion to increase the complexity of both melody and harmony, and on the other an equally strong drive to free up the melody by reducing the number of chords. Constraint versus freedom: it was an old story in the history of art. Such moments of contrary tendencies are not unusual in times when arts are in transition. You could see it in bebop when Charlie Parker was thickening the mix, heaping on the notes, and expanding the vocabulary, even as Thelonious Monk was simplifying that very approach. (And you could see the same process at work in the novel when, early in the twentieth century, James Joyce was overloading its vocabulary while Samuel Beckett and Franz Kafka were pruning it back.)

Radical recordings such as Coleman's and Coltrane's might well have threatened Davis, since his own music had usually been deeply rooted in harmonic change. But along with Gil Evans and George Russell, Miles had also noticed the limitations of bebop harmony and began thinking about ways in which to minimize or slow down harmonic change to free up the improviser. The origins of the idea went back to 1947 when Miles visited Russell while he was in the hospital with tuberculosis, and later, when they continued their discussions while Russell recovered at Max Roach's mother's house in Brooklyn. Russell was on his way to becoming one of the music's most thoughtful and provocative theorists and composers, and Davis had been telling him that he wanted to be able to improvise on something simpler than chord progressions. They sat together afternoons, trading chords, and talking over new ideas about harmony, often with Miles getting excited, and jumping up to the piano: "George, listen to this . . ." "One day," Russell recalled, "I asked him, 'Miles, what is your musical aim?'"

> He answered, "To learn all the changes." But Miles was buried in changes—he was a completely vertical player. I didn't think much of it at the time, but then I had a relapse of TB, and took fifteen more months to recuperate. Sitting in the solarium at St. Joseph's Hospital in the Bronx, I realized that if Miles said he wanted to learn all the changes that everyone knows, he had to mean something else, and I had to figure out what he meant. At times Miles could be very definite, but at other times he could be really obscure. . . . Even then Miles was noted for outlining each change, identifying it with the melody. In other words, he wouldn't have needed the piano player, because Miles' melody was dictating what the chords were. He wanted a new way to relate to chords. So, I decided what he wanted was a different approach to the chords. I began by thinking that every chord has a scale associated with it. When I played the first half of the scale, I wondered why the F was where it was? The next four notes of the scale sounded much better (the first four seemed not in unity with the scale—they sounded closer to a G-major chord). How was I going to tell musicians that if you have a C-major chord you can play a G-major scale?

"The first person I showed my idea of chord-scale unity to was Miles," Russell said. "It gave him a new direction." Miles put it this way:

> What I had learned about the modal form was that when you play this way, go in this direction, you can go on forever. You don't have to worry about changes. . . . You can do more with the musical line. The challenge here . . . is to see how inventive you can be melodically. It's not like when you base stuff on chords, and you know at the end of thirty-two bars that the chords have run out and there's nothing to do but repeat what you've done with the variations.

Miles had begun his musical career by adding chordal density to the blues and complicating pop song forms he used for his compositions, but since the early 1950s he had been looking for more open forms as well as simplifying the pop tunes he played like "It Never Entered My Mind." Some of the tunes on *Porgy and Bess* such as "I Loves You Porgy" also pointed toward this new simplicity. Miles said that Gil Evans had written "a scale that I was supposed to play. No chords. He had used two chords for the other voicing, and so my passage of scales with those two chords gives you a lot of freedom and space to hear other things." (The score for the Louis Malle film also contained pieces that were extremely simple harmonically.)

Night after night during a nineteen-concert tour from late 1958 to early 1959, Miles had been gently steering his band in a new direction, playing the tapes of each night's performance back to them and telling them what he wanted. Coltrane and Cannonball were the only people he knew who could play what he wanted, and even Adderley had trouble with it. When Cannonball first came into the band and they played the blues, he said, "Man this ain't no blues, what y'all are playing!" They assumed that any decent musician would know how to play the blues, but they had forgotten they had been making small changes along the way—like staying on one scale for two bars, or maybe playing on one note four beats longer than usual, then going back to traditional blues form. It was like eye makeup, Miles said: you go from East St. Louis to New York City and they put it on thicker, but it's the same.

Miles gave Coltrane five chords to play on for the bridges of some tunes, because he knew that John could make them sound new every time, by starting in different places, and using different intervals. Coltrane had eighty or ninety different things he could play on those few chords, Miles said. This band knew how to inspire each other, one person helping raise the others up with him. Nat Adderley, Cannonball's trumpet-playing brother, said that Miles rubbed one player against the other to get what he wanted out of their music.

> Miles would go say to Cannonball, "You ought to listen to what Coltrane is doing and the way he's got a whole philosophy of sound going." Then he goes and tells Trane, "You should listen to Cannonball. He gets himself across with more utilitarian use of notes." What Miles didn't know was that Trane and Cannon would talk to each other: "What did that little son of a b—— say to you tonight?"

When Miles planned a recording session for April, 1959, he had in mind something that would bring together his new ideas about harmony, plus others that he had been considering for some time. He and Gil had recently seen Les Ballets Africains de la Republique de Guinea perform in New York, seen them three times, in fact, and he wanted to get something of the sound he had heard their musicians produce. He was especially impressed by the mbira, the finger piano, with its two different scales flowing together from the left and right hands of the player. Something about it reminded him of some of the down-home music he had heard during his summers in Arkansas. And then there was the Guinean master drummer, who followed dancers and other musicians around the stage, putting new rhythms with and against what they were doing. Miles was also thinking about the atmospherics, exoticism, and stripped-down surfaces of Ravel's music that he and Bill Evans had been listening to.

Philly Joe's drug habit was again giving Miles fits, and he fired him night after night, until Jones left on his own, and Jimmy Cobb was brought in to replace him. Miles now had a band that he thought of as capable of playing before "mixed audiences," a band that could make a crossover record, with Bill Evans, who was brought back for the session, giving them the "quiet fire," and the drummer taking care of the rest. The record would be called *Kind of Blue,* and would be based on ideas that Davis and Evans had been talking about. (If you have to have a name for it, he once said, call it "Moe's music.") The session was scheduled for March 2, in Columbia's 30th Street studios, and when Wynton Kelly—Evans' replacement on piano—arrived and saw Bill Evans, he was irritated. Miles explained that he wanted them both on the record. He wanted Kelly to play on a straightforward blues, "Freddie Freeloader," named after a colorful character from Philadelphia, a Miles hanger-on who often ran errands for him or kept people away from him, and was in turn named after a character on the Red Skelton television show. Kelly was a master accompanist on the blues, a form Bill Evans could certainly play in, but one in which Bill felt he had "nothing to contribute."

"Miles often surprised everybody," Jimmy Cobb said. "He craved change, and never thought twice about how it would affect anything or anybody, but the music. . . . I think he enjoyed hearing the consequences." It was a band undergoing change, with most of the old rhythm section gone, yet Evans and Davis reorganized it quickly. To Cobb, "It sounded more like what Bill would play than what Miles would play." As far as Cobb was concerned, "That let me off the hook, because I didn't have to play like [Philly] Joe."

In fact, in the days before the session Miles and Bill Evans had gotten together at Miles' house and sketched out some ideas. Their thought was to keep it simple, play music of the most basic order, and try to make each first take work. Evans thought that was the secret:

> There was a simplicity about the charts that was remarkable—like "Freddie Freeloader," "So What," and "All Blues"—there was nothing written out. Oh, on "So What" I think the introduction was written out single line, and Paul and I played it—and added, you know, a little harmony to it. Other than that, the charts were just spoken, just saying like, "Play this pretty." "*You* play this note." "You play *this* note." And I sketched out "Blue and Green," which was my tune, and I sketched out the melody and the changes to it for the guys. And "Flamenco Sketches" was something Miles and I did together. I think that morning before the day I went by his apartment, and he had liked "Peace Piece" that I did, and he said he'd like to do that. And I thought maybe instead of doing one ostinato, we could move through two or three or four or five different levels that would relate to each other and make a cycle. And he agreed, and we worked at it at the piano until we arrived at the five levels we used. And I wrote those levels out for the guys, you know. That was all little sketches.

Miles' strategy was to work from minimal plans so as to increase spontaneity, "just like I thought was in the interplay of those dancers and those drummers and that finger piano player with the Ballets Africains." Jimmy Cobb said that "Miles wanted more space. There were no rehearsals. Miles would rely on the individual to do what he wanted to do with the structure." Of "All Blues," Miles said that he "wrote it in 4/4, but when we got to the studio, it hit me that it should be 3/4. I hadn't thought of it like that before, but it was exactly right." (Miles told one musician that "All Blues" was "Milestones" slowed down.) This was a piece that Miles wanted to get the finger piano sound on, but Evans said he played a tremolo instead:

> That little fluttering figure I play at the beginning is just something I threw in . . . but Miles had that ability to create a kind of a simple figure . . . that still generates a complete and positive reference off of which you can play and still relate to something which is unique. . . . He would say like, "Play the chart," and before each soloist, the figure will serve as a little vamp—you know, entrance to the next soloist.

The three horns on *Kind of Blue* represent the masterful casting skill with which Davis picked his band. John Coltrane's astringency on tenor is counterpoised to Cannonball Adderley's soulful alto, with Davis moderating between them as Bill Evans conjures up the still lake of sound on which they walk. Meanwhile, the rhythm team of Paul Chambers and Jimmy Cobb seem prepared to keep time until eternity. What Davis did on "So What" is typical of what made this album unique. Gil Evans was in the studio for these sessions, and Teo Macero recalled that the introduction to "So What" was Gil's idea: it begins deceptively, out of tempo and slow; then the main theme begins, surprisingly, as a short figure played on bass. A two-note "so what" phrase answers, stated first by piano and drums and then by trumpet and saxophones. The form is the conventional pop song AABA, with the musicians beginning on a single chord, then moving up a half step to a second chord once they reach the B section, and then coming back to the first chord again. When Davis begins his solo, he makes sure that he states the tonic (concert D, E on the trumpet) of the single chord he is playing on at the beginning, then repeating it again every now and then. It's a pattern he follows once more when he shifts to the second chord. But the flow of his ideas and the elegance of his phrases never allow the listener to become overly aware of the mechanics of his thinking. (The title may have been suggested to him by Beverly Bentley, who said it sounded like his favorite dismissive remark, but folks in East St. Louis were more likely to believe that it came from Miles' brother-in-law's retort when Miles told him in 1944 that he was leaving for New York: "So what?")

It's the album as a whole that finally impresses the listener, an extended exercise in what was to become known as modal jazz, a music free of the fixed harmonies and cadences of pop songs. In Davis' musicians' hands, it was a flowing, weightless music, but one that refuses to fade into the background. In retrospect, every note seems perfect. And every track but one was a first take (except for a number of false starts—mistakes made on the melodies, adjustments to tempo, and the like). Yet this was not easy music for them to play, based as it was on new principles of harmonic organization, lacking themes as such, and each piece moving at roughly the same speed as the others (a "junkie tempo," Quincy Jones once called it). In the differences between each of the musicians' approaches to these pieces, it's possible to hear them thinking, worrying their way through such unfamiliar territory. All the more remarkable, then, that the record seems so placid, coherent, and predetermined.

In the same year that *Kind of Blue* was released, George Russell explained his conception of modality in terms of a "river trip": If the Mississippi River can be thought of as a melody, the small towns along its banks are chords, and the big towns are tonic stations (the points toward which two or more chords tend to resolve). If an older player like Coleman Hawkins can be compared to a local steamship, he makes stops in every town—that is, plays melodies governed by each chord. A later player like Lester Young is an express steamer, and makes stops only at the larger points. John Coltrane (at least while he was playing with Miles) is a rocket ship, and will make all the stops like Hawkins, but quickly, and from the chromatic universe above. In modal playing such as heard in *Kind of Blue,* the player-ships are free to pick whatever towns they want to visit but with a main tonic station always governing. This kind of playing soon became popular among younger musicians, though *modal* came to be an umbrella term for a variety of new harmonic procedures that were developing. Older musicians sometimes claimed that there was nothing new in any of this—Charles Mingus, for example, in his "Open Letter to Miles" implies that it was his idea first—and some might point further back to compositions built on single chords in the 1920s, such as Jelly Roll Morton' "Jungle Blues" or Red Nichols' "The New Call of the Freaks." Other musicians just seemed mystified by it—Dizzy Gillespie, for example:

> Miles and I played together at the Village Gate and a place in Harlem, and the last time he came up to me afterward and said, "How'd you like it?" So I said, "What is it? Explain it to me." Well, it seems like they have a basic melody and they work around that. I guess you have to know the basic tune. . . . It reminded me so much of Ornette Coleman. . . . I could follow the chords he was playing. It was difficult stuff, very complex and highly enjoyable.

For a record that went so smoothly in the recording and seemed so perfect, everything went wrong in its production. One side was recorded at the wrong speed because of a fault in the recording machine; Adderley's name was spelled wrong on the jacket; Jimmy Cobb and Wynton Kelly became James Cobb and Wyn Kelly; two of the titles ("All Blues" and "Flamenco Sketches") were reversed on the label; later, controversy developed over Bill Evans' part in the compositions when Davis claimed composer's rights to all of them; and once it got to CD, the first reissue was poorly remastered, and the second (the high-priced "MasterSound Edition") sounded very different from the LP, with an echo effect noticeable throughout. The third reissue finally corrected the speed, but it had a new mix, with some audible tape noise and the rhythm section brought up to the front for a sound much closer to that of the nineties than of the fifties. Each one of them was a very different record.

Kind of Blue was to become the jazz record everyone had to have and is the best-selling Columbia jazz record of all time, one record that defines what jazz is for many people. For some others, such as musical minimalists, it also had a very great influence. The young Terry Riley, for example, used "So What" (though, perversely, as played by Chet Baker) as material to rework and manipulate live in the recording booth for one of his first compositions, *Music for the Gift* in 1963. And John Coltrane's playing was a key influence on Riley's *In C,* as it was for some of the early compositions of La Monte Young, who began his career as a Coltrane disciple on soprano saxophone. (Steve Reich had already been impressed by the Miles of "Walkin'," and John Adams recalls writing out Davis' solos as a student.) Nonminimalists were impressed as well: British composer Mark-Anthony Turnage used "Blue in Green" as a basis for part of his 1981 "Night Dances." Duane Allman loved *Kind of Blue* and used "All Blues" as the model for the Allman Brothers' "In Memory of Elizabeth Reed." The record would pop up in novels by Kingsley Amis in the sixties and in any number of films from the 1980s on.

In the liner notes that he wrote for *Kind of Blue,* Bill Evans compared the discipline of jazz to that of Japanese parchment painting. Later, he recalled those notes in reflecting on the accomplishment of the Davis sextet: "Well, I was comparing jazz in general . . . to that kind of thing . . . it's a remarkable discipline. You know, for people that are considered to be the most unstable, undisciplined members of society . . . the fact is that they bring to bear a kind of a discipline on their work that is practically unparalleled."

In early 1959, TV producer Robert Herridge was busy putting together twenty-six half-hour films on the arts for CBS TV—programs planned on ballet, opera, theater, and music. Charles Mingus would provide music for a dance piece set to the story of Frankie and Johnny, there would be one show called "The Sound of Jazz" (with Billie Holiday, Thelonious Monk, Count Basie, and many others), as well as programs on Ahmad Jamal and Miles Davis. But Davis had no interest in doing it—something to do with a bad experience of some sort he said he had had with another TV show. The musical adviser to Herridge's jazz shows, Nat Hentoff, nonetheless talked him into it, but Miles still approached the show warily, and argued with Herridge about what he would or would not do. The producer was on edge about the show to begin with and kept the script—or the lack of one (the show had only sixty seconds of commentary)—away from the sponsor as long as he could. He told Miles that he wanted him to play a number of songs that Miles thought were all alike. "When you play a number of similar pieces," Herridge argued, "you build up intensity." Miles disagreed: "That's not intensity. When I tell you 'no' again and again for a week, and then finally tell you 'yes', *that's* intensity."

"The Sound of Miles Davis" was filmed on April 2, though it was not broadcast until July 21, 1960. For nine minutes, the Davis quintet played "So What," with most of the time spent on a solo by Miles and briefer solos by John Coltrane and Wynton Kelly (Cannonball Adderley was absent with a migraine headache). The piece ended with Davis and bassist Paul Chambers alone on the screen, and as Davis walked off camera, leaving Chambers behind to finish alone.

The rest of the program was filled with three pieces by Gil Evans' Orchestra: "The Duke," "Blues for Pablo," and "New Rhumba." After the film was completed, Miles watched it at least five times. "You always see how you would have done it differently," he told *Down Beat*. "If I play good for eight bars, it's enough for me. The only thing is, I don't tell anybody which eight bars are the good ones. That's my secret."

Riding on the success of *Kind of Blue*, Miles took the sextet on the road for a tour that lasted almost five months. The modal innovations of the band were received with little press coverage, and what there was seemed to ignore what was new about the music and focused instead on staging and performance style. During their stay at the Jazz Seville club in Hollywood in July, for example, a *Down Beat* reviewer complained that there was no ensemble work in the group, only solos, and no regard whatsoever for the audience. In their "jam session atmosphere," he said, "at no point was the entire group ever onstage, and for two sets, Cannonball Adderley was missing. In any event, this long overdue appearance by Miles and companions in Los Angeles set the locals straight on the current New York mode of jazz presentation." At the Randall's Island Festival in August, another reviewer complained that with each soloist exiting the stage after her played, leaving only the rhythm section behind, they had become a satire of themselves. Plagued with dental problems through the whole tour, with Miles begging him not to have any teeth pulled for fear it would change his sound, John Coltrane finally left the group on the West Coast. Trane had been trying to find a way out of the band since the beginning of the year, and was looking for a replacement. He had first contacted Wayne Shorter, and then Jimmy Heath, who had just been released from prison in Pennsylvania, where he had been serving time for drug possession. Miles now called Heath, who flew out to complete the tour with them. Jimmy had the same trouble with modes that most other musicians did in that period, trying to stay in one key as if it were a traditional tune, instead of reaching out and using a wider range of notes; or not knowing how to resolve the piece at the end without the usual harmonics. When Heath went home to Philadelphia to visit his family in August, his parole officer warned him that he would have to keep within a sixty-mile radius of Philadelphia or be in violation, so he was forced to withdraw from the group's appearance at an Urban League benefit performance at the Playboy Jazz Festival in Chicago. Miles played the next few engagements with only a quintet; then John Coltrane rejoined them for a week at Birdland.

On the hot night of August 26, 1959, the sextet had just finished a twenty-seven-minute recording for the Armed Forces Radio Service in front of an audience at Birdland. During the break, Miles accompanied a white woman he later identified only as Judy to a cab in front of the club. Afterward, he remained out front, having a smoke, his jacket soaking from the heat inside. Some thirty or forty other people had also come out to get some air. A beat patrolman came by at that moment and began telling people to move on and not to block the sidewalk. When he turned to Davis and asked him to move, Miles responded by telling him, "I work here." The officer then asked Miles to stand closer to the building and not block the sidewalk. But Miles continued to stand there, his head down. The officer repeated his order to move, adding that he would lock him up if he refused. "Go ahead, lock me up." This much, both men were later to agree on. What came next Miles and Officer Gerald Kilduff disputed.

Kilduff said that he told Davis he was under arrest and took his arm, but Miles pulled away from him and said he was going nowhere. "He pulled away again and I grabbed him. This time he threw himself at me and grabbed my nightstick." Davis claimed that the officer stepped back, reaching for his handcuffs, and Miles—thinking like a boxer, and expecting a blow—moved in closer to shorten the punch and absorb the blow. The officer then stumbled and dropped his equipment, and Davis once again moved in closer, waiting to be handcuffed, he said.

Three detectives who were driving by noticed a crowd gathering—about 200, they later claimed—and stopped. One of the detectives, Donald Rolker, ran up behind Davis and hit him on the head again and again with a nightstick. People were now spilling out of Birdland, among them Illinois Jacquet, Cannonball Adderley, Paul Chambers, and the influential columnist Dorothy Kilgallen, whose account of the incident made the front page of the *Journal-American* newspaper the next day. Across the street, a group of musicians was rehearsing in the Music Unlimited Studio, and the noise outside had grown so loud that they couldn't hear themselves play. When they went to the window and saw what was happening, they shoved a microphone out on a boom to record it. The tape they made lasted four minutes, on which various voices are heard (according to the *Journal-American*'s coy redactions):

> "Take him to the precinct, that _____. Don't let him get away free. Get that _____ outta here."
> "I'll punch him right in the nose, so help me."
> "Why don't we all go to the precinct. I saw what happened."
> "That _____ ain't no police. He ain't no police."

The tape shows that the crowd continued to grow, along with the shouting, the noise of sirens, horns, and then cries of, "Okay, break it up, move along, it's all over." Reporters later interviewed a dozen witnesses who said that the detective was drunk, that Davis was innocent, and that the beating was excessive. ("They beat me like a drum," Davis complained.) One woman said that when she saw what they were doing to Davis, she hit one of the policemen herself.

It was a classic urban encounter, a confrontation that could be witnessed any day, but this one took place at a time when New York City had experienced a number of violent incidents that had begun to make race relations even worse than usual: several gang members had recently been killed in interethnic clashes; an attempt by police to arrest a drunken woman in Harlem had led to a riot that Sugar Ray Robinson had to be brought in to quell; and on the day of Davis' arrest, the police had shot a handcuffed prisoner attempting to escape from Bellevue Hospital.

At the precinct, Miles was booked for disorderly conduct and assaulting an officer, and held without bail. His "temporary" cabaret card (one he received after his 1953 brush with the California police) was also lifted, preventing him from working in clubs indefinitely. A doctor from a nearby hospital put five stitches in his scalp and applied bandages. Miles claimed that while he was waiting in the station, cops kept bumping into him, trying to provoke him with remarks like, "So you're the wise guy, huh?" Dorothy Kilgallen, Miles' lawyer Harold Lovett, and Frances came to the station, and the sight of a celebrity columnist, a stylishly dressed lawyer, and a beautiful woman sobbing over him impressed the cops. "I was there at the station," Frances said, "but Miles never discussed it with me. He kept me out. He was from the old school, where you don't want your wife to know or get involved because—probably because he was embarrassed behind it all."

Miles was released on $1,000 bail and was to appear in court on September 18 on the disorderly conduct charge, and at a later date for assault. Meanwhile, the president of Local 802 of the Musicians' Union called for an investigation into police brutality. And on October 4, Miles played a "Jazz for Civil Rights" benefit for the NAACP Freedom Fund at Hunter College in New York.

When the first part of his case came to trial, the courtroom and the halls of Magistrate's Court on 151st Street were packed with fans and the press, all of them perhaps hoping for a display of Davis' fabled anger. The hearing was presided over by Magistrate Kenneth Phipps, an African American. But Miles said very little. In support of the prosecution's case, a bartender testified that he had seen Davis' arm around the officer's waist, with the nightstick in his right hand, at about "belt level." Then Davis took the stand in his own defense. At one point, the district attorney asked him, "When the policeman said, 'You're under arrest,' and you just looked at him, what did that look mean?" Miles' lawyers, Harold Lovett and Carson Dewitt Baker (himself a former Municipal Court Justice) suddenly interrupted, then called for a recess, fearing the worst in Miles' response and the court's reaction. Miles later allowed that what he was going to say was, "If I had hit him, he wouldn't be here today."

During the break, Miles claimed the judge cautioned him not to say anything, just go through the motions—"and by the way," His Honor added, "if you don't send me some of your records, I'm going to put your ass in jail!" The magistrate ultimately dismissed the change of disorderly conduct for insufficient evidence, adding that it was not unusual for musicians to gather outside places where they were working. What's more, he said, they should be free from the fear of being molested by the police, and the officers were criticized for "misguided zeal" in the arrest

On November 19, the second charge of his arrest was heard in court. Davis' lawyers cited case law that indicated that when a citizen is illegally arrested, they may resist, even violently. The judge then chose to hear testimony from only one witness, Paul Chambers, and then promptly acquitted the defendant, declaring that "It would be a travesty on justice to adjudge the victim of an illegal arrest guilty of the crime of assaulting the one who made the arrest."

For several years before, newspapers in the United States were dominated by photos of black church bombings, failed attempts at school integration, and renewed Klan violence in the South. It was all the more poignant, then, when the image of Miles Davis ricocheted across the world, his head bandaged, blood soaking into his tailored khaki jacket, and a policeman leading him by handcuffs. The next day a *New York Times* headline read, "Miles Davis Assaulted by New York Policeman," and one British paper declared, "This Is What They Did to Miles." African American papers were quick to focus on the detail of the white woman in the cab as the motivation for the whole incident with the police, which led Davis to say of her: "This is no big love affair. I just like her. And she admires my music." In any case, when one black paper described what had happened as a "Georgia head whipping," readers understood that the kind of beatings received by civil rights demonstrators in the Deep South were also possible in the North and could be suffered by even the most famous of black people.

The point was not wasted on the world of arts and letters either. Accounts of Davis' beating coursed through the nervous system of New York's art community within hours, and for many it became a defining moment in race relations in New York. In "Personal Poem," for example, Frank O'Hara memorialized the moment he first heard about it from LeRoi Jones (Amiri Baraka), while waiting at a restaurant near his office in the Museum of Modern Art:

> . . . Moriarty's where I wait for LeRoi and hear who
> wants to be a mover and shaker the last five years my
> batting average is .016 that's that, and LeRoi comes in
> and tells me Miles Davis was clubbed 12 times last
> night outside BIRDLAND by a cop

And surely some at that time must have recalled that Langston Hughes had once written that the sound of nightsticks on the heads of his people reminded him of the rhythms of bebop.

Miles took the whole matter in stride: "It ain't a Negro in America ain't had something like that happen to him in one way or another."

Miles filed papers to sue the city for $500,000, but he was out of town when the hearing came up in February, and the suit disappeared. There were hints that Miles wanted it dropped, for fear that the police would make even more trouble for him. A newspaper columnist said that Miles was willing to drop the suit if his cabaret card was fully restored—which it was. What seemed to bother him most was that his mother had called him and said, "I know you hit him."

Interlude

I called him King Tut, and sometimes King John. What else could I call him? He had that royal thing.

VERNON DAVIS

Miles is a potentate. He's also a puritan, and the combination can be pretty sadistic.

LENA HORNE

BEYOND ANYTHING ELSE he might have been, Miles Davis was the sound of his trumpet. It was a sound that was deeply personal to him, and almost mystical in its source and power to project himself through his music. Amiri Baraka once said to poets, "You have to start and finish there, your own voice . . . how you sound." Miles, similarly, could tell horn players that sound was everything: "Believe your sound."

"Voice" is a poet's metaphor, of course, an analogy between the speaking voice and the writing voice, conveying the sense that the poet is not only what he says, but how he says it. But Miles went further and added an African American dimension to the equation by declaring that the instrumental voice is analogous to the human voice. If poets can bring a vocal, tonal quality to words on a page, then the instrumental voice can signify words through its tonality and timbre. Although Miles knew the words of all the ballads he played, he had no interest in having a singer with his band: better to have sound alone, he said, so that you could make up your own "attitude," and not be put off by the body, race, age, or sex of a singer. (Love songs with words tell you how someone else makes love, he said, like stories in *Penthouse* or *Playboy:* they're for people who aren't having sex.)

You know, when a singer sings, he gives you a map of what to think when he sings a ballad with a title. But when we play we don't bother your thoughts. You use your own thoughts. What you think is yours. When you hear someone singing a ballad you have to think what he means. He gives you the route. But when you hear—I hate to say jazz—jazz musicians give you the privacy of your own head.

His sound was not a gift, but something he crafted slowly over time, extracting it like an alchemist from an alloy of breath and metal. Gil Evans was the first to tell him of the importance of that sound and was the biggest defender of him as a stylist:

He has to exert the most tremendous control to play the way he does. Aside from blowing power, the strength of the embouchure, everything. When he works it's real labor. . . . He couldn't be a musician and sound like anybody else. He didn't know that. That developed. And you go along, you try and start out, you sound like so-and-so—various players like Clark Terry and Freddie Webster.

The first trumpet player who interested Davis as a boy was Harry James—a lead player, a ladies' man, a horseman (and clothes horse), with one foot in the concert hall and the other in the circus tent, a contender for the honor of being one of the first of the cool white men. The second was Louis Armstrong, who was many things—father of modern trumpet (and, not incidentally, Miles' mother's favorite jazz performer), shape shifter, high-C-playing hot dog, modernist, broad comedian, the Walt Whitman of jazz. Miles could benignly ignore Harry James in later life, but Armstrong was a dominating presence in the mythology of jazz, his hugeness and generosity of sound on the trumpet, the richness and inexhaustibility of his ideas, the alluvium of his voice (echoed on his trumpet), the raw countryness of his stage mugging and clowning, all of them forever bound together. Dizzy Gillespie eventually came to terms with Louis the man, as did Miles (though several remarks in his autobiography would make it appear otherwise). On the death of Armstrong in 1970, Davis wrote,

To me, the great style and interpretation that Louis gave to us musically came from the heart, but his personality was developed by white people wanting black people to entertain by smiling and jumping around. After they do it they call you a Tom, but Louis fooled all of them and became an ambassador of good will.

"Everybody up until Miles Davis played an extension of Louis Armstrong," Gil Evans said. "Even though it may have been camouflaged by high style and all that, it was still the basic sound, it was still based on Louis Armstrong, and Miles Davis changed the sound." Armstrong was either a hurdle to get over or a troubling force of influence to be creatively transformed.

Miles worked hard to get a full, round tone that lurked in the middle register. He practiced across the lake on his father's farm to open his tone up, to get a cornet sound—the sound of Wagner's brass, he said. But some heard it as a naive sound, a beginner's tone on the horn. Even his chosen range was suspected of being the result of his not being able to reach high notes. But Davis said it was more a matter of not *hearing* the trumpet in that range, and for Miles, what he heard, like whatever else he felt in his body, determined what he played. The music had to resonate physically before he could articulate it. (In fact, on many records, he can be heard reaching the upper limits of the horn with apparent ease.) Though he described his own playing as free of vibrato—that wavering of pitch that listeners hear as a sign of sincerity or professionalism—he often used some vibrato at the end of long notes and phrases, much as a singer would, and his notes could crack or sob like a singer's. Sometimes the notes seemed not to be quite there—ghosted notes, jazz musicians call them, more implied than played. It was a sound that some described as tragic, vulnerable, the essence of the blues—"a man walking on eggshells" or "a little boy crying in the closet." Kenneth Tynan would call him a "musical lonely hearts club." But there were those, especially among older listeners, who were not so happy with his blues aesthetic. Critic Roger Pryor Dodge, for example, missed the rougher, louder blues of the South and Southwest, and what he heard in modern musicians like Davis was a melodramatic, "decadent" affinity with Billie Holiday and Billy Eckstine—singers he disliked for their "whining intimacy, a merging of blues with the torch song." (In later years, when Miles flirted with rock, some heard his blues in a new way—his singing tone, soft attack, and delayed vibrato; his slurred, sobbed, and bent notes; the buzzing metallic edge of his mute, together suggested to them nothing less than the sound of an electric guitar.)

He took to playing with a Harmon mute in the mid-1950s, a tin device patented in the 1920s by Dave Harmon, owner of the Dreamland Ballroom in Chicago, where trumpeter King Oliver, a great user of mutes to transform his horn's sound, first became famous outside of New Orleans. The Harmon was originally used for "wah-wah" effects, a technologically sophisticated version of the toilet plunger employed by some trumpet players for jokey or exotic sounds. It worked by covering and uncovering the stem, the small tube in the middle, by hand, yet avoided the pitch changes that plagued plunger users. Miles, however, pulled the tube out and played the mute straight, shoving the bell of his horn into the microphone to gain volume and resonance.

The Harmon had a certain mystique to it because it was hard to record. It muted so well, in fact, that trumpet players blew harder, and it subdued the fundamental of the tone, as the engineers might say, giving off high-frequency transients that disturbed the lathes that cut the masters and distorted the sound on the records. A punctuated loud note in a fast tune could rattle the metal of the mute and give it the ominous quality of an explosion in the building next door. But Miles used it more cautiously, as a mood-enhancing apparatus. "In the slow ballads," New Yorker writer Whitney Balliett once wrote, "Davis, using a mute, buzzes rhythmically and persistently at the melody, like a bluebottle." The effect was not one of calm, but of repressed emotion. "More often than not," Gil Evans observed, "when people play with mutes, everything sounds relaxed; but with Miles there's an extraordinary tension." The mute also allowed Miles to play the way he spoke, in that grainy whisper that compelled others to lean toward him—a wisp of a musical tone that could suggest delicate intimacy but also a force barely under control. And by favoring the mute, Davis stepped back from Armstrong's country brashness and exuberance, softening the gruff voice he shared with Armstrong on both horn and larynx, and thus reinforced the perception of his playing as the essence of black urbanity.

Miles was a master of phrasing—the groupings of notes or words in songs—the nexus where the voices of both the body and the horn are most clearly aligned. Like Billie Holiday, he divided and regrouped notes by means of silences sometimes of such daring length that the audience was left wondering if he had lost his way. Through phrasing and carefully chosen tempos, he could understate a melody to the point where he stripped it of its romantic character ("All of Me"); or giving it a different turn, he could make a straightforward show tune take on a sense of poignancy ("The Surrey with the Fringe on Top") or, again, play a blues so slowly that it dissolved into a romantic ballad ("Basin Street Blues"). He might erase or hold back some of the notes from the original tune in order to work against its familiarity (as in the four held notes that speak the title of "Bye Bye Blackbird," which he effaced after a few years of playing the tune). Even if the song were well known, Miles could make listeners feel as if he were creating its melody afresh.

It was the kind of phrasing that caught the imagination of the literati. When poet Robert Creeley heard Davis' "But Not for Me" in 1954, he wondered how musicians were able to create phrases different from those in the original songs without composing them in advance. In Jack Kerouac's *Visions of Cody*, Jack Duluoz muses over the structure of Miles' phrases (and maybe mimics them as well):

> And meanwhile Miles Davis, like the sun; or the sun, like Miles Davis, blows on with his raw little horn; the prettiest trumpet tone since Hackett and McPartland and at the same time, to flesh some of its fine raw sound, some wild abstract new ideas developed around a growing theme that started off like a tree and became a structure of iron on which tremendous phrases can be strung and hung and long pauses goofed, kicked along, whaled, touched, with hidden and active meanings; to come in, then, like a sweet tenor and blow the superfinest, is mowed enow [more than enough].

Kerouac might be forgiven his excesses, because in Miles' playing the missing note, the auditory ellipsis, the sense of breath being held rather than sounded, the choked-back note—all of them *are* literary in feel, something akin to the rhetorical device called meiosis—understatement in the service of something less than the truth, a form of withholding that said that you were being asked to feel something that couldn't be explained literally. It signified that you would have to believe more than what you were being offered. Philosopher Philippe Lacoue-Labarthe, the author of *Musica Ficta*, a philosophical meditation on Wagner's operas, said that during a performance he had once seen, Miles Davis had stopped, midphrase, to utter an expletive: "In the caesura not of speech but of music, filling in with an empty word for a musical phrase he could not find, Miles shows how music is simultaneously inside the body, of the subject, and beyond."

> Frank Sinatra taught me how to phrase, when [he] sings . . .
> "Night and Day"; the way Orson Welles used to phrase . . .
> the heavy accent that would stop short.

Orson Welles and Frank Sinatra, two men whose careers began shortly after the development of the microphone, and who knew how to use it like a musical instrument. Before them, most performers used mikes as megaphones, as a means of making themselves heard at a distance. When he was a child, Miles heard Welles' voice on the radio in many roles, as the pure and disembodied voice of the Shadow ("Who knows what evil lurks in the hearts of men?"), the omniscient narrator in *The War of the Worlds* ("We know now that in the early years of the twentieth century this world was being watched closely by intelligences greater than man's"), but also as a speaker in other dramatic settings in which Welles' voice brought a sense of the body with it, making him seem a physical presence. Welles had a powerful, mellifluous voice, and he could use the mike to convey intimacy through whispers and murmurs.

Sinatra, the man they called "The Voice," phrased conversationally, closely, at moderate volume, emphasizing words rather than melody. He stretched vowels and de-emphasized consonants, allowing musical phrases to extend beyond their normal length. Moving into and away from the microphone, shifting position in relation to the hearer and the band, Sinatra learned to avoid the sibilants and pops of microphone use. At the peak of his career, he could record in a studio with a twenty-five-piece orchestra and a hundred guests and still make it sound intimate.

Like Welles and Sinatra, Davis grasped the potential of the microphone to set the body free. He sensed that a mike could be used like a close-up lens in motion pictures, focusing and amplifying small gestures and emotions, making histrionics and grand stagecraft unnecessary. With a microphone, singers and musicians could join the new naturalistic stage rhetoric that was developing in the wake of the Russian director Stanislavsky's plea that actors should cease *portraying* emotions to the audience and begin communicating them directly. In the same era when audiences were becoming accustomed to closer and more intimate looks at actors on film, the mike removed the need for musicians and singers to struggle to close the physical distance between themselves and the audience. Performers were finding new ways to position themselves on stage, assuming new attitudes (to use the word with which dancers describe the position of their feet and hands). The strongest position on stage—the three-quarter profile that allows the audience to see actors' expressions while the actors maintain the fiction that there is no audience there—could be replaced by any number of so-called weaker positions, such as performing while walking into the corners of the stage or with the actors speaking with their backs to the audience. (By the beginning of the twentieth century, the actors of the Moscow Art Theatre and the Abbey Theater had already redefined dramatic naturalism by performing back-to-audience in the United States.) The concept of a fourth wall could be realized by performing as if there were no audience in the theater at all, an illusion in which the performance element could be concealed.

Musicians and their audiences were slower than those in the theater to grasp the possibilities offered to them by the microphone and new forms of theatrical practice. At the heart of jazz performance was the demand that musicians play for an audience's entertainment, whether for listening, dancing, drinking, or various forms of coupling. They were to come onstage in character, so to speak, dressed in band uniforms or business suits, and play with a lively, expressive stage manner just short of choreography. When not playing, they were to stand in place and engage the audience with eye contact, gracious smiles, perhaps even some clowning.

Miles rejected these shibboleths. He not only resented the showbiz elements in Louis Armstrong's performances, but also the clowning of Dizzy Gillespie and the stage foolishness of Charlie Parker. At Juilliard, he had learned what an artist could demand of an audience, and it was he who would correct the music, who would purify it of its brothel and tent-show origins, and present it as the art it was. And in an era in which a night's gig in a club could constitute another chapter in the discourse on race and manhood in America, this had the weight of a mission.

He was a small man, five feet six, around 150 pounds, but the way he moved, the short cut of his coats, and his slim-profile pants made him seem larger. He dressed like a model and walked with a dancer's grace and economy, but with a detachment that hinted at a secret vulnerability. His large, round eyes seemed never to blink, and it was said by some of those in awe of him that he never closed them as he slept. When he played, he stood motionless, like a still life painting, with knees flexed, head bent forward, indulging in the vanity of the slouch. And unlike other musicians who played their trumpets like weapons, horns erect and at the ready, he pointed his down. In a time when the trumpet player symbolized a certain kind of modern man—a high, loud, and virile player, technically proficient, a master of this piece of instrumental machinery—Miles played soft and low, turning the trumpet into an organic extension of himself, hitting wrong notes along the way as though to remind the audience that it was a human performance and not a didactic essay on modernism. He brought to mind the Hollywood jazz trope in which sexual impotence is symbolized by missed high notes on a horn in movies such as *Young Man with a Horn* or *Mo' Better Blues*. But Davis instead turned such errors (if indeed they were errors) into art, making them seem like sobs and whispers from an introverted, interior monologue being carried out on the bandstand. Despite his *Playboy*-like appearance, there was a cry of loneliness in his music that, even if it came from deep within himself, spoke to a condition many felt in the 1950s.

He abandoned the banter that kept the audience quiet and engaged between pieces, and ceased to announce song titles altogether, shocking critic Whitney Balliett, who complained, "It's like a minister neglecting to reveal his chapter and verse." With Davis, there were no smiles, no bows, no recognition that an audience was even present. Nor did he acknowledge applause, at either the completion of a solo or the end of the tune. In fact, he sometimes scarcely allowed time for applause, beginning one piece almost on top of another.

In 1957, a young writer named Joyce Johnson went to the Cafe Bohemia to see Davis play and to hang out in a club beloved of artists and writers. Afterward, she wrote to her new boyfriend, Jack Kerouac, and described one occasion on which Davis did thank his audience:

> The place was packed, but silent as a cathedral. . . . Then—all of a sudden, a car smacked up across the street between a house and a lamppost. . . . A man at the bar cried "Crazy!" threw up his arms and ran out into the street, followed by everybody except Miles who kept playing. He finished and said quietly, "Thank you for the applause," and walked off. It was like a dream.

Of all Davis' mannerisms, the one that really got to fans and press was what they called "turning his back on the audience." Though he never actually played with his back turned—films from the 1950s show him standing fully forward to the microphone, or at most, playing into it with an actor's three-quarter profile—when he finished a solo, he often walked to the back of the band or left the bandstand for the bar or a table. (Jazz singer Eddie Jefferson immortalized this demeanor by putting words to "So What": "Miles Davis walked off the stage! / That's what folks are saying.") Whatever he *was* doing was enough to have the audience whispering, and the meaning of their reaction was clear: a performer—and a Negro performer, at that—was refusing to follow the fundamental etiquette of performance. He was declining to display graciousness and appreciation for the audience's attention and applause, refusing to acknowledge the special nature of their relationship—refusing to show, in a word, humility.

And what resonance that simple gesture had! During a wind-up doll joke craze in the early 1960s, George Crater, a humorist with *Down Beat* magazine, asked the question: What does a Miles Davis doll do if you wind it up? Answer: It turns its back on you. Even in the global backwaters of the jazz world, they had heard of Miles' behavior. In *Portrait of India*, Ved Mehta describes the vocalist with a Bombay jazz band singing

"My Funny Valentine" with her back to the crowd because of the disdain in which she held Indian audiences. When Birdland seemed to be on the verge of eliminating jazz for rhythm and blues in 1964, *New York Daily News* columnist Robert Sylvester quoted bartender Oscar Goodstein on "these icebox artists" who were not entertaining anyone. But if Birdland does close out jazz, Sylvester said, "It's at least one less place in which the arrogant and hostile can turn their backs on people who made them rich and sputter through their sour, slobbering horns." With the civil rights movement beginning in the same era, such a gesture took on added symbolism, that of a refusal to placate whites; and with the appearance of the black arts movement of the early 1960s, Miles could be seen as turning his back on all of Western civilization. Asked about why Miles left the stage after soloing, Dizzy Gillespie once said, "Why don't you ask him? And besides, maybe we'd all like to be like Miles and just haven't got the courage." By the 1990s this gesture was still emblematic, though of what was not so clear by then. Poet Nathaniel Mackey gently mocks the obsession with Davis' behavior by imagining a social scientist who attempts to scrupulously analyze Miles' movement:

> This clicked with an idea Derek had been carrying around for some time—namely that people weren't being precise enough in discussing Miles Davis turning his back on his audiences, that sufficient note had yet to be made of the fact that the angle at which his back addressed the audience tended to vary in relation to a host of contextual factors and coefficients. The upshot was that he set about quantifying and chronologizing based on photographs, films, secondhand accounts and firsthand observation—the positional/propositional variables attendant upon Miles' posture, or, as he himself puts it, the "semitemporal calculus of Miles' postural kinematics."

Journalists began to let readers know whenever Davis turned away from them when they asked for interviews. Newspaper headlines and club marquees now proclaimed Davis "the prince of darkness," "the angry young man of jazz," "the evil genius." *Evil* was a word whose black meanings resonated well beyond the obvious: bad humored, ominous, unnatural, angry, but also thrillingly dangerous. Despite Davis' distrust of most critics and journalists, he offered a select few of them various reasons for his behavior: he turned away from the audience when he wasn't playing because he wanted to hear the band like a conductor; he didn't want to distract from other musicians' solos when he wasn't playing; some spots on the bandstand were better than others for sound; he wanted to be close to the rhythm section; or, while playing at the Village Vanguard, he couldn't stand looking at the flicker of the candles on the tables. Since he normally played with his eyes open, this last explanation is not as strange as it might sound. Musicians who are reading music focus on the page, while those who are playing from memory or improvising have the choice of playing with eyes open or shut. Eyes open in front of an audience presents serious distractions to many players, and Miles' solution was to minimize the presence of the audience.

Charlie Parker often said that Miles was shy, as did Dizzy Gillespie: "You'd never think it, but I've been watching him for so many years. There must always be reasons for actions. So I think that the reasons for some of his actions are a natural result of his being shy." Dizzy told of the time that they were both playing at the Village Vanguard, and Sugar Ray Robinson and Archie Moore walked in the club while Miles' band was on the stand. Miles came over to Dizzy and asked him to introduce them when his set started. Knowing Miles was a huge fight fan, he said, "Hell, you're on now. You introduce them. You've got it." But Miles was too shy to do [it], and left it to Dizzy. Sonny Rollins agreed: "I hate to use that word *shy*, but he is a shy guy. Which is why he turned his back sometimes, and then people would say, 'Oh, gee, he's arrogant.' Miles wanted to hear the music, and he'd play something that he didn't want the public to hear, because we were getting the music together. It was more the feeling of a workshop, and Miles would take the time to change a note or chord. We were all experimenting, and Miles encouraged it." "Miles sometimes played into the curtain at the Vanguard," according to the club's manager, Lorraine Gordon, "but people didn't seem to mind."

James Baldwin, who said of Miles that he was the only person he knew who was shyer than he, once compared Miles' shyness to Floyd Patterson's reticence, his "will to privacy":

He lives gallantly with his scars, but not all of them have healed—and while he has found a way to master this, he has found no way to hide it; as, for example, another tough and tender man, Miles Davis, has managed to do. Miles' disguise would certainly never fool anybody with sense, but it keeps a lot of people away, and that's the point.

"Miles' way of coping with shyness," wrote Nat Hentoff, "is to affect fierceness:

"Like all of us," a musician who has known him for many years explains, "Miles only has a certain amount of energy, and he finds it difficult to meet new people. Rather than subject himself to what is for him a tiring discomfort, he tries to create so forbidding an image of himself that he won't even be bothered."

And Miles could be hurt. In early summer 1956, David Amram was at the bar in Birdland with Gil Coggins, and Miles walked in with his dark glasses and a certain look on his face, and Gil said, "Uh oh, he's not feeling too sociable tonight." David said that "this sort of wave of fear suddenly went through all the musicians, the people who loved him and admired him."

> There was this terrible kind of freeze that used to happen at Birdland. I mean it was a terrible kind of cold feeling, because without Charlie Parker being alive, it was almost like a temple named after some religious figure, and that god had died. At the same time there were these big tables where hustlers and gamblers sat who appreciated jazz. It was a combination of a gangster vibe, along with connoisseurs and snobs—if you can imagine that—all those combined.

Instead of walking to the expensive tables, Miles went in slow motion and started to go to the outer edges, the cheap seats in the bull pen and the bar where the musicians stood.

> As he got closer, I kind of tried to make myself invisible so I wouldn't offend him. And when he was about five feet away I thought to myself, "I better not even say hello." So he went *really* slow, and just when he got almost right in front of me I saw through the left side of his dark glasses a bloodshot eye, the left eye, and it flashed over for a second. And I didn't make any effort to say hello like I always would. I just acted like I didn't know he was there—and I knew in that millisecond I saw, and I *felt*, this hurt. And it completely freaked me out, because that was the last thing that I thought that I or anybody would be capable of doing, of hurting his feelings or rejecting him since I felt like a nobody in his presence. . . . I understood at that moment why he would often be the way he was when he was rude with people, or when his behavior was erratic: he could actually sense what other people were feeling and thinking. So the point was, that he had a sensitivity that was so acute that it made it impossible for him to let things slide, and they sometimes became unbearable to him. . . .
> A lot of his toughness on the outside came from a combination of pride, understanding his value as an artist, and not being able to deal with the way he was treated in some of the environments that he had to be in.

Whatever Miles meant by leaving the stage, and whether it ultimately derived from his shyness or not, his behavior and his explanations asked the audience to focus on the music, not on the performers or the audience's relation to them.

A joke went around about Miles, David Amram said, one that Miles liked so much he even told it about himself:

> A guy said, "I've been waiting to hear Miles Davis all my life. I've saved up a month's salary just to be able to stay the whole night for all the sets. I go there," he said, "and Miles comes in wearing this beautiful suit, turns his back on the audience for the whole set, doesn't play a note." He said the second set the same thing happened, so he turned to his friend who had introduced him to Miles' music, and said, "He hasn't played a *note!*" He said, "I want my money back. This is a bunch of bullshit." And his friend said, "No, man, it's not what he's *playing,* it's what he's *thinking!*"

Offstage, Miles was a sight to see. Sunglasses worn against the night, he aestheticized his vision, turning himself into an artwork, into a minor deity of some sort, a Greek *daemon* perhaps, silently observing humanity's foolishness from his seat at an empty table or at the end of the bar, or merely observing his band's behavior. Trumpeter Eddie Henderson sat beside him at the Blackhawk in 1961, and whenever saxophonist Hank Mobley squeaked or fluffed a note, Miles would half-humorously feign hitting Hank over the head with a trumpet. Mike Zwerin said that Miles complained to him about the rhythm section one night at Birdland in 1959, "What's Paul doing with the time?" But Zwerin could hear nothing wrong.

Another Miles joke: a jazz fan dies and reaches the other world and meets St. Peter, who takes him to a club with bad lighting, crowded tables, and bored waitresses. But when he sees that the customers include Lester Young, Billie Holiday, Monk, and Bird, he cries out to St. Peter, "This *is* heaven!" Then he notices a figure sitting at the end of the bar, dressed all in black, his back turned to the audience. "Who's that?" asks the fan. "Oh," says St. Peter, "that's God. He thinks he's Miles Davis."

Throughout the 1950s, Davis continued to develop a set of distinctive stage gestures, tilting his head to one side, or rocking his head left or right; pressing a forefinger underneath his ear; wiping his tongue with his fingers to dry it; or removing sweat from his brow with a sweep of one finger, flicking it to the floor. A master of the subtext, every move he made was immediately seized on, linked with the others, and studied by fans. Even friends and sidemen puzzled over his behavior and sometimes asked him what he was up to. He told them that he never made the usual announcements because music should speak for itself, or that he might decide to change the tune at the last minute. Besides, classical musicians didn't do stage banter, so why was it required of jazz? He didn't smile or bow because he associated such stage manners with Uncle Tomming. Tomming for him was a pandering performance style that knew no race lines.

Offstage he could be diffident, aloof, even hostile. (When Coleman Hawkins chided him about his stage manners, Davis reminded him of their time together on 52nd Street, and asked him, "What kind of example were you? Sometimes you didn't show up at all.") He said he didn't like to speak to customers since he was wary of them because of his drug habit and didn't know who to trust. He said he was a musician and nothing more, and in this he was apparently sincere. He seemed never to grasp what people wanted from him other than music, why they cared what he had to say about things, or why they even bothered to talk to him.

If you were insulted by Miles Davis, ignored, or treated rudely, he said it wasn't personal: some days he could answer some questions, some days he couldn't. And when he couldn't, he got angry, and his energy and creativity drained away. After a nasty confrontation, he said he could see the results in the wrinkles in his face. Some of what he felt in these encounters was embarrassment for himself, but also embarrassment for those who approached him—fans, journalists seeking interviews, would-be lovers—they were all the same. Afterward, he could feel bad for hours, and he went to any length to avoid these skirmishes.

When Miles took up the discipline of boxing, he did so as a corporeal virtue, as a way of expressing masculinity. Like one of his models, Sugar Ray Robinson, Miles was "a sybarite who enjoyed the sensual experience, was indeed a connoisseur of it," as Gerald Early has observed. Yet Davis also sought that most basic of epicurean goals, the avoidance of suffering. And if there was a contradiction for Miles between self-denial and total gratification, it was not apparent. His body was the root of his consciousness, and like a computer directing his mind, he did what it compelled him to do. In bad health and pain for much of his life, addicted in one way or another for more than half of his years, he could suffer as much as or more than any pugilist. Davis would muse that he could have been a contender, but he avoided actual fighting so as not to injure his mouth and hands. (Once, though, he said he sparred a few rounds with Roberto Duran, the man with *manos de piedra*, hands of stone.) Like Berry Gordy, who switched from professional boxer to jazz drummer and later became the emperor of Motown, Miles understood that the boxer must finally lose his title, by either retirement or defeat, while the musician can remain king forever. But, again, as Early suggests, boxers and musicians are both itinerant workers in the arena of individualism, both pay the dues of a brutal meritocracy, and though public figures, both are embedded in a shadowy elite with its own code of values under the spotlights.

Before performances, Miles stayed away from others and often drove away anyone who might approach him. Like a boxer preparing for a fight, he denied himself food and sex before playing, believing that a musician should perform hungry and unsatisfied. He said that like Joe Louis and Sugar Ray Robinson, he avoided shaking hands before the main event, or he offered his left hand. In the dressing room before the gig, he worked to get his hands to have the right feel—not too dry, not too wet. He wanted nobody else's oil on his hands. And like a fighter, he tied his shoelaces as tightly as he could bear, on shoes that were already a size smaller than his size 7 feet, so that he would feel firmly in place. Asked if he had stage fright, he answered that he was afraid of nothing, then allowed that he had "butterflies" before every performance and would often be sick to his stomach before he played. When asked if he was shy, he admitted he was, but not with what he called a white shyness; rather, it was an artistic shyness, a shyness of those who were aware. He made a similar racial distinction between confidence and arrogance: white people, he said, get confidence mixed up with arrogance. If people of any color other than white are confident, they are called arrogant.

David Amram sometimes ran into Davis at boxing matches at one of the many small boxing clubs of the 1950s:

Miles didn't go there to be *seen*. He went there to watch—watch the box-ing, and to see that *courage* and *loneliness* of what it's like to be doing that, and at the same time the only spontaneity and ensemble sense that you have even in that violent sport that somehow in its own terrible way has a certain beauty and nobility to it. It wasn't so much that he was *pugnacious*, I think, as it was that he was a very proud person.

Boxing could make you graceful, could help shape your body. But more important, boxing and music were intimately connected. Miles played from the legs, bending his knees so as to not break his embouchure. In an interview with *Down Beat* editor Don DeMicheal, Miles drew out that connection:

Davis: You notice guys when they play—and this is some corny stuff they play and they breathe in the regular spots; so, there-fore they play the regular thing.

DeMicheal: You're talking about two- and four-bar phrases, things like that?

Davis: Yeah. . . . You're playing in a pattern. Especially if the time is getting mucked up, and you're playing in a pattern, it's going to get more mucked up 'cause you're going to start drop-ping the time when you drop your horn down, 'cause whoever is playing behind you will say, "Well, he's resting." You never let a guy know when you're gonna rest. Like in boxing, if I jab a guy, I won't relax, 'cause if I jab him, that's a point for me. If I jab him, then I'm gonna do something else. I mean, you've got to keep something going on all the time.

DeMicheal: If when you move, you break your embouchure, why move at all?

Davis: You keep getting your balance back. Certain things jerk you. Say, like last night I was playing triplets against a fast 4/4. . . . You got to keep getting your balance. . . .

The things of music you just finish. When you play, you carry them through till you think they're finished or until the rhythm dictates that it's finished and then you do something else. But you also connect what you finished with what you're going to do next. So it don't sound like a pattern. So when you learn that, you've got a good band, and when the band learns that, it's a good band.

DeMicheal: A lot of times you'll let, say, eight bars go by during a solo without playing anything. . . . Doesn't that break the flow you talked about?

Davis: It doesn't break the flow because the rhythm section is doing the same thing they were doing before. . . . Whatever's been happening has been happening too long; if it dies out, you can start a whole different thing. . . . Sometimes if you do the same thing [you ended with], it hits the spot.

Though it was not apparent to his audience at first, Davis was slowly turning the bandstand into a stage, changing it from the work area of the help into an expressive and dramatic site. Bandstands had been used as vaudeville stages, as exotic sets, and sometimes even for neominstrel shows. But Davis was using his stage in much the way as did a new generation of American male actors who arrived at the same postwar moment—notably Marlon Brando, James Dean, and Montgomery Clift, all midwesterners—actors who learned the principles of Stanislavsky as filtered through the innovations of film directors and American popular style. Practicing what was called the Method, these actors broke with customary theatrical practice and became known for a form of intimate yet emotionally charged acting, carried off with the liberating sense that everything was improvised, and therefore real. Their personae, on stage and off, were often brooding, rude, and inarticulate. Yet their inarticulateness was understood to be part of their rebellion, their unease and restlessness a part of their incomplete commitment to the existing society. And behind a mask that seemed incapable of expressing anything, one sensed sensitivity and strength as well as a deeper level of expressivity. Small gestures, no matter how studied, expressed their awareness of their bodies and drew attention to their provocative sexuality, together conveying a new form of American naturalism.

These gestures, the relaxed posture, the studied inarticulateness, a calculated detachment, a certain angle of descent, merge with elements of the cool, a powerful metaphor for twentieth-century life. Cool has its roots in West and Central African philosophy, where beauty and character are joined in self-possession free of anger. But it also resonates with a nineteenth-century European sense of the artful self, the dandy, a type of aristocratic bohemian intellectual delineated by Baudelaire: "The distinguishing characteristic of the dandy's beauty consists above all in an air of coldness which comes from an unshakable determination not to be moved; you might call it a latent fire which hints at itself, and which could, but chooses not to, burst into flame." The motivation of the dandy "is the burning need to create for oneself a personal originality. . . . It is the joy of astonishing others, and the proud satisfaction of never oneself being astonished." Rooted in opposition and revolt, the dandy is driven by a need to "combat and destroy triviality." "That is the source in the dandy of that haughty, patrician attitude, aggressive even in its coldness."

It was not always easy for Miles to be cool, to slow down, to wait a few beats to understand better what something meant. He could become angry, violently so, or be hurt by criticism. And cool posture or no, he was not relaxed when he played. There is a school of thought about jazz that honors the physical and sees corporeal effort as an indication of aesthetic greatness. Such players were once rewarded with cries of "Work, man!" or "Sweat, brother!" This is what composer Anthony Braxton has called the phenomenology of the sweating brow, a celebration of the physical through an erasure of the intellect. There was an unmistakable intensity about Davis' playing, but it was not bodily. As saxophonist George Coleman said, "Miles used to sweat profusely—but it was not so much physical energy as it was mental energy. There was lots of concentration."

Being cool did not mean that he could not be verbally hot, yet he was selective, choosing the moment of his words for maximum effect. Certain men and women among his friends never heard him utter a vulgar word. But others who did knew him for his sometimes wild and chaotic use of "motherfucker" (or "mother*fuck*er," since he stressed the third syllable). Charles Mingus, for example, said that in the mid-1940s Miles used it "every other word." A term with complex origins and weight, a noun that can imply the most profane form of address, "motherfucker" can also express an affectionate or collegial relationship, or even serve as a term of praise or a description of a situation of great misfortune or great success. He was not alone in using it, of course, as it can be seen in the writings of Ralph Ellison, Billie Holiday, James Baldwin, William Burroughs, and any number of others in the 1940s and 1950s who sought to bring the language of the streets into their discourse. It was also a word that could get you beaten, or tossed out of a club in those days, and its use in public required considerable daring to pull off. But Miles used it so flagrantly and vociferously, that he personified it, made it his own, and moved it to a new level of performance. When it was turned on him, however, he could be shocked by its use. Once when a road manager told him to do an encore by yelling, "Get back on the stage, motherfucker!" Miles was incensed: "This wasn't like any motherfucker I'd ever heard before. It was a white motherfucker with too many Rs in it."

Such language clashed violently with his clothing. In the mid-fifties, Miles took to the Ivy League look in fashion, having his clothes made at the epicenter of preppy fashion, the Andover Shop in Cambridge's Harvard Square, where tailor Charlie Davidson dressed him in jackets of English tweed or madras with narrow lapels and natural shoulder, woolen or chino trousers, broadcloth shirts with button-down collars, thin knit or rep ties, and Bass Weejuns loafers. It was a look that redefined cool and shook those who thought they were in the know. Some, like *Boston Herald* columnist George Frazier, reacted badly. Calling him "the Whilom War Lord of the Weejuns," he accused Davis of no longer being cool, but of merely showing off—in fact, of having become a "fink." But as always with Miles, there was something extra about his clothing, something that the discerning could spot and know that he was set apart from the obvious. For one, his coats were cut with a ¾ inch higher rise in the back so as to gracefully accommodate the slump he assumed when he played. The chest was cut close, as were the waist and back of the coat; the pockets were piped and slightly slanted; and the buttons on the sleeves buttoned and unbuttoned, allowing for freedom of movement when playing the trumpet, but also exposing their silk lining when turned back. His shirts were high-collared and skin-tight, just as his trousers were slim and close, so close that some wondered aloud about his intentions, and whether those intentions could be sustained by his physique. But he had their attention.

He had the attention of the fashion press as well. By 1960, his tastes had shifted toward Italian-made coats of an even trimmer cut, and *Esquire,* in its September issue, picked him as one of the best-dressed men in America, side by side with Clark Gable and Dean Acheson, as well as two of his boyhood models, Fred Astaire and Cary Grant. And by April 1961, GQ chose him as a "Fashion Personality of the Month," noting that they had never seen a jacket made like the one he wore from Joe Emsley, his New York tailor. There were no seams in the shoulders, and the sleeves and body were cut in one piece; in fact, there were only two seams—under the sleeve and down the jacket's side. It was the sort of thing that gave a press agent inspiration. A press release for the Randall's Island Jazz Festival in 1961, for example, spelled out in loving detail Davis' clothing itinerary for the festival:

Before his performance, Mr. Davis will wear a single-breasted (one button) beige pongee suit, combining the French and Italian influence on pants and jacket. When Mr. Davis is playing on stage, he will be wearing a double-breasted gray imported silk (two buttons) featuring only two pockets to create an extra slim line.

After his performance, Miles will relax in a pink, single-breasted seersucker jacket with matching pants, hand-made loafers of doeskin, and white sports shirt worn with a pink silk square.

But fame can be as local as it is fickle. "Miles came home to East St. Louis wearing a continental suit," Eugene Redmond said, "but the fashion hadn't reached here yet, and at the Ringside Pool Room they teased him about his clothes being 'country,' coming in there wearing that too-tight jacket and those too-short 'highwater pants'!" And try as he would, color could trump fame in much of America. At his tailor's in Harvard Square, while Miles was being fitted in the finest fabric in the highest style, another customer bet that he could guess Miles' occupation: "tap dancer, right?"

He wore his cars like his clothes—expensive, imported, stylish, and unique. In the 1950s, imported high-performance cars were rare, driven only by the very privileged and elite, not by all of those who might be able to afford them—certainly not by hustlers, players, pimps, and gangsters, who then feared drawing *too* much attention to themselves. But Miles relished the attention and drove fearlessly on streets that could not reasonably accommodate his speed. Running cars to their limits allowed him to focus on the moment, to be free of time, of past and future, free of the body and pain, caught up in the ecstasy of pure speed.

Still, the car offered no antidote to race. As a symbol of wealth and of manhood, in fact, it was something of a red flag to those who would demean him. On one occasion he drove his Ferrari down to Philadelphia (he drove everywhere in those days) and picked up Jimmy Heath. As they sped along the wide expanses of Broad Street talking about music, Miles complaining that Sonny Stitt was messing up "So What" every time they played it, he suddenly bet Jimmy that he could make every light. He geared down and the car was whistling past lights at 60-some miles an hour (in a 25 mph zone), when one of the lights suddenly changed and he had to brake. But he knew what the car could do, and when he downshifted, it stopped smartly . . . alongside two undercover narcotics cops in an unmarked car. "It's Miles Davis and Jimmy Heath!" one of them shouted as they jumped out of the car. After a fruitless search for drugs, they grudgingly let them go. In Philadelphia on another occasion, Miles was in the Ferrari with a white woman, when a police-man pulled him over. Before the cop could speak, Miles said, "You take the girl, and I'll keep the car, okay? That's the problem, right?"

Miles was fond of jamming down on the pedal and sending the car into a slow spin. "I drive my yellow [Ferrari] in New York, police don't bother me 'cause it looks like a cab. *Wssshhhtt!* They figure, Oh shit, that's just a taxi. I did that shit once in front of a brother. I did one of those funny things that only a Ferrari can do. He stopped me and said, '*Goddamn*, Miles, why do you do that shit?' I said, 'What would *you* do if you had this motherfucker?' And he said, 'Okay, go ahead.' The shit was outrageous, though. Only a Ferrari would do that shit. I love a Ferrari, man. The white cops, they all know me by now. Motherfuckers say, 'Oh, that's just him.'"

"That car," according to a musician friend, "was his way of saying to white people, 'I'm not supposed to have this, huh? I drive a $58,000 car,' a yellow Ferrari, he says, 'and white people look at me like I'm crazy. You must be an entertainer. I say no,' says Mr. Davis, with a wide-eyed glare. 'Are you Miles Davis?' 'No,' he says, he answers, 'I'm a janitor.'"

The effectiveness of Davis' persona depended on a clash of interests and perspectives, on a series of small but effective offenses, all of which implied that the lines between white and black, male and female, per-former and audience might need to be redrawn. In his routine, he often came to work at the last second, parking his sports car in front of the club—once even having it towed to the club when it wasn't running. He entered looking good, better dressed than his audience, dressed so fine yet speaking to no one, heading first to a phone, maybe to call his stock-broker to check on his portfolio. Then, lighting a cigarette, he walked resolutely to the stand, picked up his horn, and quickly moved into the first number, usually the softest of songs, a murmur of a ballad that would halt the cocktail blender, hush the audience, and freeze the whole room. Never for a second did he allow anyone to believe that he was there to entertain. He would never let himself be received as only a black musi-cian, but neither would he permit you to think of him as one who aspired to disappear into white society. (Ornette Coleman once trenchantly acknowledged that although Miles Davis *was* a black man, he lived like a white man.)

On one occasion he might come on with the hauteur of royalty; on another, he might appear as the artist of principled violence, like

Howard Roark in Ayn Rand's *The Fountainhead*. Or, turning his shyness into a weapon of strength, he could wilt the audience with the calculated understatement of a mime. "He was jazz's Marcel Marceau," critic Albert Goldman observed:

> With a single gesture he could signal an attitude; with a single note, precipitate a deep mood. Listening to him was like watching Balinese shadow puppets. Everything was a dark profile, a tenebrous outline, a stylized stretch-and-dip that closed into itself with ritualistic finality.

Sometimes that single note was all he would play. Shirley Horn recalls a night when she was opening for Miles at the Village Vanguard in the early 1960s:

> Miles was late. . . . The club was packed and people were spilling out onto the street. I felt bad for Max Gordon, the owner: He kept worrying, pacing back and forth, chewing on his cigar. Then suddenly Miles came in, grabbed his trumpet, and counted off a blues. He played just one note, and went back out the door! As he went past the bar, I asked him, "What's the matter Miles?" He said, "I've got to make a run. . . ." And he never came back that night. It was amazing: people sat there, saying to each other, "He only played one note!"

Whatever else it was, it made for good theater of a sort. Ralph Ellison, however, was one of the first to register his complaint against it:

> The result was a grim comedy of racial manners, with the musicians employing a calculated surliness and rudeness, treating the audience very much as many white merchants in poor Negro neighborhoods treat their customers, and the white audiences were shocked at first but learned quickly to accept such treatment as evidence of "artistic" temperament. Then comes a comic reversal. Today the white audience expects the rudeness as part of the entertainment. If it fails to appear the audience is disappointed.

But if things were not right, if the crowd hadn't read his press clippings, or if it wasn't a scene he knew how to control, he could come off as merely cranky, unhappy, bitchy, or an insufferable prick. And as the collective amnesia of the sixties washed away memories of the fifties, some aspects of his persona began to seem oddly dated, and his part like that of an out-of-it hero such as Mike Hammer, the confused, anachronistic private eye in Robert Aldrich's film, *Kiss Me Deadly*. The hero, Emerson said, is at last a bore. But nothing is more boring than a hero left over from an era that people have already forgotten.

Miles' early life stretched across several difficult eras, including the Depression and World War II. By the 1950s, America had become aware of subtle shifts in social and gender roles. Sociologists and psychiatrists were talking about men trapped in gray flannel suits, the age of conformity, the weakening of the superego, the other-directed person. The fear was that a new postwar economy was creating a society in which people were externally motivated, too well adjusted, too sociable. Scarcely concealed behind the jargon of social science was the fear that it was not women who were changing, but men, who were becoming soft, emotional, and expressive—that is, more like women rather than like the rational and task-oriented patriarchs who had built and protected America. More often than not, such ideas were dressed up as if they were the received wisdom of the ages, but their sources were transparently pop.

Elsewhere, *Playboy* magazine was wrestling with the same anxieties and assuaging them with a particular kind of male hedonism, promoting the good life for the single man: money, imported cars, circular beds, top-of-the-line stereos, chicks. And like *Esquire* before it, *Playboy* championed jazz, as a male music, to be sure, but the music of a certain kind of male, as the couture, decorations, and genderized illustrations of the jazz life in its pages made clear. Then there were the Beats, detested by *Playboy*, but sharing some of its fantasies by celebrating freedom, male bonding, drugs, art, and the hip lifestyle, one of their inspirations being the nightlife of the black jazz musician. On another continent, Jean-Paul Sartre was creating an existentialist ethics that pleaded for authenticity and argued against the self-deception of bad faith—the man who impersonates himself or who plays the role in which others cast him. Sartre stood against self-estrangement through the predominance of the Other, or allowing one's past to limit the possibilities of the future.

In the midst of this maelstrom of ideas, these crisscrossed, heightened sensibilities and exaggerated claims for male selfdom, in walked Miles: inner-directed to a fault and authentic as all hell, with the material aspirations of a *Playboy* man and the drive for self-expression of the Beats. There were many at the time who saw such a configuration in Davis, or projected it onto him. Norman Mailer, for one, was drawn to him as a natural existentialist, alienated because of his color, yet out there every night, grabbing his freedom, making choices, risking everything in his solos. Mailer's essay "The White Negro" was one of several in which he purported to understand blackness through the concept of the hip—of which Davis was the avatar.

Miles was becoming the coin of the realm, cock of the walk, good copy for the tabloids, and inspiration for literary imagination. Allusions to him could turn up anywhere. There was the muted post horn, the symbol of the Tristero, the society of isolates in Thomas Pynchon's *The Crying of Lot 49* (a group bound together in part by what they didn't know about each other and bearing the slogan, "Don't ever antagonize the horn"). Tributes to him sprang up in poems by Langston Hughes ("Trumpet Player: 52nd Street"), and Gregory Corso, a poet who put him on a level shoulder to shoulder with Jackson Pollock, Lana Turner, James Dean, Errol Flynn, and Botticelli.

The breakups of Miles' groups were discussed with the passion of baseball trades, and the radical stylistic shifts that inevitably followed were dissected like great movements in painting. Young people ostentatiously carried his albums to parties and sought out his clothing in the best men's stores. In person, his every action was observed and read for meaning. They watched in silence his whispered comments to sidemen on the bandstand, and when the musicians laughed, they laughed too, envious of that confidence. A discourse developed around him, one that bore inordinate weight in matters of race—Miles stories—narratives about his inner drives, his demons, his pain, and his ambition. Invariably, the stories climaxed with a short comment, crushingly delivered in a husky imitation of the man's voice, capped by some obscenity. Whenever Miles took one of his many respites from work and disappeared from public view, the stories spread in number and variety: he was injured, sick, fat, dead, or dying; he was unable to play; he was in jail; he was coming back with some breakthrough innovation that was more than his fans could bear.

He was the man.

CHAPTER SIX

He's like everybody else except that he's . . . there's a difference in ratio of the various things and when they occur and
all that.

GIL EVANS

Me, I'm basically a quarter horse.

MILES DAVIS

AS WITH ALL WORKS OF ART of the scale and the success of Davis' and Gil
Evans' recording of *Sketches of Spain*, many people have a legitimate
claim to have been part of its origins. George Avakian, for one. His job at
Columbia also involved producing records for an international market,
and he regularly received 78 rpm singles from Columbia's overseas affili-
ates. In the 1950s, ethnic recordings of music were hard to find outside
of specialty shops, and even most of them were limited to music of one
language, nationality, or ethnic group. Listening to some of the records
that turned up on his desk, Avakian got the idea of having Gil Evans do
arrangements of music from all over the world, something like Cyril
Scott's early twentieth-century orientalist composition "Lotus Land."
He began giving Gil some of these records, such as an album of flamenco
songs called *La Niña de los Peines* by the great Andalusian singer Pastora
Pavón.

When Beverly Bentley came back from a film shoot in Spain in 1958,
she brought Miles the *Anthology of Flamenco*, an album of guitar music.
But at around the same time, Frances Davis says that though he didn't
want to go, she took Miles to see Roberto Iglesias' company of Spanish
dancers. The fire and physicality of the flamenco reached him, and on

the way home, they stopped at the Colony record store on Broadway, where "he bought every flamenco record in the place." And there were other possible sources for some of the music in *Sketches of Spain*: the *saeta* (a religious song) could have been heard in a processional of *penetentes* in Orson Welles' 1955 film *Mr. Arkadin*. An even more likely source, since it was produced under Avakian's direction, was *The Columbia Library of Folk and Primitive Music: Spain*, a collection of folk music (including *saeta* and panpipes), assembled by Alan Lomax for the Columbia World Library of Folk and Primitive Music.

But even without specific sources, Spanish culture was everywhere in the late 1950s, from the bullfighter posters in Greenwich Village apartments to the continuing buzz about Ernest Hemingway's *Death in the Afternoon*. Federico García Lorca's poetry had been translated by Langston Hughes, and García Lorca's essays on the folklore of southern Spain and of Spanish Gypsies resonated with the 1950s craze for Spanish guitar and flamenco dancing. (Miles, like Charlie Parker and many other jazz musicians, was a great fan of Andrés Segovia the classical guitarist whose recordings brought Spanish music to a broad audience in the United States and Europe.) It was García Lorca who first took the composer Manuel de Falla to hear folksongs that the composer later worked into his ballet *The Three-Cornered Hat* (and from which Gil Evans in turn borrowed for his "Blues for Pablo"). And it was the poet's essays on deep song (*cante jondo*) that fed a widespread belief that in some way, Gypsy songs could be equated with the blues. (One of the singers García Lorca most admired and wrote about was Pastora Pavón.) It was while García Lorca was studying at Columbia University in 1929, making nightly jaunts to Harlem clubs to hear jazz and blues, that he popularized the Spanish folk concept of *duende*—the capacity to convey great emotion to an audience—an ability shared by both matadors and performers of flamenco. *Duende*, like the blues, was personified as a demonic spirit capable of troublemaking and bringing with it irrationality, earthiness, a strong sense of death. And yet if you sought it out and struggled with it, it could help to communicate great emotional art. *Duende* was the inexplicable in art, the source of what García Lorca called "the black sounds," the power of music. (As if on cue, critic Kenneth Tynan declared in 1962 that Miles Davis had *duende*.)

Jazz had already mirrored the Spanish craze. In 1956, for example, Lionel Hampton recorded *Jazz Flamenco* in Barcelona, with some Spanish musicians added to his own band. Charles Mingus recorded *Tijuana Moods* with a singer and dancer in 1957, and even as Miles and Gil were working on what they were then calling their "Spanish concerto," J. J. Johnson had accepted a commission from the Monterey Jazz Festival to compose "El Camino Real."

When they began to think about recording *Sketches of Spain*, Gil and Miles pored over scores by Spanish composers and spent hours listening to folk recordings. "Miles started reading into Spanish culture and the role blacks had played in it," Frances said. "He had big ideas for this, and it could have gone on and on." Davis had discovered the creole nature of Spain, the Moorish connection, and the black history of southern Spain; and whether he read Lorca, histories of Spain, or even the jazz scholar Ernest Borneman's *An Anthropologist Looks at Jazz,* he would have seen that other side of black history, one that roots the connection between Africa and the Americas much more deeply, through a prior meeting in Spain in the eighth-century. Davis and Evans both surely knew about the Spanish tinge, the element of Africa-by-way-of-Spain that Jelly Roll Morton insisted was always part of true jazz.

With the departure of Avakian and Cal Lampley from Columbia, Irving Townsend and Teo Macero were both assigned to the production of *Sketches of Spain*, though Teo did the work. Following this, he was to be Miles' producer for the next fifteen years. Macero was a trained musician who had paid his way through a B.A. and M.A. at Juilliard by working in the school's sound engineering department, where he collaborated with experimental composer Edgard Varèse on *Poème électronique*, a three-track tape of electronic music that was played through hundreds of loudspeakers at the Brussels Exposition in 1958. (It was Varèse whom Charlie Parker had sought out as a teacher in the late 1940s.) Macero had taught at the New York Institute for the Education of the Blind for several years and received two Guggenheim Fellowships, but he was also a talented saxophonist who performed and recorded with people like the Sandole Brothers, Charles Mingus, and Teddy Charles, then some the most advanced thinkers in jazz. Avakian hired him because of his musical range and his engineering knowledge, and when he began to work with Davis, he was perhaps the only producer in the country who could make it possible for Miles to take his music where he was going. An odd pairing, to be sure—the two of them arguing, joking, cursing, conspiring, coming to blows—and all the while developing a hard-won, sometimes bitter respect for each other. Miles was hardly the only big-name artist that Teo would ever work with, but he was the one who would keep him in front of the music world as it changed. And in Teo, Miles would get a producer, editor, and advocate, all functions that would be sorely needed with Davis' and Evans' *Sketches of Spain*.

The first thing agreed on for the album was Joaquín Rodrigo's *Concierto de Aranjuez*, at the time perhaps the most popular piece in the guitar-and-orchestra repertoire. Miles first heard a recording of it through Los Angeles bassist Joe Mondragon, who suggested that Davis could play the guitar part on trumpet. After Gil heard it, he copied it off the record and rescored it. "We didn't start out to make an all-Spanish record, but it gradually worked into one," he said. Evans used only the adagio, the second movement of the *Concierto* (with Davis' trumpet substituting for the guitar, brass and reeds replacing the original strings), and an added middle section that Evans wrote, which had the feel of an orchestral improvisation. Although there are some quasi-guitar effects here and there, Davis' trumpet is more vocal than instrumental, the tightly choked effects showing just how much he had immersed himself in the music of southern Spain. And on some of the other pieces on the album—"Will o' the Wisp" from de Falla's *El Amor Brujo*, and "Saeta"— the trumpet is pointedly substituting for vocal parts. Trumpeter Marvin Stamm remarked that Davis' playing was so personalized on this recording that the listener never thought about what instrument he was playing. Evans had spent much of his life writing for singers, and his sensitivity in creating settings for voice is evident in the record.

> Now that was the hardest thing for me to do on *Sketches of Spain*: to play the parts on the trumpet where someone was supposed to be singing, especially when it was ad-libbed, like most of the time. The difficulty came when I tried to do parts that were in between the words and stuff when the singer is singing. Because you've got all those Arabic scales up there, black African scales that you can hear. And they modulate and bend and twist and snake around. . . . What really made it so hard to do was that I could only do it once or twice. If you do a song like that three or four times you lose that feeling you want to get there. . . . After we finished working on *Sketches of Spain*, I didn't have *nothing* inside of me. I was drained of all emotion and I didn't want to hear that music after I got through playing all that hard shit. Gil said, "Let's go listen to the tapes." I said, "*You* go listen to the tapes."

This was not artistic overstatement. On March 10, 1960, they completed four of the five pieces that appeared on the record, plus one not used, and various outtakes. And on this day, one of the pieces they recorded was "Solea," on which Miles played a ten-minute trumpet solo, one perhaps longer than anyone had ever attempted on record.

With me, if I read it and play it, it's not going to have that much feeling in it. But if I just listen to it and play it, it's going to have a lot of feeling in it. What I found I had to do in *Sketches of Spain* was to read the score a couple of times, listen to it a couple of times more, *then* play it. For me, it was just about knowing what it is, and then I could play it.

As always, Evans and Davis picked the musicians for these sessions with care, drawing on new people if they thought they could bring something to the recording, but mostly sticking with musicians they trusted and whom Evans knew as good readers and interpreters of his work. Miles was especially involved in the choices this time, holding out for a few people he wanted. He used his own rhythm section (though without the piano), and some of the musicians from the *Birth of the Cool* sessions were back. Lead trombonist Frank Rehak, who had been on *Miles Ahead* and *Porgy and Bess*, was one of them. When Rehak told Gil that he wasn't available for *Sketches of Spain*, he received a call at 3:30 A.M.: "'Hey, mother, what are you doing to me?' It was Miles . . . and I said, 'Man, there's no way I can do these dates,' and he said, 'Listen, I'll give you double money, I'll give you whatever you need.'" Rehak explained that it was not a question of money. He was already booked for a number of sessions, and canceling would be bad for his career. "We haggled and haggled for about fifteen minutes, and he called me several different kinds of names, and there was nothing I could do." He was available only three hours on one day, three on another, and a few hours on a third. At seven the next morning, Teo Macero called Rehak, wanting to know what he had on Miles, since he was refusing to do the record without him. In the end, nineteen musicians and several engineers all had their schedules changed to fit Rehak's on the date.

In his autobiography, Miles says that at the beginning of the November 1959 sessions in which the *Concierto* was recorded, they were using classically trained trumpet players who stuck too closely to the score. They changed the trumpet section, but the jazz players were "turning blue" from the difficulty of the parts. Gil then reorchestrated the parts to get a better feel from the music. Lead trumpet Bernie Glow was another musician whom Miles had insisted on, because he relied on Glow to give the whole band a sound with which he felt comfortable. "Miles loved Glow's lead trumpet on 'Will o' the Wisp,'" Marvin Stamm recalled. There was a solo part, high, to be played in a Harmon mute, and an improvised solo. At the end of a long day, Miles suggested that Bernie take the muted solo. 'Bernie sounds more like me than me.'"

For the percussion on the *Concierto*, Miles wanted "the snare drum to sound like paper tearing, those little tight rolls. I had heard that sound back in St. Louis at the Veiled Prophet Parades with those marching legit drummers they had back then. They sounded like Scottish bands. But they're African rhythms, because that's where the bagpipes come from, too, Africa." To get a freer sound from the drums, they turned to jazz drummers Elvin Jones and Jimmy Cobb, later adding Latin percussionist Jose Mangual.

Miles had in mind, as he often did, a mix of musicians who could read music well and play with "no feeling or a little feeling, and some others who could play with real feeling." The idea was to approach the music somewhat as a black preacher approaches the Bible for a sermon—to know the text through reading, then to know it by ear and voice, and finally to play it from the heart.

At least five sessions had to be canceled before they actually began recording because Miles was sick with the flu, and on the first day they were in the studio—Tuesday, November 10—he was still too sick to play. Most of the day was used for rehearsals to find the right tempos for the adagio section. Only near the end did Miles arrive, just as the orchestra was recording a small part of the score.

Nat Hentoff was there on that second day of recording, and he described the setup of the orchestra as being a point of contention, with Fred Plaut, Columbia's chief classical recording engineer, wanting the drums closer to the reeds and Macero wanting them nearer the brass. Teo got his way, and the musicians were spread across nine microphones, with Davis, the French horns, and the bass in the middle. Miles paced around the engineer's booth, nervously muttering to himself: "I always manage to put my foot in it. I always manage to try something I can't do. I'm going to call myself on the phone someday and tell myself to shut up." Throughout the session, Miles sipped vodka and complained that he hadn't been able to eat, and that he was hearing the music in his sleep, so there was nothing left to do but drink: "Me and Buddy Bolden," he laughed, alluding to the New Orleans trumpeter's decline into alcoholism and madness.

It was a day filled with takes, the best of which was twelve minutes long, but the engineers were already complaining about the edits needed. "This," said Fred Plaut, "is a lifetime project." Under the best of circumstances, recordings like this one are difficult, a balancing act of soloist, conductor, musicians, producer, and engineers. But with Gil Evans conducting, there were other problems: the music was hard to read, written too high, too hard to count, and Gil was so scrupulous in his work that it was a long time into the production before he heard anything he liked. For Miles, the discipline of having to work up to the same level take after take, maintaining emotional continuity throughout, was something like the experience of acting in films. But everyone seemed ecstatic with the results, and as the tapes were played back, there was a giddy atmosphere in the booth. "This," Gil pointed out, "is where the heroine is crying for the dead bullfighter." "Really?" said a visitor. "No," Gil joked, "it's just an old Spanish vamp."

> "That melody," Miles was still marveling at the piece, "is so strong that the softer you play it, the stronger it gets, and the stronger you play it, the weaker it gets." "Yes," says Gil, "it's a distilled melody. If you lay on it too hard, you don't have it." [A melody so strong, Miles also said, that "if you tried to play bebop on it, you'd wind up being a hip cornball."]
>
> "When Gil and I start on an album," Miles was relaxing, "we don't know how it's going to wind up. It just goes on and on out there. Gil," he turned to Evans, "our next record date will be silence."

Once again, the recording went over budget, and Macero had to call the president of Columbia for permission to have extra sessions. After it was approved, they did seventeen sessions in all. "Gil always wanted 'four more bars,'" said Macero, "but I finally ended the session because I thought it sounded like we had them." Miles said that he never listened to any of the takes again until the record was released.

After the record went on sale, Teo Macero got a call from Rodrigo's music publisher in Paris saying that Columbia should not have recorded it in a jazz version, and threatening to kill the project. Macero told them to wait until they saw the royalty statements before they objected.

In recent years, some have criticized the Davis-Evans collaborations as mood music, easy listening, elevator music, as mid-cult schlock better suited to TV commercials. And there were those who had similar qualms when the records were issued almost fifty years ago. An uneasiness seemed to be rising even then among some jazz fans about these recordings since, in their view, Evans would dilute the genius of Davis' contribution. Though that complaint is not so often heard today, there is reason to believe it is not far beneath the surface; the symbolism of black and white in the mythology of jazz is never very subtle or well considered and is always corrosive. What Davis had done here was to go well beyond jazz territory, in both his own playing and the company he kept. He had been moving this way since his days with Parker. What complicated it all was that he also kept a small group at work—a *jazz* group by anyone's definition—which apparently had little to do with the Evans-Davis collaboration.

Miles took the quintet to Europe in 1960, and when they played the Olympia in Paris on March 21, Coltrane was the unknown quantity for the audience. But he played as if they had been listening to him for years and held nothing back, unafraid to work the same startling phrase or figure over and over, and eager to splinter and shred notes, oblivious to the slowly growing hiss rising from an aggitated continental crowd.

The next night, in Stockholm, the quintet had been advertised as a sextet, as Miles had been trying out vibraphonist Buddy Montgomery off and on for the last month, but Montgomery did not appear on stage. Coltrane continued to push into new directions, playing even longer solos. Miles had given him the freedom and space to explore his own ideas, and he was taking it. Though the audience was more reserved than the French, many were angry about what they heard. "Coltrane didn't play one note that swung," a critic complained the next day.

In late April in Philadelphia, Coltrane performed for the last time with Davis, and Miles suddenly grabbed the mike and whispered that Coltrane would be leaving the band. The audience was stunned. It was unclear whether they were shocked more by the announcement that a hometown musician was leaving the premier band, or by the fact that Miles was actually speaking to them. Within two months, Miles had replaced Coltrane with Sonny Stitt.

When Davis' upcoming tour of the United Kingdom in September, 1960, was first announced, the British promoter told the media that Miles would not be available to photographers, press, or fans during the tour and that he would be traveling with a bodyguard. The newspapers bristled, and when Miles heard about the announcement, he said, "What do they think I am, the Congolese Ambassador or something? I'd just as soon call off the tour." As he had often done before, Leonard Feather mounted an apologia for Davis in the British music magazine *Melody Maker* under the headline, "Miles Davis Angry? Only If Provoked." By the time the band appeared at the first performance in Britain, the audience had fretted itself into a state, and what they expected to see was Davis the angry black man stalking the stage. In a review of Miles' performance at the Gaumont, Hammersmith, Humphrey Lyttelton observed that "whenever Miles turned to stroll offstage, his slightly hunched shoulders positively radiating disdain, a tremor went through the audience.

When the flow of improvisation was suddenly interrupted by some impatient by-play with the mute, we quaked in our seats. And on the single occasion in the second house on Saturday when he flicked a smile in the direction of Sonny Stitt, a nervous titter rustled through the house as tension suddenly slackened. On the steps afterwards, theory and conjecture were lobbed to and fro. Was it genuine? Does he really hate us all so much? Or is it just another presentation gimmick?

A well-known trumpet player himself in the United Kingdom, Lyttelton was suspicious of Davis' stage business: "All that angry scratching out and screwing in of a mute which seemed perfectly secure in the first place . . . and the recurrent trouble with the right ear, calling for some ferocious prodding with the forefinger and despairing gestures to the rhythm section." Lyttelton's theory was that improvisation was so easy for Davis that he had become indifferent to the melody-solo-melody formula of bebop and simply wandered offstage out of boredom.

Harold Davidson, his tour manager in London, was also Paul Robeson's agent. Miles had first become interested in Robeson from reading about him in the *Daily Worker* and playing benefit concerts in the Audubon Ballroom in Harlem put on for the *Worker* by the dramatist Douglas Turner Ward. After Miles' performance at Finsbury Park in Astoria, Robeson came back to the dressing room: "I like the way your band sounds—the modal music." Miles was impressed that he had understood what they were doing musically, and later he exploded when Davidson told him that he could get Robeson a lot more work if he would just shut his mouth about politics.

Hiring Sonny Stitt to replace Coltrane was something of a risk. Not that he couldn't play, Lord knows: Stitt was a contemporary of Charlie Parker and sounded like him, though he claimed to have found his own way into bebop without Bird. Stitt was a gladiator of the road, able to play with anyone, anywhere. He was also much overrecorded and had long ago found his role in music, and was now typecast. Stitt was known as a heavy drinker, but drunk or sober he played the same—professionally, but not always with fire. Without Coltrane, Miles was going to have to carry some weight this time out.

No rehearsals were held for Stitt ("Miles just gave me one record to listen to"—probably *Kind of Blue*), and he had the same trouble with modes that a lot of other musicians had, playing them as if they were pop tunes in fixed keys, often failing to negotiate the modal shifts that were the whole point of playing them. Miles gave him some featured numbers of his own, such as "Stardust," on which he could play in his own style. As usual, Miles walked off the stage, leaving Stitt alone with the band to smile and graciously acknowledge the applause.

Davis was by now a success by even the most cynical of show business standards. Each of his three records with Evans quickly sold over 120,000 copies, he filled concert halls, articles were written about him from one end of the media spectrum to the other—from *Ebony* to *Esquire*, the *Chicago Defender* to the *New York Times*, from men's magazines like *Oui* to culture journals like *Horizon*. He had become a big property for Columbia, even if he was not paid accordingly. Still, the record business does not run by standards that the rest of the business world would recognize as rational, even if profitable. The system of advances, where recording artists are given money against which certain production costs will be charged, can be compared only to sharecropping. It encourages friction and distrust between artist and company, with each threatening the other. Columbia gave Davis advances against sales of records, as well as interest-bearing loans, and the advances often went to pay for the loans. It was confusing at best, and at worst a constant source of irritation on both sides. Typical is this memo from producer Irving Townsend, then in Hollywood, to Goddard Lieberson, president of Columbia, on November 8, 1960:

> I talked to Miles Davis this morning and he asked if his current earning status has improved enough so that he can get another loan. . . . I pointed out to him that from our standpoint the only way this financing makes sense was for him to record and that the album pacing I originally worked out with him of one large band per year and a couple of small group albums would make the earnings rise on Columbia and justify future loans much more readily. He promised to do something about this immediately.
>
> I would appreciate your having his situation reviewed in New York and contacting him if a loan is possible.

"Davis," Townsend said, "had asked for $15,000," but "would accept $10,000 with only a mild oath."

It fell to the producers to explain, interpret, or shield the artists from the executive, and vice versa. This memo of several months later (February 16, 1961) finds Irving Townsend explaining Miles' slow productivity to Goddard Lieberson:

> Apparently we are all involved with our poll-winning friend Miles Davis. . . . I think the best way to handle him is by keeping in touch mutually with what we hear. . . . Miles tells me that he plans an album in March with Gil Evans. I hope this is true. He also is willing for me to record him out here in Hollywood on location. . . .
>
> Miles' delay in recording is based on nothing else but his feeling that only when he has something new to say musically should he make a record, but without at least 2 albums a year from Miles his earning capacity will not continue.

Back in New York, Miles and Frances were married on December 21, 1960, and Miles seemed happy. His parents liked her, her parents were pleased, he was proud of her. (Irene said that he introduced Frances to her by telling her how beautiful she was and singling out her features for praise.) *Ebony* featured Miles with his sister and brother in the January 1961 issue, the first time an African American magazine had recognized his accomplishments.

Sonny Stitt left the quintet after a December 8 performance at the Howard Theater in Washington, D.C., and as Miles, Frances, and the children were leaving for Illinois to spend Christmas, Miles had to hustle to find another saxophonist. When they opened on December 26 for a two-week stay at the Cloister in Chicago, it was tenor saxophonist Hank Mobley, another Philadelphia musician, whom he chose to as a replacement. Though Mobley lasted only a year with Miles, there was a hipness to his playing that reinforced Davis' popularity in black communities across America. Mobley had come up through Art Blakey's Jazz Messengers and Horace Silver's Quintet, and established himself as a central player in the Blue Note Records school of hard-edged post-bebop. And since he had already recorded with the members of Miles' rhythm section, the public was familiar with him. There was no shock factor with Mobley as with Coltrane's angularity and hyperspeed excursions, no kind-of-floating modal experiments. This band played for the rhythm, reestablished its blues credentials, and was not ashamed to swear allegiance to hard bop, that catch-all term that if nothing else signaled blackness. It was as if "Freddie Freeloader," that funky enigma of a tune that sat strangely in the middle of *Kind of Blue*'s gravity-free universe, had come back to take control. Pianist Wynton Kelly was back as well. Where Bill Evans' piano aesthetic leaned toward harmonic ambiguity, with some chords seemingly unrelated to what had come before, Kelly's chords were dramatically well made, clearly linked, and always resolved.

Miles took his new group into the studio in New York for three days in March, 1961, to record an album that was to be called *Someday My Prince Will Come*. Davis had decided that liner notes were unnecessary: "I got rid of all them stupid liner notes which I had been trying to do for a long time. See, I never thought there was nothing nobody could say about an album of mine," and as a result, some of the titles on this record were puzzling. "Pfrancing" played with Frances' first name, but when it was recorded again a month later, it was known as "No Blues." The same thing happened to "Teo" when it was changed to "Neo." "Drad-Dog" was Goddard Lieberson's first name spelled backward. Without notes for each cut of the record, there was no indication of who was playing where, and the listing of two tenor saxophonists, Hank Mobley and John Coltrane, and two drummers confused some listeners (Coltrane had been called in for just two tunes, and Philly Joe appeared in place of Jimmy Cobb only on one tune).

It was a relatively quiet session, leaning heavily toward Miles' introspective side, and despite the shifts in personnel, it produced a consistent, single-minded album. Mobley fashioned some fine blues-inflected tenor solos, but when you hear guest John Coltrane (on what turned out to be his last recording with Davis), especially on the modal "Teo" and on the alternate take of the title song on the reissue CD, it's understandable why Davis was shaky about recording without his old group: Coltrane plays with a confidence and a bravura that few other saxophonists could have mustered at that time, and he lifts the band on the two tracks he appears on. And when Philly Joe Jones sits in on "Blues No. 2," playing with his usual clarity and volatility, you know that this new working group of Davis' heard on the other tracks was not quite up to his best. Still, it was an accessible album, and one on which Miles played with grace and emotion.

Davis continued to press Columbia for more and more control over his records and asked them to release some of his material for jukebox play just as Prestige had done. In a memo from Irving Townsend to Teo Macero on April 4, 1961, however, Townsend doubted that there was that much sales potential, but suggested that some tunes from *Kind of*

Blue and *Jazz Track* might be good to release. Miles also insisted that Frances's picture be on the cover this time, with only a small red silhouette of himself in the upper right corner. (Throughout the photo shoot, Miles kept calling in with advice for Frances and the photographer, and when she wasn't paid a modeling fee by Columbia, he pushed her to ask for one until she got it.) A black model on a mainstream recording company's record was almost unheard of at the time, and Miles' efforts were a significant victory. But with Miles, the personal was always political, and for the rest of his career, his private life usually found its way onto his album covers one way or another.

Columbia threw its weight behind *Someday My Prince Will Come* when it was released, taking out full-page ads in mainstream publications, and the public reception, especially to the ballads on which Miles played, was warm.

He felt it coming on for months—an occasional twinge in his leg or hip, or small pains of the sort that people dismiss with jokes about getting old. He redoubled his efforts at training in the gym, but the pain only became worse. When the ache in his left hip became so severe that it made walking difficult, he had tests done for arthritis. The diagnosis was that his distress was caused by sickle-cell anemia, made worse by exercise, which had further reduced his oxygen and blood flow. He called it "the black disease," perhaps in both bitterness and pride, but he avoided complaining and tried to resist the symptoms, though he often became depressed, and along with medication he took for the pain, he began drinking more heavily and increased his cocaine use.

Columbia set up Davis' first live recording session at the Blackhawk in San Francisco during a two-week stay at the club in April. Live recording was pioneered by jazz record companies, but it was still a difficult and expensive proposition to move equipment into place and get good sound recording. On this occasion, the small size of the room required them to locate the recording equipment next door in the 211 Club. By the time the taping was complete, they decided to issue two LPs of the music recorded, an investment that showed Columbia's commitment to Davis.

Critic Martin Williams heard Miles' playing on these records as an effort to "reinterpret the whole range of sound of the Duke Ellington trumpets of 1939—Cootie Williams' plunger and Rex Stewart's half-valves—in a highly personal way, on a simply open or Harmon-muted horn. But more than anyone else . . . I hear . . . the same king of exuberant, humorous, committed, self-determined, and forceful joy in Miles Davis that there is in Louis Armstrong."

When bands are on the road, away from families and lovers, some musicians regress to self-destructive habits that, if not restrained by the leader, can send them spiraling off in different directions. Miles had sometimes played the role of tyrant on the road, but perhaps because he was in poor health, he ran this band rather casually, and Mobley recalled that Miles kept his distance, leaving them to their own devices, especially when they played in Los Angeles:

> I remember me and Philly Joe got to the airport five minutes before the plane left—we were both wandering all over town. . . . Wynton Kelly, he's probably over at that hotel partying . . . him and Paul Chambers. Miles is off talking to Boris Karloff—he and Miles lived in the same house down the strip in Hollywood. . . . We had to send for Harold (Lovett) the lawyer, to take care of business, tidy up the tab—after six nights, Wynton had about a $50 tab. Paul must've had $50. Miles must've had a couple hundred. We hung out, the four of us, and sometimes we'd run into Miles on the street.

One of the places where Miles was spending time in Los Angeles was saxophonist Paul Horn's. The gatherings at Horn's were fabled in Los Angeles, in part because he had a swimming pool, and musicians regularly dropped by for a swim. Miles, for example, first showed up there at 8:30 one morning and began to come back almost every day. Then the rest of his band followed, and Miles did the barbecuing. Daily seminars followed as Horn explained:

> Sitting with me at my piano, Miles got into music, showing me different voicings. He taught me how to work with fourths and augmented fourths, strange-sounding chord intervals that enable a soloist to step outside of conventional harmonic frameworks. In this context, any note is right, and no note sounds wrong. McCoy Tyner later used these intervals with Coltrane. . . . I always wondered how Impressionist voicings and tech-

niques like Ravel's could be incorporated into jazz. . . . Suddenly, there it was—Ravel with a rhythm section.

Miles felt strongly enough about Horn's musicianship that he urged Columbia Records to sign him, and in 1961 *The Sound of Paul Horn* was released. "'He plays the horn the way it should be played,' says Miles Davis," was emblazoned across the top of the record cover.

One of the things that musicians found fascinating about Davis was the seriousness with which he treated music, and though he was as sparing in his comments as he was in his playing, his observations were always memorable. In Horn's own liner notes to his album *Music of India*, for example, he says that Miles told him that "most jazz musicians, they're playing all the time." The challenge, Miles said, "was *not* to play all the notes you could play, but to wait, hesitate, let space become a part of the configuration." Hank Mobley also recounted some of Miles' minimalist and cryptic instructions:

> Miles pulled my coat to a few things. He suggested just straight ahead, hit every note on the head—it's hard to explain. It means, you can play two or three ways: you can play romantic-type, the big sound, like that; you can play mathematical, like my man Lee Konitz used to do with Warne Marsh; and the other is similar to Trane, where you hit everything sharp. Every time you try to get an idea across, you don't labor, play behind the beat, or anything like that: you *hit* it, and bring something out of it.

With increased earnings from the road and the money he'd borrowed from Columbia, Miles paid over $100,000 for a five-story former Russian Orthodox church at 312 West 77th Street in Manhattan and had it remodeled into a duplex for Frances and himself, with ten rooms on three other floors eventually to be rented out as apartments. Some of them were kept for now for their four children: Cheryl, Gregory, Miles IV, and seven-year-old Jean-Pierre (Frances' child from her previous marriage). Over the past ten years, the three Davis children had lived with Miles' mother in Chicago, or with Miles or Irene in Brooklyn or Manhattan. With the stability that Frances had brought to Miles' life, the children stayed on with Frances and Miles, while Irene moved to St. Louis.

Between the street and the house was a four-foot-high brick wall, where a bodyguard could often be seen standing. The roof was red tile, and there was a massive front door with a dome over it. Inside the duplex, the doors had been replaced by vaulted passages; the walls, made of stone and wood, were curved, since Miles detested corners and believed that "haunts" could hide in them. He said that the floors and steps were spaced so that he could see Frances' legs wherever he was, and were covered with animal skins or, in the sunken living room, with a lush blue carpet. The furniture in the living room was blocklike, with no legs. The one table had a large mobile sculpture on it that seemed to change on its own every so often. A stereo system was hidden in the walls. There was a sign that said "No Visitors" and a photo of John Coltrane on the wall. In the back was a kitchen with a large wooden table, floor-to-ceiling windows, and glass doors overlooking a small backyard with a thatched-roof gazebo.

Upstairs, there were more arches and many alcoves, a music room with a built-in spinet piano, his awards (*Down Beat* for best trumpeter in 1957, 1958, 1959, second best in 1951 and 1952; Jazz Critics Poll 1955, 1958, 1959; Four Roses Society of Jazz Chapter Award; New York Jazz Festival Award, 1958) and gold records, a bedroom with a sunken fan-shaped bed, an oversize blue-tiled bathtub, and an enormous closet. Two television sets were on day and night. Writer Kenneth Tynan described the house this way:

> Miles lives in a noisy, rambling, duplex apartment on West 77th Street in New York. With its marble-tiled floors, leopard-skin rugs, abstract paintings, white brick walls and proliferating electronic gadgets, it might be the hunting lodge of some preternaturally hip Swedish grandee. An Italian greyhound named Milo prances around the place, and upstairs there are turtles.

Frances recalled attending the closing on the house as the second big shock in their relationship:

> There I was at the round table at the signing, and the papers didn't come around to me. He said, "Oh, but you'll always be taken care of." I said, "Well, yeah, I heard that when I left *West Side*." And I didn't receive anything, you know, except for things for the house. It was our own design, and we both had excellent taste . . . but nothing belonged to *me*.

In the spring, some fifty people gathered in that sunken living room for a meeting of musicians and critics sponsored by *Metronome* magazine. The idea was to give the musicians a chance to ask questions of the critics for a change and to reach some rapprochement between performers and the critical establishment. Miles had offered his house as a site for the meeting. When Cannonball Adderley began the discussion by ask-ing, "What is jazz?" Miles was heard to mutter, "Oh, Jesus Christ . . ." as he strolled around the crowd gathered in the room. Nat Hentoff attempted to answer, but Cannonball interrupted by asking the critics—in vain, as it turned out—to rate each other, the way they rated musi-cians. The writers quickly bogged down while explaining the differences between journalists, writers, and critics, with only Martin Williams, Lou Gottlieb, and Gunther Schuller being elevated finally to the status of critics. Out from the wings again, Miles called, "Nat, when did [Schuller] become a critic? Remember J. J. [Johnson]—we gave him his first gig? . . . I gave him a record date in 1949 and created a monster." When no one paid any attention, Miles snorted, amused, "You're in my own house and you're ignoring me."

The talk continued, with Gerry Mulligan complaining about British writer Stanley Dance's claim that the popular poll winners in jazz were usually white ("since when is being Caucasian an asset in the jazz busi-ness?"). Miles continued to move along the sidelines, the somewhat gracious host, attending to drinks and snacks and chortling stage asides.

By the late 1950s Miles had become a much-sought-after subject for interviews, but he eluded most journalists, developing a mode of response that was uncooperative at best, and at worst dismissive, hos-tile, and well beyond rude. The only serious conversations he had with journalists were with Nat Hentoff, Leonard Feather, and Ralph J. Glea-son, all of whom defended him against other journalists. Then in 1960, Marc Crawford, an African American writer, launched his own defense of Davis in "Miles Davis, Mean Man of Music," written for *Tan*, a black-oriented magazine. But lacking an interview with Miles, he was forced to depend on quotes from Davis' friends and associates. Later in the year, he managed an interview with Miles and members of his family and published it as "Miles Davis: Evil Genius of Jazz" in *Ebony*.

In 1961, the young writer Alex Haley pitched the idea of an interview with Miles Davis to several magazines, including *Show*, and the short-lived *Show Business Illustrated*, for one of their projected series of "Can-did Conversations" with stars. He told the editors that it was part of his campaign to get people to stop "cussing Miles long enough to under-stand *why* he's sometimes truculent and that he's a beautiful human." And if they liked it, Haley said he could do other interviews—with TV talk show host Jack Paar, for instance. *SBI* bought the idea, and by the end of December, Haley submitted a draft. Unfortunately, the magazine folded before the article could be published, but since it was a Hugh Hefner magazine, the manuscript was kept in *Playboy*'s files. Later that year, its editors began to consider a monthly interview feature, and Haley's interview was pulled out again. Hefner was intrigued by what he saw as a conversation between two black men "about racial discord in America," and he sent Haley back to expand on what the editors regarded as a "partial manuscript." In a letter to *Playboy*'s editors, Haley described the circumstances of his first interview with Davis: Miles at first resisted him ("I don't trust people with pencils"), then grudgingly agreed to the interview and to being taped. He quickly grew impatient with the process, however, his answers becoming shorter and more difficult to hear as they went along. Haley then gave up on the idea of a formal interview and began to follow Davis through his daily routine: working the jump rope, the punching bags, and the rowing machine in his basement gym; showering; taking calls from friends, lawyer, and stockbroker; ordering groceries from the market ("I want them cutlets thin, now, thin! Why you need to know what I'm going to *do* with the damn tomatoes? Just send me six good tomatoes."). Stereo speakers throughout the house played Duke Ellington's "Suite Thursday" ("Ain't nobody writing like the Duke") or Isaac Stern's rendering of Ravel's *Tzigane*—Miles had been playing that one for three days straight ("I really *dig* this cat's sound. He's got a hell of an act!"). Miles "bedeviled" his daughter, Cheryl, and his wife, Frances, according to Haley. He roughhoused with his sons and coached them in boxing, called his doctor to arrange a vitamin shot, and when he was answered by a recorded message, yelled, "Stay the fuck in your damn office," into the phone. He watched a western on TV and swore at the villain, practiced the ballad "I'm Old Fashioned" on a guitar Gil Evans had just given him, and checked the stock market reports in the newspaper with the help of a *Standard & Poor's Stock Guide*. Up in his bedroom, he grabbed two greentinted Martin trumpets and took turns running rapid chromatic scales from the bottom to the top C ("I'm straight long as I'm able to run the scale like that"). He used the same battered silver mouthpiece on both horns: "This mouthpiece been everywhere I been—it's been mad, it's been high, it's been sick, it's been broke. I had it in my hand in my pocket when me and Frances got married."

When Haley asked for a second interview, Miles would agree to it only if Haley was willing to spar with him at the gym—and Haley made an easy target. But he persevered, and his notes began to accumulate:

Miles had very few jazz records, and only half of the ones he himself had recorded ("I can't stand most of them. You know, something I did and hear it later on, I see how it could of been better and feel like slapping myself"). There were *Ballets from Broadway*, the cast album to *Porgy and Bess*, Wagner's *Tristan und Isolde*, Khachaturian's *Spartacus*, *The Columbia Library of Folk and Primitive Music: Spain*, and John Lewis's *Improvised Meditations and Excursions*. The books on the shelves included some D. H. Lawrence novels, Katherine Dunham's autobiography, *Touch of Innocence*, Morton Thompson's *The Cry and the Covenant*, Freud's *A General Introduction to Psychoanalysis*, and the Bible, presumably reflecting his new wife's interests, since Miles said he never read books.

Haley's notebooks go on: Dizzy Gillespie is a genius; Miles loves Bill Evans and asks to have Evans' group play the Village Vanguard opposite his own; he likes singer Bob Dorough ("a progressive Hoagy Carmichael"), Dave Brubeck ("but not his group"); he is still angry with Charlie Parker ("They've never written what he did. You couldn't even print what he did!"); he is generous with his money (he gave his lawyer a Jaguar, his father a Mercedes); he has no time for the National Association for the Advancement of Colored People (when they asked him to attend a $100-a-plate fund-raising dinner, he sent them a check, but didn't go—"They dumb as hell. They should get white talent. White folks started this crap."). He had a fawn-colored miniature greyhound which he loved. He didn't rehearse ("I rehearse every night on the stand").

A vivid image of Davis at the beginning of the 1960s slowly emerges from Haley's notes. Miles is a man who seems confident about his place in music history, financially comfortable, urbane, a man eager to sustain family life. At the same time, race is a constant in his musings, much as it was for the rest of the country at that time:

> White people are responsible for my success. They make it so hard for you that a long time ago I got mad and made up my mind to be two, three times as good at whatever I decided to do. If I was white I probably wouldn't have had no drive.

> When a writer asked my opinions on the South, I told him, 'Just leave space for three long blank paragraphs. None of it would be printed.'

Miles was often lonely (he was known to call people at 3:00 A.M. and tell them, "You're the best friend I have," and hang up); he was ironic (he received a letter to attend a stockholders' meeting in Atlanta and broke out laughing: "Now, just suppose I had gone? They'd been so shook up, there might not of been no dividend. And they would feel like, that I had come down there to cause trouble"); his generosity was often tempered by anger (when jazz organist Jimmy Smith was sick, Miles sent him a $20 bill, and wrote on it, "Now you know what it's like to have some money, you broke son of a bitch"); he was disillusioned with the music business ("I got to give this shit up. Buy me some property and collect rents. Sick of these dumb-ass club owners. I don't even look at my horn. I don't even know if it's in the case or not"). Family was important to him (when Nat Hentoff lost his parents in an auto accident, he said, "Yeah, man, I know. One time my grandfather died, I was looking for him for three years, man").

At the time the *Playboy* interview was published—September 1962—Haley wrote another article that closely followed the content of the interviews, but expanded on them. Written in the first person, it opens with Miles defending himself:

> Somebody's complaining about me every time I turn around. Some critic with nothing else to do started this mess. I don't announce numbers, don't look at audiences, I don't bow for applause, I walk off the stage and all that. Look, I only can do one thing—play my horn. All kinds of lies go around about how I think and what I do. Everything I do, I have a reason, and nobody knows what I think except Miles Davis.

This article, like the *Playboy* interview, contains a litany of complaints: he rails against angry racists and drunken reporters; *Playboy*'s refusal to use black models; the embarrassing clichés of whites attempting to demonstrate their egalitarianism; the arrogant assumptions of whites attempting to advise blacks on what they should or should not do to advance their race; the stereotyping of blacks in the media and racism in the music business. He tells why he doesn't like playing concerts (too confining) and makes a plea for the return of the jam session. He decries the odiousness of comparing musicians to determine "the best" and suggests that the State Department send Louis Armstrong on goodwill tours to Mississippi or Alabama rather than overseas. Miles justifies his behavior onstage, deplores the ignorance of critics, and declares that he won't play in the South or in any clubs that attract tourists, drunks, or squares, or any that discourage blacks. He has something to say about everything: the American cult of personality; his fear of the Cold War (the Kennedy brothers he likes—"they're swinging people") and of traveling by airplane; his pride in his family's heritage and in his boyhood paper route, his cooking, his stock portfolio, his children, his wife, his Ferrari.

As the first of a long series of celebrity interviews published in *Playboy*, and one that appeared in the middle of a critical period of the civil rights struggle, the Davis interview took on a weight far greater than that of the usual journalist's chat with a musician. With the passing of time, it would turn out to be the source of much of the writing on Davis that was published for years to come. The interview was sampled again and again, the same quotations floating through countless other interviews, suggesting that some journalists were "cooking" them—pirating Haley's material, rephrasing Davis' answers, filling in the blanks on their own.

But there were problems with the interview itself. In his autobiography, Davis complained that Haley "made up some things, although it was good reading." For example, there was the quote from Miles about losing trumpet competitions in high school to white boys of lesser ability that was widely quoted, but which Miles denied, as did Irene and his teacher, Elwood Buchanan. He also denied another quote—that when he was a child, a white man chased him, calling him "nigger," which led to his father chasing the man with a shotgun. Some of the material Haley attributes to Davis may have first appeared in the article in *Ebony* written by Marc Crawford, drawn from an interview with Miles' father. And some of it seems confused with his father's comments, as with this sentence, quoting from Miles: "My father, Miles the first, was born six years after the Emancipation." This surely is Davis' father talking about his father. What's further confusing is that just a few months before the *Playboy* interview was published, *Esquire* printed a series of Miles' answers to questions—presumably from the magazine's editors—that provided some different material, but also seemed to rework the same answers given in *Playboy*. Whatever the problems, the Davis interview was important enough that Haley was commissioned to do others—notably with American Nazi Party leader George Lincoln Rockwell and with Malcolm X, whom he had been interviewing at the same time as Miles.

On May 19, 1961, Miles played his first Carnegie Hall concert under his own name, using both his quintet and a twenty-one-piece orchestra conducted by Gil Evans. It was a big event, a declaration of his importance to those who were not in the know, and a reiteration of his accomplishments to those who were. Before the performance, Miles was nervous, massaging his lips, pacing, trying to focus and to forget the masses assembling. This was nothing new for the ever-anxious Davis, but compounding his anxiety was Gil, who was conducting his new arrangements for Miles in public for the first time. Drummer Jimmy Cobb remembers that "Gil said that he was petrified":

> He was really scared to do that concert. So he was drinking corn whiskey he had brought down from 125th Street. He had never been in front of that many people before. Gil said that he would rather do a lot of other things rather than go out on that stage. . . . It was a big deal for all of us. It was a social event.

And for a night that should have been a great triumph, it was fraught with one problem after another.

Jean Bach had learned that Davis wanted to do a big concert and needed financial backing. She mentioned it to someone she thought might be able to help—Dr. Tom Rees, a prominent plastic surgeon in New York City. In addition to his Manhattan practice, Rees was one of a small group of "flying doctors," who were building a corps of medical workers in Africa with the sponsorship of the African Research Foundation (later renamed the African Medical Education and Research Foundation). Just at this moment, the foundation was looking to stage a fund raiser, and jazz musicians had emerged in recent years as willing participants in benefits and tributes (just two months before, Dizzy Gillespie had performed a piece at Carnegie Hall dedicated to the newly emerging African nations). Rees went to Davis' house to propose the concert to him. Although at first suspicious and inhospitable, when Miles learned that Rees knew Doug Mettome, a white trumpet player Miles had known in the Eckstine band, he opened up a bit, and after several other visits and meetings with Rees, Davis agreed to the idea of a benefit concert at Carnegie Hall. Soon everything was in line, including the promise of a live recording for Columbia.

Shortly before the concert, Max Roach showed up at Miles' home with a delegation of activists in the cause of freedom in South Africa, who believed that despite its noble goals, the foundation was a South African front, just another colonial institution dominated by whites. They urged Miles not to perform for them. When he told them that what he had learned after his beating at Birdland was that freedom could be bought if you had enough money, they were stunned by his cynicism. And of course he was going to play, he said. His decision may or may not have been affected by the fact that only two weeks before, a benefit he had planned to do for the NAACP in San Francisco's Masonic Memorial Temple had had to be canceled when the management decided that he might draw "an inappropriate audience."

As the day of the concert arrived and the truck carrying the recording equipment was about to leave for Carnegie Hall, Miles suddenly called producer Teo Macero and told him he had decided not to record because he already had done the same compositions in the studio and they had been issued on record. The plans to record were canceled, but Macero did not give up easily. When he got to Carnegie Hall, he asked one of the staff if they had any kind of recording equipment. What they had was a small Webcor tape recorder that could record in mono on half-tracks and seven-inch reels, and a mixer that could handle up to four microphones. Teo hooked it all up so that it could not be seen, and from the left side of the hall, he stubbornly prepared to do a home recording of the concert, like some bootlegging jazz freak from the bebop years.

It was one of those New York evenings when the energy of the moment leaps from person to person on line, and the importance of the occasion seemed scrawled on the sidewalk. Chic crowds of whites and blacks streamed down 57th Street and clustered around the doors to Carnegie Hall. Each woman attending was given a single red rose, as if to assure that this was something other than the usual men's-night-out-with-jazz. But with Miles Davis playing, every woman already knew that.

Symphony Sid, hipster as social climber, out of Birdland for the night on good behavior, was the master of ceremonies and let the full house know just how lucky it was. The music began with "So What," with Bill Evans' piano introduction from the original Davis recording now orchestrated for the full band, but played so slowly that bassist Paul Chambers took off on his signature bass line too soon and too fast, and for a moment it appeared that they would all crash. But that was all that Gil Evans had written out for the piece, and the quintet then took over, moving it up to speed. Miles especially was flying, surging with energy, showing his newfound eagerness for playing long solos, trying out some tricks with sliding and falling off notes, pulling ahead of the rhythm, then dropping behind, catching himself in his own slipstream.

All of the quintet's pieces were ones they were playing nightly, and all of them had just been recorded a month earlier, during two nights at the Blackhawk Club in San Francisco. The pieces with Gil Evans were from the *Miles Ahead* record of 1957, with the exception of a new arrangement of "Spring Is Here" (again, orchestrated in part from a piano trio recording by Bill Evans) and the adagio from Rodrigo's *Concierto de Aranjuez*.

During the first tune after intermission, "Someday My Prince Will Come," Max Roach and two other men suddenly appeared, all three nattily attired, and sat down on the floor in the middle of the stage with small signs made from shirt cardboards, protesting the sponsorship of the concert. Roach had two of them, which read "Africa for the Africans" and "Freedom Now." Miles abruptly stopped the band and walked off the stage. (On the live recording, the tune ends just after Davis' truncated solo, with Chambers playing a repeated bass note that should have cued in the next soloist.) Several security people lifted the demonstrators off the floor and carried them out. An *Amsterdam News* reporter heard Max Roach shouting back through the stage door, "Tell Miles I'm sorry."

Tom Rees went backstage and was told by Frances (who was there with Miles' mother) that Miles would not go back on, but Gil Evans would complete his portion of the concert—the piece from *Sketches of Spain*—without the soloist. Davis told Rees that he resented being lied to by a racist organization and tricked into appearing. Rees vehemently denied it, begging him to look at the equally black and white audience as proof. Miles took his point—but Max was his friend, and he felt that he could not in good conscience play after this demonstration. He later said that what bothered him was not the politics of the situation or Max's convictions, but "him fucking with the music like he did by coming up and sitting on the stage as we were about to play, holding up those goddamn signs. . . . It just fucked me up"—and undoubtedly embarrassed him. How was he to get himself and the audience back into the spirit of the concert after that?

Rees managed to get Miles and the protesters together outside the hall, where he passionately explained the flying doctors and their purposes, and attempted to throw the weight onto Roach by suggesting that Miles' career would be hurt if he didn't finish the concert and the public came to know what had happened. Somehow Rees managed to convince Roach enough that Max agreed that Miles should go back in and play, and they'd talk about it later. Miles still didn't want to play, but considering what Gil Evans was going to have to do to finish the concert, he agreed to go back out.

It was a bad night for Max all around. He and his wife, Abbey Lincoln, had just broken up that day, and she had left for the West Coast that night. He, meanwhile, went downtown to catch Lenny Bruce at the Vanguard, and when he walked into the club, still in his immaculate Panama suit and carrying his signs, Lenny built a whole bit on it: "Ladies and gentlemen, Max Roach, one of the founders of bebop is here, dressed for a sit-in," and continued on with a little lecture on the importance of jazz.

Like a fighter who had been knocked down but not out, Miles came back onstage steaming with "Oleo" and "No Blues," then dropped to a whisper with "I Thought About You." The audience was his again, and after the *Sketches of Spain* piece, it was erupting in applause. It was a night that would be talked about for years to come.

But it was not over yet. After the concert, Teo went backstage with the recorded tapes that Miles did not know about, and as he was coming down the hallway, Teo threw them at him: "You son of a bitch! This could have been a great recording!" Miles took it in stride and continued greeting and introducing everyone he saw as "Bob." Frances brought his mother backstage to congratulate him, but he had already left.

At three o'clock the next morning, Teo was awakened by Miles on the phone: "I want to put that out." That meant that Teo would have to get Columbia back on board for a record made below its usual standards, not an easy thing to pull off; and he would have to get permission from the African Research Foundation, Carnegie Hall, the Musicians Union, and the Recording Engineers Union. Later, Miles sent Max Roach a message telling him that they would never work together again.

The weight of making music was continuing to tell on Miles. In April, during his stay at the Blackhawk, he told Russ Wilson, a reporter for the *Oakland Tribune,* that he was thinking of retiring. "I'm not considering it—I'm going to retire. I've got $1,000 a week coming in now so I don't have to work. And I've been playing for twenty-two years—a long time." But then Ralph Gleason said that Miles had been announcing his retirement every time he came to town for the past three years. Miles seemed a bit less sure of his plans when he later spoke to writer Gilbert Millstein, this time drawing an analogy between drugs and his commitment to music:

To Davis, music is "a disease, a divine disease." Lying on a bed in his home not long ago, an arm over his eyes against the light, he remarked that he feels weak and irritable until he gets on the stand to perform. "Music is like having a habit," he said. "Only this one you can't break. You never feel like other people." He raised himself on an elbow and rolled over. "I know one of these days I'm going to walk off the stand and never play again. Something's going to touch me. And when that happens, I'll divorce myself from the trumpet." He thought about the prospect for a moment. "But not music, not the disease," he conceded with a faint smile. "I could spend the rest of my life listening, day and night, and be busy."

Booked to play two weeks at the Jazz Workshop in San Francisco, Miles missed three nights and cut his playing short on several others. The owner, Art Auerback, wanted $1,000 of his advance back, and he kept Miles' trumpet for security.

When Miles was visiting the farm in Millstadt in 1960, his father casually mentioned that he had been hit by a train at a rural railroad crossing. His father had called his brother Leonard to come out to take him to the hospital because he said the white ambulance company would not come for him. After that accident, his balance and control were affected, his walk was unsteady, and he was no longer able to work. Miles brought him to New York to have him examined by a neurosurgeon, but the results were inconclusive. When he saw his father again in 1962 on his way to Kansas City, he seemed much the same. But as Miles was leaving, his father gave him a letter, which he passed on to Frances to keep, and forgot about it. Three days later, on May 27, word reached Miles in Kansas City that his father was dead. When he finally read the letter, it said, "In three or four days after you read this, I'll be dead." Miles understood it to mean that his father had wanted to tell him that he was going to die so that his death wouldn't come as a shock.

The profitable sales of the three Davis-Evans albums kept Columbia pressuring them to do more, and in July, August, and November 1962, they were back in the studios for four more sessions toward a project vaguely defined as "a Latin-American album with a large dance band." It was Columbia's attempt to benefit from the bossa nova craze which had already put Stan Getz on the hit charts that year.

According to Macero, Evans never completed the arrangements for an album (to be called *Quiet Nights*), and because Miles was sick, less than twenty minutes of solid material was recorded during the four sessions. The resulting album shows signs of the producer's desperation. One piece is unacceptably short, another fades abruptly, and "Corcovado," only 1:18 long, is spliced onto an alternate take of "Aos Pes da Cruz" in order to get a full-length piece. Teo said that he had done the best he could with it:

> There hadn't been too many records put out. I wanted to keep his career going, so I thought I'd put this record out. I put two different tunes

together—like a medley. There's nothing wrong with that. But the critics criticized it. They said, "Well, what happened?" The tunes were only a minute long! I mean that's it, and he'd stop!

None of this was denied by Miles, who admitted they had failed: "The last thing Gil and I did on *Quiet Nights* in November just wasn't happening. It seemed like we had spent all our energy for nothing and so we just let it go." But he had no idea that Columbia would try to issue the scraps they had completed:

> I didn't talk to Teo Macero for a long time after that. He just fucked up everything on that record, looking over the musical score, getting in the way of everybody, trying to tell people what they should play and shit. He should have just kept his ass in the recording booth and got us some good sound instead of fucking around with us and fucking up everything. I started to get that motherfucker fired after that record. I called up Goddard Lieberson. . . . But when Goddard asked me if I wanted Teo fired, I just couldn't do him like that.

From Macero's perspective, Miles was not fulfilling his contract, and he was jeopardizing the efforts put forward on his behalf:

> If I interfered with the recording it was to save it, because you're sitting there as a producer and you see all these musicians out there . . . you just couldn't sit there, you know, and turn in half an album.
>   . . . I must have conducted the band. I probably did. Because I've done it on a couple of occasions where—you know, Gil, for whatever reason, couldn't do it. . . . He used to write complicated things with the rhythm, and they couldn't follow him . . . so I probably went there and conducted. And I probably saved the day.

The final track on the record was "Summer Nights," a piece recorded by a different Davis group five months later, which was added in to get the record up to what still amounted only to less than twenty-eight minutes. Reviews ranged from the unenthusiastic to the outright bored. And there were objections even from within CBS over the short length of the album. Some buyers complained about what they called "bloopers" on the record (Miles' voice could be heard saying, "I'll do it again, Teo, but let me hear this one"). Purchasers of Columbia records were apparently not as open to experimentation as those of Prestige Records. Still, everything considered, some parts of *Quiet*

Nights are fascinating and quite beautiful in the still sonic cloud they generate. It was as if having almost achieved the sort of effect that the Claude Thornhill band had wanted, both Miles and Gil gave up the effort and were now free to set off in a new and very different direction.

In the midst of the *Quiet Nights* recording sessions, Evans and Davis began several other projects, one of them built around the songs of Bob Dorough. Miles had been asked to contribute something for a Columbia Records Christmas compilation album called *Jingle Bell Jazz*. Unable to face recording yet another carol, Miles wanted something new written for him. He had first met Dorough in Hollywood, after the singer-pianist moved back from Paris, where he had been working as an accompanist for Sugar Ray Robinson's nightclub act. Robinson gave up on his nightclub career and came back to the United States, but Dorough stayed on in France for a while, came back to New York and worked with Lenny Bruce, and then moved to Los Angeles.

> I was friends with Terry Morell, a singer who lived in the attic of Roberta Bright, the widow of Robert Bright, the trumpet player. Roberta knew Miles, and he liked Roberta's place and liked to crash there when he was in town. Miles was chatting with Terry, who showed him the cover of my Bethlehem LP *Devil May Care*, and played a track for him. The next night Miles was back and asked to hear the whole LP. Terry then suggested I go with her to see Miles perform. When we were introduced, Miles asked me to sing "Baltimore Oriole" for him, which I did with just drums and bass. So we became friends while he was in L.A. for the month, and went to afternoon parties and picnics that Paul Horn threw.

Dorough had seen Miles when he lived in New York before and made an effort to speak to him, but "I didn't try to break that bubble he kept over him: I'd praise him at a club and he'd keep on walking." But now both were back in New York City, and Miles helped him in getting gigs, booked him to open for him at the Village Vanguard, and often had him as a guest at his house.

Miles asked his lawyer to see if Dorough would write a Christmas song for him to be used on the Christmas album. Dorough said:

I worked hard to get something that sounded like Miles ("Bah, humbug"), then Gil sketched it out and they recorded it with me on piano. They did the same with my "Nothing Like You," which I thought was done too hastily. The instrumental version was recorded without me knowing it.

After it was finished, Miles wanted the Christmas song issued as a single, but Teo Macero wrote Irving Townsend that "nobody likes it." "Nothing Like You" also received little attention and remained unissued for five years, eventually being stuck onto *The Sorcerer*, an album with which it shared little beyond the participation of saxophonist Wayne Shorter at the two recording sessions.

Miles thought that these two tunes could work for jukebox play because his 1954 recordings of "Old Devil Moon" and "Four" on Prestige were now on jukeboxes. As he traveled across the country, he had kept track of where they were being played. When he was back in East St. Louis, he dropped by one of the local bars, and when he asked the owner why he didn't have any of his records on the jukebox, his answer, hometown cold, was, "Maybe if you learn to play a little trumpet, I'll put your records on it!"

Hank Mobley left the band at the end of 1962, and Miles briefly replaced him with Rocky Boyd, a student of John Coltrane. After being in Chicago for Christmas, Wynton Kelly and Paul Chambers wanted to play their own music and left to form a trio. Miles was then forced to cancel engagements for the first month or so of 1963, which cost him $25,000 to pay off the losses of club owners. (He had already canceled a Detroit engagement to protect Paul Chambers from arrest in a marital suit, which resulted in Davis' being sued by the club owner.)

Between painkillers, drinking, and cocaine, Miles was becoming increasingly reclusive by 1963, and his paranoia was growing. When he and Frances went anywhere that he wasn't known, it was she who had to go in and see to reservations or a table; he wanted to avoid being turned away because of his color. He became difficult to talk to, and when she said anything that he said sounded like something his mother had said to him a long time ago ("when he couldn't do anything about it," as he put it), he'd slap her. Miles was missing gigs again, and club owners scrambled to replace him. When he failed to show at the Village Vanguard one night, the popular harmonica player Larry Adler came out of the audience to play with the band in Miles' style.

Two new styles of music were on the rise in the mid-1960s, both threatening to change the mainstream of American popular music, of which Miles Davis was now clearly a part. One of them, rock and roll, was emerging from the grass roots of the United States and England and beginning to make the executives of major record companies pay attention to what was being recorded on the otherwise disreputable regional and mom-and-pop labels. Rock was something that Miles, like most other jazz musicians, had mocked for its repetitiveness, its musicians' lack of chops, and its vulgarity. It was as if white country music, rhythm and blues, English music-hall songs, and fifties pop songs had all been laminated under the heat and pressure of the civil rights movement to fill the void created by the winding down of the swing era and the waning of the American popular art song. The other menacing music, free jazz, then still called the "new thing," sounded as if it had zoomed in from outer space, played by musicians who often seemed to have completely escaped the jazz recruitment process. They were classically trained virtuosos and musical illiterates, intellectuals and street rebels, and highbrows disguised as primitives. The center of jazz gravity quickly shifted to the Five Spot when Ornette Coleman's quartet came in from the West Coast playing what some were calling the change of the century. (Pianist Paul Bley said that "everybody was there including Miles, who stood talking to the bartender with his back to the stage, as though he was thirsty and just happened to stop in for a drink.") Miles, like many other established musicians, then promptly dismissed Coleman as "fucked up" psychologically. He would resist these new jazz movements, just as he had funk and soul music in the late 1950s. If he didn't create them, he didn't play them. For the moment, at least, Miles could stay above the threat of these contending forces because he still had the ear of all jazz musicians, and even many young people respected his music (Marianne Faithfull, for example, said it was *Sketches of Spain* she bought when she was fifteen, not pop records.)

Once he was booked for a tour of the West Coast in 1963, Miles began holding tryouts in New York to form a new quintet. Memphis tenor saxophonist George Coleman had been recommended to Miles by Coltrane, and Coleman in turn suggested some other hometown friends of his from Memphis, alto saxophonist Frank Strozier and pianist Harold Mabern. To these, Miles added Ron Carter, a bassist with a rich sound, a strong sense of countermelody, great harmonic knowledge (from his classical training), and the ability to take chances and still hold the beat. Jimmy Cobb was now the only musician remaining from the sextet. After they'd played for a few weeks, Miles scheduled a recording session on the West Coast to make *Seven Steps to Heaven* (though the title changed several times in the process: at one point it was called *So Near, So Far*). Miles didn't use Strozier on the session, and replaced Mabern with Victor Feldman, a British pianist who was active in studio work in Hollywood and who arranged five of the compositions: "So Near, So Far," "Joshua," "Seven Steps to Heaven," "I Fall in Love Too Easily," and "Basin Street." The last two songs and "Baby, Won't You Please Come Home" had been suggested to Miles after he heard Shirley Horn sing them when she opened for him at the Vanguard in 1961. He had been struck by how slowly and majestically Horn could sing a ballad, how she could space out notes, making a single note work for her, letting it hang in the air.

After six weeks on the road they returned to New York, Jimmy Cobb left, and Miles dropped Strozier and Mabern. "I thought what he really wanted was a quintet," Coleman felt, "because he used to complain about the lengthy solos. And what he would do, he'd say (in a whisper), 'Hey, Frank, go tell George he's playin' too long'; and then he'd come to me and say the same thing—'Tell Frank he's playin' too long.'"

Miles was seeking a new pianist and a new drummer by the method he preferred: put out the rumor that he needed someone and then wait to see what happens. This way, he avoided the embarrassment of rejection and also was able to hear about younger musicians he didn't know (Coleman Hawkins had told him that the secret of success was always to hire people younger than yourself). Jackie McLean soon called him about Tony Williams, a seventeen-year-old drummer he had brought down from Boston to play on the stage with him in *The Connection*, Jack Gelber's play about jazz and addiction. Miles had literally gone shopping for drummers with Philly Joe, and Tony was the only one whom Joe would approve. Miles then invited Williams to come over to his house with bassist Ron Carter and George Coleman, and meanwhile called up pianist Herbie Hancock, who was then playing with Donald Byrd, and asked him to join them. Miles listened to Herbie play for a few minutes, said, "Nice touch," then went upstairs and listened to them rehearse over his intercom. He asked them to come back the next day and auditioned them again from a distance. Gil Evans and Philly Joe came around to hear them on the third day, and this time Miles joined them, but only for three or four notes of playing. Later, he called them and told them to come in the next day to record what turned out to be the rest of the *Seven Steps* album. Tony Williams said he had memorized all of Miles' recorded solos, and he played as if he had, following Miles' playing closely, echoing him, crisscrossing him, sometimes even finishing his phrases. Miles often said that he himself played as a member of the rhythm section, punching out short phrases, breaking up the flow of the melody line so that the rhythm could be heard through it, and Williams seemed a combination of all the drummers he had played with before, but with greater fire and energy.

Jazz musicians will tell you that every drummer plays time differently, but Tony Williams could make you hear what wasn't there rhythmically, or feel the incremental pulse of rock inside the pliancy of swing by subdividing the four beats of conventional jazz rhythm into the eight of current pop and manipulating them. He could accelerate within the beat, scatter the pulse across the drum set, stomp down on every beat with the high hat, shift gears in midphrase, and send the band flying off into any number of new rhythmic worlds. Miles trusted Tony and counted on him to give his quintet its character. He respected his seriousness, his focus, his ability to listen to records and memorize every minute of them. Miles said it was Tony, not he, whom the members of the quintet were listening to. It was Tony who signaled the rhythm and tempo changes in the band by maintaining eye contact with Herbie Hancock and Ron Carter.

Ornette Coleman once said that when the drummer is playing with everyone else, it's jazz, but when everyone else is playing with the drummer, it's rock. His words had the weight of prophetic authority, but Williams mocked such dictums. You either played with Tony, adapting to his rhythms, or you played alone. Bassist Dave Holland said that Williams was immovable: you had to go to him. When he became disgusted with what another musician was playing, he would stop altogether, or play the cymbals the rest of the night, sending the rest of the rhythm section scurrying to fill in for him. He was also a young disciplinarian, criticizing players when they drank too much, chastising them for not caring enough (Tony even dared to criticize Miles for not practicing and for missing notes); but he also had no patience with players who he said *didn't* make mistakes, such as George Coleman. He wanted someone who was reaching, risking everything. His idea of serious music was free jazz, and Ornette Coleman and drummer Billy Higgins were his heroes. But he also came to like rock groups such as Cream, Hendrix, the

MC5, the Beatles. In fact, he later tried in vain to talk Miles into opening for the Beatles in 1965.

Herbie Hancock was college and conservatory educated, something of a prodigy in classical music. He played with a light, nonpercussive touch and a flowing lyrical style closer to Bill Evans than to Wynton Kelly. He had broad tastes and had investigated the full range of music, from classical to avant-garde to funk, and was open to playing them all. If he had a problem as far as Miles was concerned, it was that he was *too* good a pianist. Miles' instructions to him (such as "Try sitting on your left hand" or, "It's 'My Funny Valentine,' not a concerto") are fabled. With Hancock and Williams in place with Ron Carter's harmonic knowledge and his innovative bass patterns, the three of them felt free to experiment and to pass the rhythms from person to person.

Hancock had played with Eric Dolphy, and Williams had come from Sam Rivers' band, so the two of them were used to some of the most advanced playing in jazz. But Miles was still playing standards like "I Thought About You," so Hancock said that he and Williams tried to stay out of Miles' way whenever he soloed. But when they accompanied George Coleman, they went further out, shifting the time around, altering the harmonies. Once while they were playing in Detroit, Miles asked the rhythm section why they didn't play behind him the way they did with Coleman. Later that night, they talked it over and began to wonder if he was really serious. The next night they tried it. They began to move the accompaniment in a new direction, and—as Herbie remembered it—Miles began to bob and weave, sweating and struggling to stay with them. When he said nothing about it, they continued the same way the next night, and again Miles tried to find some way to fit in. But by the third day, Hancock said it was *he* who was trying to catch up: Miles had taken his playing to another level. It was during the first set that third night that Miles told Herbie, "I don't want to play chords any more." What he meant, according to Hancock, was that he didn't want to play conventional chords anymore. He wanted the kind of chords that were either so close together or so spread apart that it would be difficult to tell what they were. From that point on, the music changed. There were chords still there, but they were much more transparent.

The learning in this band went both ways, however. George Coleman was impressed by Miles' extensive knowledge of music.

Miles had a lot of harmonic depth. He was well trained. The first version of "Milestones," for example, is filled with intricate harmony, but he could play right through it with ease. He could do so much with those simple tunes like "Gal in Calico" or "Bye Bye Blackbird."

He also had a very sharp sense of humor—in the middle of my solo he might say, "You don't have to play all those notes." Or he might growl, "I wish I had eight bars of Sonny Rollins."

Hancock was also taken to school by Miles. He expected his musicians to write material that the band could play, and when he was given new compositions, he took them and instantly changed them by breaking them down to their elements and creating a framework that offered opportunities for improvisation. As Herbie put it, "He had the talent to draw out the best solos by ventilating the compositions." His directions—the few he gave—were cryptic. Herbie recalled a time when his own playing was growing stale, and he seemed to be playing the same thing every night. Miles leaned over to him and said, "Don't play the butter notes."

I was thinking, butter is rich, what are the rich notes? The sounds that determine the character of a chord—major or minor—so I struggled and tried to leave them out. The solo I played was jagged and too sparse, but I got it in two weeks.

Sometimes he'd say, "Put an F in the bass." It would sound strange, then I'd hear something and say, "Look at this Miles," and he'd say, "See?" He didn't want to stifle your creativity and tell you what to do. He wanted to stimulate you to think.

The recording they did for the second half of *Seven Steps to Heaven* shows this new group at work, still taking shape, but their effect on Miles is already clear: he is energized, and his solos are louder, higher, faster, and full of risk. George Coleman felt the same artistic rush: "When I came in the band they upped everything—all the tempos. Miles knew I could play fast, so he pushed them up. With Miles I got everything—up tempos, harmonic situations, taking chances . . . and I began to get this adventurous spirit."

As they progressed, it was George who often played more adventurously than Miles. On "Stella by Starlight" (on the February 12, 1964, concert recording titled *My Funny Valentine*), Coleman breaks up the four eight-bar symmetrical sections of the ballad by transforming them with a variety of rhythmic and affective means. He begins with a double-time feel that shifts back and forth to the time with which they began, but moves further and further away from the ballad's melody, becomes more abstract, then takes on a blues feeling before finally returning to the melody. The rhythm section telepathically goes in and out of double-time, Latin rhythms, and moments of suspended rhythm behind him. Tony Williams on his own could also stop playing suddenly, then start up again in surprising places. Though they were playing ballads and pop tunes that were still recognizable, they had begun to take the form of these melodies apart, restructuring them, making them new.

But Tony, according to Coleman, was unhappy with what George was playing. "He was always complaining to Miles that I wasn't hip enough for him." And Miles began to echo him. Herbie Hancock recalls that "Coleman had worked out these tricky little figures in his hotel room, and during the night he'd find a place to put these things. Miles got angry and said 'I pay you to practice *on* the bandstand.'" George, for his part, was growing tired of the whole Miles Davis experience. As the rhythm section became more adventurous, George was unhappy with the way they played broken rhythm when Miles left the stand, with no concern for keeping time. "So when we were playing at the Jazz Workshop, and Miles was off the stand, I played *out*, to show them I could do it if I wanted to. Miles said, 'What the fuck was *that?*'" Miles' behavior was also getting to him: "Miles was living too fast for me. In Europe he was self-centered, greedy, and he spent time by himself. He was centering on his own ego, rather than on the music. His priorities were with himself. He was insecure. He demanded a lot for himself—champagne, women, cars . . . or whatever else he might want." But he was also sick, and it was George who had to drag him out of bed many nights.

Miles was ill during that time—a lot of times he wouldn't make the gigs and it was frustrating. I would be standing out front and a lot of people thought *I* was Miles Davis, if you can believe *that*. And I used to stand out front and make a gig some nights after the first set, 'cause he would split . . . 'cause he was hurting, you know. His hip was bothering him—and there was a lot of pressure on me, and sometimes the money would be late and I'd get it in a check and have to try and get it cashed, so I really got tired of it; so I just decided to leave. But it didn't hurt business any: Miles could miss one night at a club, and when he came in the next night the lines would be even longer.

In early fall, Gil and Miles were invited to write and perform incidental music for *Time of the Barracudas*, a play by Peter Barnes starring Elaine Stritch and Laurence Harvey, which was premiering at the Curran Theater in San Francisco and then moving on to Los Angeles and New York. Harvey was a big Miles Davis fan, and the two had met a number of times after Miles' club performances on the West Coast. Miles and Frances and Gil and Anita Evans were flown out to Los Angeles and put up at the Chateau Marmont, the Davises staying in a suite with a piano that overlooked the famous high-stepping ceramic cowgirl on a rotating pedestal; below her was the glitter of Sunset Strip. For two weeks, Miles worked with Gil on the music in the daytime, and on October 10 and 11, he and Gil went into a recording studio in Hollywood with the finished material.

Michael Macdonald was staying at the Chateau Marmont at the time that Miles was there, working as casting director for the film *Lord of the Flies*. He first ran into Miles in an elevator. "Davis was cool and compact: black alligator shirt, tight black pants, the muscular arms of a longtime amateur boxer, and that personality: a man of very few words, and those in a gravelly, intimidating whisper. . . . Fatuously, I gushed about endlessly playing *Miles Ahead* at Harvard. 'Yeah, I had an uncle at Harvard, once . . .' came the accurate, neat put-down."

The next time he saw Davis

> was at a pleasant gathering of Davis family friends, including Gil Evans and Anita, Claude Thornton, a lawyer named "Spook" [Harold Lovett], a doctor who'd gone to Andover, Fran in striped little booties—and Miles, stripped to the waist, stretched out on the floor, eyes mainly closed, apparently mesmerized by his tapes for *Time of the Barracudas*. Blaring handsomely away, his incidental music featured a long sequence involving drums and a double bass: "Don't show me the pictures 'til the play's right," he'd told Elaine Stritch, when she tried showing him some production stills.

On another evening, he ran into Miles in the Chateau's underground garage:

> It was 1:30, we'd just returned from our long evening . . . and there were the Davises. They'd been out together and, in a merry mood, asked us up for a nightcap. Now a loving husband, Miles upstairs spoke volubly and above a whisper. This time, when I drunkenly raved about his music, he raised a glass, we exchanged toasts.

On yet another night, Macdonald called the Davises' suite to invite Fran to a Motion Picture Academy screening of *Lord of the Flies:*

> I got Miles. "She isn't here, motherfucker," said he. I hung up, then lifted the phone again to ring [another number]. "Gee," I told [Elaine]. "Miles called me a motherfucker." "No," came a gravelly whisper over the phone. "I called you a *cock sucker.*"

Time of the Barracudas, a grim comedy, opened on October 21 to bad reviews. Under the headline, "See 'Barracuda,' Hear Miles Davis," Ralph J. Gleason's "On the Town" column in the *San Francisco Chronicle* read:

> Miles' music is used in "Time of the Barracudas" all right, and it's a good thing it is, since the play at the Curran has little else to recommend it. The trouble is that, as director Anthony Page frankly said before the opening, "Miles' music is too good." You get to hear it, played from a tape made in Los Angeles, in tiny bits. . . . Miles himself doesn't get much to play until the second act when there are several moments of perhaps 18 or 20 bars, where he plays a moody series of variations. . . . Little as it is, it is a distinct delight to hear the Miles Davis–Gil Evans music coming through.

Gleason went on to dismiss the play and describe the incidental music during the first act as being rhythm only, with Ron Carter's bass and Tony Williams' drums, with the second act having only eighteen to twenty bars of Davis. (The music that played before the curtain went up was not by Davis and Evans.)

When the play moved on to the Huntington Hartford Theater on Vine near Sunset in Los Angeles, things did not go much better. In addition, Local 47 of the American Federation of Musicians objected to a tape being used in a performance and insisted on eight of their musicians being in the pit at least for the overture. "Miles' incidental music for scene changes was obscured by noisy scene changes," Macdonald recalled, "reducing it to Muzak. 'White comedy,' Miles had sniffed, one Chateau night; now his score was its white noise."

The play closed on November 23 after a few performances in Los Angeles, but the twelve minute and forty-five second recording of the various cues remains, with several interesting themes. Evans said he got the idea for one of them, "Hotel Me," from a blues figure he heard pianist Otis Spann use accompanying Muddy Waters on one of the tracks on *The Best of Muddy Waters.*

Outside the It Club at four in the morning, where Miles had been sitting in, Gil had gotten a parking ticket, and a policeman searched everyone as they approached the car—Miles, Fran, Anita, Gil, Harold Lovett, and Laurence Harvey—because they were a mixed-race group. "The policeman took it upon himself to be the cultural dictator besides the social director of the city," Gil said.

Following the passage of the Civil Rights Act of 1964, political organizing and voter registration moved into high gear, and musicians and actors were often asked to appear at benefits and protest gatherings, with half a dozen national groups and hundreds of local ones seeking support and help. A coordinated fund-raising event was scheduled for Lincoln's birthday, February 12, 1964, to benefit the defense funds of the NAACP Legal Defense Fund, the Congress of Racial Equality, and the Student Non-Violent Coordinating Committee in their efforts to register voters in Mississippi and Louisiana. Miles had been asked by CORE to appear at another event a year or so before, but he had just lost his rhythm section and had not yet organized a new quintet. This time, a letter to potential donors was sent out in advance on Miles' own stationery, and phone campaigns were used to urge people to attend the concert.

The quintet hadn't worked for months, so when they were asked to play for free (and at the last minute), they were upset. Ron Carter, for one, refused to play unless they were each paid separately and could make up their own minds on whether they wanted to contribute to the various causes. Miles agreed. Although attendance was sparse at Lincoln Center's Philharmonic Hall, some of Miles' best music came from the concert, and two albums resulted, *My Funny Valentine* and *Four & More*.

A few weeks later, on February 28, Miles learned that his mother had died. She had been in pain from cancer for some time, but she kept the degree of her suffering to herself, which deeply resonated with Miles. He and Frances got on a plane to St. Louis, but after it took off, mechanical problems forced them to return to New York. Miles—who feared flying anyway, always taking Seconal before he even got on a plane—saw it as an omen and refused to go again. Frances went on alone, and Miles said he went back home and cried for hours.

When the quintet was scheduled for a Japanese summer tour arranged by George Wein, George Coleman told Miles he wouldn't be going with them, and Tony began campaigning for Sam Rivers as his replacement. Rivers was an adventuresome player, an acknowledged figure in the avant-garde, a name often mentioned just behind John Coltrane's, and he had the potential to move the group somewhere else musically. Miles gave Sam a call in the Midwest, where he was playing with the rhythm and blues guitarist T-Bone Walker, and asked him to come on the tour in July. Before their arrival, word spread in Japan that Miles would not show; he had hinted that he was suffering from pain caused by calcium deposits on his hips. But they all arrived on time and set out, first class, with limousine, to play six concerts in four cities. Frances even came along this time.

Since Sam Rivers already knew the Davis book, he was ready to play with Miles. But like George Coleman, once he was on the job, he was not happy: Miles kept his distance from the band, leaving Herbie Hancock to handle things. None of Rivers' compositions were ever played, and Sam was never sure what he was supposed to play. Rivers wanted to loosen up the music and play more arrhythmically than they did, but Davis was not ready for that, and Sam was disappointed. "I believe that the musicians who went through Miles' bands were just as impressed with his lifestyle as they were with the music," he said. "You're not going to have it while playing at the frontiers of music." When they got back from Japan, Miles took another few months off from work, while Rivers played on Tony Williams' own record *Spring,* as well as with pianist Andrew Hill's band. But Miles never asked him to come back.

Davis' home was the site of a champagne reception to honor Robert F. Kennedy in his bid to become senator from New York on October 29. The party was arranged by Miles' friend Buddy Gist, who had an office in 866 United Nations Plaza, where Kennedy also had an office. Sixty-some guests gathered in the house and spilled out into the canopied backyard, including politicians such as New York City mayor Robert F. Wagner and Manhattan Borough president Edward R. Dudley, and friends of the Davises like Sammy Davis, Jr., Harry and Julie Belafonte, James Farmer, Diahann Carroll, and Quincy Jones. Kennedy never showed up, but the party was a success anyway, and folks were still hanging around at one o'clock in the morning when Miles asked them all to leave.

By the mid-1960s, Miles was tired of playing jazz clubs. His popularity, record sales, and success with concerts forced people to take his complaints seriously, and when Max Gordon offered him a week or two at the Village Vanguard, as he had done many times before, Miles said he could no longer stand it. "I knew what he was talking about," Gordon said:

> The unemployed musicians and ex-musicians; the pundits; the reviewers, columnists, and salesmen promoting fly-by-night jazz mags; the writers of liner notes on album covers; the record collectors; the heavyweights from Harlem; college kids bearing cassette recorders; the gossips, punks, and freeloaders who hang out in rooms where jazz is played.

The struggle not to drink, to stay off drugs, to be clean and healthy was tough. Max recalled Miles complaining to him around this time:

> You know what I mean, Max. . . . I can't stand the whole fuckin' scene. The cats comin' around, the bullshit, the intermissions. I hate intermissions. And you looking sore because I ain't up on the bandstand. And the people? "Play 'Bye Bye Blackbird!'" Shit! . . . On a college concert I do two short sets and I'm through. I don't have to hang around, listen to a lot of bullshit!

Miles was unable to reconcile his pride in Frances and a jealousy made worse by paranoid outbursts following heavy bouts of cocaine use. He loved to watch her, see the grace of her legs and hips, the flow of her movement. "He loved the fact that I had been in these places and done these things, a ballerina and all that, but he couldn't handle it. Especially when I hit Broadway. He never wanted me to dance when we went out."

> We were at a party at the Shapiros', Ben and Mickey Shapiro—Ben was his West Coast agent-manager—and I danced, and he couldn't stand it! He couldn't stand me having this attention. I'll never forget Lena Horne gave a party that I went to. Miles didn't go, but he called up and said, "Tell Frances not to dance." We were in Paris, in a club on the Left Bank, and I danced because he said it was okay. But when I came off the floor, he was so angry that he left me there, and I didn't have a franc, and I had to somehow get back to the hotel. Fortunately, I knew the owner of the club, and he gave me the money to get back to the Right Bank. And then Miles was ready to kill me.

Early in their marriage, his jealousy turned violent. One night when they were at Birdland together, Quincy Jones joined them for drinks:

> When we got home, I said, "Quincy Jones is handsome." He hit me, and it was the first time in my life that I'd ever been knocked down. Then he put me out of the apartment—with no clothes on. We weren't even married yet. I was living right across the hall from where Diahann Carroll and Monty Kay lived. I was too frightened to knock on their door, standing there nude. And the elevator was right there. I thought, "Any minute, someone's going to come." And here I am: a debutante ballerina brought up, you know, the *right* way. I knocked quietly on their door. . . . Finally, he let me back in, and said, "You won't say *that* again!"

"I was ducking punches coming at me, avoiding him burning me with his cigarette—it was a B horror movie. *I* was the one walking on eggshells!" On another occasion he put her out of the house at two in the morning, and she fled to the garage where he kept his Ferrari and called Gil Evans.

> "'Get in a taxi,' Gil said, 'and I'll pay for it.' I went to Gil's, and he called Miles to let him know I was there."
>
> And of course the next day when I came home, here come the gifts— every time he'd do something wrong like that, he'd buy me clothes and this, that, and the other. It got to a point when I told my girlfriend who owned Jax, "I don't want any more clothes. Send him to David Webb!" He was one of the top jewelers.
>
> That's the way he'd apologize. He would never openly apologize. He would just get a whole bunch of clothes or something. Then he would treat me nicely . . . until the next time.

He was obsessed with Frances, had been obsessed with her since he first saw her, and wanted to know where she was every minute of the day. If she was late coming home from anywhere, he started making calls or looking for her.

> I couldn't go *anywhere*. I couldn't have *friends*. If I had a birthday party for my son, he would be upstairs in the bedroom, and I'm downstairs enter- taining my guests and every two minutes there was a whistle. That's the way he'd call me, because of his nose and throat troubles. I was very out- going, you know, so it was difficult. I was just a jewel in my own kingdom.
>
> The best thing about him was love. He was a fabulous lover. There's no

two ways about that. But his jealousy wrecked everything. I kept thinking it would get better. For someone to be so talented and with so much love, and then to turn it into so much ugliness, as he did, just blew my mind! But I continued to feel that this too shall pass, you know, because I was brought up in Christian Science. And I fell in love with this man, so he couldn't be *that* horrible. I mean, something had to change! But of course, it didn't.

And then there were his ladies, as Frances called them—the women who called him at home. "Miles would become embarrassed when they called our home, but he wouldn't take it out on them; he'd take it out on me because I answered the phone at the wrong time, you know, and I'd be the one that got—that got knocked out. He liked a silent woman . . . he liked women to be in the background."

Miles wanted the best for his children, wanted to steer them away from the life he had led, and was living. But what Frances described as his paranoia and jealousy drove them away:

> He could be a warm, loving soul as a father, and then he could just turn off and make the children crazy. Little Miles wanted to be a musician. He wanted to play the violin. But, no, Miles wanted him to box. So, these children—their dreams were destroyed because Miles probably didn't want them to go in the direction that *he* was going in. I mean Miles was—how do you put it? He was for himself. And not anybody else around him in the limelight, so to speak. Miles was jealous of anybody around *me*—my child, his children, friends, it didn't matter, he was extremely jealous. So, he failed the children, I believe. And I don't think Miles gave them the incentive to do what they wanted to do. I think Miles kept them back.
>
> Little Miles, who was so sweet, when I left, little Miles said to me, "You know, when you were there, it was a family. But when you left, it all fell apart." And in the end, Miles put them both [Gregory and little Miles] out . . . out on the streets. In their early and late teens.

Quantities of cocaine were driving him further into fantasy and paranoia, and he seemed to be beyond help.

I definitely believe that a lot of it was drugs. But I was very naïve. I didn't even know that he was on cocaine. His mother told me. Everybody said I should leave him. And I kept saying, "No," and my doctor and everybody's saying we should put him in a sanitarium until he gets over this drug addiction. And we almost got him to rehab, and in the middle of the drive over, he turned around and said, "No, we're not going." My dad was with me, and the doctor, and Miles said, "No!"

The end came in 1965 on a holiday weekend when Miles disappeared on a cocaine binge for two or three days, and came home hallucinating, still on crutches from a recent hip operation:

There was nothing more frightening than hearing crutches coming after you. I mean, he came into the house and he was looking for this imaginary man that he said I was supposed to be sleeping with. Under the bed, in the closet. But, of course, there was no one there. He had a butcher knife and he took me downstairs in the basement because he thought he heard someone. And there was no one there. He had me by my wrists. We came upstairs, and I thought—you know how the light comes on in your head, and you say: "How am I gonna get out of this?" And something came to me at this moment, and I said to him, "There *is* somebody in this house! Let me call the police!" And I tried to make it to the door. But he said, "You're not going anywhere."

But eventually Frances called the police, and while they were there, she slipped out to the house of a friend, a Katherine Dunham dancer, who lived in the Village.

After I left Miles I was in hiding for a while, first at Nancy Wilson's in Columbus, Ohio. But somehow he found out that I was there, and he called and said, "When I come out there, if I find you, there'll be nothing left but bullets." And then I hid at the Shapiros', in West Hollywood.

When threats of violence failed, he threatened to kill himself if she didn't come back. But this time she was gone for good.

CHAPTER SEVEN

The power of a Miles Davis was that he always seemed to be waving back from the other side of Black culture's transcendable horizon, from the post-liberated side of Black potentiality. That other shore was not emblematic of emancipation. What was over there was freedom from fear of a Black romantic imagination.

GREG TATE

"YOU CAN ALWAYS GET ANOTHER WOMAN." Or another saxophonist. When Miles heard that Wayne Shorter might be willing to leave the Art Blakey group, he called him in the middle of a rehearsal and offered him the job. But leaving Blakey was no small matter. Art was one of the great post-bop drummers, and the bands he led all developed deep ties to the history of jazz. Still, Shorter was growing restless in that group. Playing with Blakey was something like being in a show, he said. There was a fixed structure to every piece, with no room for variation except in the solos, and even they were determined by the structure.

> I had a chance [to hear the Miles Davis Quintet] one night at the Regal Theater in Chicago and we had played before Miles. . . . Then I went into the audience and sat and waited until Miles' band came on. . . . I was listening to the power of individualism and subjectivity that was going on with all the players. Cannonball, Coltrane, and whoever was playing piano at the time, probably Wynton Kelly, and Paul Chambers on bass. They opened with a song called "All Blues" and what I heard and felt was this penetrating . . . it was not a sudden blast with a showlike . . . bang! . . . you know. Instead they opened with a tremolo on the piano. The tremolo sounded like a Ravel thing. This tremolo threw a hush over the audience

that was different from the Messengers' kind of opening impact sound of "bang!" . . . The music seemed to transport the audience to some place they don't usually go in their everyday life.

"Miles was the man," Ron Carter said. "Guys were killing to get that gig. . . . They would flatten your tires, put sugar in your gas tank . . . 'cause that was *the* gig!" And once Shorter was in it, this was a band that could even rival Miles' quintet with Coltrane, maybe even surpass it. It was what Amiri Baraka called the "all-time classical hydrogen bomb and switchblade band."

The new quintet's first studio recording was *E.S.P.,* completed in Los Angeles in January 1965. It announced its uniqueness in the Davis catalogue by not including any pop songs or ballads. Every piece was written by someone in the band, and most of them were either collectively reworked at the session or changed by Davis. Herbie Hancock recalled Miles' minimalist techniques as he revised Ron Carter's composition "Eight-One":

Miles took the first two bars of melody notes and squished them together, and he took out other areas to leave a big space that only the rhythm section would play. To me, it sounded like getting to the essence of the composition. He'd take the inherent structure and leave us room to breathe and create something fresh every night. There were the basic elements of the song, but not used exactly as they were in the composition.

The mixture of the abstract and the earthy that Davis had so often seemed to be reaching for began to take shape with this record. Wayne Shorter's ease with indeterminate melodies and his eagerness to join the rhythm section in churning up the music to the point that it threatened to break loose from the traditions of jazz gave Davis the space he needed to reexamine his own playing.

Although at the time there were other musicians redefining the idea of what forms jazz could be played in, or minimizing the harmonic constraints and expanding the importance of the rhythm section, this music was perhaps heard by many as more radical than it was because the record was issued only six months after *My Funny Valentine,* a live recording of familiar Davis repertoire by the previous quintet with George Coleman. (Only three months after *E.S.P.,* even more material from the *Valentine* concert was released under the title *Four & More.*) When Kenny Dorham, the trumpet player who replaced Miles in Charlie Parker's group, reviewed *E.S.P.* in *Down Beat,* his comments were cautiously worded, but like a food critic, he praised the presentation and damned the meal. Because Miles was having trouble with the melody of the title song, Dorham slyly hinted that the co-composer credits for Miles and Shorter on this composition may not have been correct and that Shorter was the real author. Dorham also found most of the music emotionally lacking. But what really worried him was that this group was edging toward the jazz avant-garde, and he concluded, "It's not for me." Given the verbal distance that Davis had already put between himself and free jazz, it's revealing to learn that a contemporary of his was unable to hear the difference.

The cover photo for *E.S.P.* showed Miles on a chaise longue in his garden, gazing quizzically up at Frances, who is looking out of the picture at the viewer. "And that little face," she said, " . . . you would not believe that about a week after it was taken I was running for my life."

A gap was beginning to open up between what Miles played live and what he recorded in the studio. It was customary for most jazz groups to work out a program they wanted to record while they were on the road, learning the material, getting it in shape. But he was introducing new music on the day of the recording session, scarcely rehearsing it or not rehearsing it at all; then it usually disappeared from their repertoire, leaving only their older material for live performances. It was also becoming clear that Miles, the master of converting popular ballads into jazz material, was losing interest in playing ballads. He now seemed to be looking for compositions that would not be dependent on the breath limits of singers and the restrictions of word phrases. On the first live recording done with this new quintet, *Miles in Berlin,* from September 25, 1964, some of this new direction was already apparent in "Autumn Leaves," when, near the end of Shorter's solo, Hancock ceased playing the song's original chords and instead continued to hammer out the same chord repeatedly. This was not a totally free interpretation, for the solo continued within the number of bars remaining in the song's original form, but the implication was that they could have gone on this way, free from conventional harmony and song structure, for some time. The new quintet's own compositions tended to have no conventional harmonic progression, no bridges—in fact, no clear structure at all. The pianist often stopped playing, completely removing harmonic guidelines for long stretches of time. And even when they played more conventional songs at live performances, their tempos became faster, their meters shifting around between 4/4, 2/4, 6/8, and 5/4, with one tune running into the next without interruption:

> I started not even bothering to have breaks in between tunes but playing everything without breaks, segueing from one tune right into the next. My music was stretching out from scale to scale, so I don't feel like breaking up the mood with stops and breaks. I just moved into the next tune, whatever tempo it was, and just played it like that. My performances were becoming more like musical suites, and this allowed for more and longer periods of improvisation.

It was a practice that had been hinted at before in the bridging passages between songs Gil Evans wrote for *Miles Ahead*. Now Miles would not find it necessary to explain why he refused to speak or acknowledge applause between tunes, because there was no longer any "between."

The pain in his hip had become so severe that he was unable to walk, and on April 14, he was admitted to New York Hospital for what was diagnosed as calcium deposits in the left hipbone, and he underwent surgery to replace his hip ball with bone grafted from his shin. Miles left the hospital before they were ready to release him and was in a wheelchair and on crutches for eight weeks, with one leg in a cast. All of his engagements were canceled for the next three months. In August, he broke the same leg while wrestling with one of his sons, and was unable to play for another month. When it was discovered that the operation hadn't worked, he was back in the hospital to have a plastic hip joint implanted. Altogether he was out of work for almost seven months, confined most of the time to a daybed on the first floor, overlooking the tiny backyard. More painkillers were added to his drug regimen, and he counted on the maid, his sons, girlfriends, and sometimes even visiting journalists to get him through the day.

Once he began to recover, Miles scheduled a few concerts to get the band in shape and see if he could last through the evening. He booked a live recording during a two-week stay at the Plugged Nickel for his usual Christmas gig in Illinois. Trucks of recording equipment were driven to Chicago and were set up to go on December 21, when Miles suddenly announced that the sessions were off. He was still not well, but the reason he gave was that Tony Williams didn't want to record—and if it was true, Williams' reasons were never made clear. Teo recommended to Columbia management that they should charge the expenses of the failed session against Miles' royalties, and if he refused to record on December 22 or 23, he should be charged again. But at that point, Miles or Tony, or both, gave in, and everything they played on those two days—seven sets altogether—was finally recorded.

It's unusual in any form of music to record an artist or group so intensively, but one of the payoffs is the discovery of performance practices not apparent in single studio recordings. In this case, what it revealed is a group in the act of rapidly transforming itself and the traditions of jazz. Ron Carter said that it gave the listener an opportunity "to hear all the clunks, all the train wrecks, and all the rockets take off, too." During this time, Miles was talking about what he no longer wanted to do—no more "songs" or chords, no fixed bar lengths or phrases. Yet he was not ready to go as far as some free jazz musicians had in attempting to abandon harmonic structure totally, and he was certainly not ready to give up on rhythmic pulse. He talked instead of "controlled freedom." It was left to Herbie Hancock to elaborate:

> What I was trying to do and what I feel they were trying to do was to combine—take these influences that were happening to all of us at that time and amalgamate them, personalize them in such a way that when people were hearing us, they were hearing the avant-garde on the one hand, and they were hearing the history of jazz that led up it on the other hand—because Miles was that history. He was that link. We were sort of walking a tightrope with the kind of experimenting we were doing in music, not total experimentation, but we used to call it "controlled freedom."

Hancock said they were thinking in terms of "anti-music" and wanted to play against expectations. Shorter spoke of "taking chances" and of "struggling" with music. Live, they were still operating with a repertoire drawn largely from pop songs, but they had found a way to create collective impressions of those songs, rather than play solo variations of the sheet music. From one set to the next over two nights at the Plugged Nickel, they were changing these tunes, shifting their tempos around, and stretching their forms to the breaking point. At times, it became messy and chaotic, but thrillingly so. Miles' playing was not always his best, and the line of his musical thought is not always clear. And Tony Williams' role in the shaping of the form—the rapid alterations, his sudden swells of volume and clatter, the occasional disappearance of the beat—borders on the eccentric. Yet it was all accomplished with a mutuality, confidence, and openness to chance that is rare in music and life.

Bassist Gary Peacock filled in for Ron Carter at times during this period and said that Miles sometimes did tunes like "Oleo" with just bass and trumpet (except for the bridge where everyone came in) for a half hour at a time.

> Or he would do things like, he would play a line and he'd be listening to me. And I realized that when he ended his solo he didn't end it with the sound of the trumpet—he let the bass end the solo. The bass would continue to play and then he'd come back in.
> He'd listen so hard that it was deafening. He didn't miss *anything*.

Like some other musicians at this time, Miles was looking into the heart of jazz and questioning its intentions. He might have gone further and gotten there faster if the group had played more of their original compositions, such as those they had recorded in the *E.S.P.* studio sessions, but at this point he was not willing to risk cutting himself loose from his audience. He knew how far out not to go.

By the time they reached the Plugged Nickel, the quintet was full of the excitement of knowing that they were the best and the sense that they were capable of doing anything they wanted. In the off-hours at the hotel, they talked music among themselves, and by the time they reached the bandstand, they were exhilarated, Wayne Shorter said.

> At the Plugged Nickel we were raising so much hell [musically] that when we came off we couldn't say nothing to each other. We were lethargic in a princely way. We weren't trying to put on airs . . . it was like, "let's not touch this." You were in the royalty of the moment, and such royalty need never be tampered with.

"Miles wanted to play with people who knew more about music than he did," according to Shorter. "He wasn't looking for that, but he wasn't afraid of it." This was a time in which Davis began to feel more at ease as a performer—maybe not at ease enough to talk to an audience or graciously accept applause, but enough to introduce some new and subtle theatrics into his shows. Gary Peacock said that he became very impressed by Miles' willingness to satisfy the public without coming to depend on it:

He knew exactly what to do to make the audience faint. One night, in the middle of one of his solos, he whispered to me, "Watch this!" and then played a long descending note "Pfiooowuuuh!" The first ten rows leaned back and murmured "Aaahoowuuuuh!" He looked back to me as if to say, "Did you see that?"

On one occasion during the Plugged Nickel sessions, Miles began his usual serene approach to "I Fall in Love Too Easily," leaving long spaces between each phrase. A drunk at a nearby table can be heard on the record groaning out what he thought Miles should play next in the solo, and Miles obliged him by playing precisely that.

Success ensured that Miles was now playing in better-paying clubs, which meant expensive clubs in white neighborhoods, and he was beginning to miss the black audiences, whose response he understood and needed.

Now, did you see last night. I was playing a blues and I go and bend down to play to that fat woman in the second row. She says, "That's right, Miles, come on over here, you can *stay* over here." So then I play something real fast, and she says, "Not like *that,* though. Go back over there if you're gonna play that shit." Now, do you think a white person would tell me that? They don't even know what she's talking about. She's talking about the *bluuuenesss.* In my hometown, if you don't play the blues, shit, them motherfuckers go to ordering drinks, but if you play the blues, they'll stay right there. That fat bitch, she'd have me blowing all night.

Yet the course his music was on guaranteed this separation, and his ambition and the speed with which he changed his music made the luxury of playing for any distinct audience, much less a black one, difficult.

When he returned to New York at the start of 1966, Miles' health problems were growing worse, and he was hospitalized again on January 31, this time for a liver infection. For the next three months, he was at home recuperating. Though he was by now generally thought of as unapproachable, he could be seen in his neighborhood almost any day, drinking a beer and sitting on the curb in front of his house, leaning against a lamppost, or walking in Riverside Park, much as he had done ever since he first came to the city. It was on one of those walks that he ran into actress Cicely Tyson, whom he had met some years before when she was working in the theater in New York. Miles said that she asked him if he came to the park every day, and when, and from that began a relationship that lasted over an eleven-year period, one that literally kept him alive during various illnesses.

Illnesses or no, Columbia was once again considering punishing Davis for not recording the Davis-Evans album for which he had received an advance. In a memo to Jack Weidenman on May 4, Howard Roberts complained about the arranger's fees already advanced to Gil Evans and said that Evans was asking for even more, although they hadn't as yet seen any work at all from him.

> I understand that Columbia is $40,000 in the red as of now with Miles Davis, but Teo informs me that there is enough in the can to put out one or two albums. Perhaps we should take that route.
>
> I certainly would appreciate hearing your thoughts on the entire matter.
>
> P.S. By the way, I was under the impression that Miles and Gil had been working on the concept of that album for over a year. However Gil told me flatly that only three tunes were ready and they still had to decide about the rest of the material.

But on July 28, Davis was notified by M. M. Drosnes, the senior attorney for CBS, that his contract with Columbia had been suspended for not completing the promised record. "Suspension," in fact, meant his contract was being extended by an additional amount of time, so that he still owed the same number of recordings to Columbia and was also prevented from recording with anyone else.

When he did record again, in October, it was the album, *Miles Smiles*, a quintet record that gave the clearest indication yet of where he wanted to take his music. When he discussed it a few months later with Ralph Gleason, Miles said that he made the piano lay out more on this record so that the rhythm could be heard. And what could be heard was an extraordinary drummer and bassist in the process of finding a new role for the rhythm section.

Jazz rhythm sections have always operated on different principles from European conceptions of rhythm. Musical time or pulse in jazz is conceived far more flexibly. The history of this music has been one of expanding rhythmic elasticity, with the roles of drummers, bassists, and pianists becoming increasingly independent from each other, while still interrelated. Bassists became more melodic, eventually strumming and arpeggiating their lines; drummers played freer from the beat, sometimes toying with the time, playing around it, or commenting on it; and pianists became more percussive and drumlike or, as in the Davis Quintet's case, they might at times disappear altogether.

On *Miles Smiles*, the quintet's new approach to rhythm could be heard in compositions like Wayne Shorter's asymmetrical "Delores," a thirty-eight-bar piece in five sections of unequal length, the first, third, and fifth sections having melodic lines for the horns, the second and the fourth being nothing more than stretches of open space for bass and drums alone. Hancock's piano disappears when the horns play, and the soloists do not adhere to any harmonic structure. Asked about this piece, Shorter said that "everyone took a certain characteristic of the song and . . . you can stay there. And you can do eight measures of it, and then you can make your own harmonic road or avenue within a certain eight measures. But not counting out the eight measures, it's like whatever fancied you. But you keep the flavor."

> We were actually tampering with something called DNA in music in a song. Each song has its DNA. So you just do the DNA and not the whole song. You do the characteristics. You say, "Okay, I will do the ear of the face, I will do the left side of the face. You do the right side of the face."

The only piece on *Miles Smiles* that was not written by a member of the quintet was "Freedom Jazz Dance," a tune first recorded the previous year by saxophonist Eddie Harris on his album, *The "In" Sound*. In its original form, it was a ten-bar, poplike melody that hovered around a single tone, B-flat, though Herbie Hancock complicated it on Miles' recording by emphasizing B-natural in his accompaniment. In this new drum-driven version, with Tony Williams playing triplets against the melody's eighth notes, Harris' tune becomes harder-edged, taking on greater angularity and swing, demonstrating just how volatile music can be made to sound even when it has minimal harmonic content.

Miles' many layoffs for illness were beginning to tell, and he was badly in need of money in late 1966. He continued to pressure Columbia for advances, and in a memo to Walter Yetnikoff on November 3, 1966, Bob Ciotti requested a $5,000 interest-bearing loan for Davis. The loan was approved, but this only increased the company's resolve to force Miles to produce faster. Irving Townsend wrote Columbia's chief counsel Walter Dean on March 17, 1967, about the difficulties he saw looming with Miles' recorded output. His memo also reveals that Bob Thiele, John Coltrane's producer at Impulse Records, was asking for permission from Columbia to allow him to record Miles with Coltrane. It was something of a strange idea, because Coltrane had moved into a very different kind of music at that point. It also made little sense for Columbia to allow one of its stars to record for another label, no matter what the financial arrangements were. Townsend wrote:

> I'm sure you're tired of the MILES DAVIS problem, but I would like to tell you what I know of it as of now.
>
> On the album with Coltrane, I discussed this with Bob Thiele and after I found out that involved our participation as well, including an advance, I told Bill Gallagher that I thought it was a poor idea and I also told this to Miles. Miles then said he would just as soon not record with Coltrane if we would do something with him where he'd get some money. He apparently has an album ready to go with Gil Evans and wants to record.
>
> I have conveyed all this to all concerned in New York. If he calls me again, I will tell him that you will pay him an advance for his new album when he has made it. I think he will do it. I will urge him to get going, but I want you to know that I did not convey this to anyone concerned that I was in favor of the Impulse deal.

By 1967, Columbia Records had a new president, Clive Davis—Harvard Law, new breed, and, at thirty-five, one of the youngest executives in the entertainment business. Unlike many previous presidents and executives at Columbia, he was not a trained musician, not even a record collector, but he knew how the business worked and saw that it wasn't working properly at a time when pop music had begun to transform the industry. Clive thought in terms of albums instead of singles, promoted stars instead of artists, spent time hanging out in the nightclubs, and was looking for a way to narrow the gap between classical and popular music audiences. He wanted nothing to do with traditionalists, jazz or pop;

instead, he was interested in stars who knew how to communicate to new audiences, by whatever means. How, for example, could he get Bill Evans to go beyond the small pool of jazz fans and reach other people? A restless, bored, ready-to-move Miles Davis was a perfect example of what he was looking for. On October 13, 1967, Teo sent Clive a memo that repeated the usual story about Miles' recalcitrance and warned that a record might be slow in coming: "The other day I discussed the possibility of doing a Miles Davis album with Miles and, as of the moment, it's only a possibility. They have been working on this possibility for three and a half years." Clive returned a handwritten reply on the same letter that hinted at why Miles would soon escape the upcoming purge of "traditional" jazz musicians from the roster at Columbia: "He is one of the few giants who appeal to the youth—we must keep after him." Getting his drift, three days later, Teo followed up with another memo to Clive:

I have just had the pleasure of being with him this morning. He is very enthusiastic about doing a *Dr. Doolittle* album with the possibility of doing something from *Camelot*, with arrangements by Gil Evans.

It's difficult in a few paragraphs to discuss the value of his work and the scale and scope of it in terms of the present market. . . . Would appreciate meeting with you.

Miles actually considered this project and surprisingly saw some possibilities in it, or at least stalled the company a bit longer with it, but at the moment his thoughts were elsewhere. He was bored with the sound of the bebop quintet and had heard in rock music an electronic element that from then on would seem to him an audible absence in jazz. It was not that he was interested in creating a music based merely on pop sensibilities. Nor did noise or distortion interest him. At that point at least, he had no desire to break rules for the sake of doing so, or produce music that roared. He had already rejected that side of free jazz. Davis, after all, was familiar with the tradition of the classical or experimental avant-garde, which viewed noise as an element to be organized musically; he and Gil Evans had pored over Cage, Partch, and others. Instead, Miles developed his taste for electronics slowly, and by his own standards: "When I started playing against that new rhythm—synthesizers and guitars and all that new stuff—first I had to get used to it. At first there was no feeling. . . . You didn't hear the sound at first. It takes time." What he seemed to be looking for was a textural element, a new pattern of musical relationships, and a sonic dimension that could enrich the music, perhaps even enrich it spiritually. Though no one would have dared say it at the time, judging by his earliest amplified works, he seemed to be seeking what might be called the electronic sublime.

In this moment of transition, Miles tried several new directions. For a short time, he added a second tenor saxophonist, Joe Henderson. Next he considered the idea of forming a big band. But he also began to cut back his work schedule, so as not to get bored, he said, playing mostly on weekends, avoiding clubs when he could, and doing concerts at colleges. Because the quintet was working less, Ron Carter began to play with other groups, and though he always made it back to the quintet for recording sessions, Miles often had to find substitutes for him. Over the next five years, he filled the bass spot with Gary Peacock, Miraslav Vitous, Marshall Hawkins, Reggie Workman, Paul Chambers, and Buster Williams. When Williams was his working bassist in the spring of 1967, he was surprised to discover that Miles was playing his older tunes much faster than he had on his records—so fast that at first Williams couldn't keep up. But Miles was tolerant, Williams said, and his playing was always astonishing: when Miles soloed, "Things could come to him like a dart out of heaven." For a band that did not often articulate its methods verbally, Buster's outsider's view of how things worked is important. The quintet's live repertoire overall leaned toward the music done on *E.S.P.*, and they opened every set with "Agitation," "the only thing that resembled a melody," Buster said.

> From then on, it was out there. I listened to Tony, and when I found that I couldn't figure out anything from Tony, I listened to Herbie. But Herbie was laying out half the time. Wayne just seemed to float on the periphery of everything, and Miles would just make his statement and go to the bar. I didn't know what I was supposed to do, man, except play the bass. . . . The guys were so beautiful, they adjusted to me.

Buster Williams saw the quintet as bringing new meaning to the concept of "faking it," by implying a certain musical reality without actually playing it.

> I learned how to keep a structure in mind and play changes so loosely that you can play for some time without people knowing whether the structure is played or not, but then hit on certain points to indicate that you have been playing the structure all the time. When you hear these points being played, you just say, "Wow! It's like the Invisible Man. You see him here and then you don't. Then all of a sudden you see him over there and then you see him over here." And it indicates that it's been happening all the time.

At every recording session, innovation reigned, traditions were shattered, and at least one of the new compositions always became the topic of public discussion—at least until the next record came along. In May, the session that resulted in the curiously unfocused album *Sorcerer* (which had a photo of Cicely Tyson on the cover) contained tunes like Tony Williams' composition "Pee Wee," on which Miles did not play, the very slow and harmonically decentered "Vonetta," and "Nothing Like You," which had been recorded by an entirely different group of musicians back in 1962.

At the June 1967 session that produced the album *Nefertiti*, it was the title tune by Wayne Shorter that got the attention. When they ran through it together for the first time, Miles told Shorter, "Wayne, we ain't gonna put no solo on this—we just gonna play the melody over and over again." There was nothing a soloist could add to this composition, he said. Just play it over and over again, like Coltrane's "A Love Supreme." But every time they played it again, it was different. Tony kept adding something, doing something to make it sound new, and they responded to him; the volume rose or fell, the horns played in unison or echoed each other, or they dropped out altogether. (Quincy Jones remarked that during this period, the roles became reversed in the group: Miles played trumpet percussively, while the rhythm section took off on its own.) The complexity that always characterized bebop melody lines was now being transferred to the rhythm section, leaving the melody instruments free to float on top of the tumult.

For most jazz groups, the improvised solo is the ultimate goal, the highest level of achievement. The composition on which they improvise and the accompaniment that frames the solos are both secondary. Typically, the leader is the best improviser, or at least the featured soloist, and the rest of the group exists to enhance the soloist's mastery. What was different about the Davis group was Miles' attitude toward the individual musicians and how they should work together. Tony Williams said that Miles hired people who were good, but he encouraged them to be better, to take chances, even to go beyond him if they chose. "He wants to hear stuff he's not in control of," Tony said. "He wants to hear something that he wouldn't think of. I mean, when he walks off the stage, he's not just going to go and, you know, read a book or something. He wants to hear the music still going on at a level that he left it at or something better."

Davis was famous among musicians for the opaqueness of his musical discussions, his paradoxical and often indecipherable mutterings. "I think Miles doesn't like to overexplain things, or to explain things to the point where it becomes crystallized in your head and you'll do only that," said Herbie Hancock. "He wants to give impressions so that you have a wider range of discerning what he wants. You know, if he tells you specifically something, you'll do that and only that, see. . . . He wants to point you in a direction, and your talent and creativity will let you do maybe five things."

Miles may have wanted each player to operate on his own resources, but as Tony Williams suggests, he also insisted that their music be a collective creation. "We never rehearsed any of that stuff, any of those things you hear on those records. I mean those changes or going from one thing to another. . . . It was just things we knew we could do and we would try them out and I would do something, and Herbie would hear me do it and he would play something with it or to complement it or play over against it to create tension, and Ron because of his massive knowledge of harmony, he knew when Herbie played a substitution what to play in the bass."

This level of group interaction and Miles' love of first takes at recording sessions were part of an aesthetic of discovery that was given priority over a finished, perfected performance. For many musicians, this kind of playing could be terrifying, since it risked mistakes. But in Miles' conception, even errors were a matter for the group to correct. "I remember," said Hancock, "one time we were playing in Germany, I think, and we were playing this song and we got to one chord and I played the chord way too soon: it clashed with everything that was going on. Miles played—it was during his solo—he played something on top of my chord to make it sound right. He made it fit and it blew my mind because I didn't even know where those notes came from. . . . He didn't hear it as a clash, he heard it as 'this is what's happening right now so I'll make the most of it.'"

Miles' ability to hear those moments in which the music was becoming unraveled and to correct them instantly was part of what Hancock thought was the magic of playing with him. "Sometimes the rhythm section would not know what they were doing," according to Herbie, "and Miles would find the notes to make it work. . . . When Miles' eyes roll back in his head, the next statement you hear come out of his trumpet, it would be a phrase that could stop you dead in your tracks [as] it would seem to come from the heavens. For instance, during 'So What' in Stuttgart, after Wayne's solo we would build things in the rhythm section and Miles was leaving space. We had to build to a climax and Miles' eyes rolled back and he played something. . . . I couldn't play for two hours! Nobody can do that. You could work a lifetime and be lucky to find a phrase like that!"

The pressure to remain creative in a group operating at this level could be daunting. Each player must be willing to continually rethink the principles that underlay what he thought he knew. Hancock, for instance, found that when they recorded, the individual musical composition no longer seemed adequate for what they were attempting and that something larger was becoming necessary: "I had to find sounds (not so much chords) so that when the information came, I wanted to leave room for more to happen, to provoke you and stretch yourself— the whole story should not be told in the song itself. The value is in the *whole* record in jazz."

Like Hancock, Wayne Shorter began to feel that the composition was an inadequate conceptual unit: "Playing with Miles, importance was placed on everything you did, even when you weren't soloing. There was that tendency to think that the whole evening was the composition. As far as everybody in the group thinking that way, it was up to each individual to be on his own to help create images and illusions." Shorter also began to question the very existence of the chord: "In a certain chord— in any one chord exists all other chords. Why go through all the other chords and keep repeating a song form over and over again. . . . So we started doing something that some people called experimental . . . some called it modal, some people called it . . . taking chances." "By the late sixties," he said, "we knew we were on the verge of something:

> Herbie said, "I don't know what to play no more." So Miles says, "Don't play nothin'. Only play when you feel like it." So we'd be playing a piece of music, and Herbie's sitting there with his hands in his lap . . . then all of a sudden he'd play one sound, and Miles said, "That one sound you made was a bitch." So everybody saw *something* happening . . . and we began playing songs without chords.

After a tour of Europe, Miles took the band into the studio on December 4, 1967, for a new round of experimentation. He'd been thinking about the use of the guitar in blues bands and James Brown's groups and how a guitar might create a new ensemble sound for him.

> When I used to listen to Muddy Waters in Chicago down on 33rd and Michigan every Monday when he played there and I would be in town, I knew I had to get some of what he was doing up in my music. You know, the sound of the $1.50 drums and the harmonicas and the two-chord blues. I had to get back to that because what we had been doing was just getting really abstracted.

Though it seemed he might be thinking of forming some kind of funk band, his first steps in a new direction were much more modest. He began by adding Joe Beck, an electric guitarist whom Gil Evans had been using. Next, he expanded the band's sonics even further by giving Herbie Hancock a celeste to play, while he himself began to toy with a set of chimes in the studio. These were interesting departures from his normal practice, though not unprecedented: many of the free jazz pioneers, such as the Art Ensemble of Chicago, were also using unusual instruments in that period. The real innovation of this session was that he chose not to record in complete takes, but in segments or sections, which would later be edited and reassembled to form a single take. The music would be partly improvised and partly composed through editing.

What they produced that day in December was "Circle in the Round," a twenty-six minute and seventeen-second piece assembled from thirty-five separate short recordings, twenty-eight of which were used in the final mix. Although Davis' recordings had been getting longer over the past seven or eight years, this one was more than four times longer than his average piece (and an earlier unissued version was even nine minutes longer). In the issued edit, a twenty-six-bar "Spanish"-type melody in 12/8 meter built on several scales is repeated again and again amid the skirls and washes of the celeste and the chattering of the drums. No solos occur for more than seven minutes. Underneath, meanwhile, bass and guitar maintain a simple repetitive drone. The piece might have been too long for some tastes, somewhat unfocused, and modal to the point of exhaustion, but it nonetheless served to sum up some of Davis' past ventures such as the exoticism of *Sketches of Spain* and the incremental repetition of "Nefertiti." It also provided a clue to what was to come in a few years with *In a Silent Way*. But since "Circle in the Round" was not issued for another eleven years, audiences were unaware of Davis' current thinking.

In several weeks, the band returned to the studio, and Hancock was startled to find a Fender Rhodes electric piano waiting for him, an instrument he had no interest at all in playing. But Miles insisted, and when Herbie sat down at the Rhodes, his reservations began to vanish as he found that he could now be heard even over Tony Williams' drums.

The electric piano was an instrument that Miles had wanted to use ever since he had heard Joe Zawinul play a Wurlitzer model on Cannonball Adderley's 1967 jazz hit, "Mercy, Mercy, Mercy." (Zawinul had begun using electric piano after he first heard Ray Charles play it and saw how it gave his music a soulful, funky edge.) The Fender Rhodes electric piano offered even greater possibilities. It was more portable than an acoustic piano, louder, and stayed in tune better; and when its ringing, watery, shimmering sound was passed through motorized, whirling Leslie loudspeakers, a wah-wah pedal, a ring modulator, and a variable-speed tape-delay device like the Echoplex, its tone could be bent and vocalized like an electric guitar's.

The first time that George Benson met Miles was in a muffler shop. Davis sidled up to him like a spider: "You George Benson? You play the *baddest* guitar, man!" Having gone through a couple of guitarists over the past two months without finding what he was looking for, Miles invited George to play on part of what was to become the album *Miles in the Sky*.

When Benson arrived at the studio in January 1968, he was stunned to see Davis leave within five minutes: "Miles came . . . played three or four notes, packed up his horn, and left." The next day, the same thing happened. When it happened again on the third day, George called Miles and told him that he didn't see any sense in coming in and taking his money if they weren't going to record. No, Miles assured him, they'd make a record, and on the fourth day Davis began by telling Tony to move his drums into the farthest part of the studio. So: it was about playing too loud, Benson thought—Miles was not yet into volume, and Tony Williams, with those extra-heavy sticks of his, was *loud*. But Benson was not particularly happy with Williams anyway, because Tony—"graduate of the Berklee College of Music and a genius," as George put it—kept giving him advice on what chords to play, until Miles had to tell him to stop it. Why did he hire Tony, George wondered; for that matter, why Herbie Hancock. These musicians did not fit the Miles Davis mold, as far as he could see. Nor was Benson happy with what he had played. He tried different things, but Miles only kept the takes on which Benson played rhythm, doubling the bass line as on a Motown arrangement (much as Joe Beck had done on "Circle in the Round") or on which he merely shadowed the bass line. Only much later did Benson see what Miles was trying to do in this music and how a guitar was supposed to fit in.

During the session, Davis got into an argument with Teo that Benson said made the musicians cringe with embarassment. Still, Miles turned right around and talked to them about having pride in their music as black men and about the importance of making a contribution to the tradition created by their race, so George said that he ended up leaving the studio filled with confidence.

Gil Evans was also at the sessions, with arrangements he had done of several of the pieces, as was Martin Williams, who was there part of the time to write up the occasion for *Stereo Review*. When Miles arrived, he began complaining about the guitar player on his last session, Bucky Pizzarelli, but they then quickly moved into rehearsing Herbie Hancock's "The Collector" (wrongly titled "Teo's Bag" on the record). Next came Wayne Shorter's piece "Paraphernalia," on which Hancock started on the electric harpsichord, then switched to the piano at Miles' suggestion. Martin Williams remarked that the piece didn't sound difficult to him, though George Benson overheard Miles say to Wayne Shorter, "I think you wrote this just to hang me up." The tricky part was a spot where the piano and bass stay on one chord until the soloist chooses to move on. Miles gave out some advice as they rehearsed, telling Hancock to stay out of the upper third of the piano, then signaled the engineers that they were ready to record. When Williams later reviewed *Miles in the Sky*, he proclaimed that Davis was now a member of the avant-garde.

After the session, Miles asked Benson if he wanted to join the band. He considered it, but finally decided against it after his manager warned him it might make it more difficult for him to hold his own band together and keep his own recording contract. Later, rather portentously, Miles said, "I'm going to tell you what I told Jimi Hendrix . . . *Play loud!*" No way was Benson going to play loud, but he interpreted Miles' advice to mean that it was time for him to come out and be his own man.

A short time later, soon after the death of guitarist Wes Montgomery, Benson ran into Miles at Count Basie's club in Harlem. Miles whispered to him, "Did you kill Wes so that you could take his spot, man?"

Two months after his divorce from Frances Taylor in February 1968, became official, Miles suddenly stopped seeing Cicely Tyson and became involved with Betty Mabry, a twenty-three-year-old from Homestead, Pennsylvania, who seemed to be everywhere in New York in a way that was possible only in the late 1960s. She was quintessentially sixties, all funky chic and an exploding Afro, with talent to burn: she had studied fashion design; written "Uptown" for the Chambers Brothers on their *The Time Has Come* album; appeared on the *Dating Game* TV show and as a model in *Ebony, Glamour, Jet,* and *Seventeen*; was co-owner of the Cellar, a club for teenagers in New York City; and was beginning a singing career. She was yet another talented woman in Miles' life, but this time a much younger one and wired into a scene that Miles had witnessed only from afar. Betty knew many of the new black rockers like Sly

Stone and Jimi Hendrix, and she introduced Miles to them and a club scene he had never been part of. She even became his dresser, taking him on shopping trips to flash and funk boutiques in the Village and steering him away from the tailored suits that he so proudly wore.

Following a Plugged Nickel performance in Chicago, they were quickly married in Gary, Indiana, on September 30, 1968, with Vernon and Dorothy as witnesses. In an interview probably better suited for *Jet* than *Down Beat*, Betty said that she had "never really been a jazz fan, because I lean to R&B and pop, but Miles' *Sketches of Spain* and *Kind of Blue* really sock it to me. But Miles is the teacher, so I'm going to be in the background, and back up my man." Though the marriage lasted only a year, their relationship sent both sailing off in new directions. Betty's picture was on the cover of Miles' *Filles de Kilimanjaro,* and he helped her with a demo single ("Live Love Learn"/"It's My Life") for Columbia backed by Hendrix musicians Mitch Mitchell and Billy Cox, with horn parts arranged by Hugh Masakela. (An album that was to be a collaboration between her and Miles was later shelved, but as late as March 1970, Miles was still planning it, and calling it *Zonked.*) Betty continued to record under the name of Davis, doing three LPs over the next five years. (One of them, *Nasty Gal* in 1975, even had a tune arranged by Gil, "You and I," with a Miles Davis sound-alike trumpet obbligato.)

With a new wave of younger black pop performers eclipsing jazz, and his own band sometimes playing to fewer than a dozen customers, Miles grew angry about the way in which black performers were marketed by white corporations and by the companies' failure to reach out to black audiences. He was dissatisfied with the African American response to his music and saw his situation as only a single case of a much larger problem. In interviews, he began to lecture journalists about the selling of music—about white salespeople in the record industry making decisions about marketing to black people. What they did was sell white skin, white hair, white voices, make *them* glamorous, creating positive opinions about whites. He told Hollie West of the *Washington Post* that he was going to Columbia Records with a proposal to set up a special marketing program with talent and promotional agencies to reach the black community through concerts, records, and nightclub appearances. He was going to suggest a range of possibilities, including sponsoring talent shows on black college campuses to find new entertainers and recruiting people who knew how to market black performers to black media. Later, he would tell his promoters that they should give away several thousand concert tickets to young African Americans and that he would be willing to play for black colleges for free: "I would like for black people to look at me like Joe Louis. Maybe it will never happen, maybe it's just wishful thinking." In fact, the younger fighters at Gleason's Gym no longer knew who he was.

In a period in which racial strife was penetrating almost every aspect of American life, reopening old grievances and long-suppressed anxieties, Miles and Gil Evans defied the times and drew even closer together. Miles once said that Gil was the only serious musician he'd ever known. But in truth, both were equally preoccupied with music and shared the sense that its melodic and rhythmic architecture organized their lives and expressed their thoughts and emotions in ways words could never do. Musical reality was intensely palpable to them both, and their conversations—low key and verbally sparse as they were—were built on this shared sense of zeitgeist. One of them might play a bit of a musical idea over the phone for the other, a riff, a chord, or bring up something more abstract (Miles to Gil: "I had this dream last night . . . what would that sound like?"). They might talk about their kids, or the two of them might watch the same TV show together, sitting alone in their respective homes in complete silence. Every project they worked on they talked over together at length beforehand, and Gil visited Miles when he was recording or working in the clubs, sometimes even going to other cities to watch him work. "They were really family," Gil's wife, Anita, said, "and I sometimes thought of Miles as my brother-in-law." Gil even named one of his sons after Miles (though Miles had kept after him to do it for months before he was born). Frances had used the Evanses' apartment as a refuge from Miles' abuse, and he used it "as a cover for his affairs with women," something Anita detested.

Miles and Gil still hoped to complete some kind of big project together for Columbia, but the last thing they did was a strange session in Columbia's studios back in February, 1968, with a sixteen-piece orchestra. The only result was "Falling Water," a short, sketchy piece that provided a base on which Miles improvised, but without a melody as such. It was not long enough for an album or usable as a single, so the tapes were stored away and remained unissued until 1998. Gil's interests were drifting elsewhere. He too was becoming interested in new developments in rock, perhaps even more so than Miles at the time; he was fascinated by Jimi Hendrix's first recordings. Miles and Gil met with Hendrix several times, trading ideas for different projects, and Jimi's influence turned up later in Miles' work when Gil reworked "The Wind Cries Mary" into "Mademoiselle Mabry." Later, Davis would incorporate small Hendrix touches by using the bass line from "Fire" in "Inamorata," and turning "Message to Love" from Hendrix's *Band of Gypsys* into "What I Say," both on *Live/Evil*. (After Hendrix's death, his hairdresser, James Finney, went to work for Miles as dietitian and hairdresser, and continued with him until Miles' death.)

Miles asked Hendrix's producer, Alan Douglas, to set up some kind of project between them. According to Douglas, "Miles wanted to work with Jimi very badly."

Jimi was probably the only musician that Miles could not fully understand. He couldn't figure out where Jimi was coming from, because he wasn't writing any music, he was just flowing. *Bitches Brew* was the result of Miles hanging out with Jimi for two years. Not that there wasn't a mutual admiration, but Jimi had the contemporary edge and Miles was always reaching out for that.

For four months Douglas worked on a deal between Columbia and Warner Brothers, and the record was set to come out on Warners. There were to be four songs, with the money split four ways among the musicians. The night of the session, Miles' agent called Douglas a half hour before it was to start and told him that Miles wanted $50,000 before he would enter the studio:

So I called Miles at home and when he finally agrees to come to the phone he says something like, "Come on, you know you got it, you know you can do it." I just hung up the phone, turned to Jimi and said, "Let's go get something to eat." We're just about to walk out of the door when the phone rings again. I thought, that must be Miles ringing back to apologize. I pick up the phone and it's Tony Williams. Tony says, "I heard you're giving Miles $50,000, so I want $50,000, too!"

"Miles had this enormous ego," Douglas said. "I was prepared for it not to work out."

Davis decided to call his next record *Girls of Kilimanjaro,* in part to acknowledge his investment in Buddy Gist's Kilimanjaro African Coffee, a company that imported beans from Kenyan coffee cooperatives. (Lena Horne and Peggy Mellon Hitchcock were also investors in the company). The title was also designed to establish a theme that would justify using Betty's picture on the cover of the record. Miles still had in mind doing some kind of African-based music, and the saxophonist Steve Potts remembers that when he was at Miles' house one night, he saw him writing "Filles de Kilimanjaro" on an African thumb piano. (Just before the record was to be released, Miles decided he wanted all the titles in French—an exotic touch but an odd one, given that French is not one of the languages of Tanzania. But it was enough to set off a scramble at Columbia as they tried to find somebody on the staff who knew how to change "Brown Hornet" to "Frelon Brun," or "Little Stuff" to "Petits Machins.") Elements of rock and soul music were scattered everywhere in this album, but so transformed and reworked as to constitute something of a reinvention of both. "Petits Machins" has a rocklike urgency, but with swirling electric piano and polymetric drumming, and solos played over the simplest of pedal devices. But what rock group in 1968 (or even since) played like this? What soul-jazz group could play with such dry sound and elliptical phrasing, or with this much rhythmic freedom and detail? And for that matter, what jazz group could maintain such an astonishing discourse among players?

Recording for this album began in June, 1968, and was to finish in September. Meanwhile, Miles asked Teo to get him a $10,000 advance for it, but Teo suggested $5,000 now and the rest on completion, since they were only three-quarters of the way through by the end of summer. When they were ready to record again at the end of September, Herbie Hancock missed the session because he had become sick on his honeymoon in Brazil. Miles promptly fired him and replaced him with Chick Corea, who was then known as something of an avant-gardist, and whom Tony Williams had recommended after playing with him in Boston. Ron Carter had in the meantime decided that he did not want to play electric bass as his regular instrument, so Miles replaced him with Dave Holland, a British bassist who said he was more open to what Davis was trying to accomplish:

> The acoustic bass wasn't holding up in the music enough, in a way the bass guitar can. Having played bass guitar before, I volunteered to do it. It was a culmination of Miles setting up a situation where it was the right thing to do. . . . Miles would set up the circumstances and then that would steer you in a certain direction.

Chick Corea, on the other hand, was hesitant to switch to electric piano for many of the same reasons as Herbie Hancock:

> I really resisted it at first because I really wanted to play the piano with Miles, but I quickly saw that this was something he was going after, so I made the best of it, but felt as though I was at a disadvantage because the quality of the instrument was not really that of an acoustic instrument. It was kind of a toy, sort of. So I started to try to get a sound out of it, fooling around with attachments that distorted the sound. I kind of got into electronics from there, fooling around with a ring modulator and an Echoplex, various echo devices, different amplifier settings, that sort of thing.

Corea, like other musicians, was shocked by the indirectness of Miles' leadership: "With Miles, there is no sitting down and discussing the music: 'Hey I'd like you to play a little more of this or that.' No instructions, no analytical conversation. There were grunts, glances, smiles, and no smiles. Miles communicated, but not on a logical or analytical level." Though Corea and Holland recorded only two tracks for the album—"Frelon Brun" and "Mademoiselle Mabry"—it was clear that Miles had found the musicians he needed for the next phase of his transition. The music so far had been relatively quiet, but Miles would soon begin making changes in the sonics. When Tony Williams heard that Miles might want to hire another drummer to intensify the polymetric rhythms in the band, he told Miles that he wanted no part of it and began thinking about leaving.

Gil Evans was deeply involved with the production of *Kilimanjaro*, arranging bass lines and voicing horns, and was the uncredited co-composer of Davis' "Petits Machins," a piece in 11/4 time that Evans later recorded himself under the title of "Eleven," with Davis listed as co-composer. But Gil's business sense was at one with his personal metaphysics. Once music was played, he thought it belonged to everyone; it was in the air and thus beyond claim. If Miles didn't pay him for his music and his arrangements, it was because Miles needed the money more than he did in order to get the things he needed to feel good about himself. Gil said he needed nothing. He was above the pettiness of it all—the music was always more important than money. (Their relationship was such that Miles gave Gil some of his old suits.) Still, Gil complained to Anita about

Miles' not paying him. And if she reminded him that he had two children to support and that they were five months behind in rent, and urged him to ask Miles for money, he would reluctantly agree, though he sometimes had to walk from Greenwich Village up to West 77th Street to see Miles because he couldn't afford a subway token. Gil's kids became his way of dealing with Miles about money—the kids needed this or that—so that it was never about Gil's needs or wants.

But it was not just Gil's help that Miles wanted to downplay publicly. Before 1960, production credits were not listed on the jackets of recordings, with the exception of two or three small jazz companies. Instead, recordings were treated as innocent, pure representations of reality—as something that just happens. In 1962, Teo Macero became one of the first producers on a major label to put his name on a record—*Quiet Nights*. Teo had been making recording history, but this credit nonetheless rankled Miles. When *Filles de Kilimanjaro* was issued, Miles insisted on having "Directions in Music by Miles Davis" put on the front of the record. "It means I tell everybody what to do," he told *Down Beat*. "If I don't tell 'em, I ask 'em. It's my date, y'understand? I get tired of seeing 'produced by this person or that person.' When I'm on a date, I'm usually supervising everything." Using *music* instead of *jazz* was also a first step toward eliminating the latter word from his vocabulary altogether.

It was no secret to those who knew him that Miles could be confrontational and argumentative, but now he had begun taking his personal and professional grievances to the press, even at the same time as he berated journalists and dismissed them as irrelevant. This change in his public persona is particularly obvious in the "Blindfold Test," a feature that Leonard Feather ran in *Down Beat* magazine. Musicians were played records without being told who or what they were listening to and then were asked to rate them from one to five stars. The point was to draw them out and get them to discuss music and musicians in a way the public seldom got to hear. Miles did four of these tests over a thirteen-year period, and his comments were discussed for months afterward, and often quoted in articles about him to demonstrate his perversity. But in his first test, in 1955, he liked everything that he heard and generously tossed the stars around in praise of Clifford Brown, Swedish pianist Bengt Hallberg ("so clean, and he swings"), Roy Eldridge, Dizzy Gillespie, Buck Clayton, dixieland jazz, Louis Armstrong, and Duke Ellington ("I think all musicians should get together on a certain day and get down on their knees and thank Duke"). By 1958, his responses were saltier: he called a Buddy Collette arrangement "an old modern picture with skeletons," and dismissed Thelonious Monk as the wrong accompanist for Sonny Rollins. He reserved his enthusiasm for records by John Lewis and Bobby Hackett.

By the time of his third test, in 1964, his remarks were sharply critical and often bitter. Of Les McCann and the Jazz Crusaders, he said, "What's that supposed to be? That ain't nothin'." He called Eric Dolphy ridiculous and sad, and the young Cecil Taylor, he said, made him apoplectic. He abused his mentor Clark Terry, and even Duke Ellington for his trio recording with Max Roach and Charles Mingus, *Money Jungle* ("Somebody should take a picket sign and picket the record company"). Of all the records he was played, only Stan Getz's bossa nova album with João Gilberto interested him.

When Leonard Feather visited Miles in his hotel in 1968 for the last of his tests, Feather seemed shocked to find records by the Byrds, James Brown, Dionne Warwick, Aretha Franklin, Tony Bennett, and the Fifth Dimension scattered around his room (Feather apparently was unaware that Alex Haley had found virtually no jazz records in Davis' apartment ten years earlier). Miles seemed to have lost all interest in what was then considered jazz, for his remarks about the samples he was offered were withering. Of trumpeter Freddy Hubbard: "I wouldn't put that shit on a record." Of a live recording by the Thad Jones and Mel Lewis Band: "It makes me feel broke and wearing a slip that doesn't belong to me, and my hair's combed the wrong way." He confused Archie Shepp with Ornette Coleman and then dismissed them both ("there sure ain't nothing there"). The Sun Ra Arkestra was called a "European group," experimentalist Don Ellis was "just another white trumpet player," and Al Hirt was "a white Uncle Tom" ("For a guy to shake his unattractive body and think somebody thinks it's funny—it ain't funny, it's disgusting"). What *did* excite him that day was the Fifth Dimension's recording of Jim Webb's "Prologue to the Magic Garden" (which he favorably compared to what he and Gil had done with *Porgy and Bess*), and he admired records by Diahann Carroll, Mel Tormé, and the Electric Flag. Feather rather weakly explained all this away by saying that when an artist has reached the highest mountaintop, there is no place to look but down.

Despite his interest in pop ("*rock* is a white man's word," he proclaimed), Miles' movement toward exploring this music was slow and cautious, his efforts less on getting pop rhythms in place and more on how to get a certain sound he was beginning to hear in it. Gil Evans was adopting rock elements much more quickly than Davis, and by early 1969 he had recorded with electric piano, electric bass, and electric guitar on *Blues in Orbit*. Teo Macero, meanwhile, was slow to acknowledge Miles' new interest in rock and was still thinking about him in traditional jazz terms. He told *Music Maker* that he wanted to record Dave Brubeck, Miles, and Charlie Byrd together on the same album.

The outline of the making of *In a Silent Way* is shown very simply in the Columbia Records expense sheets for February 18, 1969. For that day's work, Miles Davis received a union scale payment of $173.34 as leader, plus a $100 arranger's fee and $10,000 "on completion" (the remainder of an advance). Five musicians were paid $86.67 each, and two others who were neither U.S. citizens nor union members were paid $65 each as "consultants" in order to bypass the Musicians Union's rules. (There was one other musician who received $65 as a consultant in addition to his performance fee because he was already a well-known leader.) Two Fender Rhodes electric pianos were rented for the day, and an electric organ was wheeled into the studio. The five musicians were Miles' regular quintet, with Herbie Hancock back as a second keyboardist and "consultant." (Dave Holland was also a "consultant," since he was not yet a member of the union.) At the very last minute, Davis brought in two more musicians, two additional "found" elements who more than anything else gave the record its character: English guitarist John McLaughlin and Austrian keyboardist Joe Zawinul.

Tony Williams had formed his own group, Lifetime, by bringing McLaughlin over from England (at Holland's suggestion) and then hiring organist Larry Young. As a teenager in Boston, Tony had worked with organ trios like Johnny "Hammond" Smith's, and his plan was to update that idea. "It was a jazz trio," Tony said, "but playing electric music; then it was an organ trio playing some stuff that organ trios don't play." Larry Young had found a way to bring the sound of contemporary saxophonists like John Coltrane to the electric organ, and McLaughlin could seemingly adapt to any type of music. Their first recording together was *Emergency!* ("It was an emergency for me to leave Miles and put that band together," Tony said), a snarling, nasty talisman of a record that teetered on the line between jazz and rock. Through an engineer's error, it was recorded with a gauzy sound, a murky patina that kept it from becoming just another well-made record and ensured its place as one of the permanent mysteries of the rock era. As he had done with the Davis quintet, Williams played so fully and powerfully that his drum patterns enveloped the trio and created a new kind of form for them to play in.

Guitarist John McLaughlin was no neophyte. He was twenty-seven and had been playing on the British music scene for years, working with Jack Bruce and Ginger Baker in Graham Bond's group long before Eric Clapton, and recording with the Rolling Stones, Georgie Fame, and David Bowie. Only the month before, he had completed his own first LP, *Extrapolation*, which some considered the finest jazz record ever made in Britain. On his first night in New York, McLaughlin jammed with Tony at Count Basie's in Harlem before an audience that included Larry Coryell, the Cannonball Adderley band, and Miles. The next day, John went along with Tony to Davis' house, where Miles, to Tony's annoyance, asked his guitarist to come to the studio the next day.

McLaughlin had grown up with a different kind of Miles Davis music, so he was nervous, though as Wayne Shorter said, he arrived like Prince Valiant to the rescue. Since Miles had already gone through a handful of guitarists and not found what he wanted, McLaughlin knew that Miles was looking for "something else," and since he didn't really know what it was he was searching for,

> I didn't know, nobody knew, and so when he started giving me these obscure suggestions like play the guitar like you don't know how to play. . . . Well, he cooled me out when he started to do the thing in E, "In a Silent Way," and I played the whole thing very open in E-major. Miles didn't even wait, he had the recording light on and I just started playing these real simple things, and then Wayne came in with the melody and then Miles and Wayne together. But when Miles had Teo Macero play the take back, I was really in shock at how Miles had made me play in a way that I had not been aware of.

It also surprised McLaughlin that Davis was able to get musicians to play what he wanted to, even when nothing in particular had been prepared in advance. His directions about what to play might be no more than to just "make a growling noise—with no pitch, no notes." "Sometimes he'd come in," McLaughlin said, "and not have a clear idea of what he wanted himself, not even a concept. Or maybe just a concept and no notes. So we'd go in there and he'd write something on a bag on the way over in a taxi and at the session, he just sang something. Just a sound." This kind of last-minute planning was part of the tradition of the bebop recording session, the scrap of a melody on the back of an envelope, a chord or two scribbled on a paper napkin. But the musicians Miles was bringing together did not share the same aesthetic background or even know the same tunes. Nonetheless, he was counting on them to find the resources in themselves for a kind of collective composition.

The other eleventh-hour addition to the session was Joe Zawinul. Miles called him shortly before they were to start and asked him to come in as a keyboardist. A few minutes later he called again and asked him to bring some of his music with him. One of the pieces that Zawinul showed up with was one he had written in 1967, when he and his wife were visiting his parents in Austria for Christmas. They were in Vienna for an evening, and after dinner and a couple of slivovitzes, he watched through the hotel room window as snow began to gather on a statue of Johann Strauss. Somewhere between that vision of the waltz king and some pastoral thoughts he had of himself as a shepherd boy in the Austrian mountains was the genesis of a composition that took him only a minute to sketch out. Nat Adderley named it "In a Silent Way," and the Adderley brothers wanted to record it, but Zawinul thought it would work better with Miles. Once he'd played it for Miles, they made plans to record it, but nothing had come of it until the day Joe was called for this session. Miles neglected to tell Joe that there were two other electric pianists on this date, so when Zawinul got there, he decided to play organ instead. The band began with a run-through of Zawinul's piece that stuck close to the original conception. But as they prepared to record it, Miles decided not to play the introductory part and to erase most of the harmonic structure, leaving only an E chord on guitar for McLaughlin to play—part of his "play like you don't know how to play" suggestion. Chick Corea, on the other hand, heard nothing about the piece being simplified, and his music still had the original chords on it. But this was part of Davis' pattern, moving around the studio, whispering different instructions to each player or telling them nothing. "Miles has an interesting way of getting creations to happen," Corea said.

> When we recorded "In a Silent Way," he passed around a chart with a certain number of bars and chord symbols, and that was all. He never said a word to me.
>
> He gave us just a taste of a direction and we played the tune. I thought it was just a run-through, and so did Herbie and Joe Zawinul. But it turned out to be the finished product. He'd allow the musicians to create what they heard or felt. He'd allow it to be, and there it was.

For bassist Dave Holland, there was something strange about the whole studio process. "It wasn't a specific record date. I didn't know the different pieces were going in that direction. It was a very relaxed, very casual session, a surprise because there was no sense of a countdown to the red light. The rehearsals blended into the takes."

Zawinul was not happy with the changes that Miles made to his piece— he was no fan of minimalism in harmony and thought that Miles had eliminated the climax to the piece by cutting out several critical chords—but he knew that was the way Miles arranged music, by simplifying, leaving something out. It was Miles' way of setting up a style, a method he also used in his own playing. Miles' approach in the studio was very experimental, according to Zawinul: "Start on the fourth beat instead of the first." "Leave that note out." "Forget about the bar lines." (Afterward, Miles asked that his name be added to Zawinul's in "In a Silent Way" for copyright purposes, but it was too late, and Joe received the royalties.)

A year after Miles recorded "In a Silent Way," Joe recorded the piece again on his own album, *Zawinul*, with Woody Shaw on trumpet, Herbie Hancock as the second keyboardist, and a group similar to Miles', but with the original chords back in place. When producer Joel Dorn asked Miles to write some liner notes for Joe's record, what he wrote gives a hint of what Miles was trying to do on his own recording:

Zawinul is extending the thought that we've both had for years. And probably the thoughts that most so-called now musicians have not yet been able to express.

Miles Davis

P.S. Dig the two drummers and Herbie with the Echoplex—and the clear funky black soprano sound—and the setting that Woody has to play in. All these musicians are set up. Joe sets up the musicians so that they have to play like they do, in order to fit the music like they do. In order to fit the music you have to be "Cliché-Free." In order to write this type of music, you have to be free inside of yourself and be Josef Zawinul with two beige kids, a black wife, two pianos, from Vienna, a Cancer and "Cliché-Free."

The first piece they worked on that morning in February was essentially a number of short sections that were played while the tape recorder ran. Without an obvious melody to work with, they developed their solos over a steady, shuffling beat, with an electric piano (and later, the organ) doubling the bass line. These short pieces were then edited, assembled, and ultimately titled "Shhh/Peaceful." The session tape boxes and Teo's notes show, however, that as of February 18, the entire record was supposed to be called *Mornin' Fast Train from Memphis to Harlem,* and this track had the same title (though on the session sheet it was simply marked, "Choo-choo train"). As of June 20, it still had the same title, but on June 26, Teo authorized a name change for side 1 of the LP to be "Shhh/Peaceful" (though a Canadian pressing of the record was somehow released with the original title on it).

"It's About That Time," the third piece recorded, was also done in at least eight short segments that contain three different harmonic and melodic elements (which Zawinul has said he wrote). Miles' solos suggest the blues in F but in a highly simplied form—"abstracted," as Ian Carr suggests. At one point, Miles had talked about abandoning the blues: "I was telling Herbie the other day: 'We're not going to play the blues anymore. Let the white folks have the blues. They got 'em, so they can keep 'em. Play something else.'" Here he may have abandoned the form of the blues, but the blues feeling remains completely intact. Once again, Teo edited pieces togther to create this section, moving a short solo by Miles to the front of the piece to form a beginning, then repeating the same solo for an ending.

Macero's approach to assembling this record was to develop two stacks of eight-track tapes of the recording they had done, each stack to be used to make up a single piece, one for each side of an LP. Afterward, Miles took copies of a set of the tapes home and listened to them for hours, as did Teo, who excitedly told Ralph J. Gleason that they were something totally new, something even the musicians couldn't hear in the studio: the music was producing overtones that couldn't be heard until it was on tape. There had been "nothing like it since the 16th century," Teo said. It was "pure intuitive music," he declared, in virtually the same words [*musique intuitive*] that German composer Karlheinz Stockhausen was using at the same time to describe the higher consciousness or channeling of "cosmic spirit" he aimed for in music such as *Aus den sieben Tagen*—music he was producing in a studio in Europe without a score.

Miles came in for the editing session—an increasingly rare occurrence—and he and Teo went to work on the raw tapes. The problem was that the sessions were filled with solo after solo from each of the musicians, Teo recalls, "and we were selling Miles, not all those soloists." So he and Miles began cutting the tapes down until they ended up with 8 ½ minutes of music for one side of the LP and 9 ½ minutes for the other. At that point, Miles said, "That's an album," and went home. An 18-minute album? Teo had warned him that they could never get away with a record that short—Miles would be suspended and he'd be fired. But Miles was gone.

Two days later, the band was back in the studio, this time with drummer Joe Chambers substituting for Tony Williams. This music was listed to be part of the same "In a Silent Way" project, but the two pieces recorded ("The Ghetto Walk" and "Early Minor") were not used, and not issued, until 2001 (though they may have been part of the original piles of tapes considered for the record).

Teo spent several days editing the material by hand—cutting the tape with razor blades and piecing it back together. For "Shhh/Peaceful" some parts were moved around, but most of it remained roughly in the order in which it had been recorded. "In a Silent Way" begins with four minutes and eleven seconds of material, then a portion of Miles' second solo was moved to lead into eleven minutes and twenty-seven seconds of "It's About That Time," and then the same first four-plus minutes of "Silent Way" were repeated again to create an ending. Only thirty-three minutes of music were finally used to make an almost forty minute album.

The music on this album was surprisingly soft and dreamlike, closer to Ravel than to post-bop, or even rock and roll, for that matter. It still retained something of that snowy evening in Vienna, now captured in the snow globe of a recording. From the first note, an organ chord that sounded like something out of a 1950s soap opera, it should have been clear than this was not rock as anyone understood it. The three keyboardists (there were actually four of them there, but Larry Young did not play) were forced to accommodate each other beyond their usual roles as accompanists, and in the process a fastidious attention to detail emerged among them. (Zawinul said that the whole session was characterized by "restraint.") The bass and drums were assigned very different functions from the keyboards and created a muted pulse that surged quietly underneath the horns and guitar. Davis, Shorter (now playing only soprano saxophone), and McLaughlin took turns playing over this slow-moving fog of sonority, but there were no solos in the jazz sense of the term, and only the slightest of themes were played or developed. Instead there was texture, grain, and the faint scent of sixty cycles of electricity.

Much of what was then heard by listeners as elements of rock and roll had been developing slowly at Davis' recording sessions over the previous decade, though some of it had not yet been issued. Vamps and repetitive rhythm figures could be heard as far back as "Milestones" in 1958 and became more pronounced in later recordings like *Miles Smiles*. The disappearance of orthodox jazz solos had begun on "Nefertiti" in 1967 and "Circle in the Round" in 1968. And electric instruments were in place by 1968's *Miles in the Sky*. What was different was the degree to which these techniques and devices were used, the scale and length of the production, and the editing. (A much better case for Miles playing a kind of jazz-rock fusion can be made for 1968's "Directions," a furious, backbeat-driven composition with drummer Jack DeJohnette drawing his inspiration from Ginger Baker, Buddy Miles, and Greg Errico, the drummer with Sly Stone. But it was not issued until 1981.) But whatever they were hearing, it was enough to unsettle much of the jazz establishment.

When the record was issued, Martin Williams declined to review it in the *New York Times* and warned readers that "the editing, annotating, and packaging are horrendous. Through faulty tape splicing, a portion of the music even gets inadvertently repeated at one point!" He implored his readers not to blame the musicians. It was only the first of many Luddite complaints to be leveled at Davis and Macero over the next five years, for many critics not only disliked the music, they also rejected the very use of electric instruments and postproduction editing. Yet a reaction like this to *In a Silent Way* in the jazz world seems strange in retrospect. No question that it was very different from mainstream jazz. But in a year in which Pharoah Sanders recorded *Karma*, one of his longest and most hermetic recordings, and in which Tony Williams formed his trio, Lifetime, the redefinition of jazz seemed imminent anyway. With the pop charts then favoring Sly and the Family Stone's "Everyday People," the Beatles' "Come Together," the Archies' "Sugar, Sugar," and Peter, Paul, and Mary's "Leaving on a Jet Plane," it seems bizarre that Davis was accused of attempting to cross over to pop for producing a record whose two sides each contained eighteen-plus unbroken minutes (that alone guaranteeing it no radio airplay) of relatively somber material, with no vocals, no guitar rave-ups, and drums that were modest by both jazz and rock standards. Yet that was the charge hung around Davis' neck, and for the next few years he would be rebuked for "selling out."

Like many other adventurous men in their mid-forties who stray from the path, Miles was accused of trying to relive his youth and escape frustrated upward mobility and the failure of creativity. But Miles might have answered that he had no youth—he spent those years as a professional musician trying to maintain a family and serving in thrall to drugs. Once asked what his childhood was like, he said he didn't remember. The best way to stay young, he told pianist Keith Jarrett, is to have a bad memory. What did it mean to be an adult in the sixties, anyway? Defending a losing war in Vietnam? Arguing for law and order against the civil rights movement? Embracing discredited institutions? Being adult meant doing the same things over and over. There was nowhere to go within the conventional modes of adult authority.

From their position on the fringes of the commercial music world, jazz musicians had always assuaged themselves with the belief that they were superior musicians, that they had chosen the more difficult road with their art. As they watched the current boom in pop music, many harbored the faith that if they wanted to, they too could sell out and make best-selling pop albums. Yet the truth is that they seldom had anything to sell a pop market and no idea about how to make a pop record, and when they were offered the chance, the results were often comic or dreadful. Dizzy Gillespie, for example, took a stab at pop a few months before *In a Silent Way*, with *It's My Way*, an album of tunes like "Games People Play," "This Girl's in Love with You," and a medley from *Hair* played over strings and a flaccid rock rhythm section. Produced by Richard Carpenter with arrangements by swing-era great Jimmy Mundy, it was doomed to be a shallow, ill-fitting, and strange piece of work. Miles, on the other hand, seemed deadly serious about what he was doing, and therein lay part of the outrage.

Other objections to Davis' new direction came from some African Americans, especially black militants and some in the middle class, who thought of what he was playing as merely a white derivative of black music, as a cheapening of what they felt was the highest level of black art and sophistication, maybe even a weakening of blackness itself. Miles was too central to their aspirations and too emblematic of their successes for them to accept his shift of direction.

Yet there were some who got it. *Rolling Stone* tossed the job of reviewing *In a Silent Way* to the iconoclastic Lester Bangs, who saw it as "neither jazz nor rock. . . . I believe there is a new music in the air, a total art which knows no boundaries or categories, a new school run by geniuses indifferent to fashion." It *was* a new style of music—fusion, some called it, or jazz-rock, but these names overdetermined the sources while never quite capturing what was going on. Worse, they ignored its foundations in Davis' earlier music. The similarities to what he had already done with Gil Evans seem to have been lost in the heated discussions over electronics. The real change in this music was in the methods by which it was created, especially in the editing process itself, where Davis and Macero were taking an enormous leap forward.

The idea of editing sound—of moving music around, of replacing notes with other notes, creating new contexts, abbreviating, expanding, or laminating one sound on top of another—had its origins in film, a strip of celluloid bearing images in sequence that when cut, reordered, and pasted back together could interrupt and transform the narrative flow of life through the placement of different images up against each other. When the Russian film director Sergey Eisenstein began to theorize about montage—the conjunction of different film images through editing to create new images—he found his inspiration in music, making visual analogies to intervals, overtones, polyphony, breaks, elements in the rhetoric of music that hold notes together or keep them apart.

The other early theorist of film editing and montage was Dziga Vertov, another Russian, who found his inspiration in the theory of relativity, especially where Albert Einstein used the motion of a railroad train as an illustration. Not surprisingly, some of the first Russian experiments with film montage used railroad trains as an easily grasped visual subject, reversing their direction, speeding them up, making them decelerate, all in the service of what Sergey Eisenstein called visual fusion. Similarly, when Pierre Schaeffer, the French pioneer of tape-recorded sound, began to edit celluloid strips of sound in the early 1950s, it was the sounds of trains that he manipulated, reversing whistles, changing their pitch, or orchestrating the rhythm of wheels on tracks in order to create what he called *musique concrète*. It should not have been a surprise then when Teo Macero, colleague of one the first composers of taped electronic music, Edgard Varèse, took his first steps in serious tape manipulation with a piece of Miles Davis' music and called it "Mornin' Fast Train from Memphis to Harlem." In the process, the old African American folk music tradition of the train song was merged into a technique developed by the Russian and French avant-gardes.

With the invention of multitrack technology, sound recording moved beyond the limits of film. It was now possible for each microphone to pick up a different source of sound in the studio, for every source to be recorded separately on a different track, and then for each track to be manipulated, edited, altered separately, and put back together. It was even possible to bring together recordings made at different times to create a new one, which would appear to have a life of its own. With recordings now existing in multiple parts and available for infinite recombination, it was no longer possible to talk about *an* original, and even the intent of the artist became a question. In this new process, the editor and the producer came to assume roles that could be almost as important as the performer's, and sometimes even more important.

Sound tape editing presents problems that the film editor never has to face. First, there is no script, no story line, and there may be no form that the editor can follow. The story and the form may have to be developed during the editing, and the editor in the process becomes a co-composer. By the time the editing is complete, other mixes and edits carried out in the process may only be the faintest of memories to the editor and are likely never to be heard by the audience. Second, deciding what is "best" or "worst" becomes more difficult when editing from an ongoing flow of sound. What might sound "best" by itself may not work when put together with something else, and vice versa.

Macero described to author Ian Carr some of the new techniques by which he was now working:

> The recording machine doesn't stop at the sessions, they never stop, except only to make the playback. As soon as he gets in there, we start the machines rolling. Everything that's done in the studio is recorded, so you've got a fantastic collection of everything done in the studio. There isn't one thing missed. Probably, he's the only artist in this whole world, since I've handled him, where everything is intact. Normally, we used to make master reels, but then I stopped with the advent of three-track and four-track and so forth. We don't do that anymore; I just pull out what I want and copy what I want, and then the original goes back into the vaults untouched.

The "original," in this case, is the raw material on different tape tracks, and not the finished work of art. It might seem strange that a musician like Davis who favored first takes as a matter of principle would take so quickly to editing. But what was being edited *were* first takes, and editing was being used not to correct faulty or weak solos, but to compose a work that was often larger and more formally complex than what was imagined as they recorded. The focus of music making was now on the process, on the emergence and revelation of ideas in performance. The performance, however, now included postproduction—the editing process—as well, and the long, continued takes played by the musicians acknowledge that the tape might catch something the musicians didn't hear: art imitates technology.

Teo ended his comments to Ian Carr with words he has no doubt lived to regret: "So whoever doesn't like what I did, twenty years from now they can go back and redo it."

Columbia Records was finally beginning to sense Davis' sales potential with a younger group of buyers, and on April 1, 1969, Bruce Lundvall, the new president of the Jazz Division, sent a memo to his staff suggesting that "*Filles* should interest rock buyers and ads should be placed in the underground newspapers." When *In a Silent Way* was released later that year, it entered the *Billboard* hit charts at number 134 with a bullet.

CHAPTER EIGHT

I don't play rock, I play *black*.

MILES DAVIS

WITH BETTY AS HIS MUSE, Miles began training at the gym again, even as
the pain in his hip and legs worsened. He stopped smoking, turned to
health food, and traveled with his own trainer. He and Betty and several
of her friends visited some of the new oversize discotheques and pop
nightclubs, where he heard how loud and completely enveloping dance
music could be with high-powered sound systems. At such volume, it
was possible to feel sound even deeper in your body, as when an
acupuncturist uses needles with an electric charge, Miles said. It was a
new way of feeling about music. There, in a flash, he saw the solution to
the problems of balance in acoustic groups he had been putting up with,
such as the pianist having to play with the loud pedal down in order to be
heard. Miles had been worrying about sound ever since a night when he
was listening to Art Blakey's Jazz Messengers in one of the jazz clubs:
with sound that bad, he thought, if you couldn't see the players, you
couldn't really hear them. It was as if the musicians were miming the
music. Jazz records had begun to sound the same way to him—sonically
thin and weak, especially when compared to what he was hearing in
rock. Miles told producer Bill Laswell that he'd been listening to Hendrix and Sly, and he wasn't getting that big bottom-end sound from Teo's
production. A different era required a different way of hearing and making music. Plastics and new kinds of metals made people hear differently.
Even an accident in a car no longer created the familiar crunch of metals; now there was the new sound of plastics cracking and shattering.

He bought a cheap sound system of his own and tried it out in a few
clubs. Then his musicians began to complain that now *they* couldn't hear,

and he had to buy monitors. He had heard how much Joe Zawinul's electric piano had changed Cannonball Adderley's sound, especially on recordings like "74 Miles Away," and it was something he had to have. (He once flew all the way to Mexico just to hear Joe play it with Cannonball.) The only directly amplified instruments he now had were the electric bass and the electric piano, but then *he* couldn't be heard, so he bought a wireless mike for his trumpet, and later added an Echoplex tape-delay device and a Crybaby wah-wah foot pedal to allow him to get a guitar effect like Jimi Hendrix's. With all this new equipment to carry, he bought a VW minivan, and with Betty riding with him, he drove to gigs like any other sixties road band. (Meanwhile, as a memo from February 26, 1969, attests, CBS began to complain that what was left of his most recent advance would not cover his purchases of new electrical equipment.)

When he first started playing electrically, he got no particular feeling from it, and it was something of a disappointment. It wasn't like a hit of cocaine, he said—electronics grow on you gradually. There was a rush, but a slow rush. Then he discovered that it was possible to play longer if you weren't straining to be heard. But some adjustments had to be made. If he played too fast, the sound ran together like too many colors mixed on a palette, so he had to learn to phrase all over again, now keeping himself to two bars at a time, something that made sense anyway, because he wanted to hear even more rhythm coming through the melody.

A sold-out thirteen-concert tour of Japan was planned for January 1969, but it had to be canceled when the Japanese government refused to issue visas to the band because of Tony Williams' prior arrest in Japan for narcotics possession. Miles' manager, Jack Whittemore, offered to replace Williams (on his way out of the band anyway) with Jack DeJohnette, but the Japanese still refused. "I just found out that South Africa now recognizes the Japanese as white," Miles later told *Down Beat*. "Maybe this is it."

After a couple of tryout gigs in the New York area in the spring, Miles felt this new quintet of Corea, Holland, DeJohnette, and Shorter (sometimes called the "lost quintet" because they were so little recorded) was ready. They were certainly something to see. Chick, in his purple headband and blue corduroy pants, a stick of incense burning on his keyboards; Dave Holland with his curly long hair and velvet fringed shirt; and Miles, pacing the stage in leather or suede, maybe in a jumpsuit or a silk pirate's blouse and spaceman's sunglasses. The jolt of seeing them in their new finery was doubled by the dissonance of hearing them still playing some of the tunes associated with the previous quintet, though now through heavy amplification. Dave Holland said that "a lot of people went into shock when they heard the group because what we were doing with electronics just wasn't a familiar sound. It was like having someone talk to you in a foreign language." Miles began to rent the Village Gate in New York City to produce his own performances and brought in comedians such as Richard Pryor and musicians like Monk to alternate with him. By the middle of summer, the band was mixing its older repertoire with the new compositions that would be on their next album.

The music was volatile. Jack DeJohnette was going beyond Tony Williams' sly hints at pop by accenting every beat. Chick Corea played electric piano relentlessly, using Echoplex and a ring modulator to give his melodies a fluid and unstable sound. Dave Holland set up swirling rhythm vamps that drove the band but also kept it grounded on a single tone or scale. It was beginning to sound like free jazz with a strong rhythmic base, a music that on a given night alternated from the giddy recklessness of discovery to plodding nomadic treks in search of a common groove. Chick Corea believed that they succeeded only when Miles was on and leading the way:

> It was weird because of the disorganization of the group. The only organization was Miles' spearheading. He'd go out and play, and you'd follow; whenever he'd stop playing, he never told the group what to do, so we all went and did whatever. We always took the audience on a roller-coaster kind of trip. When Miles would play, everything would get very concentrated and to the point, and I'd see the audience come up because there'd be one line of thought being followed: Miles would play a melody, and then another melody that made sense after it, and suddenly a composition was being formed and there was an accompaniment that made sense. It would be happening, and the audience would get into it, and he'd stop playing, and the whole thing would blow up; and the audience would go down and not understand it.

But from Miles' perspective, he was always in charge of organizing the music:

> Sometime you subtract, take away the rhythm and leave just the high sound. Or take out what you know belongs to somebody else and keep the

feeling. I write for my group, for something I know Jack can do, or Chick. Or would want to do. What they've got to do is extend themselves beyond what they think they can do. And they've got to be quick. A soloist comes in when he feels like it. Anyway that's what he's being paid for. If it's not working out I just shut them up. How? I set up obstacles, barriers like they do in the streets but with my horn. I curve them, change their directions.

Whenever Miles left the stage, the remaining four would begin their own explorations, drawing on everything from free jazz to world musics. They might abandon all harmonic and formal structures and play beyond the boundaries of jazz; or they might all put down their instruments and begin playing wooden flutes; Chick might then switch to drums as DeJohnette took over the piano. Miles put no limits on what they did, as long as they returned to a framework he was comfortable with when he returned to the bandstand. The gap was so great that one night in the Vanguard, he watched the band from a table with Jimmy Heath, and when he got ready to go back on the bandstand, he asked, "Do you know where they're at, Jimmy?"

"It's your band, Miles," Jimmy replied, "you ought to know!"

This was Miles' riskiest move yet, one that might find him left with no audience at all. He was playing music that confounded most younger people. Though they saw the band's clothing as a gesture of solidarity, they knew it was not rock. To an older group who thought of themselves as part of the outsider elite in the 1940s and 1950s, neither the music nor the clothes made any sense. It was not cool. "Miles was an embarrassment to hear," said Annie Ross. "He was no longer hip." Even for jazz writers who might have otherwise been sympathetic, Miles' iconoclasm was threatening. Critic Gary Giddins once remarked of a younger Miles that if he was playing both cool jazz and hard bop at the same time, jazz history would have to be rethought. But now Miles was simultaneously embracing both free jazz and jazz-rock, either one of which was heretical enough to bring the jazz house down.

On June 3, Columbia studio time was scheduled for Betty Mabry to do a demo session backed by John McLaughlin and perhaps one other guitarist, Joe Zawinul and Larry Young, keyboards, Harvey Brooks on electric bass, and Mitch Mitchell (from Jimi Hendrix's trio) as the drummer, but without Miles (who was in the booth with Teo and engineer Stan

Tonkel). Three songs were recorded, "Ready, Willing, and Able," "Politician Man," and "Down on the Bayou," and for the last one, a number of takes were recorded with just the band. It was an unabashed funk session, and if the songs were undistinguished, the band worked, and locked into a groove quickly. Nothing would come from these recordings, but Miles at least knew that he had musicians who would be up to taking his next step with him.

In a memo to Clive Davis on June 18, Teo passed on a request from Miles for a $20,000 advance. He enclosed the note which Miles had given him:

> [Tell Clive Davis] I need $20,000. My albums are doing well. I am a star. I am going to do three more albums for him this year and I need money.
>
> Miles

Teo's note to Clive suggested that Miles should be paid the advance he asked for, though a note in an unknown hand added to the memo says, "Wait until September to see accounts," implying that Miles had already drawn more than he had earned.

More live recordings were planned for August 6 and 7 at the Village Vanguard and August 15 at the Philadelphia Spectrum, and an October release date was set for the new record that would result, with the title *Live at the Village Vanguard and the Spectrum*. But both the recording dates and the record idea were canceled without comment. Instead, studio time was set aside for three days beginning on August 19—the day after the end of the Woodstock Festival—to produce a single LP with the working title of *Listen to This*. Four months later, it still had that name, when it was suddenly changed to *Pharaoh's Dance*. At the very last moment, it was released as a two-LP album titled *Bitches Brew*.

Miles said that he been writing some simple things, just one chord and maybe a rest, then another chord, just some skeletons of compositions, and when he began to discuss them with the musicians he wanted to use, he told them they could do anything they wanted to do with the music, but he had to hear that chord. As simple as it was, when even the three electric keyboardists played it, he noticed it sounded different every time, and different everywhere. It was different in New Jersey, say, than it was in New York. It was nothing you could just write out for an orchestra and get them to play, he said. When you improvise and the weather changes, it changes your attitude, and your attitude becomes the music.

(In part to explain his changes in musical thinking, Miles sometimes mentioned that Stravinsky had also turned to simpler forms of writing in his neoclassical period, never mentioning that in the 1960s, Stravinsky changed again, this time turning toward complexity and serialism, perhaps racing to keep up with the Next Big Thing, as he came closer to the end of his life.)

From the way Miles ran his recording session, his plans might have appeared scattered and ill thought out. But he had prepared. Both Zawinul and Shorter had brought him some pieces beforehand, and Miles had picked out a few of them and made his own reduced sketches from them, which the keyboardists ran through at his house. Samples of these rehearsals were sometimes sent to Teo Macero for his suggestions about how they should be approached once they got into the studio. Three of the six pieces that made up the final record—"Miles Runs the Voodoo Down," "Spanish Key," and "Sanctuary"—had also been played on the road by Miles' regular quintet, all of whom were on the session. Drummer Lenny White recalls being told by a mutual friend that Miles wanted him to come to his house for a final rehearsal the night before. Only Miles, Dave Holland, Chick Corea, and Wayne Shorter were there, and they briefly ran through only the theme of "Bitches Brew," then watched fight films and sat around and talked, and were told to be at the CBS studios the next morning at ten.

This time Miles chose to expand his ensemble well beyond the one he had used on *In a Silent Way* by doubling most of the instruments, perhaps following the leads of John Coltrane and Ornette Coleman, both of whom had recorded with double quartets. The two bassists were Dave Holland and Harvey Brooks, the latter a staff producer at CBS who had also played on some of Bob Dylan's recordings and with the rock big band the Electric Flag; the two drummers were Jack DeJohnette and Lenny White; Don Alias and Jumma Santos (Jim Riley) were the percussionists; the reeds were Wayne Shorter on soprano saxophone and Bennie Maupin on bass clarinet; and there were two keyboardists, Joe Zawinul and Chick Corea (on two other pieces recorded at the same time, Larry Young was also added).

In Columbia's Studio B, drummer DeJohnette and Young were seated next to each other but separated by a baffle, with the other percussionists positioned nearby. (Miles said he wanted Jack to be the leader of the rhythm section, because he was the one wearing sunglasses.) Across from them, the keyboardists and the rest of the musicians were in a semicircle with Davis in the middle at a tall music stand from which he conducted or directed the music being made. Miles was excited and happy, and, violating his own rule about bringing lovers to the gig, Betty was there. He kept his eyes on her throughout for her approval. As Freddie Freeloader once said, the time to talk to Miles was when he was in love.

Miles spoke only a few words to each player about what they were going to do, talking rather generally about voicing and tone color, but nothing very specific. "I got the sense," Dave Holland said, "that if he felt he had to explain to someone too much then he had the wrong musician for the project." There were music stands with some lead sheets with a few motifs on them for each piece. With two drummers playing, one of them set the groove and the other played around it, while the two other percussionists added enriching detail. Something similar happened with the two bassists—one setting the beat, the other playing off it. Chick Corea and Joe Zawinul had played together on *Silent Way*, and already had their own ideas about how to make their parts fit together. Once the band was in motion, Miles signaled individual players to start or stop by pointing. The whole process would then begin again, creating stretches of tape to be edited together later. This was the way they worked for three or four hours each day.

The engineers were recording in eight-track and also in quadraphonic format, and they were taking Miles' sound from three sources: the mike attached to his horn, an input through an amplifier, and one wired directly into the mixing board. This way, all three sources could be drawn on and then mixed in several ways. Various machines built by the Columbia engineering department were also brought in afterward to create delay, echo, and other effects.

In a complete reversal of recording tradition, the tape recorders were rolling throughout the sessions, even more so than in *In a Silent Way*, picking up everything the musicians said or did. This new approach to recording would come to change the way musicians thought about their work. Recording sessions had always been somewhat strange occasions for musicians. They were locked away in a room for long stretches, usually at odd hours, with deadened acoustics, caged in by glass, cut off from life. Still, at recording sessions in the past, there were at least short, distinct takes and an immediate sense of accomplishment or failure. But with the Davis-Macero method, the results never seemed to relate to the performance as the players remembered it, and the procedure was far from what they experienced nightly in the neatly timed, well-structured environment of a club set. They recorded short pieces of music, stopping often, listening to what had just been played, sometimes with Miles writing out something he had heard on the tapes and wanted them to play again. Chick Corea, for one, recalled the *Bitches Brew* recording sessions as amorphous:

My memory of those specific dates is kind of vague and you can imagine that it would be, because during the time between 1968 and 1971 . . . those sessions took maybe two or four hours each, maybe six, tops. So they were kind of wispy, they just passed right by. The recordings themselves, from my remembrance, felt more like rehearsals. . . . There's not much romance or drama to it for me.

Miles moved around the studio as they played, weaving through the musicians, waving his hand up and down to lower or raise the volume. Even when he was in the booth listening, he continued giving signals through the window. Outside the studio Miles talked with the musicians, but normally said very little once he was inside. He was also usually quiet when he was inside the control booth, seldom telling Teo what he was doing. Sometimes he and Teo just sat together without talking. But during the *Bitches Brew* sessions, Teo and Miles got into several arguments, one concerning Teo's secretary, whom Miles suddenly wanted fired. When Teo refused, Miles threatened to hit him. There were frantic calls to Goddard Lieberson to explain what the situation was, and for a moment it appeared that the whole project would be stopped. But Teo decided to go on. Miles taunted him to come out of the booth into the studio, and Teo threatened to throw up on him if he did. Then, at one point when they were recording, Teo came into the studio and leaned against Miles as hard as he could while he was playing.

"Bitches Brew" was the first thing recorded, a roiling, lurching piece that opened (according to Wayne Shorter) with Miles playing off one of Betty's own songs (from the June 3rd demos), while he looked at her. But as his solo developed, he also alluded to Columbia pop artists Blood, Sweat and Tears' hit record, "Spinning Wheel." "Bitches Brew" was intended to be a five-part suite, but only the first and second parts were kept for the record. The third part was treated as a separate piece and called "John McLaughlin." Miles' role as director-composer can be heard by what he plays throughout, shaping the sonic environment, sometimes by the placement of only a single note. But his verbal directions are also there; close listening reveals when he gives instructions to the players several times some seven minutes into the piece. But Macero's work is also evident, since "Bitches Brew" has at least fifteen edits, including several tape loops used to repeat material to create short musical themes. It was collective improvisation and collective composition.

On the second day they completed "Miles Runs the Voodoo Down"(a title that Miles said he did not choose, and subsequently hated). Looking for something funky, Davis asked Lenny White, the youngest drummer, to set the beat, but he froze, and Don Alias moved to the drum kit and took over. As he did on "Bitches Brew," Miles played some exceptionally well-formed ideas.

Joe Zawinul's composition, "Pharaoh's Dance," was intended as programmatic music that would evoke the building of the pyramids. It begins in a busy, animated spirit, with separate instrumental lines staggering in one after the other, overlapping, piling waves of sound on top of quietly bustling percussion, while Bennie Maupin's bass clarinet bubbles up from below. Zawinul rehearsed the group for this piece, and Miles directed it, playing every note that Joe had written, but phrasing it differently each time, and bringing in other soloists to change the feel. "Spanish Key," like "Miles Runs the Voodoo Down" and "Sanctuary," had been shaped on the road by Miles' regular group, so both are relatively unedited. Live, Miles often started Wayne Shorter's "Sanctuary" by segueing into it from the ballad "I Fall in Love Too Easily," since both of them open with roughly the same notes. But on the record, the pop tune is only hinted at.

Collective composition on this scale had been tried from time to time by the likes of Bob Dylan and classical composer Stefan Wolpe, but usually with little success. The key to Miles' process was the power of his own horn as an organizer. "We realized that Miles was looking for a collective improvisation thing with all these different people who had different styles," Jack DeJohnette said. "Miles was going for unity in the collective. And his sound was so powerful that whatever he played over it galvanized everything and really gave it validity." The way he directed the music, encouraging things he liked and cutting those he didn't, indicates that he had some kind of plan before he entered the studio.

After three days of recording, there were almost nine hours of music to be edited. Engineer Ray Moore worked on it between September 22 and October 24, and Miles came in five times during the work. Teo told Ray where to make the edits, some on an eight-track mix, others on a two-track, but they were often difficult to do because Miles had insisted on having John McLaughlin right next to him in the studio, so that the guitar and the trumpet tracks often spilled over onto each other. "I listened to all the session reels," reissue producer Bob Belden said. "There were some low moments, some starts and stops. But with all that music, what we know as *Bitches Brew* could have been assembled twenty different ways, and Teo found logical, and musically interesting, ways to present it."

For this album, Miles involved himself in all phases of the production. He wanted it titled *Bitches Brew*, according to Carlos Santana, as an allusion to Betty Davis and her girlfriends Collette, Monica, and Devon (also known as "the cosmic ladies"). But Miles said that it came from the menu at Serendipity, the East Side New York eatery famous for its ice cream and sweets. The title was something of a shock for an old and respected company like Columbia and caused some trepidation. But the music was also shocking, as was the double size of the album and the cover art. Miles clearly wanted to make a statement about the importance of this music. It was his *Sgt. Pepper's Lonely Hearts Club Band*, his *There's a Riot Goin' On*.

For cover art, Miles turned to Mati Klarwein, an Israeli artist whom he had met through Alan Douglas' wife, Stella, who owned a Moroccan clothing boutique frequented by Jimi Hendrix, Brian Jones, Santana, and Miles himself. Klarwein had studied art in Paris and was befriended by Salvador Dalí. He was often seen on the free jazz scene in New York in the 1960s, and had already done album covers that mixed surrealism with psychedelic imagery for Santana and Hendrix. Miles had no suggestions for the art, so Klarwein was on his own. The front cover depicts what might be two African women embracing as they watch a thunderstorm out at sea against a blue sky. The hair of one of the women soars into the sky and disappears in the clouds. A black face looks toward the two women from the far side of the cover. When the cover is opened, a pink-white face looks in the opposite direction on the back cover at two more African women, now seen against a clear night sky. White and black hands join together to swirl off to form the two faces on both covers. A tropical blossom on fire wraps around both sides of the album.

Joe Zawinul, once again, was not entirely happy with the musical results. "It's a good album with a nice atmosphere. I don't think there's anything earthshaking about that record. When we got out of a session, Miles drove me home and he asked me why I didn't say anything during the ride and I said, 'I didn't like what we did and what is being done.' It's a good-sounding record. There's a lot of power on those sessions. Everyone had respect for each other and no one overplayed. It could have been utter chaos, but it was pretty organized. Let it be as it is. The past is a done deal. That's for sure." Chick Corea, for his part, thought *Bitches Brew* was a slower, more conservative version of what they were doing live.

Miles had been paid $20,000 for *Bitches Brew* when it looked as if it was going to be a single LP. When it turned into a two-record set, Teo communicated to Walter Deane that Miles wanted another $20,000 but would accept $10,000. Deane wanted to pay him no more than $5,000 because Davis already owed them $90,000 in advances and $30,000 in loans. Though Miles had come up with a record that would quickly sell over 500,000 copies in spite of its double size and price, he would still be in debt to Columbia.

Teo sent Ralph Gleason some advance tapes of *Bitches Brew,* and Gleason, one of Miles' greatest defenders and apologists, mock-complained about them: "No wonder jazz is dead, guys like you are killing it." Teo responded: "I may have killed jazz, but I have established a new kind of music. What have you done lately?" Once the album was released in April 1970, some who puchased it wrote to Columbia, complaining that it was not what they expected from Miles. Teo took it on himself to answer them personally and offer them packages of other Columbia LPs in exchange. To make sense of this recording, listeners' would have to abandon their belief in the improvised solo as the apotheosis of jazz. Form would have to be rethought, suspending the weight put on balanced, narrative-like compositions that resolve to well-made endings. If there was form in *Bitches Brew,* it was through-composed, repetitive, but slowly unfolding—"like Chopin," said Teo.

Reviewers like Martin Williams heard this album as an unfocused, rhythmically redundant, regressive work, one missing the true elements of jazz: coherent, developed solos and the feel of swing. Many critics had an investment in being adult, in resisting the rising tide of rock. To them, *Bitches Brew* was a foolish and desperate attempt by an aging man to attract a young audience by creating a new genre of music, jazz-rock. (Proof for them that it was a shameless attempt to cash in on the pop market was that two 45 rpm singles were prepared from edited-down versions of "Miles Runs the Voodoo Down" and "Spanish Key.") But was it a rock record? With subtle dynamics and elaborate rhythmic shifts, but again without a singer or even a true lead guitar with long solos? Was Miles selling out? With a double album (which guaranteed some loss in sales) that had radio-play-proof tracks of at least ten minutes each (with a single exception), and some with as much as twenty minutes? Miles never thought of *Bitches Brew* as rock. When accused of hiring a rock guitarist, John McLaughlin, he rightly answered: "I didn't use John as a rock player . . . but for special effects. John's no more a rock player than I'm a rock trumpet player." Nor was Miles even the inventor of jazz-rock. Others were there before him—Gary Burton, Jeremy Steig, Soft

Machine, the Free Spirits, Gabor Szabo, Tony Williams' Lifetime, and even the Byrds, with "Eight Miles High," a group that Miles helped get recorded.

Bitches Brew was something of a Rosetta stone for a wide array of people, opening up the potential of the studio to everyone from Henry Mancini to ambient musician and producer Brian Eno. What fascinated Eno was the whole procedure of putting people together in a studio who had not played together before and having them play for hours with nothing more than scraps of written music to work from. Then, from out of the piles of tapes they developed, the producer took short sections, fitted them together, sometimes repeated them, to create something never heard by the musicians. "But what really interested me in those things," Eno said, was that

he did something that was extremely modern, something you can only do on records, which is, he took the performance to pieces, spatially. Now, those things were done by a group of musicians in a room, all sitting close to one another . . . but they were all close-miked, which meant that their sounds were quite separate from one another. And when Teo Macero mixed the record, he put them miles apart. So this is very interesting to listen to a music, where you have the conga player three streets down the road here, you have the trumpet player on a mountain over there, the guitar player—you have to look through binoculars to see him, you know! Everybody is far away, and so the impression that you have immediately is not that you are in a little place with a group of people playing, but that you're on a huge plateau and all of these things are going on sort of almost on the horizon, I think. And there's no attempt made by Teo Macero to make them connect with one another. In fact, he deliberately disconnects them from one another.

While *Bitches Brew* was in some respects a reaffirmation of jazz as a collective process, it was one that had been accomplished in a studio, both live and through editing. The irascible critic Phillip Larkin once asked if studios could kill jazz. At the time, it was largely a rhetorical question. But now that there are new forms of recording and electronics, the whole history of live acoustic instruments played in real time is beginning to seem archaic, if not endangered. The new studio procedures even put the act of recording into question. What might be called the classical style of recording had developed sophisticated means of disguising the fact that sound had been recorded, obscuring the decision-making process that lay behind the production, hiding the technology, and creating a seamless flow of sound that seemed at once natural and other-worldly. *Bitches Brew* perversely drew attention to itself as a technological artifact, forcing listeners to take an extramusical position on what they were hearing, and asking them to say simply whether they approved of the process. Miles had been expressing this new attitude toward recording during the years he worked with Prestige, leaving on the records scraps of counting off, false starts, hostile exchanges, inane conversation, and musical criticism. Now his music was beginning to find a way to balance the spontaneous with the completely composed, resolving—at least for him—the problem of live creativity versus the artificiality of the studio.

Miles was once asked if the time in which he did *Bitches Brew* was one of his most creative periods. It was *their* creative period, was his response—Joe Zawinul's, his muscians'. All he did, he said, was to make it possible for them to play together. It was also a creative period for other bands, some of which were normally thought of as merely playing pop music. Between 1969 and 1971, James Brown had one of the most experimental bands in the country, as did Frank Zappa, whose rhythms had gone far beyond rock, and it was the rare younger jazz musician who did not pay close attention to what all three of these groups were doing. Suddenly, new possibilities in music were opening up everywhere. What Miles' band had played on *Bitches Brew* now inspired Wayne Shorter and Joe Zawinul to think about forming their own group, and three months later, Shorter left to form their new band, Weather Report.

Another lost saxophonist, another lost wife. Miles' relationship with Betty turned bad quickly and came to an end before their marriage was a year old. Their careers had become entangled, the two of them even sharing the same agent at one point, with Miles claiming that she had been using his sound equipment without his approving it and charging things in his name that he knew nothing about. He accused her of lying, of having an affair with Jimi Hendrix, and found some of her behavior "too young and wild" to fit in with friends of his like Camille and Bill Cosby. (Betty once embarrassed him while she was dancing by stepping on Camille's jumpsuit and ripping it.) Miles had divorce papers drawn up and talked her into signing them. In an interview in 1975, he implied that he tricked her into signing them. In any case, it was a settlement that cost him nothing.

By then he was already involved with two other women, Marguerite

Eskridge and Jackie Battle, both very different from Betty but both very young. Jackie was an art student, bright and self-confident, who worked as an assistant to Buddy Gist in the coffee-importing business, and it was she who organized some of Buddy's parties that Miles attended. He had known her since 1966 and had come to know her family and enjoyed being around them, especially her mother, Dorothea Merchant. Marguerite was a quiet, calm woman, with a Lakota Indian background; he thought of her as very spiritual and nurturing. Her relationship with Miles was such that she accepted his being with other women, and though Miles said he kept her from knowing about Jackie, Jackie said that Marguerite always knew about her relationship with Miles. "That didn't bother me a lot," Marguerite said. "But Miles had a great need to have someone at his side whenever he needed them or wanted them there. That meant you could not be terribly involved in your own career, because you could always get a call that you needed to come to this or that place and get on this flight this afternoon. I knew this was not something I could do for a long period of time. However, Miles' return to drug use was the main reason we parted."

On the night of October 9, 1969, after playing at the Blue Coronet Club in Brooklyn, Miles drove Marguerite home to her apartment. On the way, she noticed that he was constantly glancing in the rearview mirror. At one point, he told her that a gypsy cab was following them. He wound through the narrow Brooklyn streets until he thought he had lost it, but as they were kissing good night in the car in front of her building, he saw the cab coming up from behind and told her to duck. When it pulled alongside, a gunman fired at them five times. Most of the bullets lodged in the car, but Miles was slightly wounded on his left side near the hip. They drove to the hospital, where Miles was treated and released, and when they came out, the police arrested them without giving a reason. At the precinct station, they learned they were being charged with possession of marijuana, which had been found when the car was searched. But when Miles' lawyer later argued the car had recently been driven from California for him and that it was not possible to ascertain how the drug got there, the district attorney agreed, and refused to press charges.

The incident with the police was in a sense business as usual with Miles, but what was more disturbing to him was that four days earlier, he had been anonymously warned in a phone call not to appear again at the Blue Coronet. The caller had attempted to shake him down for part of his salary from a recent appearance at the club. Mati Klarwein remembers talking to Davis shortly after that incident: "Miles sat next to me with a huge line of coke and the tapes that would eventually become *Bitches Brew*. He had me open the door all the time, 'cause he was afraid he'd get shot. He was saying that the mafia was after him because he had refused to do a show at one of their clubs. They had already taken a pot-shot at him just to scare him." Davis offered a $5,000 reward for anyone helping to convict the gunman, and though there were no immediate results, he said that he later heard that the shooter had been killed.

Letters from Columbia Records to Miles in December offer a glimpse into Davis' finances and the confusion that the company's method of compensation had created. On December 9, Columbia advanced Miles $20,000, but at the same time deducted $8,000, applied to a previous unpaid loan. Also deducted was $2,185.43 in equipment rental charges he had incurred, leaving him $9,814.57. On December 31, he was sent a letter from Walter Deane, administrative vice president, telling him that Columbia's books showed that somehow they had paid him too much. In 1969, they claimed, the following payments had been made to him:

February 26	$10,000 to complete *In a Silent Way*
April 17	$7,500 to complete ¾ of an unnamed album [presumably never completed]
July 7	$10,000 for *Bitches Brew*
September 18	$10,000 for *Bitches Brew*
November 4	$25,000 for an unnamed 2-record set
Total	$62,500

Since two of these albums had never been completed, they felt that he had been overpaid and he was being denied further advances. Miles said that he didn't know what they were talking about—and apparently with good reason, since these figures did not square with some of the numbers mentioned in previous memos.

In November, many of the same musicians from *Bitches Brew* were back in the studio, but now with Billy Cobham as the only drummer, saxophonist Steve Grossman replacing Wayne Shorter, and Ron Carter in for Dave Holland. The surprise this time was the ethnic music instrumentalists brought in without any explanation. Brazilian percussionist Airto Moreira, for example, got a call from Miles' manager to come in one day before the session. Moreira played a number of percussion instruments, but especially the *cuica*, the talking, barking drum from Brazil by way of Angola, with which he answered other players' phrases, and even took occasional solos. Airto had never performed professionally in the United States before, and at most had only jammed a bit with Cannonball Adderley and Joe Zawinul. His one previous meeting with Miles had ended disastrously, with his being shunted aside as an annoying fan.

When Airto arrived at the studio, he was surprised to find the room filled with musicians, including Khalil Balakrishna on electric sitar and Bihari Sharma on tamboura. When the time came to start playing, Airto said, "I couldn't get into the music. It was new music to me that I didn't really understand, and anyway there was nothing to play because everybody was playing so much." Two hours into it, Miles cried out, "Stop, Teo, stop! This sounds like shit! I'm going home. Cancel it!" and he left. On November 19, Miles tried again, and this time, they produced "Orange Lady" and "Great Expectations." Afterward, Miles added Airto to his quintet, and they headed for Washington, D.C., to play their first job together.

Clive Davis was determined to bring Columbia into the rock and roll era and had already dropped jazz legends Dave Brubeck and Thelonious Monk. Miles was not making the kind of money that the company wanted, but Clive saw him as bringing a certain prestige to the label (much like Vladimir Horowitz, the only other person now on a retainer from Columbia), and he still saw possibilities for turning Miles into a jazz superstar. If in the meantime, it was going to cost them more than they were making, they could live with it up to a point. But Miles continued to call in search of even more advances. Clearly, he was becoming a nuisance to Clive Davis, who wrote in his autobiography, *Inside the Record Business,* that

> he has a raspy, low voice—a fiery whisper that conveys heat over the telephone while you are straining to find out how much money he wants. He is spellbinding, and he can talk. . . . Then one day Miles called me to complain about his record sales. He was tired of low sales, and angry about it. Blood, Sweat and Tears and Chicago had borrowed enormously from him—and sold millions. These young *white* artists—he was in a rather militant frame of mind—were cashing in while he was struggling from advance to advance. If you stop calling me a *jazz* man, he said at one point, and just sell me alongside these other people, I'll sell more.

Miles was not merely tossing around black nationalist rhetoric. He knew—as did Charles Mingus, Ornette Coleman, and maybe every other black jazz musician in the country—that "jazz" at that time was an ethnic label, one that may have carried a certain dignity as a marker of the greatest African American artistic tradition, but one that also got records placed in the bins with those that don't sell. Miles had survived and prospered as long and as well as he had by a mixture of scuffling and dominating, pleading and threatening, but it was not the life a dentist's son from East St. Louis was prepared to endure much longer, especially when what he thought of as unmusical white performers with long hair and paramilitary clothes were raking in the money.

As so often with Davis, his most self-serving schemes still made a good deal of business sense. But to broaden his audience, as Miles wanted, Clive Davis would have to get him to change his performance venues, get him to appear in places where those young white kids drew masses of other white kids, like the Fillmore East and the Electric Factory, those cavernous new spaces that were springing up across the country. This might have suited Miles, since he was sick of the club circuit, the "toilets" (as Lenny Bruce called them) where the jazz life was led. But instead, he exploded at Clive's suggestion: "He wasn't going to play for 'those fucking long-haired white kids,'" Clive said. "He would be 'ripped off'; Bill Graham wouldn't pay him enough *money*." Miles told Clive he wanted off the fucking label!

If Miles was going to continue to take his music in this new direction, he had to face not only the critics, club owners, and record producers who didn't like it, but his family and friends as well. When he called Vernon and played him parts of *Bitches Brew* over the phone, Vernon said, "I don't care for it." "Miles wanted to know why, and told me it won an award or something. I told him that a woman I worked with at the IRS had every record Miles did, but she said 'now he done lost us.' Miles said, 'Tell her that I don't have time—I can't stay in one place. They got to get on board.'"

CHAPTER NINE

In Xanadu did Kubla Khan
A stately pleasure dome decree

SAMUEL COLERIDGE

Music is like dope. You use it until you get tired of it.

MILES DAVIS

MILES WAS DRUNK ON LIFE. Unable to sleep, he sometimes stayed up for three or four days, until he crashed from exhaustion or pills. On the road, the band was playing long, unbroken sets that dazzled, confused, or stupefied audiences. The music seemed to owe so little to what he had already put on record that it appeared to come from nowhere, and at such levels of intensity, scale, and volume that it defied whatever laws of jazz still existed.

For the first half of 1970, Miles was either in the studio or recording live every month with a constantly shifting group of musicians, and what they recorded was reaching the public slowly, scattered through various albums, or sometimes not appearing for years. Tunes like Joe Zawinul's "Lonely Fire" and David Crosby's "Guinnevere" (which Miles recorded on January 27, 1970) were long, atmospheric meditations on the slimmest of melodic materials, played by what was essentially the *Bitches Brew* band with the addition of Khalil Balakrishna on sitar. "Feio" and "Double Image," recorded the next day by a slightly smaller group, followed a similar course.

When *Big Fun* was issued in 1974, it contained a confusing mixture of previously unreleased material from 1969, 1970, and 1972. Though Teo Macero was listed as the producer, nothing in the packaging told the listener just how large a role he had played. On "Go Ahead John" from 1970, for example, Teo had edited a long blues in between two loosely improvised passages, and then put Davis' solo through an "instant play-back" device that allowed him to sound as if he were playing a delayed second version of his solo behind himself and behind the beginning of Steve Grossman's solo, which followed. Next, John McLaughlin's solo was put through a device called an electronic switcher that made his heavily distorted solo sound as if two different guitars were playing side by side. (The drums were treated the same way, with the sound from the drum kit bouncing from left to right.) The success of this almost half-hour track depends on how one reacts to electronics: they *are* gimmicks and they did date the material, but to some listeners, that is part of the charm. Aside from the bravura editing, Miles plays one of his best solos on the blues, and McLaughlin's accompanying figures behind him are inventive and compelling.

Miles was sitting in his red Ferrari with a young woman in a no-standing zone on Central Park South on March 3, 1970, dressed in a turban, sheepskin coat, and cobra-skin pants, when he was approached by a patrolman who asked him to move on. This was a scene that Miles knew all too well. When the officer noticed the car had no inspection sticker, he asked for the license and registration. As Miles rummaged through his bag, brass knuckles fell out. (He had taken them away from his son, he said later.) He was booked on a weapons violation, a felony, and for driving an unlicensed, uninspected, and unregistered car. After a night spent in a cell, he was cleared of all charges except for having no driver's license, and paid a $100 fine. Miles told *Newsweek*, "It wouldn't have happened if I hadn't been a black man driving a red car. On the way to the station the cop keeps saying, 'I've got Miles Davis' like I was Jesse James. . . . If I could say on my record jackets that these albums couldn't be sold to the police or their relatives and friends, I would."

Two days later, Miles played his first engagement in a rock arena when he opened for the Steve Miller Band, and Neil Young and Crazy Horse at Fillmore East, where Columbia recorded him. The new sextet was incen-diary, with electronics and rhythms wilder than any rock band then dared to play. The crowd of stoned young people was not sure what to make of it all, especially as *Bitches Brew* had not yet been released, but they were at least attentive. Steve Miller dedicated "Stormy Monday" to Miles on stage, and Laura Nyro, whom Clive Davis and her manager David Geffen were both pushing hard, and thinking of recording with Miles behind her, brought him a box of red roses when she came to see him on Saturday night.

In April, 1970, Miles brought in a new bassist to record with him, Michael Henderson, an eighteen-year-old who had most recently toured with Stevie Wonder and Aretha Franklin. Henderson had never heard of most of the people in Davis' band and wasn't *that* impressed by being recruited by Miles, until others told him that he should be. Filling in for Dave Holland, with his impressive jazz and rock credentials, Henderson seemed to many of Miles' older fans an all-too-ready symbol of Miles' decline as a leader: here was another one-dimensional pop electric bassist vamping his way through the funk tunes and unable to play the ballads. And vamp Henderson did, creating focused grooves that could run in place forever. He could also create monster riffs (especially when in the company of John McLaughlin), change his tunings midstream, and erect a powerful sonic bottom that enclosed the whole band and (Miles liked to hope) put bodies in motion on the floor. With a bassist like this, Miles dared to think he might yet rule the world of those young brothers who had no idea who he was.

Only one day after Henderson arrived—not surprising for Miles—they were in the studio to record *A Tribute to Jack Johnson*. Bill Cayton, a fight manager and president of the Big Fights, Inc., was directing a documentary (*Jack Johnson*, aka *Jack Johnson: Breaking Barriers*) on the black heavyweight champion's life, and had asked Miles to do the music for it. Davis went to work on it enthusiastically, reading everything he could about Johnson and boxing history, watching films of classic matches, and sleeping with a photo of Johnson near his bed. "He would discuss boxing with an intensity you couldn't imagine," said Cayton. "He'd come to our offices and ask for a bunch of films. He'd put the spool on the projector himself, threading the projector, then sit there and watch for hours. Every once in awhile he'd come running up to me and say, 'Bill, why'd this happen? How come Joe Louis got hit with that shot?'"

The saga of Jack Johnson resonated personally with Davis, and when Teo Macero later edited the new parts of the soundtrack into a record, Miles wrote the liner notes himself, stressing Johnson's mastery as a boxer, his fondness for fast cars, jazz, clothes, and beautiful women, his unreconstructed blackness, and the threat he posed to white men:

> Johnson portrayed freedom—it rang just as loud as the bell proclaiming him champion. He was a fast-living man, he liked women—lots of them and most of them white. He had flashy cars because that was *his thing*. That's right, the big ones and the fast ones. He smoked cigars, drank only the best champagne and prized a 7 ft. bass fiddle on which he'd proudly thump jazz. His flamboyance was more than obvious. And no doubt mighty Whitey felt "No Black man should have all this."

Near the end of his notes he wrote, "Dig this—The fight he lost (1915) in Havana was rumored to be thrown—Jack Johnson died like he lived in a fast car (1946—age 68)." It was a reference to the loss of his championship to Jess Willard, where Johnson was said to have accepted money from white promoters to take a dive. Miles may have seen the irony of a connection with himself here as well, since he was now being accused of playing rock at Clive Davis' request, only for the money.

"We gave Miles a rough, rough cut of all the scenes in the movie, and he just loved it. He laid down some music. And when he was done, he handed three boxes of tapes to me and said, 'Bill, I never been better.'" Cayton made it sound simple, but Miles took this project as seriously as he had any others he had done, maybe more so, and he worried especially about the effect of his music on the film: "The question in my mind after I got to this was, well, is the music black enough, does it have a black rhythm, can you make the rhythm of the train a black thing, would Jack Johnson dance to that?" His own feel for the movements of a boxer came across clearly in the soundtrack, where he tried to make the rhythms mime the grace and confidence of fighters like Sugar Ray Robinson. (Only the month before, Miles had recorded a tribute to Roberto Duran.)

He wanted a drummer who could execute exactly what he had in mind for this record, and called Buddy Miles, then with Jimi Hendrix's Band of Gypsys. But when Buddy didn't show up for the sessions that began on April 7, Miles used Billy Cobham instead. "'I want this and I want that,'" he told Cobham, sitting at the drum kit, trying to play it for him:

> I didn't do it the way he wanted me to do it, and then he just let me alone.... But then I heard the record, man—if you can't make the adjustment to him, he will adjust to you quite naturally. It was really a *relaxed*

session; as a matter of fact, everybody seemed as if they were totally out to lunch in one respect! It's just that on a Miles Davis session, everybody's very reserved. Sort of a cloud-cover comes over, and business gets taken care of!

The core group for the recording was Herbie Hancock, Cobham, Henderson, McLaughlin, and Steve Grossman, who said that rehearsals were held before they recorded. But when they got to the studio, everything changed:

> He might keep one line from a rehearsed piece of music, or maybe nothing at all. Ninety percent of the tunes we rehearsed were never used in the studio. It seemed like everyone just felt each other out and got used to being with each other and playing with each other. Rehearsal was just hanging out together and creating something like an intimate "family" atmosphere, a support thing.

Jack Johnson was one of Miles' favorite recordings for a long time, and it's obvious why from the first note. Guitarist John McLaughlin steps out and strides across a shuffling groove that is close to barroom rhythm and blues; Davis enters with a clipped but plaintive sound that reminds that no matter what music he's playing, it will always sound like Miles. McLaughlin changes keys to accommodate Davis' entry, but bassist Michael Henderson continues to play in the old key, creating a delicious tension that he releases only after he finds out where they are. And midway through the first of two long jams, Herbie Hancock muscles his way into the mix—on organ, of all things—with a series of stabbed notes, which he repeats several times for emphasis.

What happened, Cobham said, was that McLaughlin had started warming up on a boogie figure in the studio, and Michael Henderson joined in on bass while the engineers set up mikes for a sound check. Miles came out of the booth several times to tell them to be quiet. But what they were playing was so infectious that Cobham joined in on drums, and then Miles gave in, said, "Press the red button," grabbed his horn, and came into the studio.

The final recording was full of many such "found" elements, accidents, last-minute insights, and editorial daring. Late in the session, for example, Herbie Hancock dropped by the studio with a bag of groceries to see how things were going. The music was under way and being recorded, but Miles gestured at a Farfisa organ and said, "Play." Herbie said, "I can't do this, I've got to get these groceries home." "Play!" And he said it with a vibe like, "Either you play or you die!" Herbie dropped his groceries and plunged into the mix. Once edited, the album also contained bits of music from "Shhh/Peaceful," an unissued version of "Willie Nelson," and, near the end, according to Teo, "something we had done for a TV show—'The Man Nobody Saw,' about a black man trying to get a job: Miles played solo and I put chords to it."

Jack Johnson continued ideas first formed in *Filles de Kilimanjaro*, merged them with Motown bass lines and elements of Funkadelic and James Brown's "Say It Loud, I'm Black and I'm Proud," and laid out a schematic for the true fusion groups to come. Miles saw melody beginning to shift to the drum and the bass in the new rhythm and blues groups that were emerging, and heard "those Shortnin' Bread rhythms" like he'd heard in the Sactified Church turning up in Sly and the Family Stone's music. In James Brown's music, he noticed that the bass "stayed in one place," according to Wayne Shorter, "and then moved to another place." This echoed and reinforced what he had already done on "So What."

The record was not without its problems. Miles maintained that the wrong cover was put on it when it was first issued (instead of a photo of Miles playing bent backward, it had a stylized, period illustration of Jack Johnson in his car), and had to be corrected in a later issue, with Miles' name appearing first, before Jack Johnson's. What's more, guitarist Sonny Sharrock always insisted that he was the second guitarist on parts of this record, though he is not credited on the jacket. He said that Miles later called to ask him if he wanted to tour Japan with the band, and when Sharrock agreed, Miles told him he'd have to audition first. It was silly, Sharrock said, since he'd already played with him. That was the end of the discussion, except that when Miles returned from the tour, he told him they had waited for him at the plane—he'd only been joking about an audition.

Three days after the last session, on April 10 and 11, 1970 Miles opened for Laura Nyro at the Fillmore in San Francisco. The first night's performance was recorded by Columbia and issued as *Black Beauty: Miles Davis at Fillmore West* on a double-LP album. Each side of the two records was titled "Black Beauty," although at least ten separate tunes were played during an unbroken medley. (An internal memo showed that six years later Columbia was still identifying a number of tunes that had been played in those sets, checking to see if royalties had been paid on them.) These records offered a chance to hear Miles poised between past and present, doing material from the fifties ("I Fall in Love Too Easily"), the sixties ("Masqualero"), and the post–*Bitches Brew* repertoire (with Dave Holland back on bass). It is music that honors the past, respecting space, solos, form, and fixed rhythms, though there are also hints throughout that they will soon find some other way to organize this music to play it live.

The late 1960s and early 1970s were something of an archival period in American music, a time for rummaging around in the domestic past and the exotic present. The latest chapter in the history of the diffusion of African American music among whites, which came with the rise of rock and roll, had barely begun when it was followed by the folk and blues revivals of the early 1960s. These were exercises in crypto-memory, bringing back the dead and the almost dead, and with them the origins of the music that most had mistakenly thought had been freshly forged in their own overheated moment of history. After the blues and country music had been reincorporated in pop music, some musicians began searching further afield for something else to the shock the system. The Beatles, John Coltrane, and even Duke Ellington used up the music of India in a couple of weekends.

Miles was late in beginning to borrow from exotic musics, but nevertheless approached them cautiously, incorporating the hum and buzz of the sitar or the barking commentary of the *cuica* as texture in the projects he was already working on, rather than using them as masks to alter the identity of his music. Nor was it was surprising, then, that when on May 19 he recorded something so elementally blues-based as "Honky Tonk," it would never surrender itself to the pleasures of pure revival, but rather would conceptually flirt with boogie and blues by chopping up rhythms, dropping breaks in unexpected spots, and pulling in the funk elements from the electro-ether. True, Miles played as straightforward a blues solo as he would ever record on "Honky Tonk," but the group behind him only flirted with bodily rhythms and never fully committed to them. Instead, they created a grand abstraction of the dance music that Miles said he had heard years before at those rural roadhouses in southern Illinois. This record should have turned some heads around, but it was not released for another four years, and then it was well hidden in *Get Up with It*, a wonderful but seldom-heard collection of pieces done between 1970 and 1974.

New on "Honky Tonk" was keyboardist Keith Jarrett, a classically trained, omnivorous prodigy fresh from his own acclaimed avant-garde experiments. Miles was fascinated by Keith's music (he once took his whole band in to see Jarrett's trio in Paris) and by his claim to be able to create music from nothing. Jarrett (like all of Davis' other keyboardists) professed to hate electronics; more than that, he said he disliked the band itself. (Yet he also claimed that they had developed from "pseudo-intellectual shucking and ego-tripping to a really healthy, round, bouncing band" while he was with them.) Whatever his true feelings, Jarrett threw himself into their project, playing simultaneously on multiple keyboards (alongside Herbie Hancock, brought in for the day of the recording), and for the brief time he was with them, became one of Davis' most exciting electric keyboardists.

By June, there was talk of a new supergroup to be launched at the Randall's Island Festival in New York, July 17–19: Miles with Jack Bruce and Eric Clapton of Cream, and John McLaughlin, Larry Young, and Tony Williams of Lifetime. But before that could happen, Eric Clapton was quoted in *Rolling Stone* as saying, "I don't understand what Miles is doing. . . . But I don't suppose that matters too much. Miles wants to be a pop star in the sense that he wants exposure in the pop world, and feels that he can turn on hip people if he has that exposure. . . . If everyone digs it, it would be nice to play in Europe." But by July 9, *Rolling Stone* was retracting the story, admitting that its hearsay reporting had almost wrecked the upcoming gig on Randall's Island. Then the magazine made things worse by seeking out Miles for quotes about Clapton. He was angry about Clapton's remarks about his wanting more exposure. He had never met Clapton and said that the only way *he* could get more exposure was by killing someone. Never one to leave a good closing line alone, he added that Bruce and Clapton played too loud, and if they played that loud, he would have to amp himself up. Asked if he enjoyed playing in a widening circle of musicians, he said, "You know yourself, when you're fucking a lot of different bitches instead of the same one, sure it's more fun." The supergroup, needless to say, never happened. ("What's a rock and roll band? The only rock I know is the rock of cocaine.")

Adding to the thickening discord, *Jet* magazine's "People Are Talking" column complained that Miles was playing second fiddle to marginal white rock groups by opening for them. (Leonard Feather quickly rushed in to explain that Miles had always wanted to open for other groups so that he could get home early.) Next, saxophonist Eddie Harris was quoted as saying that Miles' use of white musicians was cutting black players out of jobs. But even as these sour notes were still hanging in the air, Miles was decrying the word *rock* as a "white man's word," as *blues* is a white man's word, terms used only to mark the ethnicity of music.

Miles Davis, his
sister, Dorothy,
his brother,
Vernon, and his
mother, Cleota
Davis.
(Edna Gardner)

Miles Davis, ten
years old.
(Edna Gardner)

The Davis family home at 17th Street and Kansas
Avenue, East St. Louis, Illinois, 1999. *(John Szwed)*

Miles' first pro-
fessional job,
with Eddie
Randle's Blue
Devils in 1944.
Miles is at far
right, rear.
*(Frank Driggs
Collection)*

The Charlie Parker Quintet at the Three Deuces on 52nd Street, 1947. From left: Tommy Potter, Charlie Parker, Miles Davis, and Duke Jordan (not shown: Max Roach). *(Frank Driggs Collection)*

The *Birth of the Cool* band in the studio on January 21, 1949. From left: Junior Collins (French horn), Bill Barber (tuba), Kai Winding (trombone), Max Roach (drums, not shown), Gerry Mulligan (baritone saxophone), Davis, Al Haig (piano), Lee Konitz (alto saxophone), Joe Shulman (bass). *(Frank Driggs Collection)*

The hip, the beat, and the fashionable. From left: Gregory Corso (reclining), Allen Eager, unidentified model, and Miles Davis in the mid-1950s. *(Institute of Jazz Studies, Dana Library, Rutgers University, Newark, New Jersey)*

Recording *Miles Ahead* in the Columbia Records studios in May 1957. Producer George Avakian standing (at left), Gil Evans conducting (to the right of Avakian). *(Don Hunstein/Sony Music Photo Library)*

Gil Evans, Cal Lampley, and Davis at the *Miles Ahead* recording sessions. *(Don Hunstein/Sony Music Photo Library)*

The Miles Davis Sextet at the Newport Jazz Festival, July 3, 1958. From left: Bill Evans, Jimmy Cobb (partly obscured), Paul Chambers, Cannonball Adderley, Davis, John Coltrane. *(Sony Music Photo Library)*

Davis during the recording of *Porgy and Bess*, July 1958. *(Don Hunstein/ Sony Music Photo Library)*

Paul Chambers, Cannonball Adderley, Bill Evans, Davis, and John Coltrane discuss *Kind of Blue* at the recording sessions, 1959. *(Fred Plaut/The Fred and Rose Plaut Archives, Yale University Library)*

Miles and wife Frances Davis at the *Sketches of Spain* recording sessions, 1960. *(Fred Plaut/The Fred and Rose Plaut Archives, Yale University Library)*

Teo Macero and Davis in the recording booth.
(*Fred Plaut/The Fred and Rose Plaut Archives, Yale University Library*)

Miles and Wayne Shorter, London, 1967. (*©Val Wilmer*)

Miles and the rhythm section of his 1960s quintet: Herbie Hancock (piano), Tony Williams (drums), and Ron Carter (bass) at the Berlin Philharmonie, September 25, 1964. (*Jan Persson*)

Davis and Columbia president Clive Davis. (*Don Hunstein/ Sony Music Photo Library*)

Miles with Betty Mabry (left) and Jackie Battle (right) at
the funeral of Jimi Hendrix, 1970. *(Bob Peterson/*Time)

The Davis band at a
recording session in March
1978 (as yet unissued on
record). From left: Teo
Macero, Larry Coryell (guitar), Masabumi Kikuchi
(keyboards), T. M. Stevens
(bass), Davis, George Pulis
(keyboards), Al Foster
(drums).
*(Don Hunstein/Sony Music
Photo Library)*

Miles Davis and gui-
tarist Mike Stern,
New York City, 1985.
(Alan Nahigian)

Meanwhile, jazz musicians looked on in amazement at what Miles had wrought. They fell into camps, like the fans, with perhaps most of them offended by what he was doing. Many old friends, like Dizzy and Clark Terry, either damned him with faint praise or were outright critical. Charles Mingus, for example, during an interview on WKCR-FM in 1971, was asked about Miles' new music:

> Mingus: Who?
>
> Interviewer: Miles Davis.
>
> Mingus: Never heard of him. I knew a guy by that name who used to play with Bird, but I thought he was dead.
>
> Interviewer: You don't like his playing?
>
> Mingus: I don't think he's around anymore, unless you mean this guy who had a trumpet that I saw with pictures of naked white girls. I gave a trumpet to my four-year-old nephew, and he made better sounds than this guy.

By now, the musicians who regularly worked with Miles had come to expect that anyone at all might turn up when they recorded: amateurs, classical cellists, poets, Eskimo frame drummers, maybe Patagonian mouth harpists. His recording sessions were like Faulkner country. . . . the forest primeval. This time, May 27, 1970, when they gathered to record, it was Hermeto Pascoal who arrived, a multi-instrumentalist and composer with the reputation of being something of the Sun Ra of Brazil. His musical background had led him from *choros,* the northern Brazilian equivalent of New Orleans jazz, to sambas and free jazz, some of which he had explored with Airto Moreira in nightclubs in Rio. For Miles' purposes, Hermeto served in the role of Joe Zawinul, bringing along a stack of his own compositions. Miles wanted to record every one he brought, but Hermeto would only agree to two, "Igrejinha" (Little Church) and "Nem Um Talvez" (Not Even a Maybe). But when these tunes appeared later on the album *Live/Evil,* Hermeto was not given composer's credits. And by March 27, 1972, Hermeto's lawyers figured out that another piece on the album, "Selim," had the same melody as "Nem Um Talvez." In fact, it was simply another take of the same song.

Miles Davis at Fillmore was recorded over four nights between June 17 and 20, 1970, in New York City, this time at the eastern branch of the

San Francisco club. Again, medleys of tunes that had been recorded in the studio for *Bitches Brew, In a Silent Way,* and other sessions were played every set, but the Columbia production staff seemed unaware of it, since they made up new working titles for existing songs ("Fires," "Electjuicifing," "Mirror-Like," and "Physically Flying") during editing. Miles attended the editing sessions for three hours and decided that everything should be released. Then, while he was still in the editing room, he gave Teo a fright by suggesting that they release the recordings he had done at Fillmore East with those from Fillmore West in an expensive four-record package as a Christmas set.

When *Miles Davis at Fillmore* was released (as only a two-record set), the titles were simply "Wednesday Miles," "Thursday Miles," and so forth. Even the musicians didn't know the names of the tunes they were playing, for they were being cued into them by a series of signals and coded phrases that Miles used to thread together his medleys. By playing the first notes of a tune, or introducing a bass vamp associated with it, or stating the distinctive voicings of the harmonic progressions associated with it, he could begin one piece before the other was ended or abut one against another. Later, he would use similar signals to join together the bass lines, rhythms, or themes of two different pieces at the same time to create a completely new composition.

With Keith Jarrett on organ and Chick Corea playing electric piano, Chick complained that Miles' insistence on placing Jarrett's organ on one end of the stage and Chick's own keyboard on the other kept them from hearing each other. But in spite of this—or because of it—there are some spectacular and unruly keyboard effects as they ricocheted off each other, especially on the long version of "The Mask" (in "Thursday Miles") before it resolves into a fascinating revisionist view of how to play against a walking bass line. On "Directions," the opening track of the album (in "Wednesday Miles"), Teo edited in a small section of the live recording of "Bitches Brew," thus continuing some of the confrontational ideas he was using on the studio recordings.

Late in July, Teo received a note from the Talent Payment office at Columbia asking about the high costs of Miles' sessions. Teo replied that he wasn't aware that their office was handling production, but if they were, he'd give them Miles Davis' phone number, and if they hadn't yet spoken with him, they "were in for a treat when they called Miles."

Saxophonist Gary Bartz replaced Steve Grossman in August 1970. He came to Miles' group straight from his own band, Ntu Troupe, originally organized around a mission to bring a strong sense of ancient Africa into its music and which did its best to play without mikes, amplification, or even piano. Now Bartz was innocently stepping into a forrest of electricity. Miles' band could go all the way out or all the way in—returning to the heart of the music, or moving outside it altogether—and this was not something that Bartz felt comfortable with initially. He recalled one night in Boston when Tiki Fulwood, the drummer from George Clinton's Parliament-Funkadelic band, appeared with the group and played everything in funk style, with Miles perversely calling ballads like "Green Dolphin Street" and "Bye Bye Blackbird": "It was really horrible." On the other hand, at most performances Miles never played ballads, even in Yugoslavia, where the audience screamed at the group for not performing "My Funny Valentine" and "Someday My Prince Will Come."

Davis had his house done over again, this time with designs by Lancelot Haye, a Los Angeles interior decorator. Now there was an Egyptian mural on the patio walls, Mediterranean arches between each room, fur rugs on the floor, and black faux marble in the bathroom and kitchen. In the living room was an animal-skin sofa, a tiger's head, and a sign that said "No Visitors." His son Gregory was home from the army and living with him again, as was Miles IV, who had been medically discharged from the navy. Marguerite still had an apartment upstairs, and she was now pregnant with Miles' third son, Erin.

Miles continued his struggle to stay in shape. He stopped drinking, and avoided meat and fish. The battle he had with heroin was now being repeated with other substances and foods that he should avoid, and he was resisting them as part of his daily combat. Sometimes he won, sometimes not, but personal skirmishes like these kept him edgy and volatile for the rest of his life.

At the end of August, the band traveled to the Isle of Wight Festival, following freaky vocalist Tiny Tim on stage, and followed in turn by Joni

Mitchell, in front of hundreds of thousands of people, the largest audience it had ever faced. (Columbia recorded Miles' performance but issued only a small fraction of it as "Call It Anythin'" in an *Isle of Wight* anthology on which Jimi Hendrix was the main attraction.) After more than a year had passed, Miles called the British music magazine *Melody Maker* from Milan and asked to speak to Chris Welch, the reviewer of his performance at Isle of Wight. "What kind of man can call me arrogant?" Miles said. " . . . Oh, I know where you're at. . . . You shouldn't be a critic. You are a white man looking for white excitement, but there are more subtle forms of excitement. How can you say we were arrogant? . . . You must be out of your fucking mind!" He talked about Eric Clapton stealing solos from B. B. King records, *Melody Maker* covering only white performers, and the importance of *listening* to music ("Don't look at music, listen to it"). Welch printed Miles' comments, and told his readers that it *was* wrong of him to call Davis arrogant. "What I called arrogance, I sensed, was contempt for the entire rock set-up—rightly, as it transpired, from Miles' comments. But then why did he play a rock festival?"

In the fall, Chick Corea and Dave Holland left the band to form the quartet Circle, with saxophonist Anthony Braxton and drummer Barry Altschul. "Chick and Dave were exultant about the experience of playing with Miles," Braxton said. "*Everyone* wanted to play with Miles—I certainly did—but at the same time, they were reacting against the old man a bit, and wanting to become involved in some of the new music the AACM [Association for the Advancement of Creative Musicians, the heart of the avant-garde in Chicago] and I were playing." Circle was short-lived—a sometimes austere, sometimes explosive experiment, the essence of what was known as avant-garde jazz at the time. Writer Greg Tate would later say that he finally understood that two bands had been fighting for control of Miles' band: Miles' and Circle.

Between the fall of 1970 and April 1971, Davis took a band on the road that included Airto, Keith Jarrett, Michael Henderson, and Gary Bartz. (It was the period in which Miles had taken to wearing canary yellow boots with clear plastic heels filled with goldfish that had long since passed on.) The sound and monitor mixer for the tour was Scott Ross, a twenty-year-old who had already toured with the Allman Brothers, Johnny Winter, and Dreams. But this was something else: sound mixing for Miles was a nightmare because there was nothing obvious about what they were doing. There was no head-solo-head form, and one tune flowed into another with no warning. Miles was facing the musicians most of the time, so it was tough to know when anyone was going to solo and when the volume should be brought up on someone's mike. The band was playing several nights at each club it worked, but even after hearing the music over three nights, Scott still didn't understand how the sets were organized: "It was like the first time with Chinese food, or sex—you knew it was good, but didn't know how or why." But then, life with Miles at this point was something only a group of twenty-year-olds could handle. Every night was an occasion for some new weirdness:

> I was doing monitor mixing on the stage, and while they were performing Miles came to me and put his mouth to my ear. I could barely understand him over the music. What he said was, "My wah-wah doesn't work." It needed a battery, and once it was corrected, Miles played six or seven notes and then said to me, "Now get me some spaghetti; mushrooms is cool."

In 1970 the group played Constitution Hall in Washington, D.C., to a sold-out house. During the sound check, the Daughters of the American Revolution women who controlled the hall were startled by what they heard, and when they began to object, according to Ross, Miles hit one of the white-haired ladies on the head with his green trumpet. Things were becoming stranger.

On another occasion Ross said:

> We were traveling by bus, and most of the band was listening to Jimi Hendrix's *Electric Ladyland* and *Band of Gypsys*. No one was listening to jazz. Keith Jarrett was a loner who sat by himself in the back of the bus playing the Melodica. Everyone had a problem with him. With me, it was that he demanded that his Fender 88 had to be tuned every night. Then, there was Miles, treating the whites in the crew like second-class citizens.

Davis now had a band that was fully in tune with the racial climate and moving with a black nationalist wind at their backs. The electronic equipment was painted red, green, and black, courtesy of Yamaha. Miles had replaced Jack DeJohnette with Ndugu Leon Chancler on drums, and intensified the rhythm by adding Don Alias and M'tume (aka M'tume Heath and James Mtume Forman) on percussion. M'tume especially became a force for blackness in the group, keeping Miles in touch with current thinking. Yet there in their midst sat Keith Jarrett, who, despite his Afro and colorful clothing, was undeniably Caucasian. "At the Village Gate," Keith said, "the band was getting off on being Black Muslims, changing their names, etc."

A *Time* reporter walked in the dressing room like he was hip and asked for an interview. "Get the fuck out of here, motherfucker!" The band was in ecstasy. I'm sitting there being the only white person in the band (though everybody seemed to think I was black). And then Miles returned to being nice and quiet. A black man came into the room and asked Miles to play a benefit. The band was hopeful that they were about to see something they could tell their grandchildren. Miles said, "Get the fuck out of here, motherfucker!" And the band felt like, "Who are we? Should we even be in this dressing room?"

Declaring he was only along for the ride with Miles, Jarrett never hid his distaste for the music the group was playing and for some of the musicians in the group: "The funk and the non-knowledge of the past was beginning to take a toll on the band. Miles and I were like a duo with a group who had no idea of what they were doing."

[Miles] did get back to the old tunes once in a Boston club and it was terrible. I was the only one who knew them. The bass player was playing notes like he didn't know how to play the bass. The rest of the band were aliens. [Miles] was in bad shape.

One night Miles asked Keith if he knew why he never played ballads any more. It was because he loved them so, Miles said. Jarrett has interpreted this comment several ways. At one point, he understood Miles to mean that he'd rather play second-rate music with a second-rate band than play ballads poorly. But he also thought that Miles meant, "You have to want to struggle. And what most leaders are a victim of, is the freedom not to struggle." Miles did indeed say many times that it was a mistake to keep doing what you love, because you would never develop or progress. Besides, as he told David Amram, he detested the idea of growing old and finding himself in a room filled with twenty-five other Miles Davises.

This band was intensely rhythm driven, Henderson's bass acting as a giant drum to anchor the others, Jarrett using multiple keyboards to produce distorted riffs that rattled the groove. Michael Henderson said that Miles hired him to do what he did, and warned him not to "learn any of that old shit," that is, not to follow any of the other members of the band into music they used to play. "Keith Jarrett used to get off on being innovative and doing off-the-wall stuff. But Miles used to come over to my side, and whisper to me, 'Don't follow that motherfucker.' I don't think the other guys understood, because Keith Jarrett sometimes got frustrated when I didn't follow. The others in the band didn't know why I was in the band, but Miles knew exactly what he wanted from me." Leon Chancler said that, in order to get musical tension, "Miles told the group that 'when Keith starts playing that Catholic school shit, lay out, don't play, don't follow him.'" But Miles was also fascinated by Jarrett's sense of freedom in the music, asking him, "How do you start from nothing and play with no framework?"

Live/Evil, another double album, a patchwork of live recordings from the Cellar Door in Washington, D.C., from December 19, 1970 (with John McLaughlin back in the band for this occasion), and with the studio recordings done in February 1971 and those from June with Hermeto Pascoal, was released by Columbia. It was a dense, dark, and at times incoherent record, but one that often showed Miles at his best. He told Airto not to play rhythm all the time, but to produce sounds and colors, so Airto used the *cuica* to "tease him," to respond to Miles' playing. "What I Say?" is built on the simplest of rock drum-and-bass grooves—one chord and boom-boom-bat—but with Jarrett's hectoring figures added and taken at a ridiculously fast tempo, they go well beyond whatever it was that anyone meant by "rock." There are the meditative compositions by Pascoal, a somewhat overdriven "Funky Tonk," and "Inamorata," with a short poem written and narrated by Conrad Roberts that was crudely dubbed over the tune sometime later. There was something there for everyone to wonder about.

Mati Klarwein was again asked to do the cover art for this album, and this time Miles had a suggestion for the content: "I was doing the picture of the pregnant woman for the cover," said Mati, "and the day I finished Miles called me up and said, 'I want a picture of life on one side and evil on the other.'"

And all he mentioned was a toad. Then next to me was a copy of *Time* magazine which had Edgar Hoover on the cover, and he just looked like a toad. I told Miles I found the toad. But the funny thing was, after I painted him in drag with a wig and with tits for *Live/Evil*, a couple of years ago they published a picture of Hoover going around the streets in drag. He was a

horrible looking drag queen, just like my picture and obviously I didn't
know that at the time.

Early in 1971 there were reports that Miles was going to retire by mid-
summer, and in fact he was not playing much, though he continued to
book concerts. Troubles were piling up around him: he complained that
the IRS was harassing him over taxes (because he was black, he said—he
had already paid $40,000 last year alone); he had traded his Ferrari for a
new $20,000 Lamborghini, but then was immediately rear-ended by a
drunk, who forced him onto the sidewalk and into a brick wall on 79th
Street. Though a headlight and the grille were the only parts damaged,
somehow the repairs cost him $11,000, and he wound up in a dispute
between the insurance company and the body shop, during which the
insurance company went out of business. Next, Philadelphia DJ Georgie
Woods sued Miles for $13,000 in damages for missing a concert with
Aretha Franklin (though Miles claimed that he told Woods in advance
that he was sick). When he played the opening of the Beacon Theatre as
a favor to Jeannie Clarke (an executive secretary at NBC who had put her
life savings into the theater) on a bill that included comedian Richard
Pryor and the British progressive rock group Soft Machine, they were
unable to fill more than 40 percent of the 2,600 seats for four shows over
two nights. (Then two men robbed the box office and took most of the
money.) Miles also suffered a gallstone attack that was severe enough to
require surgery, and while he was recovering he began using drugs and
alcohol again, sometimes so heavily that that he was unable to work. On
those occasions he had to be led off the stage and apologized for by his
musicians. He made no new records for the next year and a half.

On April 29, his third son, Erin, was born. And though Erin's mother,
Marguerite, had broken with Miles, she remained upstairs in his house,
but would soon be leaving, taking their son with her.

The music called fusion was beginning to break into the pop charts. Tony
Williams' Lifetime and John McLaughlin's Mahavishnu Orchestra were
formed just the year before, as was Zawinul and Shorter's Weather

Report; Herbie Hancock had rapidly organized several different funk bands in succession (Mwandishi, the Headhunters, and the psychedelic jazz of his record *Sextant*); Chick Corea organized Return to Forever. Every one of them was having more commercial success than Miles. He complained that they copied him—*everyone* was copying him! Even John Lennon, Miles joked (maybe), had told him he was getting his hair cut to look like Miles. And his older musicians—Bill Evans, for instance—were now world famous and demanding top dollar. Miles also groused that all of these musicians played their best when they played with him, and it was an arguable point, at the least. It galled him that their successes came just when his plans were not working. At the Grammy Awards in 1972, Miles joined a walkout in protest over what he perceived as biased judging. He told *Jet* that

> the reason I didn't win is because the recording industry is 99 percent white. . . . So I'm helping to organize the Mammies for Black recording artists. We sent letters to all the Black disc jockeys and the only way a white group can get in is if it's mixed with Black musicians. There shouldn't be any prizes for any kind of art because all art is different. So we'll present awards and then tear them up in front of the cameras.

Miles still made short-lived efforts at renewing his health, but they were quickly erased by binges of various sorts. One reporter noted that after drinking cream soda and eating chocolate Easter eggs, Miles called room service for a piece of strawberry cheesecake and two dishes of vanilla ice cream. Then his hairdresser came in with twelve packs of gum, a bag of jelly beans, and another of hard candy, which he immediately began eating, insisting that it was good for the liver. Within a few years, most of his teeth had had root canals.

As Miles prepared for his next recording, his surprise guest was Paul Buckmaster, whom he had met in London six months earlier. Buckmaster was a cellist with an extraordinarily wide musical background: he had classical training, played with experimental improvisation groups like the Third Ear Band (which did the music for Roman Polanski's *Macbeth*), had written arrangements for David Bowie, Leonard Cohen, the Rolling Stones and others, and would go on to do the scores for films such as *Murder in Mind* and *12 Monkeys*. Miles sent a limo to pick him up at JFK Airport on May 17, 1972, and had him stay in his house for the next eight weeks. When Buckmaster arrived, Miles was in the midst of overdubbing "Red China Blues," a straightforward instrumental that had been recorded earlier by a group of studio musicians along with M'tume and Michael Henderson. Despite its being a throwaway performance, it was Miles' first time in the studio in almost two years.

"When I came to New York," Buckmaster said, "Miles wanted me to write some pieces, but he was also rather vague about what he wanted. I never really got a clear idea." But he had brought with him from London a couple of records by Karlheinz Stockhausen, then the most controversial and acclaimed avant-garde composer in Europe (his picture was even included in the crowd of notables on the cover of *Sgt. Pepper's Lonely Hearts Club Band*), and a man comfortable with the use of the studio and electronics in the composing process. The two records included "Mixture," "Gruppen," and "Telemusik," three long compositions completely free of conventional song structure, all of which existed only in the electronics of the studio. "Mixture" calls for four groups of musicians to play into microphones, and four engineers to balance the parts and feed them to ring modulators, which in turn are "played" by four more musicians—all of it against another group of musicians, the percussionists. The goal of the work, Stockhausen said, was to develop new kinds of musical textures and compositional methods. "Gruppen" was a piece for three separate orchestras that either play against each other or come together, often in different tempos. "Telemusik," according to Stockhausen, was inspired by Varèse's *Poème électronique* and was a kind of abstract "world music," incorporating "found" musics from Japan, Bali, North Africa, Spain, Hungary, Vietnam, and elsewhere on tape that were overlapped with manipulated electronics. Like jazz, it was music that could be thought of as ancient and modern at the same time. All three were long pieces built up from small, identifiable cells of music, each involving dense textures of sound—sound used for its own sake—and all of them edited either during the performance or afterward or both. There was a strong spatial component to Stockhausen's music, allowing players to move in spirals, in effect composing as they played within his own composition. Miles said that what impressed him most about Stockhausen was the "idea of music as a continuous process."

Since Miles and all of the musicians around him at the time were also listening to James Brown, Sly, and Hendrix, Buckmaster thought he might alternate street rhythms with Stockhausen-like abstractions—a total rhythm suddenly interrupted by floating passages. "I remember describing this to Miles," said Buckmaster.

The whole idea was based on creating a kind of "cosmic pulse" with great abstractions going on around it. I said something to Miles like, "Things are either off or on. Reality is made of a sequence of on and offness." A crazy idea. But what I meant was that a sound doesn't mean anything unless it has a silence preceding it or coming after it, or next to it. Silence makes up part of the music, it is in music, and that's what I was trying to get at. Like Stockhausen once said, "Play something next to what you hear." So here I was talking to Miles about "street music, with the cosmic pulse going on or off." Miles took that idea and used it for the title and the cover, with the front saying "On" and the other side "off."

A European avant-gardist might seem like a strange inspiration for Davis at this point in his music, but as Gil Evans said to Miles, "Stockhausen sounds like *you*." It was not much of a stretch. Both musicians were pioneers in using found music in their recordings. They used new electronic devices in performance, and made editing the principal means of creating form. Both valued the use of space and silence in their work, and shared an openness to the use of alien musics in the name of universality. Miles was no stranger to the avant-garde: he once borrowed from writer Gene Lees the entire set of recordings of commissioned works of contemporary music by the Louisville Symphony Orchestra, and he was often seen at avant-garde events. At one, after a concert of Luciano Berio's work, the *New York Times* reported that Miles asked Berio to "give me some chords." Berio replied, "You don't need them."

Stockhausen, for his part, had grown up hearing jazz, and as a pianist had even played with John Lewis at Birdland in 1958, later saying that "I learned a great deal, above all, from their instrumentation and technique . . . also the way they played, their gestures, their level of sympathy." His taste for the instruments of the jazz band surfaced in his compositions, especially in his frequent use of muted trumpet, normally featuring his son, Markus, who himself recorded with Miles' former bassist Gary Peacock and for a while had his own jazz-rock group.

While he was staying with Miles, Buckmaster often practiced the Prelude to Bach's *Cello Suite No. 1,* and Miles loved it, and asked him to work it into something for him to play. Though Buckmaster never did anything with it, Miles' interest in the Prelude shows that he could be drawn to music that was primarily made up of rhythm, texture, color, and structure and was without a real melody as such. This is all the more interesting because Miles later said that Bach made him hear what Ornette Coleman meant by "harmolodics"—a system by which all instruments of a group are liberated to solo simultaneously.

Saxophonist Dave Liebman was at his doctor's office when a call came from his mother: Teo Macero had phoned to say that Steve Grossman couldn't make a recording session that day with Miles. Could Dave? Liebman immediately drove to 52nd Street, left his car double-parked, and ran up to the studio, where they were already in the middle of a recording. Miles told him to get his horn out and play. But the other musicians were all wired up, and Dave had no earphones: all he could hear was the faint sound of a piano and a "chick-a-chick" beat in an otherwise silent studio. Miles pushed him to a mike and signaled him to play, though he had no idea of where they were in the tune or what key they were in. For two to three minutes he soloed into the silence. After another half hour passed, the session was over, and the musicians left without saying much to each other.

In most recording sessions, a musician gets to play for only a few minutes every hour, the rest of the time being taken up with playbacks, planning, and restarts. But with the tape rolling continuosly at Miles' sessions, a musician might be required to play for one or two hours out of every three or four that he was in the studio. Yet there were no beginnings, no endings, no takes, just the continual buzz of rhythm vamps beneath the horns, keyboardists, and guitarists. Liebman received no guidance other than "play what you know." What they played was polyphonic and richly reticulated music like Coltrane's *Ascension*, Liebman said, but all of it over a rock beat. It was not so much like recording as it was like boxing, "coming in and out, stop and go."

After they were finished recording, Miles listened to some of the playback, turned to Liebman, and said, "Join my band." Having fired Steve Grossman, he began to recruit Liebman like a star, later sending a limo to pick him up and bring him to his house, and offering him more money than Miles was paying the other musicians. Liebman was tempted, but finally said no because he thought that Miles was sick and a bit crazed at the time—he was heavily medicating himself with Percodan, cocaine, and assorted uppers. In addition to his other physical pains, Miles was coughing and spitting from walking pneumonia, which had become chronic over the past few years without his paying attention to it.

When Dave Liebman first went over to Miles' house, he said he walked in on a weird scene: it was almost completely dark and impossible to tell whether it was day or night. But that mattered little to Miles; he had been up for several days, obsessively playing Sly and the Family Stone's "In Time" which would later appear on the album *Fresh*. Downstairs, instruments and amplifiers were scattered around the floor. Upstairs in his bedroom, where he spent most of his time, Miles was living in total disorder, his closet overflowing with clothing and at least 1,000 pairs of shoes.

Miles' hairdresser, various hangers-on, and several women friends seemed to go and come in the house, and there were whispers that Cicely Tyson, or Richard Pryor, or Dick Gregory was staying in one of the upstairs apartments. "He did not like to be alone," Liebman concluded, and Miles was generous to them all, though he "exacted quite a price for it in what they had to do for him."

On the Corner was the record they were making when Liebman first entered the studio, a title that alluded back to that corner Miles could see from his window when they lived behind his father's dental office in East St. Louis: "I was trying to play the music I grew up on now, that roadhouse, honky-tonk, funky thing that people used to dance to on Friday and Saturday nights." In the postproduction work, Teo emphasized Davis' use of the wah-wah pedal: "Miles was just learning to use the pedal. . . . If he made a mistake, I'd take the tapes and, when I did the editing, I'd use the wah-wah pedal and punch it in. Wah-wah them to death."

Miles next made his biggest move yet to take control of his records and wrest them from the conventions imposed by Columbia. When *On the Corner* came out, there were no liner notes with the record, and more surprising, no list of instruments or players, or any pictures of Miles. The idea was that if he even revealed who the performers were on the album, opinions would be predetermined by it. He wanted the record listened to, not read. But this caused some of the musicians to complain to the company about being anonymous, and Liebman even wrote a letter to *Down Beat* with his own list of personnel. When the next issue of the recording appeared, there was a list, though it was incomplete. The 2000 reissue of *On the Corner* on CD lists sixteen musicians playing on one track or the other, including John McLaughlin on guitar, Colin Walcott and Khalil Balakrishna on acoustic or electric sitars, Badal Roy on tabla, and three drummers (Al Foster was on only part of the record because Miles hadn't been able to find his phone number); but there were likely at least six more missing from the list, including Paul Buckmaster on cello, M'tume and Don Alias on hand drums, guitarist Reggie Lucas,

Cedric Lawson on synthesizer, and organist Lonnie Liston Smith. Miles was looking to thicken the groove by filling in the space where harmonic variation would have been in conventional jazz, and he was seeking to complicate and fire the rhythmic imagination of the group. But he insisted that it was not a particular ethnic sound he wanted. Badal Roy, fresh from Calcutta and new to jazz, tuned his tabla drums to the scales the band was using, and when he asked Miles what he should play, Miles answered, "Play like a nigger," then pointed at him to start. Herbie Hancock cried, "Oh, yeah!" and they were off.

It seems that almost no one liked the record: not Dave Liebman, not Paul Buckmaster, certainly not the jazz writers or Miles' older fans. Teo Macero even had to fend off complaints from within the company. He received a letter from Richard Asher, managing director of CBS UK, about Miles Davis playing less and less on his records as time went on. Teo responded by counting Miles' playing time on *Bitches Brew* (24:43), *Live/Evil* (26:40), *Black Beauty* (33:39), and *On the Corner* (26:38).

The young, black pop-music crowd that he was aiming for never got to hear it, even though Columbia made some small efforts to market it as a pop record. One magazine ad showed no pictures of Miles, just a gathering of black folks on an urban stoop. The text that went with it was aimed at those who did not live in the neighborhood:

> Take a walk down a city street with Miles Davis and listen to the language of the people on the sidewalk.
> Listen to music that captures the joy, the pain, the beauty of people who live on "The Block."
> Listen to one of the most beautiful places in the world.

But overall, Columbia marketed *On the Corner* as another jazz record by Miles Davis, and that meant that it would never be played on black, youth-oriented stations (most record companies at the time still believed that African Americans were interested only in singles and would never buy albums). Nor was it clear that a record as radically independent and idiosyncratic as this one would have interested those caught up in the black music of the day.

Davis' anger over the record's lack of sales spread outward from Columbia to his own management, and he demanded that he work with Neil Reshen, another manager in the Shaw Agency, instead of Jack Whittemore:

They don't do anything for you unless you're white or Jewish. Except when I got out a new album or something. By now I don't even talk to them anymore. For instance: when I showed 'em the new cover by Corky McCoy, they told me it won't help sell any albums. And I told 'em how to merchandise nigger music, man. . . . Put niggers on the covers, put brothers and sisters on 'em, whatever they're gonna call us next, that's what you put on the covers to sell us.

It would take more than twenty years for history to redeem this music, until the time came that looping, growling, and bass- and drum-driven repetitive musics would rule the streets.

Miles missed what would have been his biggest performance of the year, a double concert shared with Sonny Rollins and McCoy Tyner at Carnegie Hall on July 4 during the first Newport Jazz Festival to be held in New York City. The festival itself was already in trouble: unsure of its success in New York City, it was hit by a counterfestival organized by younger black musicians. Since Newport had promised 55 percent of its profits to the National Urban League, things were going to be financially tight. Miles claimed that he had no agreement with George Wein and that his name was being used just to get more people to attend. Wein in turn said that he had sent Miles a deposit. Having already accused Wein of exploiting musicians, Miles was never one to let things lie. The festival was interested only in older-style musicians, he claimed, like Sarah Vaughan and Dizzy Gillespie. After this outburst against his old friends, there were those who said that Miles' life was out of hand, or that the reason he had failed to appear was that he had no band ready to play, or that he had laid off too long to play himself.

Only five days after the festival, Davis was charged by police with unlawful imprisonment of a woman in his house. A Mrs. Lita Merker, they said, was prevented from leaving the house by Mr. Davis. He denied any wrongdoing. Later, he would say that the newspapers had left out the fact that she lived in an apartment upstairs in his house, that he "had his woman with him" when all of this happened, and that what it was about was that Merker had been caught with hashish in customs and was now taking it all out on him. Whatever was going on between the two of them was settled out of court, apparently with apologies all around.

If there were those who thought Miles was moving too far beyond jazz with *On the Corner*, when he recorded "Rated X" in September, they surely would have felt he had now gone beyond the pale. Once Columbia heard it, it didn't want to release the recording, according to Teo, and it was shelved until it appeared two years later in the 1974 anthology *Get Up with It*. The Miles whom fans had come to know so well had literally disappeared from the record; he seemed to have abandoned the trumpet for the Yamaha electric organ. Even the jangle of electric pianos had disappeared, replaced by a polytonal mass of pulsing sound. The background had been moved into the center of the picture—like an abstract expressionist painting—with drums, bass, and sitar holding the pulse together while congas, tabla drums, and rhythm guitar were given freedom to make slight variations, as the keyboards sustained long chords as drones. The instruments entered separately at times, staggered in the old African and African American tradition, audibly building up the groove from its elements. "We had a five-hour rehearsal one day, and I gave the band a certain rhythm and told them to stay there. Not to react. To let me do all that."

Once a groove was established on "Rated X," at several points it was interrupted or suspended by the engineer's abruptly cutting off the rhythm tracks, leaving nothing but the sustained, floating sound of the held keyboard chords. A sudden loss of sound like this can feel like a physical leap into space, or something like a gravity-free move into another kind of music. It was very different from breaks in traditional jazz: if heard live, the listener could see that the musicians were still holding their instruments and would continue playing once the break ended, and through repeated listenings to recordings in the jazz tradition, one knew that the musicians would always start up again after the break. But this was something new. Using four recording machines in postproduction, the engineer switched from one tape to another, and some of the musicians were made to disappear—instantly, with no sonic residue or echo remaining. Adding to the indeterminacy was that "the organ track came from Miles' contribution to a different song," according to Teo. "It had nothing to do with the song 'Rated X' originally. You hear this band drop out, right? The organ just sits on it. That was a loop. I brought the band in one or two bars later. That track was done in the editing room."

Coming after the relentless tumult of the groove, the effect of the loss of rhythm is heart-stopping, if not apocalyptic. The return of the rhythm calls attention to the groove and forces the listener-dancer to attend to it, even in its absence. Once again, Miles had bared some of the work that went into the making of the recording and foregrounded the point at which the musicians end and the technology begins. Miles had been dropping free-floating passages into his music ever since "Deception" in 1950, but this was more radical in intent and effect. He once spoke of doing music such as he had heard in Alban Berg's opera *Wozzeck*, where during the performance, "A window is opened, suddenly the orchestra stops and you hear a marching band outside. When it's closed, the orchestra starts again. That's the kind of thing I want to do, open some windows."

In September 1972, Miles took a stripped-down version of the *On the Corner* band out for a series of concerts and festivals in Ann Arbor, Boston, Philadelphia, and New York City, where they were taped on September 29 for a somewhat disappointing album called *Miles Davis in Concert: Live at Philharmonic Hall*. Some of the musicians were young and new to the band (Cedric Lawson on synthesizer and Reggie Lucas on guitar); the sound mix was murky, with some instruments being lost altogether, while others, such as some of the percussionists, were far too prominent; and only occasionally (as on "Black Satin") did their grooves hold together as well as they did in the studio. Miles, however, could be heard clearly throughout, especially where his wah-wah pedal suffers from overuse and lack of expression. Still, listened to casually, even as background music, *In Concert* at times has an almost otherworldly musicality about it that, if not completely engaging, is at least intriguing.

Back in New York on October 9, Miles started uptown in his Lamborghini in search of drugs, when he missed the turn off the West Side Highway at the 125th Street exit and crashed into a barrier rail on a traffic island, breaking both his ankles. His performances were canceled for the rest of the year, beginning with an Apollo appearance with Johnny Nash at the start of November. He was in serious pain, hobbling about on crutches, and, as a result of his accident combined with his hip problems, one of his legs was now an inch shorter than the other. More than ever before, he was in need of drugs of various sorts just to stay mobile. "Everything started to blur after that car accident," he said.

It was Jackie Battle who received the call from the hospital and then asked his sister, Dorothy, to come to New York to help her with his recovery and with the cleaning of his apartment while he was in the hospital.

Jackie's relationship with Miles was different from that of most of the other women involved with him, and it had the potential to reverse his decline in health. He trusted her, often listened to her, and, as his autobiography reveals, thought of her as an exceptional person. To Jackie, Miles was "a very innocent, pure person, who had been made worse by bad people around him."

> Anything he did was pure—he saw nothing wrong with doing anything if you didn't feel bad about it. He really didn't fit into this world—and he took ill because the world was so deceptive and hypocritical. He had little trust in people, and had to take tranquilizers just to be able to bear listening to the bullshit around him.

Miles drew her out, encouraging her to paint and to write. He was an inspiration to her because of his concentration and his devotion to music. "He heard music all the time, in dripping faucets, the sounds of the house, in the leaves . . . but the music also consumed him. Everything he did or saw had a musical meaning. It was the cost of being a musician."

To protect himself, she thought, he cultivated a persona and a way of being that ended up attracting the very forces that were beginning to destroy him. He was fearless and constantly put himself in danger. "When I told him that he seemed miserable, he said, 'What looks like misery to you, could be happiness to me.' He was at his worst in the 1970s, and there were people in his house day and night, dealers, hustlers, hangers-on of all kinds. It was a full-time party. When it became too crazy for him, he'd leave his house and go to someone else's to be quiet and watch TV. When he came over to my place he might be hallucinating: he'd look in the closet and under the rug to see if anyone was there. Then he'd feel safe. And after a few days' rest, he'd go back to the party at his house."

> He was lonely, and tried to get people to do things for him, and stay with him. When I was in art school, trying to study, he'd call me all night long. Sometimes he didn't talk, and I fell asleep on the phone. Several times when I wanted to leave his house he put a handful of sleeping pills in his mouth and threatened to swallow them if I left. I reached in his mouth and took them out. But once when he did that I gave him a glass of water and told him to go ahead and kill himself. Another time he lay on the floor and pretended to be dead—when I started to leave he reached out and grabbed my leg, and yelled at me for leaving him. He'd get himself

admitted to the hospital just so that he could have visitors—a doctor would call me and ask me to come to see him. When I got there, there'd be a party in the hospital room, a VCR, his paints set up, him holding court, and someone would have brought him some drugs.

"What he got from me," Jackie said "was stability. He had different needs, and I wasn't going to fill all of them. I let other people take care of them. He needed a caretaker, and if he thought he was losing me, he'd offer to marry me. He had no idea of how good he was, or how good he looked: 'I'm just a nigger who plays trumpet.' He wanted to paint, but he didn't want to work alone. My brother Todd Merchant is a painter, and he tried to get him to paint with him."

"He tested everyone, challenged them. If you were good, he could make you better; if you were bad, he made you worse. He loved women, loved being around them. But in general, he thought women were dogs, and that he could get a woman to do anything he wanted. Yet he had no respect for anyone who did everything he wanted. Sometimes he even tried to get other women to call me, and tried to connect them with me."

But Miles finally became too much for her. "I had to protect myself, or life with him would have killed me. His needs were so intense they devoured you. I never got enough sleep, never enough food, or enough nurturing. I couldn't keep up with him. He was never comfortable just talking or being sociable for a long time. After a few minutes he had to get up and cook, play music, do something. When he was mean or rude to people, I think he thought of it as being true to himself. Sometimes he showed off by being rude to me in front of his musicians, but then he'd apologize for it."

While he was recovering from his accident on the West Side Highway, Jackie set up a hospital bed in the back overlooking the garden, and she slept beside him on a small bed to keep watch on him. "I'd wake up, and he'd be gone on crutches looking for drugs. You couldn't stop him from doing the things he did that were destructive. His sister, Dorothy, called me many times asking me to check on him. But there was no stopping him if he needed drugs. He once hired a plane to fly him from the Monterey Jazz Festival to San Francisco to get drugs." In his autobiography Miles wrote, "One time we were on a plane in San Francisco, this stewardess walked up and handed me a matchbox full of coke ["which had been given to her by a doctor," Jackie added] that I just started snorting right there in the seat."

"And that," Jackie said, "on top of the eight or nine Tuinals he took to get him past his fear of flying. He tried to talk you into things, and if that didn't work, he'd trick you into doing them. He asked me to go to Jimi Hendrix's funeral with him, and when I said no, he asked me to ride with him to the airport. Then he wanted me to walk with him to the plane. And before I knew it, I was on the plane with him without any luggage."

When Miles was able to play again, in January 1973, Dave Liebman decided to join the band and stayed for the next year and a half. When he first worked with the group, he expected to get at least some direction from Miles, though very little was forthcoming. Still, what Miles did say provided clues to his own playing: "Break up the phrases, stop in the middle."

Miles was a rhythmic player, playing off the beat, often on the upbeat, breaking up his phrases, or suddenly inserting an exceptionally rhythmic phrase into his solo to get the attention of the band. "With Miles, this thing was about rhythm," Liebman said, "get in between the beats."

> In a way it really relates to his interest in boxing, the thing of a jab, quick jab, feinting, going, looking, left coming at you, then the right coming at you; this kind of movement and ballet. He had a lot of interest in ballet, which is all about physical movement. When you think about Miles' playing and you listen to it, if you see it in that respect, it is a very physical way of playing. It's a ballet. It's a dance.

With rhythmic sensibilities such as his, Miles needed to be surrounded by players who understood his focus and catered to it. His rhythm sections from the late 1950s through the mid-1960s were attuned to his phrasing within the context of ballads or bebop tunes modeled on pop songs. Now, with open-ended forms and minimal melodies and little more than drones and pedal points, he wanted percussionists who could construct forms out of rhythm itself on the fly. M'tume played the conga drums tunefully and lightly, without the usual Latin patterns, and he contributed so melodically to the grooves the band was building that Miles himself would sometimes play rhythm on the trumpet for short stretches. Michael Henderson could quickly pick up the rhythms that M'tume or Miles was beginning and extend them, tossing them back and forth with others in the band, taking turns keeping the rhythm going. When they were at their best, a volatile, shifting, emergent flow was kept moving beneath them, instead of the usual recycling grooves of rhythm and blues.

"Finish before you're done." It was a remark that Liebman understood as Miles' trademark way of ending a statement, in the middle of the air.

> He doesn't go to the end of the 32nd bar and resolve to the beginning. In the old days, he'd stop and go and maybe leave four bars out or eight bars out. Then he'd come in on the third bar of a phrase instead of the first bar. He had unusual starting and ending points, unusual places to begin and end a phrase. I realized that what he was thinking about was the rhythm section, that they need the space to be inventive. If you leave the space, they will fill it up. Then you will have them to play off of.

Though Miles never explained Liebman's role in the group, over several months Dave began to understand the music to be what he called "a polyphonic bizarre combination of Sun Ra, Duke Ellington, and James Brown." Lost in the swirl and deafening roar of the band, at first he had no idea what to play and asked Miles why he even wanted a saxophone in this group. Miles' response was that "people like to see saxophone players move their fingers."

> Now, what did he really mean by that? To me what he meant was, "You play fast, I play slow. It's a good thing. It's a foil to my style. That's what Bird was and that's what Trane and Wayne Shorter were and that's what you're going to be. You're going to be the fast stuff that the saxophone does so well, and I'm going to play the slow stuff." . . . I realized that everything he does is using opposites against each other: tension and release, loud to soft, cut the band out or put the band in, drums only, then just the bass, play loud then soft, play here, don't play there, stop and go, fast and slow. . . . When you listen to Miles' music, almost from any period, you get this constant up-and-down cycle. It's in two-beat with Philly Jo[e] Jones. Suddenly it goes up and comes down again. You listen to it in the 60s with Tony Williams, Ron Carter, Wayne, and Herbie, and it's the same thing. . . . He plays spacious, Wayne comes in, it burns. . . . That was not Coltrane's way. My whole influence from Coltrane was straight down the path, two hours solo, beat it to the ground, stay there with Elvin [Jones], etc. This thing was about up and down, up and down. Once you see that about Miles, you get one of the big keys to his playing, and to the way he leads a band.

In the mid-1970s, liberated by the cordless mike, Miles' back was turned to the audience for real. When he wasn't playing, he faced the musicians, acting as director, referee, and audience. It was not about disrespect, but a seriousness about the music. "Before you went on the bandstand with him and you were in the dressing room," Liebman said, "it was silence. He was looking down and maybe saying a few words, and then he'd say, 'Let's go,' and he'd be on the stage. It was deep. Amazing concentration. Absolutely no fooling around. He was always on the case." He now stayed on the stage throughout the set, cueing soloists, raising and lowering the volume, adjusting the color of the sound (maybe putting the sitar against the organ or the congas), working toward a group sound harder than ever before. Davis' ability to hear his own playing in relation to that of the group's was astonishing. He could hear the bass, drums, and piano independently and as a section, and could respond to what any one of them was playing. It was all part of Miles' legendary power as a bandleader, his ability to draw in other players and make them a part of what he was playing, to signal what he wanted wordlessly, by the choice of a single note, or the smallest of gestures. He had the sensibilities of an auteur, the ability to draw together the sound, the look, the feel of a musical production and create a mise-en-scène that was felt and visualized as well as heard.

At this point in his life as a performer, Miles was no longer thought of as lacking technique or the ability to awe an audience with a bravura display. Instead, Liebman said,

> The thing about Miles' trumpet playing . . . is the aspect of color, which means that every tone, every pitch, every time you play it can have, should have, must have, a different expressive nuance behind it—a color. There's no such thing as the same red twice in a row. If it's a red and you look closely, it's not the same red. It may be more pink red or blue red. It's very much like painting. There are six primary colors, and there are thousands of shades. Miles' thing is that he never played the same note the same way twice. . . . [He had] the ability to make every note have some kind of different innuendo, feeling, nuance, expressive shape, color, vibrato, [and this] means that he's somehow expressing every moment of the way.

Though he got along well with Liebman, Miles was not easy for everyone to work with, and he could intimidate some of the musicians as much as he did his audience:

> What I could see was that this was a guy, in my judgment, who was basically a very shy person and talented musician who got the limelight very

quickly. He became super well known at a young age. He really did not know how to handle it, and turned on a certain defensive attitude. That became hardened and affected his personality, because deep down this guy is a nice and caring human being, very nice, aware of dance and boxing, etc. But his persona became so hardened by the jazz life and being black. Even though you're a star, you're still black. . . . I think that he got into this state, and he didn't know sometimes how to be a human being. He would be very, very rough.

"What day you saw him on determined how he *was*." The exception was race: "Miles . . . was not personally prejudiced. That I will definitely say."

In late February 1973, neighbors on West 77th Street called the police when they heard pounding on the front door of 312. When the cops arrived, they found the front door lock broken and Miles in front of a third-floor apartment with "his girlfriend, twenty-three-year-old Jody Fisher" inside. Both were arrested and charged with possession of cocaine and a weapon, a .25 caliber automatic. The drug charge was dropped, but Davis was fined for illegal possession of the gun. Next, a concert in Dallas had to be canceled when he went over the high wall in his backyard in a fit of cocaine-induced jealousy and paranoia and broke his ankle again when he fell into the next yard. When he took the band to Canada and the Northwest coast a few weeks later, he performed in a cast while seated on a stool.

Miles added guitarist Peter Cosey to the band while they were playing in Portland in April. Pete came from a strong rhythm and blues background and had played with everyone in Chicago—backed the stars of soul music on recordings, worked with the AACM, played with Muddy Waters (on the infamous *Electric Mud* album), and had been a member of the Chess Records house band. He brought an extraordinarily inventive edge to Miles' band, playing his guitar in his own exotic tunings, going well outside Hendrix or any other guitarist at the time. Like a deity from some alternative rock and roll world, he played seated on stage behind a desk covered with electronic gadgetry, his dark glasses, enormous Afro, flowing beard, and robes giving him a distant and forbidding mien.

Cosey joined at a time when Miles was growing more serious about doing extended works, wanting to make records that went well beyond the usual limits, putting the LP record to full use. He wanted to record a suite of arias from *Tosca*, for example, with his horn as the principal voice and Gil's arrangements behind him. He loved Leontyne Price's recording of the opera and praised her work ("I'd drink her bathwater! She never wastes any phrases . . . neither does Frank [Sinatra]"). But he was also talking about doing something more open, which could be developed slowly as they played—a record with only one piece, forty-five minutes long, to be called "Calypso." Though *Tosca* was never recorded, "Calypso Frelimo," (named after the Frente de Liberacion de Mozambique, one of the parties seeking Mozambique's independence from Portugal in the early 1970s) was completed on September 17, 1973. "Frelimo" was a thirty-two-minute-long study in Afro-diasporic rhythms of the moment. A "dub fugue" is what Greg Tate called it, because of its antiphonal construction and its echoed elements. With its cheerful riff-melody, it manages to out-"Afro" African pop and out-dub reggae over its three contrasting movements.

Miles was often seen during this time with Sly Stone of Sly and the Family Stone, and often drove over to Sly's apartment on 25 Central Park West in the new white Ferrai Dino he had bought to replace the Lamborghini. Miles had first heard them perform the same day that he played at the Newport Jazz Festival on July 6, 1969, and he was immediately taken by their look and their sound—part gospel, part rhythm and blues, yet also deriving from rock and roll and big band arrangements. They radiated freedom, summer nights, and both the celebratory and the forbidden poles of life. But more than this, for Miles they unified everything in his past: church, roadhouses, dance halls, farm fields, and music schools. Nothing was forbidden, nothing was too black—or white, for that matter.

Sly was Miles' entrée to a new generation of musicians, those whose associates and representatives kept them supplied with endless quantities of drugs, food, ladies, and friends, simply because, as stars, they believed they deserved it. It was a life that was rapidly doing Sly in, but still the recording company was accommodating. Since he so often failed to show up at the studio sessions scheduled for him, the company had a sixteen-track tape recorder set up in his apartment, with engineers coming in shifts to record him whenever he felt like it. Miles and Sly sometimes played together over some of the tracks that Sly's group had recently recorded, and there was some talk about Miles producing Sly's next record. Although nothing came of it, Miles did turn up at the studio a few times during the recording of Sly's album *Fresh*, along with Herbie Hancock, Ike Turner, and Johnny "Guitar" Watson. Bass player Rusty Allen recalled one night at Sly's apartment when Miles was there and "got on Sly's organ and started to voice these nine-note ethereal chords."

> Sly was way back in the bedroom and he came out yelling, "Who in the fuck is doing that on my organ?" He came in and saw. "Miles, get your motherfucking ass out," he said. "Don't ever play that voodoo shit here. Get the fuck out." Miles left and I said, "Sly, that was Miles Davis you was talking to." "I don't give a fuck," he said, "playing that shit on my organ."

Sly's friend Hamp "Bubba" Banks added, "Miles didn't care. Miles was back the next day." Miles often turned up at punk clubs with other Columbia artists. Members of the Stooges, Iggy Pop's band, recall Miles coming to see them at Ungano's, joining them backstage, praising their originality and spirit, and cheering on Iggy's antics. (Alan Vega of the duo Suicide remembers Miles' amusement when Iggy jumped on top of blues guitarist Johnny Winters at another performance.)

Davis took the concept of bringing ringers or unknowns into recording sessions to a new level on March 30, 1974. Into a group that had been performing and recording together for a year, he invited two new players—saxophonist Azar Lawrence and guitarist Dominique Gaumont—for what was in effect an audition, but in front of an audience at a concert at Carnegie Hall being recorded by Columbia. He was either crazy or very shrewd, concluded Dave Liebman. Perhaps both. Lawrence was not asked back, but Gaumont, a virtual unknown from France and Bahia, Brazil, who aspired to make a Hendrix-like impact, was hired as a third guitarist. When some of the musicians raised questions about Gaumont's ability to play with a band of that quality, Miles allowed that he had hired him "to mess with Pete." A funny comment, but Miles never took the music *that* lightly, and he later explained some of his thinking about this mix of guitarists:

> I would try exploring one chord with this band, one chord in a tune, try-
> ing to master these small little simple things like rhythm. We would take a

chord and make it work for five minutes with variations, cross rhythms, things like that. Say Al Foster is playing in 4/4, M'tume might be playing in 6/8 or 7/4, and the guitarist might be comping in another time signature, or another rhythm altogether different. There's a lot of intricate shit we were working off this one chord. But music is real mathematical, you know? Counting beats and time: shit like that. And then I was playing over and under and through all of this, and the pianist and bass were playing something else. Everyone had to be alert to what everyone was doing. At the time, Pete gave me that Jimi Hendrix and Muddy Waters sound that I wanted, and Dominique gave me that African rhythmic thing.

A rebalancing of musical elements was taking place, with rhythm being brought to parity with melody and harmony by eroding the hierarchy that kept them in place. *Dark Magus* was the title suggested for this Carnegie concert recording by Tatsu Nosaki, general manager of International A and R of CBS/Sony Japan who were producing the record. He explained that "Magus . . . is the founder of the ancient Persian religion, Zoroastrianism. The titles of [each of the LP's sides] 'Moja,' 'Wili,' 'Tatu,' and 'Nne' are Swahili for 'one,' 'two,' 'three,' and 'four.'" Given the times they were living in, that somehow may have all made sense. But these titles managed to conceal other tunes within them: "Moja" also included a theme from "Nne"; the second part of "Tatu" was "Calypso Frelimo"; and the first part of "Nne" was "Ife."

"Tatu" was typical of where they were headed. Building off a monster bass riff close to one heard on B.T. Express's "Express," Miles used hand signals to stop the band from time to time much as the engineer had occasionally erased the band on "Rated X." The empty spaces that this created were too long to be traditional jazz breaks—so long, in fact, that they begged to be filled by soloists playing cadenzas, which they did, often outrageously. There were moments when all three guitars and the two saxophonists were in dense and exalted free improvisation together, and Pete Cosey's tunings, effects, excess, and sheer inventiveness took the guitar to the point where Hendrix, free jazz, and rhythm and blues proudly merged together. Engineering fades abound in this concert recording, reminding us that there was more here than CBS/Sony was willing to set loose on the world.

The release of these new Miles Davis records was now beginning to overwhelm even those who professed to know the music. Columbia sometimes issued them out of chronological order, often with the wrong personnel listed, or none at all. To those who didn't know that Miles was sometimes playing organ, he often seemed to be disappearing in the record, and to those who did know, he sometimes appeared to be playing trumpet and organ at the same time. The writers were as stymied as the fans. The music that Miles' band was playing was becoming denser, richer, and more reticulated. It was now also louder than any jazz band had ever been, and probably louder than any rock group as well. "Just listen to it," Miles told journalist Harriet Choice. "It's so breathtaking. You can't know how terrifying it is to be in the middle of all that. It's endless sound. Music is a curse. I'm so into it that I have to have other things to get away from it." In order to play in the depths of dark funk they were seeking, Miles had to modify his tone and phrasing, or else risk sounding like a mariachi trumpeter who had somehow wandered into a B.T. Express record. As Greg Tate put it, Miles, like e.e. cummings, was making poetry out of punctuation. He was shortening his phrases, often playing pure rhythm figures. Pete Cosey said, "That music was about life. It dealt with cleansing. It dealt with rising and falling. It was extremely cerebral, but it was earthy at the same time. We were into creating moods, taking people through different experiences, and both projecting and receiving thoughts from the audience."

Live, the band was playing sets of about an hour without a break, moving from one tune to the other by means of Miles' signals. He thought of these sets as one unit, one composition, and chose not to name the different themes, even if they had already been recorded separately under one name or another. These were the longer forms he had been aiming for. Their length would be their form: "[Through] Stockhausen I could see that I didn't want to ever play again from eight bars to eight bars, because I never end songs; they just keep going on." This meant that live recordings would replace those done in the studio and that editing would become less important.

Throughout a tour of South America in May, Miles grew sicker every day, though he continued "drinking Bloody Marys all day and scotch and milk at night," according to his road manager, Jim Rose. His hip was causing him deep pain, along with his bleeding ulcer, and he was spitting up blood. Rose was treating him as if he were Miles' doctor; checking on him every few hours at night and keeping his throat clear. But just after the first show in São Paulo, Miles had a heart attack. He was admitted to the hospital but checked himself out quickly. His health, plus the news that Duke Ellington had died on May 24, 1974, sent him into deep depression. A Christmas card Ellington had sent him the previous December (signed, "Love you madly") he now understood as Duke's good-bye to him.

When they returned to New York, Miles immediately scheduled a studio session for June, and they recorded Miles' tribute to Ellington, "He

Loved Him Madly" (issued as part of *Get Up with It*, which itself was dedicated to Ellington), a thirty-two-minute piece of darkly flowing sonics filled with real or maybe only imaginary references to the Duke. Sustained guitar tones and Miles' organ chords centered the piece in C minor over funeral drums one-third of the way through, after which the rhythmic pulse quickened. Miles never discussed the piece with the group before it played it, never mentioning Ellington. Teo said that during the recording, a reverb machine they were using was causing difficulty, operating erratically, cutting off and on. When they played the tapes, they heard something in the background that sounded faintly like the Ellington band. "It was as if Duke was in the studio!" To many, this track was a deeply moving memorial to Ellington's influence, as well as a breakthrough into a new type of music. Producer Brian Eno, for one, saw it as the first truly modern ambient piece. But several members of the band—Dave Liebman and Dominique Gaumont—thought it was all rather aimless.

Liebman decided to leave the Davis group in late June to form his own band, Lookout Farm. Then in a brilliant (but doomed) act of casting, Pete Cosey recommended the little-known saxophonist Kalaparusha Maurice McIntyre as his replacement. Kalaparusha, an extreme free player, highly regarded in Chicago's AACM circle, walked onstage for his audition in Chicago without warning while the band was playing Al Green's hit "Thinking of You," and uncoiled a long in-the-spirit, explosive solo. Miles, who had forgotten about Cosey's recommendation, saw him as someone who had bum-rushed the stage and tried to stop him. But Kalaparusha was unstoppable. He continued playing when the band played over him, when the band stopped playing, even when they all left the stage. In the tumult that followed, Kalaparusha reminded Miles that Pete had asked him to audition. Miles fired Pete in a rage, though he later rehired him after he calmed down. Liebman was ultimately replaced by saxophonist Sonny Fortune, a player with impeccably straight jazz credentials (he'd recently played with Buddy Rich and McCoy Tyner), and whose age and conservative dress gave him the look of a substitute teacher dropped into a class of incorrigibles.

Not long after they had recorded the Ellington tribute, Miles was interviewed at length by Sy Johnson, a pianist, composer, and arranger who had worked with Charles Mingus and Ornette Coleman. It was a contentious meeting, though Miles seemed to relax after Johnson parried back at him. Miles was in pain and complained that the medication he had been given was so strong that he wasn't able to feel his legs and feet. He was angry because *Big Fun* had just been released, and the music on it no longer represented what he was doing. But he also talked at length about his loneliness, and how much he missed the musicians from his youth, whom he no longer saw.

> Why doesn't somebody write an article about musicians who are really close friends and don't have time—Thad Jones, Elvin Jones, Hank [Jones]. . . . We *never* see each other. . . . Nobody comes to see me. None of the guys, you know. All the young guys do, but Thad and all my friends like that never do. I like them, but they don't like me. Dizzy asks me to teach him. I say, "Yeah, come by. I'll show you everything we're doin." It'll be my pleasure." And *he* don't come by.

Gregory Davis, Miles' oldest son, had his own problems with drugs and with the law and was now on parole in Chicago. But he had become a Black Muslim and pulled his life back together. He was about to enter college when he got a call from Pete Cosey. "Rahman [Gregory's Muslim name], your father's really ailing. You all could help each other. When Miles came to the door I saw that someone had beaten him up." Gregory told Cosey that if he came to New York, he would be risking parole violation and would have to put off college—but he would be there. When he got to 77th Street, he found his father sick, Gregory said, "and lost in drugs, especially cocaine. He hated heroin—just thinking about it made him sick. But cocaine gave him a little more energy, psychophysically."

> And he really was in bad shape. Along with the fact that he had just had this operation on his hip, he was doing coke, and dealers and women were going in and out like a revolving door, like it was 42nd Street. And so I said, "Wait a minute: this is a war. These creeps are playing off this man, off his greatness. He's an artist, and he's like a fish out of water, and these people are taking advantage of him."

"He gave me the studio apartment on the roof, and I moved in to take care of him. When he'd whistle, I'd go downstairs and we'd go out to after-hours spots. He'd put his arm around me, and hop on one leg, and we'd go out."

When Miles went back out on the road, Gregory went with him, as both confidant and bodyguard. "I protected him with my life. Once I had to knock out a guy in an after-hours spot, and the guy could have had a gun, anything, but I put myself in between my sick father and this guy he had taken some drugs off of and didn't pay for."

Davis was sick with pneumonia throughout a three-week tour of Japan in early 1975. His bleeding ulcer was growing worse and his hip sometimes slipped out of its socket without warning. Unable at times to work the wah-wah and volume pedals because of the pain in his legs, he went down on his knees to press them with his hand. But he managed to keep going on the codeine and morphine he was taking for his pain, and he continued smoking and drinking large quantities of Heineken beer. Several times he managed to do two concerts in one day, as he did on February 1, where both the afternoon and the evening concerts at Festival Hall in Osaka were recorded by Sony, with Teo in charge. The first concert began at 4:00 P.M. and had two sets, the first of which included "Tatu," "Agharta Prelude," and "Maiysha" (which were titled "Prelude (Part 1)," "Prelude (Part 2)," and "Maiysha" when they were released on record in Japan only as *Agharta*); the second set included "Right Off" (with "So What" appearing for a half a minute or so at the end), and "Ife" and "Wili" (titled "Interlude" and "Theme from Jack Johnson" on the record). "Prelude" (or "Tatu") continued the heart-stopping groove dropouts of the earlier recordings of "Tatu" and "Rated X," but the bass riffs underneath were this time similar to the Ohio Players' "Fire," the tonality was more clearly pronounced, and Miles' playing was even more minimalist and repetitive and threatened again to disappear into the rhythm section. The cadenzas now were dominated by Pete Cosey, squeezing out dissonance and feedback wherever possible, and Sonny Fortune, playing as if his life depended on it.

Agharta was not released in Japan for a year and a half, as there was some discussion about whether it was strong enough to put out. The title, proposed by Sony Japan, was first conceived by the nineteenth-century French thinker Louis Jacolliot, as a land ruled by an Ethiopian ruler. Alexandre Saint-Yves d'Alveydre, the Christian hermeticist, described it as "drowning in celestial radiances all visible distinctions of race in a single chromatic of light and sound, singularly removed from the usual notions of perspective and acoustics." In the original notes to the record (written by Kiyoshi Koyama, the editor of Japan's *Swing Journal*), Miles said that "music is strange. Why does it change so frequently? Is it because my life is always changing? My life could never be an open book, so there are many secrets in my music. People don't understand mode[s], Dorian mode, Phrygian mode, electronics, etc., just like they don't understand us. But it's okay, since they don't understand my music, they get surprised. Isn't it great that you can experience surprise through music?"

That evening's concert at Osaka had two sets, the first with "Moja," "Willie Nelson," "Nne," and "Zimbabwe" (all of them titled "Zimbabwe, Parts 1 and 2" on the record), and the second set including "Ife" and "Wili" (both titled "Godwana" on the record). They were released under the title of *Pangaea*, after the mythological primordial continent (surrounded by Panthalassa, the original ocean) from which all present continents were derived through drift. It would be the last music of Davis' that would be issued on record for the next five years. Like *Agharta*, *Pangaea* was not released in the United States until 1990.

This was music that polarized audiences, provoking boos and walkouts amid the ecstasy of others. The length, density, and unforgiving nature of it mocked those who said that Miles was interested only in being trendy and popular. Some have heard in this music the feel and shape of a musician's late work, an egoless music that precedes its creator's death. As Theodor Adorno said of the late Beethoven, the disappearance of the musician into the work is a bow to mortality. It was as if Miles were testifying to all that he had been witness to for the past thirty years, both terrifying and joyful.

That's one opinion. Another was received by Teo Macero on April 23 from the accounting department at Columbia, complaining that Miles was getting $2,500 an arrangement when nothing he recorded seemed arranged.

The *Agharta/Pangaea* band went into Columbia's Studio B one last time on February 27. H. G. La Torre, a writer with *Modern Recording* magazine, attended that session and described it from the point of view of those interested in the technical processes of record making. It was a high-ceilinged room, big enough to hold one hundred musicians, with drapes on the walls; Miles' musicians were arrayed in a semicircle ten to twelve feet in front of the control room's glass window; there were twenty-four microphones; a rhythm machine was running alongside M'tume's congas. As they were setting up, Miles was complaining about Columbia's allocation of time and money for recording other artists. He considered most of them a waste. Herbie Hancock, for example: "What would anybody do in a studio that costs or is worth $65,000? I know it ain't the music on the album. That sure isn't worth $65,000." Both he and Teo agreed that rehearsing in the studio was a waste of money, and that overdubbing was a sterile and expensive process. La Torre said nothing about the music they played that day, a fifteen-or-so-minute piece called "Turn of the Century," which has never been released.

As ill as he was on the Japanese tour, Miles nonetheless took the band back out on the road again with scarcely any rest at all, opening for Herbie Hancock's funk group, Headhunters, which was riding on a series of hit jazz records that had reached that very audience of young blacks whom Miles had failed to attract. Throughout the tour, Miles grew increasingly annoyed with the acclaim that Hancock was receiving. When Herbie dropped by Miles' dressing room before their concert at Hofstra University on Long Island, Miles ordered him out: "I told him he wasn't in my band and that the dressing room was off-limits to anybody who wasn't in the band."

At a homecoming concert in March at Kiel Opera House in St. Louis, the very concert hall where his parents had taken him as a child, Miles left the stage sick at his stomach, again spitting up blood, then went back out to play. A party was thrown for him afterward, and Irene turned up uninvited: "Miles had been slipping in and out of East St. Louis whenever he was in town, and he wouldn't even answer the phone. So I had a showdown with him when he was playing St. Louis. I went to where he was staying, and told him, 'Shit, I don't think you're so wonderful.'" Miles vividly recalled that encounter in his autobiography:

> She just started putting me down in front of my family and friends and musicians. It brought tears to my eyes. I remember the look on everyone's faces, like they were waiting for me to just to knock Irene out. But I couldn't do that because I knew where her pain was coming from, from the fact that both our sons were failures and she was blaming me for that. Although it was embarrassing for me to hear it like that, I also knew that some of the things she was saying were true. I was crying because I knew I had to accept a lot of the blame. It was a very painful experience.

Irene disputes his emotional account: "He didn't cry: he wanted sympathy. I had been waiting for this chance." She was not impressed by what attracted others to Miles. "'Cool' to me means intelligent, natural, without having to work at it. It doesn't mean being out on the streets. It's just being up on things. I always knew what Miles was capable of, but I had to tell him. And I always thought he would at least be fair with the kids."

Miles was hospitalized the next day with what was diagnosed as bleeding ulcers and was forced to cancel his next concert in Chicago. He was barely out of the hospital when he had to go back in again in April for new surgery for nodes on his larynx.

Miles appeared in print again when Ralph J. Gleason died that year, and *Rolling Stone* solicited tributes to him, which they published in their July 11, 1975 issue. Miles simply said, "Give me back my friend."

The Davis band was booked to play the Newport Jazz Festival in Newport's Fort Adams State Park, with Sam Morrison now replacing Fortune on saxophone. Miles chartered a yacht to travel there in style. In July they played the Newport Festival in New York at Lincoln Center, and the Schaefer Festival in Central Park in August. But Miles' health caught up with him again, and he canceled a performance in Miami, and then a live recording planned for the Keystone Korner in San Francisco in October. He retreated to his house and lay in bed for months, depressed and in pain. Another hip replacement was scheduled for December, but was canceled when Miles contracted pneumonia.

With Jackie no longer around him, Davis had been seeing two women, Sherri "Peaches" Brewer, a dancer who later married Edgar Bronfman, and Sheila Anderson, a model and actress. It was Sheila, along with his road managers, who took Miles to Montego Bay, Jamaica, for him to recuperate, and got him back to New York in time for his rescheduled hip surgery.

The operation took over ten hours, and Cicely Tyson once again came to stay with him. As he was recovering in early 1976, he said the morphine and codeine prescribed for him left him with no will to play. Though he had been booked for an eleven-city U.S. tour and was scheduled to leave for Japan, where he would make $700,000, he canceled both gigs. There was an attempt at a recording session on March 30, with Miles playing organ, and several new pieces were recorded, including Pete Cosey's "Mother Dearest Mother," but nothing was ever issued.

For the first time, the music in his head had stopped. Miles was often unable to get out of bed and even lost interest in cooking, sometimes not eating at all, or counting on neighbors to bring him food, or hoping for someone to come by that he could send out to bring him some fried chicken. For two years he withdrew, at one point never leaving the house for six months. He became something of a neighborhood character, hanging at the front door, or sitting on the curb, watching the street. In the shuttered house, he sat in total darkness, except for a huge-screen projection TV with one bulb burned out and a blurred picture that drove visitors crazy. He kept it on all day, not to watch it but to keep him company, to fill the house with talk. All those threats made over the years about retiring were finally becoming reality.

Once in a while someone would make an effort to clean up the house and get him on his feet. Mary Lou Williams, the pianist and composer he once asked to join his group in the 1950s tried to help, and was rejected. Another woman who offered him help he chased out of the house with a knife. "He was totally out of control," Teo said. "He went to clubs occasionally, stoned out of his mind. The house was filled with bugs and rats, he was drooling. . . . I didn't know what to do. He'd call me and ask for $10, $20, $35 or $40. . . . Miles, I'm ninety miles away!" George Wein said he used to drop in and give him small amounts of money: ". . . I went over there one time and it was really terrible. He'd been beaten up; he'd actually been hurt. Some guys had come in and beaten him up because I think he owed them money and he was sitting in the bathroom and he had a pistol in his pocket. It was a macabre scene."

Miles was still under contract to Columbia, drawing a regular salary whether he recorded or not. Columbia's Bruce Lundvall said that "Miles had made a lot of money for Columbia. His previous deal was very low. His new deal was fair. But then he became sick and I got a lot of heat for making that deal. . . . We had a large bunch of recorded material, and we released some of it and kept his name alive." But his contract was coming up for renewal, and the pressure was increasing for him to show that he could still play.

Musicians came by to see him, some merely paying respects, but others, like Jimmy Heath, concerned for his state of mind and body. Heath asked him to "come out and play again. 'Play what?' he said. 'I played it all before.'" Gil Evans made several efforts to get him out of the house and playing again. He even lined up a tour for him with Kasamabumi Kikiuchi on keyboards, Pete Cosey, Jack DeJohnette, and Sly Stone on bass. But Sly never showed for rehearsals, and a leg infection kept Miles from playing on his feet. He did manage to appear in December at two brief recording and film sessions, which resulted in a short film for TDK recording tape that was used as a commercial in Japan. But he did little else. He was no longer listening to music, and he lost touch with new developments in jazz, such as Ornette Coleman's Prime Time and the new recordings of James Blood Ulmer and Ronald Shannon Jackson. Soon none of his old friends was coming by.

Julie Coryell interviewed Miles at the time for *Jazz-Rock Fusion: The People, The Music,* a book she was writing with Laura Friedman. While conducting the interviews, she saw how fragile he had become and the conditions under which he was living, and she and her friend Elena Steinberg talked him into moving to Elena's house in Norwalk, Connecticut, where he could be looked after while he recovered. While he was there in early 1978, he began working on some music and asked Julie's husband Larry Coryell, then a very hot fusion guitarist, to help. The composition Miles was developing began slowly, like an adagio, Coryell said, with a few chords and some bits of melody, then moved on to a section with two ninth chords a half step apart over several "jungle fragments of melody" for Larry to play on guitar over a shuffle rhythm. When Miles was convinced it could work, a session was set up with Teo in charge for March 2 at Columbia with Masabumi Kikuchi and George Pulis on keyboards, Coryell, and drummer Al Foster, who brought along bassist T. M. Stevens. Elena Steinberg asked Larry to be sure to take Miles' trumpet to the studio, but Miles played the organ instead. During what the band thought was a rehearsal, Miles abandoned the adagio and played the whole piece up-tempo. After two times through it, he said they were finished, as it all had been taped without their knowing it.

Afterward, T. M. Stevens asked Miles what he thought of his bass playing, and Miles responded, "It was cool." Stevens snapped back: "Cool? I played everything perfectly." "That's the problem," Miles said, "the brilliance comes in your mistakes—that's how you discover new things. And the only way to make mistakes is to stretch and take chances. If you play it safe, you'll never progress. . . . Music is like a conversation. When you play the bass, make a question—then wait a minute and answer it."

Miles loved the recording, according to Larry Coryell, and he called people to play it for them over the phone. He then gave the tape to Coryell and told him that he'd get Columbia to sign him, and asked him to join a new band he wanted to put together. But Larry said no; he could see that Miles was in no condition to do any serious work. The music they recorded was never released.

Davis returned to New York and disappeared again into the darkness of his house, surrounded by all the plaques and awards he had won and disavowed, and by photos of Charlie Parker, Coltrane, Max, and Dizzy. The man who said that the only way to stay young was to have a bad memory, the man who had mocked his own past achievements, was now living in the past, like Norma Desmond in *Sunset Boulevard*. Hiding in a dark so intense that it erased time itself, he lay in bed, calling his sister in Chicago just to ask her what time it was. Watching old fight videos, attempting to stop the pain fluttering in his ears by shooting drugs into his leg with dirty needles, doing coke—four, five grams a day—drinking cognac and Heineken at first, then anything with alcohol in it, staying up for a day and half, sometimes three days, without sleeping, smoking four packs of cigarettes a day, alternating Percodan with Seconal to get to sleep.

His hallucinations were becoming more vivid and threatening. He jumped through a window of his house when he imagined several people coming at him; he mistook snow on the ground for cocaine, an elevator for his Ferrari. "I was nuts . . . so bored that you can't realize what boredom *is*. I didn't come out of my house for four years."

"Miles was one of the most bored people I've ever seen," Dave Liebman agreed. "And he got more so as things went well for him and people took care of him." Some said he was deeply depressed, but he denied it: "*Bored* is the word. I wasn't doing nothing." And it may well have been that simple. Boredom. Doing nothing. Boredom and nothingness . . . forms of anxiety that drove him wild. The press dreamed up new names for him: "the Howard Hughes of jazz," or "the Charles Addams of jazz . . . but without the humor."

Yet Miles never completely lost his sense of humor. St. Louis trumpet player Lester Bowie came by to visit him one day, and before they could talk, Miles tried to get Bowie to play for him. Lester thought that this might be a bad idea and demurred, but Miles kept at him: "Play just one note for me, then . . . play a note!" Then he handed Bowie a battered trumpet, a dusty, funky, cobweb-covered horn. Lester finally played him a single note, and Miles laughed, the trickster of old once again, "Oh, man, I thought you could *play!*" Then they could relax, and drink together and talk about people they knew in common. But Miles seemed to have no plans at all for the future.

Writer Eric Nisenson got to know Miles in 1978 through Elena Steinberg and visited him regularly, doing favors for him, running errands (some of which risked arrest), hoping to be able to write his autobiography for him. Miles sometimes encouraged this project and at other times threatened him if he even mentioned it. Nisenson saw that Davis was at one of the worst points in his life. Each day was the same: he did some coke, but when it got him too high and he needed to sleep, he took sleeping pills; then, groggy, agitated, but unable to sleep, he did more coke (his habit was costing somewhere between $100 and $500 a day—Miles gave out different figures to the press years later). When he was high, he said his natural Gemini personality took hold, and expanded: listening to what his first mind said, monitoring with a second mind, the cocaine creating a third mind, or conscience—each conscience had a conscience. Four days of no sleep and sleeping pills and coke, and he could look in a glass of wine or a mirror and see a whole movie; he could see whatever he imagined. Miles said of himself that he was "Dr. Jekyll one day and Mr. Davis the next," and an allusion to the novel written by an author on a six-day cocaine binge seems right, though casting "Mr. Davis" in the role of the evil Mr. Hyde was especially ominous. In fact, on coke, Miles' anger could grow violent. "I've done everything, been everywhere, done so much shit, there's nothing to look forward to . . . except the coke," he told Nisenson. But often it seemed that what he looked forward to more than the drugs was the presence of the person who delivered them to him, a bit of human company in his otherwise empty day. Still, when celebrities occasionally dropped by, people like Waylon Jennings or Mick Jagger, he either acted bored or, as in the case of Jagger, wouldn't let them in.

There were women who drifted through Miles' life then, some of whom stayed with him for a short time. One of them was a men's clothing designer who had dressed Sly and the Family Stone for five years, and while she was with him, Miles' clothes became wilder by the day, and he began affecting an eye patch. But there were also times when he was with a different woman or several women every day, or several at the same time. He began to document their stays, some of them acting in little domestic dramas in which the women made love to each other, all of which he staged, directed, and photographed with a Polaroid camera. He was now impotent, yet obsessed by sex.

Was he having a good time? Were these people his friends? "People take advantage of you when you're fucked up. There are no friends when you're using."

CHAPTER TEN

Practicing is like praying. You don't just pray one day a week.

MILES DAVIS

SITTING BEFORE A MICROPHONE in the cramped studios of Columbia University's radio station WKCR-FM on July 1, 1979, Phil Schaap was announcing the beginning of a six-day, twenty-four-hour tribute to Miles Davis. The producers hoped to get a taped phone interview with Miles, who was lying in that darkened bedroom only thirty or so blocks away, but had heard nothing back from him. So when the phone rang, Schaap was surprised to hear Miles' voice. Not only did he not want to be interviewed or have his phone calls taped, but he warned Phil that "I'm a tough guy and I know tougher people. I'll kill you if you do!" "He was outrageous in his demands for what WKCR could provide him in exchange for the interview," according to Schaap. "This was the first of over seventy-five calls from Miles. He called persistently, alternating between rage and commentary, sometimes being complimentary, and finally showing some kind of appreciation."

Then on July 6, Miles made a helpful call. WKCR was playing the Japanese editions of *Agharta* and *Pangaea,* and he phoned to correct musicians' names, pseudonyms, and titles after some of them had been incorrectly announced. It took some time to get the spelling right because it was so hard to understand him over the phone. At the end of it, Miles said,

"You get it?"

"Yes, Mr. Davis, I think I have it."

"Good. Good. Now forget it! FORGET IT! Play *Sketches of Spain,* RIGHT NOW!"

Whatever interpretation one might give this exchange, it at least meant that Miles was once again engaged in music.

Columbia Records' jazz department had a new vice president in George Butler, the man who had overseen Blue Note Records' signing of fusion artists like Earl Klugh, Bobbi Humphrey, and Noel Pointer. Realizing that Miles' contract with Columbia would be soon coming to an end, Butler began to drop by to see him, not to talk to him about the music business, he said, but to show him "how important he was to America and that he had a friend at Columbia," in hopes that he would begin playing again. For the past four years, Miles had been on salary, and no records had been made.

For nine months, Butler stopped by and chatted with him almost every day for an hour or so about cars, boxing, clothes—anything but music. Sometimes there were long periods of no talk at all, with the two of them just looking at each other. On other days, there was only hello and good-bye. Then one day Miles told Butler he had some ideas about music: "We walked over to the piano and he played this chord . . . nothing, absolutely no sound . . . none of the keys worked." This gave Butler the idea of asking Columbia's president, Bruce Lundvall, to make Miles a present of a new piano for his upcoming birthday.

> The day came when the piano was being delivered. . . . Miles wouldn't open the door to his brownstone upon delivery of this new concert grand piano. I received a call from the manager of the piano company saying his delivery men were there with the piano, but that Mr. Davis would not open his door. He was just standing there looking out the window at them. I called Miles and asked that he open the door for they were there to make a delivery (Miles, incidentally, had no idea what was being delivered—no visible signs of a piano) and he immediately slammed the phone down, which was his usual way of terminating a call. Finally, he opened the door. . . .
>
> I was told by a mutual friend, namely Ed Williams, a popular New York City DJ at the time, who happened by Miles' place that day and noticed tears in Miles' eyes after the piano was set up. Later that day, Miles called and said, "George, thanks" . . . and slammed down the phone before I could say, "You're welcome."

Once again, Miles called on Paul Buckmaster to help him plan a new record. Paul flew in from London in July, 1979, checked into a hotel, and began working with Miles and Gil Evans. Miles wanted to record Rose Royce's "Love Don't Live Here Anymore," but he was high most of the time and distracted by the crowd hanging out in his house. Gil soon quit, according to Buckmaster, when they made no progress and found out that he wasn't going to be paid. George Butler encouraged Paul to go on, however, and he set up a recording session with bassist Marcus Miller, drummer Buddy Williams, Lou Volpe on guitar, keyboardist Onaje Allen Gumbs, George Devens on percussion, and Buckmaster himself on organ. When Miles failed to show up for the session (he said no one had told him about it), they recorded some tunes anyway and sent the tapes to him. Miles liked the material but not the group, so he sent for Pete Cosey, and they put together another band, this time with John Stubble-field on saxophone, guitarist Wayne Bingham, drum programmer Doni Hagen, and Ron Johnson on bass. Cosey had prepared several tunes, including "Electric Circle," as had Buckmaster. But once again Miles failed to show, this time because he had gotten into a scuffle with a clerk in a drugstore and wound up being hit with a phone. Seeing they were going nowhere, Columbia canceled the sessions.

Buckmaster was still in New York as August began, attempting to help Miles back to health. The power had been cut off in his house because the bills weren't paid, and without air-conditioning the heat inside was unbearable. Paul was convinced that Miles was dying. He called Miles' sister and asked her to come to New York and help. When she arrived the next day, she began straightening up, calling extermina-tors and professional cleaners. Chaka Khan, who lived nearby, got Miles out of the house. Then Dorothy called Cicely Tyson. Only a few people knew that Tyson had been visiting him at home from time to time, checking on his health. Since their breakup in 1969, she had called him every New Year's Eve. She also turned up—almost mystically, Miles said—whenever he was sick or in trouble. Now she was back with him, watching over him, bringing him food, taking him to an acupuncturist, urging him to stop smoking, throwing out his drugs, and running the freeloaders and hangers-on out of his house.

Dorothy's twenty-two-year-old son, Vince Wilburn, also began visiting him through the winter, telling Miles about his own ambitions in music. What seemed to jar Miles out of his torpor was some tapes Vince gave him of his own group, with keyboardist Robert Irving III, Randy Hall on guitar and vocals, Felton Crews on bass, and Vince himself on drums.

Miles became interested in what they were doing, gave them some avuncular advice, and even made some calls to set up a recording session for them at Columbia. He also called Dave Liebman and asked him to recommend a saxophonist. Liebman's suggestion was Bill Evans, a recent college graduate new to the New York scene. George Butler quickly reserved a studio for late April 1980 and made arrangements to bring all of Miles' suggested musicians in. But on the first day of recording, Davis himself didn't show for an hour and a half, and when he did come in, he had no horn with him. So for the next three hours, they arranged some music, with Miles playing along with them on electric keyboards. It went this way for a week, with Butler sweating as he watched the hotel expenses and room service charges pile up.

Then one day Miles walked in with his horn. When he blew the first note, nothing but air came out. He was embarrassed and shaken to discover that he had lost abilities that he thought would never leave him. But brass instruments are notoriously unforgiving of neglect by their players. Lay off a few weeks, and the horn seems heavier, the metal colder in your hands. Don't touch it for a few months, and nothing seems right—not the breath, the lips, the fingers. Ignore a horn for a year or more, and it becomes an alien machine, incapable of response. To lay off so long means starting all over again, building up the body, the embouchure, coordinating the mind with the body and the horn, a discipline that few are willing to put themselves through. As the closest observer of Davis' sound, Gil Evans was acutely aware of what it took for Miles to return:

> He has to get that sound every time he plays and that's what people don't realize about someone who originates a tone—they have to recreate that tone every time the way they did it originally, and it takes a lot of physical effort. So when Miles plays he has to put out all that energy. That's why he took a five year vacation, because he did it for thirty years and he was exhausted. His total organism told him to quit.

But Miles came back to the studio the next morning. His playing improved a bit each day, though Butler thought he still sounded weak. Teo Macero's recollection was not so benign. He said that Miles "was still very sick. He was so fucked up on drugs and everything that he could hardly play. He was breathing badly, and all bent over; it was terrible. We sometimes had to piece his playing together. It was rough. On some of those tracks we had to slow the tape recorder down to half speed during recording, so that he could reach those notes. The stuff with his nephew was pretty weak material. I didn't really dig it, but I accepted it. If that's what he wanted to do, we'd do it the best way we knew."

They took five and a half hours to record "Spaces" and "I'm Blue Without You" on May 1; and the next day they overdubbed them. On May 5 they did "Mrs. Slurpey," "Solar Energy," "Burn," "Thanksgiving," and "1980s," and on May 6 it was "Spider's Web." The session came to an end when Miles developed an abscess in his knee (which he said was caused by injections of dope) and was hospitalized for fear that he might lose the leg. When he had recovered somewhat, the musicians went back to work on June 4 and recorded "The Man with a Horn." On August 2 they did "Unconditional Love," "Wake Up," and "Shout." (Macero's notes show that "Shout" was not finished until May 6, 1981, when it took fifteen takes and a different band to get an acceptable version, and it was then edited into three other versions.) It was what Miles called his "bubblegum song." And on August 12 the band laid down some tracks to be used for "So Good," "Wake Up," and "On a Cloud." But only two of the tunes would ever be released by Columbia. Meanwhile, Butler kept the session a secret, daring not to tell Columbia executives what he was up to until he was sure that it would work.

Miles himself scuttled this project, and with the help of saxophonist Bill Evans he recruited a new set of musicians in early 1981: Barry Finnerty and Mike Stern on guitar, Marcus Miller (a cousin of Wynton Kelly) on bass, Sammy Figueroa on percussion, and Al Foster on drums. Davis' nephew's band felt abandoned, and thought that if Miles had given them more direction, they could have completed a record. But he was in no shape to give direction, and his own playing was not strong enough to carry them.

There was little direction for this new band either, mostly Miles saying, "I like this" or "I don't like that," as they struggled to put something together. Still, they completed "Back Seat Betty," "Aida," "Ursula," and "Fat Time," which, when added to the previous year's "The Man with the Horn" and "Shout," was enough to fill an LP titled *The Man with the Horn*. The album was proof to the public that Miles was alive and could play, even if somewhat tentatively. But it sounded like what it was: a struggle to come up with enough material to fill an LP. With no overall plan from Miles and two bands incoherently forced together on the disc, the record was a puzzlement. Coming after the firestorm of music he had produced between 1972 and 1975, it was also disheartening.

Miles was depressed over the recent deaths of Charles Mingus and pianist Bill Evans, and his own bad health and addiction left him dependent on others' help. Saxophonist Bill Evans and Al Foster were his guides in this period, getting him food, talking to him, telling him what had been going on in his absence, taking him out to the clubs to bring him up to date on music. It was on one of those club trips that he found his guitarist, Mike Stern, and a new percussionist, Mino Cinelu.

Despite his return to playing, Miles' life outside of music was far from stable. The New York Post reported on September 3, 1980, that a "saxophonist" named Fred Tolbert had alleged that Davis "did assault and batter him by striking him, pushing him, and causing him to fall down a flight of stairs" at Davis' home at 7 P.M. on October 5, 1979. The lawyer for the alleged victim said that they were suing Davis for $500,000 for breaking Tolbert's right leg. Tolbert said that Davis used a chair on him, then threw money at him, yelling, "Now take this!" Though the charges were apparently dropped or dismissed, it was a strange coda for the man they called Freddie Freeloader. There would be other such stories: a woman being thrown out of an upstairs window, friends and lovers being punched, broken jaws, scars, and flying drinks and drumsticks.

Miles sent George Wein tapes of what he had been recording, and they were promising enough for George to offer Miles what Wein said was $70,000 for a double concert at Avery Fisher Hall at Lincoln Center as part of the Kool Jazz Festival on July 5, 1981 (Miles told the New York Times that it was $90,000), and for George to write Miles a check for $35,000. It was something of a risk, but Wein knew that Miles' return could easily fill the hall for two performances. Many musicians doubted he would show up. But then one night in June, Miles walked into the Village Vanguard and sat in with the Mel Lewis Orchestra. Saxophonist Bob Mintzer said that he climbed up into the trumpet section and played the blues for twenty minutes while taking turns on each trumpeter's horn—Joe Mondello's, John Marshall's, and Earl Gardner's.

As a warm-up for Lincoln Center, Davis booked his band into the Kix club in Boston between June 26 and 29. The new band had widened its repertoire, now playing reggae-flavored tunes and ballads in addition to other near-pop material. For perhaps the first time, Miles had rehearsed a band. But they were still finding their way, not sure how to end some of the tunes, and many of the musicians felt shaky, especially with Miles not yet in shape. Once in a while they tried to get him to play in 4/4 jazz rhythm, but he refused: "No bebop. . . . I've already done that. That shit makes me feel old." But to many in the audience at Kix, the real surprise was not the music, but how much Miles seemed to have aged beyond his fifty-five years: the sleek, Afro-ed, muscled dude of the early 1970s appeared to have shrunk. He was now thin and stooped, his legs shaky, a cap pulled over his balding head. The hardest part about playing live was getting his timing back, and breathing, for which he had to count on an oxygen tank in the back of the theater. Yet Miles stayed onstage for the whole set, making faces, doing shtick, conducting the band, and guiding the rhythm section. He walked offstage only to play a couple of solos with his horn pointed into Cicely Tyson's lap, and then—surprising the audience, and perhaps even himself—he approached a man with cerebral palsy in a wheelchair and played a blues straight into his face. Then he reached out to the man, gripped his hand, held it, and continued to play, as the audience roared its approval.

Press and photographers from all over the world were there, as were Tony Williams, Herbie Hancock, and Ron Carter, who were playing a concert across town and came by afterward to pay respects. Columbia videotaped and recorded all four nights and put selected tunes together with some other pieces from concerts he would do in Japan over the next few months to make a double album, We Want Miles, released in the summer of 1982. It was a very different record from The Man with the Horn. He had picked this band himself, and his sound and technique were back (his one ballad, "My Man's Gone Now," was updated with a saucy bass riff from Marcus Miller), his playing once again inspired and broad ranging. Yet the transitional quality of the music itself was all too apparent: 1950s-style phrasing jostled contemporary funk rhythms, and overheated rock guitar licks threatened to unbalance Miles' new aesthetic. Still, the band's tentative approach to funk was cheerfully convincing, and Miles surprised everyone by coming up with melodies such as "Jean-Pierre," a tune that he remembered Frances' son singing when he was a child, which seemed to suggest a distant link to the little nursery melodies that Ornette Coleman sometimes played with his electric band. (We Want Miles won a Grammy in 1983, and Miles surprised many people by showing up to accept the award, though he still managed to stick out his tongue for the camera as his Grammy was awarded.)

Tickets for the Avery Fisher Hall concerts in July 1981 sold out before they were advertised—before they were printed, Bill Cosby said on the

Johnny Carson show—and at the seven o'clock concert, the house was full of musicians, cognoscenti, scene-makers, and fans from before his retirement. The first concert was delayed for almost an hour, so long that the stage manager finally told the audience they could get up and move around. When the music started while many in the audience were outside the hall and then lasted for only an hour, boos of disappointment rained down on the band as it rapidly fled the stage. Robert Palmer of *The New York Times* said it was the same old Miles, playing as well as always, but the band was uninteresting. Art Lange of *Down Beat* thought time had passed Davis by; it *was* the 1980s, after all. And Whitney Balliett made sport of the event in the *New Yorker*, mocking the band's paramilitary clothing, seeing it all as visual display, and likening Miles' spectacle to that of the film *Apocalypse Now*. Still, the years that Miles had been away had only enhanced his legend, and as he left Lincoln Center in a limousine that night, the audience knew it had been in the presence of one of the last musicians of the golden age of jazz.

It was all the more poignant, then, that when *The Man with the Horn* was released that summer, it was generally viewed as a weak recording. Those who had seen his new band were especially disappointed to hear a record by a group of musicians who seemed to have no relationship to what they had heard live.

Looking to find some way into a bigger audience than jazz provided, Miles had hired a new manager in August 1978, Mark Rothbaum, who also managed stars like Willie Nelson and Emmylou Harris. Through Rothbaum, Miles got another glimpse of how pop stardom worked and just how big success could be. At the same time, he saw that the music industry put its performers into the same kind of setup that boxers experience: you have to keep winning until you're beaten or you quit. Not that jazz didn't have its own version: for almost forty years, he had been expected to improvise every night with a level of intensity that could bring an audience to its feet shouting, and send them home dazzled. And like only a handful of other musicians, he had been widely copied in his own lifetime, his entire career scrupulously recorded, his music transcribed, parsed, and studied. His playing was caught on the wing and made permanent and repeatable by others through mechanical reproduction and mimicry. Still, every performance he gave was a test of his ability to resist self-plagiarism, a challenge to add something of significance without relying on his past successes. It was an impossible task.

Expectations were so high that audiences sometimes were led to see things as they wanted them to appear. Bassist Marcus Miller recalled one concert in Paris where the power went out onstage during Miles' solo. Not noticing what had happened, Miles continued playing along with the drummers. At one point, he stopped, turned to Marcus, and asked why he wasn't playing bass, only then learning that there was no amplification. The power suddenly came back on, and they returned to playing at normal volume. Afterward, when the audience applauded and the critics raved about that dramatic drop in volume, Marcus realized there was no way Miles could do wrong: "He creates magic even when he doesn't know what's going on!"

After a few performances in the United States, during which Miles developed pneumonia, the band left for a tour of Japan on September 28, 1981, for what was said to be $700,000 for eight shows, and a recording of the Tokyo concert of October 4 called *Miles! Miles! Miles!* released only in Japan. While on tour, he developed pneumonia again, and when he returned he was diagnosed as having diabetes. Only days later, on October 17, he was a guest on *Saturday Night Live*, and he appeared gaunt, limping, and hardly recognizable to many people who had not seen him perform recently. Too tired to attend rehearsals, he seemed nervous on camera, played overtime, and continued playing while the show cut to commercials.

On Thanksgiving Day, he and Cicely Tyson were married at Bill Cosby's home in Amherst, Massachusetts, with Andrew Young, Max Roach, Dizzy Gillespie, and Dick Gregory among the guests. Miles later joked that he was so sick he didn't remember getting married. He had blood in his urine, numbness in his right hand, and difficulty breathing.

When Cicely flew to Africa in January 1982 to make a film for the State Department, leaving Miles on his own, he became depressed and returned to chain-smoking, cocaine, and, despite his diabetes, drinking beer and brandy. This time it was his tour manager, Jim Rose, who first spotted the rapid decline in his health and put him into Southampton Hospital. Miles was warned by the doctors that he was rapidly killing himself, and to make the point, they took him to visit another patient's room, where Truman Capote lay wired to machines, in a coma. It was only a few days later that Miles had a stroke, which left his right hand paralyzed. Cicely returned as soon she was notified, and when his doctors were not promising about his recovery, she took him to a Chinese physician, who administered a series of acupuncture treatments and put him on a regimen of physiotherapy, Chinese herbs, and health food. He even saw a psychotherapist for a while (though he apparently viewed the experience as entertainment). Cicely took him swimming every day and encouraged him to use his hand in keyboard exercises. When spring came, some movement did return to his hand, and he was fitted with a device that allowed him to play by pulling his fingers back after he had pushed down the valves on the trumpet.

In spite of his weakened condition and lack of practice, he took the band on a month-and-a-half tour of Europe in April. Now playing with a cordless amplified trumpet, he was able to get by, though some nights he played from a wheelchair. When he went to London at the end of April, interviewers were warned not to ask about sex, drugs, or the extramusical aspects of his past. Instead, Miles talked to the press about his illnesses and recuperation, even showing his scars to a few. Though he chatted about his new, healthy life, often crediting Cicely, the pain he was experiencing was noticeable.

Some writers cautiously inquired about his use of the synthesizer, which they perhaps felt was unseemly for a giant of jazz. But Miles thought of the synthesizer as a big band, even though he admitted he missed the swells of volume, the highs and lows, the live interchange with musicians. "The unevenness of tone [of a big band] gives it a thrill. You might have five trumpet players, each with a different sound and attack, who make the sound you want." (The only other problem with the synthesizer, he said, was that its sampled trumpet sound was "white.") He was now playing noticeably higher, and when asked about that, he said that in the past, he had played in the lower and middle registers because that's all he could hear, but he could hear higher now (by "hear," he meant it made a sound that made sense to him and gave him pleasure).

After returning to the United States, Cicely and he spent time in Pawling Health Manor, a spa in upstate New York where he had the time to relax, dry out, and eat well. Having noticed him sketching on the back of envelopes and napkins, Cicely had brought along drawing pads and colored pencils, and encouraged him to take his drawing more seriously. Miles said that his father had taught Vernon and him to draw when they were young, and that he had always been good at it. (Vernon disagreed, saying that *he* was the one who was meant to be an artist and that Miles never took art seriously.) When Cicely and Miles went back to New York City, the limousine was loaded with pads full of Miles' spidery sketches, and cases of kiwi and papaya, bushels of corn and apples, sacks of cucumbers, carrots, broccoli, and pineapples, a tub of lettuce, and a recipe for making carrot cutlets. When a reporter asked if carrots beat pork chops, Miles, worried about the weight he was adding on his waist, said, "No, but it beats another ten pounds." (He said he was now wearing a truss because of a double hernia, though his assistant road manager, Chris Murphy, insists that it was just a girdle.)

There were more tours of the United States and Canada to come in the summer, and a trip with Cicely to Peru, where she was a judge for the Miss Universe contest. Having recently appeared in *Roots* and *The Autobiography of Miss Jane Pittman*, and having been nominated for an Academy Award, Cicely was a sought-after actress. Miles acknowledged that she was probably better known than he was. When they weren't traveling, they stayed in either of two apartments in New York City (Miles' house was being remodeled again), in Cicely's house in a gated colony of movie stars in Malibu, or at a friend's place in Montauk, on the tip of Long Island.

Miles began work in August 1982, on *Star People*, a new record that would take four months to finish. Along the way, he replaced guitarist Barry Finnerty with John Scofield, and Marcus Miller was replaced on bass first by Tom Barney and, after the record was completed, by Chicagoan Darryl Jones. Gil Evans was back at work with Miles again (though he was not listed in the credits), this time advising on tempos, writing short passages for them to play, and encouraging Miles to get everything they played on tape. When John Scofield was at Davis' apartment the night before the session, Miles had some chord changes that he said he'd gotten from a blues record by Lightnin' Hopkins, and Gil worked up a bass line on the keyboard to go with them. Scofield then improvised over them. The next day, Gil handed Scofield some music to play that he only vaguely recognized until Gil told him that the tune was what he had improvised the night before—a piece that was to be called "It Gets Better" on the record. "Star on Cicely," similarly, was a tune that came from a transcribed Mike Stern solo. Gil said that he'd been trying to get Miles to play his own improvisations as compositions for thirty years or more.

Miles thought of *Star People* as his blues record, and it did show him attempting to relocate himself in the jazz tradition while still sounding modern, though the record overall seemed crowded and murky. For the first time, he was becoming interested in the technology of recording, and some of the problems may have come from Miles' attempt to use new and unfamiliar techniques on this album. Engineer Jay Messina said that Miles was using click tracks to synchronize Al Foster's drumming, but he was impatient about setting the tempos for the track, and became agitated and nervous. What was also unusual about this record was the return of liner notes. Leonard Feather, with Miles' considerable help, took pains to explain the technical details of this music to its listeners, as if Davis feared that his new direction would not be appreciated or, worse, treated as *only* pop music. The credits for production on the record (the written equivalent of an entourage) had grown much longer and included Miles' own credit to himself: "All Drawings, Color Concepts and Basic Attitudes by Miles Davis."

Decoy was the next album, recorded during June, July, and September 1983. This one, he told Teo, he wanted to produce himself, although George Butler's name would remain on the record as executive producer, and Robert Irving III would be listed as co-producer, along with Miles' nephew Vince Milburn, Jr., as associate producer. It was the end of Miles' relationship with Macero. Teo said he still had new ideas for Miles, including recording him with the London Philharmonic, and he was hurt by being dropped, but he saw it as part of Miles' effort to save money by cutting personnel.

Herbie Hancock's single from a few months back "Rockit," was now everywhere on the radio, and Miles was thinking that he could get airplay for *Decoy*. But because its melodies were so plain, he felt they needed support from synthesizers, strong bass lines, overdubs, and help from countermelodies: "We put clothes on the melodies," he said. "Freaky Deaky" (named for Richard Pryor), for example, was Miles' own tune, putting what he thought of as a "Kurt Weill 'umpah' bass line" to a blues. Gil Evans was in on *Decoy*'s production, especially on "That's Right," but as an adviser more than an arranger, suggesting to Miles that he add chords behind his trumpet playing so listeners could better hear what he was playing against. On "Code M.D." Miles used a muted alternate take of himself behind his own open trumpet solo to expand the sound. He was intrigued with the idea of what he called a "layered approach," putting one song over another. "You know what would be nice . . . if you could play around one record to make another. Take a tune like 'Decoy' and have 'E.S.P.' playing in the background. I'm going to try that one of these days."

Despite his efforts, *Decoy* is a short album, uncomfortably pieced together from different sources and lacking a recognizable aesthetic. Two of the pieces are from a concert at the Montreal Jazz Festival that summer, and the three compositions co-credited to John Scofield were solos by John that Gil copied out for them to play as melodies. (Miles was unhappy with saxophonist Bill Evans' work on several of these pieces and edited out his playing. He then replaced him with Branford Marsalis to finish the record, though he gave him very little to do; and when Branford rejoined his brother Wynton's band, Miles brought Evans back again.) "That's What Happened" is a shorter version of "Speak" from *Star People*. Irving and Wilburn carried much of the production weight, and Miles was not always in the studio as the recording progressed. "We'd call him twenty times a day," Vince Wilburn said, "and he'd call the studio, and we'd play him things over the phone." Throughout, there is a sense that technology is filling in for the focused sensibility that underlay Davis' best records. The record showed little of what the band could do live and, as it would be for the rest of his life, the live performances were far more interesting than the records he made in studios.

Cicely's experience in show business allowed her to take a role in Miles' business life and make suggestions about his management, but this complicated his relationship with Mark Rothbaum. Early in 1983, Miles replaced Rothbaum with Lester and Jerry Blank, two attorneys from Philadelphia whom he said Cicely urged him to use. But in less than two years, Miles would accuse his new lawyers of being "incompetent" and of not being able to get him work. Whatever else went on between them, under their management, Miles did a tour of the United States and Canada in the beginning of 1983, traveled to Europe from late March through April, went to Japan for May, and played a number of concerts and festivals in the United States and Canada from June through the first half of October. Finally, he came back to Europe for the rest of that month. And 1984 was even busier. Still, he said that he was in such debt to the Blanks that he felt forced to sell his house to pay them, right after he had had it remodeled to suit Cicely, "so that she could make a fresh start there, without having to think about all the other women who had been in there before her."

At the end of the second 1983 European tour, Miles returned to a celebration called "Miles Ahead: A Tribute to an American Music Legend," organized by Columbia Records and Cicely at Radio City Music Hall on November 6. Bill Cosby hosted, Quincy Jones conducted Slide Hampton's arrangements of the Davis and Gil Evans big band pieces, and a number of Miles' former musicians played as well: Herbie Hancock, Tony Williams, J. J. Johnson, Jackie McLean, Philly Joe, and others. Efforts were made to have Miles play in one of his older styles, but he ignored them, and instead did a half-hour set with his current band. At the end of the evening, he was awarded an honorary degree from Fisk University. That, along with the dedication of a new Miles D. Davis Elementary School in East St. Louis that same year, would have made his mother proud.

Miles may have been short on money, but it was not apparent in the way he lived. He and Cicely often traveled by private jet, and visited Milan, where they dropped in at the designers' salons to update his suits by Versace and Armani. If he had to give up his house, there were still the apartments and Cicely's house in Malibu—a modern, multilevel gray box, dotted with African art and sculpture, a few of Miles' paintings, a Yamaha grand, wicker furniture, a fireplace, and a home-entertainment center in the lower den with a five-foot TV screen. "Miles wanted to enjoy being a star," John Scofield said. "He played the star role to the limit."

Miles first met Jo Gelbard in 1984 in the elevator of the apartment building at 985 Fifth Avenue where both were living. She was thirty-four, a sculptor and painter, the daughter of Lenny and Iris Kaplan, a well-known Diamond Row merchant family in New York, and married, with a young son. "Miles was broke when I met him, and in a mess. A total mess. I don't think there was one reason for him to be alive. Everything was wrong with him . . . his hips . . . his diabetes was out of control . . . his heart. . . . It was a very gloomy period." He was on crutches and spent a lot of time sketching, mostly for therapy and to distract himself in stressful situations, like cross-country airplane trips or interviews. When he learned she was an artist, he asked her to give him painting lessons, and she began teaching him. And like so many other women before her, she nurtured him, cooked for him, gave him vitamins, took him swimming. When he later separated from Cicely and moved to a new apartment, Jo redecorated it and furnished it with Memphis Group–designed furniture from Milan, with bold colors, geometric shapes, and finely etched lines that would later resonate in his paintings. She also urged him to change his life, surround himself with beauty, wear brighter clothes, and get a hair weave. She moved from being his teacher to becoming his collaborator, the two of them painting together on the same canvas, or Miles sending her canvases by mail for her to add her part. It was a rare creative relationship in the neurotically solitary world of art. Miles might start by sketching an outline, and Jo would fill it in with brushed-on color, both of them circling around the canvas lying flat before them. He was drawn to figurative painting, women's bodies—especially the legs, thighs, and rear—and totem poles, African carved figures, and masks. "It was his conception," said Jo. "I went on from what he did . . . and sometimes he might only sketch in a few lines if he was sick." It was her way of focusing him, giving him confidence. Since he trusted her talent, it worked both ways: "His art was a gift to me. He didn't need to do it, but it was his way of empowering me. He pushed me to be stronger and better."

"All of his senses were highly developed. He was very visually oriented, and attracted or repelled by the way people walked. He liked to stand and wait until you'd walked past him. His mother, he said, walked in a straight, erect posture. And when he got sick he hated his own walk. His sense of hearing was remarkable. He could hear pitches in dogs' barks. Once he asked me to get him some pills, some green ones, and I couldn't find them. 'They're all green,' I said. 'Shake the bottle . . . that's the one.'"

Miles thought of his music and his painting in similar ways. Both were about composition: it was just a question of knowing when to start and stop, always making sure that he stopped before he was finished. He might paint small details first, small groups of things. He thought of images as being generated by small effects ("Anything looks like a face if you put an eye in it"). He said he operated from the principle of opposites: if he was playing long notes, he wrote short rhythms; if he was playing a lot of notes, then the rhythm should be played at a different tempo, maybe in half time. "I like contrary motion, in music and art." But Jo felt that "his painting was not like his music. He was a musical minimalist, and he didn't leave any space on the canvas when he painted—he drowned the space with paint." Marcus Miller agreed: "You'd think somebody like Miles would paint a red line down the middle of the canvas, and a blue line across, and that would be it. But his paintings are a lot more dense. . . . Each person has, like, three legs and four heads. Wild stuff."

Jo tried to get Miles to meet other painters, to move in the art world, but he feared they wouldn't know who he was, and stayed away. He was impressed with the paintings of Jean-Michel Basquiat (another artist who sometimes did collaborative painting, in his case with Andy Warhol), but he never made an effort to meet him, even though he knew that Basquiat had worked his name into paintings such as *Discography (Two) 1983.*

Miles' hired a new assistant in October 1987, Michael Elam, a graduate of New York University who was also a painter. "Miles began by imitating Picasso," Mike said, "then Basquiat, then African art. He was very insecure as an artist. The paintings he owned were by fairly unknown artists, except for two by Basquiat." When they were on tour, Miles often sent Mike out to find interesting artists, and Elam brought their paintings back to the hotel for Miles to look over to see if he wanted to buy them. When Davis found out that Mike was a painter, he asked him to paint with him. But for the first year or so that he was with Miles, Mike didn't want to work with him on his art, despite Miles' cajoling: "You know, Mike, you got to be able to do more than five things at a time."

One night Miles was particularly insistent on getting Mike to paint for him and kept after him, even setting up a blank canvas on an easel, and asking him to do something, anything, even if it was just one brush stroke. When Miles gave up and went to bed, Mike thought it over and started to paint, eventually working through the night. By the time he awoke the next day, it was late morning, and he was afraid that Miles would be angry for not getting him up. But when he went into the living room, there was Miles, looking at the painting. "Mike, it's a motherfucker!" After that, the two of them did several paintings together, working much in the way that Miles and Jo worked.

Later, a show of Miles' art was arranged in Los Angeles by his art dealer, Joanne Nerlino, but on the night of the opening, Miles had no interest in going, even after his sister called from the gallery to say that people were waiting for him to appear. Jo and Mike begged him to go, got him dressed, and when they arrived, the gallery was mobbed. Mike was stunned to see that two of the three paintings they had done together were on display (he had left them unsigned). Afterward, Miles gave him $5,000 for the paintings, and asked Nerlino to look at Mike's work for a possible show of his own.

When Miles went on tour in 1990, Mike decided not to go with him again because he was tired of the bad treatment that he felt he had received from Miles, and told him so. But Miles meanwhile bought five of Mike's paintings for his new apartment, and Mike billed him for $14,000. Instead of paying the bill, Miles sent him a check for $5,000 and again began trying to talk him into going with the tour. Finally, Mike gave in and worked with him from February through April of that year, with Miles now treating him better, even letting him get out and see things on his own instead of having to sneak out when he was expected to stay with Miles at all times.

The acclaim he received as a painter never fooled Miles about his position in the art world. Though he speculated about making a living at it, he knew he would not earn enough without his music royalties. What he did know was that his name on a painting was enough to make it worth something. He once joked that if he kept getting sicker, his paintings would go up in value. Still, no one knew the role of the artiste better than Miles. Larry Rivers saw him "at the opening of a show of his paintings. He used a cane and had grown a high forehead, and had a beautiful wide cape draped seriously on his shoulders. It was very majestic and moving. I told him he had gotten better-looking as he got older. He said he was good-looking back at Juilliard, I just didn't notice it, and he strode majestically away."

When the Mosel und Tschechow Gallery in Munich, Germany, offered Miles a show in 1988, Jo told her husband that she was going with Miles. When her husband objected, she told him there was nothing between Davis and herself except art. Her husband threatened to not be there when she returned. Things had not been going well between Miles and Cicely Tyson either, and had become much worse once Jo entered his life.

"Miles was very needy," Jo said. "He needed women desperately, and their unconditional love. He got deeper into women than men who are more considerate. He was incredibly sensual, and very sexual, and needed to touch and be touched." Miles suffered from insomnia and often slept through much of the day. He wanted Jo to sleep with him and woke immediately if she got up. He wanted to be with her anywhere and anytime he could. When she threw a baby shower for her sister Meg, several years later, he wanted her to go with him somewhere else, and they had an argument that ended in Jo walking out. But on the day of the shower, Miles showed up at her apartment carrying bags of groceries and cooked the gathering a meal. Then he gave each of the twenty women there an autographed copy of *The Art of Miles Davis*, a book about his and Jo's painting. When Jo's son's bar mitzvah was scheduled, Miles wanted to come, but it was awkward because her divorce was still pending. Though he was upset that he wasn't invited, he sent his bodyguard with a $3,000 studded, hand-painted leather motorcycle jacket, which her son immediately put on and wore throughout the service.

When Miles was away from Jo, he sent her witty and romantic love letters, which he might write as minimalist poems, one word per line, and staggered, or they might come in the form of a quiz, beginning "Do you know how much a trumpet weighs in New York City?" followed by a series of other factoids such as "Do you know how far it is from New York to Rome?" and ending, "Do you know you could go crazy if you were away from me for three months?" Or they might be seasonal, in the form of a traveler's parody of "The Twelve Days of Christmas" ("eleven officials checking passports"). His letters were sprinkled with praise for parts of her body, with coded references to her husband, or to her having to leave his apartment at five each afternoon when her son came home from school. Even a painting might become a love letter (one of them had "I Love Jo" worked into it).

Jo longed to escape her Fifth Avenue life, to flee from the way married women dressed and were regarded at that level of society. But he insisted that she be treated like a lady by the musicians and the crew: no one was to walk in front of her; no one was to curse in her presence, and Miles himself spoke to her differently than he did to others. And when he took her to Bloomingdale's, stood in the dressing room with her, and sent the saleswoman to get things he liked, he ended up buying her $20,000 worth of exactly the kind of Fifth Avenue clothes she was trying to escape.

During the years she was with him, Miles preferred to stay at home most of the time and avoid seeing people he didn't know. "He was very middle-class. He liked to come home and cook dinner, and he was very comfortable there. He didn't like people, but he needed them around him in the apartment. He didn't like to talk, and would often just sit and look at me. We were always in the same room together, and when I had to go home, he'd call me at night, and sometimes he just wanted to watch TV together, over the phone, hardly saying anything at all."

When Miles watched movies at home, he wanted to see romantic films like *Dances with Wolves* or gangster movies. (He generally hated comedy or blaxploitation films.) "He liked men and women who were debonair and ice cold in attitude, like Edward, the duke of Windsor, or Fred Astaire, or tough guys—Bogart, Garfield, and later Robert DeNiro and Kevin Bacon, who he thought was the ultimate in cool."

"Miles' musical minimalism was also at odds with his behavior," according to Jo. "He was an addictive shopper, and bought more than he needed, especially clothes, and then often never wore them. He lost things, or they were stolen—he had no sense of possession. He hated American male sloppiness of dress; yet he could paint in his designer clothes, and by the end, everything he had was ruined." He wore painfully fitted tight shoes (even though his own feet were small and deformed by diabetes and years of wearing shoes too small for him). He never wore robes or slippers and kept his shoes on at all times. "He was very disorganized and sloppy, and dropped things wherever he was. If he spilled chili in the kitchen it stayed on the floor; if he half-ate fruit it stayed there as it rotted. And it didn't affect him at all."

The burden of the cool had become a heavy one, and he could mock what he had came to mean to his fans. Sometimes when he and Jo were dressed to go out, Miles joked that they were like Gene Wilder and Richard Pryor in *Stir Crazy*, strutting about in mismatched, dated clothing, declaring, "We bad, we bad!" "Miles sometimes longed not to be cool: to dress in shorts or baggy clothes, to let his hair become unkempt. He wasn't always Miles: sometimes he was only Dewey Davis. He might drive up to Harlem and stop at a chicken joint. People would stare at him for a while, and then come up to him shyly and he'd sit and talk, let them take his picture with them."

Despite his fabled ego and temper, Miles often resisted making reasonable requests because he had no sense of his fame or power. Once when he was playing at the Indigo Blues club in New York, he complained to Jo that the smoke was bothering him because he had just had another operation to remove nodes in his throat. When she told him that she could ask to have people stop smoking, he said they would never do that, because people have always smoked in clubs. But she talked to the club's manager, and he immediately made an announcement asking for no smoking. Miles was astonished.

His self-doubt and sense of his own inadequacy stayed with him into his sixties. In one of his sketch notebooks from the late 1980s, he described his body and posed a series of questions to himself about his perceived physical defects: "Are his arms long enough for him?" "Is his face round enough for him?" and ending resignedly with "Oh, well, he'll have to take me like this."

Off and on from January to April, 1984, Miles was recording one cover after another of current pop tunes—songs by Kenny Loggins, Michael Jackson, "Déjà Vu" by Dionne Warwick, Tina Turner's "What's Love Got to Do with It," most of which were never issued. But Cyndi Lauper's

"Time After Time" was released, provoking instant trepidation in the jazz community. Fans and critics had reconciled themselves to the idea that Miles would never perform a ballad again, and now he was doing one by a faux punk singer. But he would remind anyone who mentioned it that it was he who brought pop ballads and show tunes into jazz after the bebop era, and he had been criticized for that as well. Besides, he loved this song, and he played it almost everywhere he appeared, always consciously hewing close to the melody:

> You have to treat the song the way it should be interpreted: your way and hers. I just love how Cyndi Lauper sings it. I mean, that woman is the only person who can sing that song right—the only person who really knows what it means. The song is part of her—it's written for her heart, for her height, for the way she looks, the way she smells. She has imparted her voice and soul to it, and brought something kind of sanctified and churchly to it. Why distract from its meaning by messing around with a lot of variations and stuff? So I don't do anything to it: it's just the sound of my tone and the notes of that song, but they seem to work together in their own right. Still, when I like something, I try to give it to you in my own way—give it to you with a little *black* in it. Now, when I play it live, everybody seems to like it that way. I also think people know when they like a melody: a song like this gets people in a mass groove, like a tribe.

There were a number of retakes during the recording, and Miles complained about having to sit in the studio for so long and play the same songs over and over: "I had to do that on *Porgy and Bess*, and I swore I'd never do it again. It's not the retakes; it's the feelin' you put into it. . . . I mean, you can't say 'I love you' twice. You have to say it when you feel it. And when I play a ballad, more than anything else, it's all *me*."

Then, just when everyone thought Miles was turning into a pop star, he was awarded the Leonie Sonning Music Award, the most distinguished music prize in Europe, one that previously had gone to classical luminaries such as Igor Stravinsky, Leonard Bernstein, Artur Rubinstein, and Andrés Segovia. The Sonning Award Committee had written to Miles several times about the ceremonies in Copenhagen in December, but when they received no answer, they sent Erik Moseholm, the head of the Danish Radio big band department, to visit him in New York in April to try to convince him to accept it. Included in the award was a 100,000 kroner (more than $12,000) commission for Davis to play a piece of music at the ceremonies on December 14, and Moseholm proposed that Gil Evans write something approximately ten minutes long. Miles told him to call Gil, but he wasn't optimistic that he'd do it. In fact, Gil's reply was that he didn't write much any more and wasn't sure he *could* do it. The alternative was for Miles to play a five-minute work by Danish composer and trumpeter Palle Mikkelborg, accompanied by a large Danish group, and then do only a five-minute piece by Gil. Knowing Gil's work habits, Miles assured Moseholm that he wouldn't need the music in advance, and that he'd go over it when he got to Denmark. Just make sure it doesn't look backward, he said: he wanted to play new music. (He also suggested a bit of synergy: maybe they could use some of his artwork for a poster and on the cover of the program. Moseholm countered with an offer to do an exhibit of his art in the lobby. Then, Miles replied, why not print a small book of his art? The negotiations continued.)

Miles wanted someone else with him for this project, so he flew with John Scofield to Demark for rehearsals and the award ceremony in mid-December. Mikkelborg had prepared *Aura*, a nearly hour-long suite of pieces based on colors, using serial composition methods and some bits of material borrowed from French composer Olivier Messiaen. On the night of the concert, colors were projected in the hall as the orchestra began the suite. Miles played only in the last section, a blues called "Violet," and his solo was the climax of the work. A short award presentation followed, and he played "Violet" again as an encore. He then played it again, and several times more as the applause continued. Scofield suddenly went into "Jean Pierre," and Miles and the rhythm section joined in, and continued with "Time After Time."

Back in New York, Miles ended the year filming a Japanese TV commercial for Van Aquavit (in which he is seen blowing into a bottle and holding a glass) and starting on a new album, to be called *You're Under Arrest*. This was to be his protest album, he said, a protest first against police brutality against himself and all other black people (this was clear on the title tune, with its vaudeville-like police dialogue), but also a protest against American foreign policy. In "Then There Were None," synthesized nuclear storms accompanied Miles' trumpet until, at the end, he is heard ominously saying, "Ron [Reagan], I meant for you to push the *other* button.") But a lack of an overall vision in the production suggests that it might also have been something of a protest against Columbia, and Miles left the company as soon as the record was finished. Some of the material is recycled, from either his own older music or that of others: "Street Scenes" is drawn from one of the themes of "Speak," and "One Phone Call" is a vamp from "Right Off" on *Jack Johnson;* other songs are smooth jazz, frankly aimed at radio play (the cover versions of Michael Jackson's "Human Nature" and D Train's "Something on Your Mind"). Miles was now calling what he played "social music," instead of "jazz," and there were reports that live he was playing Huey Lewis and the News' "I Want a New Drug" and Nena's "99 Luftballons."

A few members of the band—Bob Berg (who now had replaced Bill Evans on saxophone) and Darryl Jones, in particular—were unhappy with the way this album was going, and Al Foster, the musician who had been with Miles the longest, walked out during the recording of "Human Nature," objecting to the song and the use of a click track to keep time. He was replaced on drums by Vince Wilburn, Jr., who was now co-producer of the album. Gil Evans' absence is also palpable on this recording. Robert Irving said that Miles had waited most of the year for Gil to come up with ideas and arrangements, and when he didn't, he went on without him. Gil was busier than usual and beginning to get movie score commissions (he completed his part of the British film *Absolute Beginners* that year) and high-profile engagements, and though he and Miles remained as close as ever, talking by phone almost every day, he and Miles never worked in the studio again. Miles was now recording without any of the people who had been part of his past successes.

There were some well-rehearsed arrangements in the session, but the tape still rolled throughout, and parts were still being edited together, following the practice he had developed with Teo Macero. "You're Under Arrest" was the one piece done in a single take, though it was later overdubbed with voices (Miles played himself; the police voices were Steve Thornton, Marek Olko, and Sting, who had come into the studio with Darryl Jones, who was later hired away for Sting's own group). "Katia" used a bass line from "Ms. Morrisine" and was recorded while the engineers were still getting sound levels. "Time After Time" was rushed to get a single out for sale, but the album version was worked on a bit more and used more signal processing.

In January 1985, Miles called Palle Mikkelborg and asked him to set up a recording of the whole "Aura" suite. Columbia would underwrite it, and then he would fly over to Denmark to play on most of the parts. They settled on sessions for late January and early February, and this time Miles took Vince Wilburn with him instead of Scofield. Davis made some suggestions, eliminated some of the more complex parts, and then surprised Mikkelborg by asking if he could also improvise over some taped electronic and vocal music that had been used only as background music while the audience entered the concert and was not intended to be part of the suite. It was retitled "White" for the album. When Miles learned that John McLaughlin was in town for some other work, he asked to have him on the recording, and he was brought in to play near the end of the sessions.

Miles was happy with the work, but Columbia stalled its release for four years, refusing, he said, to pay to have the record digitalized. That cost only $1,400, which he tried through another girlfriend to get the National Endowment for the Arts to fund, but he ended up paying for it himself. When *Aura* finally did come out, two tracks were wrongly banded on the disc (the second half of "Red" should have been the first half of "Green"), the notes were incomplete, and the cover of the record had no mention of Palle Mikkelborg's role in the project. Yet for those who longed to hear Miles revisit his triumphs with Gil Evans, it was good enough. And for those who only wanted proof that Davis could still play and that the electric band was not a cover for his failing chops, it was more than enough.

Miles now had an apartment at the Essex House on Central Park South, featuring a living room with raised platforms at both ends, with a couch and chairs at one end, and a sofa at the other, wall-to-wall carpeting, and everything done in dark grays and browns. His paintings were lined up along the wall. There was a telescope on the balcony and an exercise machine in one of the rooms. A fair number of journalists were visitors there, for Miles was changing his attitude toward the media. With Cicely's guidance, he had come to believe that the press could do him some good and that they were more than what Gregory said he called the "Miles maggots." He no longer spoiled his own press parties by refusing to answer questions or insulting the reporters, and he ceased deflating the hype behind his record company's moves. In fact, at the company's request, he even made calls to Columbia branch managers around the country to encourage them to sell his records (and if they didn't, he told them, he'd make sure they were "under arrest"). And for the first time, he began to appear at sound checks, often using them for rehearsals or to try out new material.

His cynicism and distrust seemed tempered by the lifestyle he had adopted. When he was reminded of his changed image and the adoration of his fans, he joked, "You mean I had a personality-lift?" He now had serious management, representation of all sorts, and had even begun to travel with an entourage—that often unmerry band of security, drivers, dressers and hairdressers, valets, girlfriends, flunkies, and gofers who flash importance even when they are protecting a star who has no trail of fans behind him from whom he needs protection.

Still, if the occasion were right, the prince of darkness could make a reappearance. During the taping of a segment of the ABC TV show *20/20* hosted by Harry Reasoner, Miles became incensed when the film crew tried rearranging his apartment. When Reasoner began to stumble naively into the world of Miles Davis (with questions such as, "Do you have to suffer to play the blues?"), Miles made his life so miserable that at the end of the segment, Reasoner said, "I'm not sure how I feel about Miles Davis." On an African American talk show on television in Baltimore, Miles hid behind a cape and a huge hat, but made a point of exposing the ignorance of the cohosts about jazz and his own career. His appearance on *The Dick Cavett Show* in 1986 found him embarrassing a young Nicolas Cage, who had bought a trumpet on the way to the show to ask Miles to give him a lesson ("Forget about it. Look at how you're holding the horn"). While Miles was on *Time Out*, a Philadelphia TV talk show, host Bill Boggs arranged to have some of the most talented local high school jazz players come on the show for Miles to offer encouragement and helpful hints. He had very little to say to them and certainly nothing encouraging, but he turned around in his seat to praise the young organist in the studio band, Joey DeFrancesco, to whom he offered a job a year later. Marcus Miller's effusive and adulatory comments on the *Night Moves* TV show hosted by David Sanborn resulted in Miles' gently squelching him (Marcus: "You must've felt the same way about Charlie Parker." Miles: "No").

Then there was the visit to the White House in 1987 for a Lifetime Achievement Award to Ray Charles. Miles had already been there the year before when he attended the Washington Charity Awards Dinner at the White House with Cicely, who was on a Celebrity Committee. For Miles, that had been a rather uneventful evening and he stayed in the background. But this time, when he arrived in a black waistcoat with tails and a red snake trimmed in sequins, leather pants, and two vests—red and white, with silver chains draped across them—he was the center of attention. Still, this was not his gig but Cicely's, and once he had surveyed the room for the scattered few African Americans invited, he assumed their presence was an act of tokenism. This had the makings of a disaster. Even the blandest of pleasantries had him snarling. So when a

Washington matron asked him what he had done to be invited, he snapped, "Well, I've changed music four or five times. . . . What have you done of any importance other than be white?" Miles whispered to Cicely, "'Let's get out of here as soon as this shit is over. You can handle this shit, I can't.' After this, I knew it was over between us and didn't want to have anything to do with her. So from that time on we basically lived apart."

Miles moved a bit more easily now in Hollywood circles and was approached to do a score for a film by Billy Friedkin. Though that project never materialized, in 1985 he did do a soundtrack with Robert Irving for a TV episode of *Alfred Hitchcock Presents* called "The Prisoner," starring Yaphet Kotto; and there was another one in 1986 with Irving for the film *Street Smart*, with Christopher Reeve and Morgan Freeman. Both scores were light on content, with Miles playing piano (though his part was edited out) or trumpet over synthesizer tracks on the first, and short cues with his band on the second. There was also a Honda TV ad in 1985 in which Miles leaned against a motor scooter, scowled, and rasped, "I'll play it now, and tell you what it is later . . . maybe" (a remarkably inside joke for television, one would have thought). Director John Schlesinger sounded him out about a role as a Santeria priest in *The Believers*, and also in 1985 he took the role of Ivory Jones, a pimp, in "Junk Love," an episode of NBC-TV's *Miami Vice*. Miles seemed remarkably at ease and very expressive on screen, though at times he was difficult to hear. He did a guest host spot on VH1's "New Visions Disk Jockey Show" in late December 1987, where he chatted with bass guitarist Joe "Foley" McCreary about current music videos, and in 1988 he appeared as a street person in Bill Murray's *Scrooged* and played "We Three Kings of Orient Are" with David Sanborn and Paul Shaffer.

Miles suddenly was in a fever of creativity, often phoning people in the middle of the night to try out new ideas. Herbie Hancock remembered Miles calling him one night with some speculations straight out of Sun Ra:

> "I've been thinking—what would happen if we were on the moon and wouldn't have any gravity and we had to play some music? 'Cause there wouldn't be no downbeat, like that," and he mimics a weightless state, the

illusion of pushing a beat against no resistance. "What would we be thinking of? The gravity's no barrier. Then everything you do has to begin with an 'and,' know what I mean?"

"In music, you say poom poom poom. It's just a natural thing down here with the gravity, you know. It doesn't go the other way. The other way is weird. It's like the back of something. I would really like to take a flight to outer space."

His ability to make rapid changes impressed even those who knew him well. He had new management again, this time hiring Cicely's manager, David Franklin, to handle his business. And for the first time he added a woman to the band, Marilyn Mazur, an African American percussionist raised in Denmark, whom he had first heard during the recording of *Aura*.

Onstage, a new performance style was now fully in place. With a cordless microphone fastened to the bell of his trumpet, he could be mixed and blended with the other instruments and could match them in volume and texture. He roamed the stage, his back now completely turned to the audience much of the time, his clothing a slowly changing kaleidoscopic panorama of outrageous patterns, textures, and colors, every garment cut and hung on him in some new configuration. Yet "Miles *was* shy," Mike Elam observed. "His turning his back was part of that, his overdressing as well. His clothes represented the essence of confidence, but with no personal connectedness. He often got sick with a stomach ache just before show time, and had to be talked into playing."

Miles strolled the stage, walking in rhythm as much as his limp would allow. The sheer force of his presence directed musicians toward some imagined but unarticulated goal that he had in mind. In addition to the signals and coded phrases he used to change tunes or rhythms, he focused on individual band members by walking up to them and touching them to have them start or stop playing. Or he communicated by eye contact. "He keeps you watching him," one keyboardist said, "keeps you on your toes, so you don't just become a player in the band, playing a tune. He doesn't want you to think you know what's going to happen." It was a method that could be exhilarating or frustrating, John Scofield said:

It was incredibly nerve-racking and made you really mad when he cut you off right before an idea. . . . But at the same time . . . I think it's fascinating, the idea of having somebody directing a band like that, where there are no choruses, where it's just sort of open, and somebody's sort of sculpting the whole musical thing.

As one trumpeter said, Miles could still body-English a whole band into shape, or electrify the audience *and* the band with a single note brilliantly chosen and skillfully placed.

As he wove his way across the stage, he also acknowledged the audience by occasionally looking at them, waving, pointing, even smiling. He sometimes introduced the band members to the audience, either by speaking through the trumpet microphone or holding signs with their names printed on them over their heads (though he sometimes held up the wrong sign or held it upside down). His playing was increasingly affected by the stiffness and pain in his hip: the slumping but still erect stance by which he was able to launch his percussive figures was no longer possible, and he found it easier to bend over to play, sometimes almost touching the floor with the horn. And like a James Brown, dramatically exiting the stage with the help of his people while feigning exhaustion, Miles often leaned on his sidemen—though in his case, the exhaustion was genuine.

In 1985, the Davis band worked almost continuously. There was a North American tour from late April through June, on to Europe for the month of July, and then off to Japan. They were back in the United States touring in August and September, and returned to Europe in October and November. Though not many knew it, Miles' diabetes was becoming worse. He was abusing sweets and had passed out several times in insulin shock: once on a flight to Japan, he had to be taken off the plane and hospitalized in Anchorage after he ate some pastries he brought with him. Though he became more careful about taking insulin, the paraphernalia he had to carry with him to inject it now got him into difficulties at airports across the world. The irony was not lost on him.

> The older you get, the more serious the disease gets; your pancreas starts fucking up and you can get cancer. It cuts off circulation anyway, especially in your arms and legs and toes, and I've got poor circulation anyway, especially in my legs, which are skinnier than anything anybody can imagine anyway. I can remember going to hospitals, and the doctors would be trying to draw blood from my arms and legs. They couldn't find any veins, first, because I used to be a junkie and had collapsed some of them, and second, because my legs and arms are so skinny. They would just be sticking me everywhere trying to find a vein.

George Butler was still working on Davis to get him back in the studio. But at the same time he was courting Wynton Marsalis for Columbia. It was Miles' impression that once Marsalis was signed, Wynton began to get more publicity than he was getting. So it was adding insult to injury when Butler told him that he wanted to market Miles' music as "contemporary jazz" while Columbia was still holding up the release of *Aura*. Then, when Butler asked Miles to give Wynton a call to wish him a happy birthday, Miles said it was too much and threatened to sign with Warner Bros. records.

At first glance, Wynton Marsalis and Miles Davis appear to have shared a great deal. Both were trumpet players, children of middle-class parents; both had studied at Juilliard and were smart and wily dealers with the music business. Though in different eras, they had been singled out for stardom by Columbia Records. But Marsalis was a new kind of jazz musician—one who talked the language of the recording industry and understood the social costs of innovation and bohemianism in the arts. He dressed like musicians of old, in tailored suits and silk ties. And now that such dress was more associated with the accountants and attorneys of the music business than with the musicians, it could do him nothing but good.

Marsalis zeroed in on Davis as a symbol for what had gone wrong in jazz. The 1970s electric band recordings and those that followed were enough for Wynton to see Davis as a central figure in the vulgarization of authentic African American culture, a dark angel in the Fall that resulted in blaxploitation, inarticulateness, and a debasement of the accomplishments of the race. Fusion was not a form of jazz, he said, because it was not based on the blues, and so was essentially nothing more than pop music. "And one example of that would be the development of its major figure, Miles Davis," Marsalis said.

> He went from some esoteric imitation of rock music, a combination of jazz and rock, to what he does today, Cyndi Lauper tunes and just blatant attempts to be . . . what the pop form of the day is. What fusion does is it relieves us, our country, of the problem of dealing with jazz and the contribution of the Negro to the mythology of America. The question in jazz has always been: is it pop music or is it a classical music?

As far as Marsalis was concerned, Davis had abdicated his role as elder master:

> By the time I came around, he had bent over so far for rock and roll that he was a hindrance. Like I would go to jazz festivals, and he would be there playing rock music or funk or something—he was always saying

something negative about jazz music. . . . He put me in a strange position, because I had to deal with representing the music and yet not turn it into anything personal between us.

He had identified the enemy and persistently needled Davis: the high-fashion Japanese robes he wore were "dresses," the mute he used was part of cool jazz's effort to hide the fact that it had nothing to say, Miles was past his prime, he was Tomming, and other jazz trash talk of the moment. When the day came that he finally met Davis, Miles greeted him with, "So here's the police."

The climax of the Davis-Marsalis conflict occurred at Expo '86 in Vancouver, Canada, where both men were playing. During Davis' set, Marsalis came out on the stage and started to join in. Miles asked him to leave, and then when Wynton refused he stopped the band. As a showdown, it was not much, but it was enough to give both men an excuse to continue to berate the other. Marsalis, for his part, said he had been dared by his band to go onstage to respond musically to Davis' remarks about him. For Miles, it was simply an act of disrespect. (Wynton was later to claim that Davis told him in private that he was "bullshitting" in his 1980s music, that he never meant it to be serious.)

Marsalis could have found vindication in Davis' presence on Quincy Jones' production of *Sun City*, a record and video put together in September, 1985, by Artists United Against Apartheid in South Africa. Miles's appearance was a result of his friendship with Quincy, but Jones could have chosen any number of jazz musicians from among his friends. Q, however, was canny enough to see the cross-over potential in Miles' music and to appreciate the use of that infamous scowl in publicity material for a project that was, after all, only half protest and the other half showbiz. When it was completed, Miles was the first person heard on a record that included Afrika Bambaataa, Pat Benatar, Big Youth, Ruben Blades, Bono, George Clinton, Bob Dylan, Peter Gabriel, Bonnie Raitt, Lou Reed, Bruce Springsteen, Ringo Starr, Peter Townshend, and dozens of other stars of the moment. Davis also accompanied Gil Scott-Heron on "Let Me See Your ID," played over speeches by Nelson Mandela and Desmond Tutu on "Revolutionary Situation," and reunited with Herbie Hancock, Tony Williams, Ron Carter, and others on "The Struggle Continues." A noble cause it was, but one that also placed Miles squarely in the middle of the pop scene.

CHAPTER ELEVEN

> The beginning and the end is everything. You've got to start
> and stop gracefully.
>
> MILES DAVIS

WHEN MILES SIGNED with Warner Bros. Records in 1985, the people at
Columbia were stunned. They saw him as part of their family. They'd
stayed with him through his darkest hours, backed his every change of
direction for thirty years. But Warners had recruited him persistently,
and Miles thought they'd give him the respect that he never felt from
Columbia. He also thought that they had better ideas for marketing him
and would record his concerts live, which he felt Columbia never really
wanted to do. But whether the deal he made was that good is not so
clear. Warner Bros. paid him well—seven figures, he said—though
Columbia might well have matched or bettered the offer. Yet to get that
much money, Miles' lawyer had agreed to give them the rights to a portion of his existing compositions, as well as the rights to all future creations with his new label. His concerts were recorded by Warners, but
none were released until after his death. And their marketing and production ideas were not always in line with his own. It was not even clear
at first what they wanted to do with him. The first thing he tried in the
studio was "Maze," a quick, harmonically recycling piece with a busy
bassline that reflected his fondness for the R&B group Maze, featuring
Frankie Beverly. But then he turned in another direction, and with the
help of Randy Hall, the singer and guitarist from *The Man with the Horn*
sessions, put together the Rubber Band, a funk group largely made of
LA-based musicians. Keyboardist Adam Holzman had been working
with Hall, and first met Miles when the Rubber Band recorded at Ray
Parker's studio in LA between October 1985 and January 1986: "Miles

wanted to do something poppy and really funky because he had just come off doing 'Human Nature' and 'Time After Time.' So he started working with Randy apart from the rest of his band or his normal circle in New York—except that he brought Mike Stern out to play some guitar on one of the tracks." They recorded at least twelve tunes, but all were set aside by Warners, apparently because they didn't fit their image of him.

For his next project, Miles approached a number of different people to compose and produce material for him. He talked to Bill Laswell about doing a few tracks (Bill's success with Herbie Hancock's "Rockit" was undoubtedly on his mind). But Laswell had no interest in doing only one or two tunes on an album with other producers. They toyed with other possibilities, such as some extended pieces that would incorporate repetitive musical figures that could be mixed into African- and industrial-style musics; the melodies would be juxtaposed and would continuously mutate into different themes that would sound endless on the record. But nothing came of it. Miles called Paul Buckmaster in London again, who sent him some ideas on tape that he never used. He then approached George Duke, a keyboardist who had taken Joe Zawinul's place with Cannonball Adderley's band, and asked him to give him something that sounded like Irakere, the Cuban pop group. Of the three tunes Duke sent him, Miles kept "Backyard Ritual," a rhythm and blues–flavored piece, which he put on his new record in its raw demo form.

It was at this point that Warner Bros.' Tommy LiPuma became involved with Miles. LiPuma had worked his way up through the business, becoming the first producer for A&M Records, and later creating hits for the Sandpipers, Barbra Streisand, George Benson, and Natalie Cole, and receiving Grammys for his work with Dr. John, David Sanborn, and others. LiPuma was apparently concerned with Davis' lack of direction, and he, if anyone, knew how to focus jazz musicians and gets hits from them. He began his association with Miles by offering Thomas Dolby or Lyle Mays as producers to work with him, but Miles suggested Prince. LiPuma agreed, and Prince sent Miles some tracks for a tune called "Can I Play with U?" Miles then returned the tape to Prince and got him to make some changes in the arrangement. But when Miles added his parts, Prince did not think it worked well. in the album's context.

Tommy then put Miles back in touch with Marcus Miller, whom Davis had not worked with since 1983. Marcus first wrote him some tunes and arrangements that were phrased behind the beat, the way Miles played, but Davis asked him to write them out straight, or otherwise he'd end up playing them even further behind the beat. When they rehearsed and recorded, Marcus' procedure was to begin a piece and point to Miles when it was his time to come in. The album *Tutu* emerged like that, as a two-person collaboration, very similar to the way Miles painted. As they began to build up tracks for the record, Marcus assumed they would be bringing in other musicians to play on them, but Miles encouraged him to keep adding parts himself, so that Miller ended up playing most of the instruments on the record. Marcus was very familiar with drum machines and knew how to give them a jazz feel, but there was still a stiffness to the rhythms that was nothing like Miles had ever worked with before. LiPuma's taste ran to a clean-sounding record, so these recordings were very different in other ways from what Miles had done for Columbia, where live recordings were sometimes included on the same album as studio works.

Miller worked hard to get a consistent sound on the album, and it was not always easy given the variety of material they were using and the way that Miles heard it. For example, Miles wanted to do Scritti Politti's "Perfect Way," wanted it to be the title tune of the album, in fact, but Marcus was uncertain about it, because the original depended so much on a certain synthesizer sound. But Miles liked it so much that they ended up following the original closely. "Full Nelson" (the title punning on Prince's last name, Nelson Mandela, and Miles' bebop tune "Half Nelson") aimed at Prince's sound. At that point Miles and Prince still planned to do a tune together, and Miller wrote "Full Nelson" to be a transition between their collaborative piece and the rest of the album. The title tune, "Tutu," was given what Miller thought of as a New Orleans feel, similar to some things he and drummer Al Foster had worked out before; and "Tomaas" was constructed from some ideas Miles had taped at home on the piano. For the first time in years, Davis had recorded an album of other people's tunes. Apparently, his solution to the problem of losing his rights to any new compositions he wrote was not to write any more.

As a musician, composer, arranger, and producer, Marcus Miller was the closest substitute Miles could find to fill the role that Teo Macero had played. For that matter, Marcus could also carry out some of Gil Evans' functions as well. But electronics are not live orchestras, and this music would never sound the way that Miles' music had before. Tracks of tape were built up one by one, with different instruments recorded at different times, so there was a pop sensibility about the process, as well as something of a colder sound. Such a procedure was abhorred by many jazz fans, much as they had disliked the editing procedures of Macero. Miller himself was very clear that he didn't think that what they recorded was jazz. Rather, *Tutu* was a one-time idea, the heavily arranged synthesizer-driven music serving to bring Miles up-to-date in contemporary music:

> When I talked to him about the forties or fifties, I got the impression that there was a direct link between the way people walked down the street and the popular music and the bebop that these guys played. The bebop was just an extension of the dance music of the time. So the music was connected with everything in Miles' life, and when you realize that, you begin to see that for a guy like him, music is just a reinterpretation of what's going on. And that's all it is. So for him it didn't make any sense to play in 1983 the same music he'd played in 1963. I learned that you should connect your music with your times. The downside being that the music might not last, because there's been plenty of music that was connected to its time and just stayed there. You can only hope that at a certain point it will also transcend its time. But you can't think about that: You have to concentrate on making your music relevant to what's going on.

Warners backed *Tutu* heavily, giving the record a stark cover photo of Miles done by Arthur Penn, promoting the album, and commissioning a music video directed by a young filmmaker, Spike Lee. Their efforts paid off when *Tutu* won a Grammy that year.

Tommy LiPuma continued to involve himself deeply in Miles' work, even helping him to rebuild his band. He recommended that Miles hire Robben Ford, a guitarist who had worked with various blues groups and with Joni Mitchell and the Yellowjackets. From a brief example that he heard on a cassette, Miles offered him a job. Eight days later, on April 4, 1986, Ford showed up at Constitution Hall in Washington, D.C., for his first performance. There was no rehearsal, only some tapes for him to hear and new keyboardist Adam Holzman for him to talk with. Still confused as to what he was supposed to play, Ford went to Miles' dressing room, where Miles gave him a bear hug, then stared at his coat and tie, said, "Robben, what are you going to wear onstage?"

Constitution Hall was not designed for amplified music, and when the band went into its first piece ("One Phone Call/Street Scenes"), it was loud—like a jet taking off, Ford said. "The second night the sound was better at the Beacon Theatre in New York City. I felt completely at ease. He'd make faces at you. He'd bring you out front when you soloed, if you didn't go yourself. Miles' music has the spareness of the blues. His use of space is uncanny. Nobody has as large a field to explore—it's like he's walking around in space." It was that sound and his use of space that Miles leaned on, not his technique. The form of the tunes was simple, according to Ford, but it was emotional music. "You couldn't refer back to earlier Miles music and get the same thing. He was very spontaneous in everything he did. Whatever catches his attention he responds to. He'll switch from thing to thing when you talk to him."

When Ford left to get married and start his own band six months later, Miles went through a number of other guitarists over the next seven months—Garth Webber, DeWayne "Blackbyrd" McKnight, Hiram Bullock, and Bobby Broom. Then in 1987 he heard a cassette of Joe "Foley" McCreary, a bass guitarist in lounge groups and country bands in Columbus, Ohio, who dressed somewhere between a street person and the Dobro guitar players of bluegrass bands, who wore overalls and funny hats and played the eccentric role of Uncle Zeke or Cousin Clem for comedy relief. Again, after hearing only a sample on tape, Miles asked him to join his band to play "lead bass," whatever *that* was. Foley was thrilled: "Anyone who played with Miles after 1969 was lucky, lucky, lucky."

> As bad as Scofield is—I love him—he was lucky. Rick Margitza was no Coltrane. Rick was lucky. Miles had two jazz bands, period: the one with Trane and the one with Herbie, Wayne, Ron and Tony. Those guys in that period played with Miles. Miles didn't have to play with any of us. We should be glad we talked more than five minutes with him, let alone appeared with him onstage.

In early 1987, Miles fired his nephew Vince "because he kept dropping the time." When he told Dorothy, she became very upset, and said that he should have waited until after the upcoming Chicago performance, since many of Vince's friends would be there. "Dorothy, music don't have friends like that," Miles replied. Other members of the band disputed Miles' explanation for the firing, insisting that Vince was a natural drummer. What Miles wanted, they said, was a new kind of rhythm, and, as he had so often done in the past, he went shopping for a new drummer. Mike Elam's view of such changes was that "he was enamored of musicians when they first joined the band, but then lost interest. If a musician couldn't keep up with the changes he made, he tired of them. Just when you thought you were getting cool, he would change things."

> Miles chose people with talent, but green, so that he could develop them. But he didn't want them to develop so fast that they showed that they knew what was coming next. Adam Holzman was an example: if he liked what they were doing he would invite them to hang out, watch TV. The

others he'd leave on their own. Vince was an example of one who didn't keep up.

Jo Gelbard also felt that "Miles judged people immediately, hated them or didn't hate them. When a person stopped being interesting and exciting to him—a musician, a woman—the relationship was over. He was easily bored."

With money behind him, Miles had reached a higher level of celebrity in the late eighties. He was even affable toward the audience and the press, and often gossiped with journalists (now it was sometimes hard to get him to *stop* talking). He flirted with women in the audience, smiled, even *beamed* at everyone. There was no end to the theories that promised to account for this change: it was Cicely's star-making influence, or his better health and habits, or he simply saw the end coming—the door coming closer, as Wayne Shorter put it.

Even Miles' birthday parties were social events (with a bit of help from his PR people). For his sixtieth birthday party in 1986, for example, Cicely hired an eighty-six-foot yacht in Marina del Rey for a four-hour cruise with a steel band and flew in Dorothy, Vernon, and Cheryl for a surprise party of 125 people, including Los Angeles mayor Tom Bradley, Assembly Speaker Willie Brown, former representative Yvonne Brathwaite Burke, Quincy Jones, Whoopi Goldberg, Eddie Murphy, Burt Bacharach, Carole Bayer Sager, Lola Falana, Billy Dee Williams, Roscoe Lee Brown, the spouses of Sammy Davis, Jr., Bill Cosby, and Chick Corea, and from his other life, J. J. Johnson, Herbie Hancock, Wayne Shorter, Joe Zawinul, and Tony Williams.

Miles was now doing big media events like the Amnesty International Concert in New Jersey's Meadowlands Arena, where his presence surprised everyone. Even other stars were awed by him, some coming forward to pay their respects, others warily keeping their distance. He was now asked to make cameo appearances on other musicians' records: he played on Toto's *Fahrenheit* (1986), Scritti Politti's *Provision* (1988), Chaka Khan's *CK* (1988), Cameo's *Machismo* (1988), Quincy Jones' *Back on the Block* (1989), Kenny Garrett's *Prisoner of Love* (1989), and Shirley Horn's *You Won't Forget Me* (1990). After some of these recordings, many of his older fans cringed when they heard of some new enthusiasm of his—Phil Collins, Willie Nelson, Kenny Loggins. Would he record with *anyone?* Had he lost all sense of proportion? Was this a wicked test of his fans' loyalty?

Poet Quincy Troupe, himself from St. Louis, approached Miles for an interview in 1985, and it resulted in a lengthy session that was printed in the November and December issues of *Spin* magazine that year. With a certain level of trust established between them, Miles then agreed to have Troupe write his autobiography with him. Miles had made a deal with Simon & Schuster, and Troupe began the long and arduous task of following Miles from place to place, drawing out personal information from an often reticent and increasingly sick man whose capacity to survive was being tested daily.

There was another hip operation, his diabetes was worse, pneumonia was a recurrent problem, and he ended most of his tours by checking himself into a hospital—"for a tune-up," he called it. Though he was no longer using illegal drugs, the painkillers prescribed for him were a problem, leaving him edgy, fitful, and sometimes delusional. His relationship with Cicely had deteriorated, his jealousy and anger toward her even spilling into his interviews. He said that he had discovered her diary and found that she had written negative things about him, and he began to suspect that she was selling the gifts that he gave her. He told her that he didn't want her male friends and business associates calling or visiting her at home, and when one of them left a phone message, he hit her. She hid from him for two days in the basement in Malibu, and when she called the police, he said he joked them out of taking her seriously. "Women get too frisky on you. I don't like it when women get like that. . . . They want to know what you're doing, but don't want you to know what they're doing. I could never tell my mother 'I'm going down to 12th Street and I'll be there for thirty-two minutes.'"

During his travels in Japan, Miles had become fascinated with the radical stylings of the younger Japanese couturiers. He loved the drape and loose hang of the material and the high fantasy behind their designs. As he grew thinner, suits no longer looked good on him, but beyond that, they made no sense in the music he was trying to create. He now regularly wore the robelike creations of younger designers like Issey Miyake. "He hated suits," Jo said, "they reminded him of the old jazz—each one does their thing by coming out to the mike, then leaving it, like fifty years ago. He said, 'Wynton in his suit and tie! This is black music?'"

Another one of the designers he admired was Kohshin Satoh, who regularly dressed him for events like the Grammy Awards. It was this relationship that led him into becoming involved with a bizarre fashion show of Satoh's designs at the new, and soon to be notorious, Tunnel club in Manhattan in 1987, where the evening's celebrity models were Miles and Andy Warhol. One of the designs for Davis that evening was a military band jacket à la Michael Jackson, sprinkled with golden treble clefs and worn with a cape. Compared to Miles' outrageous ensemble, Warhol's crinkled black metallic shirt with a dark scarf seemed rather dowdy, especially against his spiked platinum wig ("You only wearing two layers, man?" Miles asked). In *The Andy Warhol Diaries,* Andy wrote: "They did a $5,000 custom outfit for Miles with gold musical notes on it and *everything,* and they didn't do a thing for me, they were so mean. They could've made me a gold *palette* or something. So I looked like the poor stepchild, and in the end they even (*laughs*) told me I walked too slow."

Davis took to the runway as if he were born to it: "Why do models walk like models? I can walk better. Check this out." While they waited in the dressing room, Miles was busily sketching, and Andy reached out for his pad. Andy: "Gimme." Miles: "Give me your picture and I'll trade you." When their turn came to walk, Miles took over. "Why you hanging down your head? . . . Don't you be walking in front of me." He then told Warhol to carry the end of his cape like a train while he played his trumpet down the runway, and off they went. Andy was clearly very sick that evening, and afterward almost collapsed in his friend Steve Pivar's arms. He died five days later.

Offered the job of doing a film score for director Mary Lambert's *Siesta* (with a cast of Isabella Rossellini, Grace Jones, Ellen Barkin, Martin Sheen, and Jodie Foster), Miles accepted. Then he sent Marcus Miller a tape of the film and a line of music as a model, and told him to write it. Miller finished the score in two weeks. "I'd just roll the video tape . . . and play some things on keyboard that I thought matched the scenes. Then I'd get my bass clarinet and Miles and I would react to that, then go back and see how it worked with the film. The trick was to have Miles play Spanish music and not have it be a carbon copy of *Sketches of Spain.*" But regardless of Miller's creativity, there was no way that this score would not be compared to *Sketches of Spain;* worse, since there was no orchestra involved (only synthesizers, Miller on various instruments, Miles, and a couple of other musicians used once or twice), it would be thought of as a version made on the cheap. Still, the writing was effective for the film, and Miles played it convincingly. The movie was another thing altogether, receiving poor reviews ("pretentious," "farcical," "wildly theatrical"). Several critics said that the score was the only good thing about it. Since Marcus Miller did most of the work, Miles coming into the studio only when Miller needed a trumpet, Miller's manager insisted that he get credit, and in the end *Music from Siesta* was co-credited to Davis and Miller.

There were two other film sondtracks in which Miles was later involved, both in 1990. The first was for *Dingo*, with a score written by Michel Legrand, with whom Miles had worked briefly years before. The film was a French-Australian production, inspired by "Regret," a story by Guy de Maupassant, and was directed by Rolf de Heer. There was very little to the plot: a boy grows up in the outback of Australia, where he lives as a dingo (wild dog) trapper and plays trumpet in a country band called Dingo and the Dusters. In his dreams, world-famous jazz trumpeter Billy Cross (played by Miles himself) calls Dingo (acted by Colin Friels) to come to Paris. When he arrives, Dingo finds Cross has given up the trumpet and now plays only electric keyboards. Dingo's appearance encourages Billy to play trumpet again, and he in turn inspires the Australian to new musical heights. The film is dramatically weak, the characters lackluster, the big band music by Legrand only serviceable. (Miles' role in the film was at first intended for Yaphet Kotto, who wasn't available; Sammy Davis, Jr., was the second choice, but he grew too ill to do it.) De Heer said Miles was cooperative, intelligent, a natural; he learned his lines and there were no problems.

The second score was for *The Hot Spot*, a neo-noir set in the South, directed by Dennis Hopper, and starring Don Johnson and Virginia Madsen. Jack Nitzsche, the musical director, put together a small blues band of New Orleans funk drummer Earl Palmer, Tim Drummond from James Brown's and Neil Young's bands, and blues guitarists Taj Mahal, Roy Rogers, and John Lee Hooker. Miles' job was to add a trumpet line over the band and to play a second voice against Hooker's blues moans. The band recorded for two days, and Miles came in on the third day and overdubbed what they had already done. Hooker said, "When he got done playing, he looked at me, he give me a big hug, and he say, 'You the funkiest man alive.' I said, 'What you say?' He say, 'You the funkiest man alive. You in that mud right up to your neck.' That mean the deep, *deep, deep* blues." Hopper embellished the local color of the occasion by adding this epigram to the CD's notes: "Miles Davis . . . who I have known since I was seventeen . . . punched out the heroin dealer and said he would kill me if I ever did it again."

Early in 1987, Miles let David Franklin go, and asked his lawyer, Peter Shukat, to take over his management. Then he again changed the band. There was Foley on bass guitar, Kenny Garrett (from Art Blakey's band) on alto saxophone, Mino Cinelu back on percussion, plus Ricky Wellman on drums, one of the central figures in go-go music, Washington, D.C.'s own version of funk. Marcus Miller had done some work with the go-go band E.U. (Experience Unlimited) and had written its hit "Da Butt" for the group, and Wellman was the force behind that band. Miller heard a lot of swing in go-go music, so he thought it would be interesting for Miles to try using swing phrasing over that beat. Miles himself heard it as something akin to what Max Roach had played in early bebop—what Miles called the "klook-a-mop, 'Salt Peanuts' rhythm."

Heard live, Miles' bands between 1987 and 1991 had a rich, almost theatrical sound to them. They played a slightly eccentric music, often with a jokey edge that hinted at cartoon soundtracks. Yet live they were always more straightforwardly hot than might have been expected from their records. Miles was willing to open up a space in his arrangements almost anywhere—in the middle of a piece, for example, where a bass vamp might suddenly start up, sounding vaguely reminiscent of some of the things he did years before. As always, he favored strong dynamics, often moving the band dramatically from loud to soft. Adam Holzman recalled rehearsals where they were required to play almost inaudibly:

> We would rehearse sometimes at excruciatingly low volumes. I mean we would be barely tapping our instruments, and he would play off-mike working out a part. He'd be working on a section maybe for ten minutes straight, maybe slowly start bringing us up. Onstage, like on "Time After Time," he'd have the whole band down and keep bringing us down until you could barely hear it. And that was uncomfortable.
>
> You'd have seven guys, all playing electric instruments very softly, and that creates an interesting percolation, sort of blanket of sound, while he would be several levels above that in volume level. He'd push us down, and Miles would be barely playing . . . even on the record you can hear him go "shhhhhh" into his trumpet. He's not draining out his spit valve, he's saying "shhhh."

Miles had the ability to get even large audiences involved with this music, as if they were in a small club back in the fifties. The crowds would sometimes cry out, surprised at a sudden low note on the trumpet, or delighted by an unexpected buzz out of the horn, or they might join in on the imitative trading of four bars of music between Miles and Kenny Garrett, humming along with one of the horns. Samples of this band on the job can be heard on *Live Around the World*, where on "New Blues," for example, they sound at times like a strange lounge band with blues guitar and trumpet, backed by synthesized sounds of accordion and big band explosions.

The majority of musicians Miles used over the years shared a common aesthetic, but this group was a remarkable mix. Bassist Benny Reitveld described the Miles band he was with in the second half of 1988 as including "a drummer from Baltimore who invented the go-go beat [Ricky Wellman]; a half-Danish, half-African American percussionist who wrote chamber music and danced as she played [Marilyn Mazur]; a kid still in high school who played the Hammond B-3 organ like a 1950s road warrior [Joey DeFrancesco]; and a Dutch-Indonesian bassist from Hawaii [Reitveld]." Miles had once wanted musicians to play who they were and to practice on the job, but now he was very specific about his goals and their roles in the band, and there were sometimes very detailed rehearsals, which worked toward precise effects. But even when they weren't rehearsing, Miles often met with a few of them in his room before the performance, and made suggestions in their way, the repertoire evolved slowly, with small changes being made over time.

The medleys that once were carefully built up throughout the set disappeared, and the band returned to playing distinct tunes again and accepting applause in between. On the other hand, the blues became even more important to Miles, and he sometimes now played it simply, with an open horn, and an almost Armstrong-like feel.

Gil Evans died of peritonitis following an operation in March 1988, and Miles was devastated. "Gil might have been the only person he really loved," Jo said, echoing what many others who knew Miles believed. Certainly, no one understood Miles any better than Gil. He was one of the few people whom Miles let get close to him, and now that Gil was gone, he talked about wanting no more friends. "What good was it, anyway, to have friends—they die and leave you." There were only two photos left in his house, Gil and Coltrane, both of them dead now, and he carried their pictures back and forth between New York and Malibu, along with portraits of his mother and father. Miles still depended on all of them and said he had conversations with their spirits, as well as those of Monk, Philly Joe Jones, and Charlie Parker. When he was alone in the house, he felt the presence of his mother and of Gil. Quincy Troupe said that Miles told him that their spirits talked to him. They consoled him.

Davis began an album called *Amandla* in the fall of 1988 and finished it in January 1989. His idea was to merge Ricky Wellman's go-go rhythms with those of *zouk*, the rhythmically hopping, polyrhythmic new dance music of Martinique, which merged Central African and French West Indian rhythms to create a bottom-heavy, drum-driven new music. He took special pleasure in the cover of the record, a painting that he and Jo did together of Miles' face over a free rendering of the continent of Africa.

Guitarist Jean-Paul Bourelly was brought in to spice up the recording with his funky, pan-African-American style, and he recalls the session as being "done under very controlled circumstances; no mistakes saw the light of day. There was a lot of computer automation going on, and I think they (the producers) were trying to highlight Miles' working group and Marcus as a composer." But Marcus Miller was pleased that he had been able to get Miles to play without a mute again, and to let his sound be heard more clearly than it had in years. There was also a short moment of old-school Miles on the last track of the album. "Al Foster and I were trying to get him to play 4/4 again," Marcus said, "but he thought it sounded old. I had given up. I wrote 'Mr. Pastorius,' and after the vamp, he started playing on the changes—I was playing funky rhythm, but he signaled me to play in 4. He kept playing for 7 or 8 choruses. 'How's that?' he asked. I called Al Foster and played it. 'Put me on the record,' he said."

Though his abilities may have been diminished, Miles was nonetheless playing with nuance and refinement, as even some of his detractors might have noticed. The records he made attempted connections to new musics of all sorts. Miles vainly tried to get Warner Bros. to issue the live recordings they had of him—studio recordings, he said, being only menus for what could be heard live.

At the end of 1988 he was back in the hospital with bronchial pneumonia. Miles canceled the winter tour, though his doctors recommended that he retire altogether. For the past two years, he had been traveling for ten months out of twelve, and had refused to ease up. He rejected any suggestions that meant a loss of creativity, work, or the sense of self he had created. He was a musician who lived for the nightly performance, the rush of the arrival at the gig, the music, the audience—giving it up was death itself. Though he had ceased his drug and smoking habits, he still binged on sweets and often had to sleep for two or three days afterward. "In those last few years it took superhuman effort to get him up for a concert," Jo said. "He had to be urged to get out of bed. It took so long to get ready—the hair weave, his teeth were going from the diabetes, he couldn't feel his feet. He was using speed that he had gotten from a doctor to help him perform. He set himself goals to stay alive—to try to live through this tour, or to get through Europe and back home."

He resisted dying, but in the last years, his body was failing him and the prescription drugs that kept him afloat were aging him rapidly. "Impotence was difficult for him, since part of his image was the swaggering male with women," Jo felt. "So it was so hard to be Miles, such a strain for him to keep that going. His paranoia grew and he became violent, though he was still in control. He demanded I be by his side every minute. He was convinced I was having affairs with different members of the band, and he tried to lock me in my hotel suite. And in Rome, he had a chair set on the stage for me to sit on so he could watch me throughout the performance. He had it moved whenever the band moved. At the end of the show he came over for me, and we walked off the stage without the band, saying nothing."

Another level of complexity was added to his life when the tabloid newspaper the *Star* carried an account of Miles' most recent hospitalization with the headline, "*Roots*' Cicely Tyson 'Devastated' as AIDS Strikes Ex-Husband, Jazz Legend Miles Davis." Miles denied the story, telling Leonard Feather that "I think one of my ex-wives or ex-girlfriends may have started that story." In a strange, flirtatious interview done at Thanksgiving and written up later for the December, 1991 issue of *Spin* by Jennifer Lee, Richard Pryor's ex-wife, Miles was asked about AIDS and again denied it, and instead went on to talk about his difficulties having sex and his other health problems. Lee (who was white) and Davis got into an argument while watching Liza Minnelli on TV (Miles liked her, Lee didn't), the argument turned to racial matters, and she left. Without confirming or denying the stories about his illnesses, Quincy Troupe said that Miles had been treated with AZT during his stays in hospital in the late 1980s.

In spite of his medical difficulties, a canceled tour, and a smaller number of planned concerts, everything else in his life seemed to be improving in 1989. His divorce from Cicely was complete, and he settled into a life that for the first time appeared balanced, if not exactly normal. His brother, sister, and nephew Vincent stayed with him in Malibu to help him recover, and his son Erin came to live with him for the first time. When he was back in New York, he swam in the morning, painted in the afternoon, then rehearsed the band or composed music. Malibu was reserved entirely for rest and recovery. Now feeling stronger and having been told by his doctors that he could drive and exercise more vigorously, he worked out on an exercise bicycle when he was in Malibu, went swimming at the pool at Pepperdine University, or took a drive down the Pacific Coast Highway to a stable where he kept his three horses—Kara, Kind of Blue, and Gemini. Though he was not an exceptional rider, two of his three horses were jumpers that had been shown and had won ribbons. Financially, he was now very well off, his interests watched over by Peter Shukat's law firm, and he had income from performances and recordings, as well as from his investments and his music publishing. His paintings were beginning to sell, he had been made a Knight of Malta by the Order of St. John, he'd received the Governor's Award of the New York State Council on the Arts in June, and Troupe and producer Steve Rowland began work on *The Miles Davis Radio Project*, an eight-week long documentary that took the most complete look yet at Davis' life and achievements.

Miles: The Autobiography was published in September, and was no less than what was expected from its author. Reviewers found it contradictory, full of profanity (but inconsistently so), laced with anger and blame (especially against heroes of jazz such as Charlie Parker) and misogyny (with cold descriptions of his violence against some women, yet quiet about certain others). There was something for everyone to dislike. Playwright Pearl Cleage, for example, called for destroying Miles' records "until he acknowledges and apologizes and rethinks his position on The Woman Question," and critic Stanley Crouch used the book as source material for a withering critique ("Play the Right Thing" in the *New Republic*) that touched on every aspect of Davis' life and music. There were accusations of plagiarism, including one from a Davis biographer who accused Miles himself of having plagiarized portions of the autobiography from the biographer's book. Every review raised in one way or another the problems that come with autobiography (should we expect the truth, and if so, should we be shocked?); with black autobiography (what role should race play?); with jazz autobiography (how technical should the discussion of music be?); and with autobiographies written by someone other than the subject (who is speaking?).

It could not have been an easy book for Troupe to write. Miles was a taciturn subject, sometimes resisting questions, drifting far from the subject, or suddenly dropping names, many of them only partly remembered. "Miles started enthusiastically," Jo suggested, "but he lost interest in it." Mike Elam said that when Miles read the galley proofs of the book, he seemed amazed at some of the things that were in there. He made a game of saying he hadn't read it yet, or did I say that? What page is it on? But Troupe caught his voice, his phrasing, and the rhythm of his speech and produced a very readable book. And when Miles turned his critical ear on his own music or described the jazz life, he was both evocative and revealing. The book also gave readers a tantalizing glimpse of him though the anxieties and desires that slipped past his guard.

The *Autobiography* sold well and won an American Book Award; then when *Aura* was finally issued in 1989, it won two Grammys in 1990, and Miles was given a Lifetime Achievement Award by the Recording Academy. Though he was not particularly helpful in promoting the book, he was proud of it, as he was of *Aura*. (He tried unsuccessfully to convince Arthur Mitchell of the Dance Theater of Harlem to use it as a score for a dance.)

On his sixty-fifth birthday in May 1991, Miles' relationship with Jo was reaching its breaking point. "I threw a huge party for him in the boathouse in Central Park. We weren't getting along at all. Joanne Nerlino, his art dealer, was coming between us, and I was tired of it. If she wanted to be me, she could be me, and I was out of there. So I was going to leave, and Miles hit me . . . and I left. Then his lawyer and his sister called: 'Miles won't go without you. You have to come.' I said I'd go and I went. Afterward, we got a limo and left the party, and Miles started to hit me again on Central Park West, and the limo driver got scared, and left the car. But I'm strong, a runner, so I let out a scream, a scream like in the movies, that surprised him. I took off my pumps and ran home barefoot. But I thought it over, and I wanted to get him through death and he wanted me there. . . . That was the deal I made with him. And before he died he apologized to me for the way he had treated me."

Under the best of circumstances, Miles' scheduled performances for 1991 would have been taxing: a North American tour from February to March, breaking only to act and record for *Dingo* in March and record *The Hot Spot* in May. In June and July, he toured Europe, then the United States again in August, and back to Europe in October and November. Mid-November to March were set aside for rest. But in his state of health, each day would be a challenge. In one of his last interviews, Miles told Francis Marmande of *Le Monde* that he would quit playing next year. He complained that he couldn't go to New York anymore because of the pollution. His diabetes was uncontrollable, he was losing weight, and he "had no stomach left." "I no longer have eyes, nothing. Just a face . . . severe, straight, like the face of my mother."

Ahead of him were two incredibly demanding projects: the first was a retrospective of his big band recordings from the forties, fifties, and sixties at the Montreux Jazz Festival in late July, the other a reunion with a number of his small groups in a concert in Paris in August a few days later.

Quincy Jones had been trying to get him to do the Gil Evans arrangements for fifteen years. Quincy Troupe said that Miles told him that Jones "wants me to play that old shit. I love Gil, but I ain't going to play it, I ain't going to do it." Yet when Troupe dropped by Miles' house one day in July, he found him packing to go to Montreux. "I said, 'Going to Montreux for what?' He said, 'I'm going over there to play in this festival with Quincy Jones, we going to play Gil Evans' music.'"

> So then I was joking when I said, "Man, you must be dying man, playing that old shit." And he threw a fit, man. He put me out of his house. Put me out. He was so angry, I backed out of the apartment. I didn't want to turn my back to him because I thought he was going to hit me with something. And he didn't talk to me for a month or so. Then he finally called and said how much he'd hated playing that music.

Why did he do it? Why did he revisit the past, abandoning the one tenet that above all governed his life? Was it, as some said, that he had spoken to Gil Evans' spirit and had been assured that it was all right and that he could play the music? Did he know he was dying? Or was it only the six-figure sum he had insisted on? Whatever it was, the Evans arrangements had been reconstructed by Gil Goldstein, and two complete orchestras (Gil Evans' and George Gruntz's) plus synthesizers were rehearsing to play them under Quincy Jones' direction. It was to be a career retrospective from *Birth of the Cool* through *Sketches of Spain*.

Having not attended the rehearsals that were held in New York City and having missed nine hours of rehearsal the day before the concert in Montreux, when Miles turned up at eleven that night, trumpeter Wallace Roney had already been chosen to fill in for him. And as it worked out, Roney stayed up front with Miles at the rehearsal and again at the concert, spelling him, playing some of the parts himself. The musicians themselves disagreed on exactly what happened. Some said Miles was having trouble with the music; Roney said Miles could play it with no problems. From the videotaped and recorded results (*Miles & Quincy Live at Montreux*), his spirit was willing, though he was obviously tired and plagued by respiratory problems.

Only two days later, Miles was at the JVC Festival in the Grande Halle de la Villette in Paris. Under the title of "Around Miles Davis" and in front of giant blowups of Miles' paintings, he was reunited with musicians he had played with over the years: Saxophonists Steve Grossman, Bill Evans, Wayne Shorter, and Jackie McLean; pianists Chick Corea, Joe Zawinul, and Herbie Hancock; bassists Al Foster and Dave Holland; and guitarists John McLaughlin and John Scofield, as well as his current band. For a man who said he never looked back, it was another strange event. Wayne Shorter said that "he was seeing something about maybe the reality of life which takes precedence over profession."

> I think that maybe he was finding that there is a way of bringing you to the great realization of what life is about. And when you come to the end of that road there's really no words to express it. So I think the closest thing Miles could do to expressing what he was feeling was to get together with all the people who were still alive.

Jackie McLean had idealized Miles as a boy, received his first professional job from him, but hadn't seen much of him since the last time they recorded together in 1955. Before the concert, Miles called Jackie and asked him to come to Paris to play with him. "When he called, he said,

'Jackie, "Airegin" [a Sonny Rollins composition much favored in the 1950s]—get that together.' But when I got there, Miles said, 'What we gonna play?' I said, 'I thought you said "Airegin?"' 'Nah, what was that thing you wrote when you were a kid?' 'You don't mean "Dig?"' 'Yeah, how that go?' I played it for him, and he said, 'We'll go with that.' Miles was saying good-bye to everyone." He came to the afternoon sound check and stayed on right through the concert, playing with one group after the other for hours, at what had the look of a Felliniesque reuniting and summing up of a single life.

In August, Jack Lang, the minister of culture of France, made Davis a chevalier in the French Légion d'Honneur, and declared that Miles had "imposed his law on the world of show business: aesthetic intransigence."

Miles began work on what was to be his hip-hop album back in New York. According to his executive and associate producer, Gordon Meltzer, he wanted to do an overview of contemporary rap and rhythm and blues—a double album, one CD with Prince, the other with several other producers, including Sid Reynolds, John Bigham, and Easy Mo Bee. Plus, he wanted to remix some of the Rubber Band tapes from 1985–1986 that had never been released. Miles had done some work on the eight tracks that Prince sent him that summer, and though they weren't complete, he was performing three of them live: "Penetration," "A Girl and Her Puppy," and "Jailbait." With Easy Mo Bee, he over-dubbed six other tracks. Easy Mo then took "Fantasy" and "High Speed Chase" by the Rubber Band and worked them up around Davis' solos. With a "reprise" of one of the tracks added, there was enough to get forty minutes of music out of them and create the album *Doo-Bop*. Although Miles played well throughout, it was an undistinguished hip-hop album, and despite some remixed versions that followed, it never caught on. Not surprisingly, given the circumstances of what happened before the record was complete, it received a Grammy in 1992.

On August 25, Miles played the Hollywood Bowl. Before the concert, he was visited in his dressing room by a group of friends that included Wayne Shorter and his wife, pianist Jimmy Rowles, and Joni Mitchell. Mitchell recalled that Miles talked seriously to Shorter, telling him "that he was one of the last giants left and that he was undervalued and he shouldn't let people undervalue him. . . . He kind of gave him a pep talk." It was Shorter's birthday (Miles later injected "Happy Birthday" into

"Hannibal" on stage), and Shorter remembers Miles talking to him about American culture and the role of the music within it. "He had lost so much weight from the time I saw him in Paris in July when we played together. . . . But still he had a sort of illumination around his skin, his face and everything: there was slight illumination emanating from within him—from within to without, and I could see there was something different. He looked very smooth, I can almost say like going back to a baby. I think at that point . . . it could be that he had turned the corner already between life and death and was starting to go back to another beginning."

On Labor Day weekend, Miles began vomiting blood. Jo drove him to St. John's Hospital and Health Care Center in Santa Monica where he was admitted for what was suspected to be pneumonia, just as had happened after so many previous tours. When Mike Elam spoke to him on the phone, Miles asked to have some art supplies delivered to his room. They were delivered, but Miles failed to call Mike again, as he normally did every day. When Elam visited him to take him some soul food, Miles was tired but walking around and watching TV: "Mike, when I look at your paintings I see how much you know . . . how much you've grown." Mike hoped that they would do some more paintings together, but Miles told him he wanted to rest and that he wasn't going on tour again. When he was ready to leave, Mike said that he'd be back to see him again. Call first, Miles said, because he might be sleeping. That seemed strange to Mike, since if he called him, he would wake him up.

A few days after he was admitted, Miles had a stroke that paralyzed the left side of his body. He was agitated, battling, struggling to keep from falling asleep, and saying over and over, "I don't want to die." "He was pulling the wires and tubes out of himself," Jo said, "and the situation was getting difficult to handle, even though he was down to 80 pounds." There weren't many staff around because of the holiday, but Jo went out to get the biggest male nurse she could find to help. When they got him back into bed and Jo got in with him and held him, he suddenly went limp. "I thought he'd had a stroke, and they rushed in and began life-saving efforts. They didn't seem to notice that I was still in bed with him, and they rolled the two of us into the elevator. He went into a coma. They hooked him up again, and he was still squeezing my hand. I knew the papers would be sending reporters around, so I asked to have a guard put on the door twenty-four hours a day so no one would photograph him in that state."

He remained in a coma for almost a month and died on September 28, 1991. The causes of death according to his doctor, Jeff Harris, were pneumonia, respiratory failure, and a stroke. He was sixty-five.

As so often in Miles' life, controversy and ambiguity surrounded his death. Disagreements had surfaced between Jo and some members of the Davis family, and after his passing there was a dispute over who was with him at the time of his death. Even the cause of his death came up for contention: at least one tabloid, the *Globe,* reported that he died of AIDS. Jim Rose, his former road manager, said that he had heard that Miles had twenty strokes near the end, and that he had "HIV or AIDS, but that the strokes killed him."

At the funeral, the heritage of Miles Davis was beginning to be defined. Irene said that "Gregory and I had to sit separately from 'The Estate.' But Dizzy Gillespie came over and sat with us, and said, 'Girl, I thought you were a white woman!'" A memorial service was later held at Saint Peter's Church in New York City on a rainy October 5 evening. The speakers included Mayor David Dinkins and the Reverend Jesse Jackson (neither of whom had known Miles personally). Jackson said, "He was our music man, leaning back, blowing out of his horn, out of his soul, all the beauty and pain and sadness and determination and wishful longing of our own lives. He would growl his independence and ours out of his horn. And sometimes by turning his back as he played a solitary song, he would let us hear him talking to God." Cicely Tyson was not invited, but came as a guest of Mayor Dinkins.

Miles Davis was buried in Woodlawn Cemetery in the Bronx, in a plot that is less than ten yards from the family plot of Duke Ellington. The monument reads: "In Memory of Sir Miles Davis 1926–1991," with a scrap of the music from "Solar" below it.

> [When you die they might] have a jury trial to decide whether you're going to heaven or hell. Put your assets and your faults. . . . But I think they'll say, "Well, he's the only one who can play like that; we better let him in."
>
> MILES DAVIS

For many who followed Miles' career, the 1980s were seen as his time of slowing down, his new, simpler music an emblem of his mortality. Though he may not have changed much musically in the last few years, he had changed other things—his clothes, his drug habits—and he had taken up painting. There were things he still wanted to do. "He had all kinds of plans," Jo said. "He was still thinking of recording *Tosca*, and he wanted to do a Broadway show based on his life, and star in it." There was talk of a Brazilian project with Quincy Jones or Johnny Mandel. He wanted to make a video for PBS on Irish funeral keening. And Marcus Miller said that Miles wanted to record the sound of the players' shoes on the floor of a basketball game, since he was fascinated by the rhythms of play (much as he was by the cadence of boxers' feet).

Larry Rivers recalled another plan never completed. "In 1990, after someone put the question to us, Miles and I agreed to collaborate on a project—a music box to be painted by both of us . . . and the sounds coming from inside the box to be a CD of a musical collaboration between us. I asked him, 'What will we do for the music?' 'Oh, man, we'll get a rhythm section and blow.' This elaborate collaboration didn't make the six o'clock news. His death did, and did in our project."

And then there were his retirement plans. "In the late eighties he was leading a cult," Jo said. "Everything was working for him. He was knighted, he had the Malibu place, horses. He wanted to retire and become a gentlemen farmer and raise horses in Connecticut in his seventies."

Miles' death affected many people deeply, sometimes even spiritually. Irene said that "when Miles passed, he came to me. He appeared on the TV and said, 'Come on, I'll take you home.' I said, 'Miles, aren't you supposed to be dead?' He looked behind me and Vernon was next." Miles also appeared to Jackie Battle, but in a dream a week before he died: he hugged her and said good-bye. For a year and a half, Jo woke up every night screaming. Even the press did not want to give him up, and almost two weeks later, the *New York Daily News* seemed unwilling to accept that he was gone. Under the headline, "More on Miles," a few lines of type noted that his dark blue Ferrari was still parked at his garage.

Coda

Miles plays the way he'd like to be.

ART FARMER

TO THOSE WHO KNEW HIM, Miles was an enigma, a seemingly impenetrable self, a self that retreated the closer one got to him. Even with the distance of time, he resists interpretation as tenaciously as some cool-surfaced character from a novel by Alain Robbe-Grillet. Some have tried to understand him through what they know of his formative years—an often volatile family life as a child, his parents' divorce at a difficult age, a distant and disapproving mother, a father whose accomplishments and patrician manner could make him feel insignificant, his own early fatherhood, bad health, drugs, the sting of racism—all of them necessary for understanding him, but none of them sufficient to comprehend the complexity of his character, the depth of his insecurity, his instability, his frequent brutality to women (and men). Those closest to him saw him as the consummate performer, one who played himself brilliantly in various venues and media (the *Autobiography* presumably yet another performance). Miles eschewed the usual rules and conventions of show business, but he knew how to present his own performance-of-no-performance convincingly, staging a lifestyle, making his house, cars, clothes, female companions, music, and his race the business of his personal theater. The high life as high art. Posture, stance, attitude was everything: how one walked, held the horn, or dressed and moved; and, as with boxers, all of it was calculated to impress and intimidate. He offered whites and blacks alike entrée to what they took to be a certain kind of blackness.

Miles constructed and performed an identity that would reach beyond his middle-class African American origins, and project him as a man who knew everything he needed to know, one who would never be caught by surprise. Marguerite Eskridge, for one, said that Miles always seemed to know more than he said: "I honestly couldn't say whether this was because he was searching for the right words, or didn't want to talk about it, or maybe thought something like, 'doesn't everybody also know these things and understand them?'" Some, like Philly Joe Jones, saw him as "tortured, a nonconformist conformist." To Amiri Baraka, "Miles was the most cynical man I ever met. He was even cynical about being cynical." Others, not so impressed by his anguish and contempt, merely saw him as concealing his weaknesses behind a cool and knowing mask, or worse, becoming nothing more than the Forrest Gump of jazz.

Yet Duke Ellington called Miles the Picasso of jazz, and in terms of these two men's frequent changes of style, the volume, range, and impact of their artistic output, their involvement with numerous women, it was a fair comparison. Like Picasso, Miles was an artist completely devoted to his art. But more than that, he was in it for the long run, doing whatever was necessary to stay ahead of the others—varying styles, switching media, friends, wives:

> People who don't change will find themselves like folk musicians, playing in museums and local as a motherfucker. Because the music and the sound has gone international and there ain't no sense in trying to go back into some womb where you once were. A man can't go back into his mother's womb.

There was a shrewdness to the transformations in his art, a calculus of risk that was always at work:

> The public likes starts, confusion, and happy endings. But not everything is cut-and-dried like that. And neither is my music. People will always try to direct you toward things they like, but you get stagnant that way. Then when they get tired of you, you're labeled and can't come back with anything else.

The sheer largeness of Picasso, the excess of masculinity, the excess of life itself in the name of art, all had their parallels in Davis' own experience. Perhaps Miles could also resonate to the criticism heaped on Picasso by other painters—the accusations of "counterfeiting," of stealing others' styles, of being an opportunist who was willing to turn everyday junk into art. When Picasso said that it was the achievements of his youth that protected him, that it was the blue period and the rose period that gave him the shelter of success that he needed to do what he wanted, it might have been Davis speaking. Finally, with Davis as with Picasso, it's possible to locate the threads that connect all of his styles—the choice of a certain kind of bassist and drummer; a taste for relatively open forms, or for the insertion of vamps, interludes and codas in order to unlock and extend the forms used by jazz musicians. Above all, there was the indelible sound of his own trumpet, unifying and etching whatever he played.

But Miles not only changed styles, women, and clothing, he also changed identities: from the clean, hometown boy of the early forties, he became the hip bebop novitiate of the late forties; then the junkie flaneur of the early fifties; the romantic rebel of the late fifties; a race man of the late sixties; a 1970s alchemist and soul man; brooding mad exile of the late seventies; and finally the elder pop star of the eighties. Though he could speak of change as an obsession or a curse, he also proclaimed the idea as if it were something of an ethic, persistently driving him to seek new relationships in the music. By giving his producer-editor a role equal to that of the musicians, he was able to disrupt continuity and order in the music, and unsettle the listeners' passive acceptance. By shifting the relationship between the rhythm section and the melody instruments, he altered the perspective between ground and figure, and the ratio of elements within jazz. And, as Brian Eno said, Davis created a powerful context for his music, one larger than jazz, and it was *that* context which was listened to.

Standing atop the pinnacle of the jazz world, Miles nonetheless denied that he even played "jazz." The word had come to suggest to him a certain cultural space—the hallowed club, a scene in black and white, a cool intimacy, and a way of listening that demanded what? Heroin? Scotch? Perrier? He knew that for some African Americans, jazz might have been something of a shared secret code. But he was also aware that for many whites, jazz was just another venture into the exoticism of color: "[Jazz] means that you're a nigger, and you play an instrument that you didn't study." He detested the tendency of whites to treat him as either what he called "an accident" of history, a black man who is uniquely intelligent, instead of only one of many African American creators; or as a musical "natural," a tribute in which he saw embedded the denial of creativity.

When asked about Miles' renunciation of "jazz," Wayne Shorter said, "I think he was also saying that he denied that he was playing what people were selling—what they were trying to make jazz become so that they can sell something mediocre. If something's too good, they don't support it, so I think Miles was probably using reverse psychology (whispers) '. . . support this. This is not jazz, but it's still jazz.'" He approached music as an intellectual and suffered the frustration of feeling betrayed by every record company with which he was involved. Despite the many innovations and changes of direction in his music, he lived long enough to see revisionism set in against him. In 1980, his Prestige recordings were packaged together in a somber gray box as *Chronicle: The Complete Prestige Recordings*, with his carefully preserved verbal comments and verité remarks edited out. When Columbia prepared a retrospective called *Miles Davis: The Columbia Years 1955–1985* it favored his slower tempo pieces, whether ballads or blues; and its "electric" section left out most of his adventurous post-1969 music, ignoring 1973 and 1974 altogether in favor of the milder reggae and funk tunes of the early 1980s.

Many musicians talked of Davis' approach to music in terms of its purity, an integrity that transcends style. He aimed for a music that reached beyond voice, beyond music itself, even to the unplayable: to playing what's not there. He wanted records without singers and no liner notes, since words were not good enough for the music. His musical ethic meant being afraid of nothing, and taking risks wherever they offered themselves, struggling to stay alive to play through a lifetime of pain. He might well have paraphrased Jean-Luc Godard's remark about filmmaking, and said, "to make records is to make mistakes."

Wayne Shorter thought of Miles as operating on a higher plane of music:

Sometimes when Miles was doing things we would say, "Miles is messing up." He wasn't messing up. He was trying to destroy something, a learned thing or something that he had done before or repeated. It was like he was stumbling through something. And then the stumbling became beautiful, but he wasn't actually stumbling. He was and he wasn't. It was seamless. It was a seamless process going on. What he was doing was a dramatization of struggle in life: what the hell music might be for. To another degree it's figuring out what life is for. We have so many ways to express what life is for that we have to be careful of getting hung up on the formality of something, a mold or a way of doing something, a way of doing something which is not the way of life.

For Davis, life itself stood in the way of the music. To play it, he would have to accept a brutal discipline, one that demanded cruelty to oneself and to others and required him to give up the things he loved. He told every woman he became involved with that music always came first, before family, children, lovers, friends. Some were attracted by his intensity of commitment; others heard it as nothing more than a rap. But he was serious and nothing could prepare them for the shape that commitment would take or the force with which his rejection might come.

The wreckage Miles left in his wake was not easy for anyone to understand, or forgive. Those who did forgive him, or who chose to ignore the sacrifice and costs involved, would remind each other that it was all the product of his rage for order; whatever he had done, it was all about the music. But even with this indulgence, Davis was never able to fully enjoy the success he achieved, never free to appreciate what he had accomplished. If Gil Evans knew him best, his reading of Miles is disquieting:

> When Miles plays, it takes a tremendous amount of aggression, because everything he plays is so hard. Well, if he doesn't use that aggression on the horn, he gets it out with people, fighting, with guns, all sorts of things were happening up there: kicking people down the stairs, falling down the stairs himself. One time he was wrestling with one of his sons and broke his leg. He had to find an outlet for some of those emotions he uses in his work. And I wouldn't say Miles never turned his anger against himself. He's dabbled in everything not good for you. And I think some of his illnesses were his way of turning against himself, his masochism.

The same kind of puzzled comprehension emerges in Wayne Shorter's panegyric to Davis:

> To sum up Miles, I like to call him an original Batman. He was a crusader for justice and for value. He'd be Miles Dewey Davis III by day, the son of Dr. Davis, and at night he's in his lizard-skin suits with the dark shades and he's doing his Batman-fighting for truth and justice. But Batman had to be a dual personality, too, like he knew the criminal mind. So Miles, whatever he did that was not criminal but like short-tempered or he cursed everybody out, and when he was younger he'd hit somebody, or like they say Miles treated some woman really bad, or something like that. . . . I would say that Bruce Wayne, the guy that played Batman, he was capable of doing that, too, that's why he was such a good Batman. . . . A pure person does not know what defenses to use against the Vampire!

> Bryant Gumbel: What should we tell folks, that Miles Davis has mellowed with age, or that now people are just willing to listen to what he's always been or . . . ?
>
> Miles Davis: Don't tell them nothing! Let 'em guess.
>
> Gumbel: You *like* the mystery.
>
> Davis: *They* like it. I'm cool.

NOTES

Abbreviations

TROUPE COLLECTION: Interviews of Miles Davis conducted by Quincy Troupe in the Quincy Troupe Collection at the Schomburg Center for Research in Black Culture in New York City. At the time of writing, the collection was not yet catalogued or indexed.
MACERO COLLECTION: Teo Macero Collection, Music Division, The New York Public Library for the Performing Arts, Astor, Lenox, and Tilden Foundations. At the time of writing, the collection was not yet catalogued or indexed.
AUTOBIOGRAPHY: Miles Davis with Quincy Troupe, *Miles: The Autobiography* (New York: Simon & Schuster, 1989).
ROWLAND: Interviews conducted for *The Miles Davis Radio Project*, 1990, produced by Steve Rowland.
HALEY: Materials from the Alex Haley Collection, Schomburg Center for Research in Black Culture, New York City.
CBC: *The Man with a Horn*, radio series produced for the Canadian Broadcasting Company by Ross Porter, 1994.
JAZZ CENTRAL STATION: Interviews conducted by Bret Primack posted on the Miles Davis page of the Jazz Central Station on the Web c. 2000. This site is no longer up.

All quotations not otherwise noted are based on interviews with that person conducted by the author between 1998 and 2000.

Vamp
Page
1   *"Put that down"*: Hubert Saal, "Miles of Music," *Newsweek*, 23 March 1970, 100.
2   *"The trouble with life"*: Martin Amis, *Experience: A Memoir* (New York: Hyperion, 2000), 7.

Chapter One
Page
5   *Davis' father, Miles II:* Some of the Davis family's genealogical material is from the research of Lewis Porter in the U.S. Census for 1910 and 1920 for the entry on Miles Davis in *Baker's Dictionary of Music and Musicians,* 9th exp. ed. (New York: Schirmer, 2000).

7   *Still, East St. Louis:* Interview by the author with Eugene B. Redmond.

7   *Outrage over the event:* Elliott M. Rudwick, *Race Riot at East St. Louis* (Carbondale: Southern Illinois Press, 1964).

10   *"we weren't fooled":* See also Stanley Crouch, "Miles Davis in the Fever of Spring, 1961." *Always in Pursuit* (New York: Vintage Books, 1998), 305.

11   *"I couldn't fool around":* Cheryl McCall, "Miles Davis," *People,* 20 September 1981, 77.

11   *" . . . my mother would whip":* AUTOBIOGRAPHY, 26.

13   *"I've got one of those, too":* TROUPE COLLECTION.

13   *"When I was eleven":* Ibid.

13   *Miles, Vernon, and Dorothy Mae:* Author's interview with Irene Davis Oliver.

14   *" . . . that's when I said":* Larry Grobel, "The King of Jazz: Miles Davis," *Playgirl* (November 1986), 50.

15   *But eventually the community:* "Landrace Hog Breeder," *Ebony* (November 1959), 75–79.

16   *George A. Gibbs':* George A. Gibbs, *Modern Chord Construction and Analysis* (New York: Mills Music, 1938). The title of this book is often reported as *Georgia Gibbs' Chord Analysis,* a book that doesn't exist.

16   *(Among the records:* TROUPE COLLECTION; J. Lee Anderson, "The Musings of Miles," *Saturday Review,* 11 October 1958, 58; Howard Mandel, "Miles Davis," *Downbeat* (December, 1984), 19; author's interview with Vernon Davis.

17   *Buddy Rich on drums:* Don DeMicheal, "Miles Davis," *Rolling Stone,* 13 December 1969, 26.

17   *with Helen Forrest singing:* Author's interview with Vernon Davis.

17   *Buchanan himself said that:* Letter from Elwood C. Buchanan, Sr., to David Breskin, published with David Breskin, "Searching for Miles: Theme and Variations on the Life of a Trumpeter," *Rolling Stone,* 29 September 1983, 46. The letter is reprinted in Gary Carner, *The Miles Davis Companion* (New York: Schirmer, 1996), 1–2.

17   *It was an unusually:* Clark Terry, "A Word for Shorty Baker," *Jazz Journal* (January 1967), 7; Alyn Shipton, *A New History of Jazz* (New York: Continuum, 2001), 645.

19   *After he saw a photo:* Author's interview with Charles Davidson.

20   *"I just got onto the":* Leonard Feather, "Miles Smiles," Carner, *Miles Davis Companion,* 122.

20   *"I got to thinking":* Leonard Feather, "Miles and the Fifties," *Down Beat,* 2 July 1964, 46.

20   *With Buchanan's encouragement:* TROUPE COLLECTION.

21   *"I also remember":* AUTOBIOGRAPHY, 28–29.

22   *And some blues bands:* Harriett Oppenheimer, "The Blues Tradition in

St. Louis," *Black Music Review Journal* (Fall 1989), 135–154.

24   *"Burnt meat and hair:* AUTOBIOGRAPHY, 39.

24   *Randle's Band was often compared:* Paul DeMarinis, "Eddie Randle and the St. Louis Blue Devils," *Black Music Research Bulletin* 10 (1988), 1–3.

25   *But Randle said that:* ROWLAND.

25   *"Howard started playing":* Ibid.

25   *But when Miles' mother:* Wayne Enstice and Paul Rubin, *Jazz Spoken Here* (Baton Rouge: Louisiana State University Press, 1992), 247.

26   *"When he played":* ROWLAND.

27   *Miles bought a copy:* Paul Eduard Miller, ed., *The 1944 Esquire Jazz Book* (New York: Smith and Durrell, 1994).

29   *By summer, the Eckstine:* TROUPE COLLECTION.

29   *"It was like being":* ROWLAND.

30   *" I knew all the parts":* Conrad Silvert, album liner notes to *Tune Up,* Prestige P-24077.

30   *He was good enough:* George Hoeffer, "The Hot Box: The Birth of the Cool," *Down Beat,* 7 October 1965, 24–25, 40. See also Silvert, album liner notes, and Anderson, "Musings of Miles," 59.

Chapter Two
Page

32   *"Oh man, I was so excited":* Cheryl McCall, "Miles Davis," *Musician* (March 1982), 46.

32   *He took his examinations:* Herbert Lincoln Clarke, *Youth Dauntless* (New York: Belwin, 1936).

32   *"Miles and I would":* Larry Rivers with Arnold Weinstein, *What Did I Do?* (New York: Thunder's Mouth Press, 1992), 56.

33   *"Miles was very thin":* Ibid.

33   *It was the atomic:* "New York and the Music Revolution: Robert Orr, Trumpet," interview conducted by Charles Walton. See http://www.jazzinstituteofchicago.org/jazzgram/ bronzeville/orrbronzeville.aspl.

34   *"You know the obligattos":* Author's interview with Jimmy Rushing, August 1959.

36   *All she heard:* Simone de Beauvoir, *America Day by Day* (Berkeley: University of California Press, 1954), 352.

37   *Abstract art, abstract war:* Jack Kerouac, *Visions of Cody* (New York: McGraw-Hill, 1974), 329.

38   *And standing well hidden:* W. O. Smith, *Sideman* (Nashville: Rutledge Hill Press, 1991), 151.

39   *After Parker first tasted:* Author's interview with Irene Davis; Richard Cook, "Miles Runs the Voodoo Down," *New Music Express,* 13 July 1985, 24.

39   *He received a B:* Julliard transcript on exhibit at the Missouri Historical Society's exhibition, "Miles: A Miles Davis Retrospective," St. Louis, MO., 6/2001–2/2002.

40   *Drummer Connie Kay:* Whitney Balliett, *Ecstasy at the Onion* (Indianapolis: Bobbs-Merrill, 1971), 172.

40   *Two years later:* TROUPE COLLECTION; AUTOBIOGRAPHY, 105.

40   *Charlie Parker by himself:* TROUPE COLLECTION.

40   *"We really studied":* Marshall Stearns, *The Story of Jazz* (New York: Oxford University Press, 1958), 229.

41   *"Freddie Webster and I":* Dizzy Gillespie with Al Fraser, *To Be or Not to Bop* (New York: Doubleday, 1979), 29.

41   *"Miles and I":* ROWLAND.

41   *Pianist Sadik Hakim:* Interview with Sadik Hakim, 3 July 1979, WKCR.

42   *"that the performing artist":* Ralph Ellison, "The Golden Age, Time Past," in *The Collected Essays of Ralph Ellison* (New York: Modern Library, 1995), 248.

42   *Though he was not:* Lionel Hampton with James Haskins, *Hamp* (New York: Warner, 1989), 90.

42   *"I threw Miles":* Teddy Reig with Edward Berger, *Reminiscing in Tempo: The Life and Times of a Jazz Hustler.* (Metuchen, N.J.: Scarecrow Press and Institute of Jazz Studies, 1990), 29

43   *"Herman didn't understand":* Ibid., 29.

43   *These were rather:* Hoeffer, "Hot Box," 18.

43   *But now Miles:* Later, Charlie Parker also referred to this composition in an interview only a few months before he recorded with a string section. See "The Chili Parlor Interview" with Parker conducted by Michael Levin and John S. Wilson, first published in *Down Beat,* 9 September 1949, and reprinted in the same magazine 11 March 1965.

43   *"I was going to":* Ben Sidran, "Talking Jazz," in Carner, *Miles Davis Companion,* 193.

44   *Later, Miles would say:* Richard Williams, *Long Distance Call* (London: Arum Press, 2000), 125.

44   *"So they were sad":* AUTOBIOGRAPHY, 59.

44   *And only one page after:* Ibid., 60–61.

44   *"I knew that no white":* Ibid., 59.

44   *That's how bad he sounded:* Gillespie with Fraser, "To Be or Not to Bop," 215–216.

45   *Miles . . . was at Juilliard:* Robert Rusch, "Interview with Al McKibbon, *Cadence* (March 1987): 17.

45   *"Man, you know:* TROUPE COLLECTION.

45   *He had a patient:* Grobel, "King of Jazz," 21.

46   *"He was incredibly shy":* Gilbert Sorrentino, "Remembrances of Bop in New York, 1945–1950" *Kulchur* (Winter 1963), 80.

47   *"I couldn't figure out":* TROUPE COLLECTION.

47   *"But I know he was":* Ibid.

47   *I used to play:* Hoeffer, "Hot Box," 18.

48   *Singer Annie Ross:* Interview conducted for the author by Maxine Gordon, 2001.

48   *"[Bird] played with":* Reig, *Reminiscing in Tempo,* 19.

48   *"Ross Russell, the owner":* Russell, quoted in Geoffrey Wheeler, *Jazz by Mail* (Manassas, Va.: Hillbrook Press, 1999), 396–397.

49   *If you had been:* Reig, *Reminiscing in Tempo,* 21.

49   *The anonymous* Down Beat *writer:* Down Beat, 22 April 1946.

50   *"Lugubrious, unswinging"*: Savoy MG 12079.

51   *Strange power of the record*: Julio Cortázar, "Take It or Leave It," *Around the Day in Eighty Worlds* (San Francisco: North Point Press, 1986), 134–136.

51   *If Parker's solos*: Bergerot in the album liner notes to *Miles Davis, Volume 1: Young Miles 1945–1946*, Masters of Jazz 131, p. 37.

53   *"Well, Bill, I take one note"* Clora Bryant et al., *Central Avenue Sounds* (Berkeley: University of California Press, 1998), 376.

53   *"They thought we were"*: Richard O. Boyer, "Bop," *New Yorker*, 3 July 1948, 28–37.

53   *With no other work*: Ibid.

54   *Parker started the first tune*: Barney Kessel, "Recording with Charlie Parker," *Guitar Player* 12, (September 1978), 133

54   *When they tried it*: Roy Porter with David Keller, *There and Back: The Roy Porter Story* (Baton Rouge: Louisiana University Press, 1991), 56–57.

55   *Seriously short of money*: Chan Parker, *My Life in E-Flat* (Columbia, S.C.: University of South Carolina Press, 1993), 26.

55   *"We can't play"*: AUTOBIOGRAPHY, 87. TROUPE COLLECTION.

56   *"B would call out"*: AUTOBIOGRAPHY, 154.

57   *"All I know is"*: Ibid., 96.

57   *Heroin was next*: Ibid.

57   *"I was out"*: "Miles Davis: A Life in Four Scenes," *Musician* (December 1991), 60.

58   *"He'd hand a piece"*: Interview with Duke Jordan, WKCR.

59   *And it may also be*: Douglass Parker, "'Donna Lee' and the Ironies of Bebop," in Dave Oliphant ed., *The Bebop Revolution in Words and Music* (Austin: Harry Ransom Humanities Research Center, University of Texas at Austin, 1994), 161–202.

60   *Reig later revealed*: Reig, *Reminiscing in Tempo*, 29.

60   *Dizzy Gillespie said*: Gillespie with Fraser, *To Be or Not to Bop* (New York,: Doubleday, 1979), 371.

60   *You don't learn*: Miles Davis, Columbia Records press release, 26 November 1957, quoted in James Patrick's album notes to *Charlie Parker: The Complete Savoy and Dial Recordings*, Savoy Records 92911–2, 51.

61   *"Bird would go out"*: Duke Jordan interview.

61   *He used to turn*: AUTOBIOGRAPHY, 101.

61   *Miles heard Parker*: Ibid., 102.

62   *Max Roach for example*: Max Roach interviewed by Phil Schaap, WKCR, September 1989.

62   *Bird didn't tell*: Lee Jeske, "Miles' Long Road," *New York Post*, 27 August 1988, 15.

63   *"He never did talk"*: Stephen Davis, "My Ego Needs a Good Rhythm Section," *Real Paper*, 21 March 1973.

63   *But Parker called*: Duke Jordan interview.

63   *Although Miles often*: TROUPE COLLECTION.

63   *Miles signed a letter*: Leonard Feather, *The Jazz Years* (New York: Da Capo, 1987), 89–94.

65   *On a winter's eve:* Al Aronowitz, "Column Four, 1 December 1995,"
        The Blacklisted Journalist, http://www.bigmagic.com/pages/black/col-
        umn4.html; plus other interviews.
66   *He told Duke Jordan:* Arnold Shaw, *52nd Street: The Street of Jazz* (New
        York: Da Capo, 1983 (1971)), 298.
66   *"I got two kids":* TROUPE COLLECTION.

Chapter Three
Page

67   *"The outstanding thing about":* Whitney Balliett, *Dinosaurs in the Morn-
        ing* (London: Jazz Book Club, 1965 (1962)), 142.
68   *Miles told a* Down Beat *reporter:* Pat Harris, "Nothing But Bop? 'Stu-
        pid,' Says Miles," *Down Beat,* 27 January 1950, 19.
69   *This was a liberating:* TROUPE COLLECTION. Gil Evans had known
        Partch in California—well enough, in fact, to have him write recom-
        mendations for him. He and Partch were planning to do a new ver-
        sion of "Highball" in 1961 and record it for Verve Records. See Bob
        Gilmore, *Harry Partch: A Biography* (New Haven: Yale University
        Press, 1998), 291.
70   *This meshed with:* Brian Priestly, *Mingus: A Critical Biography* (New
        York: Da Capo, 1984 (1982)), 29.
70   *"Bird and Diz played":* AUTOBIOGRAPHY, 119.
70   *"Nobody else [but":* TROUPE COLLECTION.
70   *What it was, was:* ROWLAND.
70   *Gil, in fact, had first:* Nat Hentoff, "The Birth of the Cool," *Down
        Beat: 60 Years of Jazz,* Frank Alkyer, ed. (Milwaukee: Hal Leonard,
        1995), 97
70   *Evans recognized that:* Ibid., 220.
71   *For Mulligan, Miles "was:* ROWLAND.
71   *Miles dominated that:* Leonard Feather, Gerry Mulligan quoted in
        "Miles in the Fifties," 48.
71   *"Miles did most":* ROWLAND.
72   *"He came over":* Michael Zwerin, *Close Enough for Jazz* (London:
        Quartet, 1983), 13.
72   *"Everybody was ill at ease":* JAZZ CENTRAL STATION.
72   *"These slow things":* Hoeffer, "Hot Box," 25.
73   *The session was remembered:* Pete Welding, album liner notes to *The
        Birth of the Cool,* Capitol T 1974.
73   *He had written:* Author's interview with Bill Dixon.
73   *Miles extended each of:* Shearing's "Conception" has a conventional
        pop song structure of A-A-B-A, although somewhat unusual, in that
        each A section is made up of twelve bars (instead of eight) and the B
        section of eight bars. Davis' modification extends the final A section
        by two bars and introduces a G pedal into the last five bars. See
        Enrico Merlin, Appendix 1, in "Code MD: Coded Phrases in the First
        'Electric Period'" www.wan.umd/~losinp/music/code__md.html.
73   *(Vibraphonist Teddy Charles:* Charles says that he talked to Miles in
        Birdland in 1953, and they discovered that both had independently
        decided that jazz should have unity from beginning to end, not just

playing on chords, but in the ideas, structure, and sounds of the piece. Ira Gitler, "An Interview with Teddy Charles," *Jazz: A Quarterly of American Music* (Spring 1959), 171.

74   *Miles himself, on being asked:* Gene Lees, *You Can't Steal a Gift: Dizzy, Clark, Milt, and Nat* (New Haven: Yale University Press, 2001), 42.

74   *As he put it,:* Feather, "Miles in the Fifties," 47.

74   *John Lewis got really:* ROWLAND.

75   *John Lewis would keep:* Lees, *You Can't Steal a Gift,* 90.

75   *But when Miles received:* Contract on display at the Missouri Historical Society's exhibition, "Miles: A Miles Davis Retrospective," St Louis, 6/2001–2/2002.

75   *"John . . . was [also] upset":* ROWLAND.

75   *Miles said at the time:* Miles Davis, "My Best on Wax," *Down Beat,* 23 March 1951, 7.

75   *He later commented:* Nat Hentoff, "Miles: A Trumpeter in the Midst of a Comeback Makes a Very Frank Appraisal of Today's Jazz Scene," *Down Beat,* 2 November, 1955, 2.

75   *We made twelve:* Anderson, "The Musings of Miles," 58.

75   *Yet five years after:* Nat Hentoff, "Miles Davis," *Down Beat,* 2 November, 1955, 3.

76   *He said the first:* Feather, "Miles in the Fifties," 48.

76   *So I just told them:* AUTOBIOGRAPHY, 117.

76   *"Miles wasn't cool like":* Gillespie with Fraser, *To Be or Not to Bop,* 360.

77   *"It got to be":* Nat Hentoff, "The Birth of the Cool," *Down Beat,* 2 May 1957, 221.

78   *"I knew every chord":* Jeske, "Miles' Long Road," 15.

78   *"I felt like":* TROUPE COLLECTION, 95.

79   *Evans was using:* Stephanie Stein Crease, *Gil Evans: Out of the Cool* (Chicago: A Cappella, 2002), 172.

79   *Gil simply said he:* Gene Lees, "He Fell from a Star," *Jazzletter* (August 1995), 5.

79   *If these [jazz] men's:* de Beauvoir, *America Day by Day,* 226.

81   *At rehearsals, Tadd:* Ivor Mairants, *Great Guitarists,* quoted in Ian MacDonald, *Tadd, The Life and Legacy of Tadley Ewing Dameron* (Sheffield: Jahbero, 1998), 48.

81   *(Miles allowed that:* Boris Vian, *'Round About Close to Midnight: The Jazz Writings of Boris Vian,* trans. and ed. by Michael Zwerin (London: Quartet, 1988), 88.

82   *He was also one:* Boris Vian, *Jazz in Paris* (Paris: Pauvert, 1997).

82   *While smoking weed:* Boris Vian, *Autres écrits sur le jazz,* Vol. 1, ed., Claude Rameil, (Paris: Christian Bourgois Editeur, 1981), 70. My thanks to Aaron David Greenblatt for calling my attention to this book and other work by Vian.

82   *In one of the first:* *Jazz News,* May 1949, reprinted in Vian, *'Round About,* 76–77.

83   *For the first time:* AUTOBIOGRAPHY.

83   *Or when he walked:* Fara C., "Miles: Tutu et le reste," *Jazz Magazine* (Paris) (November 1986), 21.

84   *Sartre was helping:* Ronald Hayman, *Sartre: A Biography* (New York: Simon & Schuster, 1987), 46, 61, 74, 258.

84   *Miles and Sartre:* TROUPE COLLECTION.

84   *When he introduced them:* Ross Russell, *Bird Lives!* (Charterhouse, 1973), 271; Michael Contat, "'Sartre be-bop' un anatole." *Sommaire,* no. 384 (February 2000), 32–35.

85   *It was Miles Davis:* Juliette Greco, *Jujube* (Paris: Stock, 1987), 196–197.

86   *There was even less:* Though in his *Autobiography* Davis seems to say that he did not use heroin until he returned from Paris (AUTOBIOGRAPHY, 127), elsewhere in the same book he says he began earlier. AUTOBIOGRAPHY, 96.

86   *In New York, people:* Michael Levin and John S. Wilson, "No Bop Roots in Jazz: Parker," *Down Beat,* 9 September 1949; John S. Wilson, "Bird Wrong: Bop Must Get a Beat," *Down Beat,* 7 October 1949.

86   *When he asked Bechet:* Harris, "Nothing But Bop?" 18.

86   *Eight months a year:* Ibid.

86   *Yet here was Miles:* Bill Dixon recalls seeing Miles walking down the block from his house to sit in with whoever was playing at Copa City, the local bar.

87   *Irene and I didn't:* AUTOBIOGRAPHY, 130–131.

88   *"Bird says it's like":* Sharony Andrews Green, *Grant Green: Rediscovering the Forgotten Genius of Jazz* (San Francisco: Backbeat, 1999), 61.

88   *I just know that:* ROWLAND.

89   *He had crossed:* Author's interview with Jo Gelbard.

89   *He constructed a vision:* AUTOBIOGRAPHY, 136.

89   *Though he never mentioned:* Cheryl McCall, *People,* 20 September 1981, 78.

89   *When Pauline:* AUTOBIOGRAPHY, 137; Clark Terry, Foreword to *Miles Davis and American Culture* (St. Louis: Missouri Historical Society, 2001), ix.

89   *But the mark spotted:* Babs Gonzales, *Movin' On Down the Line* (Newark: Expubidence Publishing Company, 1975), 63–64.

89   *Reflecting back on:* AUTOBIOGRAPHY, 136; Gene Santoro, *Myself When I Am Real: The Life and Music of Charles Mingus* (New York: Oxford University Press, 2000), 79.

90   *He boasted in his autobiography:* AUTOBIOGRAPHY, 148.

90   *He explained that:* McCall, "Miles Davis," 46.

90   *"I was getting by":* AUTOBIOGRAPHY, 163.

92   *Levy himself was stabbed to death:* "The First 10 Years of Birdland," *Down Beat,* 10 December 1959, 21; Fredric Dannen, *Hit Men* (New York: Vintage Books, 1991), 53.

92   *The Birdland management:* Tom Moon, "The Black Saint's Epitaph," *Musician,* June, 1985, 121.

93   *Not every celebrity:* Kingsley Amis, *Memoirs* (New York: Summit Books, 1991), 69.

94   *"I see this real black":* "Interview with Hadley Caliman, Part 1," *Cadence* (December 2001), 9–10.

95   *Miles took the teasing:* Ibid, 10.

95 *When he was released:* Ken Vail, *Miles' Diary: The Life of Miles 1947–1961* (London: Sanctuary, 1996), 34–35.

95 *According to Drinkard:* Donald Clark, *Wishing on the Moon: The Life and Times of Billie Holiday* (New York: Viking, 1994), 331.

95 *Miles' father was still:* Interview with Gil Coggins, WKCR; Vail, *Miles' Diary*, 36.

96 *Weinstock was typical:* Album liner notes to *The Prestige Records Story*, Prestige 4PRCD-4426.

96 *"We'd get into these":* James Rozzi, "Bob Weinstock: The Audio Interview," *Audio* (August 1994), 34.

97 *He and Miles became:* Though McLean remembered the part being played by Charlton Heston.

97 *"Miles was fun":* JAZZ CENTRAL STATION.

97 *More than anything:* Howard Mandel, "Sketches of Miles," *Down Beat* (December 1991), 42.

97 *"He looked and acted":* Interview with Jackie McLean at WKCR, 1979.

97 *On January 17, 1951, Miles:* Alun Morgan, "Miles Davis" in Raymond Horricks, ed., *These Jazzmen of Our Time* (London: Victor Gollancz, 1959), 49.

97 *On the other hand:* Interview with François Postif in 1959, quoted in Michael James, *Miles Davis* (New York: A. S. Barnes, 1961), 34.

97 *Miles had just recorded:* Cab Calloway, "Is Dope Killing Our Musicians?" *Ebony* (February 1951), 22–24, 26–28.

98 *Leonard Feather in:* Leonard Feather, "Poll-topper Miles has been at a standstill since Back in 1950," *Melody Maker*, 23 February 1952, 4.

98 *In spite of the dire tone:* Phil Schaap, WKCR.

99 *One night while Miles:* Interview with Jackie McLean, WKCR, 1979.

Chapter Four
Page

101 *"First they steal your money:* Julie Coryell and Laura Friedman, *Jazz-Rock Fusion* (New York: Dell, 1978), 40.

101 *It was Christmas in":* Green, *Grant Green*, 61.

101 *Within days of coming:* Author's interview with Vernon Davis.

102 *Some nights he slipped:* Ibid. Vernon Davis recalled that it was his mother who made the call: "Put him in jail before he kills himself, and keep him there."

103 *From May through:* Author's interview with Ira Gitler.

103 *At one point:* George Wein, remarks from the stage of Symphony Space, New York City, "Wall to Wall Miles," 24 March 2001.

103 *Miles was in particularly:* Author's interview with Charles Davidson.

103 *Charles Mingus' wife:* Santoro, *Myself When I Am Real*, 102.

103 *On January 30:* Interview with Jimmy Heath, WKCR, 12 April 1996.

104 *Typical of the only work:* Santoro, *Myself When I Am Real*, 106.

105 *Miles stayed in:* TROUPE COLLECTION.

106 *Along with Miles' other:* William Claxton, *Young Chet* (New York: te Neues, 1998), 16.

106 *Both projected within and across:* A few have hinted at Davis' bisexuality, but no one interviewed for this book was able or willing to be spe-

cific about it. Several of those who spent the most time with him, such as road manager Chris Murphy and Miles' assistant Mike Elam, said they saw no evidence of it.

107 *The appearance of Chet Baker*: I am indebted here to Dave Hickey's remarks on Chet Baker ("A Life in the Arts") in *Air Guitar* (Los Angeles: Art Issues Press, 1999), 73–81.

107 *"I made up my mind"*: Mark Crawford, "Memories of Miles," *Daily Challenge*, 21 October 1991, 11–17.

108 *His account was*: McCall, "Miles Davis," *Musician*, 46.

108 *Afterward, Miles looked*: AUTOBIOGRAPHY, 170.

108 *"Then one day it"*: Ibid.

108 *From late December*: Lars Bjorn and Jim Gallert, *Before Motown: A History of Jazz in Detroit 1920–1960* (Ann Arbor: University of Michigan, 2001), 117.

109 *Carl Hill, the doorman*: Ibid., 134–135.

109 *"He used to come"*: Charles Sharr Murray, *Boogie Man: The Adventures of John Lee Hooker in the American Twentieth Century* (New York: St. Martin's Press, 2000), 455.

109 *"I remember one night"*: Prophet Jennings, ROWLAND. Miles, however, said it never happened; AUTOBIOGRAPHY, 173–174. Another version of this story from musician Frank Gant appears in Bjorn and Gallert, *Before Motown*, 134.

110 *Lonnie Hilyer, a young*: Paul Berliner, *Thinking in Jazz* (Chicago: University of Chicago Press, 1994), 256.

110 *"So here's this big"*: AUTOBIOGRAPHY, 172.

110 *Miles was so afraid*: TROUPE COLLECTION.

111 *Davis returned to New York*: Michael Ullman, *Jazz Lives* (Washington, D.C.: New Republic Books, 1980), 86.

112 *"Miles' personal life may*: Silvert, album liner notes.

113 *We drove in two cars*: Ibid.

113 *Miles took seven*: Interview with Percy Heath (and Jimmy Heath), WKCR, 2 July 1979.

114 *A year later*: Nat Hentoff, "Miles," *Down Beat*, 2 November 1955, 1.

114 *Despite Miles' alleged fears*: Bjorn and Gallert, *Before Motown*, 134.

114 *Whatever was the mix*: Author's interview with Gregory Davis.

115 *Near the end of 1954*: Letter in Miles Dewey Davis FBI file, no. 100-135-34-A, 14 February 1975.

115 *On Christmas Eve*: Leslie Gourse, *Straight, No Chaser* (New York: Simon & Schuster, 1997), 96.

115 *From accounts like these*: Author's interview with Ira Gitler.

115 *In one of the most bizarre*: André Hodeir, *The Worlds of Jazz* (New York: Grove Press, 1972), 79–99.

116 *Parker's passing was*: TROUPE COLLECTION.

116 *Lovett was a stylishly*: Joe Goldberg, *Jazz Masters of the Fifties* (New York: Macmillan, 1965), 84.

116 *Once Miles was out of*: John LaPorta, *Playing It by Ear* (Redwood, N.Y.: Cadence, 2001), 125–126.

116 *This time the arrangements*: Santoro, *Myself When I Am Real*, 113.

117   *But there was trouble:* album liner notes to *Blue Moods*, Debut DEB 120.

117   *In an interview:* Nat Hentoff, "Miles," *Down Beat,* 2 November 1955.

117   *It was the kind of diatribe:* Charles Mingus, "An Open Letter to Miles Davis," *Down Beat,* 30 November 1955, 12–13.

117   *Brubeck didn't swing:* Miles' opinions on Brubeck could go in a different direction on another day. Dave Brubeck, for example, remembers a night with Miles at the Blackhawk: "One night after hours, the place closed, Ella Fitzgerald knocked on the door and came in wanting to sing some more after her gig. I accompanied her for a couple of songs and when I was finished, Miles said, 'Dave, *you* swing. Your fucking *band* don't swing!' Author's interview with Dave Brubeck.

119   *But triumphant moments:* AUTOBIOGRAPHY, 191.

119   *On Tuesday July 19:* Ibid.

119   *Miles then proposed:* Davis remembered receiving $300,000 a year. AUTOBIOGRAPHY, 200.

120   *But Sonny Rollins:* Eric Nisenson, *Open Sky: Sonny Rollins and His World of Improvisation* (New York: St. Martin's, 2000), 67–73.

120   *But once Trane joined:* Ibid., 195.

121   *Coltrane's response:* François Postif, "John Coltrane: Une Interview," *Jazz Hot* (January 1962), 12–14, as quoted and translated in Lewis Porter, *John Coltrane: His Life and Music* (Ann Arbor: University of Michigan Press, 1998), 100.

122   *"When I first recorded":* R. Cook, "Miles Runs the Voodoo Down," 1985, 24.

122   *Coltrane said he has always:* Cobb, JAZZ CENTRAL STATION, 1999.

122   *For Coltrane it was:* Coltrane quoted in Andrew Nathaniel White III, *Trane and Me* (Washington, D.C.: Andrew's Musical Enterprise, 1981), 45.

123   *Jones left Philadelphia:* James G. Spady, "Philly Joe Jones Seized the Percussionist Space in Music and Life," TYANABA *Revue de la Société d' Antropologie* (December 1993), 69–75.

124   *"And I listen to the top":* Art Taylor, *Notes and Tones* (New York: Perigee, 1977), 11–18.

124   *"Miles had this real":* Ralph J. Gleason, "The Forming of Philly Joe," *Down Beat,* 3 March 1960, 28–29.

125   *Miles sometimes wrote out:* Author's interview with Jean Bach.

125   *Jimmy Heath was with:* Jimmy Heath interviewed by Steve Rowland. ROWLAND.

126   *In October 1955, Miles had:* Lewis Porter has suggested to me that videotapes show that when Miles Davis appeared on Steve Allen's *Tonight* television show on 18 November 1955, his voice had already been affected, so that the date that Davis gives in his autobiography for his throat operation ("February or March, 1956") is not likely correct. AUTOBIOGRAPHY, 202.

127   *Worse, some thought:* McCall, "Miles Davis," *Musician,* 46.

128   *The Davis quintet:* There is no "about" in the lyrics to the song, but it had been copyrighted under that title, and the publisher insisted that it be printed that way.

129　　*"But there was always"*: Crouch, "Miles Davis in the Fever of Spring, 1961," 303.

130　　*The girl had become:* Dunbar's poetry was having something of a revival among African American actors and jazz musicians. Oscar Brown, Jr., and Max Roach, for example, had both recently recorded versions of Dunbar's "When Malindy Sings."

131　　*In 1955, Feather conducted:* Leonard Feather, "Musicians' Musician Poll," in *The Encyclopedia Yearbooks of Jazz* (New York: Da Capo Press, 1993), 60–61.

132　　*(Gillespie had served as:* Though there are not many recordings with Gillespie as pianist, in his accompaniment to Charlie Parker on "KoKo," it's possible to hear him punctuate and underline Bird's improvisation such that he creates, in effect, an arrangement to which Parker responds.

132　　*The previous year:* Nat Hentoff, "Miles," *Down Beat,* 2 November 1955, 2.

133　　*Cannonball Adderley early on:* Cannonball Adderley, review of *Ahmad Jamal,* Argo LP 636, *Jazz Review* (February 1959), 33.

133　　*On March 16, 1956, Miles:* Ullman, 117.

134　　*Adding to the flavor:* These spoken moments were edited out of *Chronicle,* the box set of all of the Davis Prestige recordings, as well as some of the reissued single albums.

134　　*Throughout 1956 Leonard:* Nat Hentoff noted that none of the musicians shown on the television show was black. "Bernstein Shows 'World of Jazz,'" *Down Beat,* 30 November 1955: 6.

136　　*Two of the pieces:* In his notes to *The Complete Miles Davis–Gil Evans Recordings on Columbia,* Phil Schaap says that Davis' trumpet was overdubbed on these recordings, though neither George Avakian nor Gunther Schuller, both of whom worked on the editing, recalls any overdubbing.

136　　*"Miles had heard my wife":* Author's interview with George Avakian.

137　　*A few years later:* Kenneth Tynan, "Miles Apart," *Holiday* (February 1963), 105.

138　　*"He was very handsome":* *Echoes of a Genius—Miles Davis in Europe,* director, Ulli Pfau, EuroArts, 1992.

138　　*When the band went out:* Yet Miles' autobiography says that he "saw a lot of Juliette and I think it was on this trip that we decided we were always going to be just lovers and great friends." AUTOBIOGRAPHY, 218.

Chapter Five
Page

139　　*He usually managed:* Author's interview with Art D'Lugoff of the Village Gate in New York City.

139　　*Now only thirty years old:* Leonard Feather quoted in Vail, *Miles' Diary,* 95.

139　　*Though John Coltrane:* J.C. Thomas, *Chasin' the Trane* (Garden City NY: Doubleday, 1975) 85; AUTOBIOGRAPHY, 207.

141　　*The 12-inch LP:* Author's interview with George Avakian.

142   *What's more:* There was also Paul Weston's *Mood for Twelve* and *Solo Mood*, which used a variety of jazz soloists; Ted Nash, Eddie Miller, Matty Matlock, and Babe Russin; and Jack Teagarden, *Shades of Night,* with Sid Feller's arrangements.

142   *Since Evans had:* Stephen H. Lajoie, "An Analysis of Selected 1957 to 1962 Gil Evans Works Recorded by Miles Davis" (Ph.D. diss., New York University, 1999), 107–109.

143   *"It was very exciting":* ROWLAND.

143   *The photo selected:* TROUPE COLLECTION.

145   *Beverly Bentley:* I am indebted to Beverly Bentley for passing this recipe on to me.

148   *Miles said that he "cut":* AUTOBIOGRAPHY, 227.

148   *Beverly and Miles continued:* Mary V. Dearborn, *Mailer: A Biography* (Boston: Houghton Mifflin, 1999), 116.

149   *Though Miles and Norman:* Ibid., 214.

149   *"Cocaine is a good drug":* Grobel, "King of Jazz," 21.

150   *It was her version:* Blossom Dearie interviewed by Terry Gross, *Fresh Air,* 3 March 1998, WHYY, Philadelphia.

150   *In the 1950s she worked:* James Gavin, *Intimate Nights: The Golden Age of New York Cabaret* (New York: Limelight, 1992), 136.

152   *"The Olympia Theatre was sold:* Zwerin quoted in Vail, *Miles' Diary,* 107.

152   *The next night was: René Urtreger en concerts,* Carlyne Music CAR 006.

152   *Yet Barney Wilen:* Alain Tercinet, album liner notes to Barney Wilen, *Jazz sur Seine,* Emarcy 548 317-2.

153   *"Malle organized a showing":* Quoted by Frederic Goaty, album liner notes to *Miles Davis,* Paris: Editions Vade Retro, 1995, 43.

153   *"In Paris, he was completely":* Echoes.

154   *"What was typical":* Ibid.

154   *"At four in the afternoon":* Ibid.

154   *As far as Miles was:* TROUPE COLLECTION.

154   *Miles thought the whole:* Ibid.

154   *"He said, 'Wait a minute'":* Quoted in Vail, *Miles' Diary,* 108.

155   *"For example, I remember":* Album notes to Miles Davis, *Ascenseur pour l'echafaud,* Fontana 835 305-2.

155   *"I insisted that in Ascenseur":* Louis Malle, "The problem de la musique du film," *Jazz Hot,* no. 155 (June 1960), 15.

155   *("Because Malle thought":* Ibid.

155   *"It was not like":* Philip French, ed., *Malle on Malle* (London: Faber and Faber, 1993), 19.

155   *Davis' muted trumpet:* Robin Buss, *French Film Noir* (New York: Marion Boyers, 1994), 51–52.

156   *"And as some painters owe":* Album liner notes to Miles Davis and Art Blakey's Jazz Messengers, *Nouvelle Vague on CD,* Phillips 822566.

156   *But it was not to happen,:* French, *Malle on Malle,* 19–20.

156   *"They had a press party":* HALEY.

157   *Miles went on to Stuttgart: Miscellaneous Davis, 1955–1957,* Jazz Unlimited 2050, CD.

157   *"The idea I had for this":* AUTOBIOGRAPHY, 220–221.

158   *It was a minor accident*: TROUPE COLLECTION; author's interview with Allen Eager.

159   *The producer suggested that*: MACERO COLLECTION.

161   *Word got around that*: AUTOBIOGRAPHY, 226.

161   *"I remember discussing"*: Dan Morgenstern, "The Art of Playing," *Down Beat*, 22 October 1964, 16.

161   *When Evans brought him*: ROWLAND.

161   *Though he mentioned only*: Miles may have confused the two Ravel concerti for piano, since he sometimes referred to the "Concerto for the Left Hand," which was never recorded by Michelangeli.

162   *Saxophonist Dave Liebman*: Larry Fisher, *Miles Davis and David Liebman: Jazz Connections* (Lewiston: Edwin Mellen Press, 1996), 137.

162   *"Miles is . . . more or less"*: Bill Evans interviewed by Bill Goldberg and Eddie Karp, WKCR, 1979; see also Gene Lees, "Inside the New Bill Evans Trio," *Down Beat*, 22 November 1962, 24–26.

162   *Teo Macero wrote back*: MACERO COLLECTION.

163   *"There were certain things"*: Ira Gitler, "Julian 'Cannonball' Adderley, Part I," *Jazz* (Summer 1959), 201.

163   *But there was always*: Ibid., 203.

163   *"I used to use the solo"*: Ibid.

163   *"He's tired of tunes"*: Ibid., 291.

163   *"He thinks a solo"*: Ibid, 292.

164   *"He said, 'Cal, I'm'"*: Ashley Kahn, *Kind of Blue: The Making of the Miles Davis Masterpiece* (New York: Da Capo, 2000), 93.

165   *There were still some rough*: Interview with Jimmy and Percy Heath, WKCR, 2 July 1979.

165   *Gil Evans used to ask*: Charles Sharr Murray, "Miles Davis: The Cat Who Walks Alone," *Shot from the Hip* (London: Penguin, 1991), 466.

165   *In a similar way*: Lajoie, 19–20.

166   *Miles said the hardest piece*: TROUPE COLLECTION.

166   *In fact, when vocalist*: Miles Davis and Gil Evans, *The Historic Collaboration in Words and Music*. Legacy/Columbia CSK 8751 (promotional CD).

166   *"And that other passage"*: Hentoff, "An Afternoon with Miles Davis," 91.

166   *At times sonic clouds*: Despite what Davis recalls in the AUTOBIOGRAPHY (p. 230), Cannonball Adderley plays on *Porgy and Bess*; he can be heard leading the saxophone section and even speaking on one of the takes included with the box set.

166   *And it was a recording*: Review of Miles Davis and Gil Evans, *Porgy and Bess*, *Down Beat*, 23 July 1959, 20.

166   *(Much later, "Here comes*: David Toop, *Ocean of Sound* (London: Serpent Tail's Press, 1995), 111.

167   *"I finally saw that"*: Ralph Ellison and Albert Murray, *Trading Twelves* (New York: Modern Library, 2000), 193.

167   *"I cannot understand for"*: Ibid., 202.

167   *The music recorded that*: MACERO COLLECTION.

167   *And according to Bill Evans*: Peter Pettinger, *Bill Evans: How My Heart Sings* (New Haven: Yale University Press, 1998), 60.

167   *The first was that:* Gillespie with Fraser, *To Be or Not to Bop*, 405.

168   *And Miles was not beyond: The Miles Davis Story*, Mike Dibb, dir., 2001

168   *Adderley said that Bill:* Cannonball Adderley interviewed by Jack Winter, KCFR-FM, 1972, audiotape in the Institute of Jazz Studies, Rutgers University, Newark. See also *Coda Magazine*, 186 (1982), and http://www.perso.club-internet.fr/barybary/coda.htm.

168   *"I have heard":* John Mehegan, "Interview with Bill Evans," *Jazz* (June 1965).

168   *"It was more of":* Paul Wilner, "Jazz Pianist: Life on the Upbeat," *New York Times*, 25 September 1977.

168   *"At the time I":* Don Nelsen, "Bill Evans," *Down Beat*, September, 1960, 17.

169   *And Motian said that:* Quoted in the booklet to *The Complete Bill Evans on Verve*, 137.

171   *"What I had learned":* AUTOBIOGRAPHY, 225.

172   *Miles said that Gil Evans* Ibid., 230.

172   *When Cannonball first came:* TROUPE COLLECTION.

172   *"Miles would go say":* Eric Snider, "Jazz Legend Hides Behind His Reputation," *St. Petersburg Times*, 28 April 1989.

173   *Something about it:* It's tempting to believe that Davis also heard in the buzz and rattle of the *mbira* the textual equivalent of the electronic feedback in the music he would play ten years later. See David W. Sanford, "Prelude (Part I) from 'Agharta': Modernism and Primitivism in the Fusion Works of Miles Davis" (Ph.D. diss., Princeton University, 1998), 34–35.

173   *Miles now had a band:* TROUPE COLLECTION.

173   *(If you have to have . . . :* Ibid.

173   *"Miles often surprised everybody":* Jimmy Cobb, album liner notes to *Miles Davis and John Coltrane: The Complete Columbia Recordings 1955–1961*, Legacy/Columbia 65833, 108.

173   *To Cobb, "It sounded":* Jimmy Cobb on NPR's segment on *Kind of Blue* on "Weekend Edition" with Scott Simon, 3 July 1999.

173   *"That let me off":* JAZZ CENTRAL STATION.

174   *"There was a simplicity":* Bill Evans interviewed on WKCR.

174   *Miles' strategy was to:* AUTOBIOGRAPHY, 234.

174   *Jimmy Cobb said that:* Cobb on NPR.

174   *Of "All Blues," Miles:* Ralph J. Gleason, "Composed for 6 Months, Then Made a Tune a Waltz," *Des Moines Register*, 20 June 1959. Bill Evans in his liner notes to *Kind of Blue* says it is in 6/8. It might be clearer, however, if it is thought of as being in 6/4.

174   *"That little fluttering":* Ibid.

175   *(The title may have:* Author's interviews with Beverly Bentley and Eugene B. Redmond.

175   *In the same year:* George Russell, *The Lydian Chromatic Concept of Tonal Organization.* (Cambridge, Mass.: Concept Publishing Company, 1959), xviii–xix; see also Sanford, "Prelude," 75–77.

176   *This kind of playing:* A mode is a scale, and all scales are modes, but the type of scale that musicians usually call modes—the Dorian, the Phrygian, the Lydian, and others—are derived from the medieval or

Renaissance periods. Sometimes *modal* also refers to improvising in a particular mode. But improvisers seldom, if ever, limit themselves to the notes in the mode, and often they play outside it, as Davis' musicians often do on *Kind of Blue*. At other times, what is called modal is limited to the accompaniment being provided behind the improvisers. For example, on "So What" the two chords that Bill Evans plays contain all the pitches of the D Dorian mode. But this is not the pattern followed consistently in all modal playing. In fact, on "Flamenco Sketches," Evans departs from the Phrygian mode. See Keith Waters, "Modal Jazz," *Jazz Educators Journal* (July 2000), 53–55.

176   *"Miles and I played together"*: Leonard Feather, "Dizzy Gillespie Blindfold Test, Part 1," *Down Beat*, 5 February 1970, 24.

176   *For a record that went*: Near the end, Irving Townsend left the postproduction work to Teo Macero.

176   *The third reissue finally*: Gary Giddins, "Miles Again," *Village Voice*, 3 August 1993, 67, 78.

177   *Duane Allman loved*: Scott Freeman, *Midnight Rides: The Story of the Allman Brothers* (Boston: Little, Brown, 1995), 63.

177   *In the liner notes*: Bill Evans interview at WKCR.

178   *"When you play a number"*: HALEY.

178   *"You always see how"*: "The Sound of Miles," *Down Beat*, 18 August 1960, 13.

178   *"In any event"*: *Down Beat*, 6 August 1959, 32.

178   *At the Randall's Island Festival*: *Down Beat*, 17 September 1959, 15.

179   *On the hot night*: The following section is reconstructed from: Dorothy Kilgallen, "Jazzman Davis Arrested After Cop Battle on B'way," *New York Journal-American*, 26 August 1959, 1; "Miles Davis Seized," *New York Times*, 26 August 1959, 16; "Jazz Man Free on Bail," *New York Times*, 27 August 1959; "Miles Davis Taking Stand in His Defense," *New York Post*, 14 October 1959, 5; "Miles Davis Cleared: Faces Second Trial," *New York Post*, 15 October 1959, 2; "The Slugging of Miles," *Down Beat*, 1 October 1959, 11; "Aftermath for Miles," *Down Beat*, 29 October 1959, 11; "Charge Dismissed," *Down Beat*, 12 November 1959, 11; "Miles Exonerated," *Down Beat*, 18 February 1960, 12; "Miles Files," *Down Beat*, 31 March 1960, 13; "This Is What They Did to Miles," *Melody Maker*, 12 October 1959, 1; "Judge Finds Miles Not Guilty," *Melody Maker*, 24 October 1959, 1; "That Birdland Beating," *Melody Maker*, 5 September 1959, 5; "Probe into That Birdland Beat," *Melody Maker*, 5 September 1959, 1; Irving Kolodin, "'Miles Ahead' or 'Miles' Head'?" *Saturday Review*, 12 September 1959, 85; "Davis and Fans Appear, Case Off Until Oct. 13," unidentified newspaper clipping in the collection of the Institute of Jazz Studies, Rutgers University, Newark; "Judges Dig Baker the Most: Free Miles Davis with Some Cool Sounds," *New York Amsterdam News*, 16 January 1960, 1, 15; other untitled newspaper clippings at the Institute for Jazz Studies, Rutgers University; and Davis' comments to Troupe in the TROUPE COLLECTION, and the author's interview with Arnold J. Smith.

179   *People were now spilling*: Chambers said he was the only witness who

claimed that it was all about Miles being with a white woman. See Valerie Wilmer, "Paul Chambers," *Jazz Journal* 14, no. 3 (1961), 16.

180   *The tape they made:* From an undated clipping without a headline, apparently from the *New York Journal-American*, "Miles Davis" file, Institute of Jazz Studies, Rutgers University, Newark.

180   *Miles claimed that:* TROUPE COLLECTION.

180   *"I was there at the station":* Author's interview with Frances Davis.

181   *"It would be a travesty":* "Miles Exonerated," *Down Beat,* 18 February 1960, 12.

182   *In "Personal Poem":* Frank O'Hara, "Personal Poem," *Collected Poems* (New York: Knopf, 1971).

182   *And surely some at:* Langston Hughes, "Bop," in *The Book of Simple* (New York: Hill and Wang, 1961), 117–119.

182   *Miles took the whole matter:* HALEY.

182   *What seemed to bother him:* TROUPE COLLECTION. In 1977, writer Arnold J. Shaw was visiting Miles' house to do an interview for a TV show, and during a discussion of Miles' arrest, Shaw says that Davis told him that "it was at least partially my fault." Author's interview with Arnold J. Shaw.

Interlude
Page

183   *"Miles is a potentate.":* Lena Horne quoted by Kenneth Tynan, *Holiday* "Miles Apart" (February 1963), 103.

183   *Amiri Baraka once said:* Amiri Baraka, "How You Sound," William J. Harris, ed., in *The LeRoi Jones/Amiri Baraka Reader* (New York: Thunder's Mouth Press, 1999) 16.

183   *Although Miles knew:* Author's interview with Vernon Davis; Willie Ruff, *A Call to Assembly* (New York: Viking, 1991), 279; TROUPE COLLECTION.

183   *"You know, when":* Steve Lake, "Miles Smiles," *Guardian,* 15 November 1986.

184   *"He has to exert":* Gil Evans interview with Helen Johnson, Oral History Project, Institute of Jazz Studies, Rutgers University, Newark.

184   *"To me, the great style":* "Roses for Satchmo." *Down Beat,* 9 July 1970, 19.

184   *"Everybody up until Miles":* Gil Evans interview with Helen Johnson.

185   *But there were those:* Roger Pryor Dodge, *Hot Jazz and Hot Dance* (New York: Oxford University Press, 1995), 274.

186   *The Harmon had:* Keith Nichols, "Muted Bass," *Storyville,* 30 August–September 1970, 203–206; Danny Barker, *Buddy Bolden and the Last Days of Storyville* (New York: Cassell, 1998), 98.

186   *"In the slow ballads,":* Balliett, *Dinosaurs,* 142.

186   *The effect was:* Leonard Feather, "The Modulated World of Gil Evans," *Down Beat,* 23 February 1967, 17.

187   *When poet Robert Creeley:* Robert Creeley, Preface to *All That Is Lovely in Men* (Asheville, N.C.: Jonathan Williams, 1955).

187   *"And meanwhile Miles Davis":* Jack Kerouac, *Visions of Cody* (New York: McGraw Hill, [1972], 1974), 323–324.

187   *Phillippe Lacoue-Labarthe:* Quoted in Felicia McCarren, "Translator's

Foreword," in Phillipe Lacoue-Labarthe, *Music Ficta* (Stanford, Calif.: Stanford University Press, 1994), xiv. I am obliged to Lance Durenfard, who called this to my attention.

187   *"Frank Sinatra taught me"*: John Ephland, "Miles to Go," *Down Beat* (October 1988), 17.

189   *He brought to mind*: Krin Gabbard, "Signifyin(g) the Phallus: Representations of the Jazz Trumpet," in *Representing Jazz* (Durham: Duke University Press, 1995), 138–159.

190   *"The place was packed"*: Joyce Johnson, *Door Wide Open: A Beat Love Affair in Letters, 1957–1958* (New York: Vintage, 2000), 17.

190   *"Miles Davis walked off"*: Eddie Jefferson, *Body and Soul*, Prestige 7619 (1968).

190   *During a wind-up*: George Crater, "Out of My Head," *Down Beat*, 14 April 1960, 30.

190   *In Portrait of India*: Ved Mehta, "Jazz in Bombay," *Portrait of India* (New York: Farrar, Strauss and Giroux, 1970), 67.

191   *When Birdland seemed*: Ira Gitler, "The Columnist and the Club," *Down Beat*, 21 May 1964, 13.

191   *Asked about why Miles*: Gene Lees, "Dizzy Gillespie: Problems of Life on a Pedestal," *Down Beat*, 23 June 1960, 17. An odd parallel to the scandal of Miles' back turning is the outrage that Rod Steiger expressed over Marlon Brando's leaving the set as soon as he completed his portion of a critical scene between the two of them in *On the Waterfront*. James Naremore, *Actors in the Cinema* (Berkeley: University of California Press, 1988), 74. Naremore's book was a great help in framing the discussion of Davis' theatrics in this chapter.

191   *"This clicked with an idea"*: Nathaniel Mackey, "Blue in Green: Black Interiority," *River City* 16, no. 2 (1995), 122–123.

192   *Charlie Parker often said that*: Ira Gitler, CBC.

192   *"You'd never think it,"*: Dizzy Gillespie, "Blindfold Test," *Down Beat*, 5 February 1970, 24.

192   *Dizzy told of the time*: Dizzy Gillespie in Ole Brask and Dan Morgenstern, *Jazz People* (New York: Da Capo, 1993 (1978)), 9–10.

192   *Sonny Rollins agreed*: Silvert, liner album notes.

192   *"Miles sometimes played into"*: Lorraine Gordon, CBC.

192   *James Baldwin, who said*: James Baldwin, "The Fight: Patterson vs. Liston," reprinted in Gerald Early, *The Culture of Bruising* (New York: Ecco Press, 1989), 327.

192   *"Miles' way of coping"*: Nat Hentoff, *Jazz Is* (New York: Random House, 1976), 137.

195   *Offstage he could be diffident*: Stanley Dance, "Coleman Hawkins," in *The World of Swing* (New York: Da Capo, 1979 (1974)), 144.

195   *If you were insulted*: TROUPE COLLECTION.

195   *When Miles took up the*: Gerald Early, "The Art of the Muscle: Miles Davis as American Knight and American Knave," in *Miles Davis and American Culture* (St. Louis: Missouri Historical Society), 7.

196   *(Once, though, he said*: Diane Goldsmith, "A Thirst for Pressure, Not Bank Notes, Has Davis Blowing His Horn Live Again," *Atlanta Journal*, 28 August 1981.

196   *Before performances:* TROUPE COLLECTION.

196   *When asked if he was shy:* Ibid.

196   *He made a similar:* Ibid.

197   *In an interview with:* Don DeMicheal, "Miles Davis, 'And in This Corner, the Side Walk Kid . . .,'" *Down Beat,* 11 December 1969, 32–33.

198   *Practicing what was called:* Miles was familiar with stage rhetoric and—through girlfriends such as Beverly Bentley—he was especially aware of the Method. On the tapes of the sessions that produced the Los Angeles (April 16–17, 1963) part of the *Seven Steps to Heaven* album, Miles can be heard chastising saxophonist George Coleman for not signaling him more clearly while they are recording. Coleman responds: "If I feel like it, I'll nod my head." Davis: "If you 'feel like it'? What's that, Method thinking?"

198   *These gestures, the relaxed posture:* Robert Farris Thompson, "An Aesthetic of the Cool," *African Arts* 7, no. 5 (1973), 41–43, 64–67, 89–92.

199   *"The distinguishing characteristics":* Charles Baudelaire, *The Painter of Modern Life and Other Essays* (New York: Da Capo, 1986), 29.

199   *"That is the source":* Ibid., 27–28.

199   *But others who did:* Moon, "The Black Saint's Epitaph," 64.

200   *When it was turned on him:* Ibid., 14

200   *Calling him "the Whilom . . . :* George Frazier, "Cool and Otherwise," *Boston Herald,* 29 May, 1962.

201   *"Before his performance":* *New Haven Register,* 27 August 1961.

201   *Running cars to their:* Milan Kundera, *Slowness* (New York: Harper, 1995), 1–2.

202   *"I drive my yellow":* Breskin, "Searching for Miles," 46.

202   *"That car," according to:* George Goodman, Jr., "Miles Davis: I Just Pick Up My Horn and Play," *New York Times,* 28 June 1981, 2:13.

203   *"He was jazz's Marcel":* Albert Goldman, *Freak Show* (New York: Atheneum, 1971), 302.

203   *The result was:* Ralph Ellison, "On Bird, Bird-Watching and Jazz," in *The Collected Essays of Ralph Ellison* (New York: Modern Library, 1995), 259–260

Chapter Six

Page

207   *"He's like everybody else":* Gil Evans, oral history, Rutgers University.

207   *Listening to some of the:* Though "Lotus Land" was never used for Miles, Gil later arranged it for guitarist Kenny Burrell, changing its "oriental" features to give it a Spanish feel.

207   *He began giving Gil:* Ralph Ellison favorably compared Pavón to gospel diva Mahalia Jackson, in "As the Spirit Moves Mahalia," *The Collected Essay of Ralph Ellison,* John J. Collahan, ed. (New York: The Modern Library, 1995), 250–251.

207   *When Beverly Bentley came back:* Anthology of Flamenco, Hispa/Vox HH 1201-2-3 [78 RPM recordings].

208   *(As if on cue, critic Kenneth Tynan:* Kenneth Tynan, "Miles Apart," *Holiday* (February 1963) 108.

209   *"Miles started reading into"*: Author's interview with Frances Davis;
       AUTOBIOGRAPHY, 241.

209   *Davis and Evans both*: Nathaniel Mackey, "Cante Moro," in Adelaide
       Morris, ed., *Sound States* (Chapel Hill: University of North Carolina
       Press, 1997), 194–212.

210   *"We didn't start out"*: CBC.

210   *Trumpeter Marvin Stamm*: JAZZ CENTRAL STATION.

210   *"Now that was the hardest"*: AUTOBIOGRAPHY, 242, 244.

211   *"With me, if I read it"*: Ibid., 244.

211   *When Rehak told Gil*: John Kafalos and Tom Everett, "Interview with
       Frank Rehak," *Cadence* (September 1984), 18–19.

211   *In his autobiography, Miles*: AUTOBIOGRAPHY, 242–243.

211   *"Miles loved Glow's lead trumpet"*: JAZZ CENTRAL STATION.

211   *For the percussion on the*: AUTOBIOGRAPHY, 243.

212   *Nat Hentoff was there*: Nat Hentoff, "In the Studio with Miles and
       Louis," in *The Jazz Life* (New York: Dial, 1961).

213   *"That melody"*: Ibid.

213   *"Gil always wanted"*: CBC.

213   *Miles said that*: ROWLAND.

213   *Macero told them to*: CBC.

214   *Though the audience*: Jan Lohmann, album notes to *Miles Davis in
       Stockholm 1960 Complete* Dragon DRCD 228/2.

214   *The newspapers bristled*: "Miles Davis Says 'Yes' to the Press," *Melody
       Maker* (September 1960); "Eight Nights in London and Seven Else-
       where" unidentified press clipping, Institute of Jazz Studies, Rutgers
       University, Newark.

214   *As he had often done before*: Leonard Feather, "Miles Davis Angry,"
       Melody Maker, 17 September 1960, 2–3.

214   *In a review of Miles'*: Humphrey Lyttelton, "Here's My Theory,"
       Melody Maker, 1 October 1960, 3.

215   *A well-known*: Ibid.

215   *After Miles' performance*: TROUPE COLLECTION.

215   *No rehearsals were held*: Humphrey Lyttelton, "Miles Davis in
       England: Boor or Businessman?" *Metronome* (December 1960), 53.

216   *"I talked to Miles Davis"*: MACERO COLLECTION.

217   *"Apparently, we are all"*: Ibid.

218   *Davis had decided that*: AUTOBIOGRAPHY, 252

218   *In a memo from Irving Townsend to Teo Macero*: MACERO COLLECTION.

219   *Critic Martin Williams heard*: Martin Williams, "Review of *In Person*,"
       Down Beat, 23 November 1961, 23.

220   *"I remember me and Philly Joe*: John Litweiler, "Hank Mobley: The
       Integrity of the Artist—The Soul of the Man," *Down Beat*, 29 March
       1973, 15.

220   *"Sitting with me at my piano"*: Paul Horn, *Inside Paul Horn* (San Fran-
       cisco: Harper, 1990), 133.

221   *In Horn's own liner notes*: Robert Palmer, album liner notes to *Paul
       Horn in India*, Blue Note BH-LA 529-H-2.

221   *"Miles pulled my coat"*: Litweiler "Hank Mobley," 30.

221   *Inside the duplex*: Author's interview with Jackie Battle.

222   *"Miles lives in a noisy"*: Tynan, "Miles Apart," 107.

222   *In the spring, some fifty*: "U.S. Jazzmen Quiz Critics—a 'Bristling' Evening!" *Melody Maker*, 18 March 1961, 10.

223   *Miles was heard to mutter*: Dan Morgenstern, "'Sippin' at Miles' or a Press Conference in Reverse," *Metronome* May 1961, 8.

223   *Out from the wings*: "U.S. Jazzmen Quiz Critics," 10.

223   *When no one paid*: Ibid.

223   *In 1961, the young*: This section is derived from notes in the Alex Haley Collection at the Schomburg Center for Research in Black Culture. HALEY.

224   *Later that year its editors*: Gretchen Edgren, *The Playboy Book: Forty Years* (Santa Monica: General Publishing Group, 1998), 92.

225   *A vivid image of Davis*: HALEY.

227   *In his autobiography, Davis*: AUTOBIOGRAPHY, 260. See also Jennifer Lee, "Last Miles," *Spin* (December 1991), 74.

227   *For example, there was a quote*: TROUPE COLLECTION.

227   *And some of it seems*: Jack Chambers, *Milestones: The Music and Times of Miles Davis* (New York: Da Capo, 1998), ix–x.

228   *Drummer Jimmy Cobb remembers*: Crouch, "Mile Davis in the Fever of Spring, 1961," 318.

228   *Shortly before the concert*: Ibid.

228   *His decision may*: Variety, 3 May 1961, 1, 75.

230   *He later said that*: AUTOBIOGRAPHY, 253.

230   *It was a bad night*: Author's interviews with Anita Evans and Charles Graham.

231   *At three o'clock the next morning*: Assembled from George T. Simon, "Miles Davis Plays Trumpet in Carnegie Hall," *New York Herald Tribune*, 20 May 1961; Crouch, "Miles Davis in the Fever of Spring, 1961"; "Roach Interrupts Davis Concert," *New York Amsterdam News*, 27 May 1961, 17; and Ingrid Monson's interview with Ronald Mass, 21 April 1995.

231   *In April, during his stay*: Russ Wilson, "Miles Davis to Retire?" *Down Beat*, 6 July 1961, 13.

231   *But then Ralph Gleason*: Ralph J. Gleason, album liner notes to *Friday Night at the Blackhawk*, Columbia 463334.

231   *Miles seemed a bit*: Gilbert Millstein, "On Stage: Miles Davis," *Horizon* (May 1961), 100.

232   *The profitable sales of*: MACERO COLLECTION.

232   *"There hadn't been too"*: Ingrid Monson interview with Teo Macero, 15 March 1995.

233   *None of this was*: AUTOBIOGRAPHY, 259.

233   *"I didn't talk to"*: Ibid., 260.

233   *From Teo Macero's perspective*: Monson interview with Macero.

235   *After it was finished*: MACERO COLLECTION.

235   *Hank Mobley left the band*: AUTOBIOGRAPHY, 261.

235   *Between painkillers, drinking*: TROUPE COLLECTION.

235   *Miles was missing gigs*: "Strictly Ad Lib," *Down Beat*, 3 January 1963, 10.

236   *(Pianist Paul Bley said*: Francis Davis, "A to Z," in *Like Young: Jazz, Pop, Youth, and Middle Age* (New York: Da Capo, 2001), 107.

237   (*Marianne Faithfull:* Marianne Faithfull, *Faithfull: An Autobiography* (Boston: Little, Brown, 1994), 15.

237   *After they'd played for:* MACERO COLLECTION.

237   *"I thought what he really wanted":* Andrew Sussman, "George Coleman: Survival of the Grittiest," *Down Beat* (March 1980), 61.

238   *Later, he called them:* Len Lyons, *The Great Jazz Pianists* (New York: Quill, 1983), 272–273.

239   *What he meant, according:* Mandel, "Sketches," 51.

239   *From that point on:* Hancock, in *Miles Ahead*, Mark Obenhaus, dir., Obenhaus Films, 1986, tapes housed at the Institute of Jazz Studies, Rutgers University at Newark.

240   *As Herbie put it:* Ibid.

240   *"I was thinking":* Ibid.

241   *Miles got angry:* Paul Tingen, *Miles Beyond* (New York: Billboard Books, 2001), 35.

241   *"Miles was ill during":* Sussman, "George Coleman," 61.

243   *"I got Miles":* Michael Macdonald, unpublished manuscript.

243   *"Miles' music is used:* Ralph J. Gleason, "On the Town," *San Francisco Chronicle*, n.d., clipping in the files of the Institute of Jazz Studies, Rutgers University, Newark.

243   *When the play moved:* "Eight Men in a Pit for Play Using Davis-Evans Recording," *Down Beat*, 5 December 1963, 14.

244   *Outside the It Club:* Gil Evans interview with Helen Johnson.

244   *The quintet hadn't worked:* Ingrid Monson, "Miles, Politics, and Image," in Gerald Early, ed., *Miles Davis and American Culture* (Saint Louis: Missouri Historical Society Press, 2001, 93.

245   *None of Rivers' compositions:* Interview with Sam Rivers, WKCR.

245   *Rivers wanted to loosen:* Ullman, *Jazz Lives*, 135.

245   *When they got back:* Interview with Sam Rivers, WKCR.

246   *"I knew what he was talking about":* Max Gordon, *Live at the Village Vanguard* (New York: St. Martins Press, 1980), 101.

246   *"You know what I mean,":* Ibid.

Chapter Seven
Page

251   *The power of a Miles Davis:* Greg Tate, "Preface to a One-Hundred-and-Eighty Volume Patricide Note: Yet Another Few Thousand Words on the Death of Miles Davis and the Problem of the Black Male Genius," in *Black Popular Culture*, Gina Dent, ed. Dia Center for the Arts Discussions in Contemporary Culture Number 8 (Seattle: Bay Press, 1992), 245.

251   *"Then I went into the audience":* Todd Coolman, "The Quintet," album liner notes from *Miles Davis Quintet 1965–68*, Columbia Legacy 67398, 1998.

252   *"Miles was the man,":* Todd Coolman, "The Miles Davis Quintet of the Mid-1960s: Synthesis of Improvisational and Compositional Elements" (Ph.D. diss., New York University, 1997), 14.

252   *"Miles took the first":* Lyons, *Great Jazz Pianists*, 274.

252   *When Kenny Dorham, the trumpet*: Kenny Dorham, Review of *E.S.P.*,
       Down Beat, 30 December 1965, 34.

253   *On the first live recording*: Teo Macero did not think this concert good
       enough for issue, so it was not released in the United States for many
       years.

254   *"I started not even"*: AUTOBIOGRAPHY, 284–285.

254   *It was a practice*: The movement toward seamless sets was underway
       well before 1964. A British fan, Roger W. Hunter, saw Davis at Bird-
       land in September 1959 and recalls that the *Kind of Blue* tunes were
       played much faster and that "there were almost no breaks between
       tunes." Letter to the author 1999.

255   *Teo recommended to*: MACERO COLLECTION.

255   *Ron Carter said that*: CBC.

255   *"What I was trying to do"*: In *Miles Ahead*, 1986.

256   *"Or he would do things like"*: "Interview with Gary Peacock," *Cadence*
       (October 2001), 6.

256   *"At the Plugged Nickel"*: CBC.

257   *"He knew exactly what"*: Frank Bergerot, *Miles Davis: Introduction à
       l'écoute du jazz moderne* (Paris: Seuil, 1996), 165–166.

257   *On one occasion during*: This incident occurred on 2 December 1964,
       during the second set. See Miles Davis, *The Complete Live at the
       Plugged Nickel 1965*, Columbia/Legacy 66956–67095. Bertram D.
       Ashe, "On the Jazz Musician's Love/Hate Relationship with the Audi-
       ence," in Gena Dagel Caponi, ed., *Signifyin(g), Sanctifyin' and Slam
       Dunking: A Reader in African American Culture* (Amherst: University
       of Massachusetts Press, 1999), 280.

257   *"Now, did you see last night"*: Breskin, "Sending for Miles," 49.

257   *When he returned to*: *Down Beat*, 24 March 1966, 16.

258   *Miles said that she asked him*: CBS Morning News, October 1998: Q:
       "Did you fall in love?" A: "I don't know what that means."

258   *"I understand that Columbia"*: MACERO COLLECTION.

258   *But on July 28*: Ibid.

258   *When he did record again*: Ralph Gleason, "The Rhythm Section," *New
       York Post*, 7 March 1967.

259   *"We were actually tampering"*: Eric Nemeyer, "An Interview with
       Wayne Shorter," *Jazz Improv*, 2, no. 3 (2001), 75.

259   *In this new drum-driven version*: Thanks to Eric Siegel, contribution to
       miles@nic.surfnet.nl, 23 November 2001.

260   *Miles' many layoffs for*: Author's interview with Teo Macero.

260   *"I'm sure you're tired"*: MACERO COLLECTION.

260   *By 1967, Columbia Records*: Dan Morgenstern, "No Jive from Clive,"
       Down Beat, 16 September 1971, 18, 46.

261   *On October 13, 1967*: MACERO COLLECTION.

261   *"I have just had"*: Ibid.

261   *"When I started playing"*: AUTOBIOGRAPHY, 323.

261   *What he seemed*: TROUPE COLLECTION.

262   *In this moment of transition*: Feather, "The Modulated World of Evans," 16.

262   *"From then on, it was"*: Berliner, *Thinking in Jazz*, 422.

262   *"I learned how to keep":* Ibid., 340.

263   *But every time they:* TROUPE COLLECTION.

263   *(Quincy Jones remarked:* Josef Woodward, "Herbie Hancock and Quincy Jones: Talking About Music of These Times," *Down Beat* (January 1990), 20.

263   *The complexity that always:* Stuart Nicholson, "Filles de Kilimanjaro," Max Harrison, Eric Thacker and Stuart Nicholson, eds., *The Essential Jazz Records, Volume 2: Modernism to Postmodernism* (London: Mansell, 2000), 583.

263   *"He wants to hear stuff":* ROWLAND.

263   *"I think Miles doesn't":* Ibid.

264   *"We never rehearsed any":* Ibid.

264   *"I remember," said Hancock:* Ray Townley, "Hancock Plugs In," *Down Beat,* 24 October 1974, 15.

264   *"Sometimes the rhythm section":* In *Miles Ahead,* 1986.

265   *Hancock, for instance, found:* Ibid.

265   *Like Hancock, Wayne Shorter:* Tim Logan, "Wayne Shorter: Double-take," *Down Beat* (June 1974), 17.

265   *Shorter also began to:* ROWLAND.

265   *"Herbie said, 'I don't'":* David Breskin, "24 Shorter Solos," in Mark Rowland and Tony Scherman, eds., *The Jazz Musician: Fifteen Years of Interviews. The Best of Musician Magazine,* (New York: St. Martin's Press, 1994), 13.

265   *"When I used to listen":* AUTOBIOGRAPHY, 288.

267   *When Benson arrived at:* Michael Zwerin, "Culturekiosque," www.culturekiosque.com/jazz/miles/rhemile18.html.

267   *During the session:* ROWLAND.

267   *Gil Evans was also at:* Reprinted in Martin Williams, *Jazz Masters in Transition 1957–69* (New York: Da Capo, 1980), 271–277.

268   *Martin Williams remarked:* Ibid.

268   *When Williams later reviewed:* New York Times, 23 March 1969.

268   *A short time later:* In *Miles Ahead,* 1986.

269   *Following a Plugged Nickel performance:* "Miles Davis Takes New Bride of Many Talents," *Down Beat,* 14 November 1968.

269   *(An album that was to be:* Saal, "Miles of Music," 100.

269   *He told Hollie West:* Hollie I. West, "Black Tune," *Washington Post,* 13 March 1969, sec. LI, 9.

270   *Later, he would tell:* Frank Alkyer, "The Miles Files," *Down Beat* (December 1991), 23.

270   *In fact, the younger fighters:* Chris Murphy, *Miles to Go* (New York: St. Martin's Press, 2001), 145.

270   *One of them might:* Author's interview with Anita Evans.

271   *Later, Davis would:* Bob Belden quoted in "Modern Jazz Axis," *Jazz Times* (August 2001), 45.

271   *"Jimi was probably the only":* Edwin Pouncey, "The Man Who Sold the Underworld," *Wire* (July 1997), 29.

271   *"So I called Miles":* Ibid.

271   *"Miles had this enormous ego":* Ibid.

272   *Miles still had in mind*: Gareth Smith, "From Miles Davis to the AUB," *Daily Star*, Beirut, Lebanon, 23 June 1998.

272   *(Just before the record was to be* . . . : MACERO COLLECTION.

272   *Recording for this album*: MACERO COLLECTION.

272   *"The acoustic bass wasn't"*: Pete Gershon, "Class of '69," *Signal to Noise* (November–December 1998), 22.

273   *"I really resisted it at first"*: Ibid.

273   *Corea, like other musicians*: Lyons, *Great Jazz Pianists*, 261.

273   *Gil Evans was deeply involved*: Author's interview with Maxine Gordon.

274   *"It means I tell everybody"*: Don DeMicheal, "Miles Davis," *Rolling Stone*, 27 December 1969, 25.

274   *Miles did four of these tests*: Leonard Feather, "The Blindfold Test," *Down Beat*, 21 September 1955, 33–54; 7 August 1958, 29; 18 June 1964, 31 (pt. 1); 13 June 1968, 34; 27 June 1968, 33 (pt.2).

276   *Teo Macero, meanwhile, was slow*: "Brubeck to Record with Miles, Byrd?" *Melody Maker*, 6 January 1968, 3.

277   *"I didn't know, nobody knew"*: Paul Stump, *Go Ahead John: The Music of John McLaughlin* (London: SAF Publishing, 2000), 51–52.

277   *"Sometimes he'd come in"*: Ibid.

278   *They were in Vienna*: CBC.

278   *Chick Corea, on the other hand*: Brian Glasser, *In a Silent Way: A Portrait of Joe Zawinul* (London: Sanctuary, 2001), 110.

278   *"Miles has an interesting way"*: Silvert, album lines notes.

279   *"It wasn't a specific record date"*: JAZZ CENTRAL STATION.

279   *Zawinul was not happy*: Paul Tingen, "From a Whisper to a Scream," *Mojo* (September 2001), 48.

279   *It was Miles' way*: CBC.

279   *Miles' approach in the studio*: In *Miles Ahead*, 1986.

279   *(Afterward, Miles asked* . . . : MACERO COLLECTION.

279   *"Zawinul is extending"*: Miles Davis, album liner notes to Joe Zawinul, *Zawinul*, Atlantic 1579.

280   *The session tape boxes*: MACERO COLLECTION; author's interview with Jack Woker of Stereo Jack's, Cambridge, Mass.

280   *"It's About That Time,"*: Tingen, "Miles Beyond, 310.

280   *Miles' solos suggest*: Ian Carr, *Miles Davis: The Definitive Biography* (London: Harper/Collins, 1998), 249.

280   *At one point, he talked*: Jack Chambers, *Milestones*, Vol. II, 135.

280   *Macero's approach to*: The producers who prepared the box-set reissue of *In a Silent Way* could find only forty-six minutes of recorded material, but Macero insists there was originally much more.

280   *Afterward, Miles took copies*: Ralph J. Gleason, "On the Town," *San Francisco Chronicle*, 19 December 1969, 41; Karlheinz Stockhausen, "Intuitive Music," in *Towards a Cosmic Music* (Dorset, England: Element Books, 1989) 35–43.

281   *Two days later, the band*: Bob Belden's album notes for *The Complete In a Silent Way*. I am indebted for Belden's careful reconstruction of this session.

281   (*Zawinul said the whole session*: CBC.
281   *The disappearance of orthodox jazz*: Sanford, "Prelude," 27–28.
281   *When the record was*: Martin Williams, review of *In a Silent Way*, *New York Times*, 18 January 1970.
283   *Yet there were some who got it*: Lester Bangs, review of *In a Silent Way*, *Rolling Stone*, 15 November 1969, 33.
284   *Not surprisingly, some*: Annette Michelson, "On Montage and the Theory of the Interval," in Matthew Teitelbaum, ed., *Montage and Modern Life: 1919–1942* (Cambridge: MIT Press and ICA, 1992), 61–81.
285   *Macero described to author*: Carr, *Miles Davis*, 243–244.
285   *Teo ended his comments*: Ibid.

Chapter Eight
Page
287   *Jazz records had begun to*: TROUPE COLLECTION.
287   *Miles told producer Bill Laswell*: Bill Laswell, "Invisible Jukebox," *Wire* (March 2000), 41–42.
287   *A different era required*: TROUPE COLLECTION.
288   *The only directly amplified*: Ironically, the wah-wah reconnected him to an older school of trumpet players who used plungers, or those who left the stem inside their Harmon mutes to get wah effects.
288   *(Meanwhile, as a memo*: MACERO COLLECTION.
288   *When he first started playing*: TROUPE COLLECTION.
288   *Miles' manager Jack Whittemore*: "Japanese Wreck Tour by Miles Davis Group," *Down Beat*, 20 February 1969.
288   *"I just found out"*: "Random Notes," *Rolling Stone*, 19 May 1969, 4.
289   *Dave Holland said that*: Album liner notes to *The Complete In a Silent Way*, Columbia/Legacy C3K65362. 59.
289   *It was beginning to sound like*: "Groove" is a commonly used but nonetheless somewhat mysterious concept. It at least refers to a repeated rhythmic configuration that reveals its structure and its variation through repetition over time.
289   *"It was weird because of "*: John Toner, "Chick Corea," *Down Beat*, 28 March 1974, 15.
289   *"Sometime you subtract"*: Saal, "Miles of Music," 99.
291   *["Tell Clive Davis] I read"*: MACERO COLLECTION.
291   *More live recordings*: Ibid.
291   *Miles said that he*: TROUPE COLLECTION.
292   *This time Miles chose*: If Davis was influenced by the use of double quartets on John Coltrane's *Ascension* and Ornette Coleman's *Free Jazz*, the influence seemed to stop with the instrumentation. *Bitches Brew* is an exceptionally textural work, whereas Coltrane's and Coleman's recordings are more traditionally solo oriented. See Sanford, "Prelude," 30.
292   *Miles said he wanted Jack*: Tingen, "From a Whisper to a Scream," 50.
293   *"I got the sense"*: Dan Oulette, "Bitches Brew," *Down Beat* (December 1999), 34.
294   *"My memory of those"*: Gershon, "Class of '69," 23.

294   *He was also usually quiet:* Macero on WKCR.

294   *But during the Bitches Brew sessions:* CBC.

294   *"Bitches Brew" was the first: Down Beat,* Oulette, "Bitches Brew," 34.

295   *"We realized that Miles":* Rick Mattingly, "Jack DeJohnette: Stretching into Infinite Time," *Drum!* (February–March 1999), 57.

295   *"I listened to all":* Tom Moon, "Bitches Back," *Guitar World* (December 1998), 94.

296   *For this album, Miles:* album notes for *Bitches Brew,* 7. Dave Brubeck, however, believes the title came from *Witches Bru,* an as yet unissued recording he did for Columbia just before Miles' album.

296   *But Miles said:* "The Prince of Darkness Also Brings Light," *Zygote,* 12 August 1970, 28–29.

296   *Joe Zawinul, once again:* www.innerviews.org/inner/zawinul.

296   *Chick Corea, for his part:* Moon, "Bitches Back," 96.

297   *Teo sent Ralph Gleason:* MACERO COLLECTION, 22 September 1969.

297   *Teo responded:* Ibid., 25 September 1969.

297   *Once the album:* Ibid.

297   *If there was form in:* Joel Lewis, "Running the Voodoo Down," *Wire* (December 1994), 26.

297   *When accused of hiring a rock:* DeMicheal, "Miles Davis," 23.

297   *Nor was Miles even:* Benny Shapiro, Miles' Los Angeles manager, heard a band called the Jet Set (aka the Beefeaters) singing on a demo of "Mr. Tambourine Man" and told Miles about them, who passed the idea on to CBS, who then signed them under the name of the Byrds. Timothy White, *The Nearest Faraway Place: Brian Wilson, the Beach Boys, and the Southern California Experience* (New York: Henry Holt, 1994), 248–249.

298   *Bitches Brew was something:* Henry Mancini interviewed by Leonard Feather in 1971, quoted in David Toop, *Exotica* (London: Serpent's Tail, 1999), 130.

298   *"he did something that":* Brian Eno interviewed by Michael Englebrecht, http://hyperreal.org/music/artists/brian__eno/interviews/me__intr4.html.

299   *It was their creative period:* TROUPE COLLECTION. Davis, however, did not meet Buckmaster until November 1, 1969, several months after *Bitches Brew* had been recorded. Tingen, *Miles Beyond,* 130.

299   *(Betty once embarrassed him:* AUTOBIOGRAPHY, 303–304.

300   *"That didn't bother me a lot":* Tingen, *Miles Beyond,* 128.

300   *The incident with the police:* "Miles Davis, Wounded by N.Y. Gunman, Posts 5G Reward for His Arrest," *Variety,* 15 October 1969, 53; "Miles Davis Shot in N.Y. Extortion Plot," *Down Beat* 13 November 1969, 13; "Miles Davis Is Shot in Car in Brooklyn," *New York Times* 10 October 1969; Tingen, *Miles Beyond,* 77.

300   *Mati Klarwein remembers:* Liner notes from *Jazz Satellites, Volume 1: Electrification,* Virgin Records, Ambt 12.

301   *Letters from Columbia Records:* MACERO COLLECTION.

301   *Brazilian percussionist Airto:* Charles Mitchell, "The Anatomical Signatures of Airto," *Down Beat,* 7 November 1974, 9, 19.

302   *When Airto arrived:* Ibid.
302   *Clive Davis was determined:* Brubeck said he was dropped because he refused to use a Fender electric piano, an instrument that was gaining emblematic importance alongside the electric guitar. Since Columbia had acquired the Fender Company in 1963, he felt it had an interest in pushing electric instruments. Miles, he assumed, began using an electric piano because he was overdrawn on his advances and needed to keep working for the company. Fred M. Hall, *It's About Time: The Brubeck Story* (Fayetteville: University of Arkansas Press, 1996), 146–147.
302   *"he has a raspy, low voice":* Clive Davis with James Willwerth, *Clive: Inside the Record Business,* (New York: Morrow, 1974), 260.
303   *As so often with Davis:* Ibid., 261.

Chapter Nine
Page
306   *Miles was sitting:* Tom Topor, "Jazzman Miles Davis Held on Weapon Rap," *New York Post,* 4 March 1970.
306   *He was booked on a:* "Days in the Lives of Our Jazz Superstars," *Down Beat,* 16 April 1970, 11.
306   *Miles told* Newsweek: Saal, "Miles of Music," 99–100.
306   *Two days later Miles:* See *Miles Davis Live at the Fillmore East (March 7, 1970): It's About That Time,* Columbia/Legacy 85192–3.
307   *"He would discuss boxing":* Dean Chang, "Miles' Blow by Blow," *New York Daily News,* 17 March 1996.
308   *"Johnson portrayed freedom":* Miles Davis, album liner notes to *A Tribute to Jack Johnson.*
308   *"We gave Miles a rough":* Chang, "Miles' Blow by Blow." A documentary film, *"I Never Been Better!" Miles Davis' Boxing Symphony,* profiling eleven of the greatest boxers of all time and including two more hours of Miles' unreleased music, was announced in 1996 but has yet to be released.
308   *Cayton made it sound simple:* Keith Jarrett, "Tape Heads," *Pulse,* May 1955, 44.
308   *But Miles took this:* AUTOBIOGRAPHY, 315.
308   *"I want this and I want that":* Brian Priestly, "Alone . . . He's Cool," *Down Beat,* 14 March 1974, 14.
309   *"He might keep one":* Tingen, *Miles Beyond,* 105.
309   *What happened, Cobham said:* Jez Nelson, BBC interview on the thirtieth anniversary of the recording of the soundtrack to *A Tribute to Jack Johnson,* April 2000.
309   *The final recording was:* In *Miles Ahead,* 1986.
310   *In James Brown's music:* CBC.
310   *Miles maintained that the wrong cover:* Chris Murphy, *Miles to Go: The Lost Years,* (New York: Thunder's Mouth Press, 2002), 10–11.
312   *(Yet he also claimed:* "Miles Davis," *Musician* (February 1987), 64.
312   *But before that could happen:* "Eric Joins Miles' New Rock Group," *Rolling Stone,* 25 June 1970, 10.

312   *Asked if he enjoyed playing:* John Burks, "Miles and a Lot of Other Bitches," *Rolling Stone,* 9 July 1970, 15.

312   *The supergroup:* Zygote, 33.

312   *Adding to the thickening:* Leonard Feather, "The Name of the Game," *Down Beat,* 15 October 1970, 11.

312   *But even as these sour notes were still:* Al Aronowitz, "Rock Is a White Man's Word, Says Miles," *Melody Maker,* 17 October 1970, 25.

313   *"Mingus: Who?":* Interview with Charles Mingus, WKCR, 1971.

313   *But when these tunes appeared:* MACERO COLLECTION.

314   *Again, medleys of tunes:* Ibid.

314   *Then while he was:* Zygote, 33.

314   *Later, he would use:* Enrico Merlin, "Code MD: Coded Phrases in the First 'Electric Period,'"

314   *Late in July, Teo:* Teo Macero, collection, 22 July 1970.

315   *He recalled one night:* ROWLAND.

315   *Davis had his house done over:* AUTOBIOGRAPHY, 314.

315   *His son Gregory was now home:* Cliff Smith, "Miles Davis," *Courier News,* 7 April 1972.

316   *After more than:* Chris Welch, "Miles and the *Melody Maker*," *Melody Maker,* 30 October 1971, 15.

317   *Yet there in their midst:* CBC.

318   *Declaring he was only along:* Ibid.

318   *One night Miles asked:* Carr, *Miles Davis,* 334–335.

318   *Michael Henderson said:* Tingen, *Miles Beyond,* 119.

319   *"Keith Jarrett used to":* Ibid.

319   *Leon Chancler said:* Ibid., 124.

319   *But Miles was always fascinated:* CBC.

319   *Live/Evil, another double:* On *Cellar Door* sessions, scheduled to be reissued by Sony/Columbia.

319   *He told Airto not:* Chris McGowan and Ricardo Pessanha, *Brazilian Sound* (New York: Billboard Books, 1991), 163.

319   *Mati Klarwein was again:* Album liner notes from *Jazz Satellites, Volume 1: Electrification,* Virgin Records Ambt 12, 1986.

320   *Though a headlight and:* Al Aronowitz, "The $11,000 Dollar Bash," *Melody Maker,* 5 June 1971.

320   *Miles also suffered:* Carr, *Miles Davis,* 331.

321   *He complained that:* Smith, "Miles Davis,"

321   *He told Jet that:* "Blacks Win 17 Grammy Awards, But Miles Davis, Motown Execs Walk Out," *Jet,* 23 March 1972, 58.

321   *One reporter noted that:* Smith, "Miles Davis."

322   *Miles sent a limo:* MACERO COLLECTION.

322   *"When I came to New York":* Tingen, "From a Whisper," 131–132.

322   *"I remember describing":* Ibid.

323   *Miles was no stranger:* Gene Lees, *Cats of Any Color* (Oxford: Oxford University Press, 1994), 214; and Anthony Tommasini, "A Modernist for the Masses," *New York Times,* 12 November 1991.

323   *Stockhausen, for his part:* Robin Maconie, *The Works of Karlheinz Stockhausen* (London: Boyars, 1976), 8.

323 *His taste for the instruments:* Barry Bergstein, "Miles Davis and Karl-heinz Stockhausen: A Reciprocal Relationship," *Musical Quarterly* 76 (Winter 1992), 502–525.

323 *While he was staying:* Tingen, *Miles Beyond,* 132–133.

324 *Miles later said that:* AUTOBIOGRAPHY, 322.

325 *Upstairs in his bedroom:* Dave Liebman, JAZZ CENTRAL STATION.

325 *"He did not like to be alone":* Fisher, *Miles Davis,* 93.

325 *"I was trying to play":* AUTOBIOGRAPHY, 316.

325 *In the postproduction work:* Michael Jarrett, "Michael Jarrett, Wah-Wah Pedal," in *Sound Tracks* (Philadelphia: Temple University Press, 1998), 177.

325 *The 2000 reissue of:* Tingen, "Miles Beyond," 323–324.

326 *One magazine ad:* MACERO COLLECTION.

327 *"They don't do anything":* Stephen Davis.

327 *The festival was interested only:* "Miles Davis Does Not Appear, Says He Never Agreed to Play," *New York Times,* 5 July 1972, 34.

327 *Only five days after:* Ellen Plesher, "Miles Davis Charged with Imprisoning," *New York Times,* 19 July 1972, 34.

327 *He denied any wrong doing:* Frederick D. Murphy, "Miles Davis: The Monster of Modern Music," *Encore American and Worldwide News,* 21 July 1975, 36–37.

328 *Once CBS heard it:* Teo Macero interviewed on WKCR.

328 *The background had been:* Sanford, "Prelude."

328 *"We had a five-hour":* Harriet Choice, "Miles Davis, Solo: Brews Concocted and Broods Forgotten," *Chicago Tribune,* 20 January, 1974, 4.

328 *But this was something new:* H. G. La Torre, "A Session with Miles Davis," *Modern Recording* (February–March 1976), 38.

328 *Coming after the relentless:* Sanford, "Prelude," 63–65.

329 *He once spoke of:* Michael Zwerin, "A Nice Guy Under Pressure," *Wire* (February 1987), 23.

329 *Back in New York:* "Miles Davis Recovering After N.Y. Auto Mishap," *Variety,* 25 October 1972, 57.

329 *He was in serious pain:* Mark Rothbaum quoted in Tingen, *Miles Beyond,* 145.

329 *"Everything started to blur":* AUTOBIOGRAPHY, 318.

331 *In his autobiography Miles wrote:* Ibid., 326.

332 *"Break up the phrases":* Fisher, *Miles Davis,* 123. Liebman (in Fisher's book) offers the most sustained and detailed account of Davis' working methods.

332 *"In a way it really relates":* Ibid.

333 *"Finish before you're done":* Ibid., 125.

333 *"He doesn't go to the end":* Ibid.

333 *Though Miles never explained:* Ibid., 111.

333 *Lost in the swirl and:* Ibid., 113.

333 *"Now, what did he really mean":* Ibid., 113–114.

334 *"Before you went on the bandstand":* Ibid., 116.

334 *"The thing about Miles' trumpet":* Ibid., 127–128.

334 *"What I could see was":* Ibid., 119–120.

335 *"What day you saw him":* Liebman on JAZZ CENTRAL STATION.

335   *In late February 1973:* "Arrest Miles Davis on Drug, Gun Raps," *New York Times*, 28 February 1973, 57.

335   *Next, a concert in Dallas:* Murphy, *Miles to Go*, 5.

336   *Though Tosca was never recorded:* To get a sense of what Davis' *Tosca* might have sounded like, listen to Enrico Rava's recording, *L'Opera Va*, Label Bleu 6559 HM 83 CD.

337   *"Sly was way back in":* Joel Selvin, *Sly and the Family Stone: An Oral History* (New York: Avon Books, 1998), xvii, 163, 166.

337   *Members of the Stooges:* Legs McNeil and Gillian McCain, *Please Kill Me: The Uncensored Oral History of Punk* (New York: Grove Press, 1996), 65.

337   *(Alan Vega of the duo:* Ibid., 66.

337   *"I would try exploring":* AUTOBIOGRAPHY, 329–330.

338   *A rebalancing of musical elements:* MACERO COLLECTION.

338   *"Tatu" was typical of:* My thanks to Tony Green for calling this to my attention. It should be noted, though, that "Express" first appeared on record only in 1974.

339   *It was now also louder:* Murphy, *Miles to Go*.

339   *"Just listen to it":* Choice, "Mile Davis, Solo," 4

339   *Pete Cosey said:* Peter Margasak, "Post No Bills: Playing with Fire," *Chicago Reader*, 29 August 1997.

339   *"[Through] Stockhausen I could":* AUTOBIOGRAPHY, 329; see also Laurent Cugny, *Electrique Miles Davis, 1968–1975* (Marseille: André Dimanche, 1993), 125–130.

339   *When they returned to New York:* Liebman, album liner notes. Miles Davis, *Get Up with It*, Columbia/Legacy 63970.

340   *Teo said that during:* Teo Macero interviewed by Bill Goldberg on WKCR.

340   *To many, this was a:* Tingen, *Miles Beyond*, 161.

340   *Liebman decided to leave:* Fisher, *Miles Davis*,

340   *Then in a brilliant:* Tingen, *Miles Beyond*, 161.

341   *"Why doesn't somebody write":* Sy Johnson, "Sparring with Miles Davis," *Changes*, no. 89 (1976), 31.

342   *Unable at times to work:* Murphy, *Miles to Go*, 84–85.

342   *Several times he managed:* Dominique Gaumont, "Comment j'ai rencontre Miles," *Jazz Hot* (September 1988), 388.

342   *"Prelude" (or "Tatu") continued the heart-stopping:* I am indebted to Greg Tate for reminding me of this connection. It should be noted, however, that "Fire" was not issued until 1974.

342   *The title, proposed:* Jocelyn Godwin, *Arktos: The Polar Myth in Science, Symbolism and Nazi Survival*, as quoted by Toop, *Ocean of Sound*, 100.

342   *In the original notes:* A translation from the Japanese is in the MACERO COLLECTION.

343   *As Theodor Adorno said of the:* Theodor Adorno, "Spatstil Beethovens—Beethoven's Late Style," *Moments Musicaux* (Frankfurt: Suhrkamp Verlag, 1964), 14; Sanford, "Prelude," 16–20.

343   *The Agharta/Pangaea band went into:* La Torre, "A Session," 34–38.

343   *Herbie Hancock:* Ibid., 37.

344   *As ill as he was on:* AUTOBIOGRAPHY, 331.

344   *"She just started putting me:* Ibid.
345   *Another hip replacement was:* Conrad Silvert, "Miles Davis Brews Up a Recovery," *Rolling Stone*, 11 March 1976, 18.
345   *There was an attempt at:* MACERO COLLECTION.
346   *Once in a while someone:* According to the research of Linda Dahl, author of *Morning Glory: A Biography of Mary Lou Williams* (New York: Pantheon, 1999).
346   *"He was totally out of control":* CBC.
346   *George Wein said he:* Interviews for Ken Burns' *Jazz:* http://www.pbs.org/jazz/about/about__transcripts.htm.
346   *Columbia's Bruce Lundvall said that:* CBC.
346   *Heath asked him to:* CBC.
346   *Gil Evans made several:* Crease, *Gil Evans*, 293–294.
347   *The composition Miles was:* Carr, *Miles Davis* 337.
347   *Afterward, T. M. Stevens:* "Interview with T. M. Stevens," *Bass Player* (June 1994).
348   *Davis returned to New York:* Michael Zwerin, "The Prince of Silence," "Culturekiosque," www.culturekiosque.com/jazz/miles/ rhemile18.html.; AUTOBIOGRAPHY, 325; Breskin, "Sending for Miles," 49.
348   *"I was nuts . . . so":* McCall, "Miles Davis," 40.
348   *"Miles was one of the most":* JAZZ CENTRAL STATION.
348   *"Bored is the word":* People, 20 September 1981.
348   *"Play just one note for me":* Interview with Lester Bowie, 3 July 1979, WKCR.
348   *Writer Eric Nisenson:* He did publish a biography, *'Round About Midnight: A Portrait of Miles Davis* (New York: Da Capo, 1996).
349   *When he was high:* Davis said that the multiple faces of one person in his paintings reflect that experience. TROUPE COLLECTION.
349   *There were women who:* AUTOBIOGRAPHY, 336.
349   *He was now impotent:* Author's interview with Nisenson.

Chapter Ten
Page
351   *"Practicing is like praying":* Zwerin, "Prince of Silence."
352   *"We walked over to the piano":* Dr. George Butler, album liner notes to *1969 Miles: Festiva de Juan Pins*, Japanese Sony SRCS 6843, 1993, 7.
352   *"The day came when":* Ibid.
352   *"Once again":* Tingen, *Miles Beyond*, 192–193.
354   *"He has to get that sound":* Zan Stewart, "Gil Evans," *Musician, Player and Listener* (January 1982).
354   *Teo Macero's recollection:* Tingen, *Miles Beyond*, 195; Fisher, *Miles Davis*, 179–181.
355   *They took five and a half:* AUTOBIOGRAPHY, 348.
355   *Miles himself scuttled:* Tingen, *Miles Beyond*, 194.
356   *Despite his return to playing:* New York Post, 3 September 1980, 2.
356   *Miles sent George Wein:* George Goodman, Jr., "Miles Davis: I Just Pick Up My Horn and Play," *New York Times*, 28 June 1981, 2:13.
356   *It was something of a:* George Wein, "Remarks From the Stage."

356 *Saxophonist Bob Mintzer said:* JAZZ CENTRAL STATION.

357 *"No bebop . . .":* Tingen, *Miles Beyond*, 201.

357 *The hardest part about:* TROUPE COLLECTION.

357 *Then he reached out to the man:* Murphy, *Miles to Go*, 141.

357 *Still, the band's tentative:* Enrico Merlin suggests that the theme of "Jean Pierre" was played by Miles in improvisations as early as 1958. Tingen, *Miles Beyond*, 202.

357 (We Want Miles *won a:* Murphy, *Miles to Go*, 203.

359 *Afterward, when the audience:* CBC.

360 *He even saw a psychotherapist:* Murphy, *Miles to Go*, 186.

360 *Some writers cautiously inquired:* Richard Williams, *Long Distance Call*, 123.

361 *When a reporter asked: New York Post*, 30 September 1991.

361 (He said he was: Murphy, *Miles to Go*, 203.

361 *Gil said that he'd:* CBC; It was a process that George Russell had already explored by orchestrating Miles' recorded solo of "So What" into a composition of its own.

362 *For the first time:* Jay Messina interviewed by Matthew Szwed for the author.

362 *But because its melodies:* Tom Moon, "Mr. Cool Can't Keep Still," *Miami Herald*, 29 June 1984.

362 *"You know what would be nice":* Ibid.

363 *Irving and Wilburn carried:* Tingen, *Miles Beyond*, 215.

363 *Cicely's experience in show business:* AUTOBIOGRAPHY, 335.

363 *Still, he said:* Ibid., 355–356.

364 *"Miles wanted to enjoy":* J. Scofield interviewed on JAZZ CENTRAL STATION.

364 *"Miles was broke when":* Jo Gelbard in ibid., 228–229.

364 *When he learned she was:* Ibid.

365 *He . . . operated from the principle:* Interview with Miles Davis in Tokyo 1985 conducted by Mr. Tamori.

365 *"I like contrary motion":* ROWLAND.

365 *"You'd think somebody like Miles":* Ted Drodowski, "Doin' the Rat Dance," *Musician* (May 1989), 44.

367 *Larry Rivers saw him:* Larry Rivers, *What Did I Do?* 57.

370 *"You have to treat the song":* Mikal Gilmore, "Miles Davis: The Lion in Winter," *Los Angeles Herald Examiner*, 26 August 1983, 302–303.

370 *There were a number of:* Howard Mandel, "Miles Davis," *Down Beat* (December 1984), 18.

370 *The Sonning Award Committee:* Erik Moseholm, "On the Master's Doorstep: A Meeting with Miles," *Jazz Changes* (Summer 1996), 26–29.

372 *A few members of the band:* Tingen, *Miles Beyond*, 219.

372 *There were some well-rehearsed:* Howard Mandel, "Robert Irving III: In the Studio with Miles Davis," *Down Beat* (August 1985), 54.

373 *When he was reminded of:* Leonard Feather, "Miles Davis' Miraculous Recovery from Stroke," *Ebony* (December 1982), 64.

374 *Then there was the visit: The Washington Charity Awards Dinner*, souvenir program, n.d.

374   *Still, this was not his gig:* Tape-recorded interview of Miles Davis by Jeff Davis of BAM magazine on 12 June 1984.

374   *Even the blandest of pleasantries:* AUTOBIOGRAPHY, 380–381.

375   *"After this, I knew it was over":* Ibid., 382.

375   *Director John Schlesinger sounded:* It was not broadcast until the next year, on November 15, 1986.

375   *"I've been thinking—what would":* Richard Harrington, "Miles Davis Makes Peace with Himself," *Chicago Sun Times,* 16 June 1985, 4.

375   *Or he communicated by:* Adam Holzman quoted in Mark Dery and Bob Doerschuk, "Miles Davis: His Keyboardists Past and Present— Bobby Irving and Adam Holzman," *Keyboard* (October 1987), 82–85.

376   *"It was incredibly nerve-racking":* Carr, *Miles Davis,* 445-446.

377   *"The older you get":* AUTOBIOGRAPHY, 364.

378   *"He went from some esoteric":* Lolis Eric Elie, "An Interview with Wynton Marsalis," *Callaloo* 13, no. 2 (1990): 281–382.

378   *"By the time I came around":* Howard Reich, "Wynton's Decade," *Down Beat* (December 1992), 17.

379   *When the day came that:* Leslie Gourse, *Wynton Marsalis: Skain's Domain* (New York: Schirmer Books, 1999), 89.

Chapter Eleven
Page

381   *"The beginning and the end":* Coryell and Friedman, *Jazz-Rock Fusion,* 40.

382   *It was at this point:* Gérard Rony and Françoise-Marie Coudert, "Miles: Un Jour mon Prince Viendre," *Jazz* (Paris) (September 1986), 20–21.

384   *"When I talked to him":* Richard Williams, "Present Continuous," *Guardian,* 27 October 1995, 13.

384   *Eight days later:* Robben Ford interviewed in *Miles Smiles.*

385   *"Anyone who played with Miles":* Dan Oulette, "Dark Prince in Twilight," *Down Beat* (May 2001), 26

385   *In early 1987, Miles:* AUTOBIOGRAPHY, 383.

385   *"Dorothy, music don't have":* Ibid.

385   *Other members of:* Tingen, *Miles Beyond,* 254.

386   *Even Miles' birthday parties:* Leonard Feather, "Los Angeles Times Calendar," *Los Angeles Times,* 8 June 1986, 2.

387   *His relationship with Cicely:* TROUPE COLLECTION.

387   *"Women get too frisky":* Ken Frankling. "Miles Davis at Age 60: All He Wants Is Respect," *Chicago Sun-Times,* 16 May 1986, 20.

387   *During his travels in Japan:* Giacomo Pellicciotti, "Mode e Mood de Miles," *Jazz Magazine* (Paris) (November 1983), 32–34.

388   *In The Andy Warhol Diaries:* Pat Hatchett, ed., *The Andy Warhol Diaries* (New York: Warner Books, 1989), 809.

388   *Davis took to the runway:* Ibid.; Koshin Satoh and Miles Davis, *The Best to Best Miles* (San Francisco: Cadence Books, 1992), 49–60.

388   *Andy was clearly very sick:* Victor Bockris, *Warhol* (New York: Da Capo, 1997), 486.

388   *Miller finished the score:* Ted Drozdowski, "Doin' the Rat Dance," *Musician* (May 1989), 44.

389   *(Miles' role in the film:* Michael Zwerin, "Miles the Movie Star— Dingo," "Culturekiosque," www.culturekiosque.com/jazz/miles/ rhemile18.html.

389   *Hooker said, "When":* Murray, *Boogie Man,* 455.

389   *Hopper embellished the local color:* Album notes to the *Original Motion Picture Soundtrack to The Hot Spot,* Antilles 422-846 813-2.

391   *Bassist Benny Reitveld described:* Benny Rietveld, album liner notes to Miles Davis, *Live Around the World,* Warner Brothers 9 46032-2.

392   *Guitarist Jean-Paul Bourelly:* Tingen, *Miles Beyond,* 243.

392   *"Al Foster and I were":* JAZZ CENTRAL STATION.

392   *At the end of 1988:* Tingen, *Miles Beyond,* 257–258.

393   *He was convinced:* See also Quincy Troupe, *Miles and Me* (Berkeley: University of California Press, 2000), 107–109.

393   *Another level of complexity:* Beverly Williston, "'Roots' Cicely Tyson 'Devastated' as AIDS Strikes Ex-husband, Jazz Legend Miles Davis," *Star,* 2 February 1988.

393   *Miles denied the story:* Leonard Feather, "Miles Davis to Take a Break at San Juan Capistrano," *Los Angeles Times,* 15 June 1989.

393   *In a strange and flirtatious interview:* In her book *Tarnished Angels* (New York: Thunder's Mouth's Press, 1991), 329–331, Lee says they met in March 1989, and she left without doing the interview.

393   *Without confirming or denying:* Troupe, *Miles and Me,* 76–78.

394   *When he was back:* Ibid., 69.

394   *Malibu was reserved:* Feather, "Miles Davis to Take a Break."

394   *There was something for:* Pearl Cleage, "Mad at Miles: A Black Woman's Guide to the Truth," in *Deal with the Devil* (New York: Ballantine Books, 1993), 19; Stanley Crouch, "Play the Right Thing," *New Republic,* 12 February 1990.

395   *"He made a game of":* Leonard Feather, "Miles Davis: Jazz Trailblazer or Racist Turncoat?" *Gannett Suburban Newspapers,* 3 October 1991, sect. B.

395   *He was proud of:* TROUPE COLLECTION.

396   *In one of his last interviews:* Francis Marmande, "Recontre à New York avec le trompettiste Américain," *Le Monde,* 20 June 1991, 18–19.

396   *Quincy Troupe said that:* Cheo Taylor Tyehimba, "Miles and Quincy: An Interview," www.africana.com, 17 March 2000.

397   *Wayne Shorter said that:* Krystian Brodacki, "Wayne Shorter Remembers Miles Davis," *Jazz Forum* 1 (1992), 28.

397   *"When he called, he said":* Jackie McLean interview with David Yaffe.

398   *In August, Jack Lang:* New York Times, 20 September 1991.

398   *Miles began work:* CBC.

398   *Miles had done some:* www.bjazz.cow.miles__pierson.dfm.

398   *Mitchell recalled that Miles:* Danie Levitin, "A Conversation with Joni Mitchell," in *The Joni Mitchell Companion* (New York: Schirmer, 2000), 179.

398   *"He had lost so much weight":* Brodacki, "Wayne Shorter Remembers," 28.

400   *Even the cause of his death:* Globe, 1 October 1991.

400   *Jim Rose, his former road manager:* CBC. *Jet* magazine reported that

before his death, Miles had made a $170,000 down payment on a $1.7 million apartment and was suing at the time of his death because he knew he was dying. "Attorney for Miles Davis' Estate Fights for $170,000 Payment Made on Apt.," *Jet* (December 1993–January 1994), 38. The exact amount of money in his estate was never made public, though it was estimated to have been in the millions. It was reportedly divided among his son Erin (40 percent), his daughter Cheryl (20 percent), his nephew Vincent Wilburn, Jr. (10 percent), his brother, Vernon (15 percent), and his sister, Dorothy Wilburn (15 percent). "Miles Davis Excludes Two of His Sons from His Will," *Jet*, 11 November 1991, 58–59.

400   *Cicely Tyson was not:* Author's interview with Jean Bach.

400   *The monument reads:* "Solar" is a melody that guitarist Chuck Wayne contended that he wrote. See "Interview with Chuck Wayne," *Cadence* (August 1996), 11–12.

401   *["When you die they might"]:* Mark Rowland, "Miles Davis Is a Living Legend and You're Not," in Mark Rowland and Tony Scherman, eds., *The Jazz Musician: Fifteen Years of Interviews. The Best of* Musician Magazine, (New York: St. Martin's Press, 1994), 151–152.

401   *There was talk of:* Oulette, "Dark Prince in Twilight," 29, and TROUPE COLLECTION.

401   *Larry Rivers recalled another:* Larry Rivers, *What Did I Do?* 56–57.

402   *Even the press:* "More on Miles," *Daily News*, 10 October 1991.

CODA
Page

403   *"Miles plays the way":* Art Farmer interviewed by Val Wilmer. My thanks to her for the quote.

403   *Margurite Eskridge for one:* Tingen, *Miles Beyond*, 19.

404   *"Miles was the most:* Author's interview with Amiri Baraka.

404   *"People who don't change":* AUTOBIOGRAPHY, 396.

404   *"The public likes starts":* Murphy, *Miles to Go*, 36–37.

405   *But he was also aware:* "The McCrary Report," WNEW (New York), 1991.

405   *When asked about Miles':* Brodacki, "Wayne Shorter Remembers," 26.

406   *"Sometimes when Miles was":* Jon Garelick, "Wayne Shorter Explains Why He Confounds His Critics," *Boston Phoenix*, November 1995, 23–30.

407   *"When Miles Plays":* Gil Evans quoted in Breskin, "Searching for Miles," 50.

407   *"To sum up Miles":* Brodacki, "Wayne Shorter Remembers," 26.

407   *Bryant Gumbel: Today*, NBC TV, June 1984.

Acknowledgments

IN MY QUEST for help on this book I was aided by hundreds of people. I surely have missed some in my thanks below, and where I have, please forgive me. Despite my best efforts, I was not able to reach everyone of importance to Miles Davis. Some could not be located, and several people declined an interview because of their own publication plans. I look forward to their books. Meanwhile, I trust they will forgive me for any errors about their roles in this story.

I am especially grateful for the generosity of Anita Evans, Miles Evans, and Noah Evans; Bob Belden, Peter Bradley, Henri Renaud, Anthony Braxton, Beverly Bentley, and Bill Laswell; Buddy Gist, Charles Graham, Adam Holtzman, Chris Albertson, Peter Shukat, David Amram, René Urtreger, and David X. Young (of New York City); George Coleman, Allen Eager, George Avakian, Gregory Davis, Jackie Battle, Jean Bach, James Jordan, and Jo Gelbard; and Gary Goodrow, Michael McDonald, Joe McPhee, Dave Brubeck, Phil Schaap, Scott Ross, Stan Levey, and Teo Macero.

Three people should be singled out as having been extraordinarily helpful to me: the late Vernon Davis, brother of Miles, who accepted me into his home, welcomed my project, and from the very beginning made me feel that it was something that I could and should do; Eugene Redman, the poet laureate of East St. Louis, who guided me through the history and culture of his hometown as he has done so many other writers, and educated me to the complexities of life in Southern Illinois; and Irene Davis Oliver, a very resourceful woman, who shared with me the story of her life with Miles Davis.

I owe much to other writers, many of whom shared their interviews and phone numbers with me, and gave me writerly advice: Francis Davis, David Yaffe, Gary Giddins, Gerald Early, Graham Lock, Greg Tate, Howard Mandel, Ira Gitler, Ingrid Monson, James Hale, Laurent Cugny, Mike Zwerin, Robert O'Meally, Stanley Crouch, Victor Svorinich, Williard Jenkins, Al Aronowitz, Val Wilmer, Nat Hentoff,

Alan Nahigian, Lewis Porter, and Mary Dearborn. Jan Lohmann, author of *The Sound of Miles Davis: The Discography: A Listing of Records and Tapes, 1945–1991*, was also helpful to me in many ways. I owe an obvious debt to Paul Tingen, Ashley Kahn, Steve Rowland, and Quincy Troupe, and, for that matter, to every writer who has ever written about Miles Davis.

For many other favors, I thank Adam Zelinka, Albert McMahill, Anna at *The Face*, Arnold J. Shaw, Ben Cawthra, Bert Sugar, David Young (of Austin, Texas), Ira Berger, Don Sinkler, Donald Lashomb, Jack Zeitz, Jerry Gordon, Jim Chiarelli, Ken Frankling, Larry Nai, Mary Schmidt Campbell, Gray Gundaker, Maryann and Harold Ince, Maurice Marouiani, Richard J. Koloda, Alain Le Roux, Robert Levey, Roger W. Hunter, Alan Trachtenberg, Stephen Lajoie, Steve Asseta, and all of those who populate the Miles Davis mailing list (http://www.wam.umd.edu/~losinp/music/md_sites.html#listserv).

I would like to call attention to the cooperation and help extended to me by Loanne Rios-Kong of the Sony Music Photo Archives. At Yale University, I am thankful to the Whitney Humanities Center and to Provost Allison Richards for support toward research expenses for this book. I also owe a special acknowledgment to all of the students in my classes on Miles Davis for their suggestions and comments.

Six libraries were especially helpful to me: the Institute of Jazz Studies, Rutgers University at Newark (where Edward Berger, Vincent Pelote, Dan Morgenstern and the staff were always invaluable); the Schomberg Center for Research in Black Culture of the New York Public Library (my thanks especially to Director Howard Dodson and Diana Lachatanere, Head Archivist, Manuscripts, Archives, and Rare Books); the Lila Acheson Wallace Library at the Juilliard School (Laura Drake, Jane Gottlieb, Associate Vice President for Library and Information Sources, and Jeni Dahmus, Archivist); the Jazz Institut of Darmstadt, where Wolfram Knauer was my guide; the New York Public Library for the Performing Arts (George Boziwick, Curator of the American Music Collection); and at my own institution, Yale University, the always patient and worthy staff of Interlibrary Loan.

Record stores are also libraries of a sort, and I appreciate the help and encouragement given to me by Ed Krech of Integrity 'N Music of Wethersfield, Connecticut; Fred Cohen of the Jazz Record Center of New York City; Jack Woker of Stereo Jack's in Cambridge, Massachusetts; Sally White of Sally's Records of Westport, Connecticut; and Bruce Lee Gallanter and Manny Maris of Downtown Records in New York City.

Maxine Gordon conducted some of the interviews for this book, but more than that, she shared with me her special knowledge of the jazz world. Lance Duerfahrd and Michael Call were my colleagues with translations, and Rebekah Grossman with interviews. In matters both musical and editorial, I benefited from close readings by Rita Putnam. At Simon & Schuster my editor Robert Bender treated me with exemplary patience, kindness, and helpful readings. He has made this the most memorable experience I have ever had in publishing. I also want to recognize the considerable help and kindness of others at Simon & Schuster, especially Johanna Li and Victoria Meyer. Thanks to Patty Romanowski for her valuable help with the discography.

My agent, Sarah Lazin, was never less than cool throughout the whole process, for which I am eternally grateful. Mathew Szwed and Marilyn Szwed, as always, helped in every way possible, including editing and even interviewing. And finally, this book is dedicated to three extraordinary individuals who I am proud to call my friends: Roger Abrahams, Dan Rose, and Robert Farris Thompson. They have taught me more than I can ever acknowledge.

Selected Miles Davis Discography

THIS DISCOGRAPHY primarily contains the principal recordings of Miles Davis in their currently available forms on CD, with more detail on recordings I have referred to in the text. Those seeking far more detailed and complete listings might consult (as I have done) Jan Lohmann's *The Sound of Miles Davis: The Discography: A Listing of Records and Tapes, 1945–1991* (Copenhagen: JazzMedia, 1992), Peter Losin's *Miles Ahead* (http://www.wam.umd.edu/~losinp/music/miles_ahead.html), Thomas Westphal's *The Missing Links* (http://www.snafu.de/~miles/music/missing.htm), and Enrico Merlin's sessionography (1967–1991) in Paul Tingen's *Miles Beyond* (New York: Billboard Books, 2001). MD = Miles Davis.

***Young Miles, Volume 1: 1945–1946* (Masters of Jazz MJCD 131)**
04/25/45: MD (tpt), Herbie Fields (ts, cl), Henry "Rubberlegs" Williams (voc), Teddy Brannon (p), Leonard Gaskin (b), Ed Nicholson (d).
    "That's the Stuff You Gotta Watch" [takes 1, 2, 3], "Pointless Mama Blues," "Deep Sea Blues," "Bring It On Home" [takes 1, 2, 3].
11/25/45: MD (tpt), Charlie Parker (as), Dizzy Gillespie (p, tpt), Sadik Hakim (p), Dillon "Curly" Russell (b), Max Roach (d).
    "Billie's Bounce [takes 1, 2, 3, 4, 5], "Now's the Time" [takes 1, 2, 3, 4] "Thriving on a Riff" [takes 1, 2, 3].
03/00/46: MD (tpt), Charlie Parker (as), Joe Albany (p), Addison Farmer (b), Chuck Thompson (d).
    "Anthropology," "Billie's Bounce," "Blue 'n' Boogie," "All the Things You Are," "Ornithology."
***Charlie Parker: The Complete Savoy and Dial Studio Recordings* (Savoy 92911-2)**
1945–1948
***Young Miles, Volume 2: 1946* (Masters of Jazz MJCD 151)**
03/28/46; 03/31/46; 04/00/46
***Bopping the Blues* (Black Lion BLCD 760102)**
10/18/46: MD (tpt), Gene Ammons (ts), Connie Wainwright (g), Linton Garner (p), Tommy Potter (d), Art Blakey (d), Earl Coleman (voc), Ann Baker (Hathaway) (voc).
    "Don't Sing Me the Blues" [takes 1, 2], "I've Always Got the Blues" [takes 1 (inc), 2, 3], "Don't Explain to Me Baby" [takes 1, 2, 3, 4] "Baby, Won't You Make Up Your Mind" [takes 1, 2, 3].

The Complete Birth of the Cool (Capitol CDP 94550)
09/04/48; 09/18/48; 01/21/49; 04/22/49; 03/09/50
Cool Boppin': Historic Broadcasts from the Royal Roost, 1948–1949 (Fresh Sound FSCD 1008)
09/04/48; 09/18/48; 02/19/49; 02/26/49
Birth of the Cool (RVG Edition) (Capitol CDP 30117) (Original: Capitol M 11026)
01/21/49: MD (tpt), Kai Winding (tb), Junior Collins (frh), Bill Barber (tuba), Lee Konitz (as), Gerry Mulligan (bs), Al Haig (p), Joe Shulman (b), Max Roach (d).
"Move," "Jeru," "Hallucinations [Budo]," "Godchild."
04/22/49: MD (tpt), J. J. Johnson (tb), Sandy Siegelstein (frh), Bill Barber (tuba), Lee Konitz (as), Gerry Mulligan (bs), John Lewis (p), Nelson Boyd (b), Kenny Clarke (d).
"Venus de Milo," "Boplicity," "Israel," "Rouge."
03/09/50: MD (tpt), J. J. Johnson (tb), Gunther Schuller (frh), Bill Barber (tuba), Lee Konitz (as), Gerry Mulligan (bs), Al McKibbon (b), Max Roach (d), Kenny "Pancho" Hagood (voc).
"Moon Dreams," "Deception," "Rocker," "Darn That Dream."
The Complete Blue Note Recordings of Fats Navarro and Tadd Dameron (Blue Note CDP 33373)
04/21/49
Sarah Vaughan in Hi-Fi (Columbia CK 65117)
03/18/50; 03/19/50
Bird: The Complete Charlie Parker on Verve (Verve 837 141)
01/17/51
Miles Davis and Horns (OJC-053) (Original: Prestige 7025)
01/17/51: MD (tpt), Bennie Green (tb), Sonny Rollins (ts), John Lewis (p), Percy Heath (b), Roy Haynes (d).
"Morpheus," "Down," "Blue Room" [takes 1, 2], "Whispering."
02/19/53: MD (tpt), Sonny Truitt (tb), Al Cohn (ts), Zoot Sims (ts), John Lewis (p), Leonard Gaskin (b), Kenny Clarke (d).
"Tasty Pudding," "Willie the Wailer," "Floppy," "For Adults Only."
Dig (OJC-005) (Original: Prestige 7012)
10/05/51: MD (tpt), Jackie McLean (as), Sonny Rollins (ts), Walter Bishop, Jr. (p), Tommy Potter (b), Art Blakey (d).
"Dig," "It's Only a Paper Moon," "Denial," "Bluing," "Out of the Blue," "Conception," "My Old Flame."
Collectors' Items (OJC-07) (Original: Prestige 7044)
01/30/53: MD (tpt), Sonny Rollins (ts), Charlie Parker (ts), Walter Bishop, Jr. (p), Percy Heath (b), Philly Joe Jones (d).
"The Serpent's Tooth" [takes 1, 2] "'Round Midnight," "Compulsion."
03/16/56: MD (tpt), Sonny Rollins (ts), Tommy Flanagan (p), Paul Chambers (b), Arthur Taylor (d).
"No Line," "Vierd Blues [Trane's Blues]," "In Your Own Sweet Way."
Miles Davis, Volume 1 (RVG Edition) (Blue Note 32610) (Original: Blue Note BLP 5013, BLP 5040)

05/09/52: MD (tpt), J. J. Johnson (tb), Jackie McLean (as), Gil Coggins (p), Oscar Pettiford (b), Kenny Clarke (d).

"Dear Old Stockholm," "Chance It (Max Is Making Wax)" [plus alt. take],
"Dig" [plus alt. take], "Woody 'n' You" [plus alt. take], "Yesterdays," "How
Deep Is the Ocean?"

03/06/54: MD (tpt), Horace Silver (p), Percy Heath (b), Art Blakey (d).

"Take Off," "Lazy Susan," "The Leap," "Well, You Needn't," "Weirdo," "It
Never Entered My Mind."

**Miles Davis, Volume 2 (RVG Edition) (Blue Note 32611) (Original: Blue Note BLP
5022)**

04/20/53: MD (tpt), J. J. Johnson (tb), Jimmy Heath (ts), Gil Coggins (p), Percy Heath
(b), Art Blakey (d).

"Kelo" [plus alt. take], "Enigma" [plus alt. take], "Ray's Idea" [plus alt.
take], "Tempus Fugit" [plus alt. take], "C.T.A." [plus alt. take], "I Waited
for You."

Blue Haze (OJC-093) (Original: Prestige 7054)

05/19/53: MD (tpt), John Lewis (p), Charles Mingus (p), Percy Heath (b), Max Roach (d).

"Smooch," "When Lights Are Low," "Tune Up," "Miles Ahead."

03/15/54: MD (tpt), Horace Silver (p), Percy Heath (b), Art Blakey (d).

"Four," "Old Devil Moon," "Blue Haze."

04/03/54: MD (tpt), Dave Schildkraut (as), Horace Silver (p), Percy Heath (b), Kenny
Clarke (d).

"I'll Remember April."

Walkin' (OJC-213) (Original: Prestige 7076)

04/03/54: MD (tpt), Dave Schildkraut (as), Horace Silver (p), Percy Heath (b), Kenny
Clarke (d).

"Solar," "You Don't Know What Love Is," "Love Me or Leave Me."

04/29/54: MD (tpt), J. J. Johnson (tb), Eli "Lucky" Thompson (ts), Horace Silver (p),
Percy Heath (b), Kenny Clarke (d).

"Walkin'," "Blue 'n' Boogie."

Bags' Groove (OJC-245) (Original: Prestige 7109)

06/29/54: MD (tpt), Sonny Rollins (ts), Horace Silver (p), Percy Heath (b), Kenny
Clarke (d).

"Airegin," "Oleo," "But Not for Me" [takes 1, 2] "Doxy."

12/24/54: MD (tpt), Milt Jackson (vb), Thelonious Monk (p), Percy Heath (b), Kenny
Clarke (d).

"Bags' Groove" [takes 1, 2].

Miles Davis and the Modern Jazz Giants (OJC-347) (Original: Prestige 7150)

12/24/54: MD (tpt), Milt Jackson (vb), Thelonious Monk (p), Percy Heath (b), Kenny
Clarke (d).

"The Man I Love" [takes 1, 2], "Swing Spring," "Bemsha Swing."

10/26/56: MD (tpt), John Coltrane (ts), William "Red" Garland (p), Paul Chambers (b),
Philly Joe Jones (d).

"'Round Midnight."

The Musings of Miles (OJC-004-2) (Original: Prestige 7007)
06/07/55: MD (tpt), William "Red" Garland (p), Oscar Pettiford (b), Philly Joe Jones (d).
"Will You Still Be Mine?," "I See Your Face Before Me," "I Didn't," "A Gal in Calico," "A Night in Tunisia," "Green Haze."

Blue Moods (OJC-043) (Original: Debut 120)
07/09/55: MD (tpt), Britt Woodman (tb), Teddy Charles (vb), Charles Mingus (b), Elvin Jones (d).
"Nature Boy," "Alone Together," "There's No You," "Easy Living."

'Round About Midnight (Columbia/Legacy 85201) (Original: Columbia CL 949)
10/26/55: MD (tpt), John Coltrane (ts), William "Red" Garland (p), Paul Chambers (b) Philly Joe Jones (d).
"Ah-Leu-Cha" [takes 4, 5], "Little Melonae" [takes 2, 3], "Budo" [take 8].
06/05/56: MD (tpt), John Coltrane (ts), William "Red" Garland (p), Paul Chambers (b), Philly Joe Jones (d).
"Bye Bye Blackbird" [take 3], "Tadd's Delight," [take 2], "Dear Old Stockholm" [take 1].
09/10/56: MD (tpt), John Coltrane (ts), William "Red" Garland (p), Paul Chambers (b), Philly Joe Jones (d).
"'Round Midnight" [take 1], "Sweet Sue, Just You" [take 8], "All of You" [take 2].

The Complete Columbia Recordings of Miles Davis and John Coltrane (Columbia C6K 65833)
10/26/55; 06/05/56; 09/10/56; 02/04/58; 03/04/58; 05/26/58; 07/03/55; 09/09/58; 03/02/59; 04/22/59; 03/20/61; 03/21/61

The New Miles Davis Quintet (OJC 006) (Original: Prestige 7014)
11/16/55: MD (tpt), John Coltrane (ts), William "Red" Garland (p), Paul Chambers (b), Philly Joe Jones (d).
"Just Squeeze Me," "There Is No Greater Love," "How Am I to Know?," "S'posin'," "Miles' Theme (The Theme)," "Stablemates."

Facets (CBS (F) 62637)
10/27/55: MD (tpt), John Coltrane (ts), William "Red" Garland (p), Paul Chambers (b), Philly Joe Jones (d).
"Budo" [take 8].
09/10/56: MD (tpt), John Coltrane (ts), William "Red" Garland (p), Paul Chambers (b), Philly Joe Jones (d).
"Sweet Sue, Just You" [take 8].
10/20/56: MD (flh), J. J. Johnson (tb), Joe Wilder (tpt), Bernie Glow (tpt), Arthur Statter (tpt), Joe Wilder (tpt), Mel Broiles (tpt), Carmine Fornarotto (tpt), Isidore Blank (tpt), Jimmy Buffington (frh), Joe Singer (frh), Ray Alonge (frh), Art Sussman (frh), J. J. Johnson (tb), Urbie Green (tb), John Clark (tb), Bill Barber (tuba), Milt Hinton (b), Osie Johnson (d), Dick Horowitz (perc).
"Three Little Feelings."
10/23/56: MD (same personnel as 10/20/56).
"Jazz Suite for Brass (Poem for Brass)."

05/26/58: MD (tpt), Julian "Cannonball" Adderley (as), John Coltrane (ts), Bill Evans (p), Paul Chambers (b), Jimmy Cobb (d).

06/25/58: Michel Legrand Orchestra. MD (tpt), Herbie Maun (fl), Jerome Richardson (cl, bar), Phil Woods (as), John Coltrane (ts), Betty Glamann (harp), Eddie Costa (vb), Bill Evans (p), Barry Galbraith (g), Paul Chambers (b), Kenny Dennis (d), Michel Legrand (arr, cond). (Mann Richardson, Woods, and Coltrane do not appear on "Django.")

"The Jitterbug Waltz," "'Round Midnight," "Wild Man Blues," "Django."

08/21/62: MD (tpt), Frank Rehak (tb), Wayne Shorter (ts), Paul Chambers (b), Jimmy Cobb (d), Willie Bobo (bgo), Bob Dorough (p, voc).

"Blue Xmas (To Whom It May Concern)."

08/23/62: MD (tpt), Frank Rehak (tb), Wayne Shorter (ts), Paul Chambers (b), Jimmy Cobb (d), Willie Bobo (bgo).

"Devil May Care."

Circle in the Round (CBS/Sony CSCS 5340/1) (Original: Columbia KC2 36278)

10/26/55: MD (tpt), John Coltrane (ts), William "Red" Garland (p), Paul Chambers (b), Philly Joe Jones (d).

"Two Bass Hit" [takes 2,5].

05/26/58: MD (tpt), Julian "Cannonball" Adderley (as), John Coltrane (ts), Bill Evans (p), Paul Chambers (b), Jimmy Cobb (d).

"Love for Sale" [take 1].

03/21/61: MD (tpt), Hank Mobley (ts), John Coltrane (ts), Wynton Kelly (p), Paul Chambers (b), Jimmy Cobb (d), Philly Joe Jones (d).

"Blues No. 2" [take 7].

12/04/67: MD (tpt, chimes), Wayne Shorter (ts), Herbie Hancock (celeste), Joe Beck (g), Ron Carter (b), Tony Williams (d).

"Circle in the Round."

01/16/68: MD (tpt), Wayne Shorter (ts), Herbie Hancock (p), George Benson (g), Ron Carter (b), Tony Williams (d).

"Teo's Bag."

02/15/68: MD (tpt), Wayne Shorter (ts), George Benson (g), Herbie Hancock (p), Ron Carter (b), Tony Williams (d).

"Side Car I," "Side Car II" [take 4], "Sanctuary" [take 7].

11/12/68: MD (tpt), Wayne Shorter (ts), Herbie Hancock (el p, el harpsichord), Chick Corea (el p, org), Dave Holland (b, el b), Tony Williams (d).

"Splash."

01/27/70: MD (tpt), Wayne Shorter (ss), Bennie Maupin (bcl), Chick Corea (el p), Josef Zawinul (el p), John McLaughlin (g), Khalil Balakrishna (sitar), Dave Holland (el b), Billy Cobham (d), Jack DeJohnette (d), Airto Moreira (perc).

"Guinnevere."

Relaxin' with the Miles Davis Quintet (Prestige OJCCD-190-2) (Original: Prestige 7129)

05/11/56: MD (tpt), John Coltrane (ts), William "Red" Garland (p), Paul Chambers (b), Philly Joe Jones (d).

"If I Were a Bell" [with chatter], "You're My Everything" [with false start + chatter], "I Could Write a Book," "Oleo" [with false start + chatter].

10/26/56: MD (tpt), John Coltrane (ts), William "Red" Garland (p), Paul Chambers (b), Philly Joe Jones (d).

"It Could Happen to You" [with closing chatter], "Woody 'n' You" [with closing chatter].

Steamin' with the Miles Davis Quintet (OJC-291) (Original: Prestige 7200)

05/11/56: MD (tpt), John Coltrane (ts), William "Red" Garland (p), Paul Chambers (b), Philly Joe Jones (d).

"Surrey with the Fringe on Top," "Salt Peanuts," "Something I Dreamed Last Night," "Diane," "When I Fall in Love."

10/26/56: MD (tpt), John Coltrane (ts), William "Red" Garland (p), Paul Chambers (b), Philly Joe Jones (d).

"Well, You Needn't."

Workin' with the Miles Davis Quintet (IJC-296) (Original: Prestige 7166)

05/11/56: MD (tpt), John Coltrane (ts), William "Red" Garland (p), Paul Chambers (b), Philly Joe Jones (d).

"It Never Entered My Mind," "Four," "In Your Own Sweet Way," "The Theme" [take 1], "Trane's Blues," "Ahmad's Blues."

10/26/56: MD (tpt), John Coltrane (ts), William "Red" Garland (p), Paul Chambers (b), Philly Joe Jones (d).

"Half Nelson."

The Birth of the Third Stream (Columbia/Legacy CK 64929) (Original: Columbia CL 941)

10/20/56: MD (flh), J. J. Johnson (tb), Joe Wilder (tpt), Bernie Glow (tpt), Arthur Statter (tpt), Joe Wilder (tpt), Mel Broiles (tpt), Carmine Fomarotto (tpt), Isidore Blank (tpt), Jimmy Buffington (frh), Joe Singer (frh), Ray Alonge (frh), Art Sussman (frh), Urbie Green (tb), John Clark (tb), Bill Barber (tuba), Milt Hinton (b), Osie Johnson (d), Dick Horowitz (perc).

"Three Little Feelings."

10/23/56: MD (flh), J. J. Johnson (tb), Joe Wilder (tpt), Bernie Glow (tpt), Arthur Statter (tpt), Joe Wilder (tpt), Mel Broiles (tpt), Carmine Fornarotto (tpt), Isidore Blank (tpt), Jimmy Buffington (frh), Joe Singer (frh), Ray Alonge (frh), Art Sussman (frh), Urbie Green (tb), John Clark (tb), Bill Barber (tuba), Milt Hinton (b), Osie Johnson (d), Dick Horowitz (perc).

"Jazz Suite for Brass (Poem for Brass)," "Pharaoh."

Cookin' with the Miles Davis Quintet (OJC-128) (Original: Prestige 7094)

10/26/56: MD (tpt), John Coltrane (ts), William "Red" Garland (p), Paul Chambers (b), Philly Joe Jones (d).

"My Funny Valentine," "Blues by Five," "Airegin," "Tune Up," "When Lights Are Low"

Miles Ahead (Columbia/Legacy CK 53225) (Original: Columbia CL 1041)

05/06/57: MD (flh), Ernie Royal (tpt), Bernie Glow (tpt), Louis Mucci (tpt), Taft Jordan (tpt), Johnny Carisi (tpt), Frank Rehak (tb), Jimmy Cleveland (tb), Joe Bennett (tb), Tom Mitchell (tb), Willie Ruff (frh), Tony Miranda (frh), Bill Barber (tuba), Romeo Penque (fl, cl, bcl, oboe), Sid Cooper (fl, cl), Lee Konitz (as), Danny Bank (bcl), Paul Chambers (b), Arthur Taylor (d), Gil Evans (arr, cond).

"The Maids of Cadiz," "The Duke."

05/10/57: MD (flh), Ernie Royal (tpt), Bernie Glow (tpt), Louis Mucci (tpt), Taft Jordan (tpt), Johnny Carisi (tpt), Frank Rehak (tb), Jimmy Cleveland (tb), Joe Bennett (tb), Tom Mitchell (tb), Willie Ruff (frh), Tony Miranda (frh), Bill Barber (tuba), Romeo Penque (fl, cl, bcl, oboe), Sid Cooper (fl, cl), Lee Konitz (as), Danny Bank (bcl), Paul Chambers (b), Arthur Taylor (d), Gil Evans (arr, cond).

"Miles Ahead."

05/23/57: MD (flh), Ernie Royal (tpt), Bernie Glow (tpt), Louis Mucci (tpt), Taft Jordan (tpt), Johnny Carisi (tpt), Frank Rehak (tb), Jimmy Cleveland (tb), Joe Bennett (tb), Tom Mitchell (tb), Willie Ruff (frh), Jimmy Buffington (frh), Bill Barber (tuba), Romeo Penque (fl, cl, bcl, oboe), Sid Cooper (fl, cl), Lee Konitz (as), Danny Bank (bcl), Paul Chambers (b), Arthur Taylor (d), Gil Evans (arr, cond).

"Springsville," "Blues for Pablo," "New Rhumba."

05/27/57: MD (flh), Ernie Royal (tpt), Bernie Glow (tpt), Louis Mucci (tpt), Taft Jordan (tpt), Johnny Carisi (tpt), Frank Rehak (tb), Jimmy Cleveland (tb), Joe Bennett (tb), Tom Mitchell (tb), Willie Ruff (frh), Tony Miranda (frh), Bill Barber (tuba), Romeo Penque (fl, cl, oboe), Eddie Caine (cl, fl), Lee Konitz (as), Danny Bank (bcl), Wynton Kelly (p), Paul Chambers (b), Arthur Taylor (d), Gil Evans (arr, cond).

"My Ship," "The Meaning of the Blues," "Lament," "I Don't Wanna Be Kissed."

The Complete Miles Davis/Gil Evans Studio Recordings (Columbia/Legacy CK 67397)

05/06/57–02/16/68

Ascenseur pour l'échafaud: Complete Recordings (Fontana 836305-2) (Original: Columbia CL 1268)

12/04/57: MD (tpt), Barney Wilen (ts), René Urtreger (p), Pierre Michelot (b), Kenny Clarke (d).

"Nuit sur les Champs-Elysées" [takes 1, 2, 3, 4], "Assassinat' [takes 1, 2, 3], "Motel," "Final" [takes 1, 2, 3], "Ascenseur," "Le Petit Bal" [takes 1, 2], "Séquence Voiture" [takes 1, 2].

Complete Amsterdam Concert (Celluloid 668 232)

12/08/57: MD (tpt), Barney Wilen (ts), René Urtreger (p), Pierre Michelot (b), Christian Garros (d).

"Woody 'n' You," "Bags' Groove," "What's New?," "But Not for Me," "A Night in Tunisia," "Four" [with closing theme], "Walkin'," "Well, You Needn't," "'Round Midnight," "Lady Bird" [with closing theme].

Milestones (Columbia/Legacy CK 85203) (Original: Columbia CL 1193)

02/04/58: MD (tpt), Julian "Cannonball" Adderley (as), John Coltrane (ts), William "Red" Garland (p), Paul Chambers (b), Philly Joe Jones (d).

> "Two Bass Hit," "Milestones" [take 3]," "Billy Boy" [take 1], "Straight, No Chaser."

03/04/58: MD (tpt, p), Julian "Cannonball" Adderley (as), John Coltrane (ts), William "Red" Garland (p), Paul Chambers (b), Philly Joe Jones (d).

> "Dr. Jackle," "Sid's Ahead," "Two Bass Hit" [alt. take], "Milestones" [alt. take], "Straight, No Chaser" [alt. take].

'58 Sessions **(Columbia CK 47835)**

05/26/58: MD (tpt), Julian "Cannonball" Adderley (as), John Coltrane (ts), Bill Evans (p), Paul Chambers (b), Jimmy Cobb (d).

> "On Green Dolphin Street" [take 1], "Fran-Dance" [take 2], "Stella by Starlight" [take 7], "Love for Sale" [take 1].

09/09/58: MD (tpt), Julian "Cannonball" Adderley (as), John Coltrane (ts), Bill Evans (p), Paul Chambers (b), Jimmy Cobb (d).

> "Straight, No Chaser," "The Theme," "My Funny Valentine," "Oleo."

Legrand Jazz **(Philips (F) 830 074) (Original: Columbia CL 1250)**

06/25/58: MD (tpt), John Coltrane (ts), Phil Woods (as), Jerome Richardson (bs, bel), Herbie Mann (fl), Barry Galbraith (g), Betty Glamann (harp), Eddie Costa (vb), Bill Evans (p), Paul Chambers (b), Kenny Dennis (d), Michel Legrand (arr, cond).

> "The Jitterbug Waltz," "'Round Midnight," "Django," "Wild Man Blues."

Miles Davis at Newport 1958 **(Columbia/Legacy CK 85202) (Original: Columbia CL 2178)**

07/03/58: MD (tpt), Julian "Cannonball" Adderley (as), John Coltrane (ts), Bill Evans (p), Paul Chambers (b), Jimmy Cobb (d), Willis Conover (announcer).

> Introduction by Willis Conover, "Ah-Leu-Cha," "Straight, No Chaser," "Fran-Dance," "Two Bass Hit," "Bye Bye Blackbird," "The Theme."

Porgy and Bess **(Sony SRCS 5699) (Original: Columbia CL 1274)**

07/22/58: MD (flh), Ernie Royal (tpt), Johnny Coles (tpt), Bernie Glow (tpt), Louis Mucci (tpt), Joe Bennett (tb), Frank Rehak (tb), Jimmy Cleveland (tb), Dick Hixon (tb), Willie Ruff (frh), Julius Watkins (frh), Gunther Schuller (frh), Bill Barber (tuba), Julian "Cannonball" Adderley (as), Romeo Penque (fl, alto fl, cl), Phil Bodner (fl, alto fl, cl), Danny Bank (alto fl, bcl), Paul Chambers (b), Philly Joe Jones (d), Gil Evans (arr, cond).

> "Gone," "Gone, Gone, Gone," "My Man's Gone Now."

07/29/58: MD (tpt, flh), Ernie Royal (tpt), Johnny Coles (tpt), Bernie Glow (tpt), Louis Mucci (tpt), Joe Bennett (tb), Frank Rehak (tb), Jimmy Cleveland (tb), Dick Hixon (tb), Willie Ruff (frh), Julius Watkins (frh), Gunther Schuller (frh), Bill Barber (tuba), Julian "Cannonball" Adderley (as), Romeo Penque (fl, alto fl, cl), Phil Bodner (fl, alto fl, cl), Danny Bank (alto fl, bcl), Paul Chambers (b), Jimmy Cobb (d), Gil Evans (arr, cond).

> "Bess, You Is My Woman Now," "Fishermen, Strawberry, and Devil Crab," "It Ain't Necessarily So," "Here Come de Honey Man."

08/04/58: MD (flh), Ernie Royal (tpt), Johnny Coles (tpt), Bernie Glow (tpt), Louis Mucci (tpt), Joe Bennett (tb), Frank Rehak (tb), Jimmy Cleveland (tb), Dick Hixon (tb), Willie Ruff (frh), Julius Watkins (frh), Gunther Schuller (frh), Bill Barber (tuba), Julian "Cannonball" Adderley (as), Romeo Penque (fl, alto fl, cl), Jerome Richardson (fl, alto fl, cl), Danny Bank (alto fl, bcl), Paul Chambers (b), Jimmy Cobb (d), Gil Evans (arr, cond).

"Buzzard Song," "Summertime," "Oh Bess, Oh Where's My Bess," "Prayer (Oh Doctor Jesus)," "There's a Boat That's Leaving Soon for New York."

08/10/58: MD (tpt, flh), Ernie Royal (tpt), Bernie Glow (tpt), Louis Mucci (tpt), Joe Bennett (tb), Frank Rehak (tb), Jimmy Cleveland (tb), Dick Hixon (tb), Willie Ruff (frh), Julius Watkins (frh), Gunther Schuller (frh), Bill Barber (tuba), Julian "Cannonball" Adderley (as), Romeo Penque (fl, alto fl, cl), Jerome Richardson (fl, alto fl, cl), Danny Bank (alto fl, bcl), Paul Chambers (b), Jimmy Cobb (d), Gil Evans (arr, cond).

"I Loves You, Porgy."

Jazz at the Plaza, Volume 1 **(Columbia/Legacy 85245) (Original: Columbia PC 32479)**

09/09/58: MD (tpt), Julian "Cannonball" Adderley (as), John Coltrane (ts), Bill Evans (p), Paul Chambers (b), Jimmy Cobb (d).

"Jazz at the Plaza (Straight, No Chaser)," "The Theme," "My Funny Valentine," "If I Were a Bell," "Oleo."

Kind of Blue **(Columbia/Legacy CK 64935) (Original: Columbia CL 1355)**

03/02/59: MD (tpt), Julian "Cannonball" Adderley (as), John Coltrane (ts), Bill Evans (p), Wynton Kelly (p), Paul Chambers (b), Jimmy Cobb (d).

"So What," "Freddie Freeloader," "Blue in Green."

04/22/59: MD (tpt), Julian "Cannonball" Adderley (as), John Coltrane (ts), Bill Evans (p), Paul Chambers (b), Jimmy Cobb (d).

"All Blues," "Flamenco Sketches" [takes 1, 6].

Sketches of Spain **(CBS/Sony CSCS 5142) (Original: Columbia CL 1480)**

11/15, 20/59: MD (tpt, flh), Ernie Royal (tpt), Bernie Glow (tpt), Taft Jordan (tpt), Louis Mucci (tpt), Dick Hixon (tb), Frank Rehak (tb), Jimmy Buffington (frh), John Barrows (frh), Earl Chapin (frh), Jimmy McAllister (tuba), Al Block (fl), Eddie Caine (fl), Romeo Penque (oboe), Harold Feldman (oboe, cl), Jack Knitzer (bssn), Janet Putnam (harp), Paul Chambers (b), Jimmy Cobb (d), Elvin Jones (perc), Jose Manguel (perc), Gil Evans (arr, cond).

"Concierto de Aranjuez (Adagio)." "Concierto de Aranjuez (Part One)," "Concierto de Aranjuez (Part Two)."

03/10/60: MD (tpt), Ernie Royal (tpt), Bernie Glow (tpt), Johnny Coles (tpt), Louis Mucci (tpt), Dick Hixon (tb), Frank Rehak (tb), Jimmy Buffington (frh), Joe Singer (frh), Tony Miranda (frh), Bill Barber (tuba), Al Block (fl), Harold Feldman (fl), Danny Bank (bcl), Romeo Penque (oboe), Jack Knitzer (bssn), Janet Putnam (harp), Paul Chambers (b), Jimmy Cobb (d), Elvin Jones (perc), Jose Manguel (perc), Gil Evans (arr, cond).

"Will o' the Wisp," "The Pan Piper," "Saeta," "Soles," "Song of Our Country."

Directions **(CBS/Sony CSCS 5135/6) (Original: Columbia KC2 36474).**

03/10/60: MD (tpt), Ernie Royal (tpt), Bernie Glow (tpt), Johnny Coles (tpt), Louis Mucci (tpt), Dick Hixon (tb), Frank Rehak (tb), Jimmy Buffington (frh), Joe Singer (frh), Tony Miranda (frh), Bill Barber (tuba), Al Block (fl), Harold Feldman (fl), Danny Bank (bel), Romeo Penque (oboe), Jack Knitzer (bssn), Janet Putnam (harp), Paul Chambers (b), Jimmy Cobb (d), Elvin Jones (perc), Jose Manguel (perc), Gil Evans (arr, cond).

"Song of Our Country" [take 5].

04/00/61: MD (tpt), Hank Mobley (ts), Wynton Kelly (p), Paul Chambers (b), Jimmy Cobb (d).

"'Round Midnight" "The Theme."

04/16/63: MD (tpt), George Coleman (ts), Victor Feldman (p), Ron Carter (b), Frank Butler (d).

"So Near, So Far."

05/09/67: MD (tpt), Wayne Shorter (ts), Herbie Hancock (p), Buster Williams (b), Tony Williams (d).

"Limbo."

12/28/67: MD (tpt, chimes), Wayne Shorter (ts), Herbie Hancock (el p, clavinet), Joe Beck (g), Ron Carter (b), Tony Williams (d).

"Water on the Pond" [takes 9, 10].

01/12/68: MD (tpt), Wayne Shorter (ts), Bucky Pizzarelli (g), Herbie Hancock (el harpsichord), Ron Carter (b), Tony Williams (d).

"Fun" [takes 28, 30].

11/27/68: MD (tpt), Wayne Shorter (ss, ts), Chick Corea (el p), Herbie Hancock (el p), Josef Zawinul (el p, org), Dave Holland (b, el b), Jack DeJohnette (d, perc), Teo Macero (perc).

"Directions" [takes 1, 2], "Ascent."

02/27/70: MD (tpt), Steve Grossman (ss), John McLaughlin (g), Dave Holland (el b), Jack DeJohnette (d).

"Duran."

03/17/70: MD (tpt), Wayne Shorter (ss), Bennie Maupin (bcl), John McLaughlin (g), Dave Holland (el b), Billy Cobham (d).

"Konda."

05/21/70: MD (tpt), Keith Jarrett (el p), John McLaughlin (g), Dave Holland (b, el b), Jack DeJohnette (d), Airto Moreira (perc).

"Willie Nelson."

Olympia 1960 **(Trema 710455/8)**

In Stockholm 1960 Complete **(Dragon DRCD 228) (Original: Dragon DRLP 90/91, DRLP 129/30)**

03/22/60: MD (tpt), John Coltrane (ts), Wynton Kelly (p), Paul Chambers (b), Jimmy Cobb (d).

"So What," "On Green Dolphin Street," "All Blues"/"The Theme," "So What," "Fran-Dance," "Walkin'"/"The Theme."

10/13/60: MD (tpt), Sonny Stitt (as, ts), Wynton Kelly (p), Paul Chambers (b), Jimmy Cobb (d).

"Walkin'," "Autumn Leaves," "So What," "'Round Midnight"/"The Theme," "On Green Dolphin Street," "All Blues"/"The Theme," "All of You," "Walkin' " "Autumn Leaves"/"The Theme," "If I Were a Bell," "No Blues"/"The Theme."

***Live Olympia 11 Octobre 1960, Part 2* (Trema 71057/9)**
10/11/60
***Someday My Prince Will Come* (Columbia/Legacy CK 65919) (Original: Columbia CL 1656)**
03/07/61: MD (tpt), Hank Mobley (ts), Wynton Kelly (p), Paul Chambers (b), Jimmy Cobb (d).
　　　"Pfrancing (No Blues)," "Drad-Dog."
03/20/61: MD (tpt), Hank Mobley (ts), John Coltrane (ts—1st "Someday My Prince Will Come"), Wynton Kelly (p), Paul Chambers (b), Jimmy Cobb (d).
　　　"Someday My Prince Will Come," "Old Folks," "Someday My Prince Will Come."
03/21/61: MD (tpt), Hank Mobley (ts—"Blues No. 2"), John Coltrane (ts—"Teo"), Wynton Kelly (p), Paul Chambers (b), Jimmy Cobb (d), Philly Joe Jones (d—"Blues No. 2").
　　　"Teo," "I Thought About You," "Blues No. 2."

***Miles Davis in Person, Friday Night at the Blackhawk, Volume 1* (Columbia CK 44257) (Original: Columbia CL 1669)**
04/00/61: MD (tpt), Hank Mobley (ts), Wynton Kelly (p), Paul Chambers (b), Jimmy Cobb (d).
　　　"Walkin' "/"The Theme," "Bye Bye Blackbird," "All of You," "No Blues," "The Theme," "Love, I've Found You."

***Miles Davis in Person, Saturday Night at the Blackhawk, Volume 2* (Columbia CK 44425) (Original: Columbia CL 1670)**
04/00/61: MD (tpt), Hank Mobley (ts), Wynton Kelly (p), Paul Chambers (b), Jimmy Cobb (d).
　　　"Well, You Needn't," "Fran-Dance," "So What"/"No Blues," "On Green Dolphin Street," "Oleo," "If I Were a Bell," "Neo (Teo)."

***Miles Davis at Carnegie Hall* (Columbia/Legacy C2K 65027)**
05/19/61: MD (tpt), Hank Mobley (ts), Wynton Kelly (p), Paul Chambers (b), Jimmy Cobb (d), Ernie Royal (tpt), Bernie Glow (tpt), Johnny Coles (tpt), Louis Mucci (tpt), Jimmy Knepper (tb), Dick Hixon (tb), Frank Rehak (tb), Julius Watkins (frh), Paul Ingraham (frh), Bob Swisshelm (frh), Bill Barber (tuba), Romeo Penque (cl, fl), Jerome Richardson (cl, fl), Eddie Caine (cl, fl), Bob Tricarico (cl, fl), Danny Bank (cl, fl), Janet Putnam (harp), Bob Rosengarden (perc), Gil Evans (arr, cond).
　　　"So What," "Spring Is Here," "Teo," "Walkin'," "The Meaning of the Blues"/"Lament," "New Rhumba," "Someday My Prince Will Come," "Oleo," "No Blues," "I Thought About You," "Concierto de Aranjuez."

***Quiet Nights* (Columbia CK 65293) (Original: Columbia CL 2106)**
07/27/62: MD (tpt), Ernie Royal (tpt), Bernie Glow (tpt), Louis Mucci (tpt), Harold "Shorty" Baker (tpt), J. J. Johnson (tb), Frank Rehak (tb), Julius Watkins (frh),

Ray Alonge (frh), Don Corrado (frh), Bill Barber (tuba), Steve Lacy (ss), Jerome Richardson (fl), Al Block (fl), Ray Beckenstein (fl, reeds), Bob Tricarico (bssn), Garvin Bushell (bssn, c bssn), Janet Putnam (harp), Paul Chambers (b), Jimmy Cobb (d), Willie Bobo (bgo), Elvin Jones (perc), Gil Evans (arr, cond).

"Aos Pes da Cruz," "Corcovado."

08/13/62: MD (tpt), Ernie Royal (tpt), Bernie Glow (tpt), Louis Mucci (tpt), Harold "Shorty" Baker (tpt), J. J. Johnson (tb), Frank Rehak (tb), Julius Watkins (frh), Ray Alonge (frh), Don Corrado (frh), Bill Barber (tuba), Steve Lacy (ss), Jerome Richardson (fl), Al Block (fl), Ray Beckenstein (fl, reeds), Bob Triscario (bssn), Garvin Bushell (bssn, c bssn), Janet Putnam (harp), Paul Chambers (b), Jimmy Cobb (d), Willie Bobo (bgo), Elvin Jones (perc), Gil Evans (arr, cond).

"Song No. 1," "Wait till You See Her."

11/06/62: MD (tpt), Ernie Royal (tpt), Bernie Glow (tpt), Louis Mucci (tpt), Harold "Shorty" Baker (tpt), J. J. Johnson (tb), Frank Rehak (tb), Julius Watkins (frh), Ray Alonge (frh), Don Corrado (frh), Bill Barber (tuba), Steve Lacy (ss), Jerome Richardson (fl), Al Block (fl), Ray Beckenstein (fl, reeds), Bob Tricarico (bssn), Garvin Bushell (bssn, c bssn), Janet Putnam (harp), Paul Chambers (b), Jimmy Cobb (d), Willie Bobo (bgo), Elvin Jones (perc), Gil Evans (arr, cond).

"Song No. 2," "Once upon a Summertime."

04/17/63: MD (tpt), George Coleman (ts), Victor Feldman (p), Ron Carter (b), Frank Butler (d).

"Summer Nights."

10/09/63: MD (tpt), Dick Leith (tb), Richard Perissi (frh), Bill Hinshaw (frh), Arthur Maeba (frh), Paul Horn (fl, alto fl, as), Buddy Collette (fl, alto fl, ts), Gene Cipriano (oboe, alto fl, ts), Fred Dutton (bssn), Marjorie Call (harp), Herbie Hancock (p), Ron Carter (b), Tony Williams (d), Gil Evans (arr, cond).

"The Time of the Barracudas."

Miles Davis & John Coltrane: The Complete Columbia Recordings, 1955–1961 (Columbia/Legacy CK 65833)

Seven Steps to Heaven (CBS/Sony 32DP 527) (Original: Columbia CL 2051)

04/16, 17/63: MD (tpt), George Coleman (ts), Victor Feldman (p), Ron Carter (b), Frank Butler (d).

"Basin Street Blues," "I Fall in Love Too Easily," "Baby, Won't You Please Come Home?"

05/14/63: MD (tpt), George Coleman (ts), Herbie Hancock (p), Ron Carter (b), Tony Williams (d).

"Seven Steps to Heaven," "So Near, So Far," "Joshua."

Miles Davis in Europe (Sony SRCS 5705) (Original: Columbia CL 2183)

07/27/63: MD (tpt), George Coleman (ts), Herbie Hancock (p), Ron Carter (b), Tony Williams (d).

"Introduction," "Autumn Leaves," "Milestones," "Joshua," "All of You," "Walkin'."

The Complete Concert 1964: My Funny Valentine + "Four" & More

(Columbia/Legacy C2K 48821)

02/12/64: MD (tpt), George Coleman (ts), Herbie Hancock (p), Ron Carter (b), Tony
Williams (d), Mort Fega (ann).

> "My Funny Valentine," "All of You," "Go-Go" (Theme and Reintroduction), "Stella by Starlight," "All Blues," "I Thought About You," "So What," "Walkin'," "Joshua," "Go-Go" (Theme and Announcement), "Four," "Seven Steps to Heaven," "There is No Greater Love," "Go-Go" (Theme and Announcement).

Miles in Tokyo (CBS/Sony CSCS 5146) (Original: CBS/Sony SOPL 162)

07/14/64: MD (tpt), Sam Rivers (ts), Herbie Hancock (p), Ron Carter (b), Tony
Williams (d), Terno Isono (ann).

> "Introduction," "If I Were a Bell," "My Funny Valentine," "So What," "Walkin'," "All of You"/"The Theme."

Miles in Berlin (CBS/Sony CSCS 5147) (Original: CBS/Sony SOPL 163)

09/25/64: MD (tpt), Wayne Shorter (ts), Herbie Hancock (p), Ron Carter (b), Tony
Williams (d).

> "Milestones," "Autumn Leaves," "So What," "Walkin'," "The Theme."

E.S.P. (Columbia/Legacy CK 46863) (Original: Columbia CL 2350)

01/20/65: MD (tpt), Wayne Shorter (ts), Herbie Hancock (p), Ron Carter (b), Tony
Williams (d).

> "E.S.P.," "R.J."

01/21/65: MD (tpt), Wayne Shorter (ts), Herbie Hancock (p), Ron Carter (b), Tony
Williams (d).

> "Eighty-One," "Little One."

01/22/65: MD (tpt), Wayne Shorter (ts), Herbie Hancock (p), Ron Carter (b), Tony
Williams (d).

> "Agitation," "Iris," "Mood."

**The Complete Studio Recordings of the Miles Davis Quintet (1965–June 1968)
(Columbia C6K 67398)**

01/20/65–06/21/68

The Complete Plugged Nickel 1965 (Columbia CXK 66955)

12/22–23/65

Miles Smiles (Columbia/Legacy CK 48849) (Original: Columbia CL 2601)

10/24–25/66

10/24/66: MD (tpt), Wayne Shorter (ts), Herbie Hancock (p), Ron Carter (b), Tony
Williams (d).

> "Orbits," "Circle," "Dolores," "Freedom Jazz Dance."

10/25/66: MD (tpt), Wayne Shorter (ts), Herbie Hancock (p), Ron Carter (b), Tony
Williams (d).

> "Footprints," "Gingerbread Boy."

Sorcerer (Sony SRCS 5708) (Original: Columbia CL 2732)

08/21/62: MD (tpt), Frank Rehak (tb), Wayne Shorter (ts), Paul Chambers (b), Jimmy
Cobb (d), Willie Bobo (bgo), Bob Dorough (p, voc).

> "Nothing Like You."

05/16/67: MD (tpt), Wayne Shorter (ts), Herbie Hancock (p), Ron Carter (b), Tony Williams (d).

"Limbo," "Vonetta."

05/17/67: MD (tpt), Wayne Shorter (ts), Herbie Hancock (p), Ron Carter (b), Tony Williams (d).

"Masqualero," "The Sorcerer."

05/24/67: MD (tpt), Wayne Shorter (ts), Herbie Hancock (p), Ron Carter (b), Tony Williams (d).

"Prince of Darkness," "Pee Wee."

Water Babies (Columbia/Legacy ACK 86557) (Original: Columbia PC 34396)

06/07, 13, 23/67: MD (tpt), Wayne Shorter (ts), Herbie Hancock (p), Ron Carter (b), Tony Williams (d).

"Water Babies," "Capricorn," "Sweet Pea."

11/11/68: MD (tpt), Wayne Shorter (ts), Chick Corea (el p), Herbie Hancock (el p), Dave Holland (b), Tony Williams (d, perc).

"Two Faced," "Dual Mr. Anthony Tillmon Williams Process,"

11/25/68: MD (tpt), Wayne Shorter (ts), Joe Zawinul (p), Herbie Hancock (el p), Chick Corea (el p), Dave Holland (b), Tony Williams (d).

"Splash."

Nefertiti (Columbia/Legacy CK 46113) (Original: Columbia CS 9594)

06/07/67: MD (tpt), Wayne Shorter (ts), Herbie Hancock (p), Ron Carter (b), Tony Williams (d).

"Nefertiti."

06/22/67: MD (tpt), Wayne Shorter (ts), Herbie Hancock (p), Ron Carter (b), Tony Williams (d).

"Hand Jive," "Madness."

07/19/67: MD (tpt), Wayne Shorter (ts), Herbie Hancock (p), Ron Carter (b), Tony Williams (d).

"Fall," "Riot," "Pinocchio."

Miles in the Sky (CBS/Sony 32DP 728) (Original: Columbia CS 9628)

01/16/68: MD (tpt), Wayne Shorter (ts), Herbie Hancock (p), George Benson (g), Ron Carter (b), Tony Williams (d).

"Paraphernalia."

05/15/68: MD (tpt), Wayne Shorter (ts), Herbie Hancock (p), Ron Carter (b), Tony Williams (d).

"Country Son."

05/16/68: MD (tpt), Wayne Shorter (ts), Herbie Hancock (p), Ron Carter (b), Tony Williams (d).

"Black Comedy."

05/17/68: MD (tpt), Wayne Shorter (ts), Herbie Hancock (el p), Ron Carter (el b), Tony Williams (d).

"Stuff."

Filles de Kilimanjaro (Columbia/Legacy ACK 86555) (Original: Columbia CS 9750)

06/19–21/68: MD (tpt), Wayne Shorter (ts), Herbie Hancock (el p), Ron Carter (el b), Tony Williams (d).

"Tout de Suite," "Petits Machins (Little Stuff)," "Filles de Kilimanjaro," "Tout de Suite" [alt. take].

09/24/68: MD (tpt), Wayne Shorter (ts), Chick Corea (el p), Dave Holland (b), Tony Williams (d).

"Frelon Brun," "Mademoiselle Mabry (Miss Mabry)."

The Complete In a Silent Way Sessions (September 1968–February 1969) (Columbia C3K 65362)

09/00/68–02/00/69

In a Silent Way (Columbia/Legacy ACK 86556) (Original: Columbia CS 9875)

02/18/69: MD (tpt), Wayne Shorter (ss), John McLaughlin (el g), Herbie Hancock (el p), Chick Corea (el p), Josef Zawinul (org), Dave Holland (b), Tony Williams (d).

"Shhh"/"Peaceful," "In a Silent Way"/"It's About That Time," "In a Silent Way," "It's About That Time," "In a Silent Way."

The Complete Bitches Brew Sessions (Columbia C4K 65570)

08/19–21/69; 01/28/70; 02/06/70

Bitches Brew (Columbia/Legacy C2K 65774) (Original: Columbia GP 26)

08/19/69: MD (tpt), Wayne Shorter (ss), Bennie Maupin (bcl), John McLaughlin (g), Chick Corea (el p), Josef Zawinul (el p), Dave Holland (b), Harvey Brooks (el b), Jack DeJohnette (d), Lenny White (d), Charles Don Alias (d, perc), Jumma Santos (perc).

"Bitches Brew," "John McLaughlin," "Sanctuary."

08/20/69: MD (tpt), Wayne Shorter (ss), Bennie Maupin (bcl), John McLaughlin (g), Chick Corea (el p), Josef Zawinul (el p), Dave Holland (b), Harvey Brooks (el b), Jack DeJohnette (d), Jumma Santos (perc).

"Miles Runs the Voodoo Down."

08/21/69: MD (tpt), Wayne Shorter (ss), Bennie Maupin (bcl), John McLaughlin (g), Chick Corea (el p), Josef Zawinul (el p), Larry Young (el p), Dave Holland (b), Harvey Brooks (el b), Jack DeJohnette (d), Lenny White (d), Charles Don Alias (d, perc), Jumma Santos (perc).

"Pharaoh's Dance," "Spanish Key."

01/28/70: MD (tpt), Wayne Shorter (ss), Bennie Maupin (bcl), Chick Corea (el p), Josef Zawinul (el p), John McLaughlin (g), Dave Holland (el b), Billy Cobham (d), Jack DeJohnette (d), Airto Moreira (perc).

"Feio."

Big Fun (Columbia/Legacy C2K 63973) (Original: Columbia PC 32866)

11/19/69: MD (tpt), Steve Grossman (ss), Bennie Maupin (bcl), Herbie Hancock (el p), Chick Corea (el p), John McLaughlin (g), Khalil Balakrishna (el sitar), Bihari Sharma (el sitar, tamboura), Ron Carter (b), Harvey Brooks (el b), Billy Cobham (d, perc), Airto Moreira (perc).

"Great Expectations," "Yaphet."

11/28/69: MD (tpt), Steve Grossman (ss), Bernie Maupin (bcl), Herbie Hancock (el p), Larry Young (org, celeste), Chick Corea (el p), John McLaughlin (g), Khalil Balakrishna (sitar), Dave Holland (b), Harvey Brooks (el b), Jack DeJohnette (d), Billy Cobham (perc), Airto Moreira (perc), Bihari Sharma (tabla, tambura).

"Trevere," "The Little Blue Frog."

01/27/70: MD (tpt), Wayne Shorter (ss), Bennie Maupin (bcl), Chick Corea (el p), Josef
Zawinul (el p), Khalil Balakrishna (sitar, tambura), Dave Holland (el b), Billy
Cobham (d), Jack DeJohnette (d), Airto Moreira (perc).

"Lonely Fire."

02/6/70: MD (tpt), Wayne Shorter (ss), Chick Corea (el p), Joe Zawinul (el p, org), John
McLaughlin (g), Khalil Balakrishna (sitar), Dave Holland (el b), Jack
DeJohnette (d), Billy Cobham (perc), Airto Moreira (perc).

"Recollections."

03/03/70: MD (tpt), Steve Grossman (ss), John McLaughlin (g), Dave Holland (el b),
Jack DeJohnette (d).

"Go Ahead John."

06/12/72: MD (tpt), Carlos Garnett (ss), Sonny Fortune (ss, fl), Bennie Maupin (bcl),
Lonnie Liston Smith (org), Harold I. Williams (el p, synth), Michael Henderson (el b), Al Foster (d), Billy Hart (d), Mtume (cga, perc.), Badal Roy (tabla).

"Ife."

Live/Evil (Columbia/Legacy C2K 65135) (Original: Columbia G 30954)

02/06/70: MD (tpt), Wayne Shorter (ss), Chick Corea (el p), Josef Zawinul (el p), John
McLaughlin (g), Dave Holland (el b), Jack DeJohnette (d), Billy Cobham
(perc), Airto Moreira (perc).

"Gemini," "Double Image."

06/03/70: MD (tpt), Steve Grossman (ss), Chick Corea (el p), Herbie Hancock (el p),
Keith Jarrett (el p), Ron Carter (el b), Jack DeJohnette (d), Airto Moreira
(perc), Hermeto Pascoal (voc).

"Nem Um Talvez," "Selim."

06/04/70: MD (tpt), Steve Grossman (ss), Herbie Hancock (el p), Chick Corea (el p),
Keith Jarrett (el p), John McLaughlin (g), Dave Holland (b), Jack DeJohnette
(d), Airto Moreira (perc), Hermeto Pascoal (voc).

"Little Church."

12/19/70: MD (tpt), Gary Bartz (ss, as), Keith Jarrett (el p), John McLaughlin (g),
Michael Henderson (el b), Jack DeJohnette (d), Airto Moreira (perc), Conrad
Roberts (narr).

"Sivad," "What I Say," "Funky Tonk," "Inamorata," Narration by Conrad
Roberts.

Miles Davis at Filmore: Live at the Fillmore East (March 7, 1970) (Columbia/Legacy C2K 85191)

03/07/70: MD (tpt), Wayne Shorter (ss, ts), Chick Corea (el p), Dave Holland (b and el
b), Jack DeJohnette (d), Airto Moreira (perc).

"Directions," "Spanish Key," "Masqualero," "It's About That Time" "The
Theme," "Directions," "Miles Runs the Voodoo Down," "Bitches Brew,"
"Spanish Key," "It's About That Time"/"Willie Nelson."

A Tribute to Jack Johnson (Columbia/Legacy CK 47036) (Original: Columbia S 30455)

04/07/70: MD (tpt), Steve Grossman (ss), John McLaughlin (g), Herbie Hancock (org),
Michael Henderson (el b), Billy Cobham (d), Unknown orchestra (conducted

by Teo Macero), Brock Peters (narr).

"Right Off," "Yesternow."

Black Beauty: Miles Davis at Fillmore West (Columbia/Legacy C2K 65138) (Original: CBS/Sony SOPJ 39/40)

04/10/70: MD (tpt), Steve Grossman (ss), Chick Corea (el p), Dave Holland (b, el b), Jack DeJohnette (d), Airto Moreira (perc).

"Directions," "Miles Runs the Voodoo Down," "Willie Nelson," "I Fall in Love Too Easily," "Sanctuary," "It's About That Time," "Bitches Brew," "Masqualero," "Spanish Key"/"The Theme."

Get Up with It (Columbia/Legacy C2K 63970) (Original: CBS/Sony 28AP 2163/4)

05/19/70: MD (tpt), Steve Grossman (ss), John McLaughlin (g), Herbie Hancock (clavinet), Keith Jarrett (el p, org), Gene Perla (el b), Billy Cobham (d), Airto Moreira (perc).

"Honky Tonk."

03/09/72: MD (tpt), Wally Chambers (hca), Cornel Dupree (g), Michael Henderson (el b), Al Foster (d), Bernard Purdie (d), James "Mtume" Forman (cga, perc), Wade Marcus (brass arr), Billy Jackson (rhythm arr).

"Red China Blues."

09/06/72: MD (org), Reggie Lucas (g), Khahl Balakrishna (sitar), Cedric Lawson (synth), Michael Henderson (el b), Al Foster (d), James "Mtume" Forman (cga, perc), Badal Roy (tabla).

"Rated X."

12/08/72: MD (org), Carlos Garnett (ss), Cedric Lawson (keyb), Reggie Lucas (g), Khalil Balakrishna (sitar), Michael Henderson (el b), Al Foster (d), James "Mtume" Forman (cga, perc), Badal Roy (tabla).

"Billy Preston."

09/17/73: MD (tpt, org), Dave Liebman (fl), John Stubblefield (ss), Pete Cosey (g), Reggie Lucas (g), Michael Henderson (el b), Al Foster (d), James "Mtume" Forman (cga, perc).

"Calypso Frelimo."

06/19/74: MD (tpt, org), Dave Liebman (fl), Pete Cosey (g), Reggie Lucas (g), Dominique Gaumont (g), Michael Henderson (el b), Al Foster (d), James "Mtume" Forman (cga, perc).

"He Loved Him Madly."

10/07/74: MD (tpt, org), Sonny Fortune (ss, fl), Pete Cosey (g), Reggie Lucas (g), Dominique Gaumont (g), Michael Henderson (el b), Al Foster (d), James "Mtume" Forman (cga, perc).

"Maiysha," "Mtume."

Miles Davis at Fillmore East (Columbia/Legacy C2K 65139) (Original: Columbia G 30038)

06/17/70: MD (tpt), Steve Grossman (ss), Chick Corea (el p), Keith Jarrett (org), Dave Holland (b, el b), Jack DeJohnette (d), Airto Moreira (perc).

Wednesday Miles: "Directions," "Bitches Brew," "The Mask," "It's About That Time," "Bitches Brew" "The Theme,"

06/18/70: MD (tpt), Steve Grossman (ss), Chick Corea (el p), Keith Jarrett (org), Dave Holland (b, el b), Jack DeJohnette (d), Airto Moreira (perc).

Thursday Miles: "Directions," "The Mask," "It's About That Time" "Bitches Brew"/"The Theme."

06/19/70: MD (tpt), Steve Grossman (ss), Chick Corea (el p), Keith Jarrett (org), Dave Holland (b, el b), Jack DeJohnette (d), Airto Moreira (perc).

Friday Miles: "It's About That Time," "I Fall in Love Too Easily," "Sanctuary," "Bitches Brew"/"The Theme."

06/20/70: MD (tpt), Steve Grossman (ss), Chick Corea (el p), Keith Jarrett (org), Dave Holland (b, el b), Jack DeJohnette (d), Airto Moreira (perc).

Saturday Miles: "The Mask"/"It's About That Time," "I Fall in Love Too Easily," "Sanctuary," "Bitches Brew," "Willie Nelson"/"The Theme."

Message to Love: The Isle of Wight Festival 1970 (Columbia C2K 62058)
08/29/70

On the Corner (Columbia/Legacy CK 63980) (Original: Columbia KC 31096)

06/01/72: MD (tpt), Dave Liebman (ss), Chick Corea (synth), Herbie Hancock (org), Harold I. Williams (el p), John McLaughlin (g), Collin Walcott (sitar), Paul Buckmaster (el cello), Michael Henderson (el b), Jack DeJohnette (d), Billy Hart (d, perc), Don Alias (cga, perc), James "Mtume" Forman (perc), Badal Roy (tabla).

"On the Corner," "New York Girl," "Thinkin' One Thing and Doin' Another" "Vote for Miles."

06/06/72: MD (tpt), Carlos Garnett (as, ts) Bennie Maupin (bcl), Herbie Hancock (el p, synth), Harold I. Williams (el p, el org synth), Lonnie Liston Smith (org), David Creamer (g), Collin Walcott (sitar), Paul Buckmaster (el cello), Michael Henderson (el b), Jack DeJohnette (d), Billy Hart (d), Don Alias (perc), James "Mtume" Forman (perc), Badal Roy (tabla).

"Black Satin," "One and One," "Helen Butte" "Mr. Freedom X."

Miles Davis in Concert (Columbia/Legacy C2K 65140) (Original: Columbia KC 32092)

09/29/72: MD (tpt, org), Carlos Garnett (ss), Reggie Lucas (g), Khalil Balakrishna (sitar), Cedric Lawson (keyb), Michael Henderson (el b), Al Foster (d), James "Mtume" Forman (cga, perc), Badal Roy (tabla).

"Rated X," "Honky Tonk," "Right Off," "Black Satin," "Sanctuary Theme," "Ife," "Right Off," "Sanctuary Theme."

Olympia 1973 (Trema 710460)
07/11/73

Dark Magus (Columbia/Legacy C2K 65137) (Original: CBS/Sony 28AP 2165/6)

03/30/74: MD (tpt, org), Dave Liebman (ss, ts, fl), Azar Lawrence (ts), Pete Cosey (g, perc), Reggie Lucas (g), Dominique Gaumont (g), Michael Henderson (el b), Al Foster (d), James "Mtume" Forman (cga, perc).

("Moja"), "Nne" ("Moja"), "Tune in 5," ("Moja"), "Funk (Prelude, Part 1)" ("Moja"), "For Dave" ("Wili"), "Tata," "Calypso Frelimo" ("Tata"), "Ife," ("Nne") "Nne," "Tune in 5" ("Nne").

Agharta (CBS/Sony SRCS 9128+) (Original: CBS/Sony SOPJ 92/3)

02/01/75: MD (tpt, org), Sonny Fortune (ss, as, fl), Pete Cosey (g, perc), Reggie Lucas (g), Michael Henderson (el b), Al Foster (d), James "Mtume" Forman (cga, perc).

"Prelude," "Maiysha," "Interlude" "Theme from Jack Johnson."

Pangaea (CBS/Sony CSCS 5350/1) (Original: CBS/Sony SOPZ 96/7)

02/01/75: MD (tpt, org), Sonny Fortune (ss, as, fl), Pete Cosey (g, perc), Reggie Lucas (g), Michael Henderson (el b), Al Foster (d), James "Mtume" Forman (cga, perc).

"Zimbabwe," "Gondwana."

The Man with the Horn (Sony Mastersound SRCS 9132) (Original: Columbia FC 36790)

05/00/80: MD (tpt), Bill Evans (ss, ts, fl), Robert Irving III (synth), Randy Hall (g, celeste, synth, voc), Felton Crews (el b), Vincent Wilburn, Jr. (d), Angela Bofill's Singers (voc).

"The Man with the Horn."

01/00/81: MD (tpt), Bill Evans (ss, ts, fl), Barry Finnerty (g), Marcus Miller (el b), Al Foster (d), Sammy Figueroa (perc).

"Back Seat Betty," "Aida," "Ursula."

03/00/81: MD (tpt), Mike Stern (g), Marcus Miller (el b), Al Foster (d), Sammy Figueroa (perc).

"Fat Time."

05/06/81: MD (tpt), Bill Evans (ss, ts, fl), Robert Irving III (el p, arr), Randy Hall (synth, arr), Barry Finnerty (g), Felton Crews (el b), Vincent Wilburn, Jr. (d), Sammy Figueroa (perc).

"Shout."

We Want Miles (CBS/Sony CSCS 5131/2) (Original: Columbia C2 38005)

06/27/81: MD (tpt), Bill Evans (ss, ts, fl, el p), Mike Stern (g), Marcus Miller (el b), Al Foster (d), Mino Cinelu (perc).

"Fast Track," "My Man's Gone Now," "Kix."

07/05/81: MD (tpt), Bill Evans (ss, ts, fl, el p), Mike Stern (g), Marcus Miller (el b), Al Foster (d), Mino Cinelu (perc).

"Back Seat Betty."

10/04/81: MD (tpt), Bill Evans (ss, ts, fl, el p), Mike Stern (g), Marcus Miller (el b), Al Foster (d), Mino Cinelu (perc).

"Jean Pierre" [two versions].

Miles! Miles! Miles! (Sony SRCS 6513/4)

10/04/81: MD (tpt), Bill Evans (ss, ts, fl, el p), Mike Stern (g), Marcus Miller (el b), Al Foster (d), Mino Cinelu (perc).

"Back Seat Betty," "Ursula," "My Man's Gone Now," "Aida," "Fat Time," "Jean Pierre."

Star People (CBS/Sony CSCS 5347) (Original: Columbia FC 38657)

08/11/82: MD (tpt, synth), Bill Evans (ss, ts, fl, el p), Mike Stern (g), Marcus Miller (el b), Al Foster (d), Mino Cinelu (perc).

"Star on Cicely."

08/28/82: MD (tpt, synth), Bill Evans (ss, ts, fl, el p), Mike Stern (g), Marcus Miller (el b), Al Foster (d), Mino Cinelu (perc).

"Come Get It."

09/01/82: MD (tpt, synth), Bill Evans (ss, ts, fl, el p), Mike Stern (g), Marcus Miller (el b), Al Foster (d), Mino Cinelu (perc).
> "Star People," "U 'n' I."

01/05/83: MD (tpt, synth), Bill Evans (ss, ts, fl, el p), Mike Stern (g), John Scofield (g), Marcus Miller (el b), Al Foster (d), Mino Cinelu (perc).
> "It Gets Better."

02/03/83: MD (tpt, synth), Bill Evans (ss, ts, fl, el p), Mike Stern (g), John Scofield (g), Tom Barney (el b), Al Foster (d), Mino Cinelu (perc).
> "Speak."

Decoy (CBS/Sony 35DP 170) (Original: Columbia FC 38991)

06/31/83: MD (tpt, synth), John Scofield (g), Darryl Jones (el b), Al Foster (d), Mino Cinelu (perc).
> "Freaky Deaky."

07/07/83: MD (tpt, synth), Bill Evans (ss, ts, fl, el p), John Scofield (g), Darryl Jones (el b), Al Foster (d), Mino Cinelu (perc).
> "What It Is," "That's What Happened."

09/05/83: MD (tpt, synth), Robert Irving III (synth, el d), Mino Cinelu (perc).
> "Robot 415."

09/10/83: MD (tpt), Branford Marsalis (ss), John Scofield (g), Robert Irving III (synth, el d), Darryl Jones (el b), Al Foster (d), Mino Cinelu (perc).
> "Decoy," "Code M.D.," "That's Right."

Live in Warsaw (Poljazz PSI-X-001)
10/23/83

You're Under Arrest (CBS/Sony CSCS 5349) (Original: Columbia FC 40023)

01/26/84: MD (tpt, voc), John Scofield (g), Robert Irving III (synth), Darryl Jones (el b), Al Foster (d), Steve Thornton (perc).
> "Time After Time."

12/26/84: MD (tpt, voc), Bob Berg (ss, ts), John Scofield (g), Robert Irving III (synth), Darryl Jones (el b), Al Foster (d), Vincent Wilburn, Jr. (d), Steve Thornton (perc), Gordon Sumner (voc), Marek Olko (voc), James Prindiville (hand-cuffs).
> "One Phone Call"/"Street Scenes," "Human Nature," "MD 1"/"Something on Your Mind"/"MD 2," "You're Under Arrest," "Jean Pierre"/"You're Under Arrest"/"Then There Were None."

01/10/85: MD (tpt, voc), John McLaughlin (g), Robert Irving III (synth), Darryl Jones (el b), Vincent Wilburn, Jr. (d), Steve Thornton (perc).
> "Ms. Morrisine," "Katia Prelude," "Katia."

Aura (Columbia/Legacy 45332) (Original: Columbia C2X 45332)

01/31/85: MD (tpt), Benny Rosenfeld (tpt, flh), Palle Bolvig (tpt, flh), Jens Winther (tpt, flh), Perry Knudsen (tpt, flh), Palle Mikkelborg (tpt, flh), Idrees Sulieman (tpt, flh), Vincent Nilsson (tb), Jens Engel (tb), Ture Larsen (tb), Ole Kurt Jensen (bass tb), Axel Windfeld (bass tb, tuba), Jesper Thilo (reeds, flute), Per Carsten (reeds, flute), Uffe Karskov (reeds, flute), Bent Jaedig (reeds, flute), Flemming Madsen (reeds, flute), Niels Eje (oboe, engl horn), John McLaughlin (g), Bjarne Roupé (g), Lillian Thornquist (harp), Thomas Clausen (p, keyb), Ole Koch-Hansen (keyb), Kenneth Knudsen (keyb), Bo Stief (el b), Niels-Henning Ørsted Pedersen (b), Vincent Wilburn, Jr. (d), Lennart Gruvstedt (d), Marilyn Mazur (perc), Ethan Weisgaard (perc), Eva Hess-Thaysen (voc).

"Intro," "White," "Yellow," "Orange," "Red," "Green," "Blue," "Electric Red," "Indigo," "Violet."

Tutu (Warner Bros. 9-25490-2)

MD (tpt), Marcus Miller (all except as indicated), Jason Miles (synth prog), Adam Holzman (synth prog, synth solo 4) Paulinho da Costa (perc 1, 3–5) Steve Reid (perc 4) George Duke (all except tpt, bg, perc 5) Marcus Miller (b g, 5) Omar Hakim (d, perc 2) Bernard Wright (add synth 2, 7). Michael Ualaniak (v 7)

02/06/86: "Backyard Ritual" (5).

02/10/86: "Splatch" (4).

02/11/88: "Tutu" (1).

02/13/86: "Portia" (3).

03/12/86: "Tomaas" (2), "Perfect Way" (6), "Don't Lose Your Mind" (7), "Full Nelson" (8).

Miles Davis/Marcus Miller Music from Siesta (Warner 925655-2)

03/00/87: MD (tpt), Marcus Miller (all except as indicated), Jason Miles (synth prog), Earl Klugh (g, "Claire"), James Walker (fl, "Los Feliz").

"Lost in Madrid Part 1," "Siesta—Kitt's Kiss—Lost in Madrid Part II," "Theme for Augustine—Wind—Seduction—Kiss," "Submission," "Lost in Madrid Part III," "Conchita—Lament," "Lost in Madrid Part IV—Rat Dance—The Call," "Claire—Lost in Madrid Part V," "Afterglow," "Los Feliz."

Amandla (Warner Bros. 925873-2)

9/88–1/89: MD (tpt), Marcus Miller (b, key 1–8, bcl 1–4, 7–8, ss 1, 3, d 1, g 1, 4, 7), Kenny Garrett (ss 1, 3–7, ss 2), Don Alias (perc 1, 3, 6), Mino Cinelu (perc 1), George Duke (key, Synclavier 2), Michael Landau (g 2), Joey DeFrancesco (key 2), Ricky Wellman (d 3, 6), Foley McCreary (g 3, 4, 6), Jean-Paul Bourelly (g 3, 5), Omar Hakim (d 4, 5), Paulinho da Costa (perc 4–5), Rick Margitza (ts 5), Joe Sample (p 6), Bashiri Johnson (perc 6), John Bigham (d prog, g 3, key 7), Billy Patterson (wah-wah g 7), Al Foster (d 8), Jason Miles (synth prog 8).

"Catembe" (1), "Cobra" (2), "Big Time" (3), "Hannibal" (4), "Jo-Jo" (5), "Amandla" (6), "Jilli" (7), "Mr. Pastorius" (8).

Miles Davis & Michel Legrand Dingo: Selections from the Motion Picture Soundtrack (Warner Bros. 7599-26438-2)

05/00/90: MD (tpt) on 2–4, 7, 8, 10, 14, 15; Chuck Findley (tpt) on 1, 5, 6, 9, 11, 13, 14, 16 Music arranged, orchestrated and conducted by Michel Legrand.

"Kimberley Trumpet" (1), "The Arrival" (2), "Concert on the Runaway" (3), "The Departure" (4), "Dingo Howl" (5), "Letter as Hero" (6), "Trumpet Cleaning" (7), "The Dream" (8), "Paris Walking I" (9), "Paris Walking II" (10), "Kimberley Trumpet in Paris" (11), "The Music Room" (12), "Club Entrance" (13), "The Jam Session" (14), "Going Home" (15), "Surprise!" (16).

Original Motion Picture Soundtrack: The Hot Spot **(Antilles 422-846 813-2) Original music composed by Jack Nitzsche**

05/05–10/90: John Lee Hooker (g, voc 1, 3, 5–8, 10–13), MD (tpt 1, 2, 5–7, 9–13), Taj Mahal (g, voc 2, 4–5, 7, 12, 13), Earl Palmer (d 1, 2, 4, 7, 12, 13), Tim Drummond (b 1, 2, 4–7, 10–13), Roy Rogers (slide g 1, 2, 4–7, 10–13), Bradford Ellis (keyb 9).

> "Coming to Town" (1), "Empty Bank" (2), "Harry's Philosophy" (3), "Dolly's Arrival" (4), "Harry and Dolly" (5), "Sawmill" (6), "Bank Robbery" (7), "Moanin" (8), "Gloria's Story" (9), "Harry Sets Up Button" (10), "Murder" (11), "Blackmail" (12), "End Credits" (13).

Miles & Quincy Live at Montreux **(Warner Bros. WB 9 45221)**

07/08/91: MD (ttpt), the Gil Evans Orchestra, the George Gruntz Concert Jazz Band, Wallace Roney (tpt, flh), Kenny Garrett (as), Quincy Jones (cond, prod).

> Introduction by Claude Nobs and Quincy Jones, "Boplicity," "Introduction to Miles Ahead Medley," "Springsville," "Maids of Cadiz," "The Duke," "My Ship," "Miles Ahead," "Blues for Pablo," Introduction to *Porgy and Bess* Medley," "Orgone," "Gone, Gone, Gone," "Summertime," "Here Come De Honey Man," "The Pan Piper," "Solea."

Doo-Bop **(Warner Bros. 9 26938-2)**

01–02, 07–08/91: MD (tpt), J. R., A. B. Money, Easy Mo Bee (rappers).

> "Mystery," "The Doo Bop Song," "Chocolate Chip," "High Speed Chase," "Blow," "Sonya," "Fantasy," "Duke Booty," "Mystery (reprise)."

Live Around the World **(Warner Bros. 7599-25490-2)**

1988–1991

Index